Interactive television

THE FUTURE OF TELEVISION is undoubtedly digital. Television or video signals can be converted from their normal analogue form (continuously varying) into a digital form, which consists of a series of definite pulses rather like Morse code. Digital signals can be transmitted, compressed, and manipulated by computers without any unwanted "noise" affecting the data. One of the advantages of digital technology is that video data can be manipulated to make interactive television possible. Interactive "video-on-demand" (VOD) services allow users to watch the material of their choice from a large central video vault. A digital server enables many users to watch the same film, starting at different times, by sending the video data in small "packets" to them. Other services include news programmes, games, music, and electronic shopping. With the latter, the user "strolls" through a virtual shop and uses a credit card to buy items, which are then delivered to the home within days.

On-screen menus

Many new set-top boxes have considerable computing power

CATEGORIES

Westminster Cable

	Drama	1
	Comedy	2
	Childrens	3
	Natural History	4
	Travel and Arts	5
	What's On	6

To return to cable TV,
press 'FIN' twice on your remote control

HELP   MAIN   BACK

SONY

VIDEO-ON-DEMAND

Allowing viewers to choose a film or television programme from a vast selection whenever desired, video-on-demand comes complete with all the flexibility of a video recorder (including fast-forward, rewind, and pause facilities). A typical VOD system consists of video vaults containing compressed digital video data, a sophisticated digital server that sends the requested material to the correct destination, and decoder and remote control units in the home.

REMOTE CONTROL
As well as offering the standard features, the remote control enables the user to operate the VOD, play games, and buy goods from home-shopping services.

The Fin button returns the viewer to normal cable television service

Video-on-demand button

Select button

Remote controls for interactive television are simple and user-friendly in format

VJB 02

SET-TOP BOX
The set-top box sends the user's choices to the digital server and decodes video data entering the home system. Depending on the system used, the digital video data from the server is converted to an analogue signal for the television either by a junction box outside the home or by the set-top box.

The television is an analogue device

Direction buttons for navigating on-screen menus

These keys allow quick selection of colour-coded, on-screen choices

Coaxial cable carries the video data as an electrical signal

NEIGHBOURHOOD NODE
The junction box, or neighbourhood node, converts the fibre-optic cable's optical signal into an electrical signal, which is transmitted via coaxial cable to different homes in the neighbourhood.

ATM stands for "Asynchronous Transfer Mode"

ATM SWITCH
The ATM switch passes data from the server to the modulator at incredible speed.

The server is the "brains" of the system

Fibre-optic cable carries the digital video data in the form of light pulses

The modulator changes the data's frequency

DIGITAL SERVER
The digital server locates the viewer's selection in the storage vaults and divides the data into "packets". It then addresses the packets before sending them back to the ATM switch.

Each vault can store enough data for over 500 movies

MODULATOR
The information received by the modulator is converted to the correct frequency for its journey to the home.

STORAGE VAULTS
Digital video data is compressed before being stored in vaults. A typical vault may house up to 100 magnetic hard drives.

DIGITAL VIDEO DISC

The video format set to replace tapes and laserdiscs in the home looks exactly like an audio compact disc (CD) – a silver platter 12 centimetres (4³/₄ inches) in diameter. (To avoid a repetition of the 1980s' VHS/Beta video-cassette war, electronics companies involved have agreed on one format.) However, the digital video disc can hold up to 9 hours of data on its 2 sides, with each side containing 133 minutes of programme time. This is compared with the 74 minutes held by a CD. In addition, DVD's interactivity means that certain programmes can be viewed from a variety of camera angles.

COMPACT DISC

DIGITAL VIDEO DISC

CD "tracks"

DVD tracks are packed more tightly

CD CROSS-SECTION

DVD CROSS-SECTION

CD has one layer of data

DVD has two layers of data on each side

CINEMA BY COMPUTER

Disney Productions' *Toy Story* (1995) was the world's first feature film to be generated entirely on computer. A team of 27 animators worked on the film, producing an average of 3¹/₂ minutes of footage per week. Some of the characters and scenes were created solely on computer, whereas others were set up with models and props before being scanned into the computer for digitization.

BUZZ LIGHTYEAR AND WOODY IN *TOY STORY*

Raising Alexandria

MAP OF ALEXANDRIA HARBOUR
(ANCIENT CITY IN RED)

IN NOVEMBER 1996, the stunning revelation was made that marine archaeologists had discovered remains of the vanished royal quarter of the ancient city of Alexandria. Founded by Alexander the Great in 331BC, Alexandria was a celebrated centre of culture and learning in ancient times, as well as the scene of legendary events between Cleopatra, Mark Antony, and the Caesars. The discovery was made just six to eight metres (20 to 26 feet) under the Mediterranean sea on the eastern side of modern Alexandria's harbour. A team of 16 divers made 3,500 dives over a period of four months and discovered some 9,000 blocks and pieces, including material from pavements, quays, columns, and statues. Using a satellite-based global positioning system (GPS), the team mapped out a two-acre area. Selected finds were then hoisted to the surface using air-filled balloons and cables lowered by cranes. Among the pieces raised were portions of the mighty Pharos lighthouse, once the tallest building on earth and one of the Seven Wonders of the ancient world.

MARINE ENCRUSTATION
Underwater archaeologists often remove marine encrustation from material while it is still on the seabed. Here, the diver begins the task of uncovering an engraved stone.

Specially adapted underwater scraping tool

A huge concave mirror reflected light up to 50 kilometres (31 miles) out to sea

Airlift hose

The total height of the building was 117 metres (384 feet)

The lighthouse was covered in white marble

RECONSTRUCTION OF PHAROS LIGHTHOUSE
Although the lighthouse was toppled by an earthquake in the 14th century, it is possible to combine historical information with the results of the search campaign to render three-dimensional computer images of its structure.

AIRLIFT HOSE
Among the specialist equipment used in the project was this airlift hose. Here, the sand is sucked away to unearth a magnificent sphinx statue.

MEASURING IN SITU
The puzzle of the sunken city was pieced together without the excavation of every find. The team precisely drew and measured material in situ, before transferring the information to computer.

The diver records the exact dimensions of the find

Scale bar

Two-tonne
sphinx

Block
inscribed with
hieroglyphics

Underwater
breathing
apparatus

Rose granite
statue head

POSITIONING THE HARNESS
Using harness equipment, the
diver prepares this statue head
for removal to the surface.

This 1.5-tonne head
completes the statue
of the Ptolemy king

THE STATUE OF THE PTOLEMY KING
The colossal bust of the Ptolemy king is
one of the great discoveries of sunken
Alexandria. The dynasty ruled Egypt
from the death of Alexander the Great
(323BC) until the death of Cleopatra (30BC).

FROM WATER TO DRY LAND
The mighty granite bust is hoisted clear
of the water and transported to the dock
using cables lowered from a crane.

SECURING THE STATUE
Even when stationary on the dock, the
priceless statue must be kept carefully
secured with sturdy ropes and cables.

EXAMINING THE STONE
Before the process of desalinization
takes place, archaeologists make an
initial examination of the stone's surface.

Kansai Airport

AERIAL VIEW OF KANSAI

OPEN FOR BUSINESS since 4 September 1994, Kansai International Airport (KIX) is one of only two artificial structures visible from space – the other is the Great Wall of China. The purpose of this project was to build Japan's first 24-hour international airport, in order to respond to the increased demand for air transport not only in Kansai but in the whole of the country. Three mountains in the southeastern part of Japan's Osaka Bay had to be levelled to provide the landmass, and transport bridges from the harbour 5 kilometres (3 miles) away also had to be built. The cost and constructional difficulties of this ambitious undertaking were outweighed by the ideal of an isolated flight-site with future expansion possibilities and without the need for noise restrictions. Although the island is fully operational, this is only the end of Phase 1. Plans for Phase 2 include increasing the size of the island and adding a further two runways.

Each year, the runway handles 160,000 take-offs and landings

Taxiing area

KANSAI

Passenger boarding bridge

Check-in points

The roof comprises 90,000 stainless-steel panels – all identical in size

CROSS-SECTION OF THE TERMINAL
In the cross-section above, the aerodynamic shape of the terminal building's roof is clearly defined. Italian architect Renzo Piano developed this design to combat the local hazard – hurricanes. The central terminal uses a tiered system, which allows passengers quick and easy transfers between flights.

The island measures 1.25 x 4.37 kilometres ($^3/_4$ x 2$^3/_4$ miles)

AIR CIRCULATION
This computer-rendered image illustrates the gentle, aerodynamic curve of the building's roof. This design is echoed on the ceiling inside the building, allowing the fresh air, introduced through vents, to move around freely.

The transport bridge from the mainland has a six-lane motorway and a two-way railway

AERIAL VIEW OF AIRPORT SITE

Control tower

THE CONTROL TOWER
The roof of the terminal building is low enough for the control tower to have a clear view of the aeroplanes' tails, while its shape means that maximum use can be made of the island for taxiing and for the runway.

Terminal building

The railway line from the mainland runs right up to the terminal building

Aeroplane parking bays

Aerofoil-shaped wing

DEPARTURE AREA
The terminal building is supported by 900 steel columns. These are repeatedly adjusted by computer-controlled hydraulic jacks, which compensate for continual site settlement.

The two departure area "wings" are identical in length

Phase 2 will see the island's area increase from 511 hectares to 1,380 hectares

Railway line

Tilting trains

ALTHOUGH TILTING TRAINS have been in use since the 1960s, it is only recent technological developments that have been able to prevent much of the passenger discomfort caused by cornering at high speeds. As a train goes into a curve, it produces substantial centrifugal force towards the outside of the curve. By tilting the train (the equivalent of leaning into a curve on a

SWEDISH TILTING TRAIN (1990)

bicycle), this centrifugal force is balanced by a force into the inner curve and passenger discomfort is reduced. Current computer-controlled active tilting systems operate from self-steering bogies (the wheeled undercarriage of the train). Improvements in bogie design enhance the operation of the train by reducing track forces, and radial self-steering bogies with "soft" suspension have been introduced. Modern tilting trains allow operators to achieve higher speeds on existing curved routes without costly track improvements or the need to consider completely new high-speed lines.

NORMAL TRAIN CARRIAGE

Centrifugal force pushes the carriage contents towards the outside of the curve

CENTRIFUGAL FORCE

As the train enters the curve, a strong centrifugal force is produced

Banking is limited to 6°

NORMAL TRAIN ON CURVE
The normal train is "banked" slightly and slows as it goes into the bend, but the carriage body does not tilt.

Track

Train approaches at an angle

Strong sideways force outwards

STIFF-WHEEL AXLES
The inability of the axles to move means that high forces are taken by the axles themselves and then by the track.

Fiat's Pendolino – "Little Pendulum" – tilting train

PENDOLINO
Fiat's Pendolino is the prototype for most recent European tilting trains. The French tilting train shown in the main diagram (opposite) will be based on similar technology.

Axle

HIGH-SPEED TRAINS

The Japanese pioneered modern high-speed rail travel with their *Shinkansen* (High-Speed Line) trains, which entered service in 1964. On a special new line between Tokyo and Osaka, they achieved speeds of up to 210 km/h (130 mph). The line was reserved for high-speed trains, so there was no slower moving, conflicting traffic to interfere with operations. The latest Bullet Train, *Nozomi*, pictured here, has also broken speed records. Since the early 1980s, similar trains have been developed in France, intitially running between Paris and Lyon and, like the Japanese train, running on priority "dedicated" tracks. German Railways have also developed high-speed links since 1991.

Pantograph to collect electric current

Single-level passenger cabin

Driver's cab has streamlined profile

TILTING TRAIN CARRIAGE

Force produced by train's tilting motion

SIDEWAYS FORCE

Passenger suffers less discomfort

Air suspension units

Pneumatic suspension

Bogie frame

Sprung wheel sets

Hydraulic system tilts carriage body on receiving signals from detector/computer

Track still banked to angle of 6°

Reduced forces lead to less disturbance

CENTRIFUGAL FORCE

Force is reduced by tilt of carriage body

Carriage body can tilt up to 8°

Wheel axles respond individually to curves, adopting a radial attitude

Forces on track are reduced

RADIALLY SELF-STEERING WHEEL AXLES
These axles reduce the greater track forces produced by the higher speeds.

Axle

Track

TILTING TRAIN ON CURVE
Signals from an accelerometer that measures train speed and curvature are analyzed by a computer, which tilts the individual cars as the first car goes into the curve. This active passenger-car tilting minimizes the passengers' discomfort and allows higher speeds (up to 30 per cent) on traditional tracks. A tilt of eight degrees will compensate for 70 per cent of the centrifugal forces.

Electronic signal/speed detection equipment in train nose

BULLET TRAIN
The train can carry 1,324 passengers and features 64 separate traction motors, each producing 285kw of power. The body shells are made of aluminium alloy.

RECORD BREAKER
The latest prototype Bullet Train has reached speeds of 345 km/h (214 mph), but the French TGV holds the world railspeed record of 515 km/h (320 mph).

Network computers

THE INTERNET LINKS MILLIONS of computers worldwide, and anybody with a personal computer (PC) and basic communication tools can become a part of it. The ever-expanding "Net" is becoming a vital resource for business, education, and entertainment. The huge multimedia database of the World Wide Web, which is one aspect of the Net, is so sophisticated that users can "meet" in "virtual worlds". As the Net evolves, so new ways of computing are made possible. Network computing is one possible development which promises greater compatibility and efficiency than personal computing. At present, the Net consists mainly of PCs with large amounts of processing power and disk space (called "fat client computers") connected to servers (other computers that distribute data). The idea behind network computing is to replace the PC, or fat client, with a network computer (NC), or "thin client". A thin client computer has a processor, like a PC, but less memory and no disk storage, and so is much cheaper. Instead of storing application programs and data on a local hard disk (as a PC does), an NC simply downloads programs and data from a server into its RAM as needed. Network computing promises economies of scale and centralization, since all the data is stored on a few servers, and any software developments that need to be made apply to these servers only.

DATA SERVER

Data server stores data from many users

JAVA APPLET SERVER

Java applet server stores a wide range of compact, downloadable programs

MODEM

High-speed Internet links via modems and other devices

Monitor

Thin client computer consists of a basic processor and input/output devices

Thin client

Mouse

Keyboard

THIN CLIENT COMPUTER
The thin client NC is halfway between a PC and a dumb terminal, used on mainframe computers. A dumb terminal consists only of a keyboard and a monitor – all processing and data storage is carried out centrally by the mainframe. Like dumb terminals, NCs have no local disk storage, but like PCs, they do have a processor. In addition to being smaller and cheaper than PCs, NCs should be more reliable, since they do not have complex peripherals with moving parts, such as disk drives.

Monitor

Applet
developers
write software
for the servers

Server

**APPLET
DEVELOPERS' SYSTEM**

*Different regions of the
network are separated
for security purposes
by firewalls*

FIREWALL

*Firewalls limit access
to authorized users*

DISTRIBUTED COMPUTING

Network computing has been made possible because
the computer industry has agreed hardware and software
standards, including a new language, Java. When a thin
client – or a fat client acting as a Java station – is switched
on, its basic boot-up software connects to a network and
downloads the full Java operating system. The user can
then download Java application programs (called applets)
and data required, paying any fee with a smart card.
High-speed links between client and server mean that
processing tasks can be distributed between computers,
so the applets can be relatively small. In network
computing, the main burden falls not on the client
machines but on the network. Whether the present
Internet infrastructure (phone lines, cables, etc.) has
the required capacity, speed, and reliability to support
network computing remains to be seen.

VIRTUAL WORLDS ON THE NET

The World Wide Web has brought multimedia –
graphics, animations, sound, and hyperlinking – to
the Internet. The Virtual World Wide Web (VWWW),
with virtual environments, is a further development
where users can interact graphically with each other.
Typical VWWW environments are spread across
sites on the Net and on a CD-ROM. The basic
program runs from the CD, but "interactions"
between users occur at VWWW sites.

VIRTUAL PARIS

3D ENVIRONMENTS
All three-dimensional virtual worlds
must first be rendered in ink, as shown
below, after which the illustrations are
digitized by a computer.

3D drawing
of Paris
buildings

*The CD-
ROM is
based on
a series of
detailed
sketches*

CITIZENS OF A VIRTUAL WORLD
When a user logs on to a virtual world, he or she chooses a graphical
identity; this is how they will appear on other users' screens around
the world. These virtual people stroll around and meet in virtual
streets – although the real users might be thousands of miles apart.

Style and
measure-
ment
categories

*Users can
choose their
appearance
and their
personality*

REAL SERVICES IN A VIRTUAL SOCIETY
Some features of a virtual world are purely fictional, like a user's
graphical identity, while the streets or environment may be based
on a real place. But, as in the real Paris, you can "walk" into a store,
shop using your real credit card, and have the real goods delivered.

*Virtual
transport
takes the
user to
other
worlds*

*Home
shopping
services are
located
around the
virtual city*

Galileo spacecraft

IN DECEMBER 1995, the Galileo spacecraft finally arrived at the planet Jupiter. More than six years after it had been launched by NASA, the spacecraft's atmospheric probe, which had separated from the orbiter four months earlier, plunged through the gas giant's intense radiation belts, and deep into its atmosphere. The onboard electronic systems had to be heavily shielded to protect them against the radiation and temperatures twice as hot as the Sun's surface. As the probe parachuted into Jupiter's atmosphere, pulled in by the enormous gravity, the orbiter passed close to the planet, receiving and storing information for later relay back to Earth. This was just the start of the Galileo mission – since 1995, the orbiter has been circling Jupiter and recording information about its weather and its planet-sized moons. Before arriving at Jupiter, Galileo photographed the impact of Comet P/Shoemaker-Levy 9 with Jupiter, the largest explosion ever seen in the Solar System. More recently, the spacecraft has photographed volcanic activity on the moon Io, and found evidence of water beneath the icy crust of another moon, Europa.

PLANET JUPITER

GALILEO'S JOURNEY

As it began its six-year flight, Galileo moved away from Earth towards Venus, then doubled back, using the gravitational fields of Venus and Earth to propel it towards Jupiter.

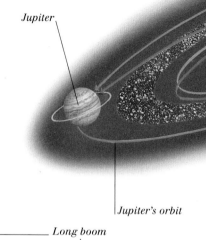

Jupiter

Jupiter's orbit

LIFE ON MARS?

Organic molecules thought to be from Mars were recently found in a 4.5 billion-year-old rock that fell into the Antarctic 13,000 years ago. Mineral features suggesting biological activity and possible microscopic fossils of bacteria-like organisms were discovered.

Composition matches Martian rock

Water-penetrated cracks

MARTIAN METEORITE

Hydrocarbon deposits

Possible microfossil

Rock structure

MICROSCOPIC VIEW OF METEORITE

Long boom carrying magnetic sensors

Low-gain antenna

Double-dish antenna

Retro propulsion module

Atmospheric sampling instrument

Atmospheric descent module

Atmospheric descent probe module

Camera package

Instruments package

Radioisotope thermoelectric generator

GALILEO

The main body of the spacecraft circling Jupiter is known as the orbiter. The probe, on the left of the diagram, descended into Jupiter's atmosphere. The probe consists of a descent module and a deceleration module; the latter protects the former from excessive heat, separating off and slowing the probe's descent.

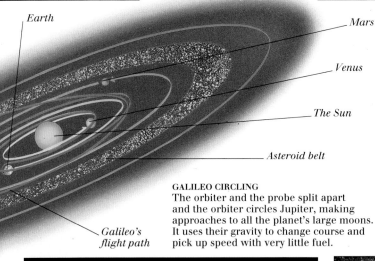

Earth

Mars

Venus

The Sun

Asteroid belt

Galileo's flight path

GALILEO CIRCLING
The orbiter and the probe split apart and the orbiter circles Jupiter, making approaches to all the planet's large moons. It uses their gravity to change course and pick up speed with very little fuel.

COMET SHOEMAKER-LEVY 9
From 16 to 22 July 1994, pieces of a comet designated P/Shoemaker-Levy 9 collided with the planet Jupiter. This was the first collision of two Solar System bodies ever to be observed. While other comets revolve around the Sun, Shoemaker-Levy 9 – named after its discoverers, Eugene and Carolyn Shoemaker and David Levy – moved around Jupiter in a very unusual elongated orbit within a period of just over two years. It became clear that the comet had recently been "captured" by the gravitational field of the planet and would soon collide with it.

Close encounter with Jupiter in 1992 broke comet apart

The gravities of Jupiter and the Sun string fragments out

Pieces consist of fragments of ice and dust

Antenna transmits data back to Earth

Erupting volcano on the moon Io

Io, Jupiter's largest moon

Jupiter

Fragment up to two kilometres in diameter

Surrounding debris cloud

Fragment a few hundred metres in diameter

TRAVELLING COMET
The comet consisted of at least 21 discernible icy fragments with diameters estimated at up to two kilometres. The fragments stretched across 1.1 million kilometres (710,000 miles) of space, almost three times the distance between Earth and the Moon.

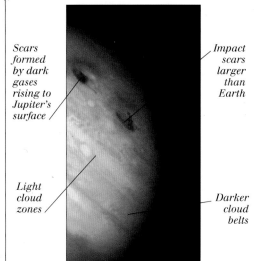

Main parachute

Descent module

Protective shield of deceleration module

THE PROBE DESCENDING
The probe descended through Jupiter's atmosphere gathering data. The descent module split from the deceleration module and a parachute slowed its rate of descent. The module descended for 57 minutes before burning out.

Scars formed by dark gases rising to Jupiter's surface

Impact scars larger than Earth

Light cloud zones

Darker cloud belts

POINT OF IMPACT
The impacts of the comet on Jupiter's atmosphere have been spectacular, with plumes thousands of kilometres high, hot "bubbles" of gas in the atmosphere, and large dark "scars".

Genetic advances

DEVELOPMENTS IN CLONING are among the most important advances in recent genetic science. A clone is a group of genes, cells, or complete organisms in which all of the group's members have the same genetic constitution. The term is also used to refer to individual members of a clone. Clones occur in nature, especially in the case of simple organisms, such as bacteria and viruses, which reproduce merely by splitting (asexual reproduction) after their DNA has replicated itself. They also occur in humans and other animals when a single fertilized egg divides and separates to form two or more identical individuals. Artificial cloning of selected genes is one of the most significant breakthroughs ever made in biology and has powerful implications for both science and industry. Once the desired gene is obtained, the cloning can be left to organisms such as bacteria, which, under suitable conditions, reproduce almost indefinitely. In this way, enormous quantities of the particular gene may be produced. Gene cloning is most commonly done in the laboratory by means of the polymerase chain reaction (PCR), which can produce millions of copies of a single gene in a matter of hours. Far more daunting an enterprise than gene cloning is the cloning of whole animals (see below right), only recently shown to be practicable. A further key genetic advance is the creation of transgenic animals, in particular pigs, which are currently being used for the "manufacture" of human-compatible organs, such as hearts.

HUMAN HEART

CREATING A TRANSGENIC ANIMAL

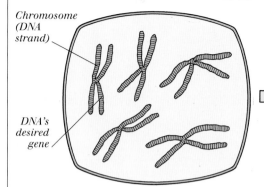

Chromosome (DNA strand)

DNA's desired gene

IDENTIFICATION
The desired gene contained within the DNA strand (chromosome) is identified.

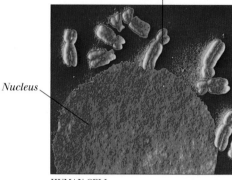

Chromosome

Nucleus

HUMAN CELL
After cell division, perfect copies of each of its chromosomes are passed to each of the daughter cells.

BSE

Among the more worrying aspects of biological research is the discovery that the brain disease bovine spongiform encephalopathy (BSE) is identical to the fatal human condition Creutzfeldt-Jakob disease (CJD). There is general agreement that the introduction of bovine tissue from affected animals into the food chain was the cause of the recent BSE epidemic. Although the genetic modification of animals is unlikely to involve the genes active in BSE, the number of unanswered questions has caused much concern about the propriety of the procedure.

GENETICALLY MODIFIED FOODS

An increasingly common practice in the food industry is the genetic modification of foodstuffs in order to extend their shelf life. This means that not only foods, for example fruit and vegetables, but also food ingredients and additives that contain genes derived from animals, fish, insects, and viruses, will appear in shops unlabelled as such.

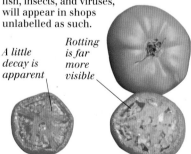

A little decay is apparent

Rotting is far more visible

GENETICALLY MODIFIED TOMATO

"NATURAL" TOMATO OF THE SAME AGE

ANIMAL CLONING

To produce a clone of an animal, a sample of its DNA must be used. Since each body cell contains a complete DNA genome, this is easily obtained. This DNA has to be introduced into an ovum (egg) of another animal of the same species after the ovum's original DNA is extracted. The egg is then inserted into a surrogate animal's womb and the pregnancy proceeds as normal. Although every body cell contains a complete genome, it will normally activate only those genes necessary for its own body part – for example kidney, brain, or bone. The other genes are not needed and are not "switched on". However, if the cell is starved of nutrients, development can be stopped at an early stage, at which point all the genes can be operative. The ovum into which the DNA is inserted will then behave as if the DNA were its own.

A donor provides the cell for cloning, e.g. mammary cell

CELL DONOR

A ewe provides an egg

EGG DONOR

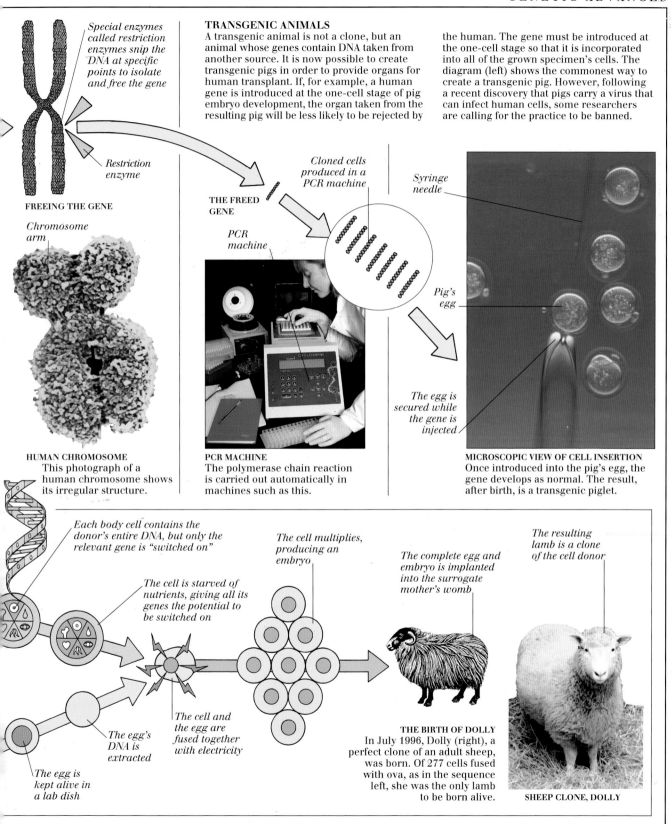

Special enzymes called restriction enzymes snip the DNA at specific points to isolate and free the gene

Restriction enzyme

FREEING THE GENE

Chromosome arm

HUMAN CHROMOSOME
This photograph of a human chromosome shows its irregular structure.

TRANSGENIC ANIMALS

A transgenic animal is not a clone, but an animal whose genes contain DNA taken from another source. It is now possible to create transgenic pigs in order to provide organs for human transplant. If, for example, a human gene is introduced at the one-cell stage of pig embryo development, the organ taken from the resulting pig will be less likely to be rejected by the human. The gene must be introduced at the one-cell stage so that it is incorporated into all of the grown specimen's cells. The diagram (left) shows the commonest way to create a transgenic pig. However, following a recent discovery that pigs carry a virus that can infect human cells, some researchers are calling for the practice to be banned.

THE FREED GENE

Cloned cells produced in a PCR machine

PCR machine

PCR MACHINE
The polymerase chain reaction is carried out automatically in machines such as this.

Syringe needle

Pig's egg

The egg is secured while the gene is injected

MICROSCOPIC VIEW OF CELL INSERTION
Once introduced into the pig's egg, the gene develops as normal. The result, after birth, is a transgenic piglet.

Each body cell contains the donor's entire DNA, but only the relevant gene is "switched on"

The cell multiplies, producing an embryo

The complete egg and embryo is implanted into the surrogate mother's womb

The resulting lamb is a clone of the cell donor

The cell is starved of nutrients, giving all its genes the potential to be switched on

The cell and the egg are fused together with electricity

The egg's DNA is extracted

The egg is kept alive in a lab dish

THE BIRTH OF DOLLY
In July 1996, Dolly (right), a perfect clone of an adult sheep, was born. Of 277 cells fused with ova, as in the sequence left, she was the only lamb to be born alive.

SHEEP CLONE, DOLLY

DNA update

ON 7 MARCH 1997, scientists from Oxford University, England, completed several months of tests and experiments and successfully extracted human DNA from a 9,000-year-old Stone Age skull. Following the DNA extraction, the scientists took samples from many staff and pupils at a school near to the skull's old resting place in a bid to identify any descendents that might still be in the area. The results of these tests exceeded all expectations when matching mitochondrial DNA was found in a local teacher.

Prehistory skull from which DNA was obtained

The complete 9,000-year-old skeleton

HISTORY TEACHER
Matching DNA was found in 42-year-old history teacher Adrian Targett, who only took part to "make up the numbers". The results show that he is linked to the skeleton via a female line of descent.

MATERNAL ORIGIN
Mitochondrial DNA derives only from the ovum and therefore can only be inherited from the mother. If it does not mutate, it can pass through countless generations.

Human cell

Mitochondrial DNA

OLDEST SKELETON
Found in 1903 in a cave in Cheddar Gorge, Somerset, the 9,000-year-old Stone Age skull is part of the oldest complete skeleton ever unearthed in Britain. The limestone in the caves helped keep the DNA intact.

ACKNOWLEDGMENTS

Editor David T. Walton
Project editor Peter Jones
Art editors Sasha Kennedy, Dawn Terrey
Senior editor Louise Candlish
Senior art editor Tracy Hambleton-Miles
DTP designer Mark Bracey

Consultants
Mukul Patel (Interactive television, Network computers),
John Coiley (Tilting trains), Giles Sparrow (Galileo spacecraft),
Dr. Robert Youngson (Genetic advances, DNA update)

Managing editor Christine Winters
Senior managing editor Sean Moore
Deputy art director Tina Vaughan

Illustrations
Nicolas H. T. Hall, Mick Gillah, Geoff Denny

Photography Andy Crawford

Picture research Angela Anderson
Production Sarah Coltman

Dorling Kindersley would like to thank:
Additional Assistance
Mike Flynn, Neil Lockley, Simon Murrell, Clare Ryder, Richard Sinclair (DK Adult); Christine Baker, Eric Pierrat (Gallimard); Sylvia Tombesi, Steve Howard

The publisher would like to thank the following for their kind permission to reproduce photographs and artworks:

ADtranz VIII tl; **Canal +** XI rt, rct, rcb, rb; **Galaxy Picture Library** XII tl, XIII br; **Genesis Space Photo Library** XII–XIII ca; **K. Hiwatashi** VI tl; **Shunji Ishiba** VI–VII cr; **Kansai International Airport Co. Ltd.** VI–VII c, VII tr; **NASA** XII bl, XII–XIII tc, cr, bc, bcl, bl; **Panasonic UK Ltd.** III tr; **Renzo Piano Building Workshop** VI l; **Press Association** XV br; **Science Photo Library** XIV–XV cr, cl, crb, c; **SNCF** VIII tr, IX tl; **South West News Service** XVI l, r; **Frank Spooner Pictures** II br; **Tony Stone Images** XIV tl; **Sun Microsystems** X bl, X–XI tc; **Sygma** I, IV–V (all except IV bl © Stephane Compoint; IV bl © Gedeon-Exmachina), XIV bl (© N. Warren Winter); **West Japan Railways** VIII bl, IX br, VIII–IX clb; **Westminster Cable** II bl, II–III cl

(t=top, b=bottom, a=above, l=left, r=right, c=centre)

Every effort has been made to trace the copyright holders. Dorling Kindersley apologizes for any unintentional omissions and would be pleased, in such cases, to add an acknowledgment in future editions.

ULTIMATE
VISUAL
DICTIONARY

**EXTERNAL FEATURES
OF A BUTTERFLY**

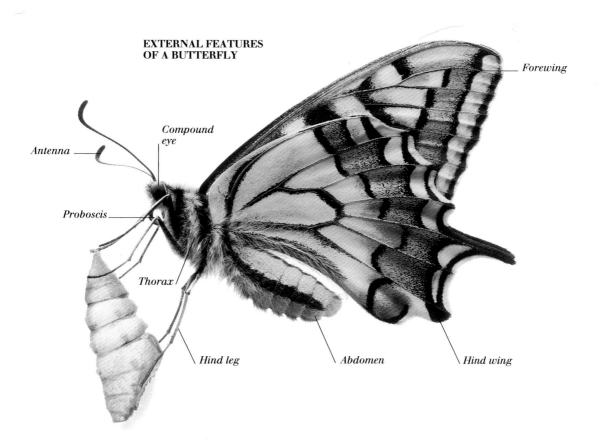

Forewing

Antenna

Compound
eye

Proboscis

Thorax

Hind leg

Abdomen

Hind wing

INTERNAL FEATURES OF BRACHIOSAURUS

First electron shell

Second electron shell

Nucleus

ANATOMY OF A FLUORINE–19 ATOM

Location of Solar System

Nucleus

OVERHEAD VIEW OF OUR GALAXY

Ovary

Bract

Pith

Cervical musculature

LONGITUDINAL SECTION THROUGH SUNFLOWER INFLORESCENCE

Lung

Fault plane

Dip of fault plane

Hade of fault plane

STRUCTURE OF A FAULT

Gizzard

Exhaust port

Floral design

VELOCETTE OHV ENGINE

MOSAIC DESIGN

Metacarpal

ULTIMATE
VISUAL
DICTIONARY

Figurehead

Cat block

Catted
anchor

Riband

Frame

BOW OF A 74–GUN SHIP

Ankle joint

COVENT
GARDEN
BOOKS

A DORLING KINDERSLEY BOOK

VISIT US ON THE WORLD WIDE WEB AT http://www.dk.com

PROJECT ART EDITORS HEATHER MCCARRY, JOHNNY PAU, CHRIS WALKER, KEVIN WILLIAMS
DESIGNER SIMON MURRELL

PROJECT EDITORS LUISA CARUSO, PETER JONES, JANE MASON, GEOFFREY STALKER
EDITOR JO EVANS

DTP DESIGNER ZIRRINIA AUSTIN
PICTURE RESEARCHER CHARLOTTE BUSH

MANAGING ART EDITOR TONI KAY
SENIOR EDITOR ROGER TRITTON
MANAGING EDITOR SEAN MOORE

PRODUCTION MANAGER HILARY STEPHENS

ANATOMICAL AND BOTANICAL MODELS SUPPLIED BY SOMSO MODELLE, COBURG, GERMANY

Sound-hole

Hollow body

Bridge

Headstock

ACOUSTIC GUITAR

FIRST PUBLISHED IN GREAT BRITAIN IN 1994
BY DORLING KINDERSLEY LIMITED,
9 HENRIETTA STREET, LONDON WC2E 8PS

REVISED EDITION © 1996

COPYRIGHT © 1994 DORLING KINDERSLEY LIMITED, LONDON

This 1998 edition published by Covent Garden Books

2 4 6 8 10 9 7 5 3

A CIP CATALOGUE RECORD FOR THIS BOOK IS AVAILABLE FROM THE BRITISH LIBRARY

ISBN 1 87185 4008

REPRODUCED BY COLOURSCAN, SINGAPORE
PRINTED AND BOUND BY STAR STANDARD INDUSTRIES, SINGAPORE.

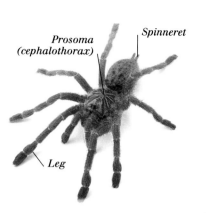

Prosoma (cephalothorax)

Spinneret

Leg

EXTERNAL FEATURES OF A SPIDER

Canopy

Fin

G-BNHB

Main landing gear

SIDE VIEW OF ARV SUPER 2 AEROPLANE

CONTENTS

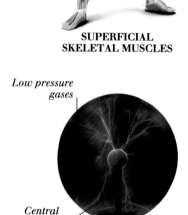

Brachialis

Frontalis

Deltoid

Rectus femoris

SUPERFICIAL SKELETAL MUSCLES

Barrel

Permanent black ink

FOUNTAIN PEN AND INK

Architrave

Podium

TEMPLE OF VESTA, TIVOLI, ITALY, c.80 BC

Sepal

Pedicel (flower stalk)

Swollen fleshy tissues of receptacle

LONGITUDINAL SECTION THROUGH A STRAWBERRY

Low pressure gases

Central electrode

BALL CONTAINING HIGH TEMPERATURE GAS (PLASMA)

Non–breakable plastic

Shock absorber

AMERICAN FOOTBALL HELMET

Introduction

THE ULTIMATE VISUAL DICTIONARY is a completely new kind of reference book. It provides a link between pictures and words in a way that no ordinary dictionary ever has. Most dictionaries simply tell you what a word means, but the *Ultimate Visual Dictionary* shows you – through a combination of detailed annotations, explicit photographs, and illustrations. In the *Ultimate Visual Dictionary*, pictures define the annotations around them. You do not read definitions of the annotated words, you see them. The highly accessible format of the *Ultimate Visual Dictionary*, the thoroughness of its annotations, and the range of its subject matter make it a unique and helpful reference tool.

***How to use the* Ultimate Visual Dictionary**
You will find the *Ultimate Visual Dictionary* simple to use. Instead of being organized alphabetically, it is divided by subject into 14 sections – The Universe, Prehistoric Earth, Plants, Animals, The Human Body, etc. Each section begins with a table of contents listing the major entries within that section. For example, The Visual Arts section has entries on *Drawing, Tempera, Fresco, Oils, Watercolour, Pastels, Acrylics, Calligraphy, Printmaking, Mosaic*, and *Sculpture*. Every entry has a short introduction explaining the purpose of the photographs and illustrations, and the significance of the annotations.

If you know what something looks like, but don't know its name, turn to the annotations surrounding the pictures; if you know a word, but don't know what it refers to, use the comprehensive index to direct you to the appropriate page.

Suppose that you want to know what the bone at the end of your little finger is called. With a standard dictionary, you wouldn't know where to begin. But with the *Ultimate Visual Dictionary* you simply turn to the entry called *Hands* – within The Human Body section – where you will find four fully annotated, colour photographs showing the skin, muscles, and bones of the human hand. In this entry you will quickly find that the bone you are searching for is called the distal phalanx, and for good measure you will discover that it is attached to the middle phalanx by the distal interphalangeal joint.

Perhaps you want to know what a catalytic converter looks like. If you look up "catalytic converter" in an ordinary dictionary, you will be told what it is and possibly what it does – but you will not be able to tell what shape it is or what it is made of. However, if you look up "catalytic converter" in the index of the *Ultimate Visual Dictionary*, you will be directed to the *Modern engines* entry on page 344 – where the introduction gives you basic information about what a catalytic converter is – and to page 350 – where there is a spectacular exploded-view photograph of the mechanics of a Renault Clio. From these pages you will find out not only what a catalytic converter looks like, but also that it is attached at one end to an exhaust downpipe and at the other to a silencer.

Whatever it is that you want to find a name for, or whatever name you want to find a picture for, you will find it quickly and easily in the *Ultimate Visual Dictionary*. Perhaps you need to know where the vamp on a shoe is; or how to tell obovate and lanceolate leaves apart; or what a spiral galaxy looks like; or whether birds have nostrils. With the *Ultimate Visual Dictionary* at hand, the answers to each of these questions, and thousands more, are readily available.

The *Ultimate Visual Dictionary* does not just tell you what the names of the different parts of an object are. The photographs, illustrations, and annotations are all specially arranged to help you understand which parts relate to one another and how objects function.

With the *Ultimate Visual Dictionary* you can find in seconds the words or pictures that you are looking for; or you can simply browse through the pages of the book for your own pleasure. The *Ultimate Visual Dictionary* is not intended to replace a standard dictionary or encyclopedia, but is instead a stimulating and valuable companion to ordinary reference volumes. Giving you access to the language that is used by astronomers and architects, musicians and mechanics, scientists and sportspeople, it is the ideal reference book for specialists and generalists of all ages.

Sections of the ULTIMATE VISUAL DICTIONARY
The 14 sections of the *Ultimate Visual Dictionary* contain a total of more than 30,000 terms, encompassing a wide range of topics:

● In the first section, THE UNIVERSE, spectacular photographs and illustrations are used to show the names of the stars and planets and to explain the structure of solar systems, galaxies, nebulae, comets, and black holes.

● PREHISTORIC EARTH tells the story in annotations of how our own planet has evolved since its formation. It includes examples of prehistoric flora and fauna, and fascinating dinosaur models – some with parts of the body stripped away to show anatomical sections.

● PLANTS covers a huge range of species – from the familiar to the exotic. In addition to the colour photographs of plants included in this section, there is a series of micrographic photographs illustrating plant details – such as pollen grains, spores, and cross-sections of stems and roots – in close-up.

● In the ANIMALS section, skeletons, anatomical diagrams, and different parts of animals' bodies have been meticulously annotated. This section provides a comprehensive guide to the vocabulary of zoological classification and animal physiology.

● The structure of the human body, its parts, and its systems are presented in THE HUMAN BODY. The section includes lifelike, three-dimensional models and the latest false-colour images. Clear and authoritative annotations indicate the correct anatomical terms.

● GEOLOGY, GEOGRAPHY, AND METEOROLOGY describes the structure of the Earth – from the inner core to the exosphere – and the physical phenomena – such as volcanoes, rivers, glaciers, and climate – that shape its surface.

● PHYSICS AND CHEMISTRY is a visual journey through the fundamental principles underlying the physical universe, and provides the essential vocabulary of these sciences.

● In RAIL AND ROAD, a wide range of trains, trams and buses, cars, bicycles, and motorcycles are described. Exploded-view photographs show mechanical details with striking clarity.

● SEA AND AIR gives the names for hundreds of parts of ships and aeroplanes. The section includes civil and fighting craft, both historical and modern.

● THE VISUAL ARTS shows the equipment and materials used by painters, sculptors, printers, and other artists. Well-known compositions have been chosen to illustrate specific artistic techniques and effects.

● ARCHITECTURE includes photographs of exemplary architectural models and illustrates dozens of additional features such as columns, domes, and arches.

● MUSIC provides a visual introduction to the special language of music and musical instruments. It includes clearly annotated photographs of each of the major groups of traditional instruments – brass, woodwind, strings, and percussion – together with modern electronic instruments.

● The SPORTS section is a guide to the playing areas, formations, equipment, and techniques needed for many of today's most popular sports.

● In EVERYDAY THINGS, familiar objects, such as shoes, clocks, and toasters, are taken apart – down to the very last screw or length of thread – to show their inner workings and to give a special insight into the language that is used by their manufacturers.

THE UNIVERSE

Anatomy of the Universe

Fireball of rapidly expanding, extremely hot gas lasting about one million years

THE UNIVERSE CONTAINS EVERYTHING that exists, from the tiniest subatomic particles to galactic superclusters (the largest structures known). Nobody knows how big the Universe is, but astronomers estimate that it contains about 100 billion galaxies, each comprising an average of 100 billion stars. The most widely accepted theory about the origin of the Universe is the Big Bang theory, which states that the Universe came into being in a huge explosion – the Big Bang – that took place between 10 and 20 billion years ago. The Universe initially consisted of a very hot, dense fireball of expanding, cooling gas. After about one million years, the gas probably began to condense into localized clumps called protogalaxies. During the next five billion years, the protogalaxies continued condensing, forming galaxies in which stars were being born. Today, billions of years later, the Universe as a whole is still expanding, although there are localized areas in which objects are held together by gravity; for example, many galaxies are found in clusters. The Big Bang theory is supported by the discovery of faint, cool background radiation coming evenly from all directions. This radiation is believed to be the remnant of the radiation produced by the Big Bang. Small "ripples" in the temperature of the cosmic background radiation are thought to be evidence of slight fluctuations in the density of the early Universe, which resulted in the formation of galaxies. Astronomers do not yet know if the Universe is "closed", which means it will eventually stop expanding and begin to contract, or if it is "open", which means it will continue expanding forever.

FALSE-COLOUR MICROWAVE MAP OF COSMIC BACKGROUND RADIATION

Pink indicates "warm ripples" in background radiation

Pale blue indicates "cool ripples" in background radiation

Deep blue indicates background radiation corresponding to -270.3°C (remnant of the Big Bang)

Red and pink band indicates radiation from our galaxy

Low-energy microwave radiation corresponding to about -270°C

High-energy gamma radiation corresponding to about 3,000°C

ORIGIN AND EXPANSION OF THE UNIVERSE

Quasar (probably the centre
of a galaxy containing a
massive black hole)

Universe one to five
billion years after
Big Bang

Protogalaxy
(condensing gas cloud)

Galaxy spinning and
flattening to become
spiral shaped

Dark cloud
(dust and gas
condensing
to form a
protogalaxy)

Elliptical
galaxy in
which stars
form rapidly

Universe today
(10–20 billion years
after Big Bang)

Cluster of
galaxies held
together by gravity

Elliptical galaxy
containing old stars
and little gas and dust

Irregular galaxy

Spiral galaxy
containing gas,
dust, and young stars

OBJECTS IN THE UNIVERSE

CLUSTER OF
GALAXIES IN VIRGO

FALSE-COLOUR IMAGE
OF 3C273 (QUASAR)

NGC 4406
(ELLIPTICAL GALAXY)

NGC 5236
(SPIRAL GALAXY)

NGC 6822
(IRREGULAR GALAXY)

THE ROSETTE NEBULA
(EMISSION NEBULA)

THE JEWEL BOX
(STAR CLUSTER)

THE SUN
(MAIN SEQUENCE STAR)

EARTH

THE MOON

Galaxies

**SOMBRERO,
A SPIRAL GALAXY**

A GALAXY IS A HUGE MASS OF STARS, nebulae, and interstellar material. The smallest galaxies contain about 100,000 stars, while the largest contain up to 3,000 billion stars. There are three main types of galaxy, classified according to their shape: elliptical, which are oval shaped; spiral, which have arms spiralling outwards from a central bulge; and irregular, which have no obvious shape. Sometimes, the shape of a galaxy is distorted by a collision with another galaxy. Quasars (quasi-stellar objects) are thought to be galactic nuclei but are so far away that their exact nature is still uncertain. They are compact, highly luminous objects in the outer reaches of the known Universe: while the furthest known "ordinary" galaxies are about 10 billion light years away, the furthest known quasar is about 15 billion light years away. Active galaxies, such as Seyfert galaxies and radio galaxies, emit intense radiation. In a Seyfert galaxy, this radiation comes from the galactic nucleus; in a radio galaxy, it also comes from huge lobes on either side of the galaxy. The radiation from active galaxies and quasars is thought to be caused by black holes (see pp. 28-29).

**OPTICAL IMAGE OF NGC 4486
(ELLIPTICAL GALAXY)**

Globular cluster containing very old red giants

Central region containing old red giants

Less densely populated region

Neighbouring galaxy

**OPTICAL IMAGE OF LARGE MAGELLANIC
CLOUD (IRREGULAR GALAXY)**

Tarantula Nebula

Dust cloud obscuring light from stars

Emission nebula

Light from stars

OPTICAL IMAGE OF NGC 2997 (SPIRAL GALAXY)

Glowing nebula in spiral arm

Spiral arm containing young stars

Galactic nucleus containing old stars

Dust in spiral arm reflecting blue light from hot young stars

Hot, ionized hydrogen gas emitting red light

Dust lane

OPTICAL IMAGE OF CENTAURUS A (RADIO GALAXY)

Dust lane crossing elliptical galaxy

Galactic nucleus containing powerful source of radiation

Light from old stars

FALSE-COLOUR RADIO IMAGE OF CENTAURUS A

Radio lobe

Red indicates high-intensity radio waves

Blue indicates low-intensity radio waves

Radiation from galactic nucleus

Outline of optical image of Centaurus A

Radio lobe

Yellow indicates medium-intensity radio waves

FALSE-COLOUR RADIO IMAGE OF 3C273 (QUASAR)

Radiation from jet of high-energy particles moving away from quasar

Quasar nucleus

Blue indicates low-intensity radio waves

White indicates high-intensity radio waves

OPTICAL IMAGE OF NGC 1566 (SEYFERT GALAXY)

Nebula in spiral arm

Compact nucleus emitting intense radiation

Spiral arm

FALSE-COLOUR OPTICAL IMAGE OF NGC 5754 (TWO COLLIDING GALAXIES)

Blue indicates low-intensity radiation

Red indicates medium-intensity radiation

Spiral arm distorted by gravitational influence of smaller galaxy

Large spiral galaxy

Smaller galaxy colliding with larger galaxy

Yellow indicates high-intensity radiation

The Milky Way

**VIEW TOWARDS
GALACTIC CENTRE**

THE MILKY WAY IS THE NAME GIVEN TO THE FAINT BAND OF LIGHT that stretches across the night sky. This light comes from stars and nebulae in our galaxy, known as the Milky Way Galaxy or simply as "the Galaxy". The Galaxy is shaped like a spiral, with a dense central bulge that is encircled by four arms spiralling outwards and surrounded by a less dense halo. We cannot see the spiral shape because the Solar System is in one of the spiral arms, the Orion Arm (also called the Local Arm). From our position, the centre of the Galaxy is completely obscured by dust clouds; as a result, optical maps give only a limited view of the Galaxy. However, a more complete picture can be obtained by studying radio, infra-red, and other radiation. The central bulge of the Galaxy is a relatively small, dense sphere that contains mainly older red and yellow stars. The halo is a less dense region in which the oldest stars are situated; some of these stars may be as old as the Galaxy itself (possibly 15 billion years). The spiral arms contain mainly hot, young, blue stars, as well as nebulae (clouds of dust and gas inside which stars are born). The Galaxy is vast, about 100,000 light years across (a light year is about 9,460 billion kilometres); in comparison, the Solar System seems small, at about 12 light hours across (about 13 billion kilometres). The entire Galaxy is rotating in space, although the inner stars travel faster than those further out. The Sun, which is about two-thirds out from the centre, completes one lap of the Galaxy about every 220 million years.

SIDE VIEW OF OUR GALAXY

Disc of spiral arms containing mainly young stars

Central bulge containing mainly older stars

Halo containing oldest stars

Nucleus

100,000 light years

OVERHEAD VIEW OF OUR GALAXY

Central bulge

Nucleus

Perseus Arm

Crux-Centaurus Arm

Dust in spiral arm reflecting blue light from hot young stars

Location of Solar System

Patch of dust clouds

Emission nebula

Sagittarius Arm

Orion Arm (Local Arm)

PANORAMIC OPTICAL MAP OF OUR GALAXY AND NEARBY GALAXIES

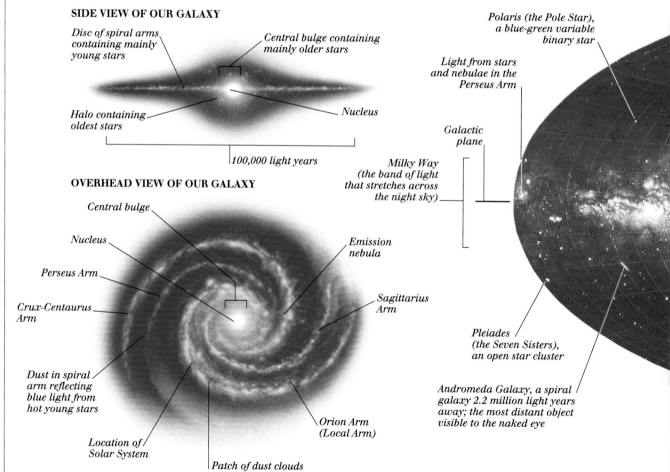

Polaris (the Pole Star), a blue-green variable binary star

Light from stars and nebulae in the Perseus Arm

Galactic plane

Milky Way (the band of light that stretches across the night sky)

Pleiades (the Seven Sisters), an open star cluster

Andromeda Galaxy, a spiral galaxy 2.2 million light years away; the most distant object visible to the naked eye

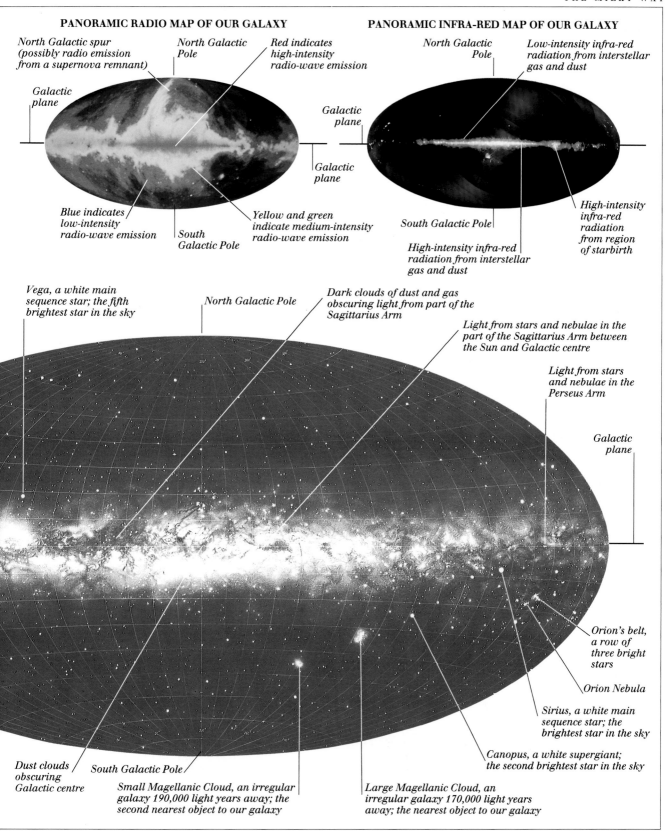

PANORAMIC RADIO MAP OF OUR GALAXY

North Galactic spur
(possibly radio emission
from a supernova remnant)

North Galactic
Pole

Red indicates
high-intensity
radio-wave emission

Galactic
plane

Galactic
plane

Galactic
plane

Blue indicates
low-intensity
radio-wave emission

South
Galactic Pole

Yellow and green
indicate medium-intensity
radio-wave emission

PANORAMIC INFRA-RED MAP OF OUR GALAXY

North Galactic
Pole

Low-intensity infra-red
radiation from interstellar
gas and dust

South Galactic Pole

High-intensity infra-red
radiation from interstellar
gas and dust

High-intensity
infra-red
radiation
from region
of starbirth

Vega, a white main
sequence star; the fifth
brightest star in the sky

North Galactic Pole

Dark clouds of dust and gas
obscuring light from part of the
Sagittarius Arm

Light from stars and nebulae in the
part of the Sagittarius Arm between
the Sun and Galactic centre

Light from stars
and nebulae in the
Perseus Arm

Galactic
plane

Orion's belt,
a row of
three bright
stars

Orion Nebula

Sirius, a white main
sequence star; the
brightest star in the sky

Canopus, a white supergiant;
the second brightest star in the sky

Dust clouds
obscuring
Galactic centre

South Galactic Pole

Small Magellanic Cloud, an irregular
galaxy 190,000 light years away; the
second nearest object to our galaxy

Large Magellanic Cloud, an
irregular galaxy 170,000 light years
away; the nearest object to our galaxy

Nebulae and star clusters

A NEBULA IS A CLOUD OF DUST AND GAS inside a galaxy. Nebulae become visible if the gas glows, or if the cloud reflects starlight or obscures light from more distant objects. Emission nebulae shine because their gas emits light when it is stimulated by radiation from hot young stars. Reflection nebulae shine because their dust reflects light from stars in or around the nebula. Dark nebulae appear as silhouettes because they block out light from shining nebulae or stars behind them. Two types of nebula are associated with dying stars: planetary nebulae and supernova remnants. Both consist of expanding shells of gas that were once the outer layers of a star. A planetary nebula is a gas shell drifting away from a dying stellar core. A supernova remnant

HODGE 11, A GLOBULAR CLUSTER

is a gas shell moving away from a stellar core at great speed following a violent explosion called a supernova (see pp. 26-27). Stars are often found in groups known as clusters. Open clusters are loose groups of a few thousand young stars that were born in the same cloud and are drifting apart. Globular clusters are densely packed, roughly spherical groups of hundreds of thousands of older stars.

TRIFID NEBULA (EMISSION NEBULA)

Reflection nebula

Emission nebula

Dust lane

Starbirth region (area in which dust and gas clump together to form stars)

PLEIADES (OPEN STAR CLUSTER) WITH A REFLECTION NEBULA

Wisps of dust and hydrogen gas remaining from cloud in which stars formed

Young star in an open cluster of 300–500 stars

Reflection nebula

HORSEHEAD NEBULA (DARK NEBULA)

Glowing filament of hot, ionized hydrogen gas

Alnitak (star in Orion's belt)

Dust lane

Emission nebula

Star near southern end of Orion's belt

Emission nebula

Horsehead Nebula

Reflection nebula

Dark nebula obscuring light from distant stars

ORION NEBULA (DIFFUSE EMISSION NEBULA)

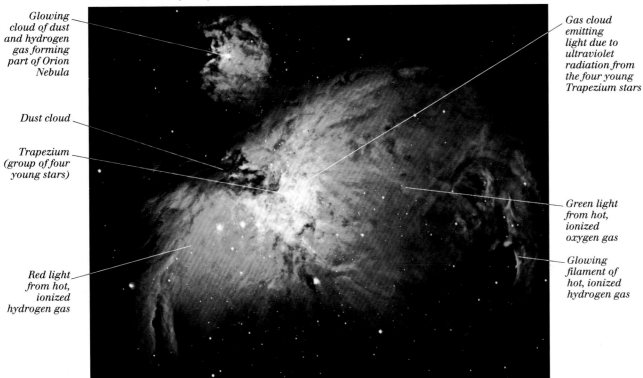

Glowing cloud of dust and hydrogen gas forming part of Orion Nebula

Gas cloud emitting light due to ultraviolet radiation from the four young Trapezium stars

Dust cloud

Trapezium (group of four young stars)

Green light from hot, ionized oxygen gas

Glowing filament of hot, ionized hydrogen gas

Red light from hot, ionized hydrogen gas

VELA SUPERNOVA REMNANT

Supernova remnant (gas shell consisting of outer layers of star thrown off in supernova explosion)

Hydrogen gas emitting red light due to being heated by supernova explosion

HELIX NEBULA (PLANETARY NEBULA)

Planetary nebula (gas shell expanding outwards from dying stellar core)

Stellar core at a temperature of about 100,000°C

Red light from hot, ionized hydrogen gas

Blue-green light from hot, ionized oxygen and nitrogen gases

Glowing filament of hot, ionized hydrogen gas

17

Stars of northern skies

WHEN YOU LOOK AT THE NORTHERN SKY, you look away from the densely populated Galactic centre, so the northern sky generally appears less bright than the southern sky (see pp. 20-21). Among the best-known sights in the northern sky are the constellations Ursa Major (the Great Bear) and Orion. Some ancient civilizations believed that the stars were fixed to a celestial sphere surrounding the Earth, and modern maps of the sky are based on a similar idea. The North and South Poles of this imaginary celestial sphere are directly above the North and South Poles of the Earth, at the points where the Earth's axis of rotation intersects the sphere. The celestial North Pole is at the centre of the map shown here, and Polaris (the Pole Star) lies very close to it. The celestial equator marks a projection of the Earth's equator on the sphere. The ecliptic marks the path of the Sun across the sky as the Earth orbits the Sun. The Moon and planets move against the background of the stars because the stars are much more distant; the nearest star outside the Solar System (Proxima Centauri) is more than 50,000 times further away than the planet Jupiter.

ORION

- Chi$_2$ Orionis
- Chi$_1$ Orionis
- Nu Orionis
- Xi Orionis
- Heka
- Mu Orionis
- Bellatrix
- Betelgeuse
- Omicron Orionis
- Orion's belt
- Pi$_2$ Orionis
- Pi$_3$ Orionis
- Alnitak
- Pi$_4$ Orionis
- Pi$_5$ Orionis
- Pi$_6$ Orionis
- Saiph
- Mintaka
- Eta Orionis
- Tau Orionis
- Orion Nebula
- Rigel
- Alnilam

VISIBLE STARS IN THE NORTHERN SKY

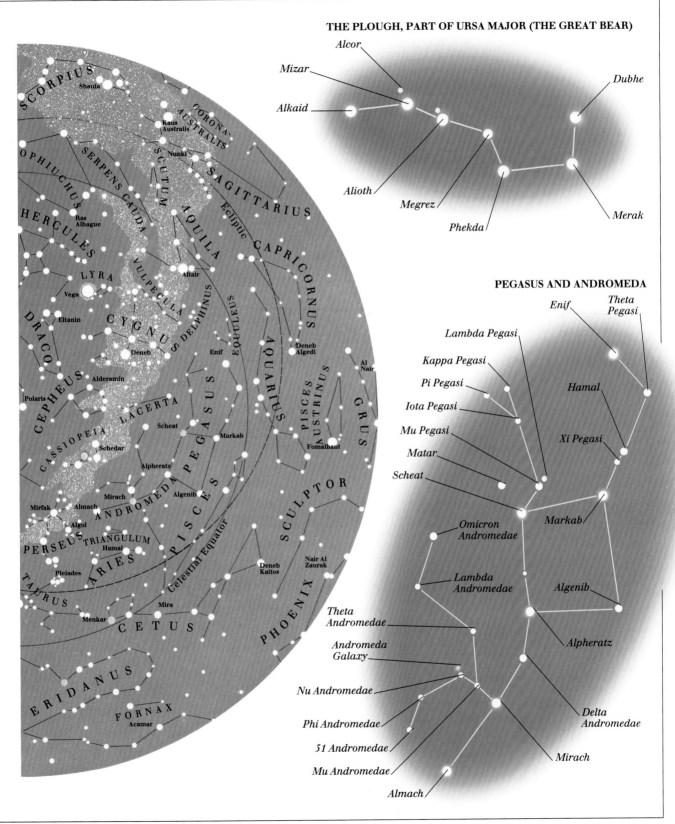

THE PLOUGH, PART OF URSA MAJOR (THE GREAT BEAR)

Alcor
Mizar
Alkaid
Dubhe
Alioth
Megrez
Merak
Phekda

PEGASUS AND ANDROMEDA

Enif
Theta Pegasi
Lambda Pegasi
Kappa Pegasi
Hamal
Pi Pegasi
Iota Pegasi
Xi Pegasi
Mu Pegasi
Matar
Scheat
Markab
Omicron Andromedae
Lambda Andromedae
Algenib
Alpheratz
Theta Andromedae
Andromeda Galaxy
Nu Andromedae
Delta Andromedae
Phi Andromedae
51 Andromedae
Mirach
Mu Andromedae
Almach

SCORPIUS
Shaula
CORONA AUSTRALIS
Kaus Australis
SERPENS CAUDA
SCUTUM
SAGITTARIUS
Nunki
OPHIUCHUS
AQUILA
Ras Alhague
Ecliptic
CAPRICORNUS
HERCULES
Altair
LYRA
VULPECULA
Vega
DELPHINUS
CYGNUS
EQUULEUS
Eltanin
AQUARIUS
Deneb
Enif
Deneb Algedi
DRACO
Al Nair
CEPHEUS
Alderamin
PISCES AUSTRINUS
LACERTA
GRUS
Polaris
PEGASUS
Scheat
Fomalhaut
CASSIOPEIA
Markab
Schedar
Alpheratz
SCULPTOR
Mirfak
Mirach
Algenib
ANDROMEDA
Almach
PISCES
Algol
PERSEUS
TRIANGULUM
Hamal
Nair Al Zaurak
Pleiades
ARIES
Celestial Equator
Deneb Kaitos
PHOENIX
TAURUS
Mira
Menkar
CETUS
ERIDANUS
FORNAX
Acamar

Stars of southern skies

WHEN YOU LOOK AT THE SOUTHERN SKY, you look towards the Galactic centre, which has a huge population of stars. As a result, the Milky Way appears brighter in the southern sky than in the northern sky (see pp. 18-19). The southern sky is rich in nebulae and star clusters. It contains the Large and Small Magellanic Clouds, which are the two nearest galaxies to our own. Stars make fixed patterns in the sky called constellations. However, the constellations are only apparent groupings of stars, since the distances to the stars in a constellation may vary enormously. The shapes of constellations may change over many thousands of years due to the relative motions of stars. The movement of the constellations across the sky is due to the Earth's motion in space. The daily rotation of the Earth causes the constellations to move across the sky from east to west, and the orbit of the Earth around the Sun causes different areas of sky to be visible in different seasons. The visibility of areas of sky also depends on the location of the observer. For instance, stars near the celestial equator may be seen from either hemisphere at some time during the year, whereas stars close to the celestial poles (the celestial South Pole is at the centre of the map shown here) can never be seen from the opposite hemisphere.

**HYDRUS (THE WATER SNAKE) AND
MENSA (THE TABLE)**

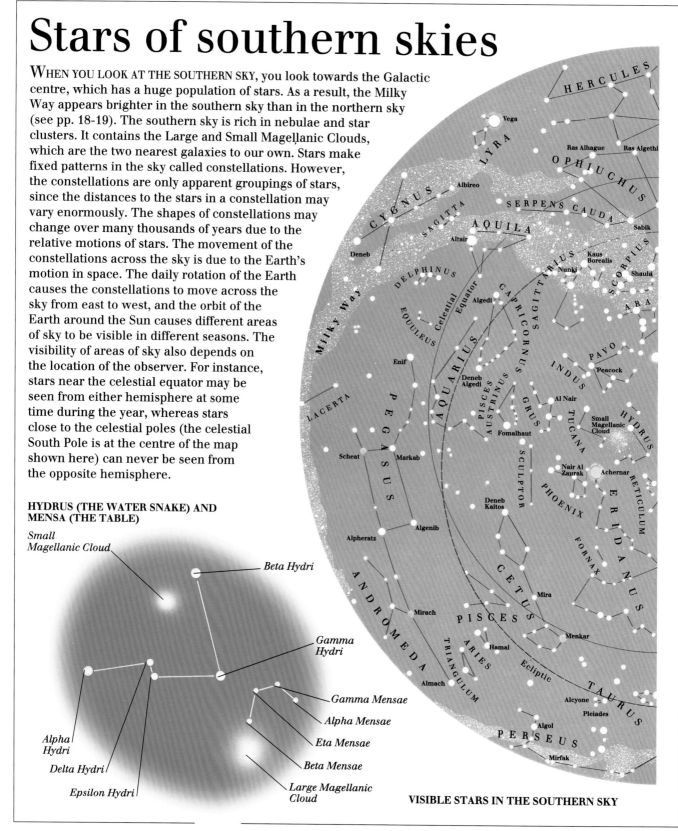

Small Magellanic Cloud

Beta Hydri

Gamma Hydri

Gamma Mensae

Alpha Mensae

Eta Mensae

Beta Mensae

Large Magellanic Cloud

Alpha Hydri

Delta Hydri

Epsilon Hydri

VISIBLE STARS IN THE SOUTHERN SKY

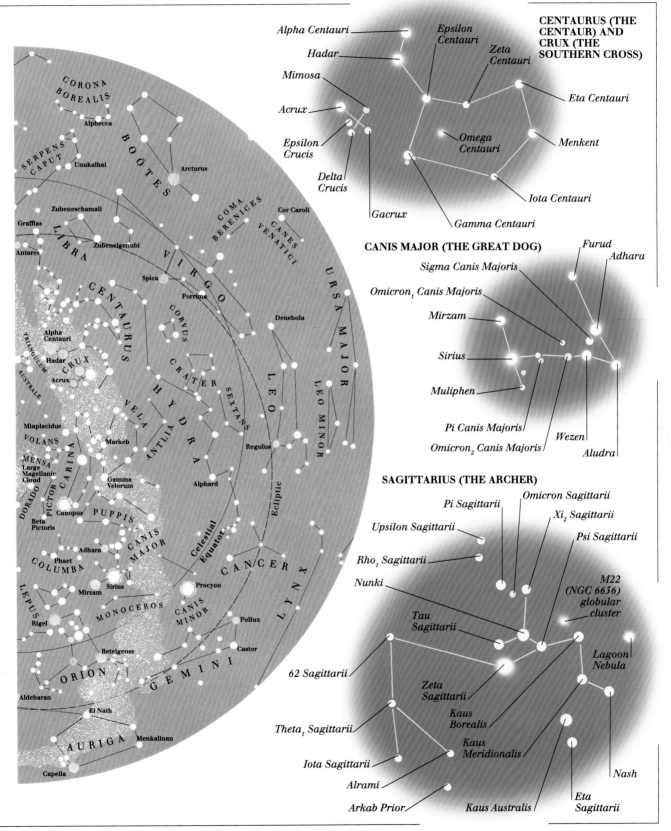

CENTAURUS (THE CENTAUR) AND CRUX (THE SOUTHERN CROSS)

Alpha Centauri
Epsilon Centauri
Hadar
Zeta Centauri
Mimosa
Eta Centauri
Acrux
Epsilon Crucis
Omega Centauri
Menkent
Delta Crucis
Gacrux
Iota Centauri
Gamma Centauri

CANIS MAJOR (THE GREAT DOG)

Furud
Adhara
Sigma Canis Majoris
Omicron$_1$ Canis Majoris
Mirzam
Sirius
Muliphen
Pi Canis Majoris
Wezen
Omicron$_2$ Canis Majoris
Aludra

SAGITTARIUS (THE ARCHER)

Omicron Sagittarii
Pi Sagittarii
Xi$_2$ Sagittarii
Upsilon Sagittarii
Psi Sagittarii
Rho$_1$ Sagittarii
M22 (NGC 6656) globular cluster
Nunki
Tau Sagittarii
Lagoon Nebula
62 Sagittarii
Zeta Sagittarii
Kaus Borealis
Theta$_1$ Sagittarii
Kaus Meridionalis
Iota Sagittarii
Nash
Alrami
Arkab Prior
Kaus Australis
Eta Sagittarii

CORONA BOREALIS
Alphecca
SERPENS CAPUT
Unukalhai
BOÖTES
Arcturus
Zubeneschamali
Grafflas
LIBRA
Zubenelgenubi
COMA BERENICES
Cor Caroli
CANES VENATICI
Antares
Spica
VIRGO
URSA MAJOR
CENTAURUS
Porrima
CORVUS
Denebola
Alpha Centauri
Hadar
CRUX
Acrux
HYDRA
CRATER
SEXTANS
LEO
LEO MINOR
TRIANGULUM AUSTRALE
VELA
ANTLIA
Miaplacidus
VOLANS
Markeb
Regulus
MENSA
Large Magellanic Cloud
Gamma Velorum
Alphard
DORADO
PICTOR
CARINA
Canopus
PUPPIS
Beta Pictoris
Celestial Equator
Ecliptic
Adhara
COLUMBA
Phaet
CANIS MAJOR
CANCER
LYNX
LEPUS
Mirzam
Sirius
MONOCEROS
Procyon
CANIS MINOR
Pollux
Rigel
Castor
Betelgeuse
ORION
GEMINI
Aldebaran
El Nath
Menkalinan
AURIGA
Capella

Stars

OPEN STAR CLUSTER AND DUST CLOUD

STARS ARE BODIES of hot, glowing gas that are born in nebulae (see pp. 24-27). They vary enormously in size, mass, and temperature: diameters range from about 450 times smaller to over 1,000 times bigger than that of the Sun; masses range from about a twentieth to over 50 solar masses; and surface temperatures range from about 3,000°C to over 50,000°C. The colour of a star is determined by its temperature: the hottest stars are blue and the coolest are red. The Sun, with a surface temperature of 5,500°C, is between these extremes and appears yellow. The energy emitted by a shining star is produced by nuclear fusion in the star's core. The brightness of a star is measured in magnitudes – the brighter the star, the lower its magnitude. There are two types of magnitude: apparent magnitude, which is the brightness seen from Earth, and absolute magnitude, which is the brightness that would be seen from a standard distance of 10 parsecs (32.6 light years). The light emitted by a star may be split to form a spectrum containing a series of dark lines (absorption lines). The patterns of lines indicate the presence of particular chemical elements, enabling astronomers to deduce the composition of the star's atmosphere. The magnitude and spectral type (colour) of stars may be plotted on a graph called a Hertzsprung-Russell diagram, which shows that stars tend to fall into several well-defined groups. The principal groups are main sequence stars (those which are fusing hydrogen to form helium), giants, supergiants, and white dwarfs.

STAR SIZES

Red giant (diameters between about 15 million and 150 million km)

The Sun (main sequence star with diameter about 1.4 million km)

White dwarf (diameters between about 3,000 and 50,000 km)

ENERGY EMISSION FROM THE SUN

Nuclear fusion in core produces gamma rays and neutrinos

Neutrinos travel to Earth directly from Sun's core in about 8 minutes

Lower-energy radiation travels to Earth in about 8 minutes

Earth

Sun

Lower-energy radiation (mainly ultraviolet, infra-red, and light rays) leaves surface

High-energy radiation (gamma rays) loses energy while travelling to surface over 2 million years

STAR MAGNITUDES

APPARENT MAGNITUDE

Brighter stars

-9

0

+9

Fainter stars

Sirius: apparent magnitude of -1.46

Rigel: apparent magnitude of +0.12

Objects of magnitude higher than about +5.5 cannot be seen by the naked eye

ABSOLUTE MAGNITUDE

Rigel: absolute magnitude of -7.1

Sirius: absolute magnitude of +1.4

NUCLEAR FUSION IN MAIN SEQUENCE STARS LIKE THE SUN

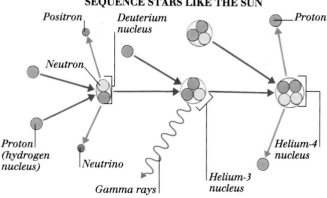

Positron

Deuterium nucleus

Proton

Neutron

Proton (hydrogen nucleus)

Neutrino

Gamma rays

Helium-3 nucleus

Helium-4 nucleus

HERTZSPRUNG-RUSSELL DIAGRAM

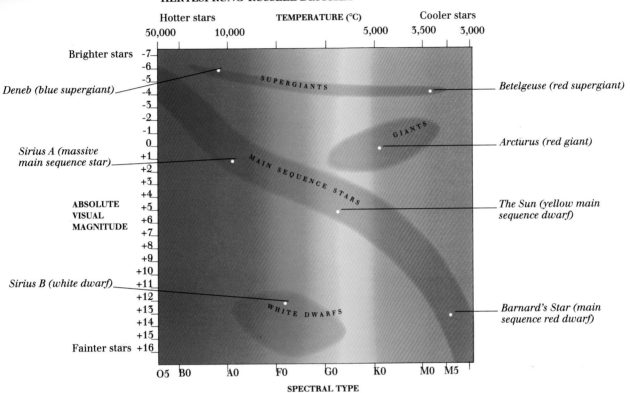

Hotter stars   **TEMPERATURE (°C)**   Cooler stars

50,000   10,000   5,000 3,500 3,000

Brighter stars -7

Deneb (blue supergiant)

SUPERGIANTS

Betelgeuse (red supergiant)

GIANTS

Arcturus (red giant)

Sirius A (massive main sequence star)

MAIN SEQUENCE STARS

The Sun (yellow main sequence dwarf)

ABSOLUTE VISUAL MAGNITUDE

Sirius B (white dwarf)

WHITE DWARFS

Barnard's Star (main sequence red dwarf)

Fainter stars +16

O5 B0   A0   F0   G0   K0   M0 M5

SPECTRAL TYPE

STELLAR SPECTRAL ABSORPTION LINES

Calcium line   Hydrogen gamma line   Hydrogen beta line   Helium line   Sodium lines   Hydrogen alpha line

STAR OF SPECTRAL TYPE A (e.g., SIRIUS)

STAR OF SPECTRAL TYPE G (e.g., THE SUN)

Hydrogen beta line   Magnesium lines   Sodium lines   Hydrogen alpha line

Small stars

REGION OF STAR FORMATION IN ORION

SMALL STARS HAVE A MASS of up to about one and a half times that of the Sun. They begin to form when a region of higher density in a nebula condenses into a huge globule of gas and dust that contracts under its own gravity. Within a globule, regions of condensing matter heat up and begin to glow, forming protostars. If a protostar contains enough matter, the central temperature reaches about 15 million °C. At this temperature, nuclear reactions in which hydrogen fuses to form helium can start. This process releases energy, which prevents the star from contracting further and also causes it to shine; it is now a main sequence star. A star of about one solar mass remains in the main sequence for about 10 billion years, until the hydrogen in the star's core has been converted into helium. The helium core then contracts again, and nuclear reactions continue in a shell around the core. The core becomes hot enough for helium to fuse to form carbon, while the outer layers of the star expand, cool, and shine less brightly. The expanding star is known as a red giant. When the helium in the core runs out, the outer layers of the star may drift off as an expanding gas shell called a planetary nebula. The remaining core (about 80 per cent of the original star) is now in its final stages. It becomes a white dwarf star that gradually cools and dims. When it finally stops shining altogether, the dead star will become a black dwarf.

STRUCTURE OF A MAIN SEQUENCE STAR

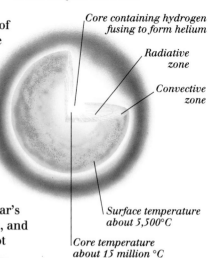

Core containing hydrogen fusing to form helium

Radiative zone

Convective zone

Surface temperature about 5,500°C

Core temperature about 15 million °C

STRUCTURE OF A NEBULA

Young main sequence star

Dense region of dust and gas (mainly hydrogen) condensing under gravity to form globules

Hot, ionized hydrogen gas emitting red light due to being stimulated by radiation from hot young stars

Dark globule of dust and gas (mainly hydrogen) contracting to form protostars

LIFE OF A SMALL STAR OF ABOUT ONE SOLAR MASS

Cool cloud of gas (mainly hydrogen) and dust

Dense globule condensing to form protostars

NEBULA

Glowing ball of gas (mainly hydrogen)

Natal cocoon (shell of dust blown away by radiation from protostar)

PROTOSTAR
Duration: 50 million years

About 1.4 million km

Star producing energy by nuclear fusion in core

MAIN SEQUENCE STAR
Duration: 10 billion years

STRUCTURE OF A RED GIANT

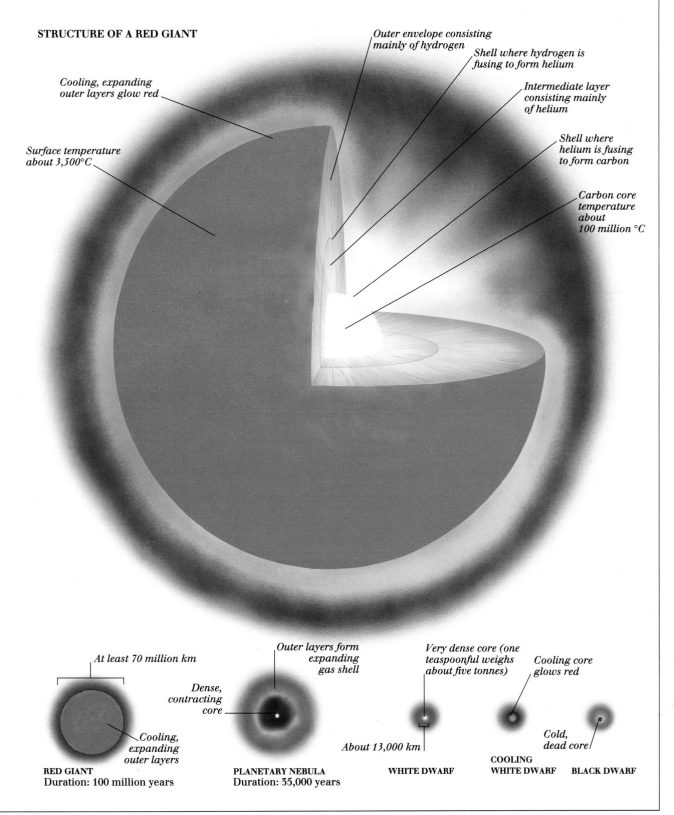

Outer envelope consisting mainly of hydrogen

Shell where hydrogen is fusing to form helium

Intermediate layer consisting mainly of helium

Shell where helium is fusing to form carbon

Carbon core temperature about 100 million °C

Cooling, expanding outer layers glow red

Surface temperature about 3,500°C

At least 70 million km

Cooling, expanding outer layers

RED GIANT
Duration: 100 million years

Outer layers form expanding gas shell

Dense, contracting core

PLANETARY NEBULA
Duration: 35,000 years

Very dense core (one teaspoonful weighs about five tonnes)

About 13,000 km

WHITE DWARF

Cooling core glows red

COOLING WHITE DWARF

Cold, dead core

BLACK DWARF

Massive stars

MASSIVE STARS HAVE A MASS AT LEAST THREE TIMES that of the Sun, and some stars are as massive as about 50 Suns. A massive star evolves in a similar way to a small star until it reaches the main sequence stage (see pp. 24-25). During the main sequence, a star shines steadily until the hydrogen in its core has fused to form helium. This process takes billions of years in a small star, but only millions of years in a massive star. A massive star then becomes a red supergiant, which initially consists of a helium core surrounded by outer layers of cooling, expanding gas. Over the next few million years, a series of nuclear reactions form different elements in shells around an iron core. The core eventually collapses in less than a second, causing a massive explosion called a supernova, in which a shock wave blows away the outer layers of the star. Supernovae shine brighter than an entire galaxy for a short time. Sometimes, the core survives the supernova explosion. If the surviving core is between about one and a half and three solar masses, it contracts to become a tiny, dense neutron star. If the core is considerably greater than three solar masses, it contracts to become a black hole (see pp. 28-29).

SUPERNOVA

TARANTULA NEBULA BEFORE SUPERNOVA

STRUCTURE OF A RED SUPERGIANT

Outer envelope consisting mainly of hydrogen

Layer consisting mainly of helium

Layer consisting mainly of carbon

Layer consisting mainly of oxygen

Layer consisting mainly of silicon

Shell of hydrogen fusing to form helium

Shell of helium fusing to form carbon

Shell of carbon fusing to form oxygen

Shell of oxygen fusing to form silicon

Shell of silicon fusing to form iron core

Surface temperature about 3,000°C

Cooling, expanding outer layers glow red

Core of mainly iron at a temperature of 3–5 billion °C

LIFE OF A MASSIVE STAR OF ABOUT 10 SOLAR MASSES

Dense globule condensing to form protostars

Cool cloud of gas (mainly hydrogen) and dust

NEBULA

Glowing ball of gas (mainly hydrogen)

Natal cocoon (shell of dust blown away by radiation from protostar)

PROTOSTAR
Duration: a few hundred thousand years

About 3 million km

Star producing energy by nuclear fusion in core

MAIN SEQUENCE STAR
Duration: 10 million years

FEATURES OF A SUPERNOVA

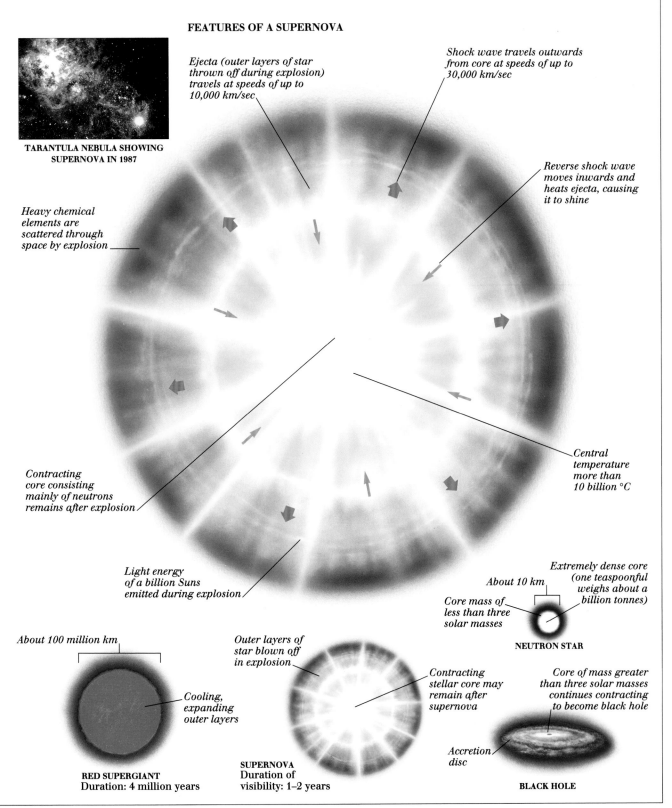

TARANTULA NEBULA SHOWING
SUPERNOVA IN 1987

*Ejecta (outer layers of star
thrown off during explosion)
travels at speeds of up to
10,000 km/sec*

*Shock wave travels outwards
from core at speeds of up to
30,000 km/sec*

*Reverse shock wave
moves inwards and
heats ejecta, causing
it to shine*

*Heavy chemical
elements are
scattered through
space by explosion*

*Central
temperature
more than
10 billion °C*

*Contracting
core consisting
mainly of neutrons
remains after explosion*

*Light energy
of a billion Suns
emitted during explosion*

*Extremely dense core
(one teaspoonful
weighs about a
billion tonnes)*

About 10 km

*Core mass of
less than three
solar masses*

NEUTRON STAR

About 100 million km

*Outer layers of
star blown off
in explosion*

*Contracting
stellar core may
remain after
supernova*

*Core of mass greater
than three solar masses
continues contracting
to become black hole*

*Cooling,
expanding
outer layers*

*Accretion
disc*

RED SUPERGIANT
Duration: 4 million years

SUPERNOVA
Duration of
visibility: 1–2 years

BLACK HOLE

Neutron stars and black holes

NEUTRON STARS AND BLACK HOLES form from the stellar cores that remain after stars have exploded as supernovae (see pp. 26-27). If the remaining core is between about one and a half and three solar masses, it contracts to form a neutron star. If the remaining core is greater than about three solar masses, it contracts to form a black hole. Neutron stars are typically only about 10 kilometres in diameter and consist almost entirely of subatomic particles called neutrons. Such stars are so dense that a teaspoonful would weigh about a billion tonnes. Neutron stars are observed as pulsars, so-called because they rotate rapidly and emit two beams of radio waves, which sweep across the sky and are detected as short pulses. Black holes are characterized by their extremely strong gravity, which is so powerful that not even light can escape; as a result, black holes are invisible. However, they may be detected if they have a close companion star. The gravity of the black hole pulls gas from the other star, forming an accretion disc that spirals around the black hole at high speed, heating up and emitting radiation. Eventually, the matter spirals in to cross the event horizon (the boundary of the black hole), thereby disappearing from the visible Universe.

X-ray emission from pulsar (neutron star rotating 30 times each second)

X-ray emission from centre of nebula

X-RAY IMAGE OF THE CRAB NEBULA (SUPERNOVA REMNANT)

PULSAR (ROTATING NEUTRON STAR)

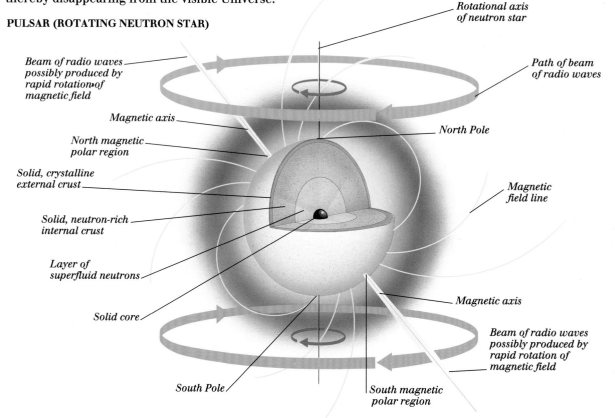

Rotational axis of neutron star

Beam of radio waves possibly produced by rapid rotation of magnetic field

Path of beam of radio waves

Magnetic axis

North magnetic polar region

North Pole

Solid, crystalline external crust

Solid, neutron-rich internal crust

Magnetic field line

Layer of superfluid neutrons

Solid core

Magnetic axis

Beam of radio waves possibly produced by rapid rotation of magnetic field

South Pole

South magnetic polar region

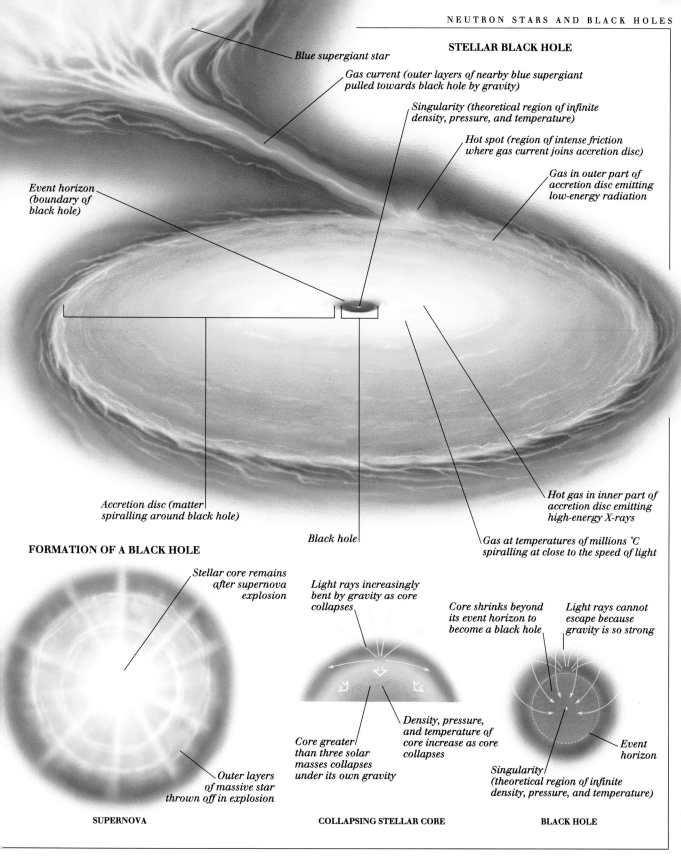

STELLAR BLACK HOLE

Blue supergiant star

Gas current (outer layers of nearby blue supergiant pulled towards black hole by gravity)

Singularity (theoretical region of infinite density, pressure, and temperature)

Hot spot (region of intense friction where gas current joins accretion disc)

Gas in outer part of accretion disc emitting low-energy radiation

Event horizon (boundary of black hole)

Accretion disc (matter spiralling around black hole)

Black hole

Hot gas in inner part of accretion disc emitting high-energy X-rays

Gas at temperatures of millions °C spiralling at close to the speed of light

FORMATION OF A BLACK HOLE

Stellar core remains after supernova explosion

Light rays increasingly bent by gravity as core collapses

Core shrinks beyond its event horizon to become a black hole

Light rays cannot escape because gravity is so strong

Outer layers of massive star thrown off in explosion

Core greater than three solar masses collapses under its own gravity

Density, pressure, and temperature of core increase as core collapses

Event horizon

Singularity (theoretical region of infinite density, pressure, and temperature)

SUPERNOVA

COLLAPSING STELLAR CORE

BLACK HOLE

The Solar System

THE SUN

THE SOLAR SYSTEM consists of a central star (the Sun) and the bodies that orbit it. These bodies include nine planets and their 61 known moons; asteroids; comets; and meteoroids. The Solar System also contains interplanetary gas and dust. Most of the planets fall into two groups: four small rocky planets near the Sun (Mercury, Venus, Earth, and Mars); and four planets further out, the gas giants (Jupiter, Saturn, Uranus, and Neptune). Pluto belongs to neither group but is very small, solid, and icy. Pluto is the outermost planet, except when it passes briefly inside Neptune's orbit. Between the rocky planets and gas giants is the asteroid belt, which contains thousands of chunks of rock orbiting the Sun. Most of the bodies in the Solar System move around the Sun in elliptical orbits located in a thin disc around the Sun's equator. All the planets orbit the Sun in the same direction (anticlockwise when viewed from above) and all but Venus, Uranus, and Pluto also spin about their axes in this direction. Moons also spin as they, in turn, orbit their planets. The entire Solar System orbits the centre of our galaxy, the Milky Way (see pp. 14-15).

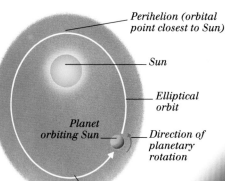

Perihelion (orbital point closest to Sun)

Sun

Elliptical orbit

Planet orbiting Sun

Direction of planetary rotation

Aphelion (orbital point furthest from Sun)

Aphelion of Neptune: 4,537 million km

ORBITS OF INNER PLANETS

Average orbital speed of Venus: 35.03 km/sec
Average orbital speed of Mercury: 47.89 km/sec
Average orbital speed of Earth: 29.79 km/sec
Average orbital speed of Mars: 24.13 km/sec

Mercury

Perihelion of Mercury: 45.9 million km
Perihelion of Venus: 107.4 million km
Perihelion of Earth: 147 million km

Mars

Perihelion of Mars: 206.7 million km

Earth

Venus

Sun

Aphelion of Mercury: 69.7 million km

Aphelion of Venus: 109 million km

Aphelion of Pluto: 7,375 million km

Asteroid belt

Aphelion of Earth: 152 million km

Aphelion of Mars: 249 million km

MERCURY
Year: 87.97 Earth days
Mass: 0.06 Earth masses
Diameter: 4,878 km

VENUS
Year: 224.7 Earth days
Mass: 0.81 Earth masses
Diameter: 12,103 km

EARTH
Year: 365.26 days
Mass: 1 Earth mass
Diameter: 12,756 km

MARS
Year: 1.88 Earth years
Mass: 0.11 Earth masses
Diameter: 6,786 km

JUPITER
Year: 11.86 Earth years
Mass: 317.94 Earth masses
Diameter: 142,984 km

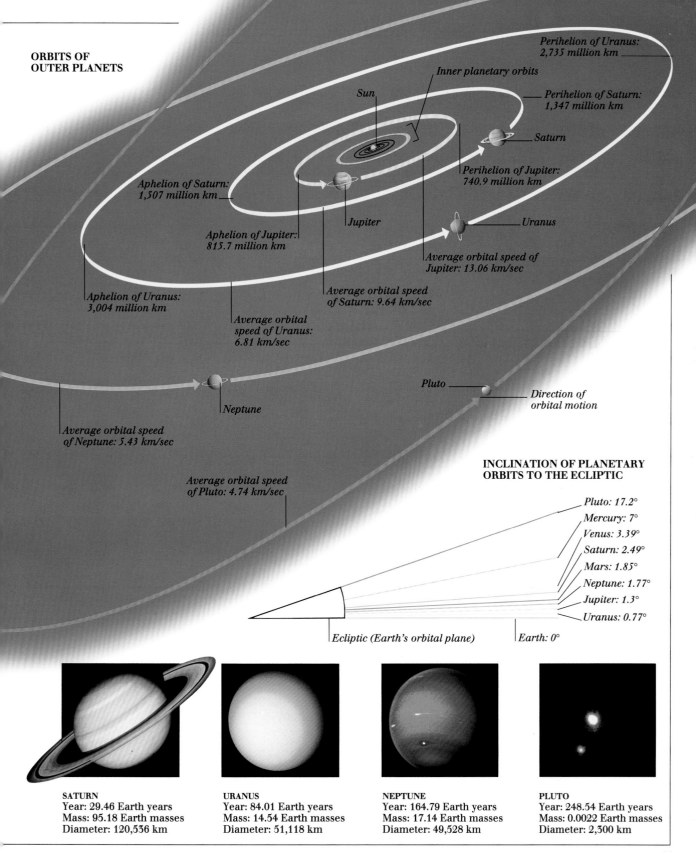

ORBITS OF OUTER PLANETS

Perihelion of Uranus: 2,735 million km

Inner planetary orbits

Sun

Perihelion of Saturn: 1,347 million km

Saturn

Perihelion of Jupiter: 740.9 million km

Aphelion of Saturn: 1,507 million km

Jupiter

Uranus

Aphelion of Jupiter: 815.7 million km

Average orbital speed of Jupiter: 13.06 km/sec

Aphelion of Uranus: 3,004 million km

Average orbital speed of Saturn: 9.64 km/sec

Average orbital speed of Uranus: 6.81 km/sec

Pluto

Direction of orbital motion

Neptune

Average orbital speed of Neptune: 5.43 km/sec

Average orbital speed of Pluto: 4.74 km/sec

INCLINATION OF PLANETARY ORBITS TO THE ECLIPTIC

Pluto: 17.2°
Mercury: 7°
Venus: 3.39°
Saturn: 2.49°
Mars: 1.85°
Neptune: 1.77°
Jupiter: 1.3°
Uranus: 0.77°

Ecliptic (Earth's orbital plane)

Earth: 0°

SATURN
Year: 29.46 Earth years
Mass: 95.18 Earth masses
Diameter: 120,536 km

URANUS
Year: 84.01 Earth years
Mass: 14.54 Earth masses
Diameter: 51,118 km

NEPTUNE
Year: 164.79 Earth years
Mass: 17.14 Earth masses
Diameter: 49,528 km

PLUTO
Year: 248.54 Earth years
Mass: 0.0022 Earth masses
Diameter: 2,300 km

The Sun

SOLAR PHOTOSPHERE

THE SUN IS THE STAR AT THE CENTRE of the Solar System. It is about five billion years old and will continue to shine as it does now for about another five billion years. The Sun is a yellow main sequence star (see pp. 22-23) about 1.4 million kilometres in diameter. It consists almost entirely of hydrogen and helium. In the Sun's core, hydrogen is converted to helium by nuclear fusion, releasing energy in the process. The energy travels from the core, through the radiative and convective zones, to the photosphere (visible surface), where it leaves the Sun in the form of heat and light. On the photosphere there are often dark, relatively cool areas called sunspots, which usually appear in pairs or groups and are thought to be caused by magnetic fields. Other types of solar activity are flares, which are usually associated with sunspots, and prominences. Flares are sudden discharges of high-energy radiation and atomic particles. Prominences are huge loops or filaments of gas extending into the solar atmosphere; some last for hours, others for months. Beyond the photosphere is the chromosphere (inner atmosphere) and the extremely rarified corona (outer atmosphere), which extends millions of kilometres into space. Tiny particles that escape from the corona give rise to the solar wind, which streams through space at hundreds of kilometres per second. The chromosphere and corona can be seen from Earth when the Sun is totally eclipsed by the Moon.

HOW A SOLAR ECLIPSE OCCURS

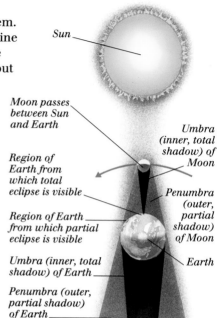

Sun

Moon passes between Sun and Earth

Region of Earth from which total eclipse is visible

Region of Earth from which partial eclipse is visible

Umbra (inner, total shadow) of Earth

Penumbra (outer, partial shadow) of Earth

Umbra (inner, total shadow) of Moon

Penumbra (outer, partial shadow) of Moon

Earth

SURFACE FEATURES

Gas loop (looped prominence)

Prominence (jet of gas at edge of Sun's disc up to hundreds of thousands of kilometres high)

Spicule (vertical jet of gas)

Photosphere (visible surface)

Chromosphere (inner atmosphere)

TOTAL SOLAR ECLIPSE

Corona (outer atmosphere of extremely hot, diffuse gas)

Moon covers Sun's disc

SUNSPOTS

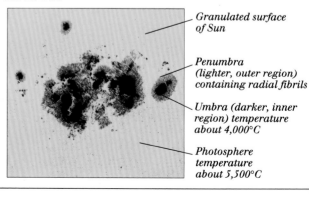

Granulated surface of Sun

Penumbra (lighter, outer region) containing radial fibrils

Umbra (darker, inner region) temperature about 4,000°C

Photosphere temperature about 5,500°C

**EXTERNAL FEATURES AND
INTERNAL STRUCTURE OF THE SUN**

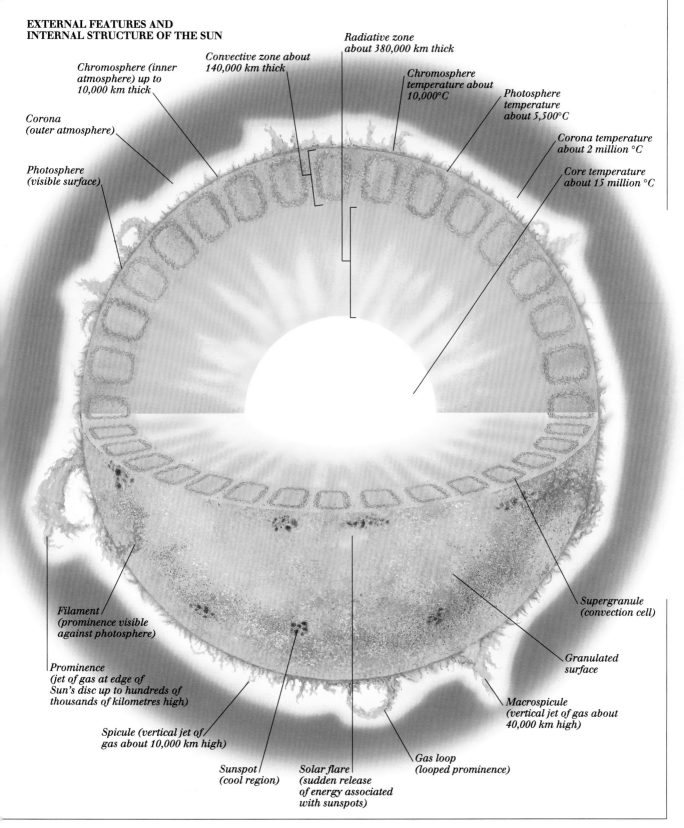

*Chromosphere (inner
atmosphere) up to
10,000 km thick*

*Convective zone about
140,000 km thick*

*Radiative zone
about 380,000 km thick*

*Chromosphere
temperature about
10,000°C*

*Photosphere
temperature
about 5,500°C*

*Corona
(outer atmosphere)*

*Corona temperature
about 2 million °C*

*Photosphere
(visible surface)*

*Core temperature
about 15 million °C*

*Supergranule
(convection cell)*

*Granulated
surface*

*Filament
(prominence visible
against photosphere)*

*Prominence
(jet of gas at edge of
Sun's disc up to hundreds of
thousands of kilometres high)*

*Macrospicule
(vertical jet of gas about
40,000 km high)*

*Spicule (vertical jet of
gas about 10,000 km high)*

*Sunspot
(cool region)*

*Solar flare
(sudden release
of energy associated
with sunspots)*

*Gas loop
(looped prominence)*

Mercury

MERCURY

MERCURY IS THE NEAREST PLANET to the Sun, orbiting at an average distance of about 58 million kilometres. Because Mercury is the closest planet to the Sun, it moves faster than any other planet, travelling at an average speed of nearly 48 kilometres per second and completing an orbit in just under 88 days. Mercury is very small (only Pluto is smaller) and rocky. Most of the surface has been heavily cratered by the impact of meteorites, although there are also smooth, sparsely cratered plains. The Caloris Basin is the largest crater, measuring about 1,300 kilometres across. It is thought to have been formed when a rock the size of an asteroid hit the planet, and is surrounded by concentric rings of mountains thrown up by the impact. The surface also has many ridges (called rupes) that are thought to have been formed when the hot core of the young planet cooled and shrank about four billion years ago, buckling the planet's surface in the process. The planet rotates about its axis very slowly, taking nearly 59 Earth days to complete one rotation. As a result, a solar day (sunrise to sunrise) on Mercury is about 176 Earth days – twice as long as the 88-day Mercurian year. Mercury has extreme surface temperatures, ranging from a maximum of 430°C on the sunlit side to -170°C on the dark side. At nightfall, the temperature drops very quickly because the planet's atmosphere is almost non-existent. It consists only of minute amounts of helium and hydrogen captured from the solar wind, plus traces of other gases.

TILT AND ROTATION OF MERCURY

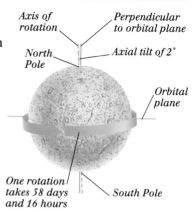

Axis of rotation

Perpendicular to orbital plane

North Pole

Axial tilt of 2°

Orbital plane

One rotation takes 58 days and 16 hours

South Pole

DEGAS AND BRONTË (RAY CRATERS)

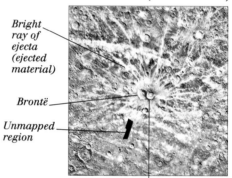

Bright ray of ejecta (ejected material)

Brontë

Unmapped region

Degas with central peak

FORMATION OF A RAY CRATER

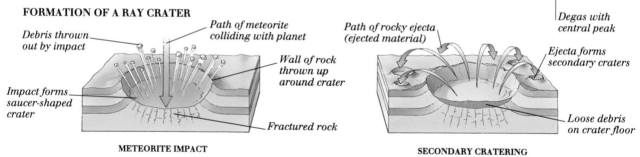

Debris thrown out by impact

Path of meteorite colliding with planet

Wall of rock thrown up around crater

Impact forms saucer-shaped crater

Fractured rock

METEORITE IMPACT

Path of rocky ejecta (ejected material)

Ejecta forms secondary craters

Loose debris on crater floor

SECONDARY CRATERING

Wall of rock forms ring of mountains

Ray of ejecta (ejected material)

Small secondary crater

Loose ejected rock

Central mountain rings form if floor of large crater recoils from meteorite impact

Falling debris forms ridges on side of wall

RAY CRATER

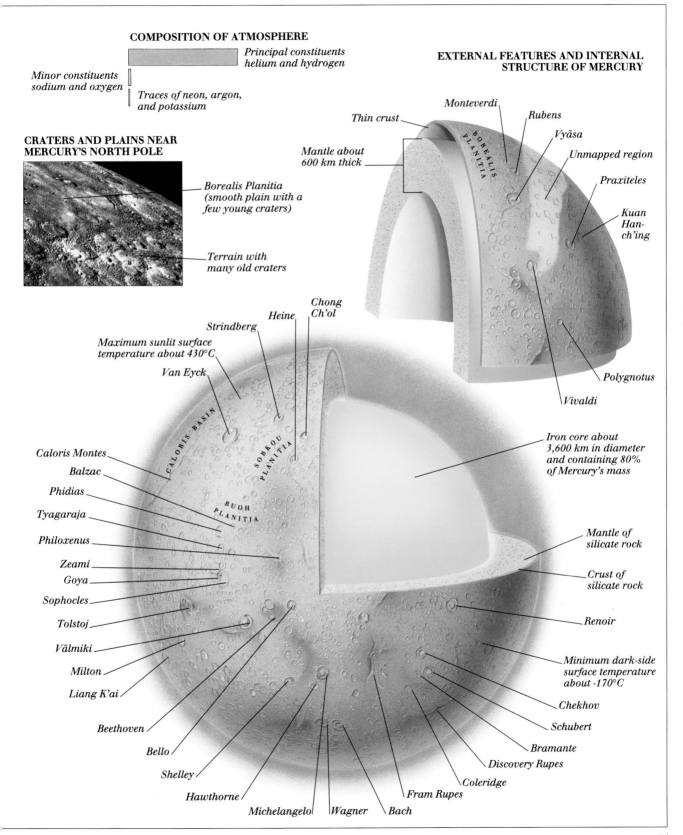

COMPOSITION OF ATMOSPHERE

Principal constituents
helium and hydrogen

Minor constituents
sodium and oxygen

Traces of neon, argon,
and potassium

**CRATERS AND PLAINS NEAR
MERCURY'S NORTH POLE**

Borealis Planitia
(smooth plain with a
few young craters)

Terrain with
many old craters

**EXTERNAL FEATURES AND INTERNAL
STRUCTURE OF MERCURY**

Thin crust

Monteverdi

Rubens

Vyāsa

Unmapped region

Praxiteles

Mantle about
600 km thick

BOREALIS
PLANITIA

Kuan
Han-
ch'ing

Polygnotus

Vivaldi

Chong
Ch'ol

Heine

Strindberg

Maximum sunlit surface
temperature about 430°C

Van Eyck

CALORIS BASIN

SOBKOU
PLANITIA

Iron core about
3,600 km in diameter
and containing 80%
of Mercury's mass

Caloris Montes

Balzac

Phidias

Tyagaraja

Philoxenus

Zeami

Goya

Sophocles

Tolstoj

Vālmiki

Milton

Liang K'ai

Beethoven

Bello

Shelley

Hawthorne

Michelangelo

Wagner

Bach

Fram Rupes

Coleridge

Discovery Rupes

Bramante

Schubert

Chekhov

Minimum dark-side
surface temperature
about -170°C

Renoir

Mantle of
silicate rock

Crust of
silicate rock

BUDH
PLANITIA

Venus

RADAR IMAGE OF
VENUS

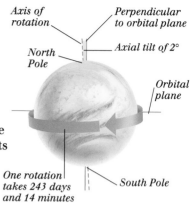

Axis of
rotation

Perpendicular
to orbital plane

North
Pole

Axial tilt of 2°

Orbital
plane

One rotation
takes 243 days
and 14 minutes

South Pole

VENUS IS A ROCKY PLANET and the second planet from the Sun. Venus spins slowly backwards as it orbits the Sun, causing its rotational period to be the longest in the Solar System, at about 243 Earth days. It is slightly smaller than Earth and probably has a similar internal structure, consisting of a semi-solid metal core, surrounded by a rocky mantle and crust. Venus is the brightest object in the sky after the Sun and Moon because its atmosphere reflects sunlight strongly. The main component of the atmosphere is carbon dioxide, which traps heat in a greenhouse effect far stronger than that on Earth. As a result, Venus is the hottest planet, with a maximum surface temperature of about 480°C. The thick cloud layers contain droplets of sulphuric acid and are driven around the planet by winds at speeds of up to 360 kilometres per hour. Although the planet takes 243 Earth days to rotate once, the high-speed winds cause the clouds to circle the planet in only four Earth days. The high temperature, acidic clouds, and enormous atmospheric pressure (about 90 times greater at the surface than that on Earth) make the environment extremely hostile. However, space probes have managed to land on Venus and photograph its dry, dusty surface. The Venusian surface has also been mapped by probes with radar equipment that can "see" through the cloud layers. Such radar maps reveal a terrain with craters, mountains, volcanoes, and areas where craters have been covered by plains of solidified volcanic lava. There are two large highland regions called Aphrodite Terra and Ishtar Terra.

CLOUD FEATURES

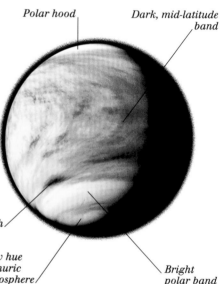

Polar hood

Dark, mid-latitude
band

Cloud features
swept around
planet by winds
of up to 360 km/h

Dirty yellow hue
due to sulphuric
acid in atmosphere

Bright
polar band

VENUSIAN CRATERS

Danilova

Ejecta (ejected
material)

Central peak

Howe

**FALSE-COLOUR RADAR MAP
OF THE SURFACE OF VENUS**

Metis Regio

Maxwell Montes

Bell Regio

Tethus Regio

Sedna Planitia

Eisila Regio

Guinevere Planitia

Phoebe Regio

Alpha Regio

Themis Regio

Lavinia Planitia

Helen Planitia

ISHTAR TERRA

APHRODITE TERRA

Atalanta Planitia

Leda Planitia

Tellus Regio

Niobe Planitia

Ovda Regio

Thetis Regio

Aino Planitia

Lada Terra

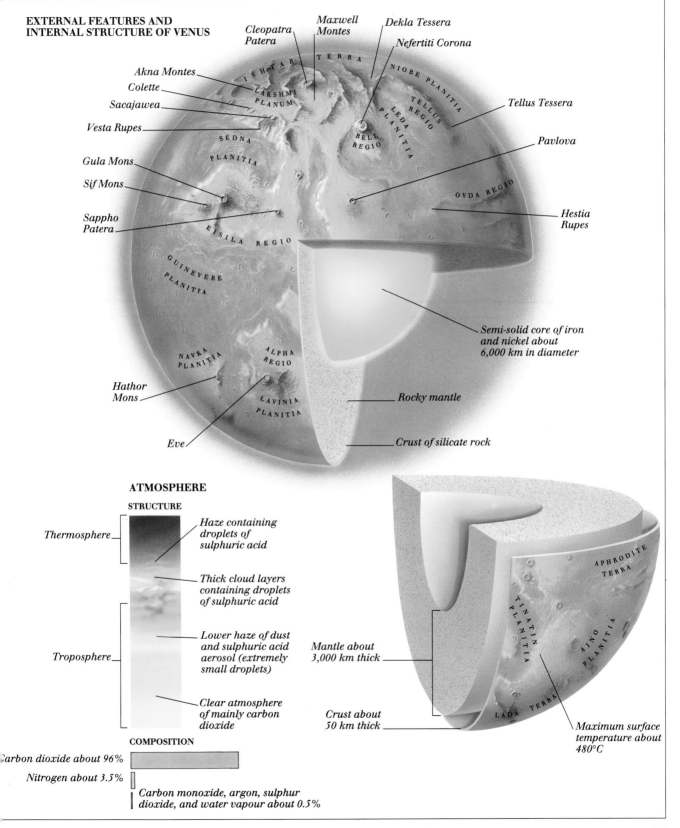

**EXTERNAL FEATURES AND
INTERNAL STRUCTURE OF VENUS**

Cleopatra
Patera

Maxwell
Montes

Dekla Tessera

Nefertiti Corona

Akna Montes

Colette

Sacajawea

Vesta Rupes

Gula Mons

Sif Mons

Sappho
Patera

Hathor
Mons

Eve

ISHTAR TERRA

NIOBE PLANITIA

LAKSHMI PLANUM

TELLUS REGIO

LEDA PLANITIA

BELL REGIO

SEDNA PLANITIA

Tellus Tessera

Pavlova

OVDA REGIO

Hestia
Rupes

EISILA REGIO

GUINEVERE PLANITIA

NAVKA PLANITIA

ALPHA REGIO

LAVINIA PLANITIA

Semi-solid core of iron
and nickel about
6,000 km in diameter

Rocky mantle

Crust of silicate rock

ATMOSPHERE

STRUCTURE

Thermosphere

Troposphere

Haze containing
droplets of
sulphuric acid

Thick cloud layers
containing droplets
of sulphuric acid

Lower haze of dust
and sulphuric acid
aerosol (extremely
small droplets)

Clear atmosphere
of mainly carbon
dioxide

COMPOSITION

Carbon dioxide about 96%

Nitrogen about 3.5%

Carbon monoxide, argon, sulphur
dioxide, and water vapour about 0.5%

APHRODITE TERRA

TINATIN PLANITIA

AINO PLANITIA

LADA TERRA

Mantle about
3,000 km thick

Crust about
50 km thick

Maximum surface
temperature about
480°C

37

The Earth

Axis of rotation

Axial tilt of 23.4°

North Pole

Orbital plane

South Pole

One rotation takes 23 hours and 56 minutes

Perpendicular to orbital plane

THE EARTH

THE EARTH IS THE THIRD of the nine planets that orbit the Sun. It is the largest and densest rocky planet, and the only one known to support life. About 70 per cent of the Earth's surface is covered by water, which is not found in liquid form on the surface of any other planet. There are four main layers: the inner core, the outer core, the mantle, and the crust. At the heart of the planet the solid inner core has a temperature of about 4,000°C. The heat from this inner core causes material in the molten outer core and mantle to circulate in convection currents. It is thought that these convection currents generate the Earth's magnetic field, which extends into space as the magnetosphere. The Earth's atmosphere helps screen out some of the harmful radiation from the Sun, stops meteorites from reaching the planet's surface, and traps enough heat to prevent extremes of cold. The Earth has one natural satellite, the Moon, which is large enough for both bodies to be considered a double-planet system.

THE FORMATION OF THE EARTH

The heat of the collisions caused the planet to glow red

The cloud broke up into particles of ice and rock, which stuck together to form planets

Micro-organisms began to photosynthesize, creating a build up of oxygen

4,600 MILLION YEARS AGO, THE SOLAR SYSTEM FORMED FROM A CLOUD OF GAS AND DUST

THE EARTH WAS FORMED FROM COLLIDING ROCKS

4,500 MILLION YEARS AGO THE SURFACE COOLED TO FORM THE CRUST

THE CONTINENTS BROKE UP AND REFORMED, GRADUALLY TAKING THEIR PRESENT POSITIONS

Solar wind enters atmosphere and produces aurora

Magnetosphere (magnetic field)

Solar wind (stream of electrically charged particles)

THE EARTH'S MAGNETOSPHERE

Van Allen radiation belt

Earth

Axis of geographic poles

Axis of magnetic poles

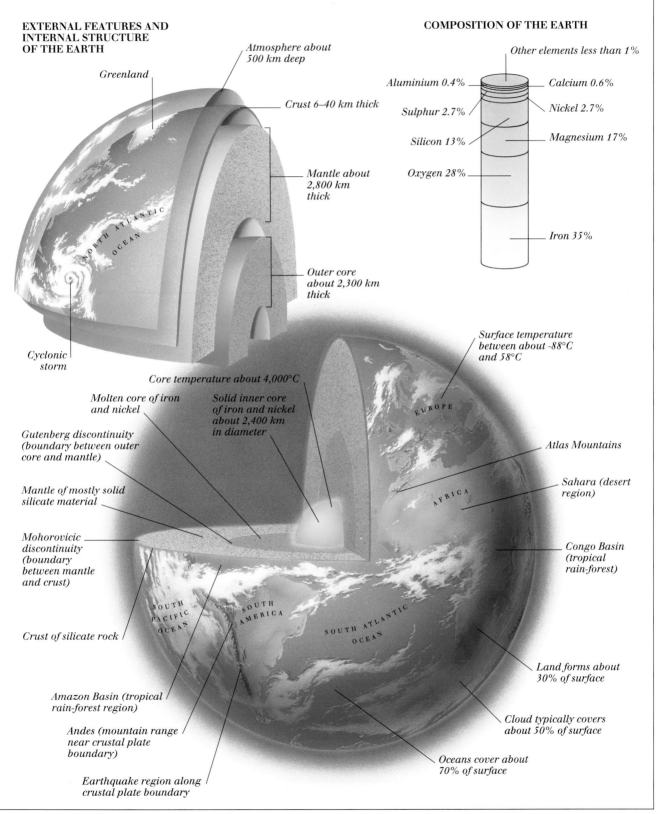

**EXTERNAL FEATURES AND
INTERNAL STRUCTURE
OF THE EARTH**

COMPOSITION OF THE EARTH

Greenland

Atmosphere about
500 km deep

Crust 6–40 km thick

NORTH ATLANTIC
OCEAN

Mantle about
2,800 km
thick

Outer core
about 2,300 km
thick

Cyclonic
storm

Other elements less than 1%

Aluminium 0.4%

Calcium 0.6%

Sulphur 2.7%

Nickel 2.7%

Silicon 13%

Magnesium 17%

Oxygen 28%

Iron 35%

Surface temperature
between about -88°C
and 58°C

Core temperature about 4,000°C

EUROPE

Molten core of iron
and nickel

Solid inner core
of iron and nickel
about 2,400 km
in diameter

Atlas Mountains

Gutenberg discontinuity
(boundary between outer
core and mantle)

Sahara (desert
region)

AFRICA

Mantle of mostly solid
silicate material

Mohorovicic
discontinuity
(boundary
between mantle
and crust)

Congo Basin
(tropical
rain-forest)

Crust of silicate rock

SOUTH
PACIFIC
OCEAN

SOUTH
AMERICA

SOUTH ATLANTIC
OCEAN

Land forms about
30% of surface

Amazon Basin (tropical
rain-forest region)

Cloud typically covers
about 50% of surface

Andes (mountain range
near crustal plate
boundary)

Oceans cover about
70% of surface

Earthquake region along
crustal plate boundary

The Moon

THE MOON FROM EARTH

THE MOON IS THE EARTH'S only natural satellite. It is relatively large for a moon, with a diameter of about 3,470 kilometres – just over a quarter that of the Earth. The Moon takes the same time to rotate on its axis as it takes to orbit the Earth (27.3 days), and so the same side (the near side) always faces us. However, the amount of the surface we can see – the phase of the Moon – depends on how much of the near side is in sunlight. The Moon is dry and barren, with no atmosphere or water. It consists mainly of solid rock, although its core may contain molten rock or iron. The surface is dusty, with highlands covered in craters caused by meteorite impacts, and lowlands in which large craters have been filled by solidified lava to form dark areas called maria or "seas". Maria occur mainly on the near side, which has a thinner crust than the far side. Many of the craters are rimmed by mountain ranges that form the crater walls and can be thousands of metres high.

TILT AND ROTATION OF THE MOON

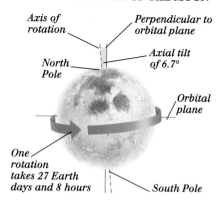

Axis of rotation
Perpendicular to orbital plane
North Pole
Axial tilt of 6.7°
Orbital plane
One rotation takes 27 Earth days and 8 hours
South Pole

CRATERS ON OCEANUS PROCELLARUM

Aristarchus
Cobra Head (head of Schröter's Valley)
Herodotus

NEAR SIDE OF THE MOON

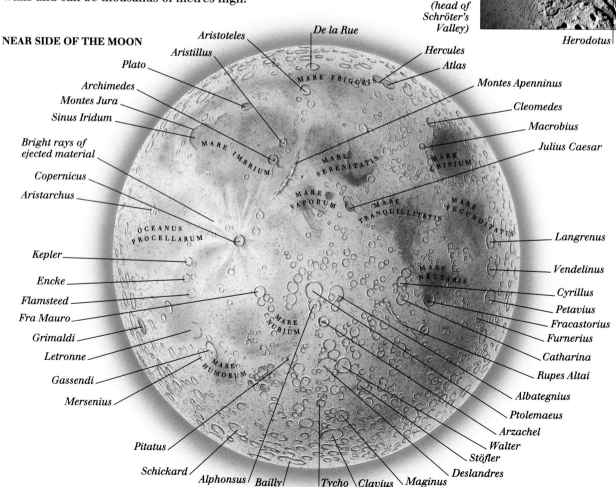

De la Rue
Aristoteles
Aristillus
Plato
Hercules
Atlas
Archimedes
Montes Apenninus
Montes Jura
Cleomedes
Sinus Iridum
Macrobius
Bright rays of ejected material
Julius Caesar
Copernicus
Aristarchus
MARE FRIGORIS
MARE IMBRIUM
MARE SERENITATIS
MARE CRISIUM
MARE VAPORUM
MARE TRANQUILLITATIS
MARE FECUNDITATIS
OCEANUS PROCELLARUM
Langrenus
Kepler
Vendelinus
Encke
MARE NECTARIS
Cyrillus
Flamsteed
Petavius
Fra Mauro
Fracastorius
Grimaldi
MARE NUBIUM
Furnerius
Letronne
Catharina
Gassendi
MARE HUMORUM
Rupes Altai
Mersenius
Albategnius
Ptolemaeus
Arzachel
Pitatus
Walter
Schickard
Stöfler
Alphonsus
Bailly
Tycho
Clavius
Maginus
Deslandres

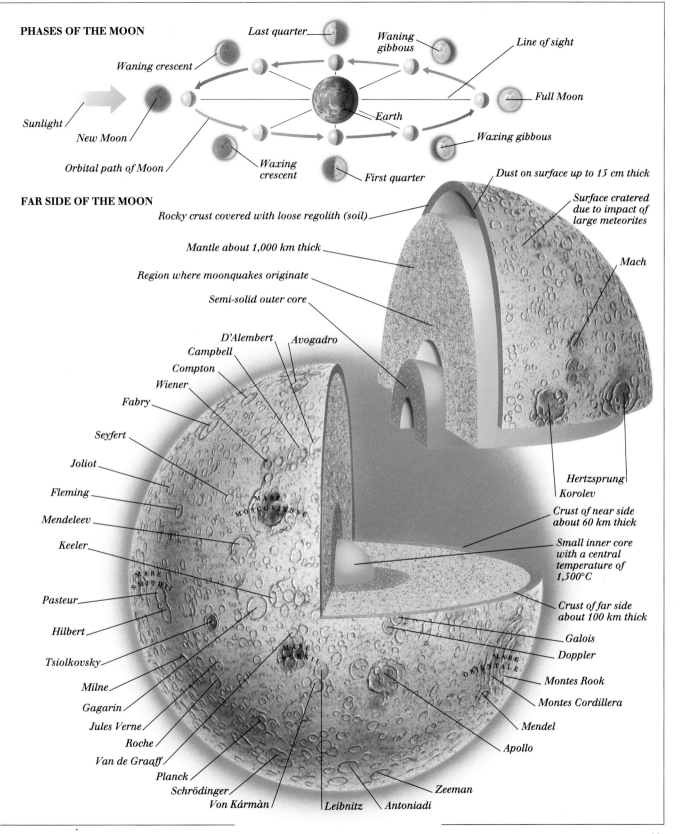

PHASES OF THE MOON

Last quarter

Waning gibbous

Waning crescent

Line of sight

Sunlight

New Moon

Earth

Full Moon

Orbital path of Moon

Waxing gibbous

Waxing crescent

First quarter

FAR SIDE OF THE MOON

Rocky crust covered with loose regolith (soil)

Dust on surface up to 15 cm thick

Surface cratered due to impact of large meteorites

Mantle about 1,000 km thick

Region where moonquakes originate

Mach

Semi-solid outer core

D'Alembert

Avogadro

Campbell

Compton

Wiener

Fabry

Seyfert

Joliot

Fleming

Mendeleev

MARE MOSCOVIENSE

Keeler

Hertzsprung

Korolev

Crust of near side about 60 km thick

Small inner core with a central temperature of 1,500°C

Pasteur

MARE SMITHII

Hilbert

Crust of far side about 100 km thick

Tsiolkovsky

Galois

Milne

Doppler

Gagarin

MARE INGENII

MARE ORIENTALE

Montes Rook

Jules Verne

Montes Cordillera

Roche

Mendel

Van de Graaff

Apollo

Planck

Schrödinger

Zeeman

Von Kármàn

Leibnitz

Antoniadi

Mars

MARS

MARS, KNOWN AS THE RED PLANET, is the fourth planet from the Sun and the outermost rocky planet. In the 19th century, astronomers first observed what were thought to be signs of life on Mars. These signs included apparent canal-like markings on the surface, and dark patches that were thought to be vegetation. It is now known that the "canals" are an optical illusion, and the dark patches are areas where the red dust that covers most of the planet has been blown away. The fine dust particles are often whipped up by winds into dust storms that occasionally obscure almost all the surface. Residual dust in the atmosphere gives the Martian sky a pinkish hue. The northern hemisphere of Mars has many large plains formed of solidified volcanic lava, whereas the southern hemisphere has many craters and large impact basins. There are also several huge, extinct volcanoes, including Olympus Mons, which, at 600 kilometres across and 25 kilometres high, is the largest known volcano in the Solar System. The surface also has many canyons and branching channels. The canyons were formed by movements of the surface crust, but the channels are thought to have been formed by flowing water that has now dried up. The Martian atmosphere is much thinner than Earth's, with only a few clouds and morning mists. Mars has two tiny, irregularly shaped moons called Phobos and Deimos. Their small size indicates that they may be asteroids that have been captured by the gravity of Mars.

TILT AND ROTATION OF MARS

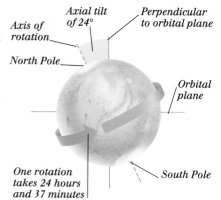

Axis of rotation
Axial tilt of 24°
Perpendicular to orbital plane
North Pole
Orbital plane
One rotation takes 24 hours and 37 minutes
South Pole

SURFACE FEATURES OF MARS

Bright water-ice fog

Fog in canyon about 20 km wide at end of Valles Marineris

Syria Planum

NOCTIS LABYRINTHUS (CANYON SYSTEM)

Summit caldera consisting of overlapping collapsed volcanic craters

Crater

Gentle slope produced by lava flow

Cloud formation

OLYMPUS MONS (EXTINCT SHIELD VOLCANO)

THE SURFACE OF MARS

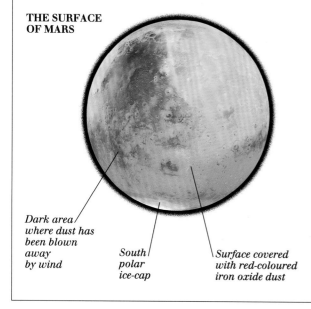

Dark area where dust has been blown away by wind

South polar ice-cap

Surface covered with red-coloured iron oxide dust

MOONS OF MARS

PHOBOS
Average diameter: 22 km
Average distance from planet: 9,400 km

DEIMOS
Average diameter: 13 km
Average distance from planet: 23,500 km

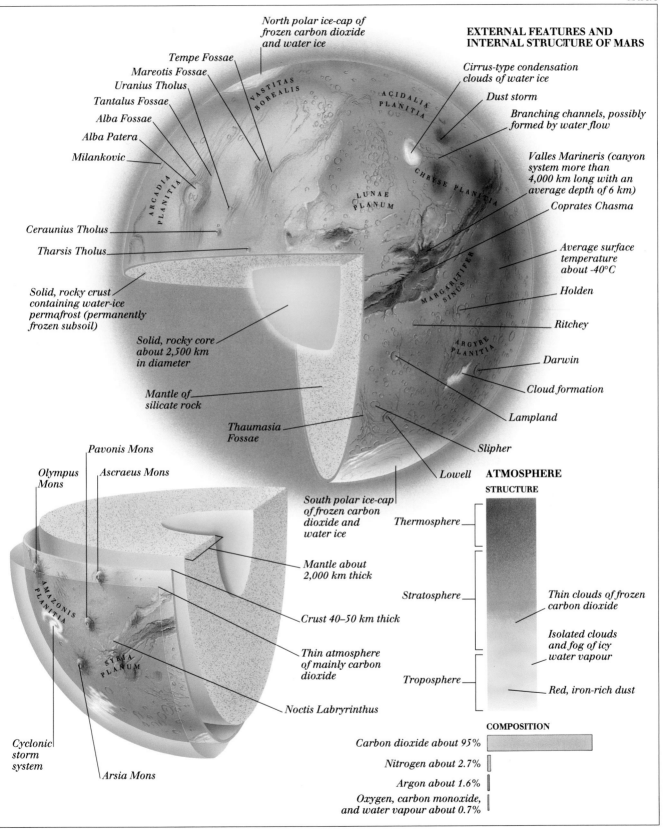

North polar ice-cap of frozen carbon dioxide and water ice

Tempe Fossae

Mareotis Fossae

Uranius Tholus

Tantalus Fossae

Alba Fossae

Alba Patera

Milankovic

Ceraunius Tholus

Tharsis Tholus

Solid, rocky crust containing water-ice permafrost (permanently frozen subsoil)

Solid, rocky core about 2,500 km in diameter

Mantle of silicate rock

Thaumasia Fossae

VASTITAS BOREALIS

ACIDALIA PLANITIA

CHRYSE PLANITIA

LUNAE PLANUM

ARCADIA PLANITIA

MARGARITIFER SINUS

ARGYRE PLANITIA

EXTERNAL FEATURES AND INTERNAL STRUCTURE OF MARS

Cirrus-type condensation clouds of water ice

Dust storm

Branching channels, possibly formed by water flow

Valles Marineris (canyon system more than 4,000 km long with an average depth of 6 km)

Coprates Chasma

Average surface temperature about -40°C

Holden

Ritchey

Darwin

Cloud formation

Lampland

Slipher

Lowell

Pavonis Mons

Ascraeus Mons

Olympus Mons

AMAZONIS PLANITIA

SYRIA PLANUM

Cyclonic storm system

Arsia Mons

South polar ice-cap of frozen carbon dioxide and water ice

Mantle about 2,000 km thick

Crust 40–50 km thick

Thin atmosphere of mainly carbon dioxide

Noctis Labryrinthus

ATMOSPHERE

STRUCTURE

Thermosphere

Stratosphere

Troposphere

Thin clouds of frozen carbon dioxide

Isolated clouds and fog of icy water vapour

Red, iron-rich dust

COMPOSITION

Carbon dioxide about 95%

Nitrogen about 2.7%

Argon about 1.6%

Oxygen, carbon monoxide, and water vapour about 0.7%

Jupiter

JUPITER

JUPITER IS THE FIFTH PLANET from the Sun and the first of the four gas giants. It is the largest and the most massive planet, with a diameter about 11 times that of the Earth and a mass about 2.5 times the combined mass of the eight other planets. Jupiter is thought to have a small rocky core surrounded by an inner mantle of metallic hydrogen (liquid hydrogen that acts like a metal). Outside the inner mantle is an outer mantle of liquid hydrogen and helium that merges into the gaseous atmosphere. Jupiter's rapid rate of rotation causes the clouds in its atmosphere to form belts and zones that encircle the planet parallel to the equator. Belts are dark, low-lying, relatively warm cloud layers, and zones are bright, high-altitude, cooler cloud layers. Within the belts and zones, turbulence causes the formation of cloud features such as white ovals and red spots, both of which are huge storm systems. The most prominent cloud feature is a storm called the Great Red Spot, which consists of a spiralling column of clouds three times wider than the Earth that rises about eight kilometres above the upper cloud layer. Jupiter has one thin, faint, main ring, inside which is a tenuous halo ring of tiny particles extending towards the planet. There are 16 known Jovian moons. The four largest moons (called the Galileans) are Ganymede, Callisto, Io, and Europa. Ganymede and Callisto are cratered and probably icy. Europa is smooth and icy and may contain water. Io is covered in bright red, orange, and yellow splotches. This colouring is caused by sulphurous material from active volcanoes that shoot plumes of lava hundreds of kilometres above the surface.

RINGS OF JUPITER

Main ring

Halo ring

TILT AND ROTATION OF JUPITER

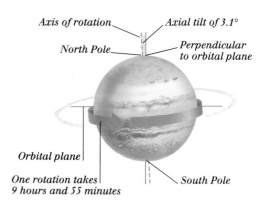

Axis of rotation

Axial tilt of 3.1°

North Pole

Perpendicular to orbital plane

Orbital plane

One rotation takes 9 hours and 55 minutes

South Pole

GREAT RED SPOT AND WHITE OVAL

Great Red Spot (anticyclonic storm system)

Red colour probably due to phosphorus

White oval (temporary anticyclonic storm system)

GALILEAN MOONS OF JUPITER

EUROPA
Diameter: 3,138 km
Average distance from planet: 670,900 km

CALLISTO
Diameter: 4,800 km
Average distance from planet: 1,880,000 km

GANYMEDE
Diameter: 5,262 km
Average distance from planet: 1,070,000 km

IO
Diameter: 3,642 km
Average distance from planet: 421,800 km

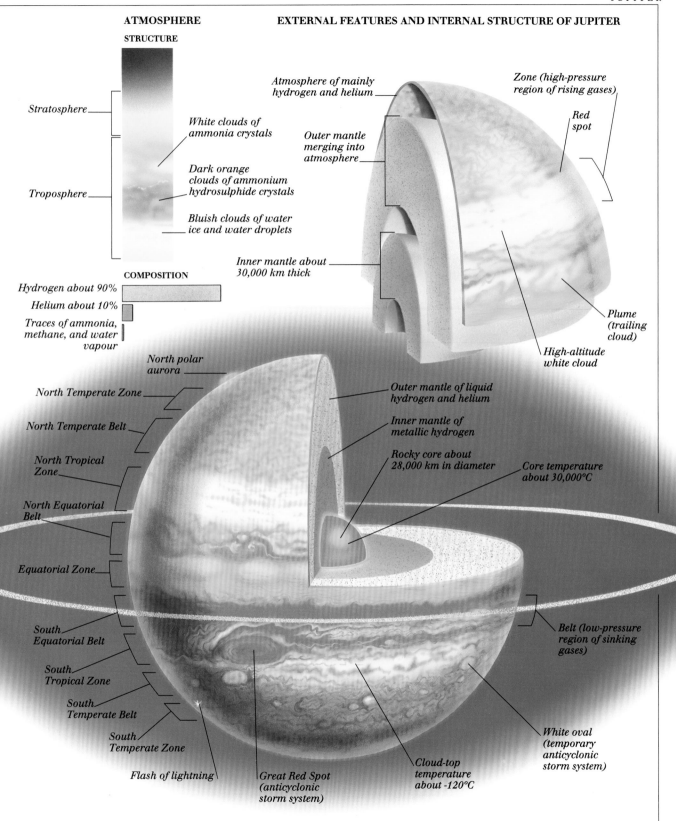

ATMOSPHERE

STRUCTURE

EXTERNAL FEATURES AND INTERNAL STRUCTURE OF JUPITER

Stratosphere

Troposphere

White clouds of
ammonia crystals

Dark orange
clouds of ammonium
hydrosulphide crystals

Bluish clouds of water
ice and water droplets

COMPOSITION

Hydrogen about 90%

Helium about 10%

Traces of ammonia,
methane, and water
vapour

Atmosphere of mainly
hydrogen and helium

Outer mantle
merging into
atmosphere

Inner mantle about
30,000 km thick

Zone (high-pressure
region of rising gases)

Red
spot

Plume
(trailing
cloud)

High-altitude
white cloud

North polar
aurora

North Temperate Zone

North Temperate Belt

North Tropical
Zone

North Equatorial
Belt

Equatorial Zone

South
Equatorial Belt

South
Tropical Zone

South
Temperate Belt

South
Temperate Zone

Flash of lightning

Great Red Spot
(anticyclonic
storm system)

Outer mantle of liquid
hydrogen and helium

Inner mantle of
metallic hydrogen

Rocky core about
28,000 km in diameter

Core temperature
about 30,000°C

Belt (low-pressure
region of sinking
gases)

White oval
(temporary
anticyclonic
storm system)

Cloud-top
temperature
about -120°C

Saturn

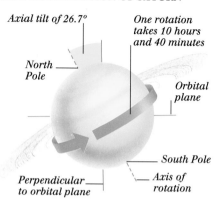

Axial tilt of 26.7°

One rotation takes 10 hours and 40 minutes

North Pole

Orbital plane

South Pole

Axis of rotation

Perpendicular to orbital plane

FALSE-COLOUR IMAGE OF SATURN

SATURN IS THE SIXTH PLANET from the Sun. It is a gas giant almost as big as Jupiter, with an equatorial diameter of about 120,500 kilometres. Saturn is thought to consist of a small core of rock and ice surrounded by an inner mantle of metallic hydrogen (liquid hydrogen that acts like a metal). Outside the inner mantle is an outer mantle of liquid hydrogen that merges into a gaseous atmosphere. Saturn's clouds form belts and zones similar to those on Jupiter, but obscured by overlying haze. Storms and eddies, seen as red or white ovals, occur in the clouds. Saturn has an extremely thin but wide system of rings that is less than one kilometre thick but extends outwards to about 420,000 kilometres from the planet's surface. The main rings comprise thousands of narrow ringlets, each made of icy lumps that range in size from tiny particles to chunks several metres across. The D, E, and G rings are very faint, the F ring is brighter, and the A, B, and C rings are bright enough to be seen from Earth with binoculars. Saturn has 18 known moons, some of which orbit inside the rings and are thought to exert a gravitational influence on the shapes of the rings. Unusually, seven of the moons are co-orbital – they share an orbit with another moon. Astronomers believe that such co-orbital moons may have originated from a single satellite that broke up.

FALSE-COLOUR IMAGE OF SATURN'S CLOUD FEATURES

Ribbon-shaped striation caused by winds of up to 540 km/h

Oval (rotating storm system)

INNER RINGS OF SATURN

D ring

C ring ("crepe ring")

B ring

Cassini Division

A ring

Encke Division

F ring

MOONS OF SATURN

ENCELADUS
Diameter: 498 km
Average distance from planet: 238,000 km

TETHYS
Diameter: 1,050 km
Average distance from planet: 295,000 km

DIONE
Diameter: 1,118 km
Average distance from planet: 377,000 km

MIMAS
Diameter: 397 km
Average distance from planet: 186,000 km

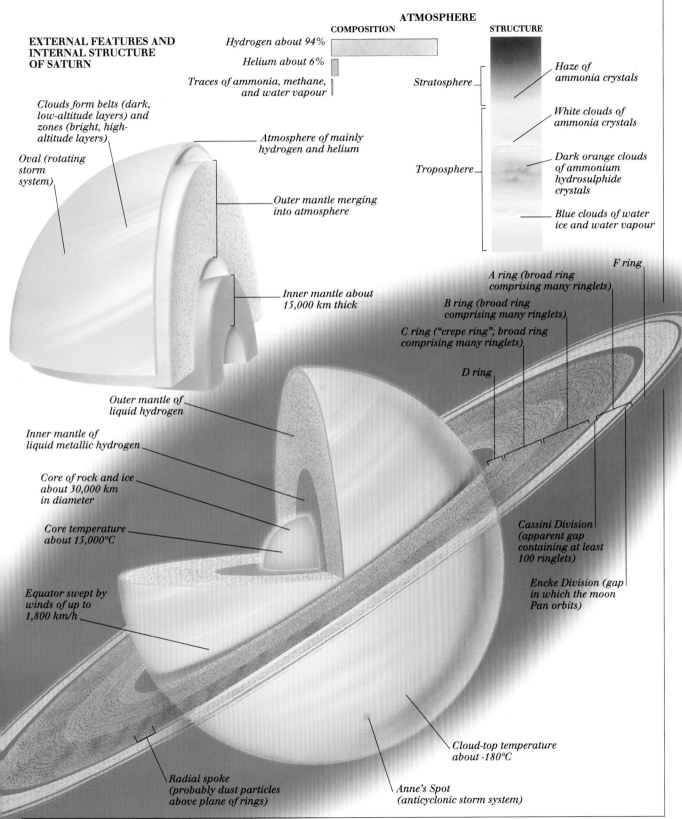

EXTERNAL FEATURES AND
INTERNAL STRUCTURE
OF SATURN

ATMOSPHERE

COMPOSITION

Hydrogen about 94%

Helium about 6%

Traces of ammonia, methane,
and water vapour

STRUCTURE

Stratosphere

Troposphere

Haze of
ammonia crystals

White clouds of
ammonia crystals

Dark orange clouds
of ammonium
hydrosulphide
crystals

Blue clouds of water
ice and water vapour

Clouds form belts (dark,
low-altitude layers) and
zones (bright, high-
altitude layers)

Oval (rotating
storm
system)

Atmosphere of mainly
hydrogen and helium

Outer mantle merging
into atmosphere

Inner mantle about
15,000 km thick

Outer mantle of
liquid hydrogen

Inner mantle of
liquid metallic hydrogen

Core of rock and ice
about 30,000 km
in diameter

Core temperature
about 15,000°C

Equator swept by
winds of up to
1,800 km/h

F ring

A ring (broad ring
comprising many ringlets)

B ring (broad ring
comprising many ringlets)

C ring ("crepe ring"; broad ring
comprising many ringlets)

D ring

Cassini Division
(apparent gap
containing at least
100 ringlets)

Encke Division (gap
in which the moon
Pan orbits)

Cloud-top temperature
about -180°C

Radial spoke
(probably dust particles
above plane of rings)

Anne's Spot
(anticyclonic storm system)

Uranus

**FALSE-COLOUR
IMAGE OF URANUS**

URANUS IS THE SEVENTH PLANET from the Sun
and the third largest, with a diameter of about
51,000 kilometres. It is thought to consist of
a dense mixture of different types of ice and
gas around a solid core. Its atmosphere contains
traces of methane, giving the planet a blue-green
hue, and the temperature at the cloud tops is
about -210°C. Uranus is the most featureless
planet to have been closely observed: only a
few icy clouds of methane have been seen so far. Uranus is unique
among the planets in that its axis of rotation lies close to its orbital
plane. As a result of its strongly tilted rotational axis, Uranus rolls on
its side along its orbital path around the Sun, whereas other planets spin
more or less upright. Uranus is encircled by 11 rings that consist of rocks
interspersed with dust lanes. The rings contain some of the darkest matter
in the Solar System and are extremely narrow, making them difficult to detect:
nine of them are less than 10 kilometres wide, whereas most of Saturn's rings
are thousands of kilometres in width. There are 15 known Uranian moons, all
of which are icy and most of which are further out than the rings. The 10 inner
moons are small and dark, with diameters of less than 160 kilometres, and the
five outer moons are between about 470 and 1,600 kilometres in diameter.
The outer moons have a wide variety of surface features. Miranda has the
most varied surface, with cratered areas broken up by huge ridges and
cliffs 20 kilometres high.

TILT AND ROTATION OF URANUS

Axial tilt
of 97.9°

Perpendicular to
orbital plane

Orbital
plane

South Pole

Axis of
rotation

North
Pole

One rotation
takes 17 hours
and 14 minutes

OUTER MOONS

MIRANDA
Diameter: 472 km
Average distance from
planet: 129,800 km

RINGS OF URANUS

Epsilon ring

Ring 1986 U1R

Delta ring

Gamma
ring

Eta ring

Beta ring

Alpha ring

Rings 4 and 5

Ring 6

Ring 1986 U2R

RINGS AND DUST LANES

ARIEL
Diameter: 1,158 km
Average distance from
planet: 191,200 km

UMBRIEL
Diameter: 1,169 km
Average distance from
planet: 266,000 km

TITANIA
Diameter: 1,578 km
Average distance from
planet: 435,900 km

OBERON
Diameter: 1,523 km
Average distance from
planet: 582,600 km

EXTERNAL FEATURES AND INTERNAL STRUCTURE OF URANUS

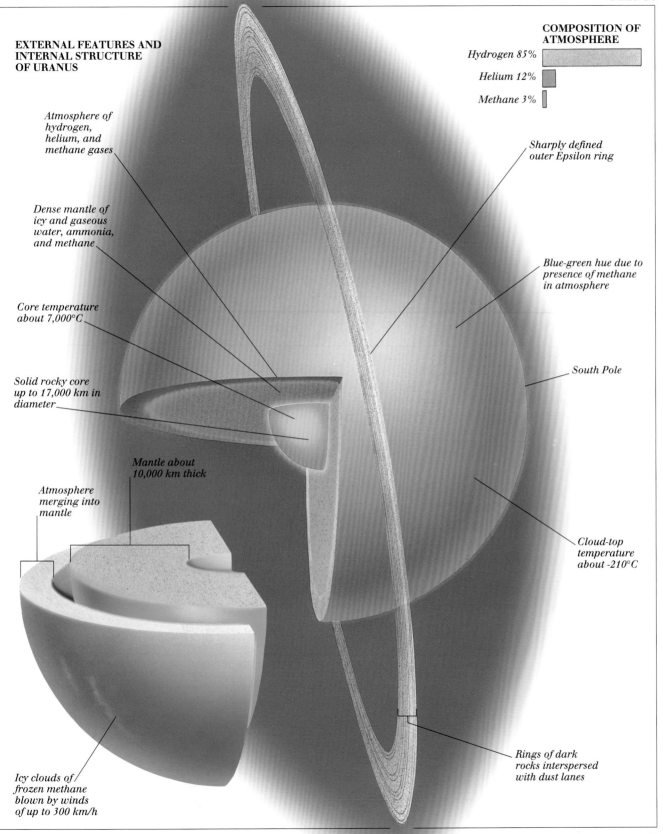

COMPOSITION OF ATMOSPHERE

Hydrogen 85%

Helium 12%

Methane 3%

Atmosphere of hydrogen, helium, and methane gases

Dense mantle of icy and gaseous water, ammonia, and methane

Core temperature about 7,000°C

Solid rocky core up to 17,000 km in diameter

Mantle about 10,000 km thick

Atmosphere merging into mantle

Icy clouds of frozen methane blown by winds of up to 300 km/h

Sharply defined outer Epsilon ring

Blue-green hue due to presence of methane in atmosphere

South Pole

Cloud-top temperature about -210°C

Rings of dark rocks interspersed with dust lanes

Neptune and Pluto

FALSE-COLOUR IMAGE OF NEPTUNE

NEPTUNE AND PLUTO are the two furthest planets from the Sun, at an average distance of about 4,500 million kilometres and 5,900 million kilometres respectively. Neptune is a gas giant and is thought to consist of a small rocky core surrounded by a mixture of liquids and gases. The atmosphere contains several prominent cloud features. The largest of these are the Great Dark Spot, which is as wide as the Earth, the Small Dark Spot, and the Scooter. The Great and Small Dark Spots are huge storms that are swept around the planet by winds of about 2,000 kilometres per hour. The Scooter is a large area of cirrus cloud. Neptune has four tenuous rings and eight known moons. Triton is the largest Neptunian moon and the coldest object in the Solar System, with a temperature of -235°C. Unlike most moons in the Solar System, Triton orbits its mother planet in the opposite direction to the planet's rotation. Pluto is usually the outermost planet but its elliptical orbit causes it to pass inside the orbit of Neptune for 20 years of its 248-year orbit. Pluto is so small and far away that little is known about it. It is a rocky planet, probably covered with ice and frozen methane. Pluto's only known moon, Charon, is large for a moon, at half the size of its parent planet. Because of the small difference in their sizes, Pluto and Charon are sometimes considered to be a double-planet system.

TILT AND ROTATION OF NEPTUNE

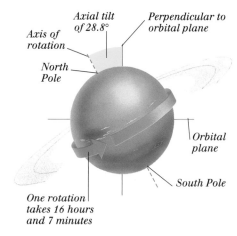

Axial tilt of 28.8°

Perpendicular to orbital plane

Axis of rotation

North Pole

Orbital plane

South Pole

One rotation takes 16 hours and 7 minutes

CLOUD FEATURES OF NEPTUNE

Great Dark Spot (anticyclonic wind storm)

Scooter (cirrus cloud)

Small Dark Spot (cyclonic wind storm)

RINGS OF NEPTUNE

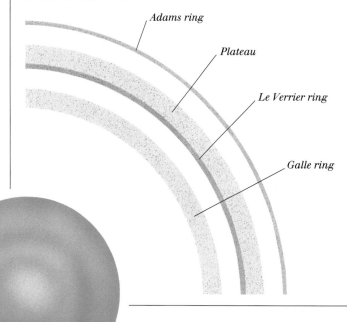

Adams ring

Plateau

Le Verrier ring

Galle ring

HIGH-ALTITUDE CLOUDS

Methane cirrus clouds 40 km above main cloud deck

Cloud shadow

Main cloud deck blown by winds at speeds of about 2,000 km/h

MOONS OF NEPTUNE

TRITON
Diameter: 2,705 km
Average distance from planet: 354,800 km

PROTEUS
Diameter: 416 km
Average distance from planet: 117,600 km

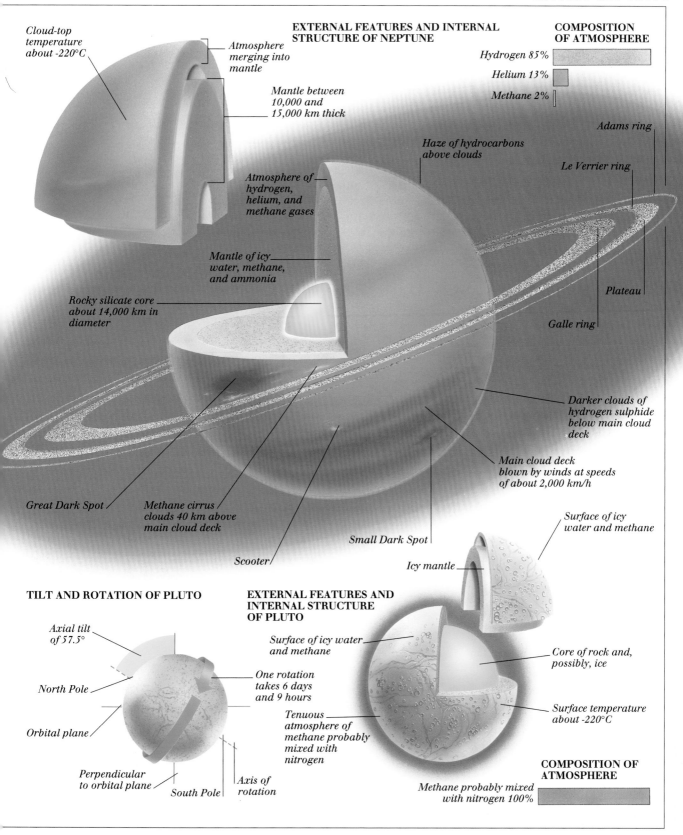

Cloud-top temperature about -220°C

Atmosphere merging into mantle

EXTERNAL FEATURES AND INTERNAL STRUCTURE OF NEPTUNE

COMPOSITION OF ATMOSPHERE

Hydrogen 85%

Helium 13%

Methane 2%

Mantle between 10,000 and 15,000 km thick

Haze of hydrocarbons above clouds

Adams ring

Le Verrier ring

Atmosphere of hydrogen, helium, and methane gases

Mantle of icy water, methane, and ammonia

Plateau

Rocky silicate core about 14,000 km in diameter

Galle ring

Darker clouds of hydrogen sulphide below main cloud deck

Main cloud deck blown by winds at speeds of about 2,000 km/h

Great Dark Spot

Methane cirrus clouds 40 km above main cloud deck

Scooter

Small Dark Spot

Icy mantle

Surface of icy water and methane

TILT AND ROTATION OF PLUTO

EXTERNAL FEATURES AND INTERNAL STRUCTURE OF PLUTO

Surface of icy water and methane

Core of rock and, possibly, ice

Axial tilt of 57.5°

North Pole

One rotation takes 6 days and 9 hours

Orbital plane

Tenuous atmosphere of methane probably mixed with nitrogen

Surface temperature about -220°C

Perpendicular to orbital plane

South Pole

Axis of rotation

COMPOSITION OF ATMOSPHERE

Methane probably mixed with nitrogen 100%

51

Asteroids, comets, and meteoroids

ASTEROID 951 GASPRA

ASTEROIDS, COMETS, AND METEOROIDS are all debris remaining from the nebula in which the Solar System formed 4.6 billion years ago. Asteroids are rocky bodies up to about 1,000 kilometres in diameter, although most are much smaller. Most of them orbit the Sun in the asteroid belt, which lies between the orbits of Mars and Jupiter. Comets may originate in a huge cloud (called the Oort Cloud) that is thought to surround the Solar System. They are made of frozen gases and dust, and are a few kilometres in diameter. Occasionally, a comet is deflected from the Oort Cloud to orbit the Sun in a long, elliptical path. As the comet approaches the Sun, the comet's surface starts to vaporize in the heat, producing a brightly shining coma (a huge sphere of gas and dust around the nucleus), a gas tail, and a dust tail. Meteoroids are small chunks of stone or stone and iron, some of which are fragments of asteroids or comets. Meteoroids range in size from tiny dust particles to objects tens of metres across. If a meteoroid enters the Earth's atmosphere, it is heated by friction and appears as a glowing streak of light called a meteor (also known as a shooting star). Meteor showers occur when the Earth passes through the trail of dust particles left by a comet. Most meteors burn up in the atmosphere. The few that are large enough to reach the Earth's surface are termed meteorites.

FALSE-COLOUR IMAGE OF HALLEY'S COMET

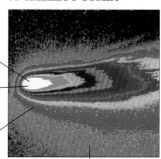

High-intensity light emission

Nucleus

Medium-intensity light emission

Low-intensity light emission

FALSE-COLOUR IMAGE OF A LEONID METEOR SHOWER

METEORITES

DEVELOPMENT OF COMET TAILS

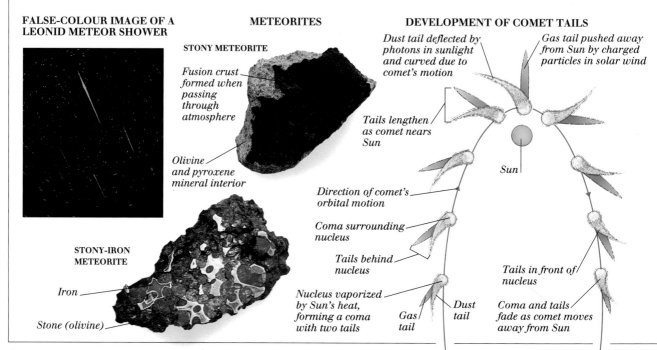

STONY METEORITE

Fusion crust formed when passing through atmosphere

Olivine and pyroxene mineral interior

STONY-IRON METEORITE

Iron

Stone (olivine)

Dust tail deflected by photons in sunlight and curved due to comet's motion

Gas tail pushed away from Sun by charged particles in solar wind

Tails lengthen as comet nears Sun

Direction of comet's orbital motion

Coma surrounding nucleus

Tails behind nucleus

Nucleus vaporized by Sun's heat, forming a coma with two tails

Gas tail

Dust tail

Sun

Tails in front of nucleus

Coma and tails fade as comet moves away from Sun

FEATURES OF A COMET

Thin, straight
gas tail

Broad, curved
dust tail

Gas molecules
heated by Sun
and emitting
light

Comet tails up to
100 million km long

Thin, straight gas
tail blown by
solar wind

Head (coma and nucleus)

Coma
surrounding
nucleus

Nucleus a few
kilometres
across

**STRUCTURE OF
A COMET**

Glowing coma up
to 1 million km
across surrounding
nucleus

Possible
core of
silicate
dust

Crust
with active
areas emitting
jets of gas
and dust

Jet of gas
and dust produced
by vaporization on
sunlit side of nucleus

Ices, including
water ice, and frozen carbon
dioxide, methane, and ammonia

Broad dust
tail curved along
comet's orbital path

Dust particles
reflecting sunlight

53

PREHISTORIC EARTH

The changing Earth

THE EARTH FORMED FROM A CLOUD OF DUST and gas drifting through space about 4,600 million years ago. Dense minerals sank to the centre while lighter ones formed a thin rocky crust. However, the first known life-forms – bacteria and blue-green algae – did not appear until about 3,400 million years ago, and it was only about 700 million years ago that more complex plants and animals began to develop. Since then, thousands of animal and plant species have evolved; some, such as the dinosaurs, survived for many millions of years, while others died out quickly. The Earth itself is continually changing. Although continents neared their present locations about 50 million years ago, they are still drifting slowly over the planet's surface, and mountain ranges such as the Himalayas – which began to form 40 million years ago – are continually being built up and worn away. Climate is also subject to change: the Earth has undergone a series of ice ages interspersed with warmer periods (the most recent glacial period was at its height about 20,000 years ago).

Small mammals appeared (e.g., Crusafontia)

Dinosaurs became extinct

Global mountain building occurred

Multicellular soft-bodied animals appeared (e.g., worms and jellyfish)

Shelled invertebrates appeared (e.g., trilobites)

Marine plants flourished

Land plants appeared (e.g., Cooksonia)

Unicellular organisms appeared (e.g., blue-green algae)

Earth formed

Coral reefs appeared

Vertebrates appeared (e.g., Hemicyclaspis)

More complex types of algae appeared

Amphibians appeared (e.g., Ichthyostega)

CRETACEOUS

ORDOVICIAN

CAMBRIAN

PRECAMBRIAN TIME

SILURIAN

DEVONIAN

GEOLOGICAL TIMESCALE

MILLIONS OF
YEARS AGO (MYA)

4,600	570	510	439	409	363	323	290

PRECAMBRIAN TIME	CAMBRIAN	ORDOVICIAN	SILURIAN	DEVONIAN	MISSISSIPPIAN (NORTH AMERICA)	PENNSYLVANIAN (NORTH AMERICA)
					CARBONIFEROUS	
	PALAEOZOIC					

EVOLUTION OF THE EARTH

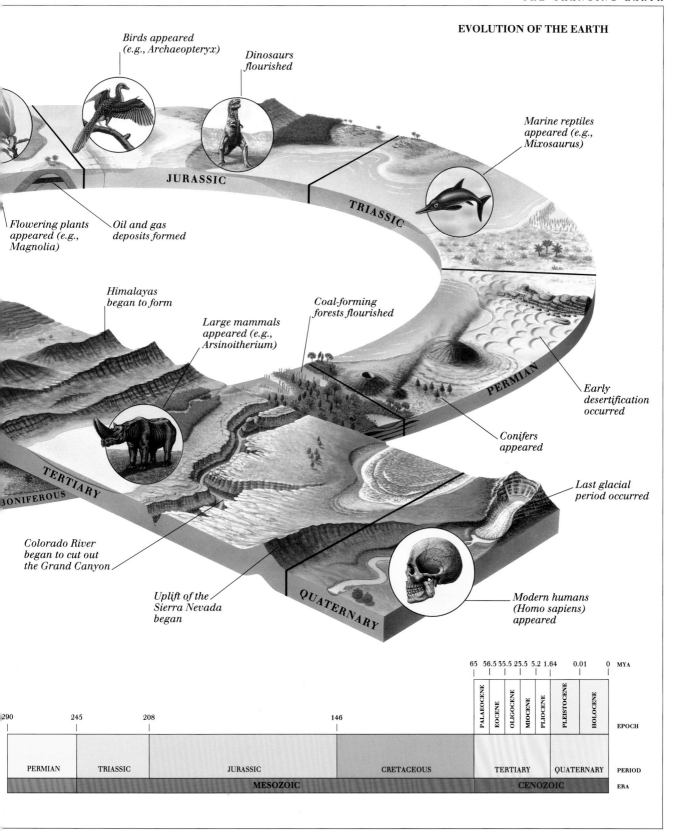

Birds appeared
(e.g., Archaeopteryx)

Dinosaurs
flourished

Marine reptiles
appeared (e.g.,
Mixosaurus)

JURASSIC

TRIASSIC

Flowering plants
appeared (e.g.,
Magnolia)

Oil and gas
deposits formed

Himalayas
began to form

Large mammals
appeared (e.g.,
Arsinoitherium)

Coal-forming
forests flourished

Early
desertification
occurred

Conifers
appeared

PERMIAN

TERTIARY

BONIFEROUS

Last glacial
period occurred

Colorado River
began to cut out
the Grand Canyon

Uplift of the
Sierra Nevada
began

QUATERNARY

Modern humans
(Homo sapiens)
appeared

	65	56.5	35.5	23.5	5.2	1.64		0.01	0	MYA
	PALAEOCENE	EOCENE	OLIGOCENE	MIOCENE	PLIOCENE		PLEISTOCENE		HOLOCENE	EPOCH

290		245		208		146					
PERMIAN		TRIASSIC		JURASSIC		CRETACEOUS		TERTIARY		QUATERNARY	PERIOD
			MESOZOIC					CENOZOIC			ERA

57

The Earth's crust

THE EARTH'S CRUST IS THE SOLID outer shell of the Earth. It includes continental crust (about 40 kilometres thick) and oceanic crust (about six kilometres thick). The crust and the topmost layer of the mantle form the lithosphere. The lithosphere consists of semi-rigid plates that move relative to each other on the underlying asthenosphere (a partly molten layer of the mantle). This process is known as plate tectonics and helps explain continental drift. Where two plates move apart, there are rifts in the crust. In mid-ocean, this movement results in sea-floor spreading and the formation of ocean ridges; on continents, crustal spreading can form rift valleys. When plates move towards each other, one may be subducted beneath (forced under) the other. In mid-ocean, this causes ocean trenches, seismic activity, and arcs of volcanic islands. Where oceanic crust is subducted beneath continental crust or where continents collide, land may be uplifted and mountains formed (see pp. 62–63). Plates may also slide past each other – along the San Andreas fault, for example. Crustal movement on continents may result in earthquakes, while movement under the seabed can lead to tidal waves.

ELEMENTS IN THE EARTH'S CRUST

Other elements 2%

Potassium 2.6%

Calcium 3.6%

Aluminium 8%

Magnesium 2%

Sodium 2.8%

Iron 5%

Silicon 28%

Oxygen 46%

FEATURES OF PLATE MOVEMENTS

Ridge where magma is rising to form new oceanic crust

Region of sea-floor spreading

Ocean trench formed where oceanic crust is forced under continental crust

Subduction zone

Rift formed where two plates are moving apart

Magma (molten rock) erupts at rift

Magma rises to form a hot spot

Volcano develops over hot spot and builds up to form an island

Volcanic island that originally formed over hot spot

Oceanic crust melts

Magma rises to form a volcano

MAJOR PLATES OF THE EARTH'S CRUST

Hellenic plate

Eurasian plate

North American plate

Plates sliding past each other

Pacific plate

Cocos plate

Philippine plate

Caribbean plate

Plates converging

Nazca plate

South American plate

African plate

Indo-Australian plate

Plates moving apart

Boundary along which two plates slide past each other

Mountain range uplifted where subducting oceanic crust compresses and deforms edge of continental crust

Lithosphere (crust and topmost layer of mantle)

Asthenosphere (upper part of mantle)

MOVEMENT OF LAND ALONG OCEANIC RIDGES

Land moves apart at a constant rate, perpendicular to ridge

STRAIGHT OCEANIC RIDGE

Land moves apart at a constant rate, perpendicular to curve

CURVED OCEANIC RIDGE

Staggered parallel ridge sections take shape of curve

Transform fault

STRESSES RESOLVE INTO SECTIONS

Faults and folds

THE CONTINUOUS MOVEMENT of the Earth's crustal plates (see pp. 58–59) can squeeze, stretch, or break rock strata, deforming them and producing faults and folds. A fault is a fracture in a rock along which there is movement of one side relative to the other. The movement can be vertical, horizontal, or oblique (vertical and horizontal). Faults develop when rocks are subjected to compression or tension. They tend to occur in hard, rigid rocks, which are more likely to break than bend. The smallest faults occur in single mineral crystals and are microscopically small, whereas the largest – the Great Rift Valley in Africa, which formed between 5 million and 100,000 years ago – is more than 9,000 kilometres long. A fold is a bend in a rock layer caused by compression. Folds occur in elastic rocks, which tend to bend rather than break. The two main types of fold are anticlines (upfolds) and synclines (downfolds). Folds vary in size from a few millimetres long to folded mountain ranges hundreds of kilometres long, such as the Himalayas (see pp. 62–63) and the Alps, which are repeatedly folding. In addition to faults and folds, other features associated with rock deformations include boudins, mullions, and *en échelon* fractures.

STRUCTURE OF A FOLD

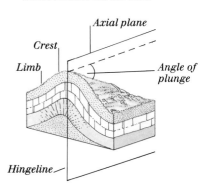

Axial plane
Crest
Limb
Angle of plunge
Hingeline

STRUCTURE OF A FAULT

Fault plane
Dip of fault plane (angle from horizontal)
Upthrow
Throw (vertical displacement of fault)
Downthrow
Hade of fault plane (angle from vertical)

STRUCTURE OF A SLOPE

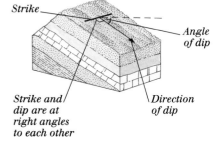

Strike
Angle of dip
Strike and dip are at right angles to each other
Direction of dip

FOLDED ROCK

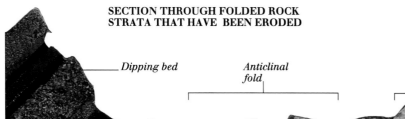

Steeply dipping limbs
Crest of anticline
Plunge

SECTION THROUGH FOLDED ROCK STRATA THAT HAVE BEEN ERODED

Dipping bed
Anticlinal fold
Monoclinal fold
Mineral-filled fault

Upper Carboniferous Millstone Grit
Lower Carboniferous Limestone

EXAMPLES OF FOLDS

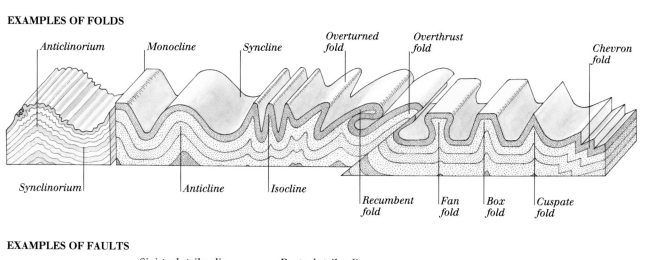

Anticlinorium *Monocline* *Syncline* *Overturned fold* *Overthrust fold* *Chevron fold*

Synclinorium *Anticline* *Isocline* *Recumbent fold* *Fan fold* *Box fold* *Cuspate fold*

EXAMPLES OF FAULTS

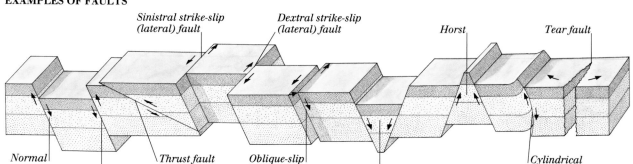

Sinistral strike-slip (lateral) fault *Dextral strike-slip (lateral) fault* *Horst* *Tear fault*

Normal dip-slip fault *Reverse dip-slip fault* *Thrust fault* *Oblique-slip fault* *Graben* *Cylindrical fault*

SMALL-SCALE ROCK DEFORMATIONS

Competent bed (rocks that break) *Tension* *Incompetent bed* *Tension* *Tension* *Tension* *Masses of rock shear past each other* *Tension* *En échelon fracture*

Tension *Incompetent bed (rocks that bend)* *Competent bed breaks into sections* *Competent bed* *Competent bed splits into prisms* *Tension* *Joint opened by stress*

BOUDIN **MULLION** **EN ECHELON FRACTURE**

Mineral-filled fault *Dipping bed* *Gently folded bed* *Horizontal bed* *Mineral-filled fault* *Dipping bed*

| Upper Carboniferous Millstone Grit | Upper Carboniferous Coal Measures |

Mountain building

THE PROCESSES INVOLVED in mountain building – termed orogenesis – occur as a result of the movement of the Earth's crustal plates (see pp. 58–59). There are three main types of mountains: volcanic mountains, fold mountains, and block mountains. Most volcanic mountains have been formed along plate boundaries where plates have come together or moved apart and lava and other debris have been ejected onto the Earth's surface. The lava and debris may have built up to form a dome around the vent of a volcano. Fold mountains are formed where plates push together and cause the rock to buckle upwards. Where oceanic crust meets less dense continental crust, the oceanic crust is forced under the continental crust. The continental crust is buckled by the impact. This is how folded mountain ranges, such as the Appalachian Mountains in North America, were formed. Fold mountains are also formed where two areas of continental crust meet. The Himalayas, for example, began to form when India collided with Asia, buckling the sediments and parts of the oceanic crust between them. Block mountains are formed when a block of land is uplifted between two faults as a result of compression or tension in the Earth's crust (see pp. 60–61). Often, the movement along faults has taken place gradually over millions of years. However, two plates may cause an earthquake by suddenly sliding past each other along a faultline.

BHAGIRATHI PARBAT, HIMALAYAS

FORMATION OF THE HIMALAYAS

Asia

Himalayas formed by buckling of sediment and part of the oceanic crust between two colliding continents

India moves north

India collides with Asia about 40 million years ago

EXAMPLES OF MOUNTAINS

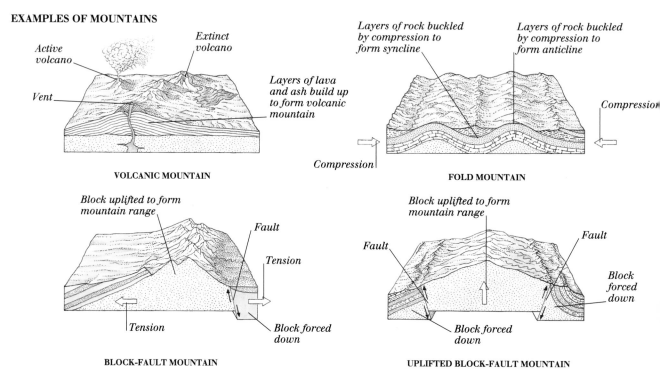

Active volcano

Extinct volcano

Vent

Layers of lava and ash build up to form volcanic mountain

VOLCANIC MOUNTAIN

Layers of rock buckled by compression to form syncline

Layers of rock buckled by compression to form anticline

Compression

Compression

FOLD MOUNTAIN

Block uplifted to form mountain range

Fault

Tension

Tension

Block forced down

BLOCK-FAULT MOUNTAIN

Block uplifted to form mountain range

Fault

Fault

Block forced down

Block forced down

UPLIFTED BLOCK-FAULT MOUNTAIN

STAGES IN THE FORMATION OF THE HIMALAYAS

Sediment

India moves towards Asia

Ocean area becomes smaller as plates converge

Sediment

Asia

Volcano

Continental crust

Continental crust

Oceanic crust forced under continental crust

Magma rises to form volcanoes

60 MILLION YEARS AGO

Sediment and part of oceanic crust folded by continental collision

India

Asia

Continental crust

Oceanic crust forced further under continental crust

Continental crust

40 MILLION YEARS AGO

Ganges plain

Sediment and part of oceanic crust folded and uplifted

India

Asia

Continental crust

Continental crust

20 MILLION YEARS AGO

Sediment and part of oceanic crust further folded and uplifted to form Himalayas

Ripple effect of collision forms mountains and plateau of Tibet

Ganges plain

India

Asia

Continental crust

Continental crust

TODAY

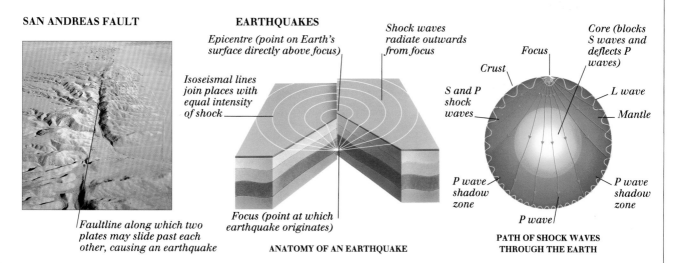

SAN ANDREAS FAULT

Faultline along which two plates may slide past each other, causing an earthquake

EARTHQUAKES

Epicentre (point on Earth's surface directly above focus)

Isoseismal lines join places with equal intensity of shock

Shock waves radiate outwards from focus

Focus (point at which earthquake originates)

ANATOMY OF AN EARTHQUAKE

Core (blocks S waves and deflects P waves)

Focus

Crust

L wave

S and P shock waves

Mantle

P wave shadow zone

P wave shadow zone

P wave

PATH OF SHOCK WAVES THROUGH THE EARTH

Precambrian to Devonian periods

MIDDLE ORDOVICIAN POSITIONS OF PRESENT-DAY LAND-MASSES

North America · Greenland · China · Australia · South America · South Africa · Africa · Scandinavia · Europe · Siberia · Central Asia · India · North East Africa

WHEN THE EARTH FORMED about 4,600 million years ago, its atmosphere consisted of volcanic gases with little oxygen, making it hostile to most forms of life. One large supercontinent, Gondwanaland, was situated over the southern polar region, while other smaller continents were spread over the rest of the world. Constant movement of the earth's crustal plates carried continents across the earth's surface. The first primitive life-forms emerged around 3,400 million years ago in shallow, warm seas. The build up of oxygen began to form a shield of ozone around the earth, protecting living organisms from the sun's harmful rays and helping to establish an atmosphere in which life could sustain itself. The first vertebrates appeared about 470 million years ago, during the Ordovician period (510–439 million years ago), the first land plants appeared around 400 million years ago during the Devonian period (409–363 million years ago), and the first land animals about 30 million years later.

EXAMPLES OF PRECAMBRIAN TO DEVONIAN PLANT GROUPS

A PRESENT-DAY CLUBMOSS
(*Lycopodium sp.*)

A PRESENT-DAY LAND PLANT
(*Asparagus setaceous*)

FOSSIL OF AN EXTINCT LAND PLANT
(*Cooksonia hemisphaerica*)

FOSSIL OF AN EXTINCT SWAMP PLANT
(*Zosterophyllum llanoveranum*)

EXAMPLES OF PRECAMBRIAN TO DEVONIAN TRILOBITES

ACADAGNOSTUS
Family: Agnostidae
Length: 8 mm (⅓ in)

PHACOPS
Family: Phacopidae
Length: 4.5 cm (1¾ in)

OLENELLUS
Family: Olenellidae
Length: 6 cm (2½ in)

ELRATHIA
Family: Ptychopariidae
Length: 2 cm (¾ in)

THE EARTH DURING THE MIDDLE ORDOVICIAN PERIOD

Siberia

Laurentia

China

Kazakstania

Gondwanaland

Baltica

EXAMPLES OF EARLY MARINE INVERTEBRATES

FOSSIL NAUTILOID
(Estonioceras perforatum)

FOSSIL BRACHIOPOD
(Dicoelosia bilobata)

TRACE FOSSIL
(Mawsonites spriggi)

FOSSIL GRAPTOLITE
(Monograptus convolutus)

EXAMPLES OF DEVONIAN FISH

RHAMPHODOPSIS
Family: Ptyctodontidae
Length: 15 cm (6 in)

PTERASPIS
Family: Pteraspidae
Length: 25 cm (10 in)

COCCOSTEUS
Family: Coccosteidae
Length: 35 cm (14 in)

BOTHRIOLEPIS
Family: Bothriolepidae
Length: 40 cm (16 in)

CHEIRACANTHUS
Family: Acanthodidae
Length: 30 cm (12 in)

PTERICHTHYODES
Family: Asterolepidae
Length: 15 cm (6 in)

CHEIROLEPIS
Family: Cheirolepidae
Length: 17 cm (6¾ in)

CEPHALASPIS
Family: Cephalaspidae
Length: 22 cm (8¾ in)

Carboniferous to Permian periods

North America
Greenland
Siberia
China
South America
Antarctica
Africa
Antarctica
Australia
India

THE CARBONIFEROUS PERIOD (363–290 million years ago) takes its name from the thick, carbon-rich layers – now coal – that were produced during this period as swampy tropical forests were repeatedly drowned by shallow seas. The humid climate across northern and equatorial continents throughout Carboniferous times produced the first dense plant cover on Earth. During the early part of this period, the first reptiles appeared. Their development of a waterproof egg with a protective internal structure ended animal life's dependence on an aquatic environment. Towards the end of Carboniferous times, the earth's continents Laurasia and Gondwanaland collided, resulting in the huge land-mass of Pangaea. Glaciers smothered much of the southern hemisphere during the Permian period (290–245 million years ago), covering Antarctica, parts of Australia, and much of South America, Africa, and India. Ice locked up much of the world's water and large areas of the northern hemisphere experienced a drop in sea-level. Away from the poles, deserts and a hot dry climate predominated. As a result of these conditions, the Permian period ended with the greatest mass extinction of life on earth ever.

EXAMPLES OF CARBONIFEROUS AND PERMIAN PLANT GROUPS

A PRESENT-DAY FIR
(Abies concolor)

FOSSIL OF AN EXTINCT FERN
(Zeilleria frenzlii)

FOSSIL OF AN EXTINCT HORSETAIL
(Equisetites sp.)

FOSSIL OF AN EXTINCT CLUBMOSS
(Lepidodendron sp.)

EXAMPLES OF CARBONIFEROUS AND PERMIAN TREES

PECOPTERIS
Family: Marattiaceae
Height: 4 m (13 ft)

PARIPTERIS
Family: Medullosaceae
Height: 5 m (16 ft 6 in)

MARIOPTERIS
Family: Unclassified
Height: 5 m (16 ft 6 in)

MEDULLOSA
Family: Medullosaceae
Height: 5 m (16 ft 6 in)

THE EARTH DURING THE LATE CARBONIFEROUS PERIOD

EXAMPLES OF CARBONIFEROUS AND PERMIAN ANIMALS

Siberia

Laurussia

China

Ural Mountains

Caledonian Mountains

Appalachian Mountains

Gondwanaland

SKULL OF AN EXTINCT SYNAPSID REPTILE
(*Dimetrodon loomisi*)

FOSSIL TEETH OF AN EXTINCT SHARK
(*Helicoprion bessonowi*)

MODEL OF AN EXTINCT CARBONIFEROUS REPTILE
(*Westlothiana lizziae*)

LEPIDODENDRON
Family: Lepidodendraceae
Height: 30 m (100 ft)

CORDAITES
Family: Cordaitacea
Height: 10 m (33 ft)

GLOSSOPTERIS
Family: Glossopteridaceae
Height: 8 m (26 ft)

ALETHOPTERIS
Family: Medullosaceae
Height: 5 m (16 ft 6 in)

67

Triassic period

THE TRIASSIC PERIOD (245–208 million years ago) marked the beginning of what is known as the Age of the Dinosaurs (the Mesozoic era). During this period, the present-day continents were massed together, forming one huge continent known as Pangaea. This land-mass experienced extremes of climate, with lush green areas around the coast or by lakes and rivers, and arid deserts in the interior. The only forms of plant life were non-flowering plants, such as conifers, ferns, cycads, and ginkgos; flowering plants had not yet evolved. The principal forms of animal life included primitive amphibians, rhynchosaurs ("beaked lizards"), and primitive crocodilians. Dinosaurs first appeared about 230 million years ago, at the beginning of the Late Triassic period. The earliest known dinosaurs were the carnivorous (flesh-eating) herrerasaurids and staurikosaurids, such as *Herrerasaurus* and *Staurikosaurus*. Early herbivorous (plant-eating) dinosaurs first appeared in Late Triassic times and included *Plateosaurus* and *Technosaurus*. By the end of the Triassic period, dinosaurs dominated Pangaea, possibly contributing to the extinction of many other reptiles.

TRIASSIC POSITIONS OF PRESENT-DAY LAND-MASSES

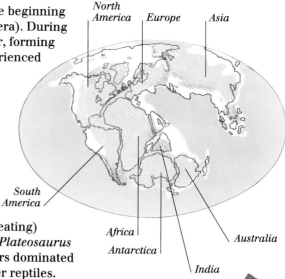

North America
Europe
Asia
South America
Africa
Antarctica
India
Australia

EXAMPLES OF TRIASSIC PLANT GROUPS

A PRESENT-DAY CYCAD
(*Cycas revoluta*)

A PRESENT-DAY GINKGO
(*Ginkgo biloba*)

A PRESENT-DAY CONIFER
(*Araucaria araucana*)

FOSSIL OF AN EXTINCT FERN
(*Pachypteris sp.*)

FOSSIL LEAF OF AN EXTINCT CYCAD
(*Cycas sp.*)

EXAMPLES OF TRIASSIC DINOSAURS

MELANOROSAURUS
A melanorosaurid
Length: 12.2 m (40 ft)

MUSSAURUS
A plateosaurid
Length: 2–3 m (6 ft 6 in–10 ft)

HERRERASAURUS
A herrerasaurid
Length: 3 m (10 ft)

PISANOSAURUS
A primitive ornithischian
Length: 90 cm (3 ft)

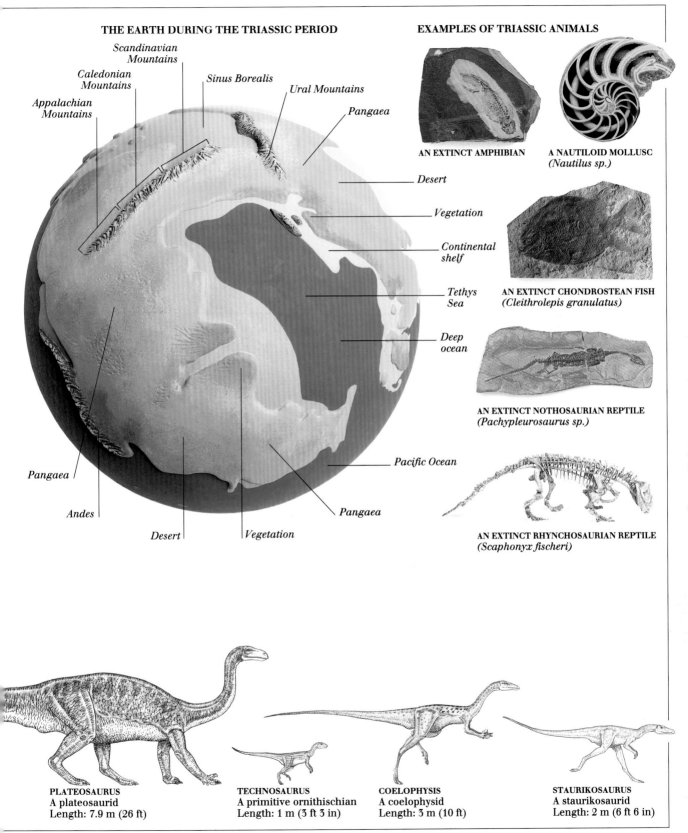

THE EARTH DURING THE TRIASSIC PERIOD

Scandinavian Mountains

Caledonian Mountains

Appalachian Mountains

Sinus Borealis

Ural Mountains

Pangaea

Desert

Vegetation

Continental shelf

Tethys Sea

Deep ocean

Pacific Ocean

Pangaea

Andes

Pangaea

Desert

Vegetation

EXAMPLES OF TRIASSIC ANIMALS

AN EXTINCT AMPHIBIAN

A NAUTILOID MOLLUSC
(Nautilus sp.)

AN EXTINCT CHONDROSTEAN FISH
(Cleithrolepis granulatus)

AN EXTINCT NOTHOSAURIAN REPTILE
(Pachypleurosaurus sp.)

AN EXTINCT RHYNCHOSAURIAN REPTILE
(Scaphonyx fischeri)

PLATEOSAURUS
A plateosaurid
Length: 7.9 m (26 ft)

TECHNOSAURUS
A primitive ornithischian
Length: 1 m (3 ft 3 in)

COELOPHYSIS
A coelophysid
Length: 3 m (10 ft)

STAURIKOSAURUS
A staurikosaurid
Length: 2 m (6 ft 6 in)

Jurassic period

THE JURASSIC PERIOD, the middle part of the Mesozoic era, lasted from 208 to 146 million years ago. During Jurassic times, the land-mass of Pangaea broke up into the continents of Gondwanaland and Laurasia, and sea-levels rose, flooding areas of lower land. The Jurassic climate was warm and moist. Plants such as ginkgos, horsetails, and conifers thrived, and giant redwood trees appeared, as did the first flowering plants. The abundance of plant food coincided with the proliferation of herbivorous (plant-eating) dinosaurs, such as the large sauropods (e.g., *Diplodocus*) and stegosaurs (e.g., *Stegosaurus*). Carnivorous (flesh-eating) dinosaurs, such as *Compsognathus* and *Allosaurus*, also flourished by hunting the many animals that existed – among them other dinosaurs. Further Jurassic animals included shrew-like mammals, and pterosaurs (flying reptiles), as well as plesiosaurs and ichthyosaurs (both marine reptiles).

JURASSIC POSITIONS OF PRESENT-DAY LAND-MASSES

North America
Europe
Arabia
Asia
South America
Africa
Antarctica
India
Australia

EXAMPLES OF JURASSIC PLANT GROUPS

A PRESENT-DAY FERN
(*Dicksonia antarctica*)

A PRESENT-DAY HORSETAIL
(*Equisetum arvense*)

A PRESENT-DAY CONIFER
(*Taxus baccata*)

FOSSIL LEAF OF AN EXTINCT CONIFER
(*Taxus sp.*)

FOSSIL LEAF OF AN EXTINCT REDWOOD
(*Sequoiadendron affinis*)

EXAMPLES OF JURASSIC DINOSAURS

DIPLODOCUS
A diplodocid
Length: 26.8 m (88 ft)

CAMPTOSAURUS
A camptosaurid
Length: 4.9–7 m (16–23 ft)

DRYOSAURUS
A dryosaurid
Length: 3–4 m (10–13 ft)

THE EARTH DURING THE JURASSIC PERIOD

North Atlantic Ocean

Laurasia

Laurasia

Ural Mountains

Turgai Strait

North American Cordillera

Vegetation

Laurasia

Desert

Tethys Sea

Deep ocean

Continental shelf

Desert

Andes

Gondwanaland

Vegetation

Gondwanaland

Pacific Ocean

EXAMPLES OF JURASSIC ANIMALS

AN EXTINCT PTEROSAUR
(Rhamphorhynchus sp.)

AN EXTINCT BELEMNITE MOLLUSC
(Belemnoteuthis sp.)

AN EXTINCT RHYNCHOSAURIAN REPTILE
(Homeosaurus pulchellus)

AN EXTINCT PLESIOSAUR
(Peloneustes philarcus)

AN EXTINCT ICHTHYOSAUR
(Ichthyosaurus megacephalus)

ALLOSAURUS
An allosaurid
Length: 11 m (36 ft)

SCELIDOSAURUS
A scelidosaurid
Length: 4 m (13 ft)

STEGOSAURUS
A stegosaurid
Length: 9.1 m (30 ft)

71

Cretaceous period

THE MESOZOIC ERA ENDED WITH the Cretaceous period, which lasted from 146 to 65 million years ago. During this period, Gondwanaland and Laurasia were breaking up into smaller land-masses that more closely resembled those of the modern continents. The climate remained mild and moist but the seasons became more marked. Flowering plants, including deciduous trees, replaced many cycads, seed ferns, and conifers. Animal species became more varied, with the evolution of new mammals, insects, fish, crustaceans, and turtles. Dinosaurs evolved into a wide variety of species during Cretaceous times; more than half of all known dinosaurs – including *Iguanodon*, *Deinonychus*, *Tyrannosaurus*, and *Hypsilophodon* – lived during this period. At the end of the Cretaceous period, however, dinosaurs became extinct. The reason for this mass extinction is unknown but it is thought to have been caused by climatic changes due to either a catastrophic meteor impact with the Earth or extensive volcanic eruptions.

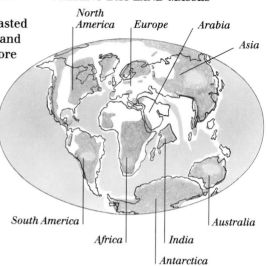

CRETACEOUS POSITIONS OF PRESENT-DAY LAND-MASSES

North America · Europe · Arabia · Asia · South America · Africa · India · Antarctica · Australia

EXAMPLES OF CRETACEOUS PLANT GROUPS

A PRESENT-DAY CONIFER
(*Pinus muricata*)

A PRESENT-DAY DECIDUOUS TREE
(*Magnolia sp.*)

FOSSIL OF AN EXTINCT FERN
(*Sphenopteris latiloba*)

FOSSIL OF AN EXTINCT GINKGO
(*Ginkgo pluripartita*)

FOSSIL LEAVES OF AN EXTINCT DECIDUOUS TREE
(*Cercidyphyllum sp.*)

EXAMPLES OF CRETACEOUS DINOSAURS

SALTASAURUS
A titanosaurid
Length: 12.2 m (40 ft)

TOROSAURUS
A ceratopsid
Length: 7.6 m (25 ft)

HYPSILOPHODON
A hypsilophodontid
Length: 1.4–2.3 m (4 ft 6 in–7 ft 6 in)

THE EARTH DURING THE CRETACEOUS PERIOD

West Africa

Africa

Greenland

Europe

Continental Sea

North America

Ural Mountains

Rocky Mountains

Desert

Tethys Sea

Asia

India

Indian Ocean

Pacific Ocean

North Atlantic Ocean

Andes

South America

South Atlantic Ocean

Antarctica

Vegetation

Australia

EXAMPLES OF CRETACEOUS ANIMALS

AN EXTINCT INSECT
(*Libellulium longialatum*)

AN EXTINCT MARINE TURTLE
(*Plesiochelys latiscutata*)

AN EXTINCT CRUSTACEAN
(*Homarus sp.*)

AN EXTINCT CROCODILIAN

AN EXTINCT HOLOSTEAN FISH
(*Lepidotes maximus*)

TYRANNOSAURUS
A tyrannosaurid
Length: 12.2 m (40 ft)

DEINONYCHUS
A dromaeosaurid
Length: 2.4–3.4 m (8–11 ft)

IGUANODON
An iguanodontid
Length: 9.1 m (30 ft)

73

Tertiary period

FOLLOWING THE DEMISE OF THE DINOSAURS at the end of the Cretaceous period, the Tertiary period (65–1.6 million years ago), which formed the first part of the Cenozoic era (65 million years ago–present), was characterized by a huge expansion of mammal life. Placental mammals nourish and maintain the young in the mother's uterus; only three orders of placental mammals existed during Cretaceous times, compared with 25 orders during the Tertiary period. One of these 25 included the first hominid (see pp.108–109), *Australopithecus*, which appeared in Africa. By the beginning of the Tertiary period, the continents had almost reached their present position. The Tethys Sea, which had separated the northern continents from Africa and India, began to close up, forming the Mediterranean Sea and allowing the migration of terrestrial animals between Africa and western Europe. India's collision with Asia led to the formation of the Himalayas. During the middle part of the Tertiary period, the forest-dwelling and browsing mammals were replaced by mammals such as the horse, better suited to grazing the open savannahs that began to dominate. Repeated cool periods throughout the Tertiary period established the Antarctic as an icy island continent.

TERTIARY POSITIONS OF PRESENT-DAY LAND-MASSES

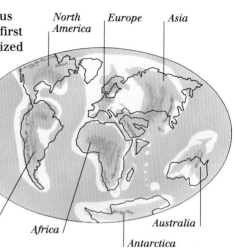

North America · Europe · Asia · South America · Africa · Australia · Antarctica

EXAMPLES OF TERTIARY PLANT GROUPS

A PRESENT-DAY OAK
(*Quercus palustris*)

A PRESENT-DAY BIRCH
(*Betula grossa*)

FOSSIL LEAF OF AN EXTINCT BIRCH
(*Betulites sp.*)

FOSSILIZED STEM OF AN EXTINCT PALM
(*Palmoxylon sp.*)

EXAMPLES OF TERTIARY ANIMAL GROUPS

HYAENODON
An hyaenodontid
Length: 2 m (6 ft 6 in)

TITANOHYRAX
A pliohyracid
Length: 2 m (6 ft 6 in)

PHORUSRHACUS
A phorusrhacid
Length: 1.5 m (5 ft)

SAMOTHERIUM
A giraffid
Length: 3 m (10 ft)

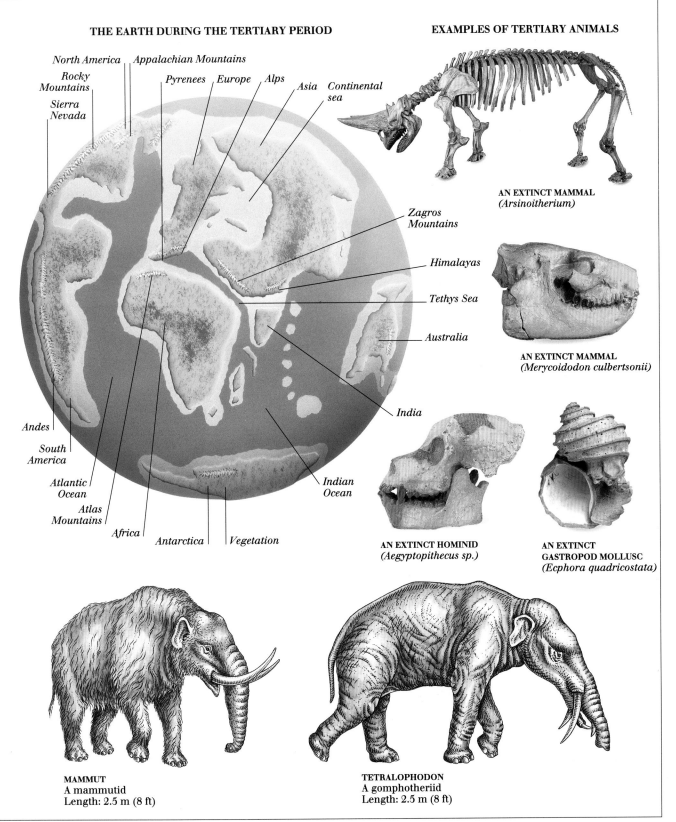

THE EARTH DURING THE TERTIARY PERIOD

North America

Rocky Mountains

Sierra Nevada

Appalachian Mountains

Pyrenees

Europe

Alps

Asia

Continental sea

Zagros Mountains

Himalayas

Tethys Sea

Australia

India

Andes

South America

Atlantic Ocean

Atlas Mountains

Africa

Antarctica

Vegetation

Indian Ocean

EXAMPLES OF TERTIARY ANIMALS

AN EXTINCT MAMMAL
(*Arsinoitherium*)

AN EXTINCT MAMMAL
(*Merycoidodon culbertsonii*)

AN EXTINCT HOMINID
(*Aegyptopithecus sp.*)

AN EXTINCT GASTROPOD MOLLUSC
(*Ecphora quadricostata*)

MAMMUT
A mammutid
Length: 2.5 m (8 ft)

TETRALOPHODON
A gomphotheriid
Length: 2.5 m (8 ft)

Quaternary period

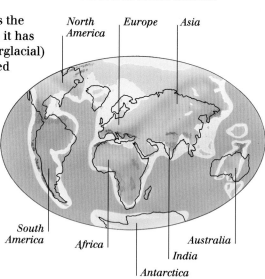

North
America   Europe   Asia

South
America   Africa   Australia
Antarctica   India

THE QUATERNARY PERIOD (1.6 million years ago–present) forms the
second part of the Cenozoic era (65 million years ago–present): it has
been characterized by alternating cold (glacial) and warm (interglacial)
periods. During cold periods, ice sheets and glaciers have formed
repeatedly on northern and southern continents. The cold
environments in North America and Eurasia, and to a lesser
extent in southern South America and parts of Australia, have
caused the migration of many life forms towards the Equator.
Only the specialized ice age mammals such as *Mammuthus*
and *Coelodonta*, with their thick wool and fat insulation,
were suited to life in very cold climates. Humans developed
throughout the Pleistocene period (1.6 million–10,000 years
ago) in Africa and migrated northward into Europe and Asia.
Modern humans, *Homo sapiens*, lived on the cold European
continent 30,000 years ago and hunted mammals. The end of
the last ice age and the climatic changes that occurred about
10,000 years ago brought extinction to many Pleistocene
mammals, but enabled humans to flourish.

EXAMPLES OF QUATERNARY PLANT GROUPS

A PRESENT-DAY BIRCH
(Betula lenta)

A PRESENT-DAY SWEEETGUM
(Liquidambar styraciflua)

FOSSIL LEAF OF A SWEETGUM
(Liquidambar europeanum)

FOSSIL LEAF OF A BIRCH
(Betula sp.)

EXAMPLES OF QUATERNARY ANIMAL GROUPS

PROCOPTODON
A macropodid
Length: 3 m (10 ft)

DIPROTODON
A diprotodontid
Length: 3 m (10 ft)

TOXODON
A toxodontid
Length: 3 m (10 ft)

MAMMUTHUS
An elephantid
Length: 3 m (10 ft)

THE EARTH DURING THE QUATERNARY PERIOD

Pyrenees

Alps

Appalachian
Mountains

Ice sheet

Rocky
Mountains

Asia

North
America

Vegetation

Carpathian
Mountains

Taurus
Mountains

Himalayas

India

Australia

Desert

Andes

Indian
Ocean

South
America

Atlantic
Ocean

Ice cap

Atlas
Mountains

Africa

Antarctica

EXAMPLES OF QUATERNARY ANIMALS

A MAMMAL SKELETON
*(Hippopotamus
amphibius)*

**SKULL OF AN EXTINCT
CAVE BEAR**
(Ursus spelaeus)

**SKULL OF AN
EXTINCT TORTOISE**
(Meiolania platyceps)

A MAMMOTH TOOTH
*(Mammuthus
primigenius)*

DEINOTHERIUM
A deinotheriid
Length: 4 m (13 ft)

COELODONTA
A rhinocerotid
Length: 4 m (13 ft)

AUSTRALOPITHECUS
A hominid
Length: 1.2 m (4 ft)

Early signs of life

FOR ALMOST A THOUSAND MILLION YEARS after its formation, there was no known life on Earth. The first simple, sea-dwelling organic structures appeared about 3,400 years ago; they may have formed when certain chemical molecules joined together. Prokaryotes, single-celled micro-organisms such as blue-green algae, were able to photosynthesize (see pp. 138–139), and thus produce oxygen. A thousand million years later, sufficient oxygen had built up in the earth's atmosphere to allow multicellular organisms to proliferate in the Precambrian seas (before 570 million years ago). Soft-bodied jellyfish, corals, and seaworms flourished about 700 million years ago. Trilobites, the first animals with hard body frames, developed during the Cambrian period (570–510 million years ago). However, it was not until the beginning of the Devonian period (409–363 million years ago) that early land plants, such as *Asteroxylon*, formed a water-retaining cuticle, which ended their dependence on an aquatic environment. About 363 million years ago, the first amphibians (see pp. 80–81) crawled onto the land, although they still returned to the water to lay their soft eggs. Not until the emergence of the first reptiles would animals appear that were independent of water in this way.

STROMATOLITIC LIMESTONE

Alternate layers of mud and sand

Layers bound by algae

Layered structure

Limestone

Long, beak-like snout

Growth line

Dorsal plate

Dorsal spine base

Fixed lateral plate

Bony dorsal shield

Glabella

Eye

Thoracic pleurae

Tail shield

Tail area

FOSSILIZED JAWLESS FISH

FOSSILIZED TRILOBITE

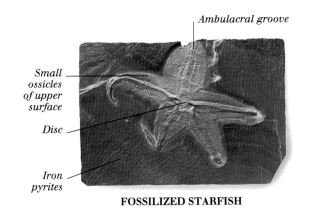

Ambulacral groove

Small ossicles of upper surface

Disc

Iron pyrites

FOSSILIZED STARFISH

Row of ossicles

Broad disc

Row of ossicles

Short arm

UPPER SURFACE OF FOSSILIZED STARFISH

LOWER SURFACE OF FOSSILIZED STARFISH

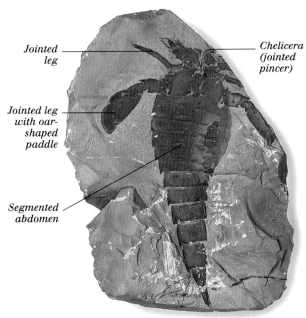

Jointed leg

Chelicera (jointed pincer)

Jointed leg with oar-shaped paddle

Segmented abdomen

UNDERSIDE OF FOSSILIZED EURYPTERID

Growing tip

Disc-shaped sporangium (spore-case)

Leaf-like scale

Stem

Telson (tail spine)

Abdominal segments

Shell contains eight somites (thoracic segments)

Hingeless, bivalved shell

FOSSIL OF AN EXTINCT SHRIMP

RECONSTRUCTION OF ASTEROXYLON

Amphibians and reptiles

THE EARLIEST KNOWN AMPHIBIANS, such as *Acanthostega*
and *Ichthyostega*, lived about 363 million years ago
at the end of the Devonian period (409–363 million
years ago). Their limbs may have evolved from the
muscular fins of lungfish. These fish can use their fins
to push themselves along the bottom of lakes and some
can breathe at the water's surface. While amphibians
(see pp. 182–183) can exist on land, they are dependent
on a wet environment because their skin does not retain
moisture and they must return to the water to lay their
eggs. Evolving from amphibians, reptiles (see pp. 184–
187) first appeared during the Carboniferous period
(363–290 million years ago): *Westlothiana*, the earliest
known reptile, lived on land 338 million years ago.
The development of the amniotic egg, with an embryo
enclosed in its own wet environment (the amnion) and
protected by a waterproof shell, freed reptiles from the
amphibian's dependence on a wet habitat. A scaly skin
protected the reptile from desiccation on land and
enabled it to exploit ways of life closed to its amphibian
ancestors. Reptiles include the dinosaurs, which came
to dominate life on land during the Mesozoic era
(245–65 million years ago).

Sculpted or pitted bone surface

Orbit

Pocket enclosing nostril

Spiracle to draw in water

Mandible

Small tooth

FOSSIL SKULL OF ACANTHOSTEGA

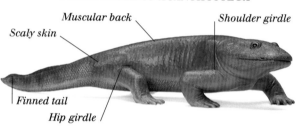

Scaly skin

Muscular back

Shoulder girdle

Finned tail

Hip girdle

MODEL OF ICHTHYOSTEGA

Dorsal vertebra

Scapula

Cleithrum

Cervical vertebra

Cranium

Orbit

Maxilla

Naris

Rib

Glenoid cavity

Humerus

Elbow joint

Mandible

Clavicle

Radius

Ulna

Sharp tooth

Phalanges

Metacarpals

SKELETON OF ERYOPS

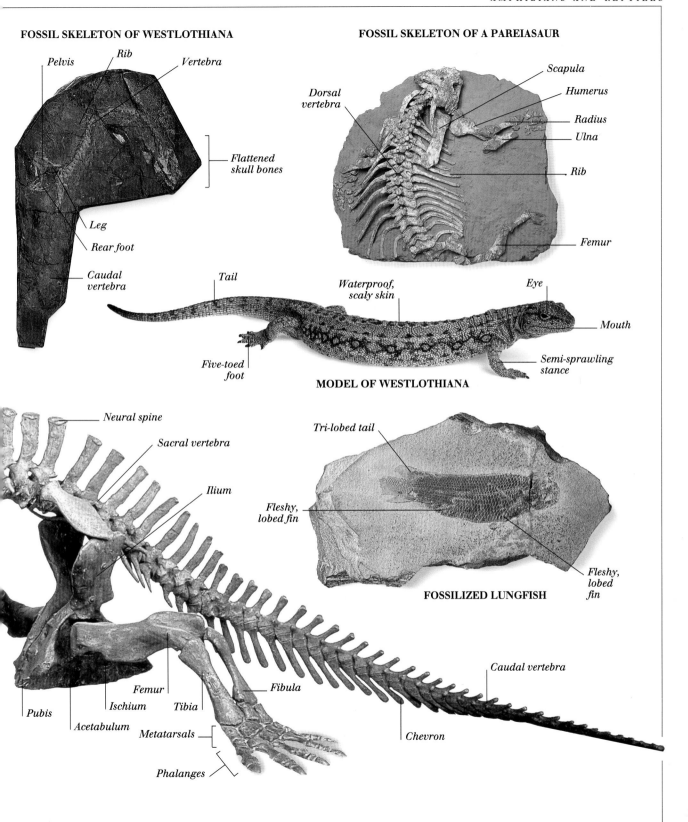

FOSSIL SKELETON OF WESTLOTHIANA

Pelvis

Rib

Vertebra

Flattened
skull bones

Leg

Rear foot

Caudal
vertebra

FOSSIL SKELETON OF A PAREIASAUR

Dorsal
vertebra

Scapula

Humerus

Radius

Ulna

Rib

Femur

Tail

Waterproof,
scaly skin

Eye

Mouth

Semi-sprawling
stance

Five-toed
foot

MODEL OF WESTLOTHIANA

Neural spine

Sacral vertebra

Ilium

Tri-lobed tail

Fleshy,
lobed fin

Fleshy,
lobed
fin

FOSSILIZED LUNGFISH

Caudal vertebra

Pubis

Acetabulum

Ischium

Femur

Tibia

Metatarsals

Fibula

Phalanges

Chevron

81

The dinosaurs

THE DINOSAURS WERE A LARGE GROUP of reptiles that were the dominant land vertebrates (animals with backbones) for most of the Mesozoic era (245–65 million years ago). They appeared some 230 million years ago and were distinguished from other scaly, egg-laying reptiles by an important feature: dinosaurs had an erect limb stance. This enabled them to keep their bodies well above the ground, unlike the sprawling and semi-sprawling stance of other reptiles. The head of the dinosaur's femur (thigh-bone) fitted into a socket in its pelvis (hip-bone), producing efficient and mobile locomotion. Dinosaurs are categorized into two groups according to the structure of their pelvis: saurischian (lizard-hipped) and ornithischian (bird-hipped) dinosaurs. In the case of most saurischians, the pubis (part of the pelvis) jutted forward, while in ornithischians it slanted back, parallel to the ischium (another part of the pelvis). The enormous variety of dinosaur species equals that of mammals. The Dinosauria were the most successful land vertebrates ever, and survived for 165 million years, until their extinction 65 million years ago.

STRUCTURE OF SAURISCHIAN PELVIS

Ilium

Hook of preacetabular process

Postacetabular process

Ilio-pubic joint

Acetabulum

Pubis

Ilio-ischial joint

Ischium

Pubic foot

GALLIMIMUS
A saurischian dinosaur

POSITION OF PELVIS IN A SAURISCHIAN DINOSAUR

STRUCTURE OF ORNTHISCHIAN PELVIS

Ilium

Postacetabular process

Preacetabular process

Ilio-pubic joint

Prepubis

Ilio-ischial joint

Acetabulum

Pubis

Ischium

HYPSILOPHODON
An ornithischian dinosaur

POSITION OF PELVIS IN AN ORNITHISCHIAN DINOSAUR

BAROSAURUS
A saurischian dinosaur

COMPARISON OF ANIMAL STANCES

SPRAWLING STANCE
The thighs and upper arms project straight out from the body so that the knees and elbows are bent at right angles.

COMMON IGUANA
(*Iguana iguana*)
A present-day reptile

ERECT STANCE
The thighs and upper arms project straight down from the body so that the knees and elbows are straight.

SEMI-SPRAWLING STANCE
The thighs and upper arms project downwards and outwards so that the knees and elbows are slightly bent.

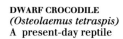

DWARF CROCODILE
(*Osteolaemus tetraspis*)
A present-day reptile

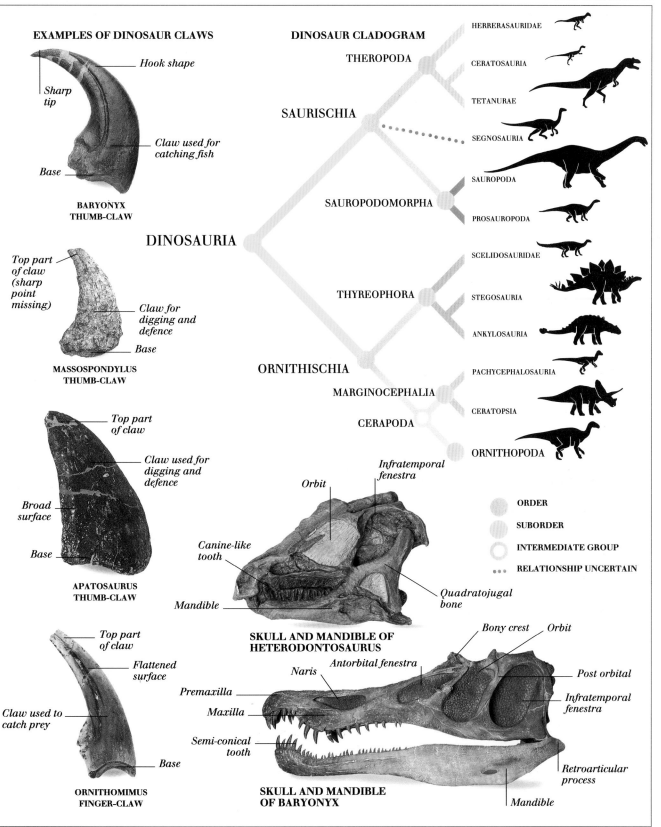

EXAMPLES OF DINOSAUR CLAWS

Hook shape

Sharp tip

Claw used for catching fish

Base

BARYONYX THUMB-CLAW

Top part of claw (sharp point missing)

Claw for digging and defence

Base

MASSOSPONDYLUS THUMB-CLAW

Top part of claw

Claw used for digging and defence

Broad surface

Base

APATOSAURUS THUMB-CLAW

Top part of claw

Flattened surface

Claw used to catch prey

Base

ORNITHOMIMUS FINGER-CLAW

DINOSAUR CLADOGRAM

HERRERASAURIDAE

THEROPODA

CERATOSAURIA

TETANURAE

SAURISCHIA

SEGNOSAURIA

SAUROPODA

SAUROPODOMORPHA

PROSAUROPODA

DINOSAURIA

SCELIDOSAURIDAE

THYREOPHORA

STEGOSAURIA

ANKYLOSAURIA

ORNITHISCHIA

PACHYCEPHALOSAURIA

MARGINOCEPHALIA

CERATOPSIA

CERAPODA

ORNITHOPODA

ORDER

SUBORDER

INTERMEDIATE GROUP

••• RELATIONSHIP UNCERTAIN

Infratemporal fenestra

Orbit

Canine-like tooth

Mandible

Quadratojugal bone

SKULL AND MANDIBLE OF HETERODONTOSAURUS

Bony crest   *Orbit*

Antorbital fenestra

Naris

Premaxilla

Maxilla

Semi-conical tooth

Post orbital

Infratemporal fenestra

Retroarticular process

Base

Mandible

SKULL AND MANDIBLE OF BARYONYX

Theropods 1

AN ENORMOUSLY SUCCESSFUL SUBORDER of the Saurischia, the bipedal (two-footed) theropods ("beast feet") emerged 230 million years ago in Late Triassic times; the oldest known example comes from South America. Theropods spanned the whole of the Age of the Dinosaurs (230–65 million years ago) and included most of the known predatory dinosaurs. The typical theropod had small arms with sharp, clawed fingers; powerful jaws lined with sharp teeth; an S-shaped neck; long, muscular hind limbs; and clawed, usually four-toed feet. Many theropods may have been warm-blooded; most were exclusively carnivorous. Theropods ranged from animals no larger than a chicken to huge creatures, such as *Tyrannosaurus* and *Baryonyx*. The group also included ostrich-like omnivores and herbivores with toothless beaks, such as *Struthiomimus* and *Gallimimus*. Many scientists believe that birds are the closest living relatives to the dinosaurs, and share a common ancestor with the theropods. *Archaeopteryx*, small and feathered, was the first known bird and lived alongside its dinosaur relatives.

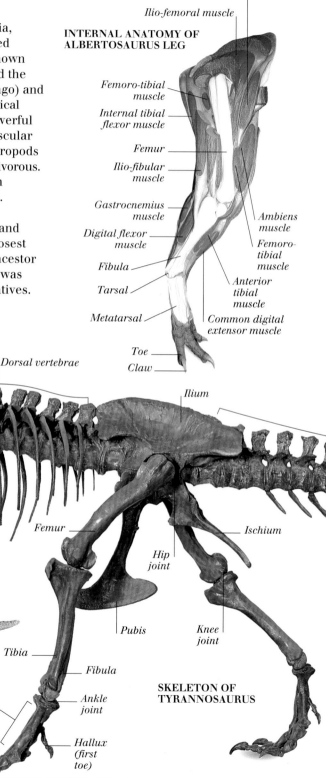

INTERNAL ANATOMY OF ALBERTOSAURUS LEG

Ilio-tibial muscle
Ilio-femoral muscle
Femoro-tibial muscle
Internal tibial flexor muscle
Femur
Ilio-fibular muscle
Gastrocnemius muscle
Digital flexor muscle
Fibula
Tarsal
Metatarsal
Ambiens muscle
Femoro-tibial muscle
Anterior tibial muscle
Common digital extensor muscle
Toe
Claw

Cranium
Orbit
Naris
Supraoccipital crest
Cervical vertebrae
Dorsal vertebrae
Ilium
Mandible
Cervical rib
Serrated tooth
Scapula
Shoulder joint
Ulna
Phalanges
Metacarpals
Wrist joint
Elbow joint
Coracoid
Rib
Humerus
Femur
Ischium
Hip joint
Pubis
Knee joint

Naris
Eye
Thigh
Scaly skin
Tail
Hand
Forelimb
Knee
Hind limb
Toe
Claw
Ankle
Foot

EXTERNAL FEATURES OF TYRANNOSAURUS

Tibia
Fibula
Metatarsals
Phalanges
Ankle joint
Hallux (first toe)

SKELETON OF TYRANNOSAURUS

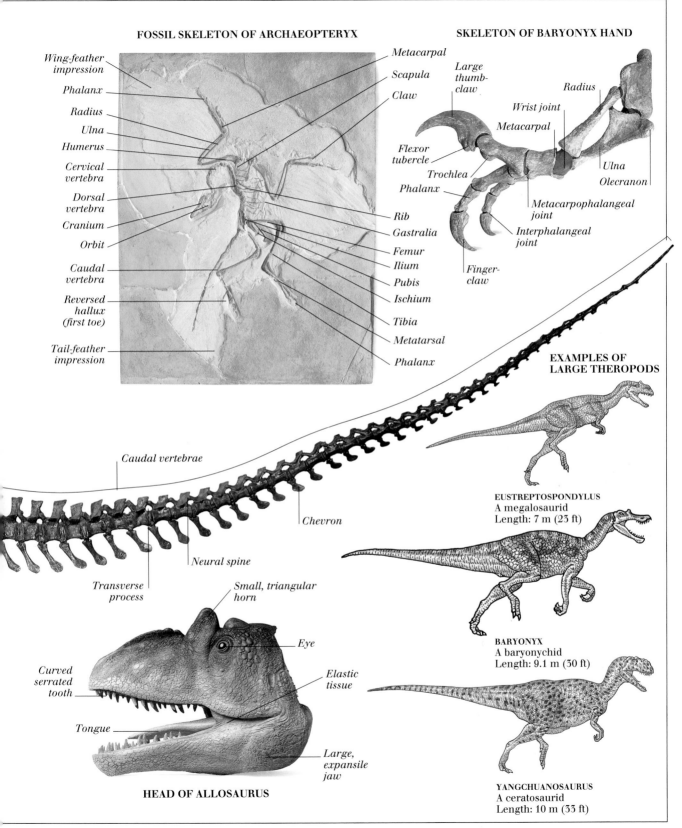

FOSSIL SKELETON OF ARCHAEOPTERYX

Wing-feather impression
Phalanx
Radius
Ulna
Humerus
Cervical vertebra
Dorsal vertebra
Cranium
Orbit
Caudal vertebra
Reversed hallux (first toe)
Tail-feather impression

Metacarpal
Scapula
Claw
Rib
Gastralia
Femur
Ilium
Pubis
Ischium
Tibia
Metatarsal
Phalanx

SKELETON OF BARYONYX HAND

Large thumb-claw
Flexor tubercle
Trochlea
Phalanx
Finger-claw
Wrist joint
Metacarpal
Radius
Ulna
Olecranon
Metacarpophalangeal joint
Interphalangeal joint

Caudal vertebrae
Chevron
Neural spine
Transverse process

EXAMPLES OF LARGE THEROPODS

EUSTREPTOSPONDYLUS
A megalosaurid
Length: 7 m (23 ft)

BARYONYX
A baryonychid
Length: 9.1 m (30 ft)

YANGCHUANOSAURUS
A ceratosaurid
Length: 10 m (33 ft)

Small, triangular horn
Eye
Curved serrated tooth
Elastic tissue
Tongue
Large, expansile jaw

HEAD OF ALLOSAURUS

Theropods 2

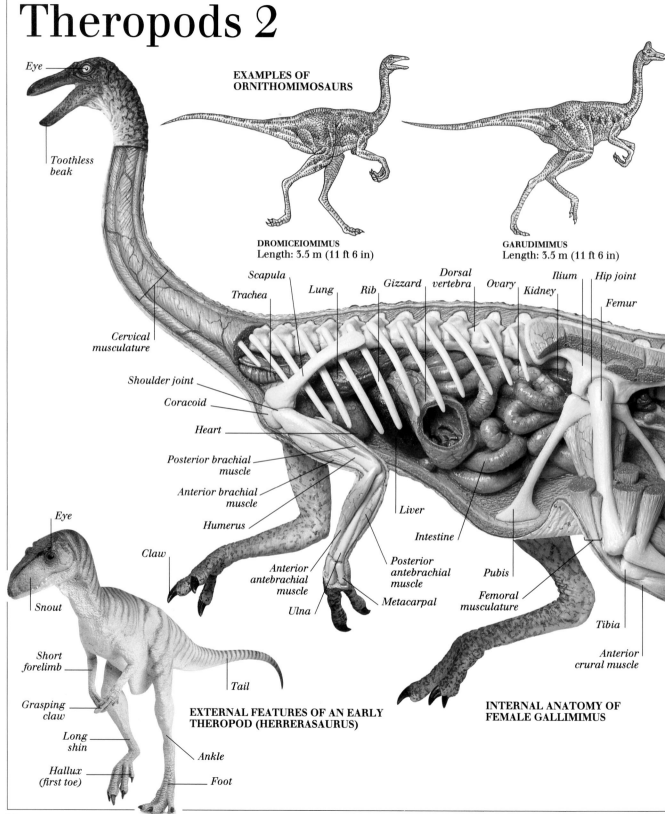

Eye

Toothless
beak

Cervical
musculature

**EXAMPLES OF
ORNITHOMIMOSAURS**

DROMICEIOMIMUS
Length: 3.5 m (11 ft 6 in)

GARUDIMIMUS
Length: 3.5 m (11 ft 6 in)

Scapula

Trachea

Lung

Rib

Gizzard

Dorsal
vertebra

Ovary

Kidney

Ilium

Hip joint

Femur

Shoulder joint

Coracoid

Heart

Posterior brachial
muscle

Anterior brachial
muscle

Humerus

Liver

Intestine

Pubis

Femoral
musculature

Tibia

Anterior
crural muscle

Eye

Snout

Short
forelimb

Grasping
claw

Long
shin

Hallux
(first toe)

Claw

Anterior
antebrachial
muscle

Ulna

Posterior
antebrachial
muscle

Metacarpal

Tail

Ankle

Foot

**EXTERNAL FEATURES OF AN EARLY
THEROPOD (HERRERASAURUS)**

**INTERNAL ANATOMY OF
FEMALE GALLIMIMUS**

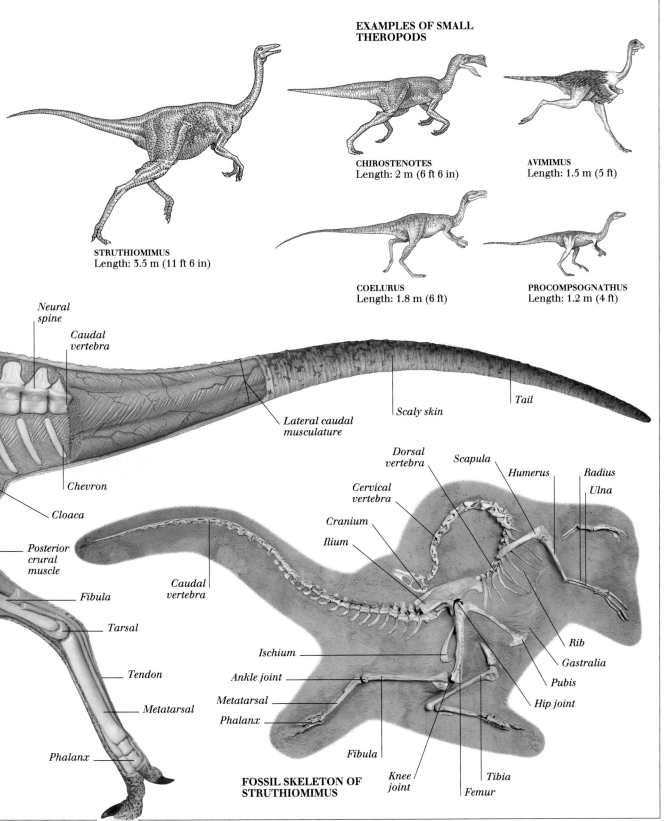

EXAMPLES OF SMALL THEROPODS

CHIROSTENOTES
Length: 2 m (6 ft 6 in)

AVIMIMUS
Length: 1.5 m (5 ft)

STRUTHIOMIMUS
Length: 3.5 m (11 ft 6 in)

COELURUS
Length: 1.8 m (6 ft)

PROCOMPSOGNATHUS
Length: 1.2 m (4 ft)

Neural spine

Caudal vertebra

Lateral caudal musculature

Scaly skin

Tail

Chevron

Cloaca

Posterior crural muscle

Fibula

Tarsal

Tendon

Metatarsal

Phalanx

Caudal vertebra

Dorsal vertebra

Cervical vertebra

Cranium

Ilium

Scapula

Humerus

Radius

Ulna

Rib

Gastralia

Ischium

Ankle joint

Metatarsal

Phalanx

Fibula

Knee joint

Femur

Tibia

Pubis

Hip joint

FOSSIL SKELETON OF STRUTHIOMIMUS

Sauropodomorphs 1

THE SAUROPODOMORPHA ("lizard-feet forms")
were herbivorous, usually quadrupedal (four-footed)
dinosaurs. A suborder of the Saurischia, they
were characterized by small heads, bulky bodies,
and long necks and tails. There were two
infraorders: prosauropods and sauropods.
Prosauropods lived from Late Triassic to Early
Jurassic times (225–180 million years ago) and included beasts such
as the small *Anchisaurus* and one of the first very large dinosaurs,
Melanosaurus. By Middle Jurassic times (about 165 million years ago),
sauropods had replaced prosauropods and spread worldwide. They
included the heaviest and longest land animals ever, such as *Diplodocus*
and *Brachiosaurus*. Sauropods persisted to the end of the Cretaceous
period (65 million years ago). Many of these dinosaurs moved in herds,
protected from predatory theropods by their huge bulk and powerful
tails, which they could use to lash out at attackers. Sauropodomorphs
were the most common large herbivores until Late Jurassic
times (about 145 million years ago), and appear to
have survived in southern continents
long after they had disappeared
from the north.

THECODONTOSAURUS

Naris

Antorbital
fenestra

Orbit

Mandible

Infratemporal
fenestra

Serrated, leaf-
shaped tooth

Paroccipital
process

Mandibular
fenestra

Dorsal vertebrae

Sacral vertebrae

**SKELETON OF
PLATEOSAURUS**

Ilium

Cervical
vertebrae

Humerus

Scapula

Shoulder
joint

Rib

Pubis

Femur

Hip joint

Ischium

Curved
thumb-claw

Elbow joint

Radius

Knee joint

Tail

Wrist joint

Ulna

Tibia

Metacarpal

Fibula

Ankle joint

Cranium

Phalanx

Metatarsals

Orbit

Mandible

Phalanges

Naris

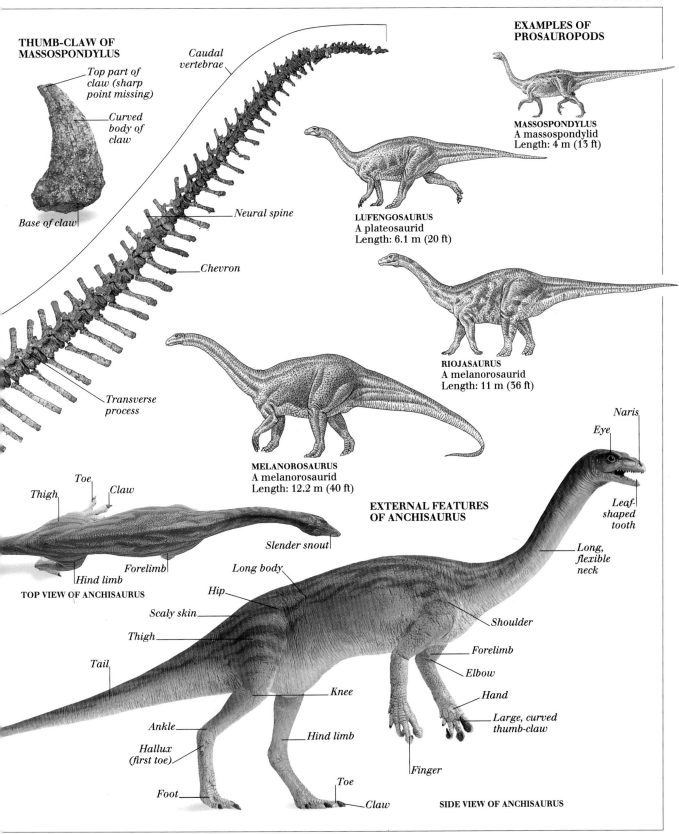

THUMB-CLAW OF MASSOSPONDYLUS

Top part of claw (sharp point missing)

Curved body of claw

Base of claw

Caudal vertebrae

Neural spine

Chevron

Transverse process

EXAMPLES OF PROSAUROPODS

MASSOSPONDYLUS
A massospondylid
Length: 4 m (13 ft)

LUFENGOSAURUS
A plateosaurid
Length: 6.1 m (20 ft)

RIOJASAURUS
A melanorosaurid
Length: 11 m (36 ft)

MELANOROSAURUS
A melanorosaurid
Length: 12.2 m (40 ft)

Naris

Eye

Leaf-shaped tooth

Long, flexible neck

EXTERNAL FEATURES OF ANCHISAURUS

Toe

Thigh

Claw

Forelimb

Hind limb

TOP VIEW OF ANCHISAURUS

Slender snout

Long body

Hip

Scaly skin

Thigh

Tail

Knee

Ankle

Hallux (first toe)

Hind limb

Foot

Toe

Claw

Shoulder

Forelimb

Elbow

Hand

Large, curved thumb-claw

Finger

SIDE VIEW OF ANCHISAURUS

Sauropodomorphs 2

Orbit

Antorbital
fenestra

Cranium

Maxillary
fenestra

Maxilla

Sclerotic
ring

Peg-shaped
tooth

Infratemporal
fenestra

Mandible

**SKULL AND MANDIBLE
OF DIPLODOCUS**

**FOREFOOT OF
ELEPHANT**

Wrist

Nail

**FOREFOOT BONES
OF ELEPHANT**

Radius

Ulna

Carpals

Metacarpals

Phalanges

**COMPARISON OF
THE FOREFEET
OF AN ELEPHANT
AND DIPLODOCUS**

**FOREFOOT BONES
OF DIPLODOCUS**

Radius

Ulna

Carpals

Metacarpals

Phalanges

Coracoid

Dorsal
vertebra

Scapula

Sacral vertebra

Ilium

Caudal
vertebra

Neural
spine

Small
intestine

Dorsal vertebra

Ovary

Kidney

Rib

Large intestine

Hip joint

Caecum

Pubis

Femur

Oviduct

Cloaca

Humerus

Rib

Hip joint

Ischium

Femur

Elbow joint

Knee joint

Ulna

Tibia

Ankle joint

Radius

Fibula

Wrist joint

Phalanges

Metacarpals

MIDDLE SECTION OF DIPLODOCUS SKELETON

Thigh
musculature

Posterior crural
musculature

Caudal
musculature

Fibula

Anterior
crural
muscle

Ankle joint

Metatarsal

FOSSIL EGG OF TITANOSAURID

Fossil eggshell fragment

Fossil egg

Fossil eggshell fragment

Outer ear

Naris

Eye

Mouth

Orbit

Antorbital fenestra

Naris

Maxilla

Cranium

Spoon-shaped tooth

Infratemporal fenestra

Mandible

SKULL AND MANDIBLE OF CAMARASAURUS

INTERNAL ANATOMY OF FEMALE BRACHIOSAURUS

Cervical vertebra

Scapula

Trachea

Oesophagus

Intercostal muscle

Scapular muscle

Shoulder joint

Lung

Humerus

Gizzard

Anterior brachial muscle

Posterior brachial musculature

Elbow joint

Radius

Ulna

Posterior antebrachial musculature

Wrist joint

Metacarpal

CETIOSAURUS
A cetiosaurid
Length: 18 m (59 ft)

SHUNOSAURUS
A cetiosaurid
Length: 10 m (33 ft)

SALTASAURUS
A titanosaurid
Length: 12.2 m (40 ft)

DIPLODOCUS
A diplodocid
Length: 27.4 m (90 ft)

Thyreophorans 1

THYREOPHORANS ("SHIELD BEARERS") were a group
of quadrupedal armoured dinosaurs. A sub-order of the
Ornithischia (bird-hipped dinosaurs), they were characterized
by rows of bony studs, plates, or spikes along the back, which
protected some from predators and may have helped others regulate
body temperature. Up to 9m (30ft) long, with a small head and small cheek
teeth, Thyreophorans had shorter forelimbs than hind limbs and probably
browsed on low-level vegetation. The earliest thyreophorans were
small and lived in Early Jurassic times (about 200 million
years ago) in Europe, North America, and
China. Stegosaurs, such as *Stegosaurus*
and *Kentrosaurus*, replaced these older
forms. The earliest stegosaur remains
come from England and China. Several genera
of stegosaurs survived into the Early Cretaceous period
(146–100 million years ago), but only in India did they persist
into Late Cretaceous times (97–65 million years ago).
Ankylosaurs, with their toothless beaks and cheek
teeth adapted for cropping vegetation,
appeared later than stegosaurs.
They originated in the Late
Jurassic period (155 million
years ago) and in North
America survived until the
extinction of the dinosaurs,
65 million years ago.

TUOJIANGOSAURUS
A stegosaurid
Length: 7 m (23 ft)

Dorsal plate

Caudal plate

Caudal spike

Small head

Beak

Cervical plate

Hind foot

Scaly skin

TOP VIEW OF STEGOSAURUS

Dorsal plate

**EXTERNAL FEATURES
OF STEGOSAURUS**

Scaly skin

Cervical plate

Outer ear

Eye

Naris

Hip

Thigh

Beak

Cheek

Neck

Shoulder

Knee

Long
hind limb

Short forelimb

Elbow

Wrist

Ankle

Nail

Forefoot

Hind foot

Nail

SIDE VIEW OF STEGOSAURUS

EXAMPLES OF STEGOSAURS

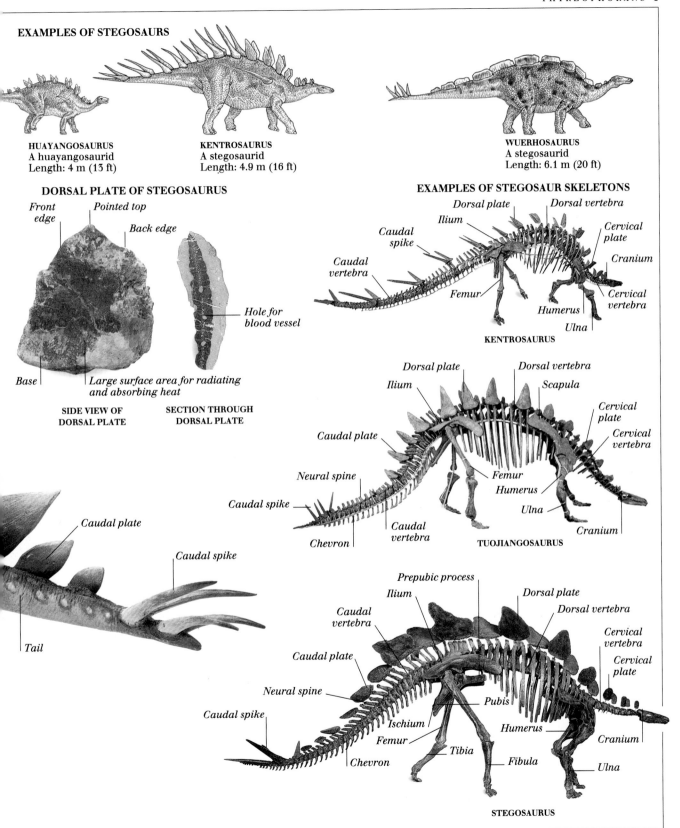

HUAYANGOSAURUS
A huayangosaurid
Length: 4 m (13 ft)

KENTROSAURUS
A stegosaurid
Length: 4.9 m (16 ft)

WUERHOSAURUS
A stegosaurid
Length: 6.1 m (20 ft)

DORSAL PLATE OF STEGOSAURUS

Front edge

Pointed top

Back edge

Hole for blood vessel

Base

Large surface area for radiating and absorbing heat

SIDE VIEW OF DORSAL PLATE

SECTION THROUGH DORSAL PLATE

EXAMPLES OF STEGOSAUR SKELETONS

Dorsal plate

Dorsal vertebra

Ilium

Cervical plate

Caudal spike

Cranium

Caudal vertebra

Femur

Cervical vertebra

Humerus

Ulna

KENTROSAURUS

Dorsal plate

Dorsal vertebra

Ilium

Scapula

Caudal plate

Cervical plate

Cervical vertebra

Neural spine

Caudal spike

Femur

Humerus

Caudal vertebra

Ulna

Chevron

Cranium

TUOJIANGOSAURUS

Caudal plate

Caudal spike

Tail

Prepubic process

Ilium

Dorsal plate

Caudal vertebra

Dorsal vertebra

Caudal plate

Cervical vertebra

Cervical plate

Neural spine

Pubis

Caudal spike

Ischium

Humerus

Femur

Cranium

Chevron

Tibia

Fibula

Ulna

STEGOSAURUS

Thyreophorans 2

EXAMPLES OF ANKYLOSAUR SKULLS

Maxilla

Orbit

Naris

Beak

Tooth

Mandible

Posterolateral horn

Cranium

Jugal plate

SKULL AND MANDIBLE OF EUOPLOCEPHALUS

Nasal bone

Maxilla

Orbit

Cranium

Posterolateral horn

Naris

Beak

Tooth

Mandible

SKULL AND MANDIBLE OF ANKYLOSAURUS

Beak

Nasal bone

Orbit

Naris

Cranium

Infratemporal fenestra

Mandible

SKULL AND MANDIBLE OF PANOPLOSAURUS

Dorsal vertebra

Rib

Small intestine

Gizzard

Ilio-tibial muscle

Reproductive canal

Scapula

Lung

Ilium

Ischium

Shoulder spike

Coracoid

Cervical musculature

Head horn

Humerus

Radius

Wrist joint

Toothless beak

Metacarpal

Ventral antebrachial muscle

Ulna

Elbow joint

Heart

Liver

Large intestine

Ilio-tibial muscle

Fibula

Digital extensor muscle

Femur

Knee joint

Gastrocnemius muscle

Ankle joint

Metatarsal

INTERNAL ANATOMY OF FEMALE EUOPLOCEPHALUS

EXTERNAL FEATURES OF EDMONTONIA

- Hind limb
- Flank spike
- Dorsal scute
- Dermal armour
- Scaly skin
- Nuchal ring
- Shoulder spike
- Broad, flat snout
- Naris
- Ankle
- Elbow
- Forelimb
- Forefoot
- Blunt nail
- Caudal vertebra
- Neural spine
- Ureter
- Chevron
- Cloaca
- Lateral caudal musculature

EXAMPLES OF ANKYLOSAURS

PINACOSAURUS
An ankylosaurid
Length: 5 m (16 ft 6 in)

MINMI
A nodosaurid
Length: 2.4 m (8 ft)

POLACANTHUS
A nodosaurid
Length: 4 m (13 ft)

- Terminal plate
- Lateral plate

FOSSIL OF ANKYLOSAURUS TAIL CLUB

- Ossified caudal vertebra
- Tail club

Ornithopods 1

IGUANODON TOOTH

ORNITHOPODS ("BIRD FEET") were a group of ornithischian ("bird-hipped") dinosaurs. These bipedal and quadrupedal herbivores had a horny beak, plant-cutting or grinding cheek teeth, and a pelvic and tail region stiffened by bony tendons. They evolved teeth and jaws adapted to pulping vegetation and flourished from the Middle Jurassic to the Late Cretaceous period (165–65 million years ago) in North America, Europe, Africa, China, Australia, and Antarctica. Some ornithopods were no larger than a dog, while others were immense creatures up to 15 m (49 ft) long. Iguanodonts, an ornithopod group, had a broad, toothless beak at the end of a long snout, large jaws with long rows of ridged, closely packed teeth for grinding vegetation, a bulky body, and a heavy tail. *Iguanodon* and some other iguanodonts had large thumb-spikes that were strong enough to stab attackers. Another group, the hadrosaurs, such as *Gryposaurus* and *Hadrosaurus*, lived in Late Cretaceous times (97–65 million years ago) and with their broad beaks are sometimes known as "duckbills". They were characterized by their deep skulls and closely packed rows of teeth, while some, such as *Corythosaurus* and *Lambeosaurus*, had tall, hollow, bony head crests.

SKELETON OF IGUANODON

Orbit · Cranium · Naris · Mandible · Cervical rib · Cervical vertebra · Scapula · Dorsal vertebra · Humerus · Sternal bone · Radius · Sacral vertebra · Ulna · Caudal vertebra · Prepubic process · Neural spine · Femur · Pubis · Tibia · Ilium · Chevron · Fibula · Ischium · Metatarsal

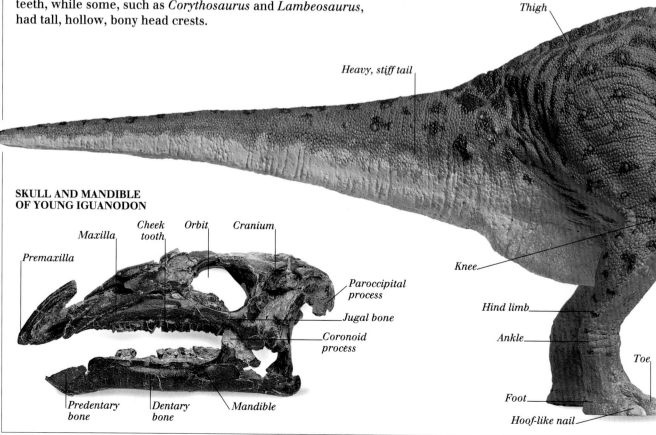

Thigh · Heavy, stiff tail · Knee · Hind limb · Ankle · Toe · Foot · Hoof-like nail

SKULL AND MANDIBLE OF YOUNG IGUANODON

Premaxilla · Maxilla · Cheek tooth · Orbit · Cranium · Paroccipital process · Jugal bone · Coronoid process · Predentary bone · Dentary bone · Mandible

EXAMPLES OF IGUANODONTS

OURANOSAURUS
An iguanodontid
Length: 7 m (23 ft)

CAMPTOSAURUS
A camptosaurid
Length: 4.9–7 m (16–23 ft)

MUTTABURRASAURUS
A camptosaurid
Length: 7 m (23 ft)

PROBACTROSAURUS
An iguanodontid
Length: 6.1 m (20 ft)

EXTERNAL FEATURES OF IGUANODON

Eye

Naris

Shoulder

Neck

Tongue

Beak

Scaly skin

Forelimb

Elbow

Thumb-spike

Wrist

Hand

Finger

Hoof-like nail

INTERNAL ANATOMY OF HIND LEG OF IGUANODON

Ilio-femoral muscle

Ilium

Ilio-tibial muscle

Ambiens muscle

Short caudo-femoral muscle

External pubo-ischio-femoral muscle

Tibial flexor muscle

Femur

Ilio-fibular muscle

Common digital extensor muscle

Gastrocnemius muscle

Anterior tibial muscle

Tibia

Fibula

Tarsal

Toe

Metatarsal

Hoof-like nail

Ornithopods 2

BRACHYLOPHOSAURUS
Length: 7m (23 ft)

LAMBEOSAURUS
Length: 14.9 m (49 ft)

Caudal vertebrae

Sacral vertebrae

Neural spine

Rounded top end of egg

Chevron

Emerging hatchling

Hatchling

Eggshell fragment

Plant material to protect and warm eggs

Ilium

Unhatched egg

Bony crest

Raised nest made of sand

Hip joint

Naris

Ischium

Prepubic process

Eye

MODEL OF MAIASAURA NEST

Femur

Cheek pouch

Neck

Knee joint

Thigh

FOSSIL SKELETON OF PARASAUROLOPHUS

Tongue

Toothless beak

Scaly skin

Shoulder

Forelimb

Elbow

Tubercle

Wrist

Knee

Hind limb

Long, thick tail

Ankle joint

Metatarsal

Nail

Ankle

EXTERNAL FEATURES OF CORYTHOSAURUS

Toe

Nail

Foot

EXAMPLES OF HADROSAURS

HYPACROSAURUS
Length: 9.1 m (30 ft)

HADROSAURUS
Length: 7.9–10 m (26–33 ft)

GRYPOSAURUS
Length: 7.9–10 m (26–33 ft)

Dorsal vertebrae

Bony crest

Air passage

Cranium

Infratemporal fenestra

Orbit

Cervical vertebrae

Mandible

Naris

Orbit

Infratemporal fenestra

Air passage

Naris

Mandible

Tooth

SKULL AND MANDIBLE OF JUVENILE LAMBEOSAURUS

Scapula

Shoulder joint

Tibia

Rib

Fibula

Humerus

Elbow joint

Radius

Wrist joint

Ulna

Phalanges

Metacarpal

Phalanges

Sclerotic ring

Cranium

Bony crest

Orbit

Naris

Infratemporal fenestra

Mandible

Premaxilla

SKULL AND MANDIBLE OF ADULT LAMBEOSAURUS

Marginocephalians 1

HEAD-BUTTING PRENOCEPHALES

MARGINOCEPHALIA ("margined heads") were a group of bipedal and quadrupedal ornithischian dinosaurs with a narrow shelf or deep, bony frill at the back of the skull. Marginocephalians were probably descended from the same ancestor as the ornithopods and lived in what are now North America, Africa, Asia, and Europe during the Cretaceous period (146–65 million years ago). They were divided into two infraorders: Pachycephalosauria ("thick-headed lizards"), such as *Pachycephalosaurus* and *Stegoceras*, and Ceratopsia ("horned faces"), such as *Triceratops* and *Psittacosaurus*. The thick skulls of Pachycephalosauria protected their brains during head-butting contests fought to win territory and mates; their hips and spines were also strengthened to withstand the shock. The bony frill of Ceratopsia would have added to their frightening appearance when charging; the neck was strengthened for impact and to support the huge head, with its snipping beak and powerful slicing toothed jaws. A charging ceratops would have been a formidable opponent for even the largest predators. Ceratopsia were among the most abundant herbivorous dinosaurs of the Late Cretaceous period (97–65 million years ago).

EXAMPLES OF SKULLS OF PACHYCEPHALOSAURS

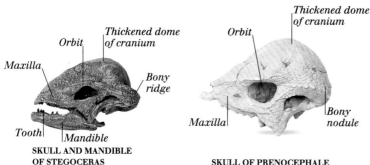

SKULL AND MANDIBLE OF STEGOCERAS

SKULL OF PRENOCEPHALE

SKULL OF PACHYCEPHALOSAURUS

EXTERNAL FEATURES OF PACHYCEPHALOSAURUS

SECTION THROUGH SKULL OF PACHYCEPHALOSAURUS

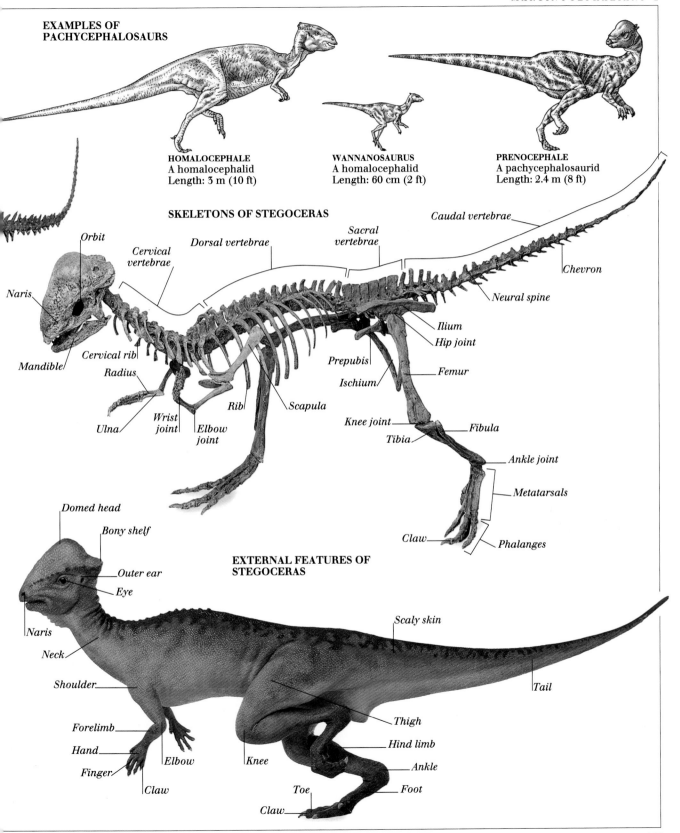

EXAMPLES OF PACHYCEPHALOSAURS

HOMALOCEPHALE
A homalocephalid
Length: 3 m (10 ft)

WANNANOSAURUS
A homalocephalid
Length: 60 cm (2 ft)

PRENOCEPHALE
A pachycephalosaurid
Length: 2.4 m (8 ft)

SKELETONS OF STEGOCERAS

Caudal vertebrae

Sacral vertebrae

Dorsal vertebrae

Orbit

Cervical vertebrae

Chevron

Naris

Neural spine

Mandible

Ilium

Hip joint

Cervical rib

Prepubis

Femur

Radius

Ischium

Ulna

Rib

Scapula

Wrist joint

Elbow joint

Knee joint

Fibula

Tibia

Ankle joint

Metatarsals

Claw

Phalanges

EXTERNAL FEATURES OF STEGOCERAS

Domed head

Bony shelf

Outer ear

Eye

Scaly skin

Naris

Neck

Tail

Shoulder

Thigh

Forelimb

Hind limb

Hand

Elbow

Knee

Ankle

Finger

Toe

Foot

Claw

Claw

Marginocephalians 2

SKULL AND MANDIBLE OF STYRACOSAURUS

Parietal fenestra
Epoccipital bone
Parietosquamosal frill
Nose horn core
Supraorbital ridge
Naris
Orbit
Cranium
Mandible

EXTERNAL FEATURES OF TRICERATOPS

Parietosquamosal frill
Epoccipital bone
Brow horn
Nose horn
Thick, scaly skin
Thigh
Tail
Ankle
Hind limb
Nail
Elbow
Forelimb
Wrist
Eye
Naris
Toothless beak

SKULL AND MANDIBLE OF PROTOCERATOPS

Parietosquamosal frill
Cranium
Postorbital bone
Nasal bone
Orbit
Lacrimal bone
Naris
Beak
Rostral bone
Predentary bone
Dentary bone
Tooth
Mandible
Parietal fenestra
Infratemporal fenestra
Jugal bone
Surangular bone
Angular bone

SKELETON OF TRICERATOPS

Prepubis
Ilium
Hip joint
Parietosquamosal frill
Dorsal vertebrae
Ischium
Femur
Knee joint
Fibula
Tibia
Ankle joint
Metatarsals
Phalanges
Caudal vertebra
Chevron
Neural spine
Rib
Scapula
Humerus
Elbow joint
Ulna
Sternal bone
Coracoid
Shoulder joint
Radius

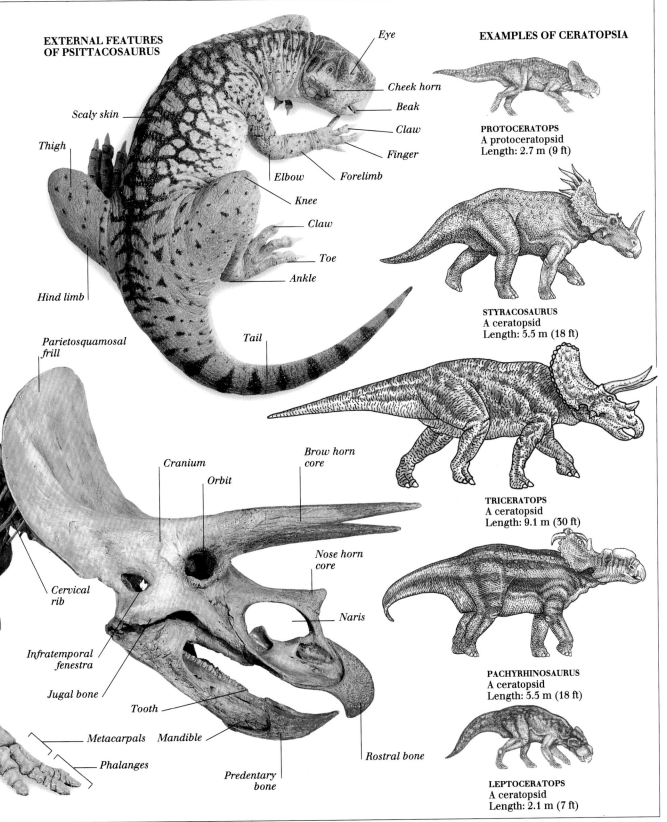

**EXTERNAL FEATURES
OF PSITTACOSAURUS**

Eye

Cheek horn

Beak

Claw

Finger

Scaly skin

Thigh

Elbow

Forelimb

Knee

Claw

Toe

Ankle

Hind limb

Tail

*Parietosquamosal
frill*

Cranium

Orbit

*Brow horn
core*

*Nose horn
core*

*Cervical
rib*

Naris

*Infratemporal
fenestra*

Jugal bone

Tooth

Metacarpals

Mandible

Phalanges

*Predentary
bone*

Rostral bone

EXAMPLES OF CERATOPSIA

PROTOCERATOPS
A protoceratopsid
Length: 2.7 m (9 ft)

STYRACOSAURUS
A ceratopsid
Length: 5.5 m (18 ft)

TRICERATOPS
A ceratopsid
Length: 9.1 m (30 ft)

PACHYRHINOSAURUS
A ceratopsid
Length: 5.5 m (18 ft)

LEPTOCERATOPS
A ceratopsid
Length: 2.1 m (7 ft)

Mammals 1

TETRALOPHODON CHEEK TEETH

SINCE THE EXTINCTION of the dinosaurs 65 million years ago, mammals have been the dominant vertebrates on Earth and include terrestrial, aerial, and aquatic forms. Having developed from the reptilian Therapsids, the first true mammals – small, nocturnal, rodent-like creatures, such as *Megazostrodon* – appeared over 200 million years ago during the Triassic period (245–208 million years ago). Mammals had several features that improved on those of their reptilian ancestors: an efficient four-chambered heart allowed these warm-blooded animals to sustain high levels of activity; a covering of hair helped them maintain a constant body temperature; an improved limb structure gave them more efficient locomotion; and the birth of live young and the immediate supply of food from the mother's milk aided their rapid growth. Since the end of the Mesozoic era (65 million years ago), the number of different mammal orders and the abundance of species in each order have varied dramatically. For example, the Perissodactyla (the order that includes *Coelodonta* and modern horses) was the most common group during the Early Tertiary period (about 54 million years ago). Today, the mammalian orders with the most populous species are the Rodentia (rats and mice), the Carnivora (bears, cats, and dogs), and the Artiodactyla (cattle, deer, and pigs), while the Proboscidea order, which included many genera, such as *Phiomia, Moeritherium, Tetralophodon,* and *Mammuthus,* now has only one member: the modern elephant. In Australia and South America, millions of years of continental isolation led to the development of the marsupials, a group of mammals distinct from the placentals (see p. 74) that existed elsewhere.

MODEL OF A MEGAZOSTRODON

Long tail aids balance

Insulating hair

Neural spine

Scapula

Cervical vertebra

Humerus

Nasal horn

Naris

Orbit

Predentary bone

Mandible

Radius

Ulna

Chisel-edged molar

Metacarpal

Phalanx

UPPER JAWBONE (MAXILLA) OF A HORSE

Molars

Premolars

HOOFBONE (THIRD PHALANX) OF A HORSE

Articular surface

Tendon insertion

Cranium

Naris

Predentary bone

Molar tooth

SKULL AND MANDIBLE OF A MOERITHERIUM

Nasal tusk

Molar tooth

Shovel-shaped tusk

SKULL AND MANDIBLE OF A PHIOMIA

Trunk

Thick hide

Short tusk used for rooting up plants

MODEL OF A PHIOMIA

Dorsal vertebra

Ilium

Ball and socket joint

Pubis

Rib

Caudal vertebra

Femur

Tibia

Fibula

Metatarsal

Phalanx

SKELETON OF AN ARSINOITHERIUM

Mandible

Cranium

Teeth

Elongated digit

Humerus

Hind limb bone

FOSSIL SKELETON OF A BAT

Mammals 2

LOWER JAW OF A BEAR

Large canine

Diastema

Articulation with skull

Low cusp

Premolar

Molar

SKELETON OF A TOXODON

Scapula

Neural spine

Cervical vertebra

Coronoid process

Zygomatic arch

Cranium

Orbit

Maxilla

Nasal bone

Canine

Mandible

Molar

Incisor

Occipital region

Humerus

Radius

Large breastbone

Ulna

Metacarpals

SKULL OF AN OPOSSUM

Orbit

Cranium

Naris

Occipital region

Canine

Infraorbital foramen

Molar

Phalanx

FOSSIL SKULL OF AN HYAENODON

Orbit

Naris

Sagittal crest

Cranium

Canine

Neck insertion

Infraorbital foramen

Mandible

Molar

LOWER JAW OF AN AUSTRALOPITHECUS

Expanded occlusal surface

Premolar

Molar

SKULL OF A SMILODON

Orbit

Muscle scar

Naris

Sagittal crest

Infraorbital foramen

Occipital condyle

Canine

Dentary bone

Slicing tooth

Zygomatic arch

Ilium

Femur

Rib

Knee joint

Tibia

Fibula

Metatarsals

Phalanx

Thick, insulating coat

Ivory tusk

Woolly underhair

Hairy trunk

RECONSTRUCTION OF A MAMMOTH

The first hominids

JAWBONE OF AUSTRALOPITHECUS (SOUTHERN APE)

MODERN HUMANS BELONG TO THE MAMMALIAN order of primates (see pp. 202–203), which originated about 55 million years ago; they comprise the only extant hominid species. The earliest hominid was *Australopithecus* ("southern ape"), a small-brained intermediate between apes and humans that was capable of standing and walking upright. *Homo habilis*, the first known human appeared at least 2 million years ago. This larger-brained "handy man" began making tools for hunting. *Homo erectus* first appeared in Africa about 1.8 million years ago and spread into Asia about 800,000 years later. Smaller-toothed than *Homo habilis*, it developed fire as a tool, which enabled it to cook food. Neanderthals, a near relative of modern humans, originated about 200,000 years ago, and *Homo sapiens* (modern humans) appeared in Africa about 100,000 years later. The two co-existed for thousands of years, but by 30,000 years ago, *Homo sapiens* had become dominant and the Neanderthals had died out. Classification of *Homo sapiens* in relation to its ancestors is enormously problematic: modern humans must be classified not only by bone structure, but also by specific behaviour – the ability to plan future action; to follow traditions; and to use symbolic communication, including complex language and the ability to use and recognize symbols.

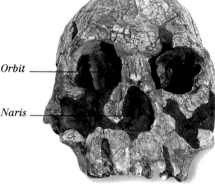

Larger jawbone than modern human

Large back tooth

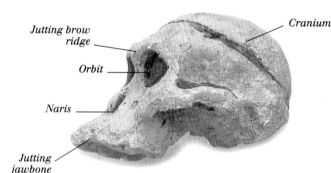

Jutting brow ridge

Cranium

Orbit

Naris

Jutting jawbone

SKULL OF AUSTRALOPITHECUS (SOUTHERN APE)

Orbit

Naris

SKULL OF HOMO HABILIS (FIRST KNOWN HUMAN)

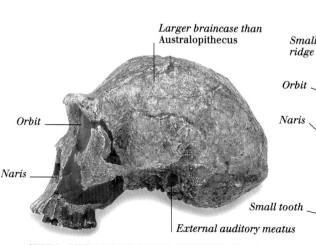

Larger braincase than Australopithecus

Orbit

Naris

External auditory meatus

SKULL OF HOMO ERECTUS (UPRIGHT MAN)

Well-rounded cranium

Small brow ridge

Orbit

Naris

Small tooth

External auditory meatus

SKULL OF HOMO SAPIENS (MODERN HUMAN)

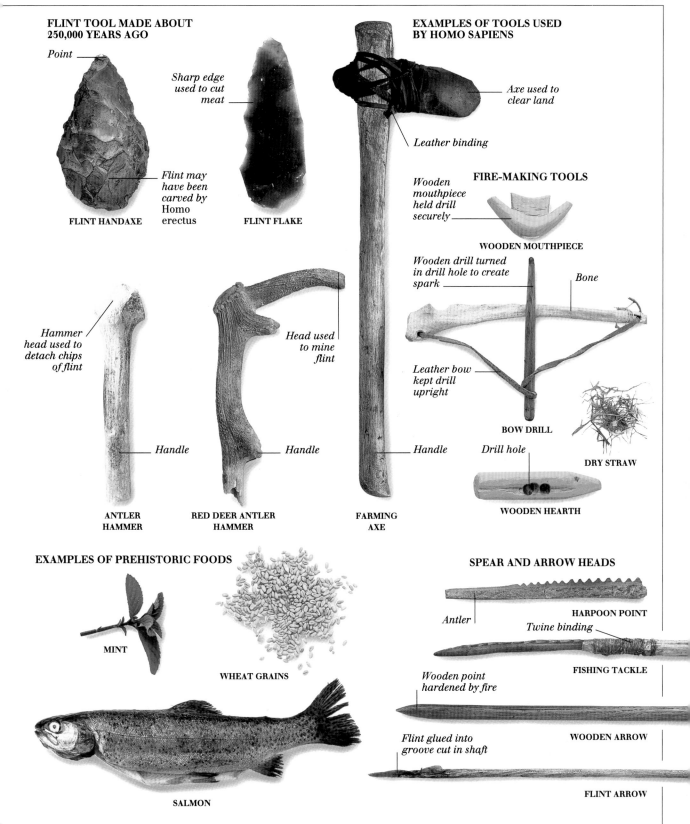

FLINT TOOL MADE ABOUT 250,000 YEARS AGO

Point

Sharp edge used to cut meat

Flint may have been carved by Homo erectus

FLINT HANDAXE

FLINT FLAKE

Hammer head used to detach chips of flint

Handle

ANTLER HAMMER

Handle

RED DEER ANTLER HAMMER

Head used to mine flint

Handle

FARMING AXE

EXAMPLES OF TOOLS USED BY HOMO SAPIENS

Axe used to clear land

Leather binding

FIRE-MAKING TOOLS

Wooden mouthpiece held drill securely

WOODEN MOUTHPIECE

Wooden drill turned in drill hole to create spark

Bone

Leather bow kept drill upright

BOW DRILL

Drill hole

DRY STRAW

WOODEN HEARTH

EXAMPLES OF PREHISTORIC FOODS

MINT

WHEAT GRAINS

SALMON

SPEAR AND ARROW HEADS

Antler

HARPOON POINT

Twine binding

FISHING TACKLE

Wooden point hardened by fire

WOODEN ARROW

Flint glued into groove cut in shaft

FLINT ARROW

PLANTS

Plant variety

Leaf

THERE ARE MORE THAN 300,000 SPECIES of plants. They
show a wide diversity of forms and life-styles, ranging, for example, from delicate
liverworts, adapted for life in a damp habitat, to cacti, capable of surviving in the desert, and
from herbaceous plants, such as corn, which completes its life-cycle in one year, to the giant redwood tree,
which can live for thousands of years. This diversity reflects the adaptations of plants to survive in a wide
range of habitats. This is seen most clearly in the flowering plants (phylum Angiospermophyta), which are
the most numerous, with over 250,000 species, and the most widespread, being found from the tropics to the
poles. Despite their diversity, plants share certain characteristics: typically, plants are green, and make their
food by photosynthesis; and most plants live in or on a substrate, such as soil, and do not actively move. Algae
(kingdom Protista) and fungi (kingdom Fungi) have some plant-like characteristics and are
often studied alongside plants, although they are not true plants.

GREEN ALGA
Micrograph of desmid
(*Micrasterias sp.*)

FERN
Tree fern
(*Dicksonia antarctica*)

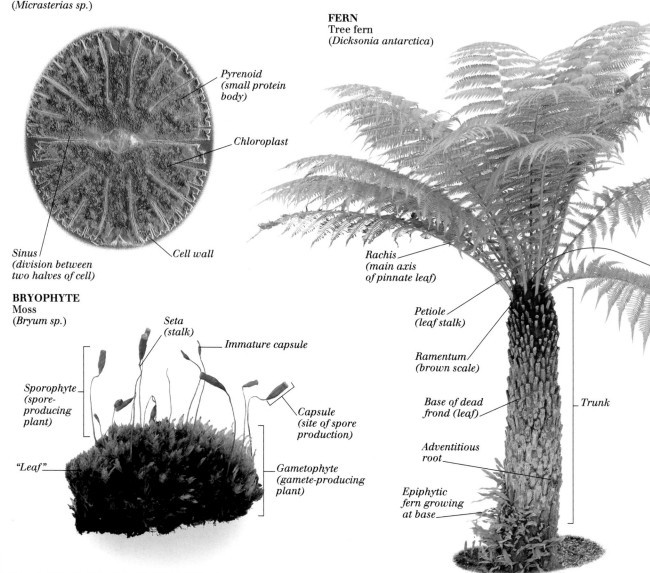

Pyrenoid
(small protein
body)

Chloroplast

Sinus
(division between
two halves of cell)

Cell wall

Rachis
(main axis
of pinnate leaf)

BRYOPHYTE
Moss
(*Bryum sp.*)

Seta
(stalk)

Immature capsule

Petiole
(leaf stalk)

Ramentum
(brown scale)

Sporophyte
(spore-
producing
plant)

Capsule
(site of spore
production)

Base of dead
frond (leaf)

Trunk

"Leaf"

Gametophyte
(gamete-producing
plant)

Adventitious
root

Epiphytic
fern growing
at base

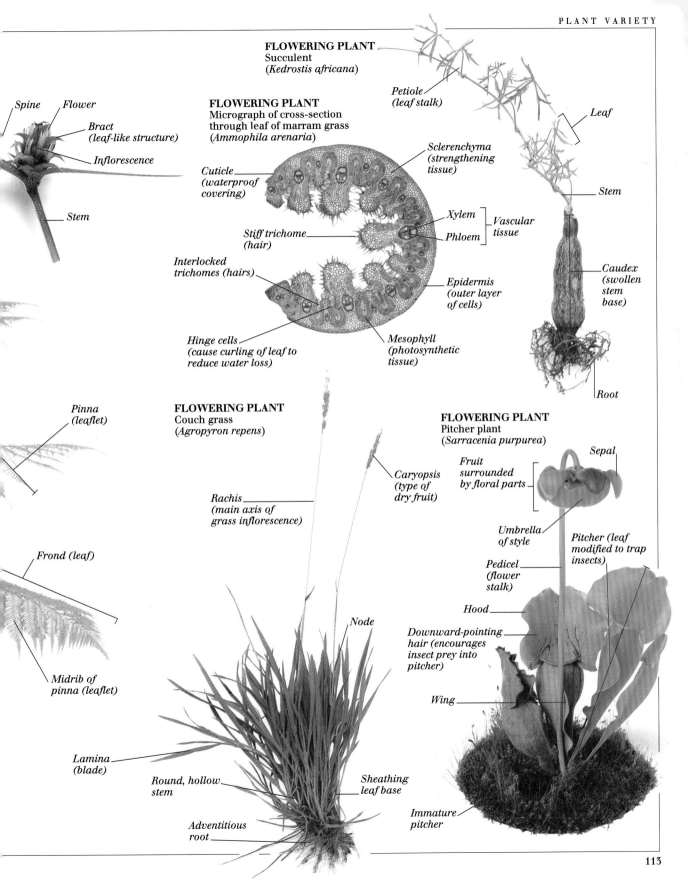

FLOWERING PLANT
Succulent
(*Kedrostis africana*)

*Petiole
(leaf stalk)*

Leaf

FLOWERING PLANT
Micrograph of cross-section
through leaf of marram grass
(*Ammophila arenaria*)

Stem

*Sclerenchyma
(strengthening
tissue)*

*Cuticle
(waterproof
covering)*

Xylem

Phloem

*Vascular
tissue*

*Stiff trichome
(hair)*

*Caudex
(swollen
stem
base)*

*Interlocked
trichomes (hairs)*

*Epidermis
(outer layer
of cells)*

*Hinge cells
(cause curling of leaf to
reduce water loss)*

*Mesophyll
(photosynthetic
tissue)*

Root

Spine   *Flower*

*Bract
(leaf-like structure)*

Inflorescence

Stem

*Pinna
(leaflet)*

FLOWERING PLANT
Couch grass
(*Agropyron repens*)

FLOWERING PLANT
Pitcher plant
(*Sarracenia purpurea*)

*Caryopsis
(type of
dry fruit)*

*Fruit
surrounded
by floral parts*

Sepal

*Rachis
(main axis of
grass inflorescence)*

*Umbrella
of style*

*Pitcher (leaf
modified to trap
insects)*

*Pedicel
(flower
stalk)*

Node

Hood

Frond (leaf)

*Downward-pointing
hair (encourages
insect prey into
pitcher)*

*Midrib of
pinna (leaflet)*

Wing

*Lamina
(blade)*

*Round, hollow
stem*

*Sheathing
leaf base*

*Adventitious
root*

*Immature
pitcher*

Fungi and lichens

FUNGI WERE ONCE THOUGHT OF AS PLANTS but are now classified as a separate kingdom. This kingdom includes not only the familiar mushrooms, puffballs, stinkhorns, and moulds, but also yeasts, smuts, rusts, and lichens. Most fungi are multicellular, consisting of a mass of thread-like hyphae that together form a mycelium. However, the simpler fungi (e.g., yeasts) are microscopic, single-celled organisms. Typically, fungi reproduce by means of spores. Most fungi feed on dead or decaying matter, or on living organisms. A few fungi obtain their food from plants or algae, with which they have a symbiotic (mutually advantageous) relationship. Lichens are a symbiotic partnership between algae and fungi. Of the six types of lichens the three most common are crustose (flat and crusty), foliose (leafy), and fruticose (shrub-like). Some lichens (e.g., *Cladonia floerkeana*) are a combination of types. Lichens reproduce by means of spores or soredia (powdery vegetative fragments).

EXAMPLES OF FUNGI

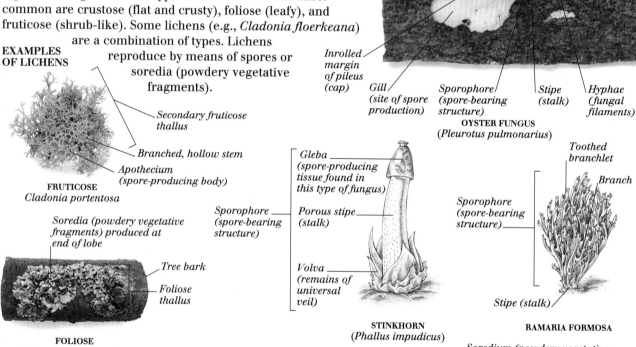

Emerging sporophore (spore-bearing structure)

Pileus (cap) continuous with stipe (stalk)

Bark of dead beech tree

Inrolled margin of pileus (cap)

Gill (site of spore production)

Sporophore (spore-bearing structure)

Stipe (stalk)

Hyphae (fungal filaments)

OYSTER FUNGUS
(*Pleurotus pulmonarius*)

EXAMPLES OF LICHENS

Secondary fruticose thallus

Branched, hollow stem

Apothecium (spore-producing body)

FRUTICOSE
Cladonia portentosa

Soredia (powdery vegetative fragments) produced at end of lobe

Tree bark

Foliose thallus

FOLIOSE
Hypogymnia physodes

Gleba (spore-producing tissue found in this type of fungus)

Sporophore (spore-bearing structure)

Porous stipe (stalk)

Volva (remains of universal veil)

STINKHORN
(*Phallus impudicus*)

Toothed branchlet

Branch

Sporophore (spore-bearing structure)

Stipe (stalk)

RAMARIA FORMOSA

Soredia (powdery vegetative fragments) released onto surface of squamulose thallus

Apothecium (spore-producing body)

Basal scale of primary squamulose thallus

Podetium (granular stalk) of secondary fruticose thallus

Moss

SQUAMULOSE (SCALY) AND FRUTICOSE THALLUS
Cladonia floerkeana

SECTION THROUGH FOLIOSE LICHEN SHOWING REPRODUCTION BY SOREDIA

Algal cell

Fungal hypha

Soredium (powdery vegetative fragment involved in propagation) released from lichen

Upper cortex

Algal layer

Medulla of fungal hyphae (mycelium)

Lower cortex

Rhizine (bundle of absorptive hyphae)

Soralium (pore in upper surface of thallus)

Upper surface of thallus

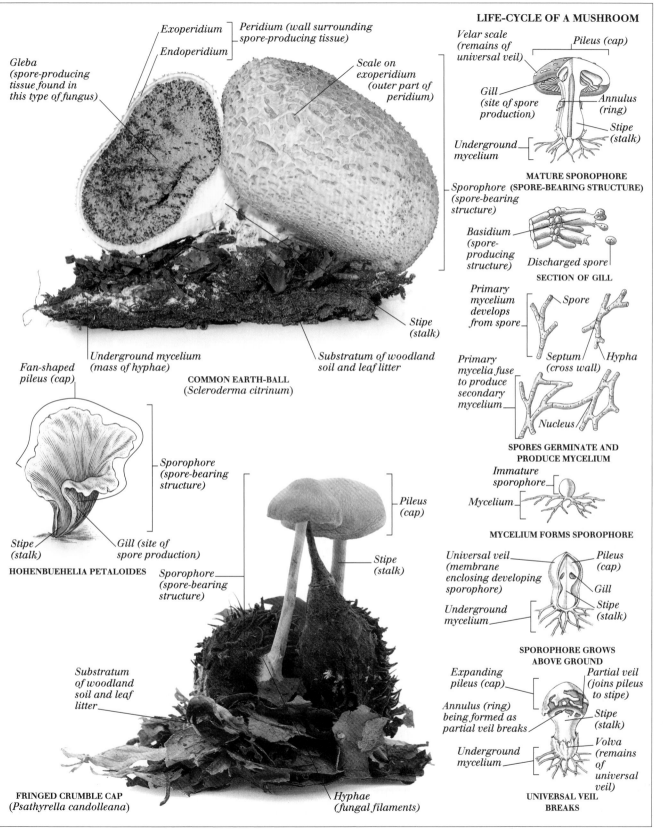

LIFE-CYCLE OF A MUSHROOM

Exoperidium

Endoperidium

Peridium (wall surrounding spore-producing tissue)

Gleba (spore-producing tissue found in this type of fungus)

Scale on exoperidium (outer part of peridium)

Velar scale (remains of universal veil)

Pileus (cap)

Gill (site of spore production)

Annulus (ring)

Stipe (stalk)

Underground mycelium

MATURE SPOROPHORE

Sporophore (spore-bearing structure)

Basidium (spore-producing structure)

Discharged spore

SECTION OF GILL

Primary mycelium develops from spore

Spore

Septum (cross wall)

Hypha

Primary mycelia fuse to produce secondary mycelium

Nucleus

SPORES GERMINATE AND PRODUCE MYCELIUM

Immature sporophore

Mycelium

MYCELIUM FORMS SPOROPHORE

Stipe (stalk)

Underground mycelium (mass of hyphae)

Substratum of woodland soil and leaf litter

COMMON EARTH-BALL
(Scleroderma citrinum)

Universal veil (membrane enclosing developing sporophore)

Pileus (cap)

Gill

Underground mycelium

Stipe (stalk)

SPOROPHORE GROWS ABOVE GROUND

Fan-shaped pileus (cap)

Sporophore (spore-bearing structure)

Stipe (stalk)

Gill (site of spore production)

HOHENBUEHELIA PETALOIDES

Sporophore (spore-bearing structure)

Pileus (cap)

Stipe (stalk)

Sporophore (spore-bearing structure)

Expanding pileus (cap)

Partial veil (joins pileus to stipe)

Annulus (ring) being formed as partial veil breaks

Stipe (stalk)

Underground mycelium

Volva (remains of universal veil)

UNIVERSAL VEIL BREAKS

Substratum of woodland soil and leaf litter

FRINGED CRUMBLE CAP
(Psathyrella candolleana)

Hyphae (fungal filaments)

Algae and seaweeds

ALGAE ARE NOT TRUE PLANTS. They form a diverse group of plant-like organisms that belong to the kingdom Protista. Like plants, algae possess the green pigment chlorophyll and make their own food by photosynthesis (see pp. 138-139). Many algae also possess other pigments by which they can be classified; for example, the brown pigment fucoxanthin is found in the brown algae. Some of the ten phyla of algae are exclusively unicellular (single-celled); others also contain aggregates of cells in filaments or colonies. Three phyla – the Chlorophyta (green algae), Rhodophyta (red algae), and Phaeophyta (brown algae) – contain larger, multicellular, thalloid (flat), marine organisms commonly known as seaweeds. Most algae can reproduce sexually. For example, in the brown seaweed *Fucus vesiculosus*, gametes (sex cells) are produced in conceptacles (chambers) in the receptacles (fertile tips of fronds); after their release into the sea, antherozoids (male gametes) and oospheres (female gametes) fuse; the resulting zygote settles on a rock and develops into a new seaweed.

BROWN SEAWEED
Channelled wrack
(*Pelvetia canaliculata*)

Receptacle (fertile tip of frond)

Thallus (plant body)

Margin of lamina (blade) rolled inwards to form channel

Apical notch

Hapteron (holdfast)

BROWN SEAWEED
Spiral wrack
(*Fucus spiralis*)

Apical notch

Conceptacle (chamber)

Receptacle (fertile tip of frond)

Lamina (blade)

Smooth margin

Midrib

Thallus (plant body)

Hapteron (holdfast)

EXAMPLES OF ALGAE

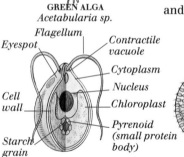

Reproductive chamber

Cap

Sterile whorl

Cell wall

Stalk

Rhizoid

GREEN ALGA
Acetabularia sp.

Flagellum

Eyespot

Contractile vacuole

Cytoplasm

Nucleus

Cell wall

Chloroplast

Pyrenoid (small protein body)

Starch grain

GREEN ALGA
Chlamydomonas sp.

Coenobium (colony of cells)

Daughter coenobium

Gelatinous sheath

Biflagellate cell

GREEN ALGA
Volvox sp.

Spine

Cytoplasm

Girdle

Vacuole

Plastid (photosynthetic organelle)

Nucleus

DIATOM
Thalassiosira sp.

Apical notch

Receptacle (fertile tip of frond)

Conceptacle (chamber) containing reproductive structures)

Lamina (blade)

Midrib

RECEPTACLE
Spiral wrack
(*Fucus spiralis*)

BROWN SEAWEED
Oarweed
(*Laminaria digitata*)

Thallus (plant body)

Lamina (blade) palmately divided

GREEN SEAWEED
Enteromorpha linza

Crinkled margin

Thallus
(plant
body)

Unbranched,
spirally twisted
frond

Small hapteron
(holdfast) attaching
seaweed to mussel

RED SEAWEED
Corallina officinalis

Branch

Branched,
hard thallus
(plant body)

Hapteron
(holdfast)

Main
stem

LIFE-CYCLE OF BROWN SEAWEED
Bladder wrack
(*Fucus vesiculosus*)

Male
receptacle

Female
receptacle

Lamina
(blade)

Air bladder

Hapteron
(holdfast)

Stipe
(stalk)

MALE AND FEMALE SEAWEEDS

Male
receptacle

Female
receptacle

Conceptacle

Ostiole
(opening to
conceptacle)

MALE AND FEMALE RECEPTACLES

Paraphysis
(sterile hair)

Ostiole
(opening to
conceptacle)

Antheridium
(male sex
organ)

Oogonium
(female sex organ)

**SECTIONS THROUGH MALE AND FEMALE
CONCEPTACLES**

Antherozoid
(male gamete)

Oogonium

Antheridium
(male sex organ)

Oosphere
(female
gamete)

PRODUCTION OF GAMETES

RED SEAWEED
Dilsea carnosa

Thallus
(plant
body)

Lamina
(blade)

Hapteron
(holdfast)

Antherozoid (male
gamete) swims
towards oosphere

Flagellum

Oosphere
(female
gamete) is
fertilized by
antherozoid
to produce
a zygote

FERTILIZATION

GREEN ALGA
Spirogyra sp.

Cytoplasm

End wall
of cell

Cell (cylindrical)

Cell wall

Filament
(strand of
linked cells)

Two filaments
linked for
conjugation
(sexual
reproduction)

Spirally
wound
chloroplast

Conjugation
tube

End wall of conjugation
tube still in place

Flexible stipe
(stalk)

Hapteron
(holdfast)

Young thallus
(plant body)

Hapteron
(holdfast)

**ZYGOTE DEVELOPS INTO
A YOUNG SEAWEED**

117

Liverworts and mosses

"Stem"

"Leaf"

Rhizoid

LIVERWORTS AND MOSSES ARE SMALL, LOW-GROWING PLANTS that belong to the phylum Bryophyta. Bryophytes do not have true stems, leaves, or roots (they are anchored to the ground by rhizoids), nor do they have the vascular tissues (xylem and phloem) that transport water and nutrients in higher plants. With no outer, waterproof cuticle, bryophytes are susceptible to drying out, and most grow in moist habitats. The bryophyte life-cycle has two stages. In stage one, the green plant (gametophyte) produces male and female gametes (sex cells), which fuse to form a zygote. In stage two, the zygote develops into a sporophyte that remains attached to the gametophyte. The sporophyte produces spores, which are released and germinate into new green plants. Liverworts (class Hepaticae) grow horizontally and may be thalloid (flat and ribbon-like) or "leafy". Mosses (class Musci) typically have an upright "stem" with spirally arranged "leaves".

A THALLOID LIVERWORT
Marchantia polymorpha

Gemma cup

Gemma (detachable tissue that produces new plants)

Thallus (plant body)

Toothed margin of cup

DETAIL OF GEMMA CUP

Archegoniophore (stalked structure carrying archegonia)
— Disc
— Lobe
— Stalk

Thallus (plant body)

Apical notch

Rhizoid

FEMALE GAMETOPHYTE

Disc

Lobe

Stalk

SIDE VIEW OF ARCHEGONIOPHORE

Lobe

Disc

Ray (radial groove)

Stalk

ARCHEGONIOPHORE FROM BELOW

Pore

Ray (radial groove)

MICROGRAPH OF LOBE

Gemma cup

Thallus (plant body)

Midrib

Archegoniophore (stalked structure carrying archegonia)

MICROGRAPH OF THALLUS
Conocephalum conicum

Position of air chamber

Pore for exchange of gases

Upper surface

Rhizoid

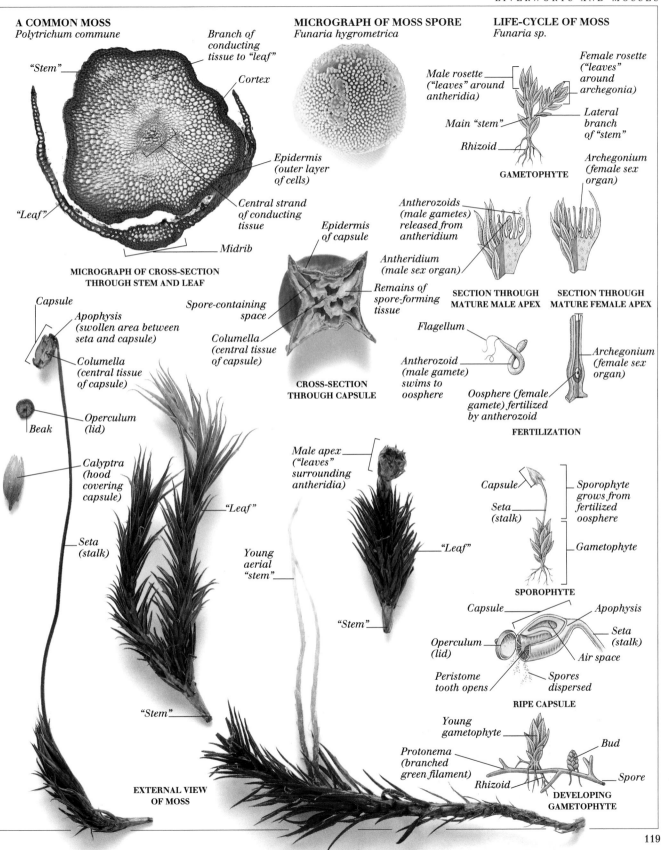

A COMMON MOSS
Polytrichum commune

"Stem"

Branch of conducting tissue to "leaf"

Cortex

Epidermis (outer layer of cells)

Central strand of conducting tissue

"Leaf"

Midrib

MICROGRAPH OF CROSS-SECTION THROUGH STEM AND LEAF

MICROGRAPH OF MOSS SPORE
Funaria hygrometrica

LIFE-CYCLE OF MOSS
Funaria sp.

Male rosette ("leaves" around antheridia)

Female rosette ("leaves" around archegonia)

Main "stem"

Lateral branch of "stem"

Rhizoid

GAMETOPHYTE

Archegonium (female sex organ)

Antherozoids (male gametes) released from antheridium

Antheridium (male sex organ)

SECTION THROUGH MATURE MALE APEX

SECTION THROUGH MATURE FEMALE APEX

Flagellum

Antherozoid (male gamete) swims to oosphere

Archegonium (female sex organ)

Oosphere (female gamete) fertilized by antherozoid

FERTILIZATION

Capsule

Apophysis (swollen area between seta and capsule)

Columella (central tissue of capsule)

Operculum (lid)

Beak

Calyptra (hood covering capsule)

Seta (stalk)

Epidermis of capsule

Spore-containing space

Columella (central tissue of capsule)

Remains of spore-forming tissue

CROSS-SECTION THROUGH CAPSULE

"Leaf"

Young aerial "stem"

"Stem"

Male apex ("leaves" surrounding antheridia)

"Leaf"

"Stem"

EXTERNAL VIEW OF MOSS

Capsule

Seta (stalk)

Sporophyte grows from fertilized oosphere

Gametophyte

SPOROPHYTE

Capsule

Apophysis

Operculum (lid)

Seta (stalk)

Air space

Peristome tooth opens

Spores dispersed

RIPE CAPSULE

Young gametophyte

Protonema (branched green filament)

Bud

Spore

Rhizoid

DEVELOPING GAMETOPHYTE

119

Horsetails, clubmosses, and ferns

HORSETAILS, CLUBMOSSES, AND FERNS are primitive land plants, which, like higher plants, have stems, roots, and leaves, and vascular systems that transport water, minerals, and food. However, unlike higher plants, they do not produce seeds when reproducing. Their life-cycles involve two stages. In stage one, the sporophyte (green plant) produces spores in sporangia. In stage two, the spores germinate, developing into small, short-lived gametophyte plants that produce male and female gametes (sex cells); the gametes fuse to form a zygote from which a new sporophyte plant develops. Horsetails (phylum Sphenophyta) have erect, green stems with branches arranged in whorls; some stems are fertile and have a single spore-producing strobilus (group of sporangia) at the tip. Clubmosses (phylum Lycopodophyta) typically have small leaves arranged spirally around the stem, with spore-producing strobili at the tip of some stems. Ferns (phylum Filicinophyta) typically have large, pinnate fronds (leaves); sporangia, grouped together in sori, develop on the underside of fertile fronds.

FROND
Male fern
(*Dryopteris filix-mas*)

CLUBMOSS
Lycopodium sp.

Stem with spirally arranged leaves

Branch

Strobilus (group of sporangia)

CLUBMOSS
Selaginella sp.

Epidermis (outer layer of cells)

Cortex (layer between epidermis and vascular tissue)

Vascular tissue
Phloem
Xylem

Lacuna (air space)

Root

MICROGRAPH OF CROSS-SECTION THROUGH CLUBMOSS STEM

Shoot apex

Branch

Rhizophore (leafless branch)

Creeping stem with spirally arranged leaves

HORSETAIL
Common horsetail
(*Equisetum arvense*)

Sporangiophore (structure carrying sporangia)

Apex of sterile shoot

Strobilus (group of sporangia)

Non-photosynthetic fertile stem

Collar of small brown leaves

Young shoot

Lateral branch

Photosynthetic sterile stem

Node

Internode

Node

Tuber

Rhizome

Adventitious root

Endodermis (inner layer of cortex)

Vascular tissue

Sclerenchyma (strengthening tissue)

Chlorenchyma (photosynthetic tissue)

Epidermis (outer layer of cells)

Parenchyma (packing tissue)

Cortex (layer between epidermis and vascular tissue)

Hollow pith cavity

Vallecular canal (longitudinal channel)

Carinal canal (longitudinal channel)

MICROGRAPH OF CROSS-SECTION THROUGH HORSETAIL STEM

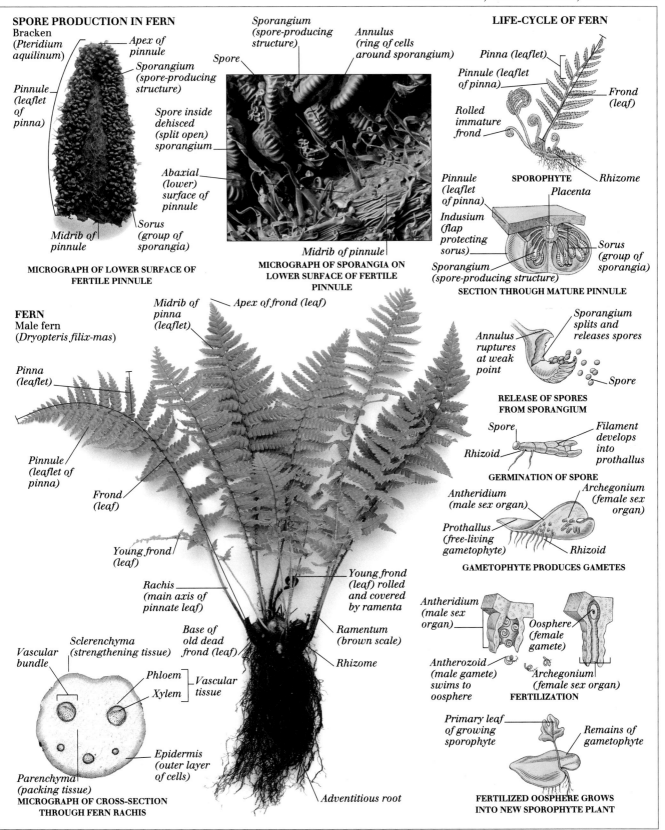

SPORE PRODUCTION IN FERN
Bracken
(*Pteridium aquilinum*)

Apex of pinnule

Sporangium (spore-producing structure)

Pinnule (leaflet of pinna)

Spore inside dehisced (split open) sporangium

Abaxial (lower) surface of pinnule

Midrib of pinnule

Sorus (group of sporangia)

MICROGRAPH OF LOWER SURFACE OF FERTILE PINNULE

Sporangium (spore-producing structure)

Annulus (ring of cells around sporangium)

Spore

Midrib of pinnule

MICROGRAPH OF SPORANGIA ON LOWER SURFACE OF FERTILE PINNULE

LIFE-CYCLE OF FERN

Pinna (leaflet)

Pinnule (leaflet of pinna)

Frond (leaf)

Rolled immature frond

SPOROPHYTE

Rhizome

Pinnule (leaflet of pinna)

Placenta

Indusium (flap protecting sorus)

Sorus (group of sporangia)

Sporangium (spore-producing structure)

SECTION THROUGH MATURE PINNULE

Sporangium splits and releases spores

Annulus ruptures at weak point

Spore

RELEASE OF SPORES FROM SPORANGIUM

Spore

Filament develops into prothallus

Rhizoid

GERMINATION OF SPORE

Antheridium (male sex organ)

Archegonium (female sex organ)

Prothallus (free-living gametophyte)

Rhizoid

GAMETOPHYTE PRODUCES GAMETES

Antheridium (male sex organ)

Oosphere (female gamete)

Antherozoid (male gamete) swims to oosphere

Archegonium (female sex organ)

FERTILIZATION

Primary leaf of growing sporophyte

Remains of gametophyte

FERTILIZED OOSPHERE GROWS INTO NEW SPOROPHYTE PLANT

FERN
Male fern
(*Dryopteris filix-mas*)

Midrib of pinna (leaflet)

Apex of frond (leaf)

Pinna (leaflet)

Pinnule (leaflet of pinna)

Frond (leaf)

Young frond (leaf)

Rachis (main axis of pinnate leaf)

Young frond (leaf) rolled and covered by ramenta

Ramentum (brown scale)

Rhizome

Base of old dead frond (leaf)

Vascular bundle

Sclerenchyma (strengthening tissue)

Phloem

Xylem

Vascular tissue

Epidermis (outer layer of cells)

Parenchyma (packing tissue)

MICROGRAPH OF CROSS-SECTION THROUGH FERN RACHIS

Adventitious root

121

Gymnosperms 1

THE GYMNOSPERMS ARE FOUR RELATED PHYLA of seed-producing plants; their seeds, however, lack the protective, outer covering which surrounds the seeds of flowering plants. Typically, gymnosperms are woody, perennial shrubs or trees, with stems, leaves, and roots, and a well-developed vascular (transport) system. The reproductive structures in most gymnosperms are cones: male cones produce microspores in which male gametes (sex cells) develop; female cones produce megaspores in which female gametes develop. Microspores are blown by the wind to female cones, male and female gametes fuse during fertilization, and a seed develops. The four gymnosperm phyla are the conifers (phylum Coniferophyta), mostly tall trees; cycads (phylum Cycadophyta), small palm-like trees; the ginkgo or maidenhair tree (phylum Ginkgophyta), a tall tree with bilobed leaves; and gnetophytes (phylum Gnetophyta), a diverse group of plants, mainly shrubs, but also including the horizontally growing welwitschia.

LIFE-CYCLE OF SCOTS PINE
(*Pinus sylvestris*)

Needle
(*foliage leaf*)

Cone

Ovuliferous scale
(ovule- then seed-bearing structure)

MALE CONES

YOUNG FEMALE CONE

Pollen grain in micropyle
(entrance to ovule)

Ovuliferous scale

Pollen grain

Nucleus

Air sac

Ovule
(contains female gamete)

POLLINATION

Integument
(outer part of ovule)

Pollen tube
(carries male gamete from pollen grain to ovum)

Archegonium
(containing female gamete)

FERTILIZATION

SCALE AND SEEDS
Pine
(*Pinus sp.*)

Ovuliferous scale
(ovule- then seed-bearing structure)

Wing scar

Wing of seed derived from ovuliferous scale

Seed

Seed

Point of attachment to axis of cone

Seed scar

OVULIFEROUS SCALE FROM THIRD-YEAR FEMALE CONE

Ovuliferous scale
(ovule- then seed-bearing structure)

Seed

Seed

Wing

MATURE FEMALE CONE AND WINGED SEED

Microsporangium
(structure in which pollen grains are formed)

Microsporophyll
(modified leaf carrying microsporangia)

Ovule
(contains female gametes)

Plumule
(embryonic shoot)

Cotyledon
(seed leaf)

Root

Bract scale

Axis of cone

Scale leaf

Ovuliferous scale
(ovule- then seed-bearing structure)

Axis of cone

GERMINATION OF PINE SEEDLING

MICROGRAPH OF LONGITUDINAL SECTION THROUGH YOUNG MALE CONE

MICROGRAPH OF LONGITUDINAL SECTION THROUGH SECOND-YEAR FEMALE CONE

WELWITSCHIA
(*Welwitschia mirabilis*)

Frayed end of leaf

SMOOTH CYPRESS
(*Cupressus glabra*)

Immature female cone

Ovuliferous scale (ovule- then seed-bearing structure)

Ovuliferous scale

Ovule (contains female gamete)

CROSS-SECTION THROUGH IMMATURE CONE

Ovuliferous scale (ovule- then seed-bearing structure)

Seed

Scale-like leaf

CROSS-SECTION THROUGH MATURE CONE

Mature female cone

Immature male cone

Woody scale

Opening between woody scales through which seeds are released

DISCARDED CONE

Stem

YEW
(*Taxus baccata*)

Single ovule (contains female gamete)

Scale

Female "cone"

Scale

Developing seed

Scale

FEMALE "CONES" AT VARIOUS STAGES OF DEVELOPMENT

Seed

Aril (fleshy outgrowth from seed)

Stem

Needle (foliage leaf)

CYCAD
Sago palm
(*Cycas revoluta*)

Pinna (leaflet)

Pinnate leaf

Scale leaf

Old leaf base

Stem covered by scale leaves

MAIDENHAIR TREE
(*Ginkgo biloba*)

Girdle scar

Stem

Petiole (leaf stalk)

Bilobed leaf

Continuously growing leaf

Site of cone growth

Adaxial (upper) surface of leaf

Abaxial (lower) surface of leaf

Frayed end of leaf

Immature cone

Stalk scar

Woody stem

Gymnosperms 2

BRANCH OF BISHOP PINE
(*Pinus muricata*)

*Needle
(foliage leaf)*

*Ovuliferous scale
(ovule- then seed-
bearing structure)*

*Bud
scale*

Cone

Cone stalk

Stem

Dwarf shoot

Scale leaf scar

**FEMALE CONE
(FIRST YEAR)**

Second-year female cone

*Ovuliferous scale
(ovule- then seed-bearing
structure)*

Apical bud

Stem

Needle (foliage leaf)

Dwarf shoot

Male cone

*Scar of
dwarf shoot*

*Upper surface
of needle
(foliage leaf)*

*Margin
of needle
(foliage leaf)*

*Needle
(foliage leaf)*

Apical bud

Stem

Dwarf shoot

TERMINAL ZONE OF BRANCH

*Stoma
(pore)*

*Female
cone*

*Woody ovuliferous
scale (ovule- then
seed-bearing structure)*

**FEMALE CONE
(THIRD YEAR)**

Vascular tissue

Phloem *Xylem*

*Mesophyll
(photosynthetic tissue)*

*Stoma
(pore)*

*Epidermis
(outer
layer of
cells)*

*Endodermis
(inner layer
of cortex)*

Resin canal

*Cuticle
(waterproof
covering)*

**MICROGRAPH OF CROSS-SECTION
THROUGH NEEDLE (FOLIAGE LEAF)**

**MICROGRAPH OF NEEDLE
(FOLIAGE LEAF) OF PINE**
(*Pinus sp.*)

CROSS-SECTION THROUGH
MATURE STEM OF BISHOP PINE
(*Pinus muricata*)

Apical bud scale

Apical bud

Shoot
apex

Needle
(foliage
leaf) bud

Bud scale

Scale leaf

Immature needle
(foliage leaf)

**MICROGRAPH OF LONGITUDINAL SECTION
THROUGH SHOOT APEX OF PINE
(*Pinus sp.*)**

Annual ring

Heartwood
(supportive,
inactive
secondary
xylem)

Branch trace
(vascular bundle
supplying branch)

Pith

Medullary ray
(extension of pith)

Cortex
(layer between
epidermis and
vascular tissue)

Secondary
xylem

Vascular
tissue

Phloem

Primary
xylem

Pith

Hypodermis
(cell layer below
epidermis)

Base of dwarf shoot

Dwarf shoot trace
(vascular bundle
supplying dwarf
shoot)

Epidermis
(outer layer
of cells)

Resin canal

**MICROGRAPH OF CROSS-SECTION
THROUGH YOUNG STEM OF PINE
(*Pinus sp.*)**

Sapwood
(active secondary
xylem)

Phloem

Bark — Periderm
(outer layer
of bark)

Cortex
(layer between
phellem and
vascular tissue)

Resin canal

Endodermis
(inner layer
of cortex)

Phloem

Phellem
(protective
outer layer)

Secondary
xylem

Primary
xylem

**MICROGRAPH OF CROSS-SECTION
THROUGH YOUNG ROOT OF PINE
(*Pinus sp.*)**

Cortex
(layer between
phellem and
vascular tissue)

Secondary
xylem

Phellem
(protective
outer layer)

Phloem

Primary
xylem

Resin canal

**MICROGRAPH OF CROSS-SECTION
THROUGH MATURE ROOT OF PINE
(*Pinus sp.*)**

Monocotyledons and dicotyledons

FLOWERING PLANTS (PHYLUM ANGIOSPERMOPHYTA) are divided into two classes: monocotyledons (class Monocotyledoneae) and dicotyledons (class Dicotyledoneae). Typically, monocotyledons have seeds with one cotyledon (seed leaf); their foliage leaves are narrow with parallel veins; the flower components occur in multiples of three; sepals and petals are indistinguishable and are known as tepals; vascular (transport) tissues are scattered in random bundles throughout the stem; and, since they lack stem cambium (actively dividing cells that produce wood), most monocotyledons are herbaceous (see pp. 128-129). Dicotyledons have seeds with two cotyledons; leaves are broad with a central midrib and branched veins; flower parts occur in multiples of four or five; sepals are generally small and green; petals are large and colourful; vascular bundles are arranged in a ring around the edge of the stem; and, because many dicotyledons possess wood-producing stem cambium, there are woody forms (see pp. 130-131) as well as herbaceous ones.

CROSS-SECTION THROUGH MONOCOTYLEDONOUS LEAF BASES

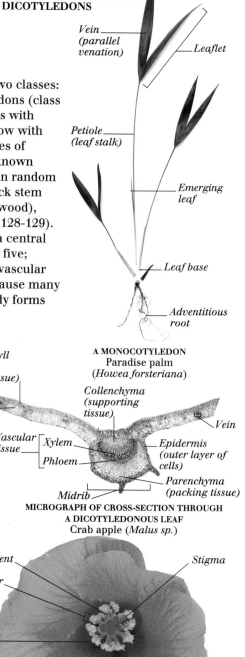

COMPARISONS BETWEEN MONOCOTYLEDONS AND DICOTYLEDONS

Vein (parallel venation)

Leaflet

Petiole (leaf stalk)

Emerging leaf

Leaf base

Adventitious root

A MONOCOTYLEDON
Paradise palm
(*Howea forsteriana*)

Water-absorbing parenchyma (packing tissue)

Mesophyll (photosynthetic tissue)

Vein

Xylem

Phloem

Vascular tissue

Sunken stoma (pore)

Cuticle (waterproof covering)

Sclerenchyma (strengthening tissue)

Epidermis (outer layer of cells)

MICROGRAPH OF CROSS-SECTION THROUGH A MONOCOTYLEDONOUS LEAF
Yucca (*Yucca* sp.)

Palisade mesophyll (tightly packed photosynthetic tissue)

Spongy mesophyll (loosely packed photosynthetic tissue)

Vascular tissue

Xylem

Phloem

Collenchyma (supporting tissue)

Vein

Epidermis (outer layer of cells)

Parenchyma (packing tissue)

Midrib

MICROGRAPH OF CROSS-SECTION THROUGH A DICOTYLEDONOUS LEAF
Crab apple (*Malus* sp.)

Outer tepal (monocotyledonous sepal)

Lateral, inner tepal (monocotyledonous petal)

Column (stamens and style)

Guide hair

A MONOCOTYLEDONOUS FLOWER
Orchid
(*Phalaenopsis sp.*)

Labellum (lip) forming landing stage for pollinator

Funnel guide for bird pollinators' beak

Stamen

Filament

Anther

Pollen on anther

Stigma

Petal

A DICOTYLEDONOUS FLOWER
Hibiscus
(*Hibiscus rosa-sinensis*)

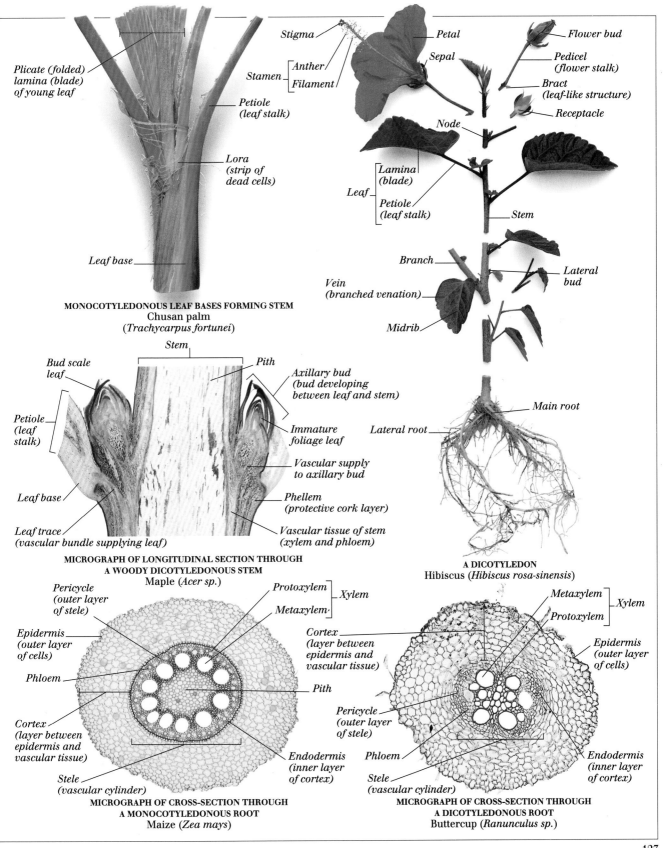

Plicate (folded)
lamina (blade)
of young leaf

Petiole
(leaf stalk)

Lora
(strip of
dead cells)

Leaf base

MONOCOTYLEDONOUS LEAF BASES FORMING STEM
Chusan palm
(*Trachycarpus fortunei*)

Stigma

Stamen { Anther
Filament

Petal

Sepal

Flower bud

Pedicel
(flower stalk)

Bract
(leaf-like structure)

Receptacle

Node

Leaf { Lamina
(blade)

Petiole
(leaf stalk)

Stem

Branch

Vein
(branched venation)

Lateral
bud

Midrib

Main root

Lateral root

A DICOTYLEDON
Hibiscus (*Hibiscus rosa-sinensis*)

Bud scale
leaf

Stem

Pith

Axillary bud
(bud developing
between leaf and stem)

Petiole
(leaf
stalk)

Immature
foliage leaf

Vascular supply
to axillary bud

Leaf base

Phellem
(protective cork layer)

Leaf trace
(vascular bundle supplying leaf)

Vascular tissue of stem
(xylem and phloem)

**MICROGRAPH OF LONGITUDINAL SECTION THROUGH
A WOODY DICOTYLEDONOUS STEM**
Maple (*Acer sp.*)

Pericycle
(outer layer
of stele)

Epidermis
(outer layer
of cells)

Phloem

Cortex
(layer between
epidermis and
vascular tissue)

Stele
(vascular cylinder)

Protoxylem } Xylem
Metaxylem

Pith

Endodermis
(inner layer
of cortex)

**MICROGRAPH OF CROSS-SECTION THROUGH
A MONOCOTYLEDONOUS ROOT**
Maize (*Zea mays*)

Metaxylem } Xylem
Protoxylem

Cortex
(layer between
epidermis and
vascular tissue)

Epidermis
(outer layer
of cells)

Pericycle
(outer layer
of stele)

Phloem

Stele
(vascular cylinder)

Endodermis
(inner layer
of cortex)

**MICROGRAPH OF CROSS-SECTION THROUGH
A DICOTYLEDONOUS ROOT**
Buttercup (*Ranunculus sp.*)

Herbaceous flowering plants

HERBACEOUS FLOWERING PLANTS TYPICALLY HAVE GREEN, NON-WOODY STEMS, and tend to be relatively short-lived. Many herbaceous plants live for only one or two years. Annuals (e.g., sweet peas) grow from seed, produce flowers and then seeds, and die within a single year. Biennials (e.g., carrots) have a two-year life cycle. In the first year, seeds grow into plants, which produce leaves and store food in underground storage organs; the stems and foliage then die back in winter. In the second year, new stems grow from the storage organs, produce leaves, flowers, and seeds, and then die. Some herbaceous plants (e.g., potatoes) are perennial. They grow back year after year, producing shoots and flowers in spring, storing food in underground tubers or rhizomes during summer, dying back in autumn, and surviving underground during winter.

Young plant forming

Petiole (stalk) of young leaf

Lateral root

Stipule (structure at base of leaf)

Trifoliate leaf

Node

Simple ovate leaflet

Root nodule

Main root

SWEET PEA
(*Lathyrus odoratus*)

STRAWBERRY
(*Fragaria* x *ananassa*)

Runner (creeping stem)

Remains of leaves

Lateral root scar

Leaf scar

Rib

Stem

Lateral root

Tap root

Leaf scar

Petiole (leaf stalk)

Leaf base

Spine (modified leaf)

CARROT
(*Daucus carota*)

Slender rhizome

Stem tuber

Adventitious root

Stem

Narrow, succulent leaf

Simple deltoid leaf

POTATO
(*Solanum tuberosum*)

ROCK STONECROP
(*Sedum rupestre*)

Adventitious root

PARTS OF HERBACEOUS FLOWERING PLANTS

*Bract
(leaf-like
structure)*

*Bracteole
(small bract)*

Midrib

*Cyme
(type of inflorescence)*

*Succulent,
simple ovate
leaf*

*Inner, tubular
disc floret*

*Outer, ligulate
ray floret*

Node

Flower bud

*Dentate
margin*

*Peduncle
(inflorescence stalk)*

Internode

**LIVE-FOR-EVER OR
ICE PLANT**
(*Sedum spectabile*)

*Simple lobed
leaf*

*Capitulum
(type of inflorescence)*

Leaf

*Peduncle
(inflorescence
stalk)*

*Flower
bud*

*Petiole
(leaf stalk)*

*Petiole
(leaf
stalk)*

Leaf base

Stem

FLORISTS' CHRYSANTHEMUM
(*Chrysanthemum morifolium*)

*Succulent
stem*

*Leaf
scar*

*Lateral
bud*

*Linear
leaf*

Prickle

BEGONIA
(*Begonia* x
tuberhybrida)

*Bract
(leaf-like
structure)*

*Capitulum
(type of
inflorescence)*

*Hollow
stem*

*Sheath formed
from leaf base*

TOADFLAX
(*Linaria sp.*)

**CEREOID
CACTUS**

*Spinose-dentate
margin*

SLENDER THISTLE
(*Carduus tenuiflorus*)

*Dentate
margin*

*Unwinged rachis
(main axis of
pinnate leaf)*

*Rachis
(main axis of
pinnate leaf)*

*Winged
stem*

*Stipule
(structure at
base of leaf)*

Tendril

*Stem
segment*

*Winged
rachis
(main
axis of
pinnate
leaf)*

*Peduncle
(inflorescence
stalk)*

Flower bud

*Pinna
(leaflet)*

HOGWEED
(*Heracleum sphondylium*)

*Petiole
(leaf stalk)*

*Margin of
cladode*

*Toothed
notch*

*Bract
(leaf-like
structure)*

Tepal

*Peduncle
(inflorescence
stalk)*

PERUVIAN LILY
(*Alstroemeria aurea*)

*Cladode
(flattened stem)*

*Stem
branch*

*Raceme
(type of inflorescence)*

CRAB CACTUS
(*Schlumbergera truncata*)

Petal

Sepal

EVERLASTING PEA
(*Lathyrus latifolius*)

Woody flowering plants

WOODY FLOWERING PLANTS ARE PERENNIAL, that is, they continue to grow and reproduce for many years. They have one or more permanent stems above ground, and numerous smaller branches. The stems and branches have a strong woody core that supports the plant and contains vascular tissue for transporting water and nutrients. Outside the woody core is a layer of tough, protective bark, which has lenticels (tiny pores) in it to enable gases to pass through. Woody flowering plants may be shrubs, which have several stems arising from the soil; bushes, which are shrubs with dense branching and foliage; or trees, which typically have a single upright stem (the trunk) that bears branches. Deciduous woody plants (e.g., roses) shed all their leaves once a year and remain leafless during winter. Evergreen woody plants (e.g., ivy) shed their leaves gradually, so retaining full leaf cover throughout the year.

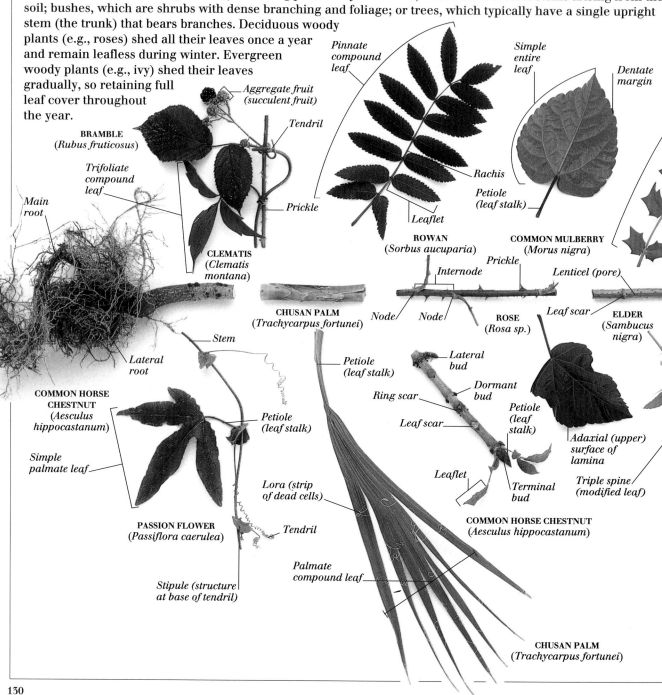

Aggregate fruit (succulent fruit)

Tendril

BRAMBLE
(*Rubus fruticosus*)

Trifoliate compound leaf

Prickle

CLEMATIS
(*Clematis montana*)

Main root

Pinnate compound leaf

Simple entire leaf

Dentate margin

Rachis

Petiole (leaf stalk)

Leaflet

ROWAN
(*Sorbus aucuparia*)

COMMON MULBERRY
(*Morus nigra*)

Prickle

Lenticel (pore)

Internode

Leaf scar

Node

Node

ROSE
(*Rosa sp.*)

ELDER
(*Sambucus nigra*)

CHUSAN PALM
(*Trachycarpus fortunei*)

Stem

Lateral root

COMMON HORSE CHESTNUT
(*Aesculus hippocastanum*)

Simple palmate leaf

Petiole (leaf stalk)

Petiole (leaf stalk)

Lateral bud

Dormant bud

Ring scar

Leaf scar

Petiole (leaf stalk)

Adaxial (upper) surface of lamina

Triple spine (modified leaf)

Leaflet

Terminal bud

COMMON HORSE CHESTNUT
(*Aesculus hippocastanum*)

Lora (strip of dead cells)

Tendril

Palmate compound leaf

Stipule (structure at base of tendril)

PASSION FLOWER
(*Passiflora caerulea*)

CHUSAN PALM
(*Trachycarpus fortunei*)

130

PARTS OF WOODY FLOWERING PLANTS

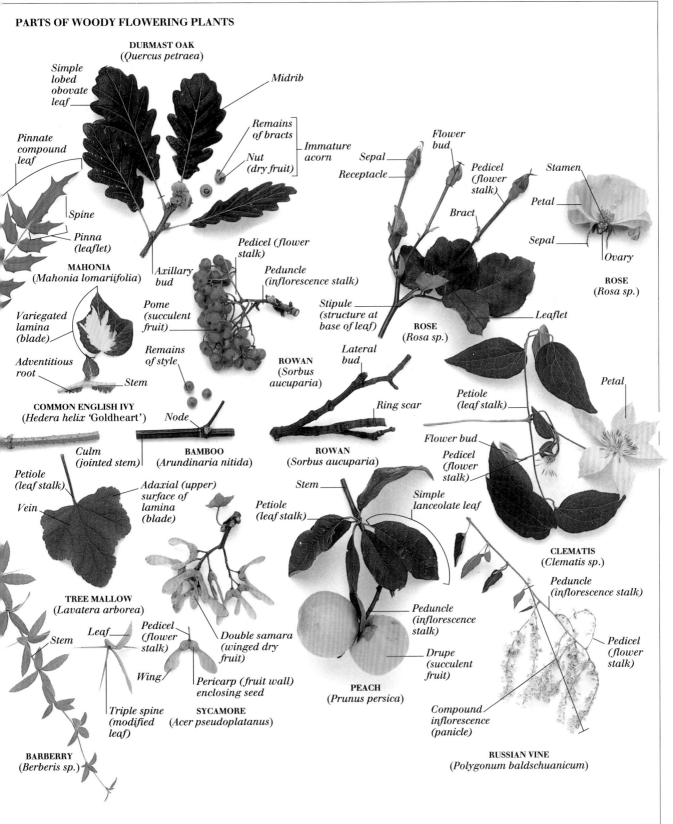

DURMAST OAK
(*Quercus petraea*)

Simple lobed obovate leaf

Midrib

Remains of bracts

Nut (dry fruit)

Immature acorn

Pinnate compound leaf

Spine

Pinna (leaflet)

MAHONIA
(*Mahonia lomariifolia*)

Axillary bud

Pedicel (flower stalk)

Peduncle (inflorescence stalk)

Flower bud

Sepal

Receptacle

Pedicel (flower stalk)

Bract

Stamen

Petal

Sepal

Ovary

ROSE
(*Rosa sp.*)

Variegated lamina (blade)

Pome (succulent fruit)

Stipule (structure at base of leaf)

Leaflet

ROSE
(*Rosa sp.*)

Adventitious root

Stem

Remains of style

ROWAN
(*Sorbus aucuparia*)

Lateral bud

Petiole (leaf stalk)

Petal

COMMON ENGLISH IVY
(*Hedera helix* 'Goldheart')

Node

Ring scar

Flower bud

Pedicel (flower stalk)

Culm (jointed stem)

BAMBOO
(*Arundinaria nitida*)

ROWAN
(*Sorbus aucuparia*)

Stem

CLEMATIS
(*Clematis sp.*)

Petiole (leaf stalk)

Vein

Adaxial (upper) surface of lamina (blade)

Simple lanceolate leaf

Petiole (leaf stalk)

Peduncle (inflorescence stalk)

TREE MALLOW
(*Lavatera arborea*)

Stem

Leaf

Pedicel (flower stalk)

Double samara (winged dry fruit)

Peduncle (inflorescence stalk)

Pedicel (flower stalk)

Wing

Pericarp (fruit wall) enclosing seed

Drupe (succulent fruit)

Triple spine (modified leaf)

SYCAMORE
(*Acer pseudoplatanus*)

PEACH
(*Prunus persica*)

Compound inflorescence (panicle)

BARBERRY
(*Berberis sp.*)

RUSSIAN VINE
(*Polygonum baldschuanicum*)

Roots

ROOTS ARE THE UNDERGROUND PARTS OF PLANTS. They have three main functions. First, they anchor the plant in the soil. Second, they absorb water and minerals from the spaces between soil particles; the roots' absorptive properties are increased by root hairs, which grow behind the root tip, allowing maximum uptake of vital substances. Third, the root is part of the plant's transport system: xylem carries water and minerals from the roots to the stem and leaves, and phloem carries nutrients from the leaves to all parts of the root system. In addition, some roots (e.g., carrots) are food stores. Roots have an outer epidermis covering a cortex of parenchyma (packing tissue), and a central cylinder of vascular tissue. This arrangement helps the roots resist the forces of compression as they grow through the soil.

CARROT
(*Daucus carota*)

MICROGRAPH OF PRIMARY ROOT DEVELOPMENT
Cabbage (*Brassica sp.*)

Split in testa as seed germinates

Cotyledon (seed leaf)

Primary root

Testa (seed coat)

Root hair

Root tip (region of cell division)

FEATURES OF A TYPICAL ROOT
Buttercup (*Ranunculus sp.*)

Pericycle (outer layer of stele)

Root hair

Air space (allowing gas diffusion in the root)

Stele (vascular cylinder)

Phloem sieve tube (through which nutrients are transported)

Companion cell (cell associated with phloem sieve tube)

Cortex (layer between epidermis and vascular tissue)

Root hair

Epidermis (outer layer of cells)

Xylem vessel (through which water and minerals are transported)

Endodermis (inner layer of cortex)

Cell wall

Nucleus

Cytoplasm

Parenchyma (packing) cell

PRIMARY ROOT AND MICROGRAPHS OF SECTIONS THROUGH ROOTS

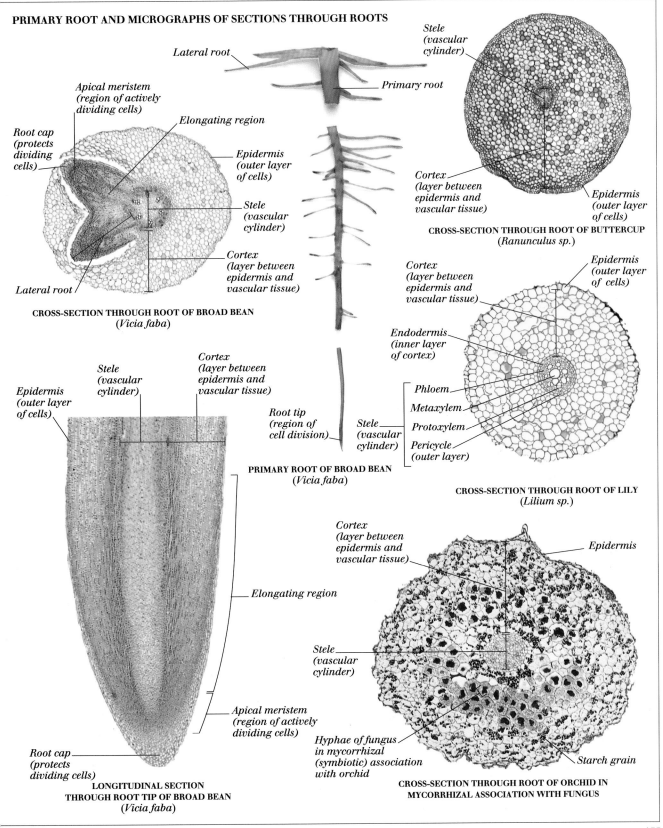

Lateral root

Primary root

Stele (vascular cylinder)

Apical meristem (region of actively dividing cells)

Elongating region

Root cap (protects dividing cells)

Epidermis (outer layer of cells)

Stele (vascular cylinder)

Cortex (layer between epidermis and vascular tissue)

Lateral root

CROSS-SECTION THROUGH ROOT OF BROAD BEAN
(*Vicia faba*)

Cortex (layer between epidermis and vascular tissue)

Epidermis (outer layer of cells)

CROSS-SECTION THROUGH ROOT OF BUTTERCUP
(*Ranunculus sp.*)

Cortex (layer between epidermis and vascular tissue)

Epidermis (outer layer of cells)

Endodermis (inner layer of cortex)

Phloem

Metaxylem

Protoxylem

Pericycle (outer layer)

Stele (vascular cylinder)

CROSS-SECTION THROUGH ROOT OF LILY
(*Lilium sp.*)

Stele (vascular cylinder)

Cortex (layer between epidermis and vascular tissue)

Epidermis (outer layer of cells)

Root tip (region of cell division)

Stele (vascular cylinder)

PRIMARY ROOT OF BROAD BEAN
(*Vicia faba*)

Elongating region

Apical meristem (region of actively dividing cells)

Root cap (protects dividing cells)

**LONGITUDINAL SECTION
THROUGH ROOT TIP OF BROAD BEAN**
(*Vicia faba*)

Cortex (layer between epidermis and vascular tissue)

Epidermis

Stele (vascular cylinder)

Hyphae of fungus in mycorrhizal (symbiotic) association with orchid

Starch grain

**CROSS-SECTION THROUGH ROOT OF ORCHID IN
MYCORRHIZAL ASSOCIATION WITH FUNGUS**

133

Stems

THE STEM IS THE MAIN SUPPORTIVE PART OF A PLANT that grows above ground. Stems bear leaves (organs of photosynthesis), which grow at nodes; buds (shoots covered by protective scales), which grow at the stem tip (apical or terminal buds) and in the angle between a leaf and the stem (axillary or lateral buds); and flowers (reproductive structures). The stem forms part of the plant's transport system: xylem tissue in the stem transports water and minerals from the roots to the aerial parts of the plant, and phloem tissue transports nutrients manufactured in the leaves to other parts of the plant. Stem tissues are also used for storing water and food. Herbaceous (non-woody) stems have an outer protective epidermis covering a cortex that consists mainly of parenchyma (packing tissue) but also has some collenchyma (supporting tissue). The vascular tissue of such stems is arranged in bundles, each of which consists of xylem, phloem, and sclerenchyma (strengthening tissue). Woody stems have an outer protective layer of tough bark, which is perforated with lenticels (pores) to allow gas exchange. Inside the bark is a ring of secondary phloem, which surrounds an inner core of secondary xylem.

MICROGRAPH OF LONGITUDINAL SECTION THROUGH APEX OF STEM
Coleus sp.

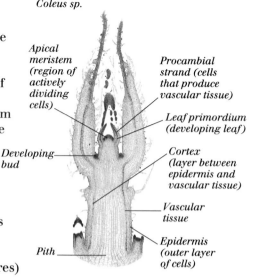

Apical meristem (region of actively dividing cells)

Procambial strand (cells that produce vascular tissue)

Leaf primordium (developing leaf)

Developing bud

Cortex (layer between epidermis and vascular tissue)

Vascular tissue

Pith

Epidermis (outer layer of cells)

YOUNG WOODY STEM
Lime
(*Tilia sp.*)

Cortex (layer between phellem and vascular tissue)

Secondary phloem

Pith

Phellem (protective cork layer)

Xylem vessel (through which water and minerals are transported)

Xylem fibre (supporting tissue)

Ray (parenchyma cells)

Phloem sieve tube (through which nutrients are transported)

Phloem fibre (supporting tissue)

Lenticel (pore)

Vascular cambium (actively dividing cells that produce xylem and phloem)

Autumn wood

Spring wood

Secondary xylem

Companion cell (cell associated with phloem sieve tube)

EMERGENT BUDS
London plane
(*Platanus x acerifolia*)

Young leaves emerging

Terminal bud

Lateral bud

Node

Internode

Inner bud scale

Outer bud scale

Node

Leaf scar

Lenticel (pore)

Woody stem

MICROGRAPHS OF CROSS-SECTIONS THROUGH VARIOUS STEMS

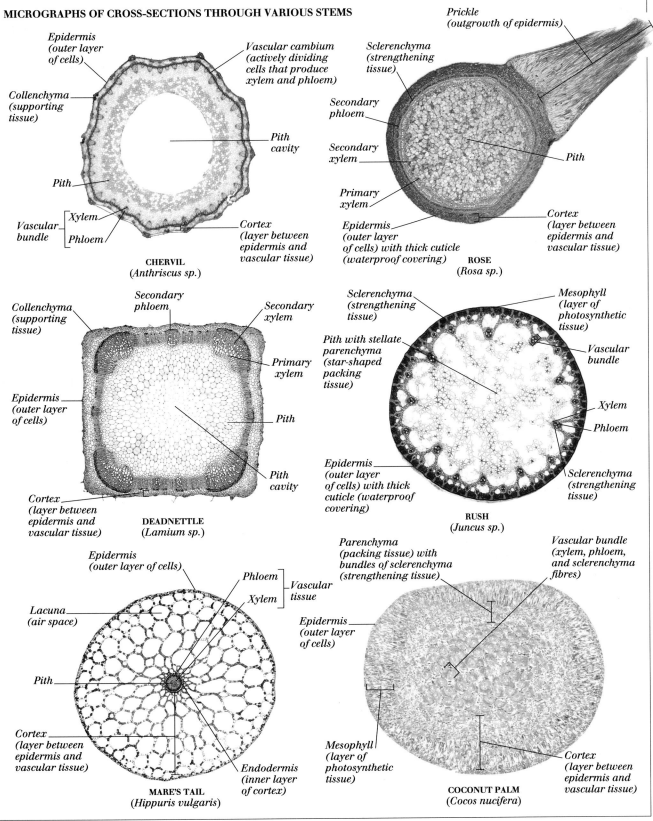

Epidermis (outer layer of cells)

Vascular cambium (actively dividing cells that produce xylem and phloem)

Collenchyma (supporting tissue)

Pith cavity

Pith

Vascular bundle — *Xylem* *Phloem*

Cortex (layer between epidermis and vascular tissue)

CHERVIL (*Anthriscus sp.*)

Prickle (outgrowth of epidermis)

Sclerenchyma (strengthening tissue)

Secondary phloem

Secondary xylem

Pith

Primary xylem

Epidermis (outer layer of cells) with thick cuticle (waterproof covering)

Cortex (layer between epidermis and vascular tissue)

ROSE (*Rosa sp.*)

Collenchyma (supporting tissue)

Secondary phloem

Secondary xylem

Primary xylem

Epidermis (outer layer of cells)

Pith

Pith cavity

Cortex (layer between epidermis and vascular tissue)

DEADNETTLE (*Lamium sp.*)

Sclerenchyma (strengthening tissue)

Mesophyll (layer of photosynthetic tissue)

Pith with stellate parenchyma (star-shaped packing tissue)

Vascular bundle

Xylem

Phloem

Epidermis (outer layer of cells) with thick cuticle (waterproof covering)

Sclerenchyma (strengthening tissue)

RUSH (*Juncus sp.*)

Epidermis (outer layer of cells)

Phloem *Xylem* — *Vascular tissue*

Lacuna (air space)

Pith

Cortex (layer between epidermis and vascular tissue)

Endodermis (inner layer of cortex)

MARE'S TAIL (*Hippuris vulgaris*)

Parenchyma (packing tissue) with bundles of sclerenchyma (strengthening tissue)

Vascular bundle (xylem, phloem, and sclerenchyma fibres)

Epidermis (outer layer of cells)

Mesophyll (layer of photosynthetic tissue)

Cortex (layer between epidermis and vascular tissue)

COCONUT PALM (*Cocos nucifera*)

Leaves

LEAVES ARE THE MAIN SITES OF PHOTOSYNTHESIS (see pp. 138-139) and transpiration (water loss by evaporation) in plants. A typical leaf consists of a thin, flat lamina (blade) supported by a network of veins; a petiole (leaf stalk); and a leaf base, where the petiole joins the stem. Leaves can be classified as simple, in which the lamina is a single unit, or compound, in which the lamina is divided into separate leaflets. Compound leaves may be pinnate, with pinnae (leaflets) on both sides of a rachis (main axis), or palmate, with leaflets arising from a single point at the tip of the petiole. Leaves can be classified further by the overall shape of the lamina, and by the shape of the lamina's apex, margin, and base.

CHECKERBLOOM
(*Sidalcea malviflora*)

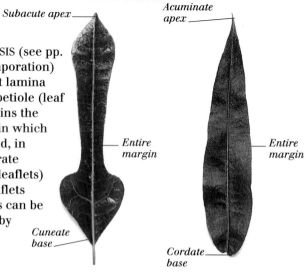

SIMPLE LEAF SHAPES

Subacute apex
Acuminate apex
Entire margin
Entire margin
Cuneate base
Cordate base

PANDURIFORM
Croton
(*Codiaeum variegatum*)

LANCEOLATE
Sea buckthorn
(*Hippophae rhamnoides*)

GENERAL LEAF FEATURES

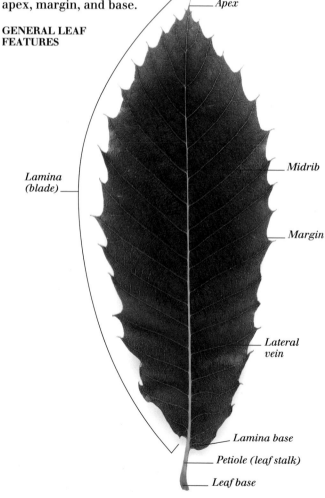

Apex
Midrib
Margin
Lamina (blade)
Lateral vein
Lamina base
Petiole (leaf stalk)
Leaf base

Sweet chestnut
(*Castanea sativa*)

COMPOUND LEAF SHAPES

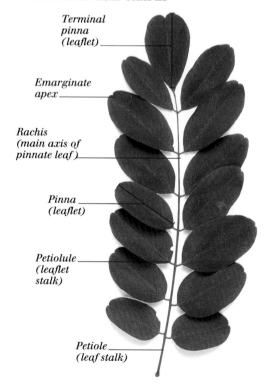

Terminal pinna (leaflet)
Emarginate apex
Rachis (main axis of pinnate leaf)
Pinna (leaflet)
Petiolule (leaflet stalk)
Petiole (leaf stalk)

ODD PINNATE
False acacia
(*Robinia pseudoacacia*)

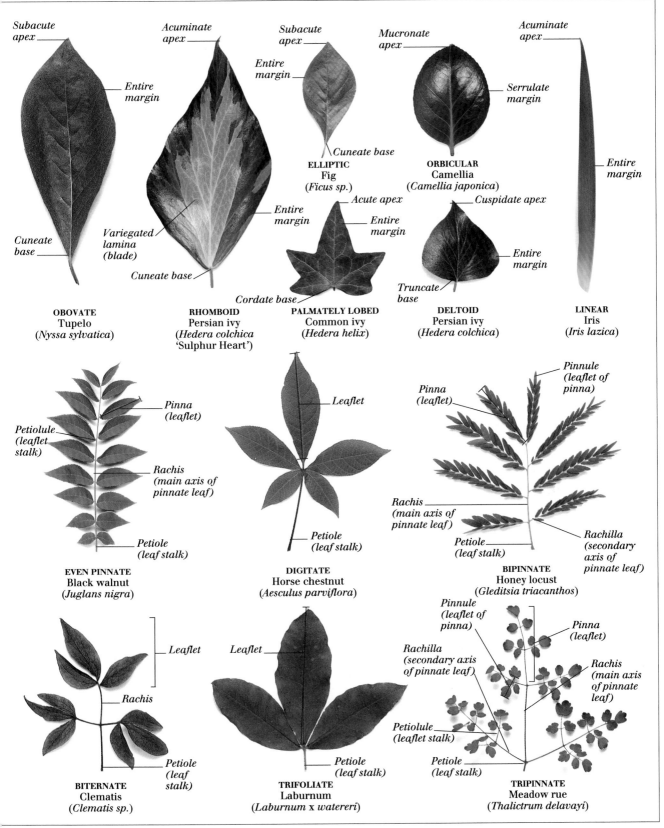

OBOVATE
Tupelo
(*Nyssa sylvatica*)

Subacute apex
Entire margin
Cuneate base

RHOMBOID
Persian ivy
(*Hedera colchica*
'Sulphur Heart')

Acuminate apex
Entire margin
Variegated lamina (blade)
Cuneate base

ELLIPTIC
Fig
(*Ficus sp.*)

Subacute apex
Entire margin
Cuneate base

ORBICULAR
Camellia
(*Camellia japonica*)

Mucronate apex
Serrulate margin

LINEAR
Iris
(*Iris lazica*)

Acuminate apex
Entire margin

PALMATELY LOBED
Common ivy
(*Hedera helix*)

Acute apex
Entire margin
Cordate base

DELTOID
Persian ivy
(*Hedera colchica*)

Cuspidate apex
Entire margin
Truncate base

EVEN PINNATE
Black walnut
(*Juglans nigra*)

Pinna (leaflet)
Petiolule (leaflet stalk)
Rachis (main axis of pinnate leaf)
Petiole (leaf stalk)

DIGITATE
Horse chestnut
(*Aesculus parviflora*)

Leaflet
Petiole (leaf stalk)

BIPINNATE
Honey locust
(*Gleditsia triacanthos*)

Pinnule (leaflet of pinna)
Pinna (leaflet)
Rachis (main axis of pinnate leaf)
Petiole (leaf stalk)
Rachilla (secondary axis of pinnate leaf)

BITERNATE
Clematis
(*Clematis sp.*)

Leaflet
Rachis
Petiole (leaf stalk)

TRIFOLIATE
Laburnum
(*Laburnum* x *watereri*)

Leaflet
Petiole (leaf stalk)

TRIPINNATE
Meadow rue
(*Thalictrum delavayi*)

Pinnule (leaflet of pinna)
Pinna (leaflet)
Rachilla (secondary axis of pinnate leaf)
Rachis (main axis of pinnate leaf)
Petiolule (leaflet stalk)
Petiole (leaf stalk)

Photosynthesis

PHOTOSYNTHESIS IS THE PROCESS by which plants make their food using sunlight, water, and carbon dioxide. It takes place inside special structures in leaf cells called chloroplasts. The chloroplasts contain chlorophyll, a green pigment that absorbs energy from sunlight. During photosynthesis, the absorbed energy is used to join together carbon dioxide and water to form the sugar glucose, which is the energy source for the whole plant; oxygen, a waste product, is released into the air. Leaves are the main sites of photosynthesis, and have various adaptations for that purpose: flat laminae (blades) provide a large surface for absorbing sunlight; stomata (pores) in the lower surface of the laminae allow gases (carbon dioxide and oxygen) to pass into and out of the leaves; and an extensive network of veins brings water into the leaves and transports the glucose produced by photosynthesis to the rest of the plant.

MICROGRAPH OF LEAF
Lily (*Lilium sp.*)

Stoma
(pore)

Guard cell
(controls
opening
and closing
of stoma)

Lower
surface of
lamina
(blade)

THE PROCESS OF PHOTOSYNTHESIS

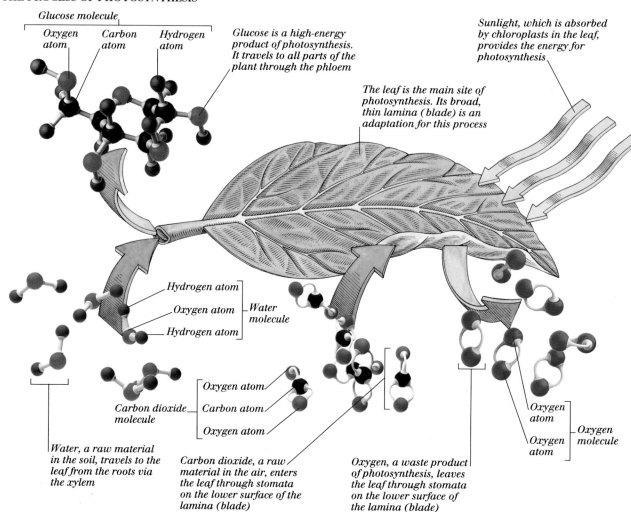

Glucose molecule

Oxygen atom Carbon atom Hydrogen atom

Glucose is a high-energy product of photosynthesis. It travels to all parts of the plant through the phloem

Sunlight, which is absorbed by chloroplasts in the leaf, provides the energy for photosynthesis

The leaf is the main site of photosynthesis. Its broad, thin lamina (blade) is an adaptation for this process

Hydrogen atom
Oxygen atom — Water molecule
Hydrogen atom

Carbon dioxide molecule

Oxygen atom
Carbon atom
Oxygen atom

Oxygen atom
Oxygen atom — Oxygen molecule

Water, a raw material in the soil, travels to the leaf from the roots via the xylem

Carbon dioxide, a raw material in the air, enters the leaf through stomata on the lower surface of the lamina (blade)

Oxygen, a waste product of photosynthesis, leaves the leaf through stomata on the lower surface of the lamina (blade)

CROSS-SECTION THROUGH LEAF
Christmas rose
(*Helleborus niger*)

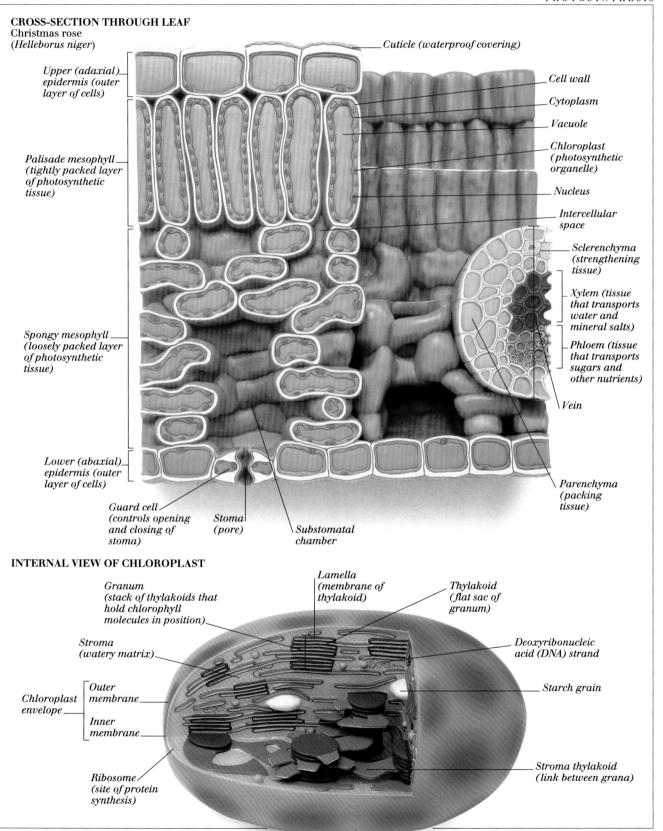

Cuticle (*waterproof covering*)

Upper (adaxial) epidermis (outer layer of cells)

Cell wall

Cytoplasm

Vacuole

Chloroplast (*photosynthetic organelle*)

Palisade mesophyll (*tightly packed layer of photosynthetic tissue*)

Nucleus

Intercellular space

Sclerenchyma (*strengthening tissue*)

Xylem (*tissue that transports water and mineral salts*)

Spongy mesophyll (*loosely packed layer of photosynthetic tissue*)

Phloem (*tissue that transports sugars and other nutrients*)

Vein

Lower (abaxial) epidermis (outer layer of cells)

Parenchyma (*packing tissue*)

Guard cell (*controls opening and closing of stoma*)

Stoma (*pore*)

Substomatal chamber

INTERNAL VIEW OF CHLOROPLAST

Granum (*stack of thylakoids that hold chlorophyll molecules in position*)

Lamella (*membrane of thylakoid*)

Thylakoid (*flat sac of granum*)

Stroma (*watery matrix*)

Deoxyribonucleic acid (DNA) strand

Chloroplast envelope

Outer membrane

Inner membrane

Starch grain

Ribosome (*site of protein synthesis*)

Stroma thylakoid (*link between grana*)

Flowers 1

FLOWERS ARE THE SITES OF SEXUAL REPRODUCTION in flowering plants. Their component parts are arranged in whorls around the receptacle (tip of the flower stalk). The sepals (collectively called the calyx) are outermost; typically small and green, they protect the developing flower. The petals (collectively called the corolla) are typically large and brightly coloured; they are found inside the sepals. In monocotyledonous flowers (see pp. 126-127), sepals and petals are indistinguishable; individually they are called tepals (collectively called the perianth). The petals surround the male and female reproductive structures (androecium and gynoecium). The androecium consists of stamens (male organs); each stamen is made up of a filament (stalk) and anther. The gynoecium has one or more carpels (female organs); each carpel consists of an ovary, style, and stigma. Some flowers (e.g., lily) occur singly on a pedicel (flower stalk); others (e.g., elder, sunflower) are arranged in a group (inflorescence) on a peduncle (inflorescence stalk).

A MONOCOTYLEDONOUS FLOWER
Lily
(*Lilium sp.*)

Syncarpous
(fused carpels)
gynoecium

Ovary

Stigma

Style

Stamen

Anther

Filament

Pollen on anther

Inner tepal
(monocotyledonous
petal)

Honey
guide

Groove
secreting
nectar

Filament

Style

Outer tepal
(monocotyledonous
sepal)

Stigma

Anther

EXTERNAL VIEW

Inner tepal
(monocotyledonous
petal)

Honey
guide

Outer tepal
(monocotyledonous
sepal)

Tepal
scar

Receptacle

Ovary
wall

Ovule

Pedicel
(flower
stalk)

Papilla
(fleshy hair)

Outer tepal
sheath

Style

Folded inner tepal
(monocotyledonous petal)

Stigma

Ovary

Receptacle

Anther

Pedicel
(flower
stalk)

Filament

**LONGITUDINAL SECTION
THROUGH FLOWER BUD**

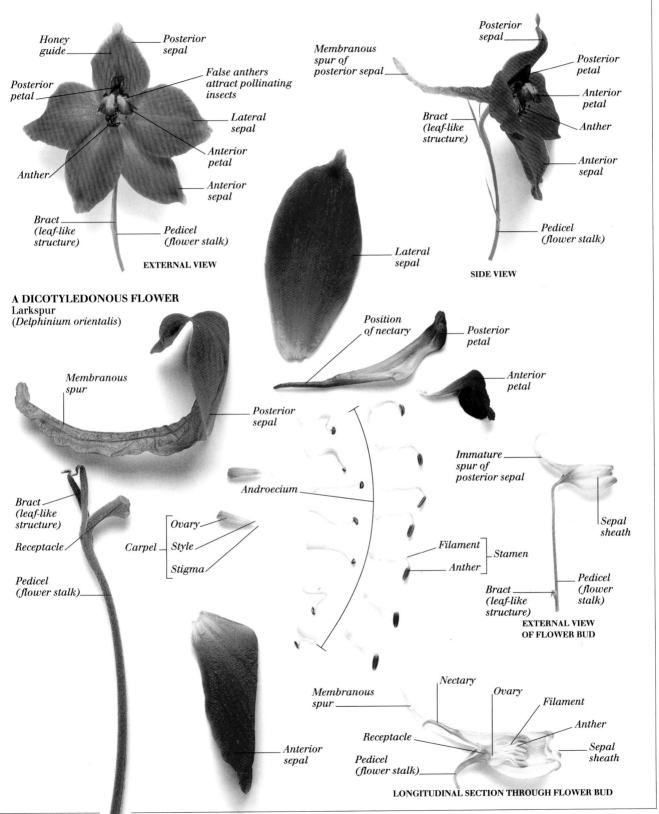

Honey
guide

Posterior
sepal

Posterior
petal

False anthers
attract pollinating
insects

Lateral
sepal

Anterior
petal

Anterior
sepal

Anther

Bract
(leaf-like
structure)

Pedicel
(flower stalk)

EXTERNAL VIEW

Posterior
sepal

Membranous
spur of
posterior sepal

Posterior
petal

Anterior
petal

Anther

Bract
(leaf-like
structure)

Anterior
sepal

Pedicel
(flower stalk)

SIDE VIEW

Lateral
sepal

A DICOTYLEDONOUS FLOWER
Larkspur
(*Delphinium orientalis*)

Membranous
spur

Posterior
sepal

Position
of nectary

Posterior
petal

Anterior
petal

Bract
(leaf-like
structure)

Receptacle

Pedicel
(flower stalk)

Carpel

Ovary

Style

Stigma

Androecium

Filament

Anther

Stamen

Immature
spur of
posterior sepal

Sepal
sheath

Bract
(leaf-like
structure)

Pedicel
(flower
stalk)

**EXTERNAL VIEW
OF FLOWER BUD**

Membranous
spur

Anterior
sepal

Nectary

Receptacle

Pedicel
(flower stalk)

Ovary

Filament

Anther

Sepal
sheath

LONGITUDINAL SECTION THROUGH FLOWER BUD

Flowers 2

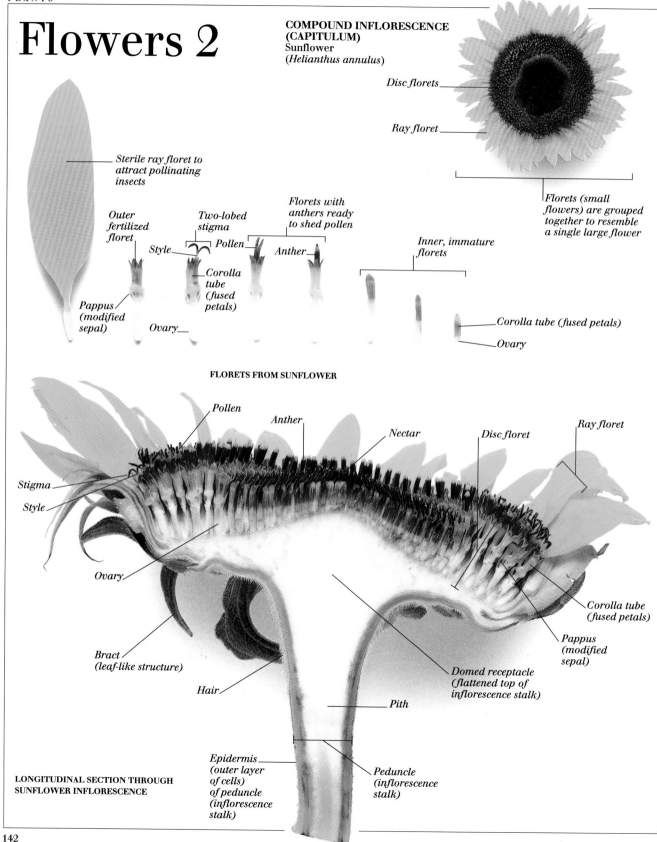

COMPOUND INFLORESCENCE (CAPITULUM)
Sunflower
(*Helianthus annulus*)

Disc florets

Ray floret

Florets (small flowers) are grouped together to resemble a single large flower

Sterile ray floret to attract pollinating insects

Outer fertilized floret

Two-lobed stigma

Florets with anthers ready to shed pollen

Style

Pollen

Anther

Inner, immature florets

Corolla tube (fused petals)

Pappus (modified sepal)

Ovary

Corolla tube (fused petals)

Ovary

FLORETS FROM SUNFLOWER

Pollen

Anther

Nectar

Disc floret

Ray floret

Stigma

Style

Ovary

Corolla tube (fused petals)

Pappus (modified sepal)

Bract (leaf-like structure)

Hair

Domed receptacle (flattened top of inflorescence stalk)

Pith

Epidermis (outer layer of cells) of peduncle (inflorescence stalk)

Peduncle (inflorescence stalk)

LONGITUDINAL SECTION THROUGH SUNFLOWER INFLORESCENCE

ARRANGEMENT OF FLOWERS ON STEM

Bract
(leaf-like
structure)

Flower

Ovary

Remains of tepals
(monocotyledonous
petals and sepals)

Peduncle
(inflorescence
stalk)

INFLORESCENCE (SPIKE)
Heliconia peruviana

Flower

Petal

Peduncle
(inflorescence
stalk)

Pedicel
(flower
stalk)

**INFLORESCENCE
(COMPOUND UMBEL)**
Common elder
(*Sambucus nigra*)

Spathe
(large bract) to
attract pollinating
insects

Spadix (fleshy
axis) carrying
male and female
flowers

Peduncle
(inflorescence
stalk)

INFLORESCENCE (SPADIX)
Painter's palette
(*Anthurium andreanum*)

Stigma

Style

Anther

Filament

Stamen

Flower
bud

Pedicel
(flower
stalk)

Bract
(leaf-like
structure)

Peduncle
(inflorescence
stalk) fused
to bract

**INFLORESCENCE
(DICHASIAL CYME)**
Common lime
(*Tilia* x *europaea*)

Three-lobed
stigma

Style

Ovary

Inner tepal
(monocotyledonous
petal)

Filament

Anther

Stamen

Outer tepal
(monocotyledonous
sepal)

Pedicel
(flower stalk)

SINGLE FLOWER
Glory lily
(*Gloriosa superba*)

Flower

Corolla

Calyx

Peduncle
(inflorescence
stalk)

Bract
(leaf-like
structure)

**SINGLE
FLOWER**

**INFLORESCENCE
(SPHERICAL UMBEL)**
Allium sp.

Pollination

POLLINATION IS THE TRANSFER OF POLLEN (which contains the male sex cells) from an anther (part of the male reproductive organ) to a stigma (part of the female reproductive organ). This process precedes fertilization (see pp. 146-147). Pollination may occur within the same flower (self-pollination), or between flowers on separate plants of the same species (cross-pollination). In most plants, pollination is carried out either by insects (entomophilous pollination) or by the wind (anemophilous pollination). Less commonly, birds, bats, or water are the agents of pollination. Insect-pollinated flowers are typically brightly coloured, scented, and produce nectar, on which insects feed. Such flowers also tend to have patterns that are visible only in ultraviolet light, which many insects can see but which humans cannot. These features attract insects, which become covered with the sticky or hooked pollen grains when they visit one flower, and then transfer the pollen to the next flower they visit. Wind-pollinated flowers are generally small, relatively inconspicuous, and unscented. They produce large quantities of light pollen grains that are easily blown by the wind to other flowers.

REPRODUCTIVE STRUCTURES IN WIND-POLLINATED PLANT
Sweet chestnut
(*Castanea sativa*)

Flower bud

Prominent stigma protrudes from flower

Female flower

Petiole (leaf stalk)

Bract (leaf-like structure)

Peduncle (inflorescence stalk)

Male flower

Part of male catkin (inflorescence adapted for wind pollination)

Peduncle (inflorescence stalk)

Filament

Anther

FEMALE

MALE

REPRODUCTIVE STRUCTURES IN INSECT-POLLINATED PLANTS

Stigma

Style

Dehisced (split open) pollen sac

Boundary between two fused carpels (each carpel consists of a stigma, style, and ovary)

Ovary

Endothecium (pollen sac wall)

Pollen grain

Anther

Filament

Stamen

Calyx (whorl of sepals)

MICROGRAPH OF CARPELS (FEMALE ORGANS)
Yellow-wort
(*Blackstonia perfoliata*)

MICROGRAPH OF STAMENS (MALE ORGANS)
Common centaury
(*Centaurium erythraea*)

MICROGRAPHS OF POLLEN GRAINS

Exine (outer coat of pollen grain)

Colpus (furrow-shaped aperture)

Exine (outer coat of pollen grain)

Pore

EUROPEAN FIELD ELM
(*Ulmus minor*)

Exine (outer coat of pollen grain)

Pore

Exine (outer coat of pollen grain)

JUSTICIA AUREA

Colpus (furrow-shaped aperture)

Exine (outer coat of pollen grain)

Baculum (rod-shaped structure)

MEADOW CRANESBILL
(*Geranium pratense*)

Equatorial furrow

BOX-LEAVED MILKWORT
(*Polygala chamaebuxus*)

INSECT POLLINATION OF MEADOW SAGE

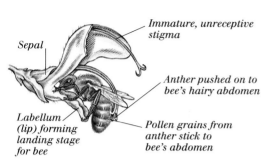

Sepal

Immature, unreceptive stigma

Anther pushed on to bee's hairy abdomen

Labellum (lip) forming landing stage for bee

Pollen grains from anther stick to bee's abdomen

1. BEE VISITS FLOWER WITH MATURE ANTHERS BUT IMMATURE STIGMA

Pollen grains attached to hairy abdomen

2. BEE FLIES TO OTHER FLOWERS

Long style curves downwards when bee enters flower

Sepal

Mature, receptive stigma touches bee's abdomen, picking up pollen

Labellum (lip) forming landing stage for bee

3. BEE VISITS FLOWER WHERE THE ANTHERS HAVE WITHERED AND THE STIGMA IS MATURE

SUNFLOWER UNDER NORMAL AND ULTRAVIOLET LIGHT

Central area of disc florets

Ray floret

NORMAL LIGHT

Petal

Ovary

Stigma

Stamen
- Filament
- Anther

NORMAL LIGHT

ST JOHN'S WORT UNDER NORMAL AND ULTRAVIOLET LIGHT

Honey guide directs insects to dark, central part of flower

Paler, outer part of ray floret

Darker, inner part of ray floret

Insects attracted to darkest, central part of flower, which contains nectaries, anthers, and stigmas

Dark central area containing nectaries, anthers, and stigmas

ULTRAVIOLET LIGHT

ULTRAVIOLET LIGHT

Pore

Exine (outer coat of pollen grain)

MIMULOPSIS SOLMSII

Trilete mark (development scar)

Exine (outer coat of pollen grain)

THESIUM ALPINIUM

Columella (small column-shaped structure)

Exine (outer coat of pollen grain)

RUELLIA GRANDIFLORA

Colpus (furrow-shaped aperture)

Exine (outer coat of pollen grain)

Tricolpate (three colpae) pollen grain

CROSSANDRA NILOTICA

Fertilization

FERTILIZATION IS THE FUSION of male and female
gametes (sex cells) to produce a zygote (embryo).
Following pollination (see pp. 144-145), the pollen
grains that contain the male gametes are on
the stigma, some distance from the female
gamete (ovum) inside the ovule. To enable the
gametes to meet, the pollen grain germinates
and produces a pollen tube, which grows
down and enters the embryo sac (the inner
part of the ovule that contains the ovum).
Two male gametes, travelling at the tip of the
pollen tube, enter the embryo sac. One gamete
fuses with the ovum to produce a zygote that will
develop into an embryo plant. The other male
gamete fuses with two polar nuclei to produce the
endosperm, which acts as a food store for the
developing embryo. Fertilization also initiates
other changes: the integument (outer part of ovule)
forms a testa (seed coat) around the embryo and
endosperm; the petals fall off; the stigma and style
wither; and the ovary wall forms a layer (called the
pericarp) around the seed. Together, the pericarp
and seed form the fruit, which may be succulent
(see pp. 148-149) or dry (see pp. 150-151). In some
species (e.g., blackberry), apomixis can occur: the
seed develops without fertilization of the ovum by
a male gamete but endosperm formation and fruit development take
place as in other species.

BANANA
(*Musa 'lacatan'*)

DEVELOPMENT OF A SUCCULENT FRUIT
Blackberry
(*Rubus fruticosus*)

Petal

Stamen — { Filament / Anther }

Carpel — { Ovary / Stigma / Style }

**1. FLOWER IN FULL BLOOM
ATTRACTS POLLINATORS**

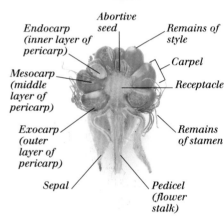

Endocarp
(inner layer of
pericarp)

Abortive
seed

Remains of
style

Carpel

Receptacle

Mesocarp
(middle
layer of
pericarp)

Exocarp
(outer
layer of
pericarp)

Remains
of stamen

Sepal

Pedicel
(flower
stalk)

**4. PERICARP FORMS
FLESH, SKIN, AND A HARD INNER
LAYER (SHOWN IN CROSS-SECTION)**

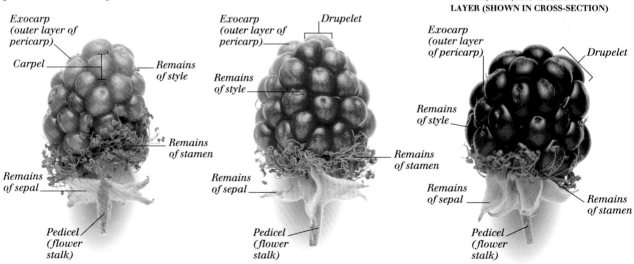

Exocarp
(outer layer of
pericarp)

Carpel

Remains
of style

Remains
of stamen

Remains
of sepal

Pedicel
(flower
stalk)

**7. MESOCARP (FLESHY PART OF PERICARP)
OF EACH CARPEL STARTS TO
CHANGE COLOUR**

Exocarp
(outer layer of
pericarp)

Drupelet

Remains
of style

Remains
of stamen

Remains
of sepal

Pedicel
(flower
stalk)

**8. CARPELS MATURE INTO DRUPELETS
(SMALL FLESHY FRUITS WITH SINGLE SEEDS
SURROUNDED BY HARD ENDOCARP)**

Exocarp
(outer layer
of pericarp)

Drupelet

Remains
of style

Remains
of sepal

Remains
of stamen

Pedicel
(flower
stalk)

**9. MESOCARP OF DRUPELET BECOMES
DARKER AND SWEETER**

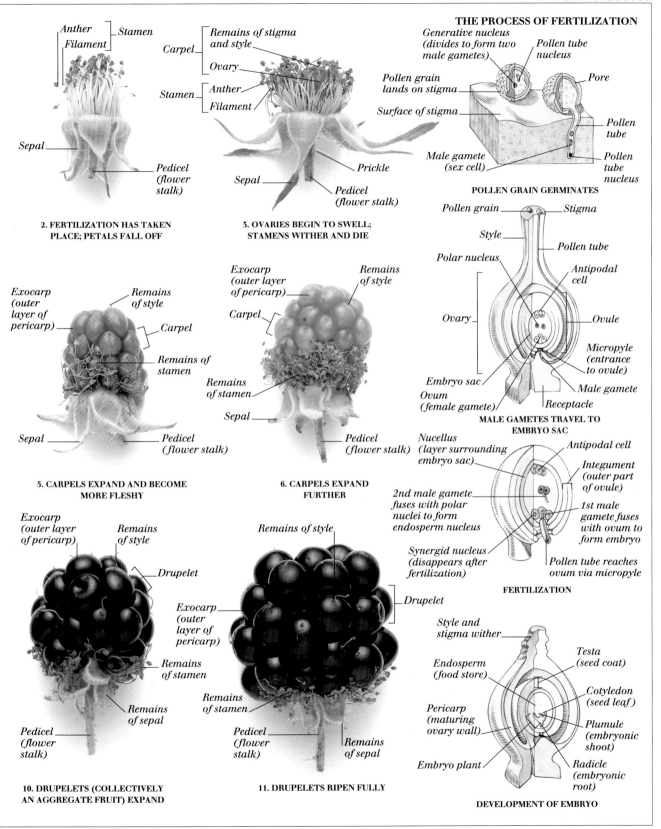

THE PROCESS OF FERTILIZATION

Anther
Filament
Stamen

Sepal

Pedicel
(flower
stalk)

2. FERTILIZATION HAS TAKEN PLACE; PETALS FALL OFF

Carpel

Remains of stigma
and style

Ovary

Anther
Filament
Stamen

Sepal

Prickle

Pedicel
(flower stalk)

5. OVARIES BEGIN TO SWELL; STAMENS WITHER AND DIE

Generative nucleus
(divides to form two
male gametes)

Pollen tube
nucleus

Pollen grain
lands on stigma

Pore

Surface of stigma

Pollen
tube

Male gamete
(sex cell)

Pollen
tube
nucleus

POLLEN GRAIN GERMINATES

Exocarp
(outer
layer of
pericarp)

Remains
of style

Carpel

Remains of
stamen

Sepal

Pedicel
(flower stalk)

5. CARPELS EXPAND AND BECOME MORE FLESHY

Exocarp
(outer layer
of pericarp)

Remains
of style

Carpel

Remains
of stamen

Sepal

Pedicel
(flower stalk)

6. CARPELS EXPAND FURTHER

Pollen grain

Stigma

Style

Pollen tube

Polar nucleus

Antipodal
cell

Ovary

Ovule

Micropyle
(entrance
to ovule)

Embryo sac

Male gamete

Ovum
(female gamete)

Receptacle

MALE GAMETES TRAVEL TO EMBRYO SAC

Exocarp
(outer layer
of pericarp)

Remains
of style

Drupelet

Remains
of stamen

Pedicel
(flower
stalk)

10. DRUPELETS (COLLECTIVELY AN AGGREGATE FRUIT) EXPAND

Remains of style

Exocarp
(outer
layer of
pericarp)

Drupelet

Remains
of stamen

Pedicel
(flower
stalk)

Remains
of sepal

11. DRUPELETS RIPEN FULLY

Nucellus
(layer surrounding
embryo sac)

Antipodal cell

Integument
(outer part
of ovule)

2nd male gamete
fuses with polar
nuclei to form
endosperm nucleus

1st male
gamete fuses
with ovum to
form embryo

Synergid nucleus
(disappears after
fertilization)

Pollen tube reaches
ovum via micropyle

FERTILIZATION

Style and
stigma wither

Testa
(seed coat)

Endosperm
(food store)

Cotyledon
(seed leaf)

Pericarp
(maturing
ovary wall)

Plumule
(embryonic
shoot)

Embryo plant

Radicle
(embryonic
root)

DEVELOPMENT OF EMBRYO

Succulent fruits

A FRUIT IS A FULLY DEVELOPED and ripened ovary (seed-producing part of a plant's female reproductive organs). Fruits may be succulent or dry (see pp. 150-151). Succulent fruits are fleshy and brightly coloured, making them attractive to animals, which eat them and so disperse the seeds away from the parent plant. The wall (pericarp) of a succulent fruit has three layers: an outer exocarp, a middle mesocarp, and an inner endocarp. These three layers vary in thickness and texture in different types of fruits and may blend into each other. Succulent fruits can be classed as simple (derived from one ovary) or compound (derived from several ovaries). Simple succulent fruits include berries, which typically have many seeds, and drupes, which typically have a single stone or pip (e.g., cherry and peach). Compound succulent fruits include aggregate fruits, which are formed from many ovaries in one flower, and multiple fruits, which develop from the ovaries of many flowers. Some fruits, known as false fruits or pseudocarps, develop from parts of the flower in addition to the ovaries. For example, the flesh of the apple is formed from the receptacle (the upper end of the flower stalk).

BERRY
Cocoa
(*Theobroma cacao*)

HESPERIDIUM (A TYPE OF BERRY)
Lemon
(*Citrus limon*)

Pedicel (flower stalk)
Endocarp
Mesocarp
Pedicel (flower stalk)
Exocarp
Leathery exocarp
Seed
Oil gland
Vesicle (juice sac)
Remains of style
Remains of style
Placenta

EXTERNAL VIEW OF FRUIT

LONGITUDINAL SECTION THROUGH FRUIT

Hilum (point of attachment to ovary)
Embryo
Seed
Carpel wall
Carpel
Testa (seed coat)
Cotyledon (seed leaf)
Placenta

EXTERNAL VIEW AND SECTION THROUGH SEED

CROSS-SECTION THROUGH FRUIT

SYCONIUM (A TYPE OF FALSE FRUIT)
Fig
(*Ficus carica*)

Remains of female flowers
Fleshy infolded receptacle
Remains of male flowers
Peduncle (inflorescence stalk)
Pip (seed surrounded by endocarp)
Skin
Pore closed by scales

EXTERNAL VIEW OF FRUIT

LONGITUDINAL SECTION THROUGH FRUIT

FRUIT WITH FLESHY ARIL
Lychee
(*Litchi chinensis*)

Pedicel (flower stalk)
Pedicel (flower stalk)
Seed
Aril (fleshy outgrowth from seed stalk)
Pericarp (fruit wall)
Pericarp (fruit wall)

EXTERNAL VIEW OF FRUIT

LONGITUDINAL SECTION THROUGH FRUIT

Remains of style
Endocarp
Drupelet
Pip
Pedicel (flower stalk)
Endocarp
Embryo
Cotyledon (seed leaf)
Testa (seed coat)

REMAINS OF A SINGLE FEMALE FLOWER

EXTERNAL VIEW AND SECTION THROUGH PIP

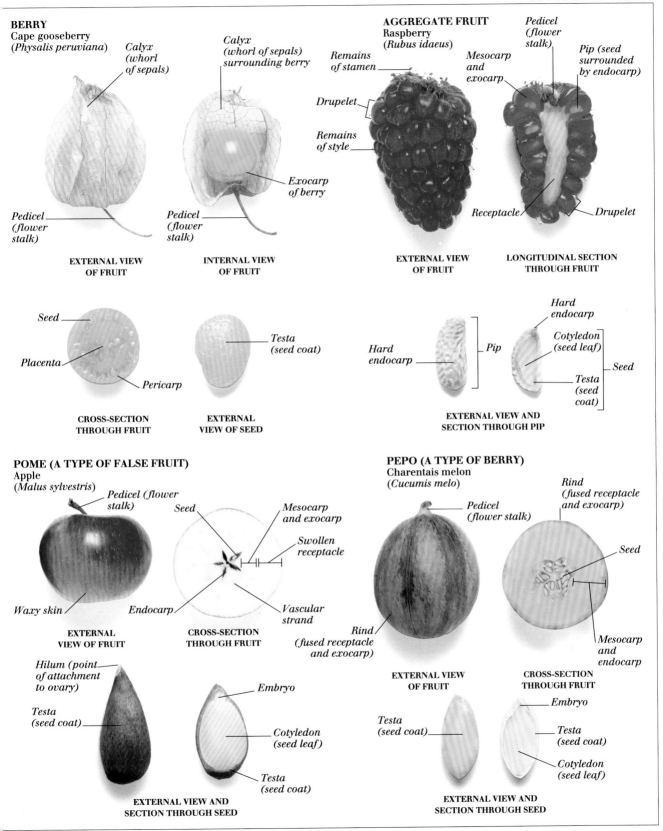

BERRY
Cape gooseberry
(*Physalis peruviana*)

Calyx (whorl of sepals)

Calyx (whorl of sepals) surrounding berry

Pedicel (flower stalk)

Pedicel (flower stalk)

Exocarp of berry

EXTERNAL VIEW OF FRUIT

INTERNAL VIEW OF FRUIT

Seed

Placenta

Pericarp

Testa (seed coat)

CROSS-SECTION THROUGH FRUIT

EXTERNAL VIEW OF SEED

AGGREGATE FRUIT
Raspberry
(*Rubus idaeus*)

Remains of stamen

Drupelet

Remains of style

Pedicel (flower stalk)

Pip (seed surrounded by endocarp)

Mesocarp and exocarp

Receptacle

Drupelet

EXTERNAL VIEW OF FRUIT

LONGITUDINAL SECTION THROUGH FRUIT

Hard endocarp

Pip

Hard endocarp

Cotyledon (seed leaf)

Seed

Testa (seed coat)

EXTERNAL VIEW AND SECTION THROUGH PIP

POME (A TYPE OF FALSE FRUIT)
Apple
(*Malus sylvestris*)

Pedicel (flower stalk)

Seed

Mesocarp and exocarp

Swollen receptacle

Waxy skin

Endocarp

Vascular strand

EXTERNAL VIEW OF FRUIT

CROSS-SECTION THROUGH FRUIT

Hilum (point of attachment to ovary)

Testa (seed coat)

Embryo

Cotyledon (seed leaf)

Testa (seed coat)

EXTERNAL VIEW AND SECTION THROUGH SEED

PEPO (A TYPE OF BERRY)
Charentais melon
(*Cucumis melo*)

Pedicel (flower stalk)

Rind (fused receptacle and exocarp)

Seed

Rind (fused receptacle and exocarp)

Mesocarp and endocarp

EXTERNAL VIEW OF FRUIT

CROSS-SECTION THROUGH FRUIT

Testa (seed coat)

Embryo

Testa (seed coat)

Cotyledon (seed leaf)

EXTERNAL VIEW AND SECTION THROUGH SEED

Dry fruits

DRY FRUITS HAVE A HARD, DRY PERICARP (fruit wall) around their seeds unlike succulent fruits, which have fleshy pericarps (see pp. 148-149). Dry fruits are divided into three types: dehiscent, in which the pericarp splits open to release the seeds; indehiscent, which do not split open; and schizocarpic, in which the fruit splits but the seeds are not exposed. Dehiscent dry fruits include capsules (e.g., love-in-a-mist), follicles (e.g., delphinium), legumes (e.g., pea), and siliquas (e.g., honesty). Typically, the seeds of dehiscent fruits are dispersed by the wind. Indehiscent dry fruits include nuts (e.g., sweet chestnut), nutlets (e.g., goosegrass), achenes (e.g., strawberry), caryopses (e.g., wheat), samaras (e.g., elm), and cypselas (e.g., dandelion). Some indehiscent dry fruits are dispersed by the wind, assisted by "wings" (e.g., elm) or "parachutes" (e.g., dandelion); others (e.g., goosegrass) have hooked pericarps to aid dispersal on animals' fur. Schizocarpic dry fruits include cremocarps (e.g., hogweed), and double samaras (e.g., sycamore); these are dispersed by the wind.

NUTLET
Goosegrass
(*Galium aparine*)

LEGUME
Pea
(*Pisum sativum*)

- Pedicel (flower stalk)
- Receptacle
- Remains of sepal
- Remains of stamen
- Placenta
- Pericarp (fruit wall)
- Remains of style and stigma

EXTERNAL VIEW OF FRUIT

- Pedicel (flower stalk)
- Receptacle
- Remains of sepal
- Funicle (stalk attaching seed to placenta)
- Pericarp (fruit wall)
- Seed
- Remains of style and stigma

INTERNAL VIEW OF FRUIT

NUT
Sweet chestnut
(*Castanea sativa*)

- Line of splitting between valves of cupule
- Peduncle (inflorescence stalk)
- Remains of male inflorescence
- Nut (indehiscent fruit)
- Spiky cupule (husk around fruit formed from bracts)

EXTERNAL VIEW OF FRUIT WITH SURROUNDING CUPULE

- Funicle (stalk attaching seed to placenta)
- Micropyle (pore for water absorption)
- Testa (seed coat)
- Cotyledon (seed leaf)
- Radicle (embryonic root)
- Testa (seed coat)
- Plumule (embryonic shoot)

EXTERIOR VIEW AND SECTION THROUGH SEED

ACHENE
Strawberry
(*Fragaria x ananassa*)

- Sepal
- Pedicel (flower stalk)
- Swollen receptacle
- Remains of stigma and style
- Achene (one-seeded dry fruit)

EXTERNAL VIEW OF FRUIT

- Sepal
- Pedicel (flower stalk)
- Swollen fleshy tissues of receptacle

LONGITUDINAL SECTION THROUGH FRUIT

- Remains of stigma
- Remains of style
- Remains of stigma
- Remains of style
- Nut (indehiscent fruit)
- Embryo
- Cotyledon (seed leaf)
- Testa (seed coat)
- Woody pericarp (fruit wall)
- Woody pericarp (fruit wall)

EXTERNAL VIEW AND SECTION THROUGH FRUIT

- Pericarp (fruit wall)
- Cotyledon (seed leaf)
- Pericarp (fruit wall)
- Testa (seed coat)

EXTERNAL VIEW AND SECTION THROUGH SEED

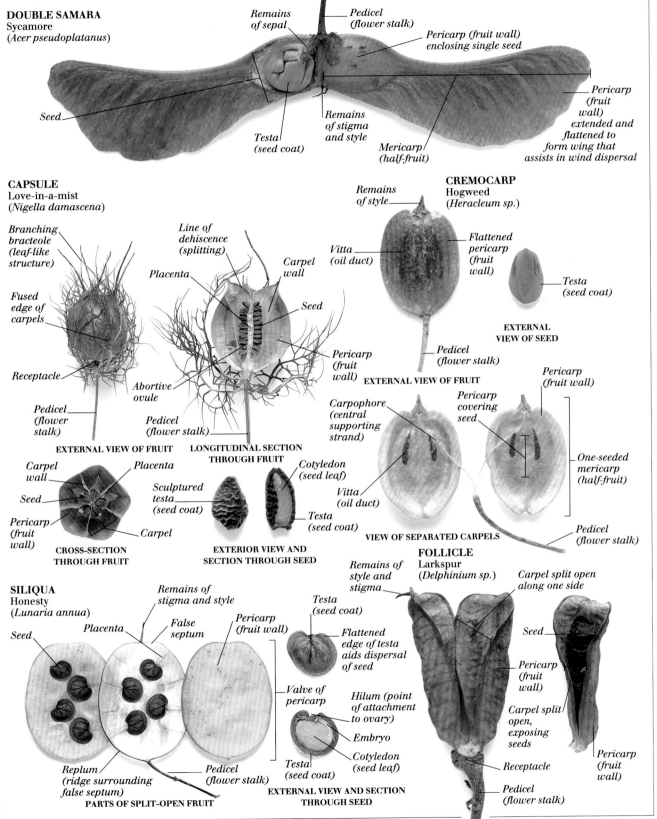

DOUBLE SAMARA
Sycamore
(*Acer pseudoplatanus*)

Remains
of sepal

Pedicel
(flower stalk)

Pericarp (fruit wall)
enclosing single seed

Pericarp
(fruit
wall)
extended and
flattened to
form wing that
assists in wind dispersal

Seed

Remains
of stigma
and style

Testa
(seed coat)

Mericarp
(half-fruit)

CAPSULE
Love-in-a-mist
(*Nigella damascena*)

Branching
bracteole
(leaf-like
structure)

Line of
dehiscence
(splitting)

Carpel
wall

Placenta

Seed

Fused
edge of
carpels

Receptacle

Pedicel
(flower
stalk)

Abortive
ovule

Pedicel
(flower stalk)

Pericarp
(fruit
wall)

EXTERNAL VIEW OF FRUIT

**LONGITUDINAL SECTION
THROUGH FRUIT**

Carpel
wall

Placenta

Seed

Pericarp
(fruit
wall)

Carpel

**CROSS-SECTION
THROUGH FRUIT**

Sculptured
testa
(seed coat)

Cotyledon
(seed leaf)

Testa
(seed coat)

**EXTERIOR VIEW AND
SECTION THROUGH SEED**

CREMOCARP
Hogweed
(*Heracleum sp.*)

Remains
of style

Vitta
(oil duct)

Flattened
pericarp
(fruit
wall)

Testa
(seed coat)

**EXTERNAL
VIEW OF SEED**

Pedicel
(flower stalk)

EXTERNAL VIEW OF FRUIT

Pericarp
(fruit wall)

Pericarp
covering
seed

Carpophore
(central
supporting
strand)

Vitta
(oil duct)

One-seeded
mericarp
(half-fruit)

Pedicel
(flower stalk)

VIEW OF SEPARATED CARPELS

SILIQUA
Honesty
(*Lunaria annua*)

Remains of
stigma and style

Pericarp
(fruit wall)

Seed

Placenta

False
septum

Valve of
pericarp

Replum
(ridge surrounding
false septum)

Pedicel
(flower stalk)

PARTS OF SPLIT-OPEN FRUIT

Testa
(seed coat)

Flattened
edge of testa
aids dispersal
of seed

Hilum (point
of attachment
to ovary)

Embryo

Cotyledon
(seed leaf)

Testa
(seed coat)

**EXTERNAL VIEW AND SECTION
THROUGH SEED**

FOLLICLE
Larkspur
(*Delphinium sp.*)

Remains of
style and
stigma

Carpel split open
along one side

Seed

Pericarp
(fruit
wall)

Carpel split
open,
exposing
seeds

Receptacle

Pedicel
(flower stalk)

Pericarp
(fruit
wall)

Germination

GERMINATION IS THE GROWTH OF SEEDS INTO SEEDLINGS. It starts when seeds become active below ground, and ends when the first foliage leaves appear above ground. A seed consists of an embryo and its food store, surrounded by a testa (seed coat). The embryo is made up of one or two cotyledons (seed leaves) attached to a central axis. The upper part of the axis consists of an epicotyl, which has a plumule (embryonic shoot) at its tip. The lower part of the axis consists of a hypocotyl and a radicle (embryonic root). After dispersal from the parent plant, the seeds dehydrate and enter a period of dormancy. Following this dormant period, germination begins, provided that the seeds have enough water, oxygen, warmth, and, in some cases, light. In the first stages of germination, the seed takes in water; the embryo starts to use its food store; and the radicle swells, breaks through the testa, and grows downwards. Germination then proceeds in one of two ways, depending on the type of seed. In epigeal germination, the hypocotyl lengthens, pulling the plumule and its protective cotyledons out of the soil. In hypogeal germination, the cotyledons remain below ground and the epicotyl lengthens, pushing the plumule upwards.

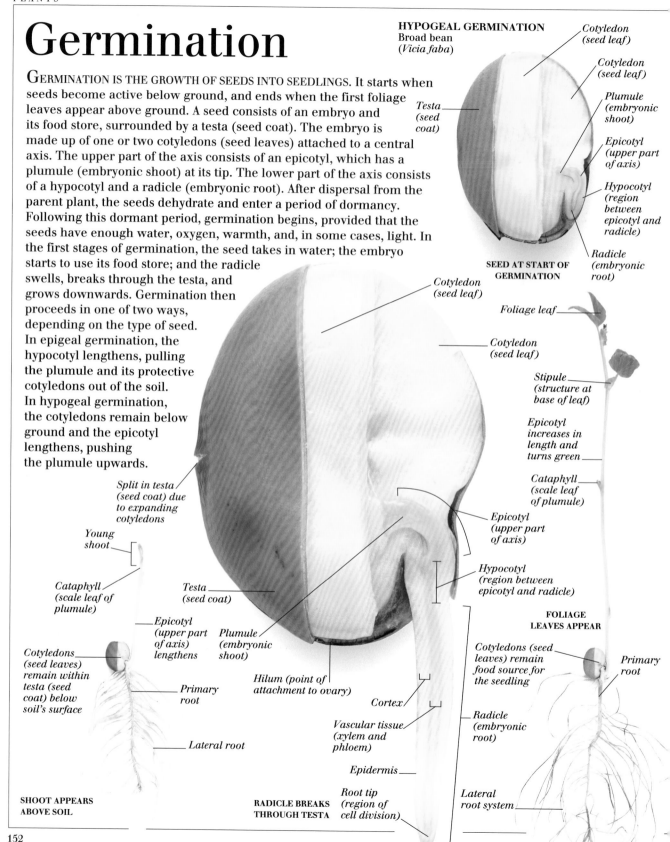

HYPOGEAL GERMINATION
Broad bean
(*Vicia faba*)

Cotyledon
(seed leaf)

Cotyledon
(seed leaf)

Plumule
(embryonic
shoot)

Testa
(seed
coat)

Epicotyl
(upper part
of axis)

Hypocotyl
(region
between
epicotyl and
radicle)

**SEED AT START OF
GERMINATION**

Radicle
(embryonic
root)

Cotyledon
(seed leaf)

Foliage leaf

Cotyledon
(seed leaf)

Stipule
(structure at
base of leaf)

Epicotyl
increases in
length and
turns green

Cataphyll
(scale leaf
of plumule)

Epicotyl
(upper part
of axis)

Hypocotyl
(region between
epicotyl and radicle)

**FOLIAGE
LEAVES APPEAR**

Cotyledons (seed
leaves) remain
food source for
the seedling

Primary
root

Radicle
(embryonic
root)

Lateral
root system

Split in testa
(seed coat) due
to expanding
cotyledons

Young
shoot

Cataphyll
(scale leaf of
plumule)

Testa
(seed coat)

Cotyledons
(seed leaves)
remain within
testa (seed
coat) below
soil's surface

Epicotyl
(upper part
of axis)
lengthens

Primary
root

Plumule
(embryonic
shoot)

Hilum (point of
attachment to ovary)

Lateral root

Cortex

Vascular tissue
(xylem and
phloem)

Epidermis

Root tip
(region of
cell division)

**SHOOT APPEARS
ABOVE SOIL**

**RADICLE BREAKS
THROUGH TESTA**

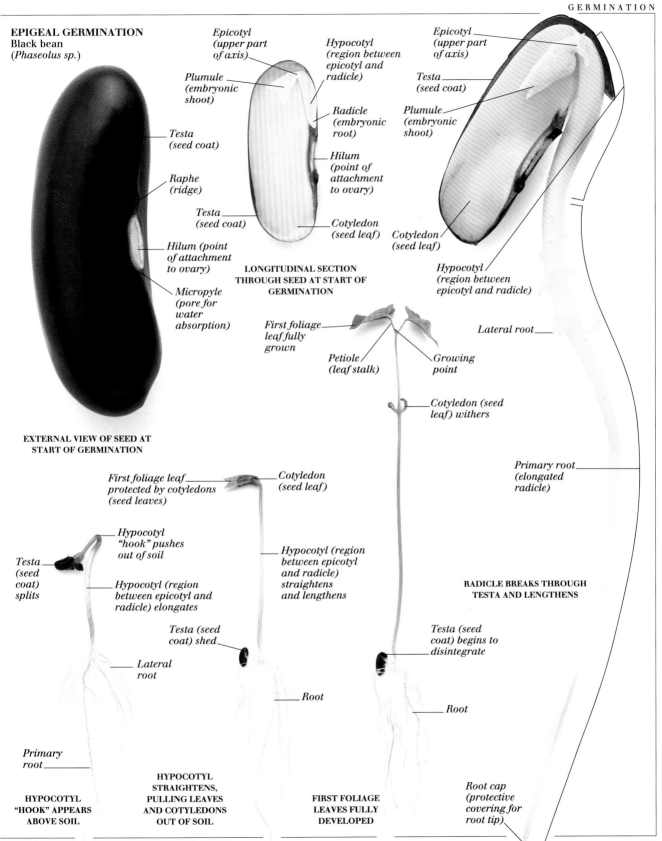

EPIGEAL GERMINATION
Black bean
(*Phaseolus sp.*)

*Testa
(seed coat)*

*Raphe
(ridge)*

*Hilum (point
of attachment
to ovary)*

*Micropyle
(pore for
water
absorption)*

**EXTERNAL VIEW OF SEED AT
START OF GERMINATION**

*Epicotyl
(upper part
of axis)*

*Plumule
(embryonic
shoot)*

*Hypocotyl
(region between
epicotyl and
radicle)*

*Radicle
(embryonic
root)*

*Hilum
(point of
attachment
to ovary)*

*Testa
(seed coat)*

*Cotyledon
(seed leaf)*

**LONGITUDINAL SECTION
THROUGH SEED AT START OF
GERMINATION**

*Epicotyl
(upper part
of axis)*

*Testa
(seed coat)*

*Plumule
(embryonic
shoot)*

*Cotyledon
(seed leaf)*

*Hypocotyl
(region between
epicotyl and radicle)*

**RADICLE BREAKS THROUGH
TESTA AND LENGTHENS**

Lateral root

*Primary root
(elongated
radicle)*

*Testa (seed
coat) begins to
disintegrate*

Root

*Root cap
(protective
covering for
root tip)*

*First foliage
leaf fully
grown*

*Petiole
(leaf stalk)*

*Growing
point*

*Cotyledon (seed
leaf) withers*

*First foliage leaf
protected by cotyledons
(seed leaves)*

*Cotyledon
(seed leaf)*

*Hypocotyl
"hook" pushes
out of soil*

*Testa
(seed
coat)
splits*

*Hypocotyl (region
between epicotyl and
radicle) elongates*

*Testa (seed
coat) shed*

*Lateral
root*

*Primary
root*

**HYPOCOTYL
"HOOK" APPEARS
ABOVE SOIL**

**HYPOCOTYL
STRAIGHTENS,
PULLING LEAVES
AND COTYLEDONS
OUT OF SOIL**

*Hypocotyl (region
between epicotyl
and radicle)
straightens
and lengthens*

Root

**FIRST FOLIAGE
LEAVES FULLY
DEVELOPED**

153

Vegetative reproduction

MANY PLANTS CAN PROPAGATE THEMSELVES by vegetative reproduction. In this process, part of a plant separates off, takes root, and grows into a new plant. Vegetative reproduction is a type of asexual reproduction; that is, it involves only one parent, and there is no fusion of gametes (sex cells). Plants use various structures to reproduce vegetatively. Some plants use underground storage organs. Such organs include rhizomes (horizontal, underground stems), the branches of which produce new plants; bulbs (swollen leaf bases) and corms (swollen stems), which produce daughter bulbs or corms that separate off from the parent; and stem tubers (thickened underground stems) and root tubers (swollen adventitious roots), which also separate off from the parent. Other propagative structures include runners and stolons, creeping horizontal stems that take root and produce new plants; bulbils, small bulbs that develop on the stem or in the place of flowers, and then drop off and grow into new plants; and adventitious buds, miniature plants that form on leaf margins before dropping to the ground and growing into mature plants.

CORM
Gladiolus
(*Gladiolus sp.*)

ADVENTITIOUS BUD
Mexican hat plant
(*Kalanchoe daigremontiana*)

Apex of leaf

Lamina (blade) of leaf

Leaf margin

Notch in leaf margin containing meristematic (actively dividing) cells

Adventitious bud (detachable bud with adventitious roots) drops from leaf

Petiole (leaf stalk)

BULBIL IN PLACE OF FLOWER
Orange lily
(*Lilium bulbiferum*)

Scar left by flower

Leaf

Pedicel (flower stalk)

Detachable bulbil formed in place of flower

Peduncle (inflorescence stalk)

STOLON
Ground ivy
(*Glechoma hederacea*)

Terminal bud

Internode

Node

Node

Parent plant

Stolon (creeping stem)

Adventitious root of daughter plant

Daughter plant developed from lateral bud

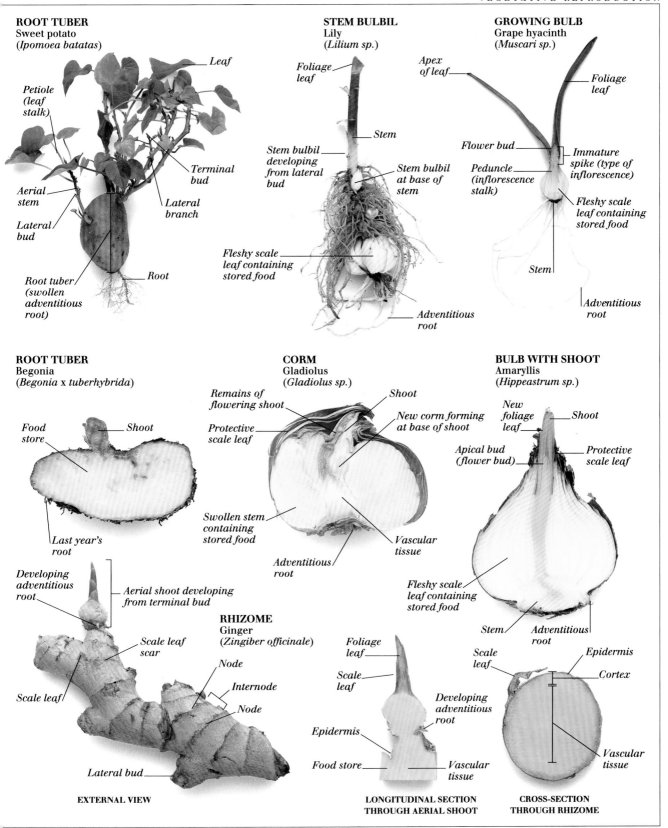

ROOT TUBER
Sweet potato
(*Ipomoea batatas*)

Leaf

Petiole
(leaf
stalk)

Terminal
bud

Aerial
stem

Lateral
branch

Lateral
bud

Root

Root tuber
(swollen
adventitious
root)

STEM BULBIL
Lily
(*Lilium sp.*)

Foliage
leaf

Stem

Stem bulbil
developing
from lateral
bud

Stem bulbil
at base of
stem

Fleshy scale
leaf containing
stored food

Adventitious
root

GROWING BULB
Grape hyacinth
(*Muscari sp.*)

Apex
of leaf

Foliage
leaf

Flower bud

Immature
spike (type of
inflorescence)

Peduncle
(inflorescence
stalk)

Fleshy scale
leaf containing
stored food

Stem

Adventitious
root

ROOT TUBER
Begonia
(*Begonia* x *tuberhybrida*)

Food
store

Shoot

Last year's
root

CORM
Gladiolus
(*Gladiolus sp.*)

Remains of
flowering shoot

Shoot

Protective
scale leaf

New corm forming
at base of shoot

Swollen stem
containing
stored food

Adventitious
root

Vascular
tissue

BULB WITH SHOOT
Amaryllis
(*Hippeastrum sp.*)

New
foliage
leaf

Shoot

Apical bud
(flower bud)

Protective
scale leaf

Fleshy scale
leaf containing
stored food

Stem

Adventitious
root

Developing
adventitious
root

Aerial shoot developing
from terminal bud

Scale leaf
scar

RHIZOME
Ginger
(*Zingiber officinale*)

Node

Internode

Node

Scale leaf

Lateral bud

EXTERNAL VIEW

Foliage
leaf

Scale
leaf

Developing
adventitious
root

Epidermis

Food store

Vascular
tissue

**LONGITUDINAL SECTION
THROUGH AERIAL SHOOT**

Scale
leaf

Epidermis

Cortex

Vascular
tissue

**CROSS-SECTION
THROUGH RHIZOME**

155

Dryland plants

DRYLAND PLANTS (XEROPHYTES) are able to survive in unfavourable habitats. All are found in places where little water is available; some live in high temperatures that cause excessive loss of water from the leaves. Xerophytes show a number of adaptations to dry conditions; these include reduced leaf area, rolled leaves, sunken stomata, hairs, spines, and thick cuticles. One group, succulent plants, stores water in specially enlarged spongy tissues found in leaves, roots, or stems. Leaf succulents have enlarged, fleshy, water-storing leaves. Root succulents have a large, underground water-storage organ with short-lived stems and leaves above ground. Stem succulents are represented by the cacti (family Cactaceae). Cacti stems are fleshy, green, and photosynthetic; they are typically ribbed or covered by tubercles in rows, with leaves being reduced to spines or entirely absent.

LEAF SUCCULENT
Lithops sp.

STEM SUCCULENT
Golden barrel cactus
(*Echinocactus grusonii*)

Areole
(modified
lateral shoot)

Trichome
(hair)

Spine
(modified
leaf)

Waxy cuticle
(waterproof
covering)

Water-storing
parenchyma
(packing tissue)

Tubercle
(projection
from stem
surface)

Vascular
cylinder
(transport
tissue)

Root

LONGITUDINAL SECTION
THROUGH STEM

Spine
(modified
leaf)

Tubercle
(projection
from stem
surface)

Root

EXTERNAL VIEW

Sinuous
(wavy)
cell wall

Stoma (pore)
controlling
exchange of
gases

MICROGRAPH OF STEM SURFACE

Spine
(modified
leaf)

Areole
(modified
lateral shoot)

Tubercle
(projection from
stem surface)

Waxy cuticle
(waterproof
covering)

DETAIL OF STEM SURFACE

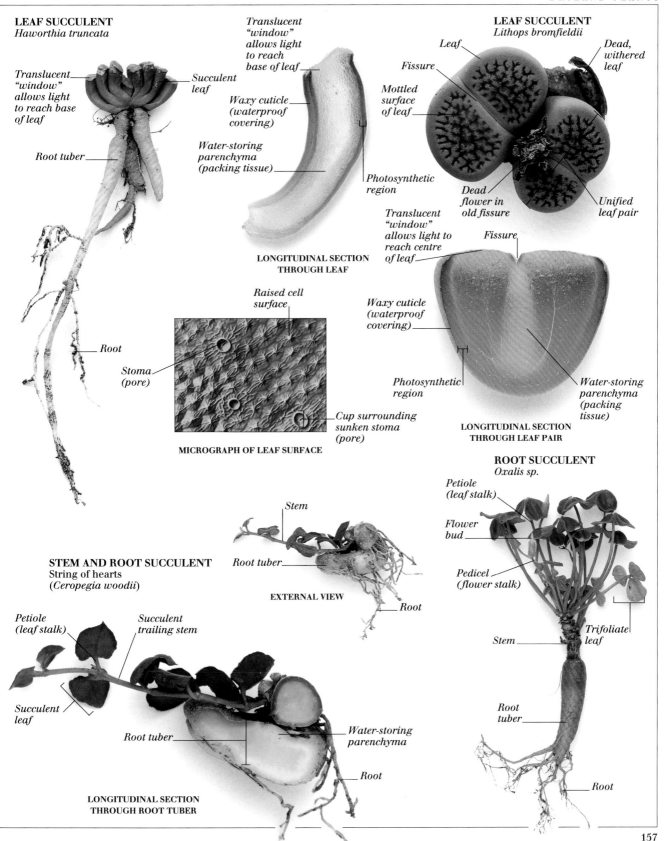

LEAF SUCCULENT
Haworthia truncata

Translucent "window" allows light to reach base of leaf

Succulent leaf

Root tuber

Root

Translucent "window" allows light to reach base of leaf

Waxy cuticle (waterproof covering)

Water-storing parenchyma (packing tissue)

Photosynthetic region

LONGITUDINAL SECTION THROUGH LEAF

Raised cell surface

Stoma (pore)

Cup surrounding sunken stoma (pore)

MICROGRAPH OF LEAF SURFACE

LEAF SUCCULENT
Lithops bromfieldii

Leaf

Fissure

Mottled surface of leaf

Dead, withered leaf

Dead flower in old fissure

Unified leaf pair

Translucent "window" allows light to reach centre of leaf

Fissure

Waxy cuticle (waterproof covering)

Photosynthetic region

Water-storing parenchyma (packing tissue)

LONGITUDINAL SECTION THROUGH LEAF PAIR

STEM AND ROOT SUCCULENT
String of hearts
(*Ceropegia woodii*)

Petiole (leaf stalk)

Succulent trailing stem

Succulent leaf

Stem

Root tuber

Root

EXTERNAL VIEW

Root tuber

Water-storing parenchyma

Root

LONGITUDINAL SECTION THROUGH ROOT TUBER

ROOT SUCCULENT
Oxalis sp.

Petiole (leaf stalk)

Flower bud

Pedicel (flower stalk)

Stem

Trifoliate leaf

Root tuber

Root

Wetland plants

WETLAND PLANTS GROW SUBMERGED IN WATER, either partially (e.g., water hyacinth) or completely (e.g., pond weeds), and show various adaptations to this habitat. Typically, there are numerous air spaces inside the stems, leaves, and roots; these aid gas exchange and buoyancy. Submerged parts generally have no cuticle (waterproof covering), enabling the plants to absorb minerals and gases directly from the water; in addition, being supported by the water, they need little of the supportive tissue found in land plants. Stomata, the gas exchange pores, are absent from plants that are completely submerged; in partially submerged plants with floating leaves (e.g., water lilies), stomata are found on the upper leaf surfaces, where they cannot be flooded.

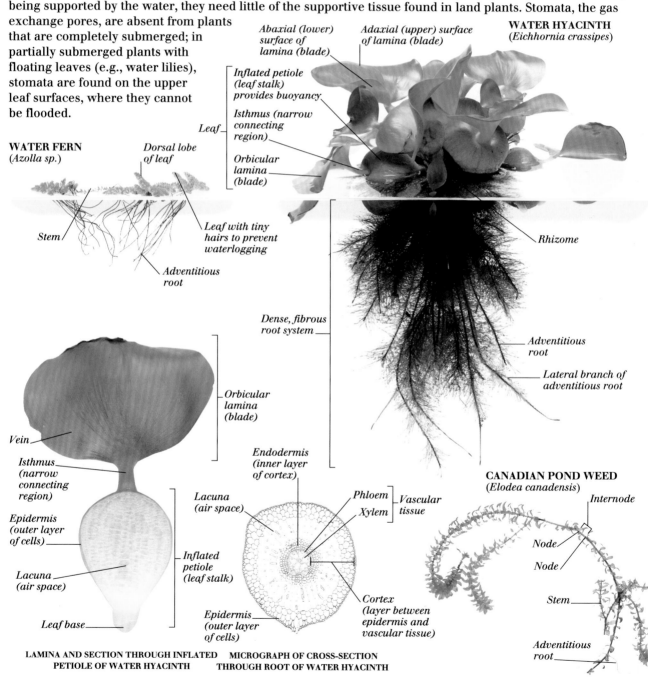

WATER FERN
(*Azolla sp.*)

Dorsal lobe of leaf

Stem

Adventitious root

Leaf with tiny hairs to prevent waterlogging

Abaxial (lower) surface of lamina (blade)

Adaxial (upper) surface of lamina (blade)

WATER HYACINTH
(*Eichhornia crassipes*)

Inflated petiole (leaf stalk) provides buoyancy

Isthmus (narrow connecting region)

Leaf

Orbicular lamina (blade)

Rhizome

Dense, fibrous root system

Adventitious root

Lateral branch of adventitious root

Orbicular lamina (blade)

Vein

Isthmus (narrow connecting region)

Epidermis (outer layer of cells)

Lacuna (air space)

Leaf base

Inflated petiole (leaf stalk)

Endodermis (inner layer of cortex)

Lacuna (air space)

Phloem

Xylem

Vascular tissue

Epidermis (outer layer of cells)

Cortex (layer between epidermis and vascular tissue)

CANADIAN POND WEED
(*Elodea canadensis*)

Internode

Node

Node

Stem

Adventitious root

LAMINA AND SECTION THROUGH INFLATED PETIOLE OF WATER HYACINTH

MICROGRAPH OF CROSS-SECTION THROUGH ROOT OF WATER HYACINTH

WATER LILY
(Nymphaea sp.)

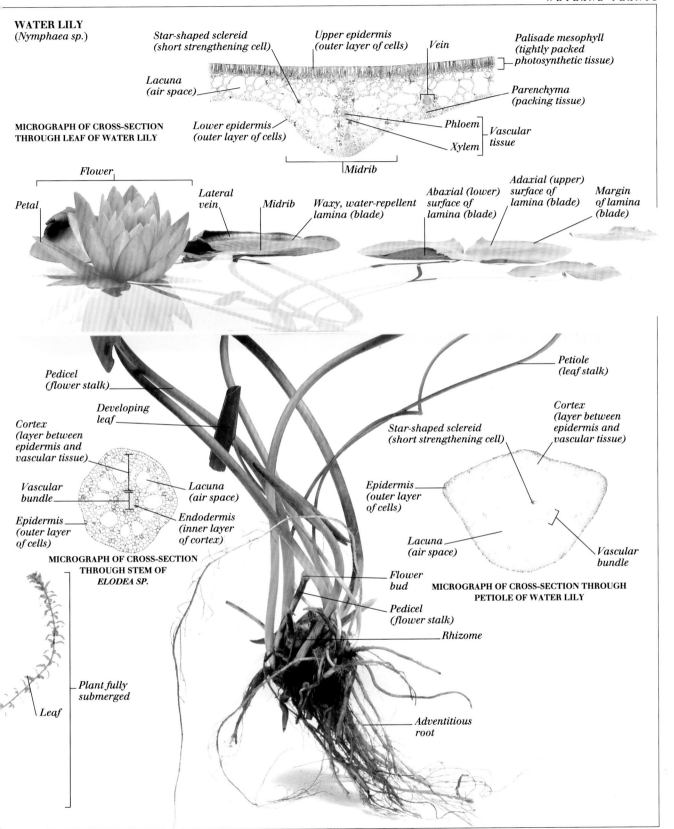

Star-shaped sclereid (short strengthening cell)

Upper epidermis (outer layer of cells)

Vein

Palisade mesophyll (tightly packed photosynthetic tissue)

Lacuna (air space)

Parenchyma (packing tissue)

MICROGRAPH OF CROSS-SECTION THROUGH LEAF OF WATER LILY

Lower epidermis (outer layer of cells)

Phloem — *Vascular tissue*

Xylem

Midrib

Flower

Petal

Lateral vein

Midrib

Waxy, water-repellent lamina (blade)

Abaxial (lower) surface of lamina (blade)

Adaxial (upper) surface of lamina (blade)

Margin of lamina (blade)

Pedicel (flower stalk)

Petiole (leaf stalk)

Developing leaf

Cortex (layer between epidermis and vascular tissue)

Star-shaped sclereid (short strengthening cell)

Cortex (layer between epidermis and vascular tissue)

Vascular bundle

Lacuna (air space)

Epidermis (outer layer of cells)

Epidermis (outer layer of cells)

Endodermis (inner layer of cortex)

Lacuna (air space)

Vascular bundle

MICROGRAPH OF CROSS-SECTION THROUGH STEM OF ELODEA SP.

MICROGRAPH OF CROSS-SECTION THROUGH PETIOLE OF WATER LILY

Flower bud

Pedicel (flower stalk)

Rhizome

Plant fully submerged

Leaf

Adventitious root

159

Carnivorous plants

CARNIVOROUS (INSECTIVOROUS) PLANTS FEED ON INSECTS and other small animals, in addition to producing food in their leaves by photosynthesis. The nutrients absorbed from trapped insects enable carnivorous plants to thrive in acid, boggy soils that lack essential minerals, especially nitrates, where most other plants could not survive. All carnivorous plants have some leaves modified as traps; many use bright colours and scented nectar to attract prey; and most use enzymes to digest the prey. There are three types of traps. Pitcher plants, such as the monkey cup and cobra lily, have leaves modified as pitcher-shaped pitfall traps, half-filled with water; once lured inside the mouth of the trap, insects lose their footing on the slippery surface, fall into the liquid, and either decompose or are digested. Venus fly traps use a spring-trap mechanism; when an insect touches trigger hairs on the inner surfaces of the leaves, the two lobes of the trap snap shut. Butterworts and sundews entangle prey by sticky droplets on the leaf surface, while the edges of the leaves slowly curl over to envelop and digest the prey.

PITCHER PLANT
Cobra lily (*Darlingtonia californica*)

Areola ("window" of transparent tissue)

Fishtail nectary

Wing

Hood

Pitcher

Tubular petiole (leaf stalk)

Areola ("window" of transparent tissue)

Dome-shaped hood develops

Fishtail nectary appears

Immature pitcher

Smooth surface

Nectar roll

Mouth

Wing

Downward pointing hair

DEVELOPMENT OF MODIFIED LEAF IN COBRA LILY

Immature trap

Interlocked teeth

Closed trap

VENUS FLY TRAP
(*Dionaea muscipula*)

Phyllode (flattened petiole)

Summer petiole (leaf stalk)

Nectary zone (glands secrete nectar)

Digestive zone (glands secrete digestive enzymes)

Tooth

Lobe of trap

Midrib (hinge of trap)

Trigger hair

Spring petiole (leaf stalk)

Trap (twin-lobed leaf blade)

Red colour of trap attracts insects

Sensory hinge

Trigger hair

Inner surface of trap

Digestive gland

MICROGRAPH OF LOBE OF VENUS FLY TRAP

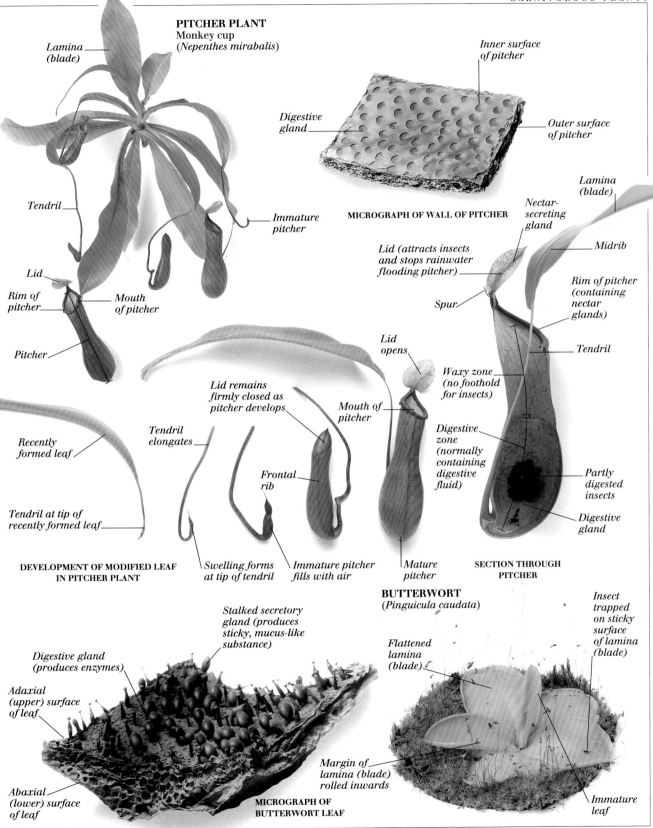

PITCHER PLANT
Monkey cup
(*Nepenthes mirabalis*)

Lamina (blade)

Tendril

Immature pitcher

Lid

Rim of pitcher

Mouth of pitcher

Pitcher

Inner surface of pitcher

Digestive gland

Outer surface of pitcher

MICROGRAPH OF WALL OF PITCHER

Lamina (blade)

Nectar-secreting gland

Midrib

Lid (attracts insects and stops rainwater flooding pitcher)

Rim of pitcher (containing nectar glands)

Spur

Tendril

Lid opens

Waxy zone (no foothold for insects)

Mouth of pitcher

Digestive zone (normally containing digestive fluid)

Partly digested insects

Digestive gland

Recently formed leaf

Tendril elongates

Lid remains firmly closed as pitcher develops

Frontal rib

Tendril at tip of recently formed leaf

Swelling forms at tip of tendril

Immature pitcher fills with air

Mature pitcher

DEVELOPMENT OF MODIFIED LEAF IN PITCHER PLANT

SECTION THROUGH PITCHER

BUTTERWORT
(*Pinguicula caudata*)

Stalked secretory gland (produces sticky, mucus-like substance)

Digestive gland (produces enzymes)

Adaxial (upper) surface of leaf

Flattened lamina (blade)

Insect trapped on sticky surface of lamina (blade)

Margin of lamina (blade) rolled inwards

Abaxial (lower) surface of leaf

MICROGRAPH OF BUTTERWORT LEAF

Immature leaf

161

Epiphytic and parasitic plants

EPIPHYTIC AND PARASITIC PLANTS GROW ON OTHER LIVING PLANTS. Typically, epiphytic plants are not rooted in the soil; instead, they live above ground level on the stems and branches of other plants. Epiphytes obtain water from trapped rainwater and from moisture in the air, and minerals from organic matter that has accumulated on the surface of the plant on which they are growing. Like other green plants, epiphytes produce their food by photosynthesis. Epiphytes include tropical orchids and bromeliads (air plants), and some mosses that live in temperate regions. Parasitic plants obtain all their nutrient requirements from the host plants on which they grow. The parasites produce haustoria, root-like organs that penetrate the stem or roots of the host and grow inwards to merge with the host's vascular tissue, from which the parasite extracts water, minerals, and manufactured nutrients. As they have no need to produce their own food, parasitic plants lack chlorophyll, the green photosynthetic pigment, and they have no foliage leaves. Partial parasitic plants (e.g., mistletoe) obtain water and minerals from the host plant but have green leaves and stems and are therefore able to produce their own food by photosynthesis.

EPIPHYTIC BROMELIAD
Aechmea miniata

Inflorescence (spike)

Peduncle (inflorescence stalk)

Flower bud

Strap-shaped arching leaf (part of rosette of leaves)

Leaf margin with spines

Overlapping leaf bases in which rainwater is trapped

Mass of adventitious roots

Stem

Bark of tree to which epiphyte is attached

EPIPHYTIC ORCHID
Brassavola nodosa

Peduncle (inflorescence stalk)

Pedicel (flower stalk)

Flower

Scale leaf

Leaf

Aerial root

Node

Stem

Bark of tree to which epiphyte is attached

Velamen (multi-layered epidermis capable of absorbing water from rain or condensation)

Exodermis (outer layer of cortex)

Cortex (layer between epidermis and vascular tissue)

Cortex cell containing chloroplasts

Pith

Vascular tissue
Xylem
Phloem

Endodermis (inner layer of cortex)

MICROGRAPH OF CROSS-SECTION THROUGH AERIAL ROOT OF EPIPHYTIC ORCHID

LONGITUDINAL SECTION THROUGH EPIPHYTIC BROMELIAD
Scarlet star
(*Guzmania
lingulata*)

Bract
(leaf-like
structure)

Leaf (part of
rosette of leaves)

Immature
bracts

Overlapping leaf bases
in which rainwater is
trapped

Stem

Immature
flowers

Swollen stem base

ROOT PARASITE
Broomrape
(*Orobanche sp.*)

Stem of host plant

Flower bud
of broomrape

Flower of
broomrape

Stem of
broomrape

Leaf of
host plant

Tuber of broomrape attached to
host plant's roots through
haustoria (penetrating organs
that absorb nutrients from host's
vascular tissue)

Shoot of
broomrape

Main root
of host plant

Lateral root of
host plant

STEM PARASITE
Dodder
(*Cuscuta europaea*)

Tip of dodder
stem showing
circular
movement
around
host plant

Inflorescence
(spike) of dodder
flowers

Point of
attachment
of dodder stem
to host stem

Leaf of
host plant

Thread-like
stem of dodder
twined around
stem of host
plant

Stem of
host plant

Haustorium
(penetrating organ that
absorbs nutrients from
host's vascular tissue)

Vascular tissue
of dodder

Union of host and dodder
vascular systems

Stem of
dodder

Vascular
tissue
of host plant

Phloem

Xylem

Stem of
host plant

**EXTERNAL VIEW OF PLANT
PARASITIZED BY DODDER**

**MICROGRAPH OF CROSS-SECTION THROUGH STEM
OF PLANT PARASITIZED BY DODDER**

163

ANIMALS

Sponges, jellyfish, and sea anemones

SPONGES ARE MAINLY MARINE animals that make up the phylum Porifera. They are among the simplest of all animals, having no tissues or organs. Their bodies consist of two layers of cells separated by a jelly-like layer (mesohyal) that is strengthened by mineral spicules or protein fibres. The body is perforated by a system of pores and water channels called the aquiferous system. Special cells (choanocytes) with whip-like structures (flagella) draw water through the aquiferous system, thereby bringing tiny food particles to the sponge's cells. Jellyfish (class Scyphozoa), sea anemones (class Anthozoa), and corals (also class Anthozoa) belong to the phylum Cnidaria, also known as Coelenterata. More complex than sponges, coelenterates have simple tissues, such as nervous tissue; a radially symmetrical body; and a mouth surrounded by tentacles with unique stinging cells (cnidocytes).

INTERNAL ANATOMY OF A SPONGE

Amoebocyte

Osculum (excurrent pore)

Choanocyte (collar cell)

Ostium (incurrent pore)

Porocyte (pore cell)

Mesohyal

Spongocoel (atrium; paragaster)

Spicule

Pinacocyte (epidermal cell)

Ostium (incurrent pore)

SKELETON OF A SPONGE

Protein matrix

Pore

EXTERNAL FEATURES OF A SEA ANEMONE

Tentacle

EXAMPLES OF SEA ANEMONES

PARASITIC ANEMONE (*Calliactis parasitica*)

JEWEL ANEMONE (*Corynactis viridis*)

PLUMOSE ANEMONE (*Metridium senile*)

MEDITERRANEAN SEA ANEMONE (*Condylactis sp.*)

GREEN SNAKELOCK ANEMONE (*Anemonia viridis*)

BEADLET ANEMONE (*Actinia equina*)

GHOST ANEMONE (*Actinothoe sphyrodeta*)

Sagartia elegans

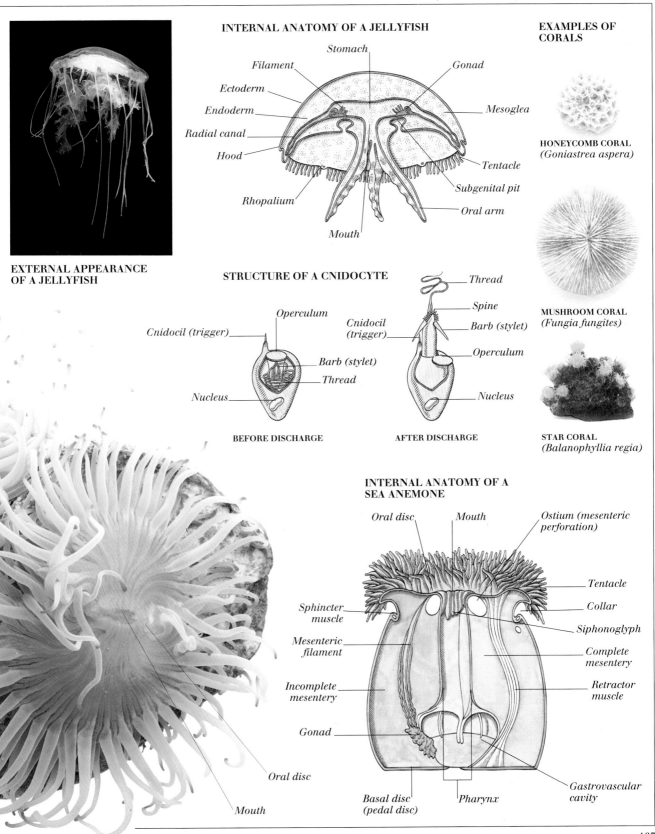

INTERNAL ANATOMY OF A JELLYFISH

Stomach

Filament

Ectoderm

Endoderm

Radial canal

Hood

Rhopalium

Mouth

Gonad

Mesoglea

Tentacle

Subgenital pit

Oral arm

EXTERNAL APPEARANCE OF A JELLYFISH

EXAMPLES OF CORALS

HONEYCOMB CORAL
(Goniastrea aspera)

MUSHROOM CORAL
(Fungia fungites)

STAR CORAL
(Balanophyllia regia)

STRUCTURE OF A CNIDOCYTE

Operculum

Cnidocil (trigger)

Barb (stylet)

Thread

Nucleus

BEFORE DISCHARGE

Thread

Spine

Barb (stylet)

Cnidocil (trigger)

Operculum

Nucleus

AFTER DISCHARGE

INTERNAL ANATOMY OF A SEA ANEMONE

Oral disc

Mouth

Ostium (mesenteric perforation)

Sphincter muscle

Mesenteric filament

Incomplete mesentery

Gonad

Tentacle

Collar

Siphonoglyph

Complete mesentery

Retractor muscle

Oral disc

Mouth

Basal disc (pedal disc)

Pharynx

Gastrovascular cavity

167

Insects

**PUPA
(CHRYSALIS)**

THE WORD INSECT REFERS to small invertebrate creatures, especially those with bodies divided into sections. Insects, including beetles, ants, bees, butterflies, and moths, belong to various orders in the class Insecta, which is a division of the phylum Arthropoda. Features common to all insects are an exoskeleton (external skeleton); three pairs of jointed legs; three body sections (head, thorax, and abdomen); and one pair of sensory antennae. Beetles (order Coleoptera) are the biggest group of insects, with about 300,000 species (about 30 per cent of all known insects). They have a pair of hard elytra (wing cases), which are modified front wings. The principal function of the elytra is to protect the hind wings, which are used for flying. Ants, together with bees and wasps, form the order Hymenoptera, which contains about 200,000 species. This group is characterized by a marked narrowing between the thorax and abdomen. Butterflies and moths form the order Lepidoptera, which has about 150,000 species. They have wings covered with tiny scales, hence the name of their order (Lepidoptera means "scale wings"). The separation of lepidopterans into butterflies and moths is largely artificial as there are no features that categorically distinguish one group from the other. In general, however, most butterflies fly by day, whereas most moths are night-flyers. Some insects, including butterflies and moths, undergo complete metamorphosis (transformation) during their life-cycle. A butterfly metamorphoses from an egg to a larva (caterpillar), then to a pupa (chrysalis), and finally to an imago (adult).

EXAMPLES OF INSECTS

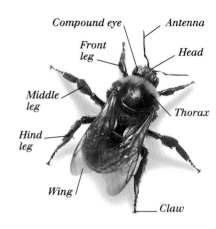

Compound eye — *Antenna*
Front leg — *Head*
Middle leg — *Thorax*
Hind leg
Wing
Claw

BUMBLEBEE

Compound eye
Stigma (spot)
Vein
Abdomen

DAMSELFLY

**EXTERNAL FEATURES
OF A BEETLE**

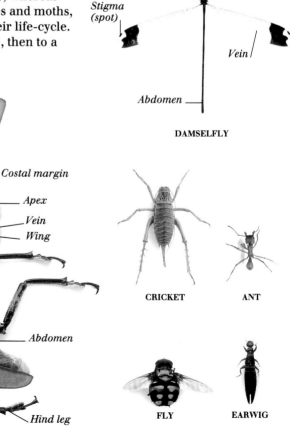

Elytron
Tarsus
Claw — *Tibia*
Pedicel
Femur *Costal margin*
Flagellum *Apex*
Trochanter *Vein*
Mandible *Scape* *Wing*
Labrum *Coxa*
Labial palp
Abdomen
Compound eye
Head
Prothorax
Front leg *Mesothorax*
Scutellum *Hind leg*
Metathorax *Middle leg*

CRICKET

ANT

FLY

EARWIG

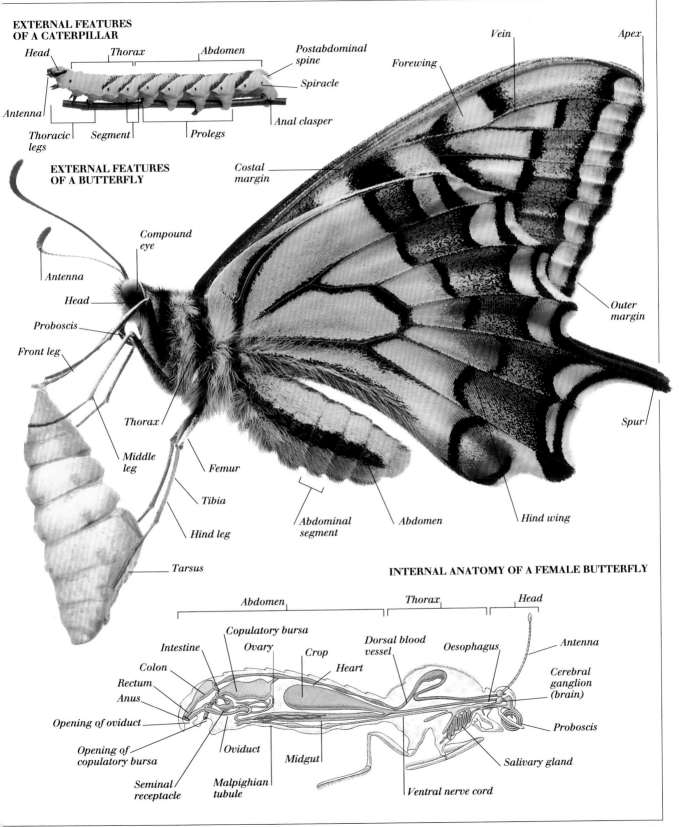

**EXTERNAL FEATURES
OF A CATERPILLAR**

Head

Thorax

Abdomen

Postabdominal
spine

Spiracle

Antenna

Thoracic
legs

Segment

Prolegs

Anal clasper

Vein

Forewing

Apex

**EXTERNAL FEATURES
OF A BUTTERFLY**

Costal
margin

Compound
eye

Antenna

Head

Proboscis

Front leg

Thorax

Middle
leg

Femur

Tibia

Hind leg

Tarsus

Outer
margin

Spur

Abdominal
segment

Abdomen

Hind wing

INTERNAL ANATOMY OF A FEMALE BUTTERFLY

Abdomen

Thorax

Head

Copulatory bursa

Intestine

Colon

Rectum

Anus

Opening of oviduct

Opening of
copulatory bursa

Seminal
receptacle

Ovary

Oviduct

Malpighian
tubule

Crop

Midgut

Dorsal blood
vessel

Heart

Oesophagus

Ventral nerve cord

Antenna

Cerebral
ganglion
(brain)

Proboscis

Salivary gland

Arachnids

THE CLASS ARACHNIDA INCLUDES SPIDERS (order Araneae) and scorpions (order Scorpiones). The class is part of the phylum Arthropoda, which also includes insects and crustaceans. Spiders and scorpions are characterized by having four pairs of walking legs; a pair of pincer-like mouthparts called chelicerae; another pair of frontal appendages called pedipalps, which are sensory in spiders but used for grasping in scorpions; and a body divided into two sections (a combined head and thorax called a cephalothorax or prosoma, and an abdomen or opisthosoma). Unlike other arthropods, spiders and scorpions lack antennae. Spiders and scorpions are carnivorous. Spiders poison prey by biting with the fanged chelicerae, scorpions by stinging with the end of the metasoma (tail).

MEXICAN TRUE RED-LEGGED TARANTULA
(Euathlus emilia)

INTERNAL ANATOMY OF A FEMALE SPIDER

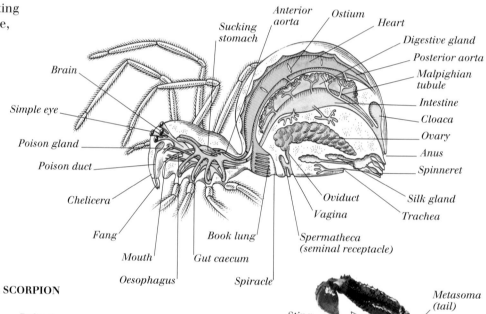

EXTERNAL FEATURES OF A SCORPION

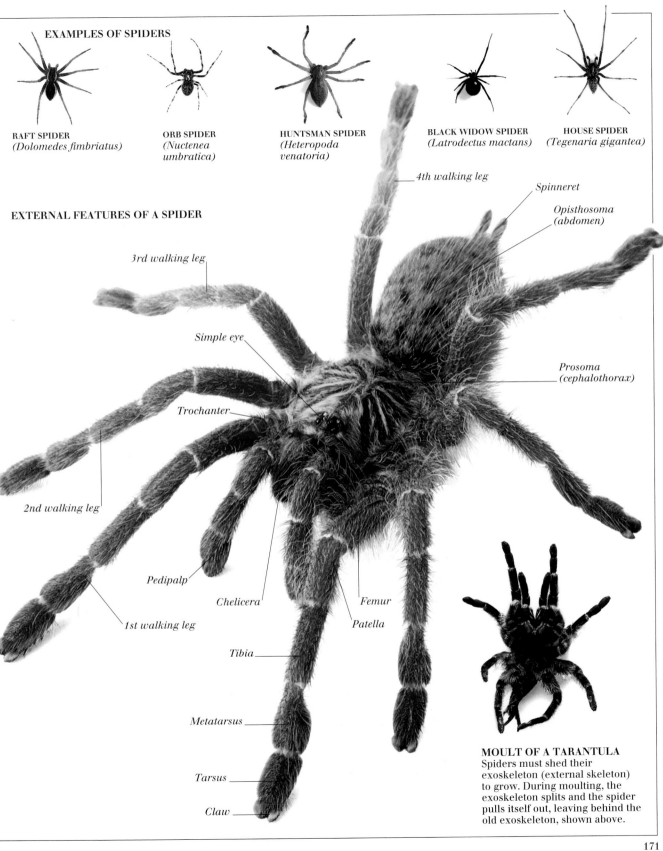

EXAMPLES OF SPIDERS

RAFT SPIDER
(Dolomedes fimbriatus)

ORB SPIDER
(Nuctenea umbratica)

HUNTSMAN SPIDER
(Heteropoda venatoria)

BLACK WIDOW SPIDER
(Latrodectus mactans)

HOUSE SPIDER
(Tegenaria gigantea)

EXTERNAL FEATURES OF A SPIDER

4th walking leg

Spinneret

Opisthosoma (abdomen)

3rd walking leg

Simple eye

Prosoma (cephalothorax)

Trochanter

2nd walking leg

Pedipalp

Chelicera

Femur

1st walking leg

Patella

Tibia

Metatarsus

Tarsus

Claw

MOULT OF A TARANTULA
Spiders must shed their
exoskeleton (external skeleton)
to grow. During moulting, the
exoskeleton splits and the spider
pulls itself out, leaving behind the
old exoskeleton, shown above.

Crustaceans

THE SUBPHYLUM CRUSTACEA is one of the largest groups in the phylum Arthropoda. The subphylum is divided into several classes, the most important of which are Malacostraca and Cirripedia. The class Malacostraca includes crayfish, crabs, lobsters, and shrimps. Typical features of malacostracans include a body divided into two sections (a combined head and thorax called a cephalothorax, and an abdomen); an exoskeleton (external skeleton) with a large plate (carapace) covering the cephalothorax; stalked, compound eyes; and two pairs of antennae. The class Cirripedia includes barnacles, which, unlike other crustaceans, spend their adult lives attached to a surface, such as a rock. Other characteristics of cirripedes include an exoskeleton of overlapping calcareous plates; a body consisting almost entirely of thorax (the abdomen and head are minute); and six pairs of thoracic appendages (cirri) used for filter feeding.

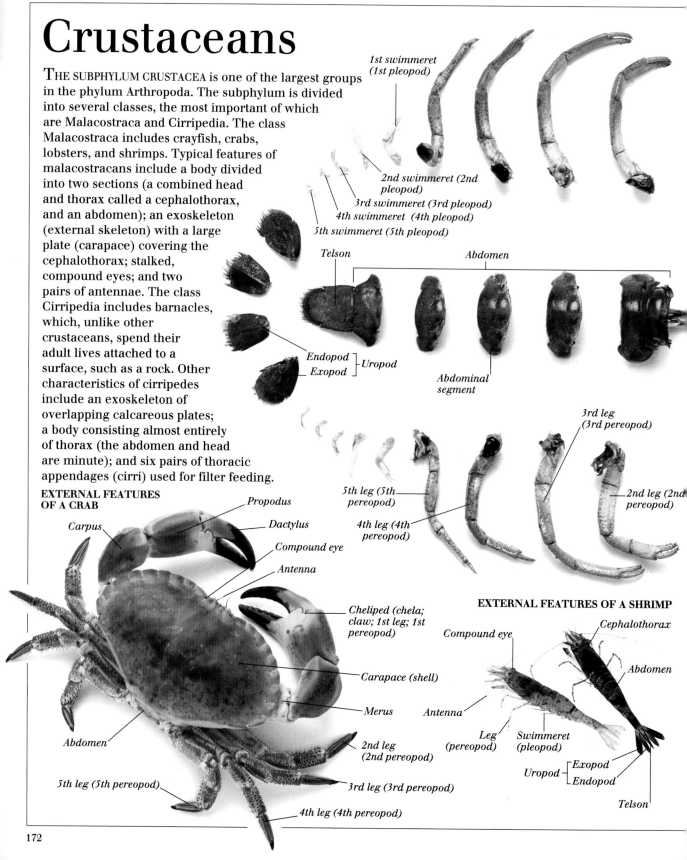

1st swimmeret (1st pleopod)

2nd swimmeret (2nd pleopod)

3rd swimmeret (3rd pleopod)

4th swimmeret (4th pleopod)

5th swimmeret (5th pleopod)

Telson

Abdomen

Endopod
Exopod } Uropod

Abdominal segment

3rd leg (3rd pereopod)

2nd leg (2nd pereopod)

5th leg (5th pereopod)

4th leg (4th pereopod)

EXTERNAL FEATURES OF A CRAB

Propodus

Carpus

Dactylus

Compound eye

Antenna

Cheliped (chela; claw; 1st leg; 1st pereopod)

Carapace (shell)

Merus

Abdomen

2nd leg (2nd pereopod)

5th leg (5th pereopod)

3rd leg (3rd pereopod)

4th leg (4th pereopod)

EXTERNAL FEATURES OF A SHRIMP

Compound eye

Cephalothorax

Abdomen

Antenna

Leg (pereopod)

Swimmeret (pleopod)

Uropod { Exopod
Endopod

Telson

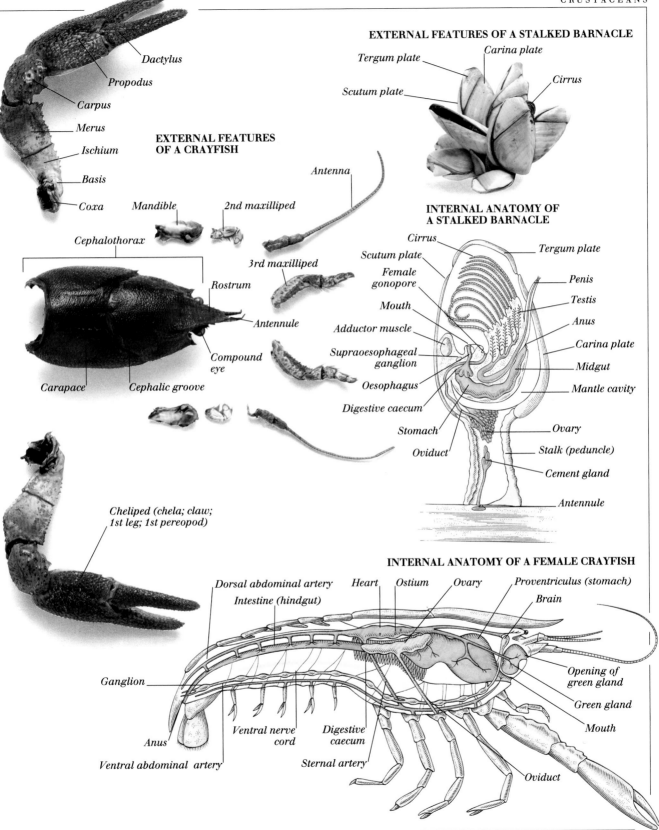

EXTERNAL FEATURES OF A STALKED BARNACLE

Tergum plate
Carina plate
Scutum plate
Cirrus

Dactylus
Propodus
Carpus
Merus
Ischium
Basis
Coxa

EXTERNAL FEATURES OF A CRAYFISH

Antenna

Mandible
2nd maxilliped

3rd maxilliped

Cephalothorax
Rostrum
Antennule
Compound eye
Carapace
Cephalic groove

INTERNAL ANATOMY OF A STALKED BARNACLE

Cirrus
Scutum plate
Female gonopore
Mouth
Adductor muscle
Supraoesophageal ganglion
Oesophagus
Digestive caecum
Stomach
Oviduct

Tergum plate
Penis
Testis
Anus
Carina plate
Midgut
Mantle cavity
Ovary
Stalk (peduncle)
Cement gland
Antennule

Cheliped (chela; claw; 1st leg; 1st pereopod)

INTERNAL ANATOMY OF A FEMALE CRAYFISH

Dorsal abdominal artery
Heart
Ostium
Ovary
Proventriculus (stomach)
Intestine (hindgut)
Brain

Ganglion

Opening of green gland
Green gland
Mouth

Anus
Ventral nerve cord
Digestive caecum
Sternal artery
Oviduct
Ventral abdominal artery

Starfish and sea urchins

STARFISH, SEA URCHINS, AND THEIR relatives (including feather stars, brittle stars, basket stars, sea daisies, sea lilies, and sea cucumbers) make up the phylum Echinodermata. A unique feature of echinoderms is the water vascular system, which consists of a series of water-filled canals from which protrude thousands of tiny tube feet. The tube feet may be used for movement, feeding, or respiration. Other features include pentaradiate symmetry (that is, the body can be divided into five parts radiating from the centre); no head; a diffuse, decentralized nervous system that lacks a brain; and no excretory organs. Typically, echinoderms also have an endoskeleton (internal skeleton) consisting of hard calcite ossicles embedded in the body wall and often bearing protruding spines or tubercles. The ossicles may fit together to form a test (as in sea urchins) or remain separate (as in sea cucumbers).

EXTERNAL FEATURES OF A STARFISH (UPPER, OR ABORAL, SURFACE)

Disc

Madreporite

Spine

Arm

INTERNAL ANATOMY OF A STARFISH

Rectum

Pyloric stomach

Madreporite

Stone canal

Anus

Rectal caecum

Tube foot

Ring canal

Lateral canal

Radial canal

Ampulla

Cardiac stomach

Pyloric duct

Pyloric caecum

Mouth

Oesophagus

Gonad

Gonopore

Tube foot

EXAMPLES OF SEA URCHINS

EDIBLE SEA URCHIN
(Echinus escelentus)

**CALIFORNIAN PURPLE
SEA URCHIN**
*(Strongylocentrotus
purpuratus)*

**PENCIL SLATE SEA
URCHIN**
*(Heterocentrotus
mammillatus)*

**INTERNAL ANATOMY
OF A SEA URCHIN**

Gonopore

Anus

Madreporite

Genital plate

Intestine

Stone canal

Ring canal

Polian vesicle

Pharynx

Nerve ring

Radial nerve   *Mouth*

Radial canal

Ampulla

Gonad

Axial gland

Siphon

Test

Spine

Tube foot

**EXTERNAL FEATURES OF A
SEA URCHIN (UPPER, OR
ABORAL, SURFACE)**

Anus

Spine

Tube foot

CUSHION STAR
(Asterina gibbosa)

COMMON BRITTLE STAR
(Ophiothix fragilis)

Tube foot

**EXAMPLES OF
STARFISH**

Mouth

Ambulacral groove

COMMON STARFISH
(Asterias rubens)

**EXTERNAL FEATURES OF A STARFISH
(LOWER, OR ORAL, SURFACE)**

Molluscs

THE PHYLUM MOLLUSCA (MOLLUSCS) is a large group of animals that includes octopuses, snails, and scallops. Octopuses and their relatives —including squid and cuttlefish—form the class Cephalopoda. Cephalopods typically have a head with a radula (a file-like feeding organ) and beak; a well-developed nervous system; sucker-bearing tentacles; a muscular mantle (part of the body wall) that can expel water through the siphon, enabling movement by jet propulsion; and a small shell or no shell. Snails and their relatives—including slugs, limpets, and abalones—make up the class Gastropoda. Gastropods typically have a coiled external shell, although some, such as slugs, have a small internal shell or no shell; a flat foot; and a head with tentacles and a radula. Scallops and their relatives—including clams, mussels, and oysters—make up the class Bivalvia (also called Pelecypoda). Features of bivalves include a shell with two halves (valves); large gills that are used for breathing and filter feeding; and no radula.

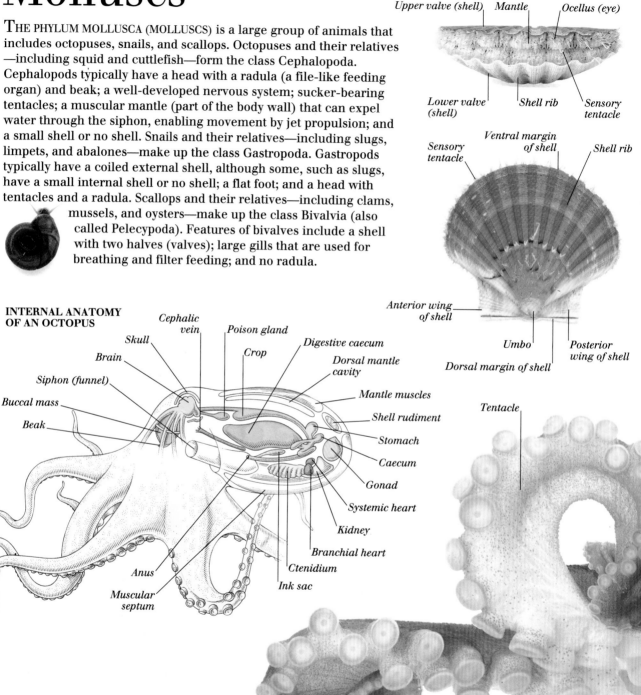

EXTERNAL FEATURES OF A SCALLOP

Upper valve (shell) Mantle Ocellus (eye)

Lower valve (shell) Shell rib Sensory tentacle

Sensory tentacle Ventral margin of shell Shell rib

Anterior wing of shell Umbo Posterior wing of shell

Dorsal margin of shell

INTERNAL ANATOMY OF AN OCTOPUS

Cephalic vein Poison gland Digestive caecum

Skull Crop Dorsal mantle cavity

Brain

Siphon (funnel) Mantle muscles

Buccal mass Shell rudiment

Beak Stomach

Caecum

Gonad

Systemic heart

Kidney

Branchial heart

Anus Ctenidium

Muscular septum Ink sac

Tentacle

Sucker

176

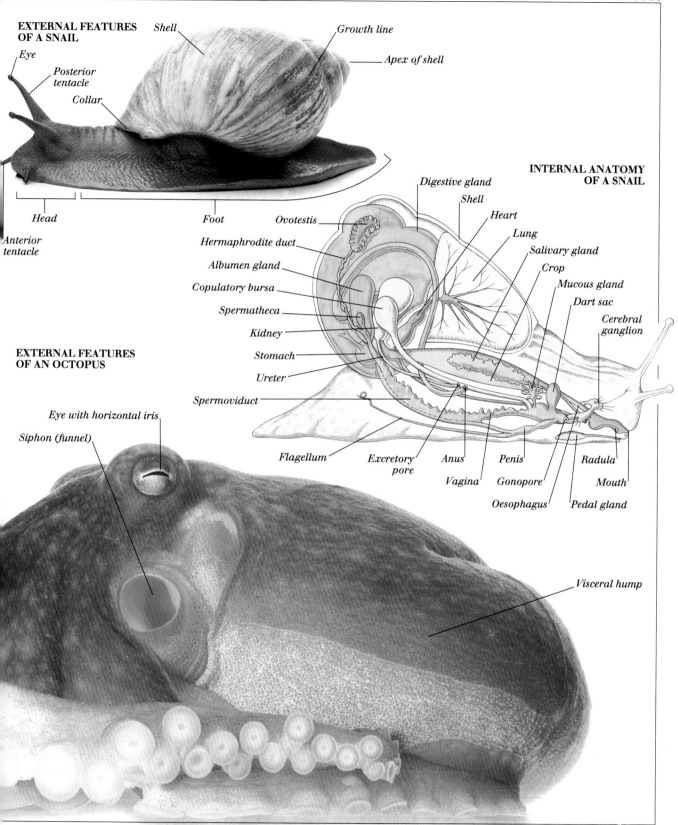

EXTERNAL FEATURES OF A SNAIL

Shell

Growth line

Apex of shell

Eye

Posterior tentacle

Collar

Head

Foot

Anterior tentacle

INTERNAL ANATOMY OF A SNAIL

Digestive gland

Shell

Heart

Lung

Salivary gland

Crop

Mucous gland

Dart sac

Cerebral ganglion

Ovotestis

Hermaphrodite duct

Albumen gland

Copulatory bursa

Spermatheca

Kidney

Stomach

Ureter

Spermoviduct

Flagellum

Excretory pore

Anus

Penis

Radula

Vagina

Gonopore

Mouth

Oesophagus

Pedal gland

EXTERNAL FEATURES OF AN OCTOPUS

Eye with horizontal iris

Siphon (funnel)

Visceral hump

177

Sharks and jawless fish

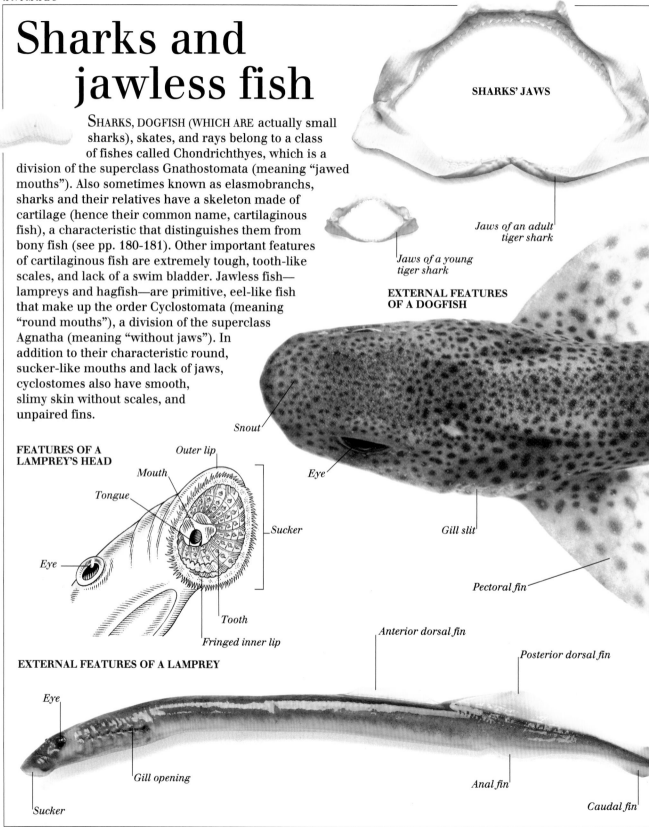

SHARKS, DOGFISH (WHICH ARE actually small sharks), skates, and rays belong to a class of fishes called Chondrichthyes, which is a division of the superclass Gnathostomata (meaning "jawed mouths"). Also sometimes known as elasmobranchs, sharks and their relatives have a skeleton made of cartilage (hence their common name, cartilaginous fish), a characteristic that distinguishes them from bony fish (see pp. 180-181). Other important features of cartilaginous fish are extremely tough, tooth-like scales, and lack of a swim bladder. Jawless fish—lampreys and hagfish—are primitive, eel-like fish that make up the order Cyclostomata (meaning "round mouths"), a division of the superclass Agnatha (meaning "without jaws"). In addition to their characteristic round, sucker-like mouths and lack of jaws, cyclostomes also have smooth, slimy skin without scales, and unpaired fins.

SHARKS' JAWS

Jaws of an adult tiger shark

Jaws of a young tiger shark

EXTERNAL FEATURES OF A DOGFISH

Snout

Eye

Gill slit

Pectoral fin

FEATURES OF A LAMPREY'S HEAD

Outer lip

Mouth

Tongue

Eye

Sucker

Tooth

Fringed inner lip

EXTERNAL FEATURES OF A LAMPREY

Eye

Anterior dorsal fin

Posterior dorsal fin

Gill opening

Anal fin

Sucker

Caudal fin

EXAMPLES OF CARTILAGINOUS FISH

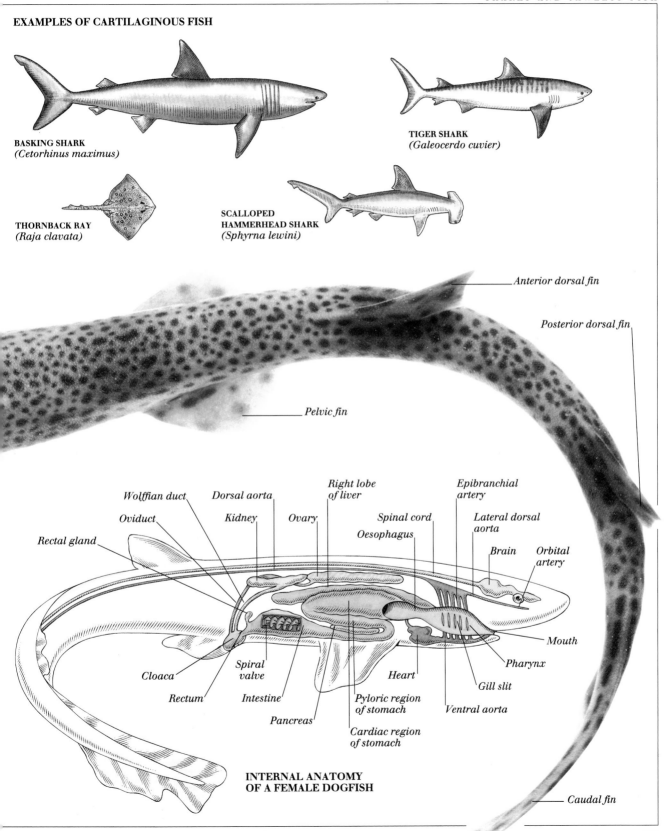

BASKING SHARK
(Cetorhinus maximus)

TIGER SHARK
(Galeocerdo cuvier)

THORNBACK RAY
(Raja clavata)

**SCALLOPED
HAMMERHEAD SHARK**
(Sphyrna lewini)

Anterior dorsal fin

Posterior dorsal fin

Pelvic fin

Wolffian duct
Oviduct
Rectal gland
Dorsal aorta
Kidney
Ovary
*Right lobe
of liver*
Oesophagus
Spinal cord
*Epibranchial
artery*
*Lateral dorsal
aorta*
Brain
*Orbital
artery*

Cloaca
Rectum
*Spiral
valve*
Intestine
Pancreas
*Pyloric region
of stomach*
*Cardiac region
of stomach*
Heart
Ventral aorta
Gill slit
Mouth
Pharynx

**INTERNAL ANATOMY
OF A FEMALE DOGFISH**

Caudal fin

Bony fish

BONY FISH, SUCH AS CARP, TROUT, SALMON, perch, and cod, are by far the best known and largest group of fish, with more than 20,000 species (over 95 per cent of all known fish). As their name suggests, bony fish have skeletons made of bone, in contrast to the cartilaginous skeletons of sharks, jawless fish, and their relatives (see pp. 178-179). Other typical features of bony fish include a swim bladder, which functions as a variable-buoyancy organ, enabling a fish to remain effortlessly at whatever depth it is swimming; relatively thin, bone-like scales; a flap (called an operculum) covering the gills; and paired pelvic and pectoral fins. Scientifically, bony fish belong to the class Osteichthyes, which is a division of the superclass Gnathostomata (meaning "jawed mouths").

HOW FISH BREATHE

Fish "breathe" by extracting oxygen from water through their gills. Water is sucked in through the mouth; simultaneously, the opercula close to prevent the water from escaping. The mouth is then closed, and muscles in the walls of the mouth, pharynx, and opercular cavity contract to pump the water inside over the gills and out through the opercula. Some fish rely on swimming with their mouths open to keep water flowing over the gills.

Pharynx

Gill raker

Water out

Gill slit

Mouth

Water in

Gill filament

Operculum

EXAMPLES OF BONY FISH

MANDARINFISH
(Synchiropus splendidus)

ANGLERFISH
(Caulophryne jordani)

LIONFISH
(Pterois volitans)

OCEANIC SEAHORSE
(Hippocampus kuda)

Vertebra

Neural spine

Hypural

Haemal spine

Caudal fin ray

Anal fin ray

Radial cartilage

STURGEON
(Acipenser sturio)

SNOWFLAKE MORAY EEL
(Echidna nebulosa)

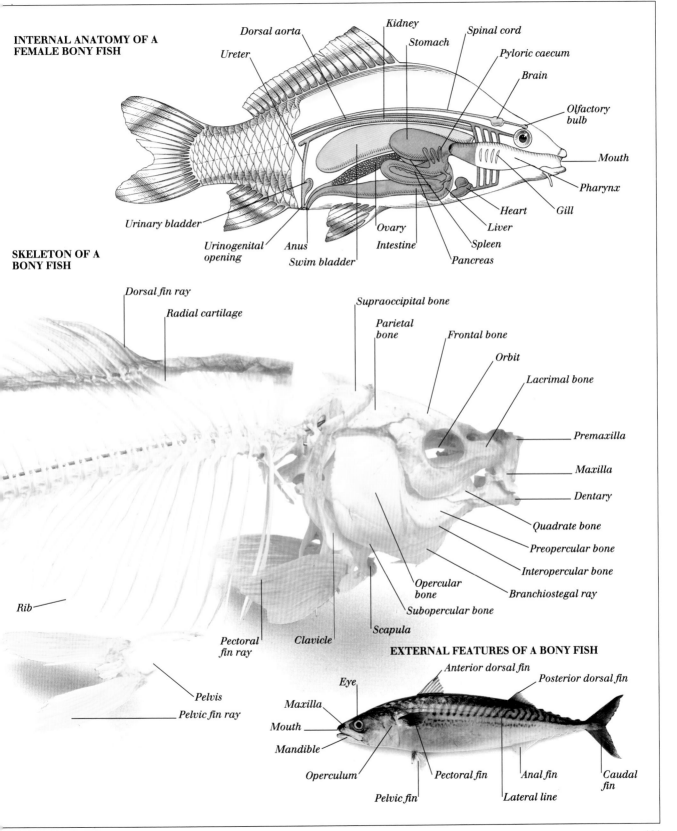

INTERNAL ANATOMY OF A FEMALE BONY FISH

Dorsal aorta

Ureter

Kidney

Stomach

Spinal cord

Pyloric caecum

Brain

Olfactory bulb

Mouth

Pharynx

Urinary bladder

Urinogenital opening

Anus

Swim bladder

Ovary

Intestine

Heart

Liver

Spleen

Pancreas

Gill

SKELETON OF A BONY FISH

Dorsal fin ray

Radial cartilage

Supraoccipital bone

Parietal bone

Frontal bone

Orbit

Lacrimal bone

Premaxilla

Maxilla

Dentary

Quadrate bone

Preopercular bone

Interopercular bone

Branchiostegal ray

Opercular bone

Subopercular bone

Scapula

Rib

Pectoral fin ray

Clavicle

Pelvis

Pelvic fin ray

EXTERNAL FEATURES OF A BONY FISH

Anterior dorsal fin

Posterior dorsal fin

Eye

Maxilla

Mouth

Mandible

Operculum

Pelvic fin

Pectoral fin

Anal fin

Lateral line

Caudal fin

181

Amphibians

THE CLASS AMPHIBIA INCLUDES FROGS and toads (which make up the order Anura), and newts and salamanders (which make up the order Urodela). Amphibians typically have moist, scaleless, hairless skin; lungs; and are cold-blooded. They also undergo complete metamorphosis, from eggs laid in water through various water-living larval stages (such as tadpoles) to land-living adults. Typical features of adult frogs and toads include a squat body with no tail; long, powerful hind legs; and large, often bulging, eyes. Adult newts and salamanders typically have a long body with a well-developed tail; and relatively short, equal-sized legs. However, newts and salamanders show considerable variation; for example, in some species the adults have minute legs, external gills rather than lungs, and spend their entire lives in water.

INTERNAL ANATOMY OF A FEMALE FROG

Larynx
Right bronchus
Stomach
Right lung
Pulmonary artery
Heart
Left lung
Liver
Pancreas
Posterior vena cava
Duodenum
Right kidney
Spleen
Dorsal aorta
Left kidney
Cloaca
Mesentery
Rectum
Small intestine (ileum)
Left ureter

EXTERNAL FEATURES OF A FROG

Hind limb
Trunk
Head
Forelimb
5 digits
External nostril
Mouth
Tympanum (eardrum)
Eye
Web
4 digits

EXTERNAL FEATURES OF A SALAMANDER

Eye
Tail
Forelimb
Hind limb
Digit

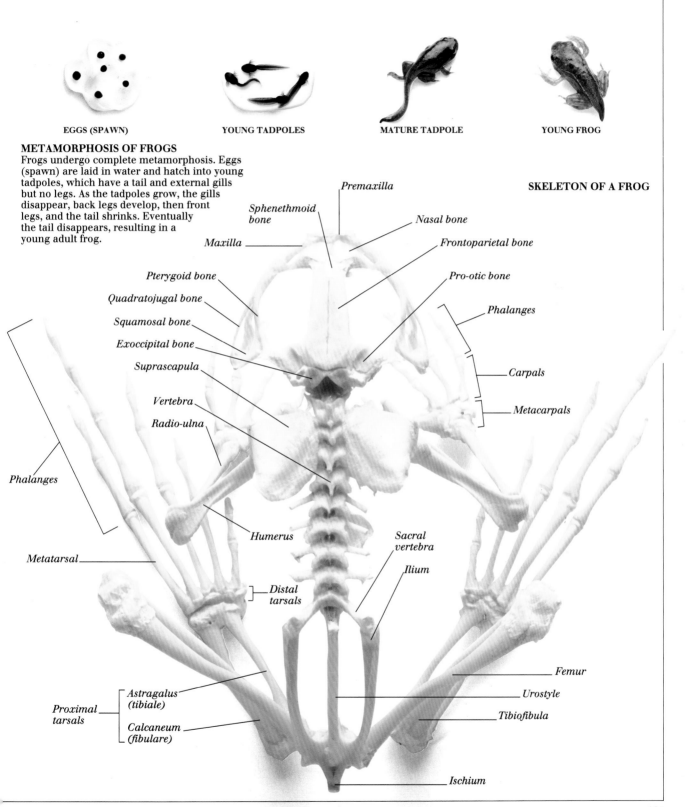

EGGS (SPAWN) **YOUNG TADPOLES** **MATURE TADPOLE** **YOUNG FROG**

METAMORPHOSIS OF FROGS

Frogs undergo complete metamorphosis. Eggs (spawn) are laid in water and hatch into young tadpoles, which have a tail and external gills but no legs. As the tadpoles grow, the gills disappear, back legs develop, then front legs, and the tail shrinks. Eventually the tail disappears, resulting in a young adult frog.

SKELETON OF A FROG

Premaxilla

Sphenethmoid bone

Nasal bone

Maxilla

Frontoparietal bone

Pterygoid bone

Pro-otic bone

Quadratojugal bone

Phalanges

Squamosal bone

Exoccipital bone

Carpals

Suprascapula

Vertebra

Metacarpals

Radio-ulna

Phalanges

Humerus

Metatarsal

Sacral vertebra

Ilium

Distal tarsals

Femur

Proximal tarsals

Astragalus (tibiale)

Urostyle

Calcaneum (fibulare)

Tibiofibula

Ischium

Lizards and snakes

LIZARDS AND SNAKES BELONG to the order Squamata, a division of the class Reptilia. Characteristic reptilian features include scaly skin, lungs, and cold-bloodedness. Most reptiles lay leathery-shelled eggs, although some hatch the eggs inside their bodies and give birth to live young. Lizards belong to the suborder Lacertilia. Typically, they have long tails, and shed their skin in several pieces. Many lizards can regenerate a tail if it is lost; some can change colour; and some are limbless. Snakes make up the suborder Ophidia (also called Serpentes). All snakes have long, limbless bodies; can dislocate their lower jaw to swallow large prey; and have eyelids that are joined together to form a single transparent covering over the front of the eye. Most snakes shed their skin in a single piece. Constrictor snakes kill their prey by squeezing; venomous snakes poison their prey.

EXAMPLES OF SNAKES

MEXICAN MOUNTAIN KING SNAKE (*Lampropeltis triangulum annulata*)

BANDED MILK SNAKE (*Lampropeltis ruthveni*)

EXTERNAL FEATURES OF A LIZARD

Eye

Mouth

Crest

Eardrum

Masseteric scale

Dorsal scale

External nostril

SKELETON OF A LIZARD

Skull

Orbit

Scapula

Cervical vertebrae

Phalanges

Carpals

Metacarpal

Humerus

Ulna

Radius

Rib

Thoracolumbar vertebrae

Pelvis

Sacrum

Femur

Tibia

Fibula

Tarsals

Metatarsal

Dewlap

Caudal vertebrae

Phalanges

Foreleg

Belly

Ventral scale

Toe

Claw

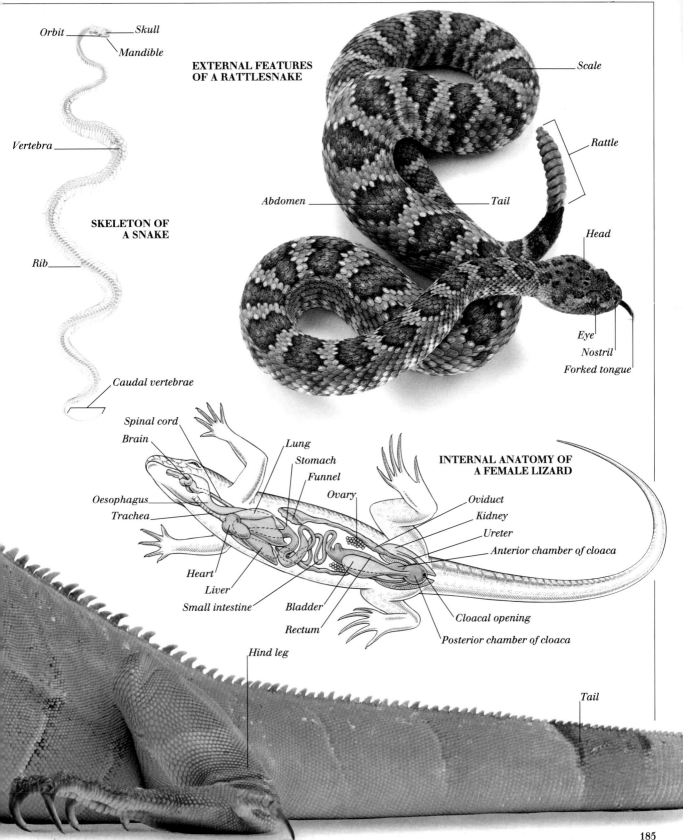

Orbit

Skull

Mandible

EXTERNAL FEATURES OF A RATTLESNAKE

Scale

Vertebra

Rattle

Abdomen

Tail

SKELETON OF A SNAKE

Head

Rib

Eye

Nostril

Forked tongue

Caudal vertebrae

Spinal cord

Brain

Lung

Stomach

Funnel

INTERNAL ANATOMY OF A FEMALE LIZARD

Ovary

Oesophagus

Oviduct

Trachea

Kidney

Ureter

Anterior chamber of cloaca

Heart

Liver

Small intestine

Bladder

Rectum

Cloacal opening

Posterior chamber of cloaca

Hind leg

Tail

185

Crocodilians and turtles

GHARIAL
(Gavialis gangeticus)

NILE CROCODILE
(Crocodylus niloticus)

AMERICAN ALLIGATOR
(Alligator mississippiensis)

CROCODILIANS AND TURTLES BELONG to different orders in the class Reptilia. The order Crocodilia includes crocodiles, alligators, caimans, and gharials. Typically, crocodilians are carnivores (flesh-eaters), and have a long snout, sharp teeth for gripping prey, and hard, square scales. All crocodilians are adapted to living on land and in water: they have four strong legs for moving on land; a powerful tail for swimming; and their eyes and nostrils are high on the head so that they stay above water while the rest of the body is submerged. The order Chelonia includes marine turtles, terrapins (freshwater turtles), and tortoises (land turtles). Characteristically, chelonians have a short, broad body encased in a bony shell with an outer horny covering, into which the head and limbs can be withdrawn; and a horny beak instead of teeth.

SKELETON OF A CROCODILE

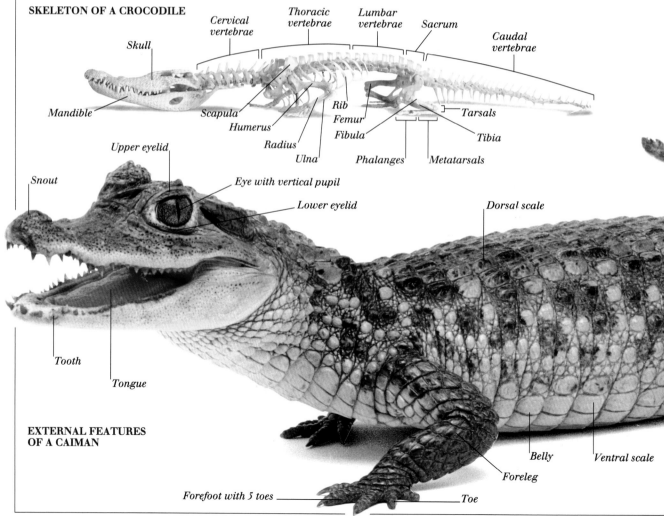

Cervical vertebrae

Thoracic vertebrae

Lumbar vertebrae

Sacrum

Caudal vertebrae

Skull

Mandible

Scapula

Humerus

Radius

Ulna

Rib

Femur

Fibula

Phalanges

Metatarsals

Tarsals

Tibia

Snout

Upper eyelid

Eye with vertical pupil

Lower eyelid

Dorsal scale

Tooth

Tongue

EXTERNAL FEATURES OF A CAIMAN

Belly

Ventral scale

Foreleg

Forefoot with 5 toes

Toe

EXTERNAL FEATURES OF A TERRAPIN

SKELETON OF A TURTLE

INTERNAL ANATOMY OF A FEMALE TORTOISE

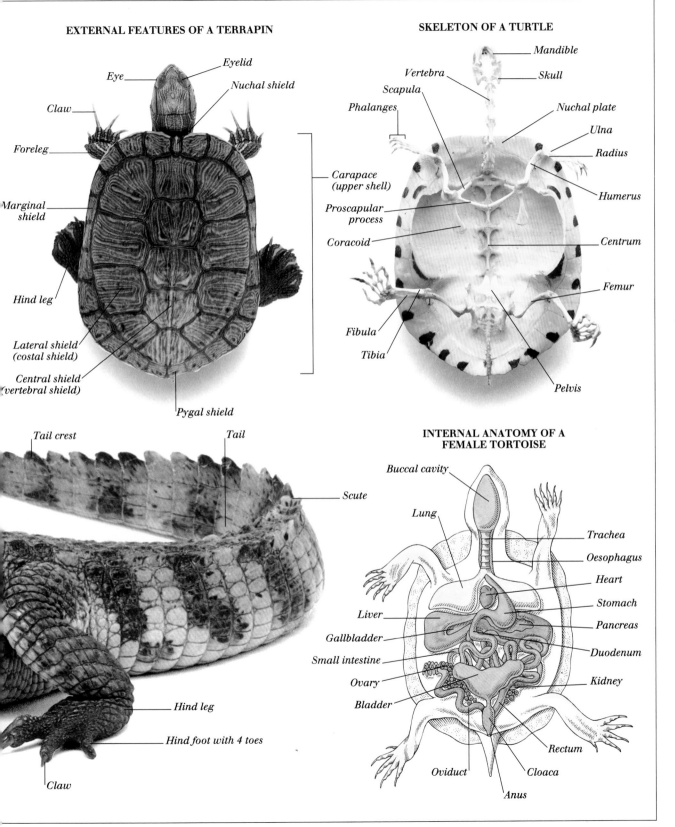

Eyelid

Eye

Claw

Nuchal shield

Foreleg

Marginal
shield

Hind leg

Lateral shield
(costal shield)

Central shield
(vertebral shield)

Pygal shield

Carapace
(upper shell)

Mandible

Vertebra

Skull

Scapula

Phalanges

Nuchal plate

Ulna

Radius

Humerus

Proscapular
process

Coracoid

Centrum

Femur

Fibula

Tibia

Pelvis

Tail crest

Tail

Scute

Buccal cavity

Lung

Trachea

Oesophagus

Heart

Stomach

Liver

Pancreas

Gallbladder

Duodenum

Small intestine

Kidney

Ovary

Hind leg

Bladder

Hind foot with 4 toes

Rectum

Claw

Oviduct

Cloaca

Anus

Birds 1

BIRDS MAKE UP THE CLASS AVES. There are more than 9,000 species, almost all of which can fly (the only flightless birds are penguins, ostriches, rheas, cassowaries, and kiwis). The ability to fly is reflected in the typical bird features: forelimbs modified as wings; a streamlined body; and hollow bones to reduce weight. All birds lay hard-shelled eggs, which the parents incubate. Birds' beaks and feet vary according to diet and way of life. Beaks range from general-purpose types suitable for a mixed diet (those of thrushes, for example), to types specialized for particular foods (such as the large, curved, sieving beaks of flamingos). Feet range from the webbed "paddles" of ducks, to the talons of birds of prey. Plumage also varies widely, and in many species the male is brightly coloured for courtship display whereas the female is drab.

EXTERNAL FEATURES OF A BIRD

Forehead

Eye

Crown

Nostril

Nape

Upper mandible

Beak

Lower mandible

Chin

Throat

EXAMPLES OF BIRDS

Minor coverts

Lesser wing coverts

Median wing coverts

Greater wing coverts (major coverts)

Secondary flight feathers (secondary remiges)

Primary flight feathers (primaryremiges)

Breast

Belly

Flank

Thigh

Under tail coverts

Claw

Tarsus

Toe

Tail feathers (retrices)

MALE TUFTED DUCK
(Aythya fuligula)

WHITE STORK
(Ciconia ciconia)

MALE OSTRICH
(Struthio camelus)

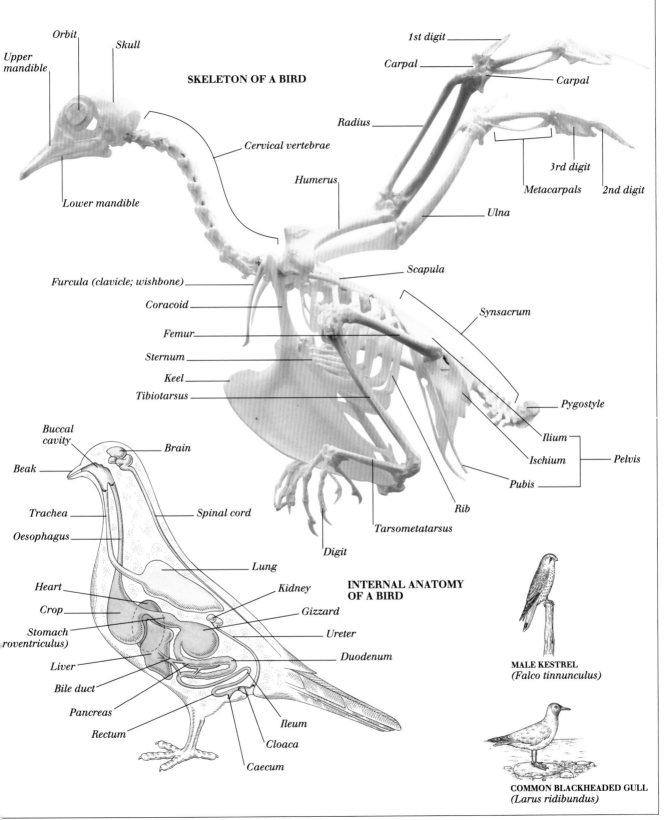

Orbit

Skull

Upper mandible

SKELETON OF A BIRD

Cervical vertebrae

Lower mandible

Humerus

1st digit

Carpal

Carpal

Radius

3rd digit

Metacarpals

2nd digit

Ulna

Scapula

Furcula (clavicle; wishbone)

Coracoid

Synsacrum

Femur

Sternum

Keel

Tibiotarsus

Pygostyle

Ilium

Ischium

Pubis

Pelvis

Rib

Tarsometatarsus

Digit

Buccal cavity

Brain

Beak

Trachea

Spinal cord

Oesophagus

Lung

INTERNAL ANATOMY OF A BIRD

Heart

Kidney

Crop

Gizzard

Stomach (proventriculus)

Ureter

Duodenum

Liver

Bile duct

Pancreas

Ileum

Rectum

Cloaca

Caecum

MALE KESTREL
(Falco tinnunculus)

COMMON BLACKHEADED GULL
(Larus ridibundus)

Birds 2

EXAMPLES OF BIRDS' FEET

KITTIWAKE
(Rissa tridactyla)
The webbed feet are
adapted for paddling
through water.

LITTLE GREBE
(Tachybaptus ruficollis)
The lobed, flattened feet
are adapted for swimming
underwater.

TAWNY OWL
(Strix aluco)
The clawed feet are adapted
for gripping prey.

EXAMPLES OF BIRDS' BEAKS

KING VULTURE
(Sarcorhamphus papa)
The hooked beak is adapted
for pulling apart flesh.

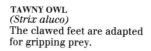

GREATER FLAMINGO
(Phoenicopterus ruber)
In the living bird, the large,
curved beak contains a
cartilaginous "sieve" for
filtering food particles
from water.

MISTLE THRUSH
(Turdus viscivorus)
The general-purpose beak is
suitable for a wide range of animal
and plant foods.

BLUE-AND-YELLOW MACAW
(Ara ararauna)
The broad, powerful, hooked beak
is adapted for crushing seeds and
eating fruit.

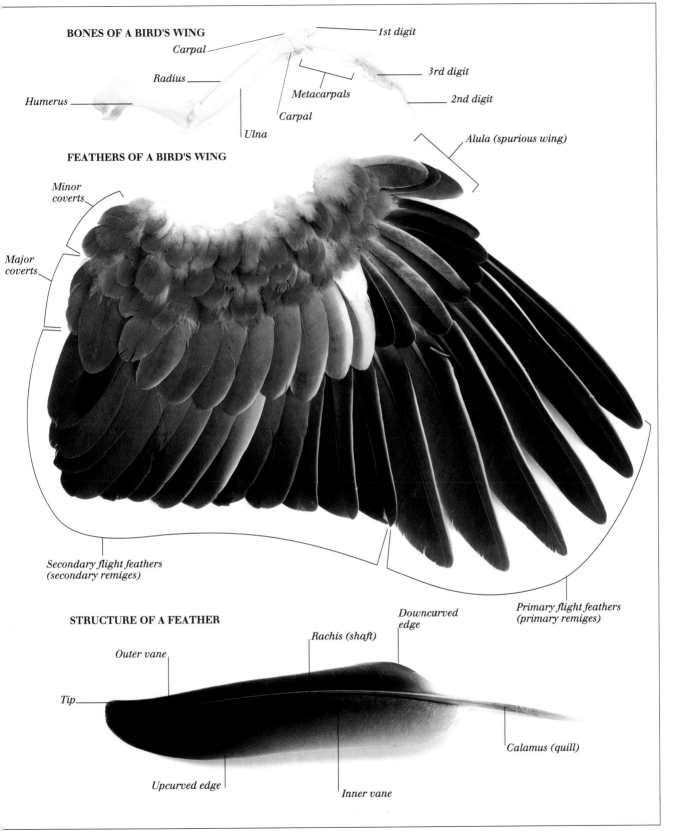

BONES OF A BIRD'S WING

1st digit

Carpal

Radius

3rd digit

Metacarpals

Humerus

2nd digit

Carpal

Ulna

Alula (spurious wing)

FEATHERS OF A BIRD'S WING

Minor coverts

Major coverts

Secondary flight feathers (secondary remiges)

Primary flight feathers (primary remiges)

Downcurved edge

STRUCTURE OF A FEATHER

Rachis (shaft)

Outer vane

Tip

Calamus (quill)

Upcurved edge

Inner vane

Eggs

AN EGG IS A SINGLE CELL, produced by the female, with the capacity to develop into a new individual. Development may take place inside the mother's body (as in most mammals) or outside, in which case the egg has a protective covering such as a shell. Egg yolk nourishes the growing young. Eggs developing inside the mother generally have little yolk, because the young are nourished from her body. Eggs developing outside may also have little yolk if they are produced by animals whose young go through a larval stage (such as a caterpillar) that feeds itself while developing into the adult form. The shelled eggs of birds and reptiles contain enough yolk to sustain the young until it hatches into a juvenile version of the adult.

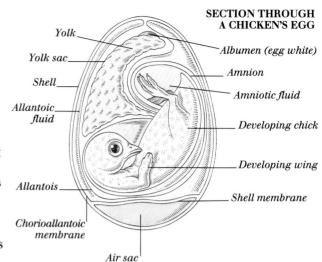

SECTION THROUGH A CHICKEN'S EGG

Yolk
Yolk sac
Shell
Allantoic fluid
Allantois
Chorioallantoic membrane
Air sac
Albumen (egg white)
Amnion
Amniotic fluid
Developing chick
Developing wing
Shell membrane

VARIETY OF EGGS

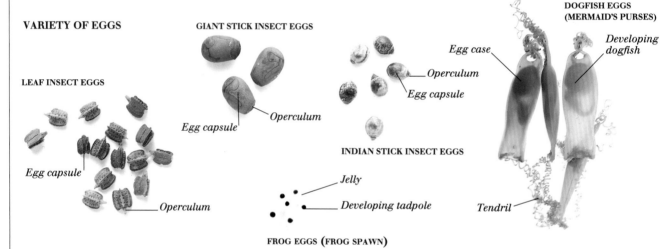

LEAF INSECT EGGS

Egg capsule
Operculum

GIANT STICK INSECT EGGS

Egg capsule
Operculum

INDIAN STICK INSECT EGGS

Operculum
Egg capsule

FROG EGGS (FROG SPAWN)

Jelly
Developing tadpole

DOGFISH EGGS (MERMAID'S PURSES)

Developing dogfish
Egg case
Tendril

HATCHING OF A QUAIL'S EGG

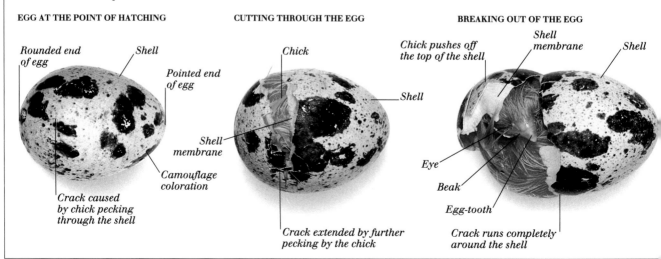

EGG AT THE POINT OF HATCHING

Rounded end of egg
Shell
Pointed end of egg
Shell membrane
Camouflage coloration
Crack caused by chick pecking through the shell

CUTTING THROUGH THE EGG

Chick
Shell
Crack extended by further pecking by the chick

BREAKING OUT OF THE EGG

Chick pushes off the top of the shell
Shell membrane
Shell
Eye
Beak
Egg-tooth
Crack runs completely around the shell

EXAMPLES OF BIRDS' EGGS

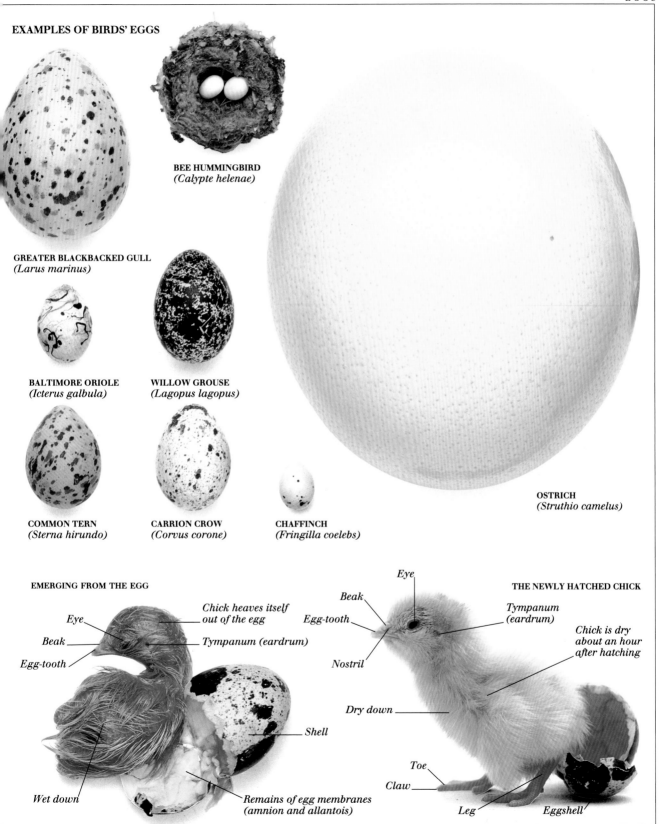

GREATER BLACKBACKED GULL
(Larus marinus)

BEE HUMMINGBIRD
(Calypte helenae)

BALTIMORE ORIOLE
(Icterus galbula)

WILLOW GROUSE
(Lagopus lagopus)

COMMON TERN
(Sterna hirundo)

CARRION CROW
(Corvus corone)

CHAFFINCH
(Fringilla coelebs)

OSTRICH
(Struthio camelus)

EMERGING FROM THE EGG

Eye

Beak

Egg-tooth

Chick heaves itself
out of the egg

Tympanum (eardrum)

Shell

Wet down

*Remains of egg membranes
(amnion and allantois)*

Eye

Beak

Egg-tooth

Nostril

THE NEWLY HATCHED CHICK

*Tympanum
(eardrum)*

Chick is dry
about an hour
after hatching

Dry down

Toe

Claw

Leg

Eggshell

Carnivores

THE MAMMALIAN ORDER CARNIVORA includes cats, dogs, bears, raccoons, pandas, weasels, badgers, skunks, otters, civets, mongooses, and hyenas. The order's name is derived from the fact that most of its members are carnivores (flesh-eaters). Typical carnivore features therefore reflect a hunting life-style: speed and agility; sharp claws and well-developed canine teeth for holding and killing prey; carnassial teeth (cheek teeth) for cutting flesh; and forward-facing eyes for good distance judgment. However, some members of the order—bears, badgers, and foxes, for example—have a more mixed diet, and a few are entirely herbivorous (plant-eating), notably pandas. Such animals have no carnassial teeth and tend to be slower-moving than pure flesh-eaters.

EXTERNAL FEATURES OF A MALE LION

Nose
Eye
Mane
Nostril
Vibrissa (whisker)
Tongue
Canine tooth
Incisor tooth
Chest
Elbow
Lower arm
Toe

SKULL OF A LION

Zygomatic arch
Coronoid process
Sagittal crest
Orbit
Nasal bone
Maxilla
Upper premolars
Upper canine
Lower canine
Mandible
Lower premolars
Occipital condyle
Tympanic bulla
Condyle
Angular process
Upper carnassial tooth (4th upper premolar)

SKULL OF A BEAR

Sagittal crest
Occipital condyle
Zygomatic arch
Orbit
Upper molars
Nasal bone
Upper premolars
Maxilla
Upper canine
Upper incisor
Lower incisor
Lower canine
Mandible
Tympanic bulla
Angular process
Condyle
Lower molars
Lower premolars

EXAMPLES OF CARNIVORES

ALSATIAN DOG
(Canis familiaris)

MANED WOLF
(Chrysocyon brachyurus)

RACCOON
(Procyon lotor)

AMERICAN BLACK BEAR
(Ursus americanus)

SKELETON OF A DOMESTIC CAT

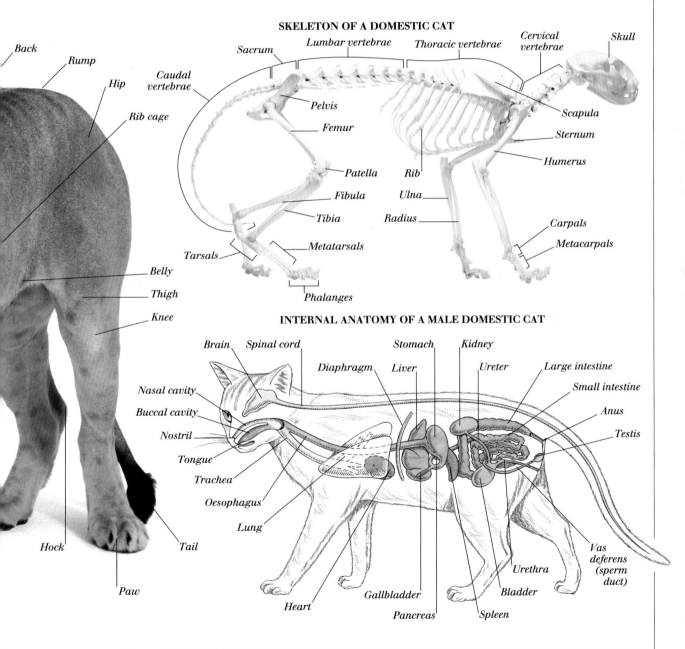

Back

Rump

Hip

Rib cage

Belly

Thigh

Knee

Hock

Paw

Sacrum

Caudal vertebrae

Lumbar vertebrae

Thoracic vertebrae

Cervical vertebrae

Skull

Pelvis

Femur

Scapula

Sternum

Humerus

Patella

Rib

Fibula

Ulna

Tibia

Radius

Carpals

Metacarpals

Tarsals

Metatarsals

Phalanges

INTERNAL ANATOMY OF A MALE DOMESTIC CAT

Brain

Spinal cord

Stomach

Kidney

Diaphragm

Liver

Ureter

Large intestine

Small intestine

Nasal cavity

Buccal cavity

Anus

Nostril

Testis

Tongue

Trachea

Oesophagus

Lung

Tail

Heart

Gallbladder

Pancreas

Spleen

Bladder

Urethra

Vas deferens (sperm duct)

195

Rabbits and rodents

ALTHOUGH RABBITS AND RODENTS belong to different orders of mammals, they have some features in common. These features include chisel-shaped incisor teeth that grow continually, and eating their faeces to extract more nutrients from their plant diet. Rabbits and hares belong to the order Lagomorpha. Characteristically, they have four incisors in the upper jaw and two in the lower jaw; powerful hind legs for jumping; forelimbs adapted for burrowing; long ears; and a small tail. Rodents make up the order Rodentia. This is the largest order of mammals, with more than 1,700 species, including squirrels, beavers, chipmunks, gophers, rats, mice, lemmings, gerbils, porcupines, cavies, and the capybara. Typical rodent features include two incisors in each jaw; short forelimbs for manipulating food; and cheek pouches for storing food.

Snout
Eye
Ear
Nose
Nostril
Vibrissa (whisker)
Neck
Mouth
Tail
Pinna (ear flap)
Forelimb
5 digits
Hind limb
5 digits

EXTERNAL FEATURES OF A RABBIT

Pinna (ear flap)
Ear
Shoulder
Eye
Nose
Nostril
Vibrissa (whisker)
Forelimb
5 digits

INTERNAL ANATOMY OF A MALE RABBIT

Brain
Gallbladder
Liver
Stomach
Kidney
Spinal cord
Colon
Ileum
Ureter
Rectum
Bladder
Anus
Urethra
Testis
Vas deferens
Appendix
Nasal cavity
Mouth
Buccal cavity
Tongue
Oesophagus
Lung
Trachea
Heart
Diaphragm
Pancreas
Duodenum
Caecum

SKELETON OF A HARE

Skull

Mandible

Cervical vertebrae

Thoracic vertebrae

Scapula

Sternum

Lumbar vertebrae

Rib

Humerus

Femur

Radius

Pelvis

Ulna

Sacrum

Patella

Carpals

Fibula

Metacarpals

Tibia

Caudal vertebrae

Phalanges

Phalanges

Tarsals

Metatarsals

Tail

Knee

Hind limb

4 digits

EXAMPLES OF RODENTS

GREY SQUIRREL
(*Sciuris carolinensis*)

PLAINS VISCACHA
(*Lagostomus maximus*)

CRESTED PORCUPINE
(*Hystrix africaeaustralis*)

AMERICAN BEAVER
(*Castor canadensis*)

CAPYBARA
(*Hydrochoerus hydrochaeris*)

Ungulates

UNGULATES IS A GENERAL TERM FOR a large, varied group of mammals that includes horses, cattle, and their relatives. The ungulates are divided into two orders on the basis of the number of toes. Members of the order Perissodactyla (odd-toed ungulates) have one or three toes. Perissodactyls include horses, asses, and zebras (all of which are one-toed), and rhinoceroses and tapirs (which are three-toed). Members of the order Artiodactyla (even-toed ungulates) have two or four toes. Most artiodactyls have two toes, which are typically encased in hooves to give the so-called cloven hoof. Two-toed, cloven-hoofed artiodactyls include cows and other cattle, sheep, goats, antelopes, deer, and giraffes. The other main two-toed artiodactyls are camels and llamas. Most two-toed artiodactyls are ruminants; that is, they have a four-chambered stomach and chew the cud. The principal four-toed artiodactyls are pigs, peccaries, and hippopotamuses.

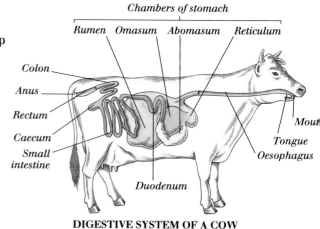

DIGESTIVE SYSTEM OF A COW

COMPARISON OF THE FRONT FEET OF A HORSE AND A COW

SKELETON OF THE LEFT FRONT FOOT OF A HORSE

SKELETON OF THE RIGHT FRONT FOOT OF A COW

EXAMPLES OF UNGULATES

MALE RED DEER
(Cervus elephas)
An even-toed ungulate
(order Artiodactyla)

BACTRIAN CAMEL
(Camelus ferus)
An even-toed ungulate
(order Artiodactyla)

GIRAFFE
(Giraffa camelopardalis)
An even-toed ungulate
(order Artiodactyla)

BLACK RHINOCEROS
(Diceros bicornis)
An odd-toed ungulate
(order Perissodactyla)

EXTERNAL FEATURES OF A HORSE

Crest

Withers

Mane

Poll

Ear

Forelock

Forehead

Eye

Muzzle

Nose

Nostril

Cheek

Throatlatch

Mouth

Chin groove

Neck

Shoulder

Breast

Elbow

Forearm

Knee

Cannon bone

Fetlock

Pastern

SKELETON OF A HORSE

Caudal vertebrae

Sacrum

Lumbar vertebrae

Thoracic vertebrae

Orbit

Atlas

Axis

Skull

Cervical vertebrae

Pelvis

Scapula

Mandible

Femur

Sternum

Fibula

Humerus

Tibia

Patella

Radius

Calcaneum

Rib

Ulna

Carpals

2nd metatarsal

Tarsals

3rd metacarpal
(cannon bone)

3rd metatarsal

4th metatarsal

Phalanges of
3rd digit

Phalanges of 3rd digit

Elephants

THE TWO SPECIES OF elephants—African and Asian—are the only members of the mammalian order Proboscidea. The bigger African elephant is the largest land animal: a fully grown male may be up to 4 m (13 ft) tall and weigh as much as 7 tonnes (6.9 tons). A fully grown male Asian elephant may be 3.3 m (11 ft) tall and weigh 5.4 tonnes (5.3 tons). The trunk—an extension of the nose and upper lip—is the elephant's other most obvious feature. It is used for manipulating and lifting, feeding, drinking and spraying water, smelling, touching, and producing trumpeting sounds. Other characteristic features include a pair of tusks, used for defence and for crushing vegetation; thick, pillar-like legs and broad feet to support the massive body; and large ear flaps that act as radiators to keep the elephant cool.

DIFFERENCES BETWEEN AFRICAN AND ASIAN ELEPHANTS

Flat forehead
Very large ears
2 "lips" at the end of the trunk
Concave back
4 toenails
3 toenails

AFRICAN ELEPHANT
(Loxodonta africana)

Twin-domed forehead
Smaller ears
1 "lip" at the end of the trunk
Arched back
5 toenails
4 toenails

ASIAN ELEPHANT
(Elephas maximus)

INTERNAL ANATOMY OF A FEMALE ELEPHANT

Spinal cord
Brain
Nasal cavity
Buccal cavity
Mouth
Tongue
Tusk
Nasal passage
Heart
Epiglottis
Oesophagus
Trachea
Lung
Diaphragm
Nostril
Stomach
Duodenum
Spleen
Vulva
Kidney
Ureter
Uterus
Rectum
Bladder
Anal flap
Anus
Vagina
Small intestine
Rump
Hind leg
Toenail

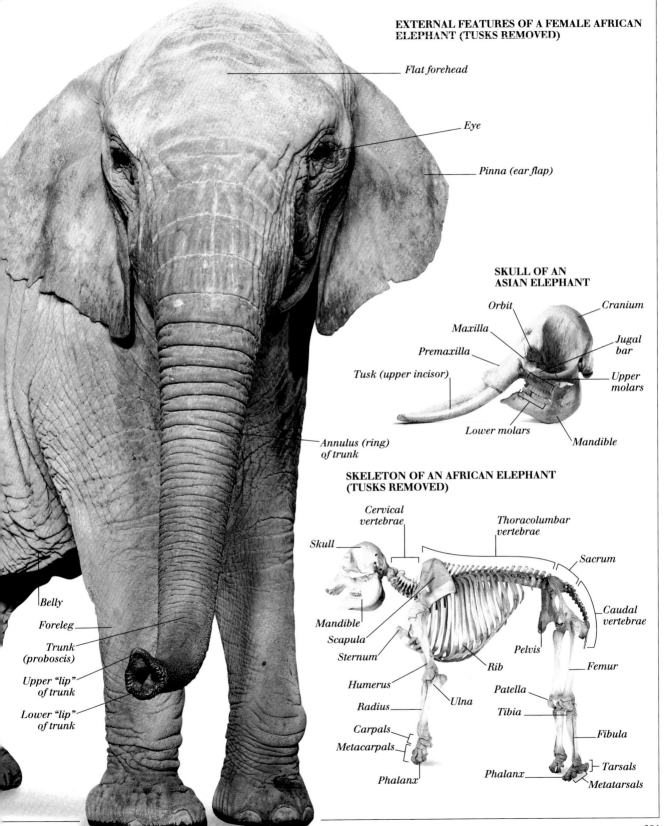

**EXTERNAL FEATURES OF A FEMALE AFRICAN
ELEPHANT (TUSKS REMOVED)**

Flat forehead

Eye

Pinna (ear flap)

**SKULL OF AN
ASIAN ELEPHANT**

Orbit

Cranium

Maxilla

Jugal
bar

Premaxilla

Tusk (upper incisor)

Upper
molars

Lower molars

Mandible

Annulus (ring)
of trunk

**SKELETON OF AN AFRICAN ELEPHANT
(TUSKS REMOVED)**

Cervical
vertebrae

Thoracolumbar
vertebrae

Skull

Sacrum

Mandible

Caudal
vertebrae

Scapula

Sternum

Pelvis

Belly

Rib

Femur

Foreleg

Humerus

Patella

Trunk
(proboscis)

Radius

Ulna

Tibia

Upper "lip"
of trunk

Carpals

Fibula

Lower "lip"
of trunk

Metacarpals

Tarsals

Phalanx

Phalanx

Metatarsals

Primates

THE MAMMALIAN ORDER PRIMATES consists of monkeys, apes, and their relatives (including humans). There are two suborders of primates: Prosimii, the primitive primates, which include lemurs, tarsiers, and lorises; and Anthropoidea, the advanced primates, which include monkeys, apes, and humans. The anthropoids are divided into New World monkeys, Old World monkeys, and hominids. New World monkeys typically have wide-apart nostrils that open to the side; and long tails, which are prehensile (grasping) in some species. This group of monkeys lives in South America, and includes marmosets, tamarins, and howler monkeys. Old World monkeys typically have close-set nostrils that open forwards or downwards; and non-prehensile tails. This group of monkeys lives in Africa and Asia, and includes langurs, mandrills, macaques, and baboons. Hominids typically have large brains, and no tail. This group includes the apes—chimpanzees, gibbons, gorillas, and orangutans—and humans.

INTERNAL ANATOMY OF A FEMALE CHIMPANZEE

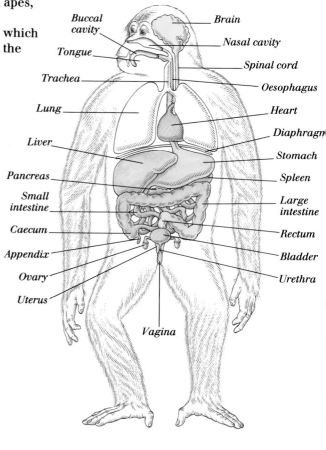

Buccal cavity
Tongue
Trachea
Lung
Liver
Pancreas
Small intestine
Caecum
Appendix
Ovary
Uterus
Vagina

Brain
Nasal cavity
Spinal cord
Oesophagus
Heart
Diaphragm
Stomach
Spleen
Large intestine
Rectum
Bladder
Urethra

SKELETON OF A RHESUS MONKEY

Skull
Orbit
Cervical vertebrae
Mandible
Thoracic vertebrae
Clavicle
Scapula
Rib
Humerus
Lumbar vertebrae
Radius
Ulna
Sacrum
Femur
Patella
Tibia
Carpals
Metacarpals
Fibula
Pelvis
Phalanges
Caudal vertebrae
Tarsals
Metatarsals
Phalanges

SKULL OF A CHIMPANZEE

Temporal bone
Suture
Frontal bone
Parietal bone
Supraorbital ridge
Orbit
Occipital bone
Maxilla
Premaxilla
Auditory meatus
Zygomatic arch
Incisor tooth
Canine tooth
Mandible
Molar tooth
Premolar tooth

EXAMPLES OF PRIMATES

RING-TAILED LEMUR
(Lemur catta)
A prosimian

MALE RED HOWLER MONKEY
(Alouatta seniculus)
A New World monkey

MALE MANDRILL
(Mandrillus sphinx)
An Old World monkey

CHIMPANZEE
(Pan troglodytes)
An ape

EXTERNAL FEATURES OF A YOUNG GORILLA

GOLDEN LION TAMARIN
(Leontopithecus rosalia)
A New World monkey

Pinna (ear flap)

Brow ridge

Eye

Shoulder

Nostril

Mouth

Upper arm

Thigh

Forearm

Chest

Elbow

Knee

Lower leg

Hand

Foot

Toe

Finger

Toenail

Dolphins, whales, and seals

DOLPHINS, WHALES, AND SEALS belong to two orders of mammals adapted to living in water. Dolphins and whales make up the order Cetacea. Typical cetacean features include a streamlined, fish-like shape; forelimbs in the form of flippers; no visible hind limbs; a horizontally flattened tail; and thick blubber under the skin. There are two groups of cetaceans: toothed whales, including sperm whales, white whales, beaked whales, dolphins, and porpoises; and the larger whalebone (baleen) whales, including rorquals, grey whales, and right whales. The blue whale—a rorqual—is the largest living animal: an adult may be up to 30 m (100 ft) long and weigh 130 tonnes (128 tons). Seals and their relatives—sea lions and walruses—make up the order Pinnipedia. Characteristically, they have a streamlined, torpedo-shaped body; forelimbs and hind limbs modified as flippers; thick blubber; and no external ears.

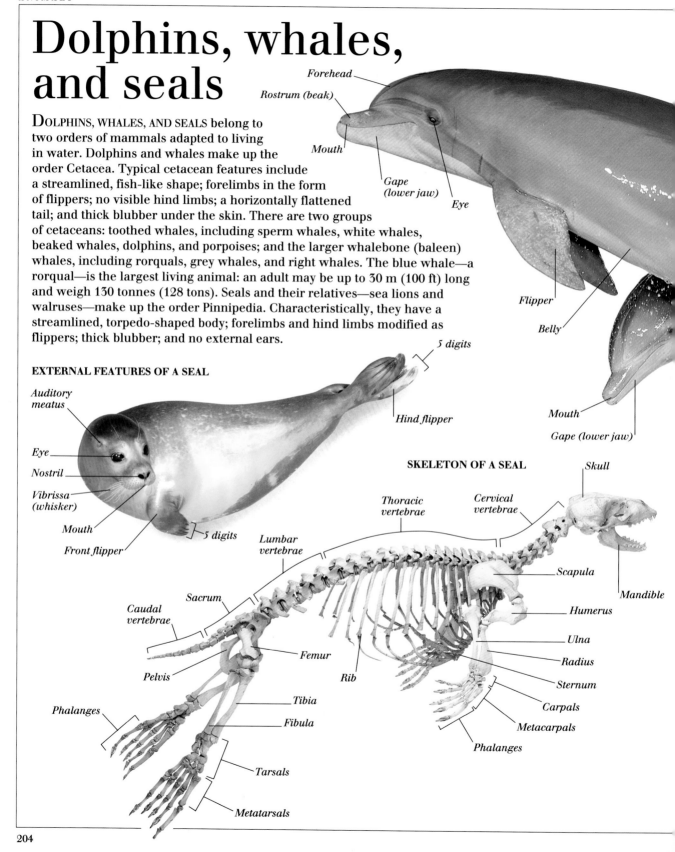

Forehead
Rostrum (beak)
Mouth
Gape (lower jaw)
Eye
Flipper
Belly
Mouth
Gape (lower jaw)

EXTERNAL FEATURES OF A SEAL

Auditory meatus
Eye
Nostril
Vibrissa (whisker)
Mouth
Front flipper
5 digits
5 digits
Hind flipper

SKELETON OF A SEAL

Skull
Cervical vertebrae
Thoracic vertebrae
Lumbar vertebrae
Scapula
Mandible
Humerus
Ulna
Radius
Sternum
Carpals
Metacarpals
Phalanges
Sacrum
Caudal vertebrae
Pelvis
Femur
Rib
Tibia
Fibula
Phalanges
Tarsals
Metatarsals

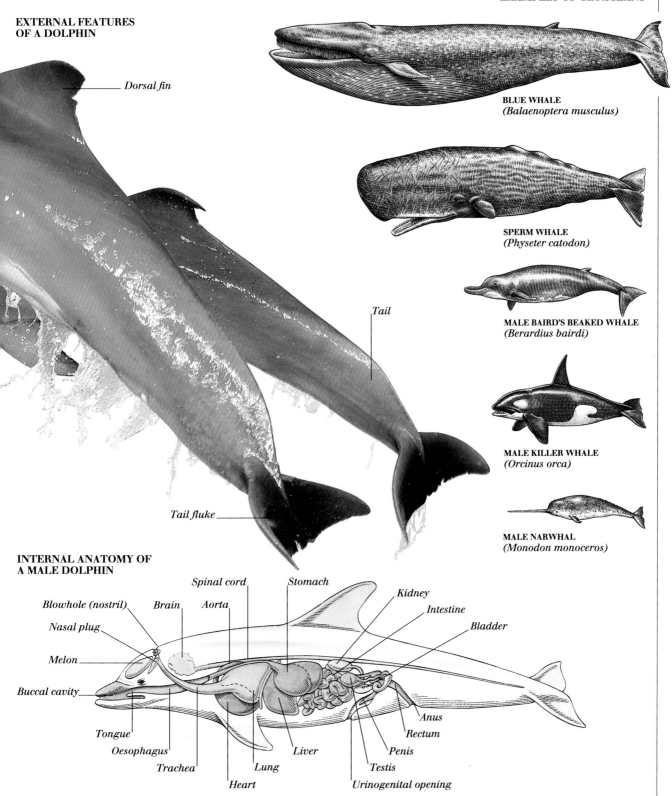

**EXTERNAL FEATURES
OF A DOLPHIN**

Dorsal fin

Tail

Tail fluke

EXAMPLES OF CETACEANS

BLUE WHALE
(Balaenoptera musculus)

SPERM WHALE
(Physeter catodon)

MALE BAIRD'S BEAKED WHALE
(Berardius bairdi)

MALE KILLER WHALE
(Orcinus orca)

MALE NARWHAL
(Monodon monoceros)

**INTERNAL ANATOMY OF
A MALE DOLPHIN**

Spinal cord

Stomach

Kidney

Intestine

Bladder

Blowhole (nostril)

Brain

Aorta

Nasal plug

Melon

Buccal cavity

Anus

Rectum

Tongue

Oesophagus

Penis

Liver

Trachea

Testis

Lung

Urinogenital opening

Heart

Marsupials and Monotremes

MARSUPIALS AND MONOTREMES are two orders of mammals that differ from other mammalian groups in the ways that their young develop. The order Marsupalia, the pouched mammals, is made up of kangaroos and their relatives. Typically, marsupials give birth to their young at a very early stage of development. The young then crawls to the mother's pouch (which is on the outside of her abdomen), where it attaches itself to a nipple and remains until fully developed. Most marsupials live in Australia, although the opossums—which are classified as marsupials despite not having a pouch—live in the Americas. The order Monotremata is made up of the platypus and its relatives (the echidnas, or spiny anteaters). The monotremes are primitive mammals that lay eggs, which the mother incubates. The monotremes are found only in Australia and New Guinea.

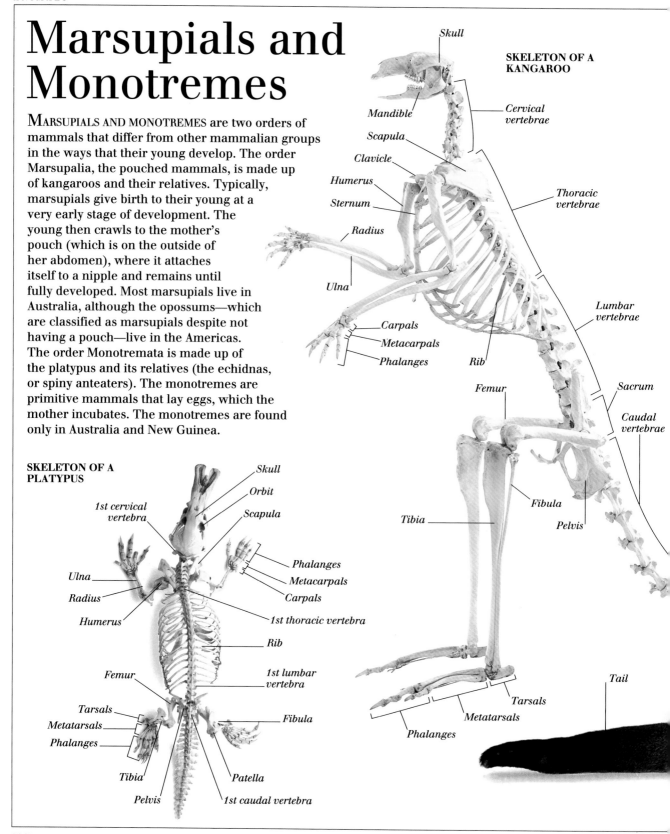

SKELETON OF A KANGAROO

Skull
Mandible
Cervical vertebrae
Scapula
Clavicle
Humerus
Sternum
Radius
Ulna
Thoracic vertebrae
Lumbar vertebrae
Carpals
Metacarpals
Phalanges
Rib
Femur
Sacrum
Caudal vertebrae
Fibula
Pelvis
Tibia
Tarsals
Metatarsals
Phalanges
Tail

SKELETON OF A PLATYPUS

Skull
Orbit
1st cervical vertebra
Scapula
Phalanges
Metacarpals
Carpals
Ulna
Radius
Humerus
1st thoracic vertebra
Rib
1st lumbar vertebra
Femur
Fibula
Tarsals
Metatarsals
Phalanges
Tibia
Patella
Pelvis
1st caudal vertebra

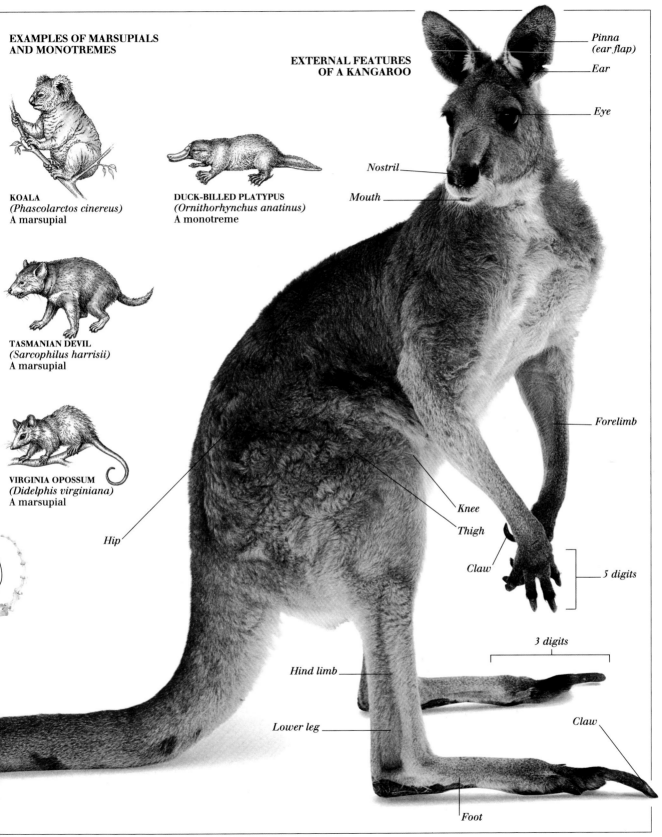

EXAMPLES OF MARSUPIALS AND MONOTREMES

EXTERNAL FEATURES OF A KANGAROO

KOALA
(Phascolarctos cinereus)
A marsupial

DUCK-BILLED PLATYPUS
(Ornithorhynchus anatinus)
A monotreme

TASMANIAN DEVIL
(Sarcophilus harrisii)
A marsupial

VIRGINIA OPOSSUM
(Didelphis virginiana)
A marsupial

Pinna (ear flap)

Ear

Eye

Nostril

Mouth

Forelimb

Hip

Knee

Thigh

Claw

5 digits

3 digits

Hind limb

Lower leg

Claw

Foot

THE
HUMAN BODY

Body features

ALTHOUGH THERE IS enormous variation between the external appearances of humans, all bodies contain the same basic features. The outward form of the human body depends on the size of the skeleton, the shape of the muscles, the thickness of the fat layer beneath the skin, the elasticity or sagginess of the skin, and the person's age and sex. Males tend to be taller than females, with broader shoulders, more body hair, and a different pattern of fat deposits under the skin; the female body tends to be less muscular and has a shallower and wider pelvis to allow for childbirth.

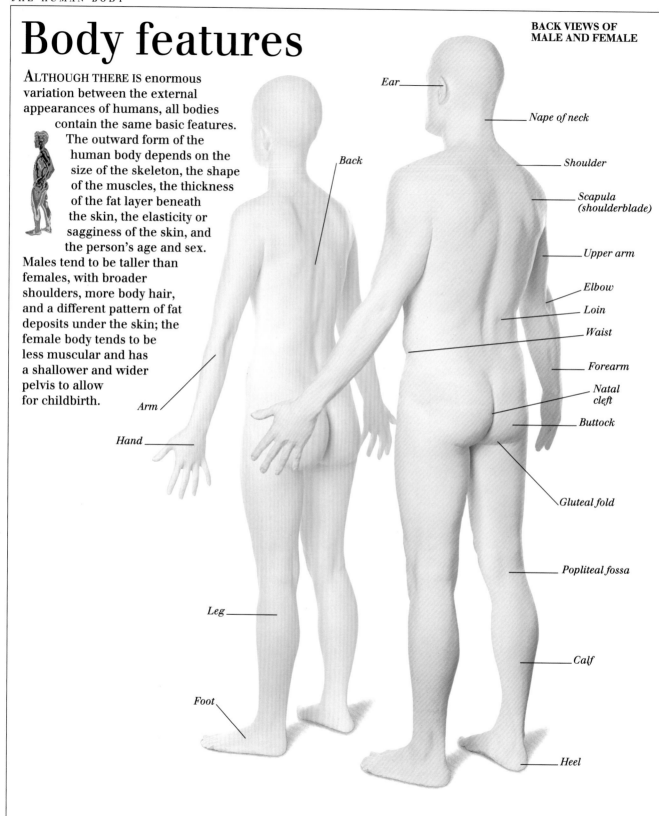

Ear

Nape of neck

Shoulder

Scapula
(shoulderblade)

Upper arm

Elbow

Loin

Waist

Forearm

Natal
cleft

Buttock

Gluteal fold

Popliteal fossa

Calf

Heel

Back

Arm

Hand

Leg

Foot

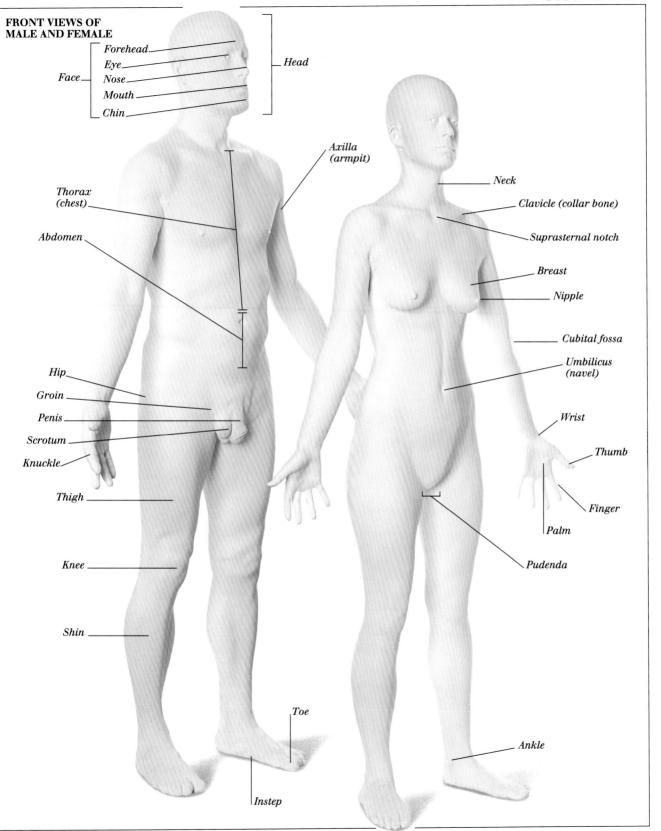

**FRONT VIEWS OF
MALE AND FEMALE**

Forehead

Eye

Face — Nose

Mouth

Chin

Head

Axilla
(armpit)

Neck

Clavicle (collar bone)

Suprasternal notch

Thorax
(chest)

Abdomen

Breast

Nipple

Cubital fossa

Umbilicus
(navel)

Hip

Groin

Penis

Scrotum

Knuckle

Wrist

Thumb

Finger

Palm

Thigh

Pudenda

Knee

Shin

Toe

Ankle

Instep

Head

IN A NEWBORN BABY, the head accounts for one-quarter of the total body length; by adulthood, the proportion has reduced to one-eighth. Contained in the head are the body's main sense organs: eyes, ears, olfactory nerves that detect smells, and the taste buds of the tongue. Signals from these organs pass to the body's great coordination centre: the brain, housed in the protective, bony dome of the skull. Hair on the head insulates against heat loss, and adult males also grow thick facial hair. The face has three important openings: two nostrils through which air passes, and the mouth, which takes in nourishment and helps form speech. Although all heads are basically similar, differences in the size, shape, and colour of features produce an infinite variety of appearances.

SIDE VIEW OF EXTERNAL FEATURES OF HEAD

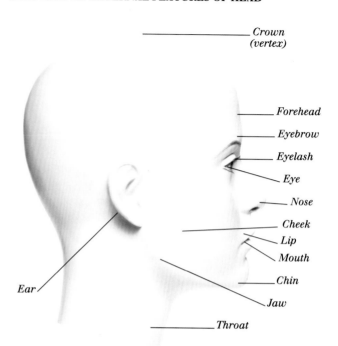

Crown (vertex)

Forehead

Eyebrow

Eyelash

Eye

Nose

Cheek

Lip

Mouth

Chin

Jaw

Throat

Ear

SECTION THROUGH HEAD

Skull

Pineal body

Pituitary gland

Cerebellum

Pons

Medulla oblongata

Pharynx

Cervical vertebra

Spinal cord

Intervertebral disc

Superior sagittal sinus

Cerebrum

Frontal sinus

Sphenoidal sinus

Superior concha

Middle concha

Inferior concha

Vestibule

Maxilla (upper jaw)

Hard palate

Soft palate

Tongue

Uvula

Mandible (lower jaw)

Palatine tonsil

Epiglottis

Trachea

Oesophagus

**FRONT VIEW OF EXTERNAL
FEATURES OF HEAD**

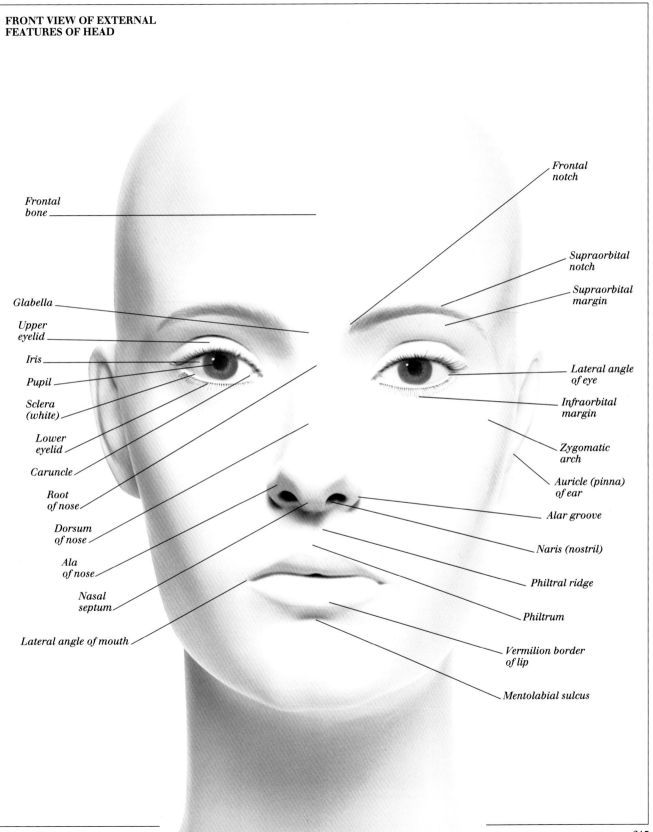

Frontal
notch

Supraorbital
notch

Supraorbital
margin

Frontal
bone

Glabella

Upper
eyelid

Iris

Pupil

Lateral angle
of eye

Sclera
(white)

Infraorbital
margin

Lower
eyelid

Zygomatic
arch

Caruncle

Auricle (pinna)
of ear

Root
of nose

Alar groove

Dorsum
of nose

Naris (nostril)

Ala
of nose

Philtral ridge

Nasal
septum

Philtrum

Lateral angle of mouth

Vermilion border
of lip

Mentolabial sulcus

Body organs

ALL THE VITAL BODY ORGANS except for the brain are enclosed within the trunk or torso (the body apart from the head and limbs). The trunk contains two large cavities separated by a muscular sheet called the diaphragm. The upper cavity, known as the thorax or chest cavity, contains the heart and lungs. The lower cavity, called the abdominal cavity, contains the stomach, intestines, liver, and pancreas, which all play a role in digesting food. Also within the trunk are the kidneys and bladder, which are part of the urinary system, and the reproductive organs, which hold the seeds of new human life. Modern imaging techniques, such as contrast X-rays and different types of scans, make it possible to see and study body organs without the need to cut through their protective coverings of skin, fat, muscle, and bone.

MAJOR INTERNAL STRUCTURES

Thyroid gland
Larynx
Heart
Right lung
Left lung
Diaphragm
Liver
Stomach
Large intestine
Small intestine
Greater omentum

IMAGING THE BODY

SCINTIGRAM OF HEART CHAMBERS

ANGIOGRAM OF RIGHT LUNG

CONTRAST X-RAY OF GALLBLADDER

SCINTIGRAM OF NERVOUS SYSTEM

DOUBLE CONTRAST X-RAY OF COLON

ULTRASOUND SCAN OF TWINS IN UTERUS

ANGIOGRAM OF KIDNEYS

ANGIOGRAM OF ARTERIES OF HEAD

CT SCAN THROUGH FEMALE CHEST

THERMOGRAM OF CHEST REGION

ANGIOGRAM OF ARTERIES OF HEART

MRI SCAN THROUGH HEAD AT EYE LEVEL

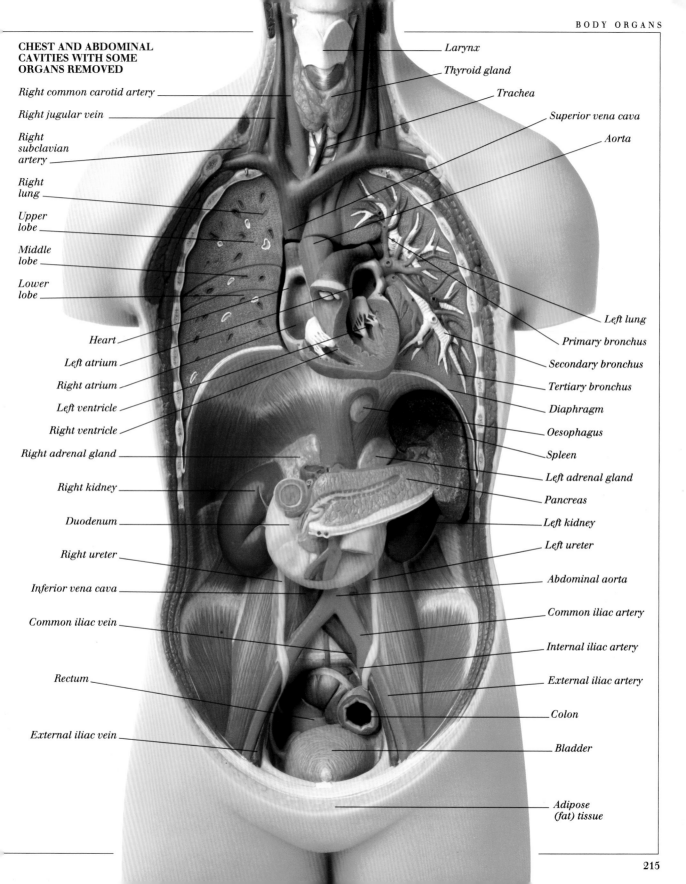

CHEST AND ABDOMINAL CAVITIES WITH SOME ORGANS REMOVED

Larynx

Thyroid gland

Right common carotid artery

Trachea

Right jugular vein

Superior vena cava

Right subclavian artery

Aorta

Right lung

Upper lobe

Middle lobe

Lower lobe

Heart

Left lung

Left atrium

Primary bronchus

Right atrium

Secondary bronchus

Left ventricle

Tertiary bronchus

Right ventricle

Diaphragm

Right adrenal gland

Oesophagus

Right kidney

Spleen

Duodenum

Left adrenal gland

Right ureter

Pancreas

Inferior vena cava

Left kidney

Common iliac vein

Left ureter

Rectum

Abdominal aorta

External iliac vein

Common iliac artery

Internal iliac artery

External iliac artery

Colon

Bladder

Adipose (fat) tissue

Body cells

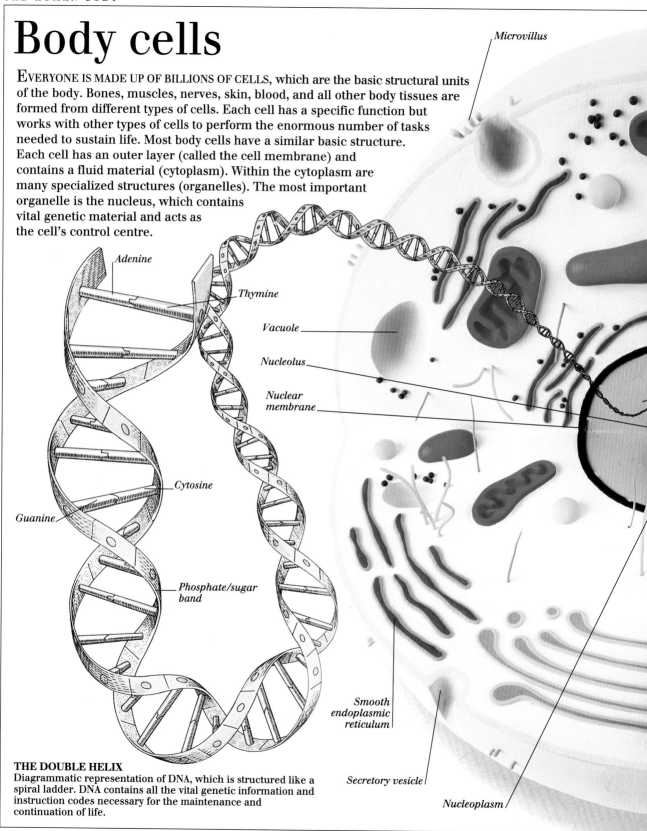

EVERYONE IS MADE UP OF BILLIONS OF CELLS, which are the basic structural units of the body. Bones, muscles, nerves, skin, blood, and all other body tissues are formed from different types of cells. Each cell has a specific function but works with other types of cells to perform the enormous number of tasks needed to sustain life. Most body cells have a similar basic structure. Each cell has an outer layer (called the cell membrane) and contains a fluid material (cytoplasm). Within the cytoplasm are many specialized structures (organelles). The most important organelle is the nucleus, which contains vital genetic material and acts as the cell's control centre.

Microvillus

Adenine

Thymine

Vacuole

Nucleolus

Nuclear membrane

Cytosine

Guanine

Phosphate/sugar band

Smooth endoplasmic reticulum

Secretory vesicle

Nucleoplasm

THE DOUBLE HELIX
Diagrammatic representation of DNA, which is structured like a spiral ladder. DNA contains all the vital genetic information and instruction codes necessary for the maintenance and continuation of life.

GENERALIZED HUMAN CELL

Cytoplasm

Lysosome

Cell membrane

Mitochondrial crista

Nucleus

Rough endoplasmic reticulum

Microfilament

Pore of nuclear membrane

Ribosome

Centriole

Mitochondrion

Microtubule

Peroxisome

Pinocytotic vesicle

Golgi complex (Golgi apparatus; Golgi body)

TYPES OF CELLS

BONE-FORMING CELL

NERVE CELLS IN SPINAL CORD

SPERM CELLS IN SEMEN

SECRETORY THYROID GLAND CELLS

ACID-SECRETING STOMACH CELLS

CONNECTIVE TISSUE CELLS

MUCUS-SECRETING DUODENAL CELLS

RED AND TWO WHITE BLOOD CELLS

FAT CELLS IN ADIPOSE TISSUE

EPITHELIAL CELLS IN CHEEK

Skeleton

THE SKELETON IS A MOBILE FRAMEWORK made up of 206 bones, approximately half of which are in the hands and feet. Although individual bones are rigid, the skeleton as a whole is remarkably flexible and allows the human body a huge range of movement. The skeleton serves as an anchorage for the skeletal muscles, and as a protective cage for the body's internal organs. Female bones are usually smaller and lighter than male bones, and the female pelvis is shallower and has a wider cavity.

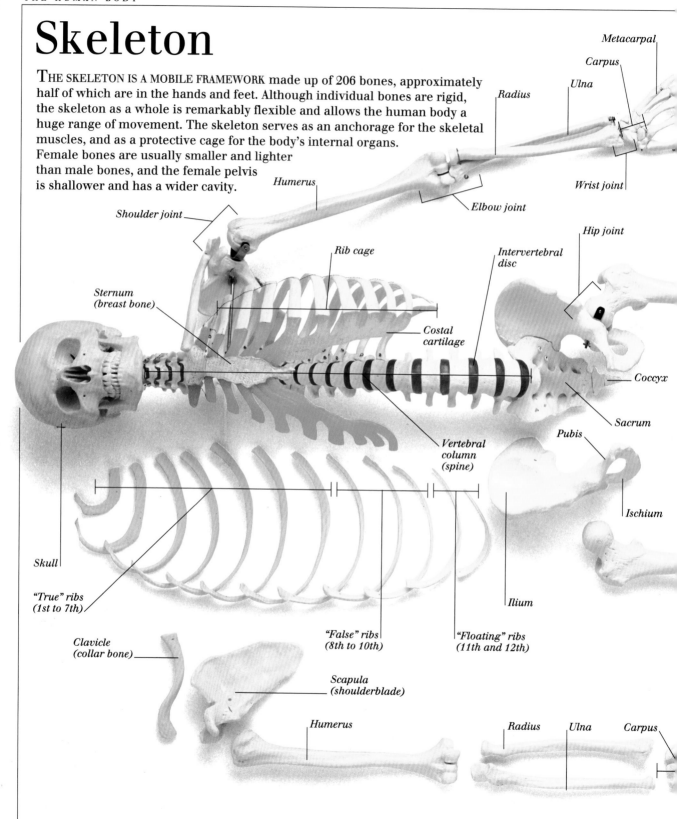

Metacarpal

Carpus

Ulna

Radius

Wrist joint

Hip joint

Humerus

Elbow joint

Shoulder joint

Rib cage

Intervertebral disc

Sternum
(breast bone)

Costal
cartilage

Coccyx

Sacrum

Pubis

Vertebral
column
(spine)

Ischium

Skull

Ilium

"True" ribs
(1st to 7th)

"False" ribs
(8th to 10th)

"Floating" ribs
(11th and 12th)

Clavicle
(collar bone)

Scapula
(shoulderblade)

Humerus

Radius

Ulna

Carpus

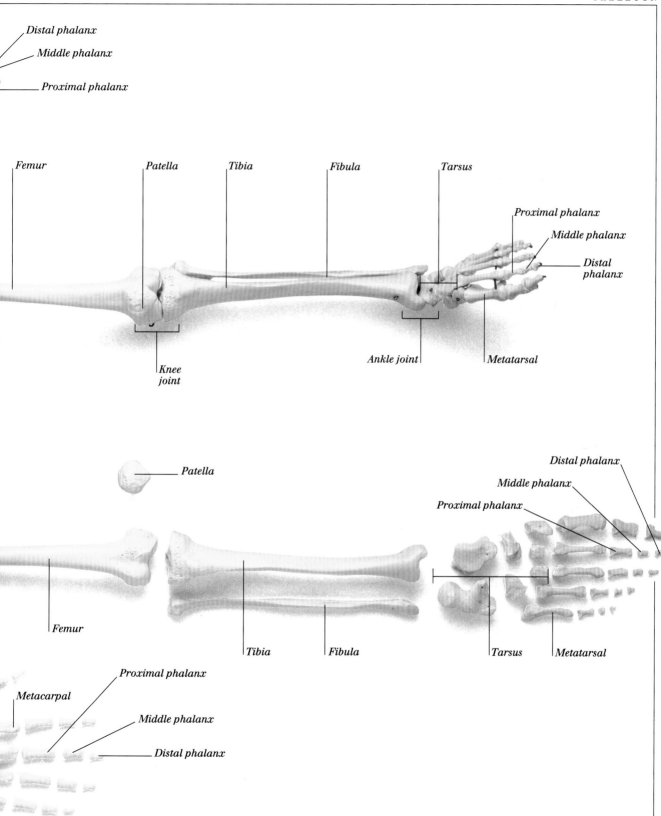

Distal phalanx

Middle phalanx

Proximal phalanx

Femur

Patella

Tibia

Fibula

Tarsus

Proximal phalanx

Middle phalanx

Distal phalanx

Knee joint

Ankle joint

Metatarsal

Patella

Distal phalanx

Middle phalanx

Proximal phalanx

Femur

Tibia

Fibula

Tarsus

Metatarsal

Metacarpal

Proximal phalanx

Middle phalanx

Distal phalanx

Skull

THE SKULL is the most complicated bony structure of the body but every feature serves a purpose. Internally, the main hollow chamber of the skull has three levels that support the brain, with every bump and hollow corresponding to the shape of the brain. Underneath and towards the back of the skull is a large round hole, the foramen magnum, through which the spinal cord passes. To the front of this are many smaller openings through which nerves, arteries, and veins pass to and from the brain. The roof of the skull is formed from four thin, curved bones that are firmly fixed together from the age of about two years. At the front of the skull are the two orbits, which contain the eyeballs, and a central hole for the airway of the nose. The jaw bone hinges on either side at ear level.

RIGHT SIDE VIEW OF A FETAL SKULL

Anterior fontanelle

Parietal bone

Coronal suture

Frontal bone

Nasal bone

Mental symphysis

Lambdoid suture

Occipital bone

Sphenoidal fontanelle

Mastoid fontanelle

External auditory meatus

RIGHT SIDE VIEW OF SKULL

Coronal suture

Frontal bone

Greater wing of sphenoid bone

Frontozygomatic suture

Parietal bone

Supraorbital margin

Squamous suture

Orbital cavity

Nasal bone

Anterior nasal spine

Maxilla (upper jaw)

Lambdoid suture

Mandible (lower jaw)

Occipital bone

Temporal bone

External auditory meatus

Mastoid process

Condyle

Coronoid process

Zygomatic bone

Mental foramen

VIEW OF SKULL FROM BELOW

External occipital crest

Foramen magnum

Occipital condyle

Carotid canal

Mastoid process

Pharyngeal tubercle

Pterygoid plate

Pterygoid hamulus

Greater palatine foramen

Posterior nasal aperture

Styloid process

Zygomatic arch

Posterior border of vomer

Concha

Mandible (lower jaw)

FRONT VIEW OF SKULL

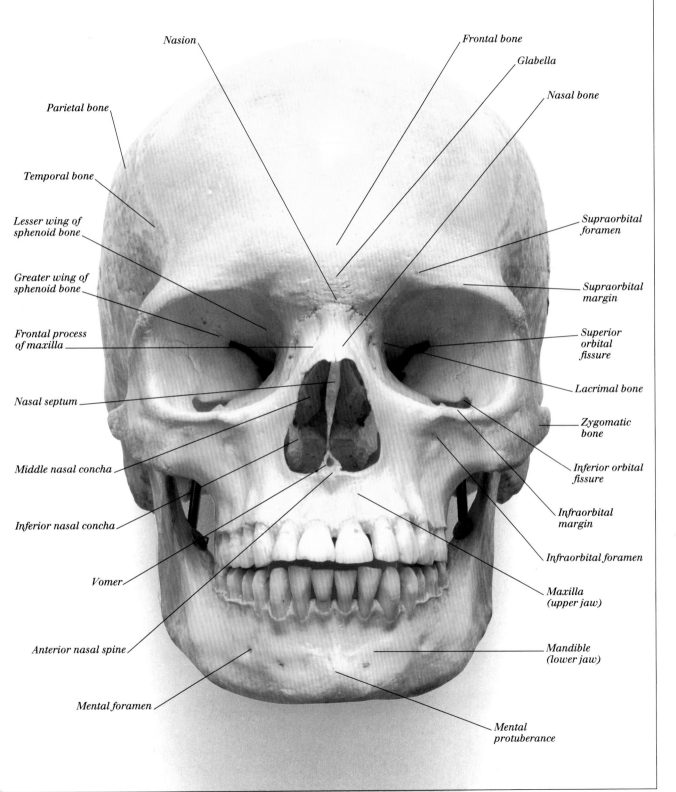

Nasion

Frontal bone

Glabella

Nasal bone

Parietal bone

Temporal bone

Lesser wing of
sphenoid bone

Greater wing of
sphenoid bone

Frontal process
of maxilla

Nasal septum

Middle nasal concha

Inferior nasal concha

Vomer

Anterior nasal spine

Mental foramen

Supraorbital
foramen

Supraorbital
margin

Superior
orbital
fissure

Lacrimal bone

Zygomatic
bone

Inferior orbital
fissure

Infraorbital
margin

Infraorbital foramen

Maxilla
(upper jaw)

Mandible
(lower jaw)

Mental
protuberance

Spine

THE SPINE (OR VERTEBRAL COLUMN) has two main functions: it serves as a protective surrounding for the delicate spinal cord and forms the supporting back bone of the skeleton. The spine consists of 24 separate differently shaped bones (vertebrae) with a curved, triangular bone (the sacrum) at the bottom. The sacrum is made up of fused vertebrae; at its lower end is a small tail-like structure made up of tiny bones collectively called the coccyx. Between each pair of vertebrae is a disc of cartilage that cushions the bones during movement. The top two vertebrae differ in appearance from the others and work as a pair: the first, called the atlas, rotates around a stout vertical peg on the second, the axis. This arrangement allows the skull to move freely up and down, and from side to side.

SPINE DIVIDED INTO VERTEBRAL SECTIONS　　FRONT

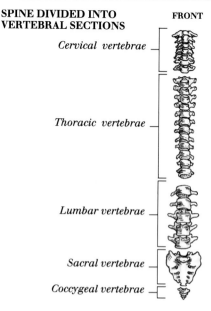

Cervical vertebrae

Thoracic vertebrae

Lumbar vertebrae

Sacral vertebrae

Coccygeal vertebrae

TYPES OF VERTEBRAE (VIEWED FROM ABOVE)

ATLAS

Lateral mass with superior articular facet

Anterior arch

Posterior arch

Anterior tubercle

Posterior tubercle

Vertebral foramen

Transverse foramen

Transverse process

AXIS

Facet

Dens

Vertebral foramen

Spinous process

Lamina

Transverse process and foramen

CERVICAL VERTEBRA

Body

Superior articular process

Anterior tubercle

Spinous process

Vertebral foramen

Posterior tubercle

Transverse foramen

SKULL AND SPINE

Skull

Cervical vertebrae

1st 2nd 3rd 4th 5th 6th 7th

Thoracic vertebrae

1st 2nd 3rd 4th 5th 6th 7th

Atlas　Axis

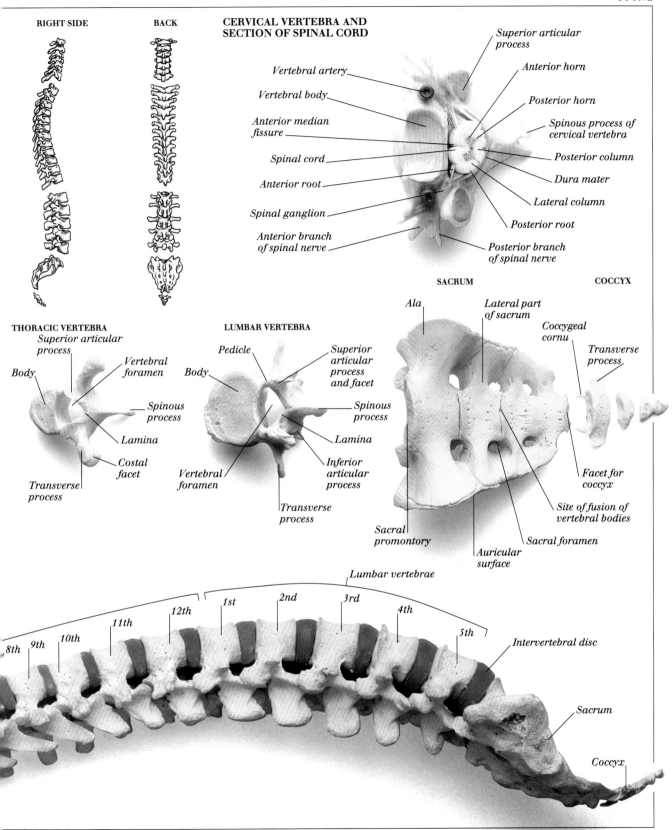

RIGHT SIDE

BACK

CERVICAL VERTEBRA AND SECTION OF SPINAL CORD

Superior articular process

Vertebral artery

Anterior horn

Vertebral body

Posterior horn

Anterior median fissure

Spinous process of cervical vertebra

Spinal cord

Posterior column

Anterior root

Dura mater

Spinal ganglion

Lateral column

Anterior branch of spinal nerve

Posterior root

Posterior branch of spinal nerve

SACRUM

COCCYX

Ala

Lateral part of sacrum

Coccygeal cornu

Transverse process

THORACIC VERTEBRA

Superior articular process

Body

Vertebral foramen

Spinous process

Lamina

Costal facet

Transverse process

LUMBAR VERTEBRA

Pedicle

Body

Superior articular process and facet

Spinous process

Lamina

Inferior articular process

Vertebral foramen

Transverse process

Sacral promontory

Auricular surface

Facet for coccyx

Site of fusion of vertebral bodies

Sacral foramen

Lumbar vertebrae

1st

2nd

3rd

4th

5th

8th

9th

10th

11th

12th

Intervertebral disc

Sacrum

Coccyx

Bones and joints

BONES FORM the body's hard, strong skeletal framework. Each bone has a hard, compact exterior surrounding a spongy, lighter interior. The long bones of the arms and legs, such as the femur (thigh bone), have a central cavity containing bone marrow. Bones are composed chiefly of calcium, phosphorus, and a fibrous substance known as collagen. Bones meet at joints, which are of several different types. For example, the hip is a ball-and-socket joint that allows the femur a wide range of movement, whereas finger joints are simple hinge joints that allow only bending and straightening. Joints are held in place by bands of tissue called ligaments. Movement of joints is facilitated by the smooth hyaline cartilage that covers the bone ends and by the synovial membrane that lines and lubricates the joint.

LIGAMENTS SURROUNDING HIP JOINT

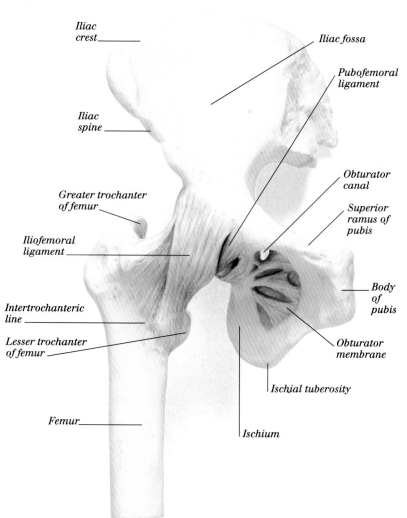

Iliac crest

Iliac fossa

Pubofemoral ligament

Iliac spine

Obturator canal

Superior ramus of pubis

Greater trochanter of femur

Iliofemoral ligament

Body of pubis

Intertrochanteric line

Lesser trochanter of femur

Obturator membrane

Ischial tuberosity

Femur

Ischium

SECTION THROUGH LEFT FEMUR

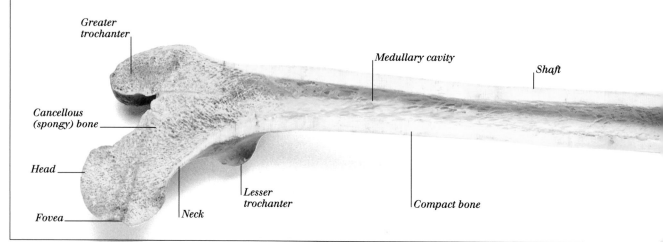

Greater trochanter

Medullary cavity

Shaft

Cancellous (spongy) bone

Head

Lesser trochanter

Compact bone

Fovea

Neck

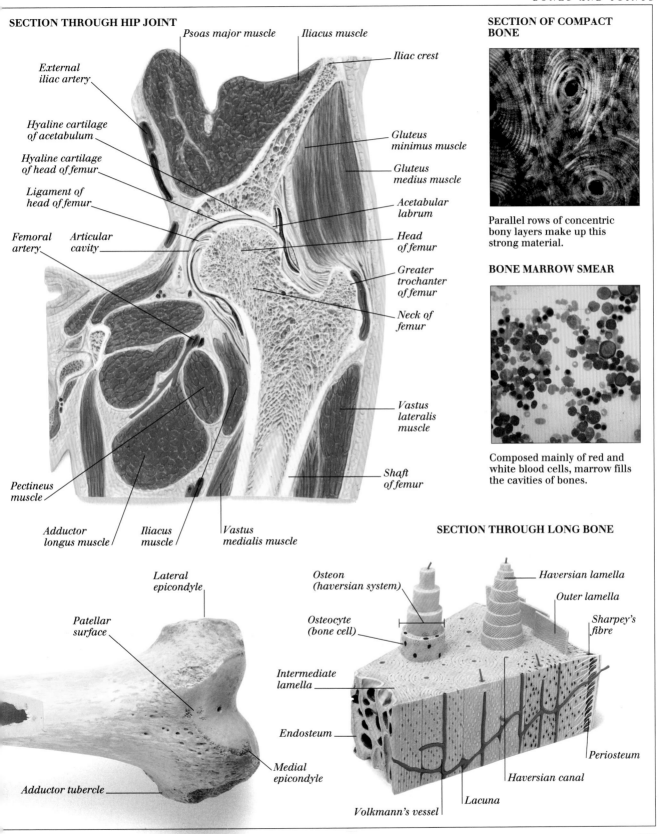

SECTION THROUGH HIP JOINT

Psoas major muscle

Iliacus muscle

Iliac crest

External iliac artery

Hyaline cartilage of acetabulum

Hyaline cartilage of head of femur

Ligament of head of femur

Femoral artery

Articular cavity

Pectineus muscle

Adductor longus muscle

Iliacus muscle

Vastus medialis muscle

Gluteus minimus muscle

Gluteus medius muscle

Acetabular labrum

Head of femur

Greater trochanter of femur

Neck of femur

Vastus lateralis muscle

Shaft of femur

SECTION OF COMPACT BONE

Parallel rows of concentric bony layers make up this strong material.

BONE MARROW SMEAR

Composed mainly of red and white blood cells, marrow fills the cavities of bones.

Lateral epicondyle

Patellar surface

Adductor tubercle

Medial epicondyle

SECTION THROUGH LONG BONE

Osteon (haversian system)

Osteocyte (bone cell)

Intermediate lamella

Endosteum

Volkmann's vessel

Lacuna

Haversian canal

Periosteum

Sharpey's fibre

Outer lamella

Haversian lamella

Muscles 1

THERE ARE THREE MAIN TYPES OF MUSCLE: skeletal muscle (also called voluntary muscle because it can be consciously controlled); smooth muscle (also called involuntary muscle because it is not under voluntary control); and the specialized muscle tissue of the heart. Humans have more than 600 skeletal muscles, which differ in size and shape according to the jobs they do. Skeletal muscles are attached either directly or indirectly (via tendons) to bones, and work in opposing pairs (one muscle in the pair contracts while the other relaxes) to produce body movements as diverse as walking, threading a needle, and an array of facial expressions. Smooth muscles occur in the walls of internal body organs and perform actions such as forcing food through the intestines, contracting the uterus (womb) in childbirth, and pumping blood through the blood vessels.

SOME OTHER MUSCLES IN THE BODY

Iris

Pupil

IRIS
The muscle fibres contract and dilate (expand) to alter pupil size.

TONGUE
Interlacing layers of muscle allow great mobility.

ILEUM
Opposing muscle layers transport semi-digested food.

SUPERFICIAL SKELETAL MUSCLES

FRONT VIEW

Brachioradialis

Flexors of forearm

Brachialis

Frontalis

Orbicularis oculi

Temporalis

Sternocleidomastoid

Trapezius

Pectoralis major

Deltoid

Serratus anterior

Biceps brachii

Rectus abdominis

Linea alba

External oblique

Tensor fasciae latae

Iliopsoas

Pectineus

Adductor longus

Rectus femoris

Sartorius

Vastus lateralis

Gracilis

Vastus medialis

Gastrocnemius

Tibialis anterior

BACK VIEW

Extensors of hand

Flexors of hand

Temporalis

Sternocleidomastoid

Trapezius

Deltoid

Triceps brachii

Teres minor

Teres major

Infraspinatus

Rhomboideus major

Latissimus dorsi

Gluteus maximus

Adductor magnus

Gracilis

Biceps femoris

Semitendinosus

Gastrocnemius

Soleus

Peroneus brevis

MOVEMENT OF THE FOREARM
Controlled movement of the limbs relies on coordinated relaxation and contraction of opposing muscles. To raise the forearm, the biceps (two-rooted muscle) contracts and shortens while the triceps (three-rooted muscle) relaxes; the reverse occurs when the forearm is lowered.

Triceps in resting phase

Biceps in resting phase

Forearm at rest

Triceps relaxes

Biceps contracts

Forearm half raised

Triceps fully relaxed

Biceps fully contracted

Forearm fully raised

Triceps contracts

Biceps relaxes

Forearm half lowered

Triceps back in resting phase

Biceps back in resting phase

Forearm back at rest

Muscles 2

SKELETAL MUSCLE FIBRE

Myofibril

Sarcomere

Motor end plate

Synaptic knob

Nucleus

Sarcoplasmic reticulum

Schwann cell

Sarcolemma

Motor neuron

Endomysium

Node of Ranvier

MUSCLES OF FACIAL EXPRESSION

A single expression is the result of movement of many muscles; the main muscles of expression are shown in action below.

FRONTALIS

CORRUGATOR SUPERCILII

ORBICULARIS ORIS

ZYGOMATICUS MAJOR

DEPRESSOR ANGULI ORIS

TYPES OF MUSCLE

CARDIAC MUSCLE

SKELETAL MUSCLE

SMOOTH MUSCLE

CONTRACTION OF SKELETAL MUSCLE

RELAXED STATE

CONTRACTED STATE

**MUSCLES OF
HEAD AND NECK**

Frontalis

Procerus

Temporalis

Corrugator
supercilii

Orbicularis
oculi

Levator labii
superioris

Nasalis

Zygomaticus
major

Orbicularis oris

Buccinator

Masseter

Risorius

Depressor labii
inferioris

Levator anguli oris

Platysma

Mentalis

Depressor anguli oris

Thyrohyoid

Scalenus medius

Sternocleidomastoid

Sternohyoid

Omohyoid

Cricothyroid

Trapezius

Hands

THE HUMAN HAND is an extremely versatile tool, capable of delicate manipulation as well as powerful gripping actions. The arrangement of its 27 small bones, moved by 37 skeletal muscles that are connected to the bones by tendons, allows a wide range of movements. Our ability to bring the tips of our thumbs and fingers together, combined with the extraordinary sensitivity of our fingertips due to their rich supply of nerve endings, makes our hands uniquely dextrous.

X-RAY OF LEFT HAND OF A YOUNG CHILD

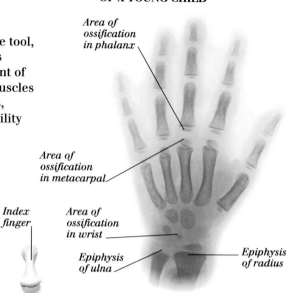

Area of ossification in phalanx

Area of ossification in metacarpal

Area of ossification in wrist

Epiphysis of ulna

Epiphysis of radius

Areas of cartilage in the wrist and at the ends of the finger bones are the sites of growth and have still to ossify.

BONES OF HAND

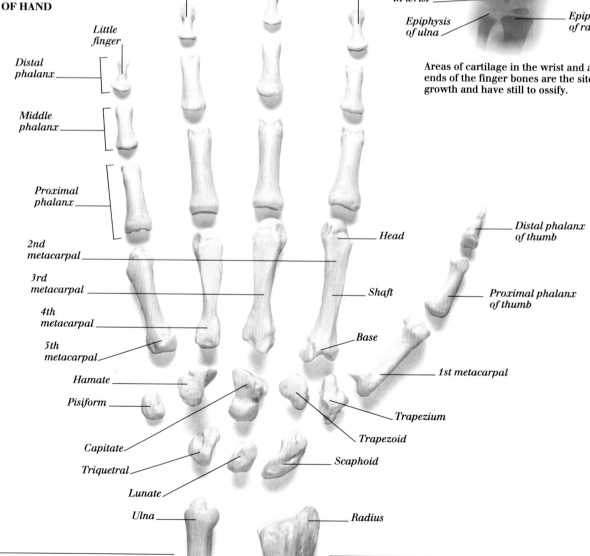

Ring finger

Middle finger

Index finger

Little finger

Distal phalanx

Middle phalanx

Proximal phalanx

2nd metacarpal

3rd metacarpal

4th metacarpal

5th metacarpal

Hamate

Pisiform

Capitate

Triquetral

Lunate

Ulna

Head

Shaft

Base

Trapezium

Trapezoid

Scaphoid

1st metacarpal

Distal phalanx of thumb

Proximal phalanx of thumb

Radius

STRUCTURES UNDERLYING SKIN OF PALM OF HAND

Flexor pollicis brevis muscle

Opponens pollicis muscle

Abductor pollicis brevis muscle

Flexor retinaculum

Radial artery

Adductor pollicis muscle

2nd lumbrical muscle

Digital artery

Digital nerve

Flexor digitorum tendon

Opponens digiti minimi muscle

Abductor digiti minimi muscle

Ulnar nerve

Ulnar artery

Palmaris longus tendon

EXTERNAL FEATURES OF BACK OF HAND

Little finger

Distal interphalangeal joint

Proximal interphalangeal joint

Extensor digitorum tendon

Head of ulna

Ring finger

Middle finger

Cuticle

Lunule

Index finger

Nail

Metacarpophalangeal joint

Wrist

Distal end of radius

Thumb

Feet

THE FEET AND TOES are essential elements in body movement. They bear and propel the weight of the body during walking and running, and also help to maintain balance during changes of body position. Each foot has 26 bones, more than 100 ligaments, and 33 muscles, some of which are attached to the lower leg. The heel pad and the arch of the foot act as shock absorbers, providing a cushion against the jolts that occur with every step.

BONES OF FOOT

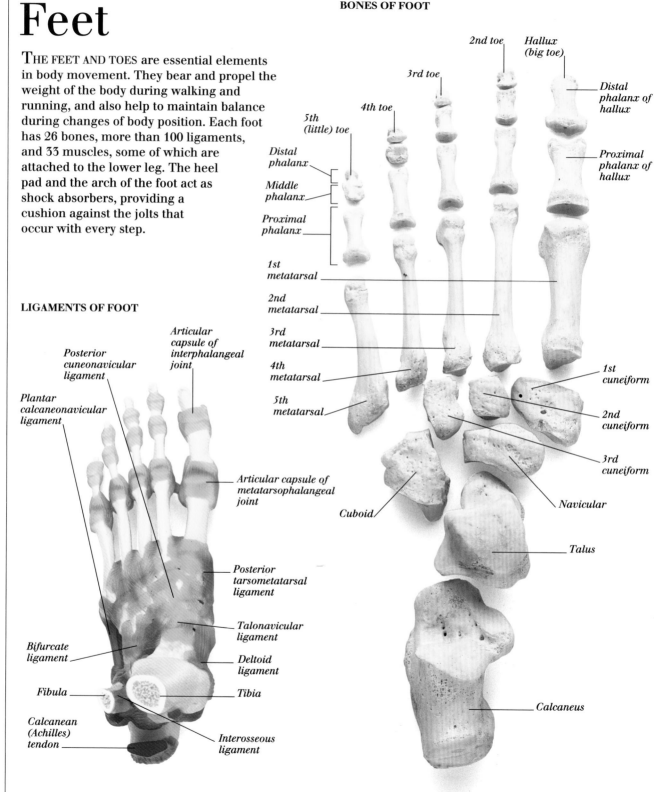

2nd toe

Hallux (big toe)

3rd toe

Distal phalanx of hallux

4th toe

5th (little) toe

Distal phalanx

Proximal phalanx of hallux

Middle phalanx

Proximal phalanx

1st metatarsal

2nd metatarsal

3rd metatarsal

4th metatarsal

5th metatarsal

1st cuneiform

2nd cuneiform

3rd cuneiform

Navicular

Cuboid

Talus

Calcaneus

LIGAMENTS OF FOOT

Posterior cuneonavicular ligament

Articular capsule of interphalangeal joint

Plantar calcaneonavicular ligament

Articular capsule of metatarsophalangeal joint

Posterior tarsometatarsal ligament

Talonavicular ligament

Bifurcate ligament

Deltoid ligament

Fibula

Tibia

Calcanean (Achilles) tendon

Interosseous ligament

STRUCTURES UNDERLYING SKIN OF FOOT

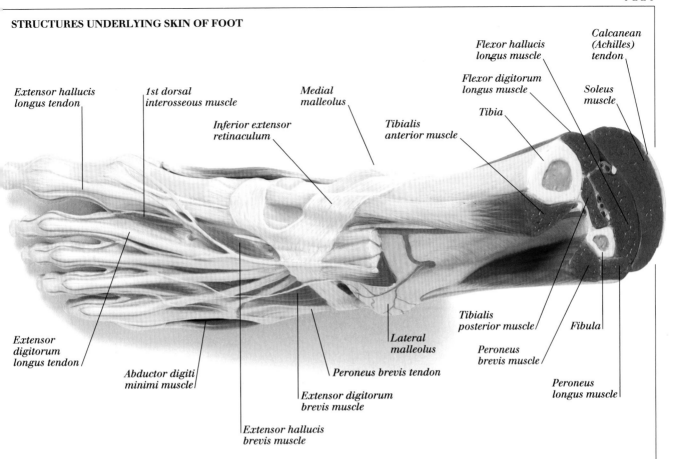

Extensor hallucis
longus tendon

1st dorsal
interosseous muscle

Medial
malleolus

Flexor hallucis
longus muscle

Calcanean
(Achilles)
tendon

Flexor digitorum
longus muscle

Soleus
muscle

Inferior extensor
retinaculum

Tibialis
anterior muscle

Tibia

Extensor
digitorum
longus tendon

Abductor digiti
minimi muscle

Extensor hallucis
brevis muscle

Extensor digitorum
brevis muscle

Peroneus brevis tendon

Lateral
malleolus

Tibialis
posterior muscle

Peroneus
brevis muscle

Fibula

Peroneus
longus muscle

EXTERNAL FEATURES OF FOOT

Toenail

Hallux
(big toe)

Interphalangeal
joint

Extensor hallucis
longus tendon

Extensor digitorum
longus tendon

Medial malleolus

2nd toe

3rd toe

4th toe

5th
(little) toe

Lateral malleolus

233

Skin and hair

SKIN IS THE BODY'S LARGEST ORGAN, a waterproof barrier that protects the internal organs against infection, injury, and harmful sun rays. The skin is also an important sensory organ and helps to control body temperature. The outer layer of the skin, known as the epidermis, is coated with keratin, a tough, horny protein that is also the chief constituent of hair and nails. Dead cells are shed from the skin's surface and are replaced by new cells from the base of the epidermis, the region that also produces the skin pigment, melanin. The dermis contains most of the skin's living structures, and includes nerve endings, blood vessels, elastic fibres, sweat glands that cool the skin, and sebaceous glands that produce oil to keep the skin supple. Beneath the dermis lies the subcutaneous tissue (hypodermis), which is rich in fat and blood vessels. Hair shafts grow from hair follicles situated in the dermis and subcutaneous tissue. Hair grows on every part of the skin apart from the palms of the hands and soles of the feet.

SECTION OF HAIR

Medulla

Cortex

Melanin granule

Cell nucleus residue

Macrofibril

Cuticle

SECTIONS OF DIFFERENT TYPES OF SKIN

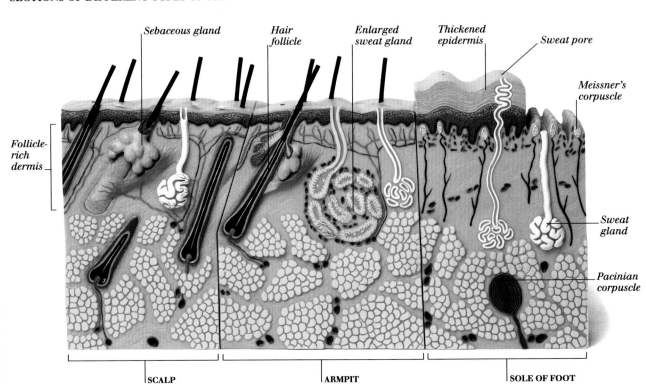

Sebaceous gland

Hair follicle

Enlarged sweat gland

Thickened epidermis

Sweat pore

Meissner's corpuscle

Follicle-rich dermis

Sweat gland

Pacinian corpuscle

SCALP

ARMPIT

SOLE OF FOOT

SECTION OF SKIN

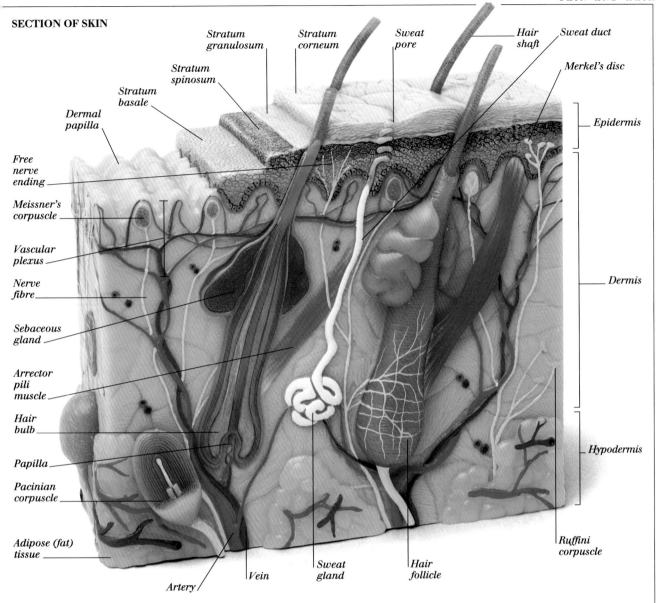

Stratum granulosum

Stratum corneum

Sweat pore

Hair shaft

Sweat duct

Stratum spinosum

Merkel's disc

Stratum basale

Epidermis

Dermal papilla

Free nerve ending

Meissner's corpuscle

Vascular plexus

Nerve fibre

Sebaceous gland

Arrector pili muscle

Hair bulb

Papilla

Pacinian corpuscle

Adipose (fat) tissue

Dermis

Hypodermis

Ruffini corpuscle

Artery

Vein

Sweat gland

Hair follicle

PHOTOMICROGRAPHS OF SKIN AND HAIR

SECTION OF SKIN
The flaky cells at the skin's surface are shed continuously.

SWEAT PORE
This allows loss of fluid as part of temperature control.

SKIN HAIR
Two hairs pushing through the outer layer of skin.

HEAD HAIR
The root and part of the shaft of a hair from the scalp.

Brain

THE BRAIN IS THE MAJOR ORGAN of the central nervous system and the control centre for all the body's voluntary and involuntary activities. It is also responsible for the complexities of thought, memory, emotion, and language. In adults, this complex organ is a mere 1.4 kg (3 lb) in weight, containing over 10 thousand million nerve cells. Three distinct regions can easily be seen – the brainstem, the cerebellum, and the large cerebrum. The brainstem controls vital body functions, such as breathing and digestion. The cerebellum's main functions are the maintenance of posture and the coordination of body movements. The cerebrum, which consists of the right and left cerebral hemispheres joined by the corpus callosum, is the site of most conscious and intelligent activities.

MRI SCAN OF TRANSVERSE SECTION THROUGH BRAIN

White matter

Grey matter

Skull

Scalp

Lateral ventricle

Longitudinal fissure

Coronal section

Sagittal section

SAGITTAL SECTION THROUGH BRAIN

Central sulcus

Fornix

Cerebrum

Parietal lobe

Parieto-occipital sulcus

Corpus callosum

Thalamus

Pineal body

Occipital lobe

Frontal lobe

Aqueduct

Hypothalamus

Cerebellum

Optic chiasma

4th ventricle

Pituitary gland

Spinal cord

Mesencephalon (midbrain)

Pons

Brainstem

Medulla oblongata

SECTION THROUGH SKULL AND BRAIN

Scalp
Epicranial aponeurosis
Arachnoid granulation
Pericranium
Skull
Lateral lacuna
Dura mater
Arachnoid mater
Superior sagittal sinus
Pia mater
Falx cerebri
Subarachnoid space
Cerebral vessel
Cerebrum { Grey matter / White matter

EXTERNAL ANATOMY OF BRAIN

Parietal lobe
Parieto-occipital sulcus
Precentral gyrus
Postcentral gyrus
Central sulcus
Frontal lobe
Lateral sulcus
Occipital lobe
Temporal lobe
Cerebellum

SPECIFIC ROLES OF AREAS OF CEREBRUM

Skilled movements
Basic movements
Sensation
Visual recognition
Behaviour and emotion
Speech
Vision
Hearing
Balance and muscle coordination

CORONAL SECTION THROUGH BRAIN

Corpus callosum
Longitudinal fissure
Grey matter / White matter } Cerebrum
Caudate nucleus
Lateral ventricle
Fornix
Lentiform nucleus
Internal capsule
Thalamus
Crus cerebri of midbrain
3rd ventricle
Pons
Medulla oblongata
Cerebellum

NERVE CELLS IN BRAIN

The dark cells are Purkinje's cells, which are among the largest nerve cells in the body.

Nervous system

THE NERVOUS SYSTEM IS THE BODY'S internal, electrochemical, communications network. Its main parts are the brain, spinal cord, and nerves. The brain and spinal cord form the central nervous system (CNS), the body's chief controlling and coordinating centres. Billions of long neurons, many grouped as nerves, make up the peripheral nervous system, transmitting nerve impulses between the CNS and other regions of the body. Each neuron has three parts: a cell body, branching dendrites that receive chemical signals from other neurons, and a tube-like axon that conveys these signals as electrical impulses.

CENTRAL AND PERIPHERAL NERVOUS SYSTEMS

Cranial nerves

Cerebrum

Cerebellum

Cervical nerves

Brachial plexus

Spinal cord

Thoracic nerves

Radial nerve

Median nerve

Ulnar nerve

Lumbar nerves

Sacral nerves

Sacral plexus

Femoral nerve

Pudendal nerve

Sciatic nerve

Cutaneous nerve

Common peroneal nerve

Posterior tibial nerve

Superficial peroneal nerve

Deep peroneal nerve

SECTION THROUGH SPINAL CORD

Spinal ganglion

Grey matter

Central canal

Posterior root of spinal nerve

Spinal nerve

White matter

Anterior median fissure

Anterior root of spinal nerve

STRUCTURE OF A MOTOR NEURON

Cell body

Nucleus

Synaptic knob

Axon hillock

Axon

Dendrite

Nucleolus

Nissl body

Schwann cell

Node of Ranvier

Myelin sheath

Mitochondrion

TYPES OF NERVE ENDING

FREE NERVE ENDING

MEISSNER'S CORPUSCLE

MERKEL'S DISC

RUFFINI CORPUSCLE

PACINIAN CORPUSCLE

STRUCTURE OF A SYNAPTIC KNOB

Presynaptic axon

Microtubule

Neurofilament

Endoplasmic reticulum

Mitochondrion

Synaptic vesicle

Neurotransmitter

Presynaptic membrane

TYPES OF NEURON

MULTIPOLAR

Motor end plate

Node of Ranvier

Schwann cell

Myelin sheath

Cell body

Axon

Nucleus

Dendrite

Receptor

UNIPOLAR

Dendrite

Axon

Cell body

Nucleus

BIPOLAR

Dendrite

Axon

Cell body

Nucleus

Dendrite

239

Eye

THE EYE IS THE ORGAN OF SIGHT. The two eyeballs, protected within bony sockets called orbits and on the outside by the eyelids, eyebrows, and tear film, are directly connected to the brain by the optic nerves. Each eye is moved by six muscles, which are attached around the eyeball. Light rays entering the eye through the pupil are focused by the cornea and lens to form an image on the retina. The retina contains millions of light-sensitive cells, called rods and cones, which convert the image into a pattern of nerve impulses. These impulses are transmitted along the optic nerve to the brain. Information from the two optic nerves is processed in the brain to produce a single coordinated image.

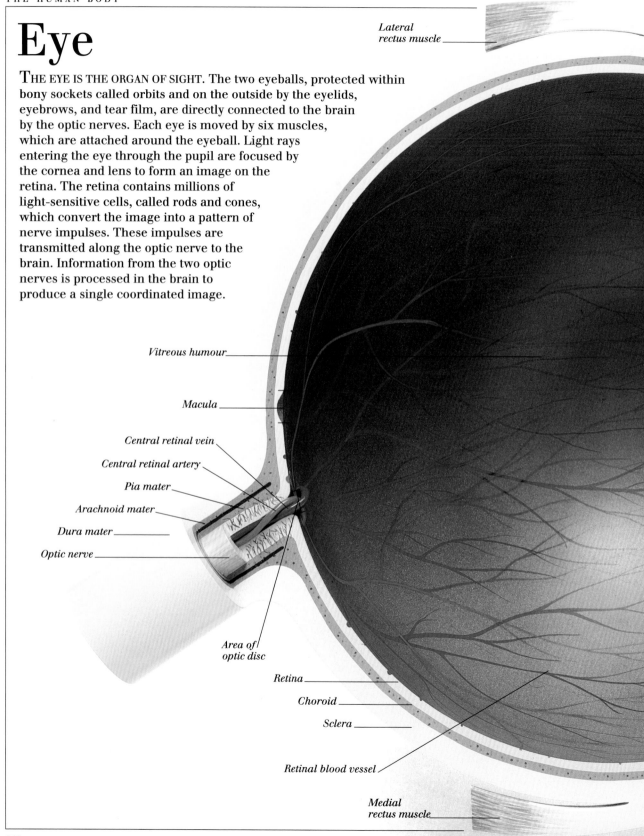

Lateral rectus muscle

Vitreous humour

Macula

Central retinal vein

Central retinal artery

Pia mater

Arachnoid mater

Dura mater

Optic nerve

Area of optic disc

Retina

Choroid

Sclera

Retinal blood vessel

Medial rectus muscle

SECTION THROUGH LEFT EYE

LACRIMAL (TEAR-PRODUCING) APPARATUS

Lacrimal sac

Lacrimal canaliculus

Lacrimal gland

Middle meatus

Middle nasal concha

Nasal septum

Inferior nasal concha

Nasolacrimal duct

Lacrimal punctum

Iris

Anterior chamber

Posterior chamber

Aqueous humour

Conjunctiva

Pupil

Cornea

Lens

Sphincter muscle

Dilator muscle

Zonular ligament

Sinus venosus sclerae

Iridocorneal angle

Ciliary body

Ora serrata

OPHTHALMOSCOPIC VIEW OF RETINA

Retinal blood vessel

Optic disc

Macula

The blind spot, where the optic nerve leaves the eye, can be clearly seen as a light circular area towards the centre of the image.

MUSCLES SURROUNDING RIGHT EYE

Medial rectus

Superior oblique

Trochlea

Superior rectus

Levator palpebrae superioris

Annular tendon

Inferior rectus

Lateral rectus

Inferior oblique

Ear

THE EAR IS THE ORGAN OF HEARING AND BALANCE. The outer ear consists of a flap called the auricle or pinna and the auditory canal. The main functional parts – the middle and inner ears – are enclosed within the skull. The middle ear consists of three tiny bones, known as auditory ossicles, and the eustachian tube, which links the ear to the back of the nose. The inner ear consists of the spiral-shaped cochlea, and also the semicircular canals and the vestibule, which are the organs of balance. Sound waves entering the ear travel through the auditory canal to the tympanic membrane (eardrum), where they are converted to vibrations that are transmitted via the ossicles to the cochlea. Here, the vibrations are converted by millions of microscopic hairs into electrical nerve signals to be interpreted by the brain.

RIGHT AURICLE (PINNA)

Upper crux of antihelix

Auricle (pinna)

Triangular fossa

Scaphoid fossa

Lower crux of antihelix

Concha

Helix

Auditory canal

Antihelix

Tragus

Antitragus

Intertragic notch

External auditory meatus

Cartilaginous part of meatus

Lobule

Lobule

Temporal bone

Cartilage of auricle

Mastoid process

OSSICLES OF MIDDLE EAR

MALLEUS (HAMMER) **INCUS (ANVIL)** **STAPES (STIRRUP)**

These three tiny bones connect to form a bridge between the tympanic membrane and the oval window. With a system of membranes they convey sound vibrations to the inner ear.

INTERNAL STRUCTURE OF AMPULLA

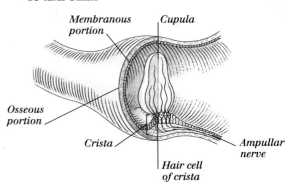

Membranous portion

Cupula

Osseous portion

Crista

Hair cell of crista

Ampullar nerve

LABYRINTH

Utricle

Saccule

Vestibular nerve

Common crus

Tympanic canal

Anterior semicircular canal

Median canal

Osseous (bony) part of meatus

Vestibular canal

Lateral semicircular canal

Tympanic membrane (eardrum)

Cochlea

Semicircular canal

Ampulla

Vestibulocochlear nerve

Cochlear nerve

Cochlea

Tensor tympani muscle

Oval window

Posterior semicircular canal

Internal carotid artery

SECTION THROUGH COCHLEA

Organ of Corti

Median canal

Vestibular canal

Vestibular membrane

Eustachian tube

Spiral ganglion

Cochlear nerve

Hair cells

Tympanic canal

Basilar membrane

Styloid process

Nose, mouth, and throat

WITH EVERY BREATH, air passes through the nasal cavity down the pharynx (throat), larynx ("voice box"), and trachea (windpipe) to the lungs. The nasal cavity warms and moistens air, and the tiny layers in its lining protect the airway against damage by foreign bodies. During swallowing, the tongue moves up and back, the larynx rises, the epiglottis closes off the entrance to the trachea, and the soft palate separates the nasal cavity from the pharynx. Saliva, secreted from three pairs of salivary glands, lubricates food to make swallowing easier; it also begins the chemical breakdown of food, and helps to produce taste. The senses of taste and smell are closely linked. Both depend on the detection of dissolved molecules by sensory receptors in the olfactory nerve endings of the nose and in the taste buds of the tongue.

STRUCTURE OF TONGUE

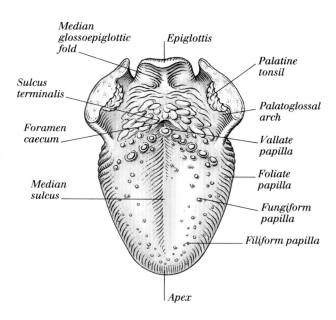

Median glossoepiglottic fold
Epiglottis
Palatine tonsil
Sulcus terminalis
Palatoglossal arch
Foramen caecum
Vallate papilla
Foliate papilla
Median sulcus
Fungiform papilla
Filiform papilla
Apex

TASTE AREAS ON TONGUE

STRUCTURES SURROUNDING PHARYNX

Lingual nerve
Tongue
Styloglossus muscle
Hyoglossus muscle
Sublingual gland
Hypoglossal nerve
Mandible (lower jaw)
Superior laryngeal nerve
Submandibular gland
Superior thyroid artery
Hyoid bone
Laryngeal prominence (Adam's apple)
Thyrohyoid muscle
Thyrohyoid membrane
Cricothyroid muscle
Cricothyroid ligament
Thyroid gland
Trachea

Bitter
Sour
Salt
Sweet

TYPES OF PAPILLAE

FILIFORM PAPILLAE   FUNGIFORM PAPILLAE   VALLATE PAPILLAE

SECTION THROUGH NOSE, MOUTH, AND THROAT

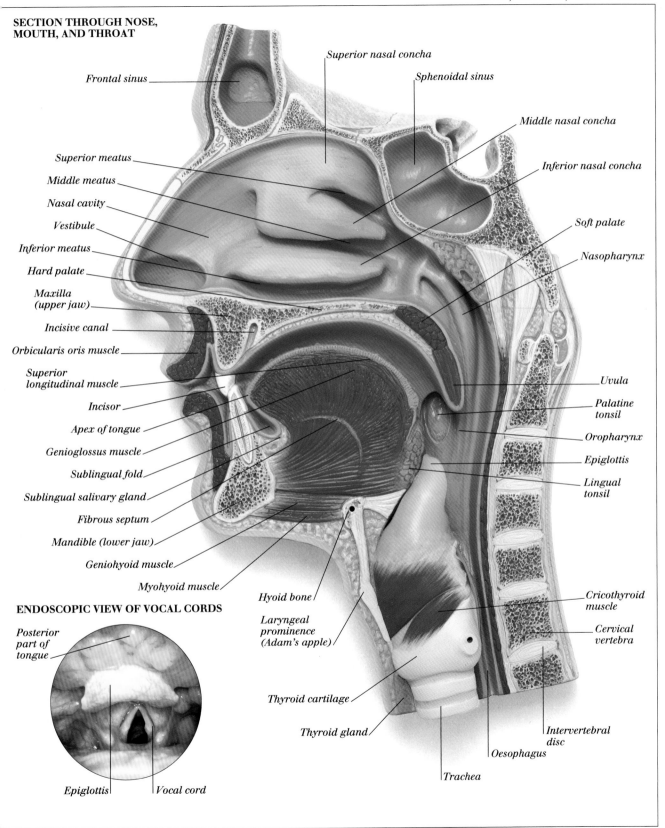

Frontal sinus

Superior nasal concha

Sphenoidal sinus

Middle nasal concha

Inferior nasal concha

Superior meatus

Middle meatus

Nasal cavity

Vestibule

Inferior meatus

Hard palate

Maxilla (upper jaw)

Incisive canal

Orbicularis oris muscle

Superior longitudinal muscle

Incisor

Apex of tongue

Genioglossus muscle

Sublingual fold

Sublingual salivary gland

Fibrous septum

Mandible (lower jaw)

Geniohyoid muscle

Myohyoid muscle

Soft palate

Nasopharynx

Uvula

Palatine tonsil

Oropharynx

Epiglottis

Lingual tonsil

Cricothyroid muscle

Cervical vertebra

Intervertebral disc

Oesophagus

Trachea

Thyroid gland

Thyroid cartilage

Laryngeal prominence (Adam's apple)

Hyoid bone

ENDOSCOPIC VIEW OF VOCAL CORDS

Posterior part of tongue

Epiglottis

Vocal cord

Teeth

THE 20 PRIMARY TEETH (also called deciduous or milk teeth) usually begin to erupt when a baby is about six months old. They start to be replaced by the permanent teeth when the child is about six years old. By the age of 20, most adults have a full set of 32 teeth although the third molars (commonly called wisdom teeth) may never erupt. While teeth help people to speak clearly and give shape to the face, their main function is the chewing of food. Incisors and canines shear and tear the food into pieces; premolars and molars crush and grind it further. Although tooth enamel is the hardest substance in the body, it tends to be eroded and destroyed by acid produced in the mouth during the breakdown of food.

DEVELOPMENT OF TEETH IN A FETUS

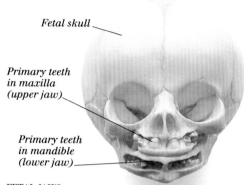

Fetal skull

Primary teeth in maxilla (upper jaw)

Primary teeth in mandible (lower jaw)

FETAL JAWS
By the sixth week of embryonic development areas of thickening occur in each jaw; these areas give rise to tooth buds. By the time the fetus is six months old, enamel has formed on the tooth buds.

DEVELOPMENT OF JAW AND TEETH

Maxilla (upper jaw)

Mandible (lower jaw)

A NEWBORN BABY'S JAWS
The primary teeth can be seen developing in the jaw bones; they begin to erupt around the age of six months.

A FIVE-YEAR-OLD CHILD'S TEETH
There is a full set of 20 erupted primary teeth; the permanent teeth can be seen developing in the upper and lower jaws.

A NINE-YEAR-OLD CHILD'S TEETH
Most of the teeth are primary teeth but the permanent incisors and first molars have now emerged.

AN ADULT'S TEETH
By the age of 20, the full set of 32 permanent teeth (including the wisdom teeth) should be in position.

THE PERMANENT TEETH

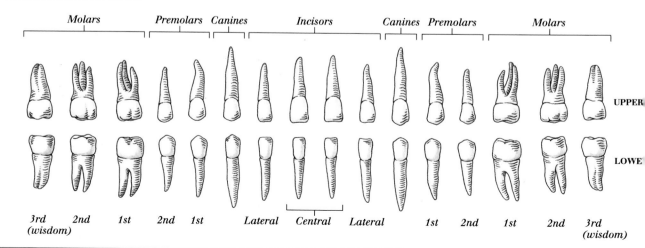

Molars — Premolars — Canines — Incisors — Canines — Premolars — Molars

UPPER

LOWER

3rd (wisdom) — 2nd — 1st — 2nd — 1st — Lateral — Central — Lateral — 1st — 2nd — 1st — 2nd — 3rd (wisdom)

STRUCTURE OF A TOOTH

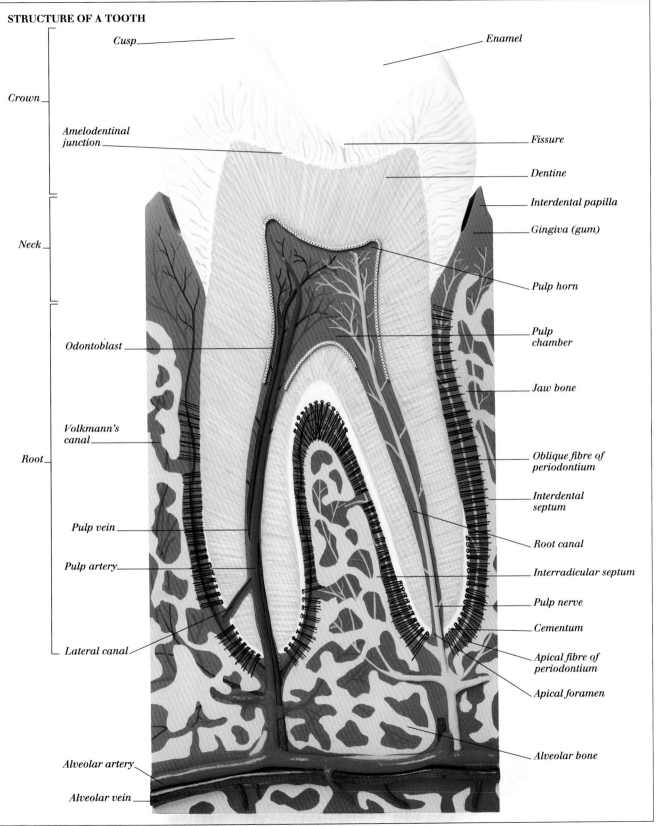

Cusp

Enamel

Crown

Ameledentinal
junction

Fissure

Dentine

Neck

Interdental papilla

Gingiva (gum)

Pulp horn

Odontoblast

Pulp
chamber

Jaw bone

Volkmann's
canal

Root

Oblique fibre of
periodontium

Interdental
septum

Pulp vein

Root canal

Pulp artery

Interradicular septum

Pulp nerve

Cementum

Lateral canal

Apical fibre of
periodontium

Apical foramen

Alveolar bone

Alveolar artery

Alveolar vein

Digestive system

THE DIGESTIVE SYSTEM BREAKS DOWN FOOD into particles so tiny that blood can take nourishment to all parts of the body. The system's main part is a 9 m (30 ft) tube from mouth to rectum; muscles in this alimentary canal force food along. Chewed food first travels through the oesophagus to the stomach, which churns and liquidizes food before it passes through the duodenum, jejunum, and ileum – the three parts of the long, convoluted small intestine. Here, digestive juices from the gallbladder and pancreas break down food particles; many filter out into the blood through tiny fingerlike villi that line the small intestine's inner wall. Undigested food in the colon forms faeces that leave the body through the anus.

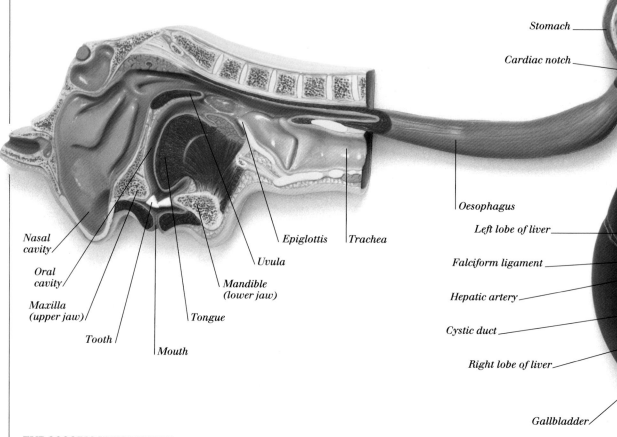

Stomach

Cardiac notch

Oesophagus

Left lobe of liver

Falciform ligament

Hepatic artery

Cystic duct

Right lobe of liver

Gallbladder

Nasal cavity

Oral cavity

Maxilla (upper jaw)

Tooth

Mouth

Tongue

Mandible (lower jaw)

Uvula

Epiglottis *Trachea*

ENDOSCOPIC VIEWS INSIDE ALIMENTARY CANAL

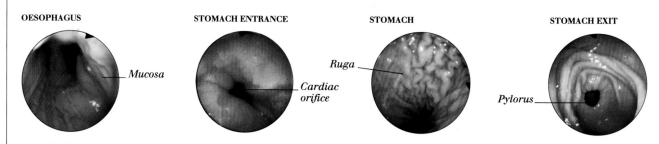

OESOPHAGUS

Mucosa

STOMACH ENTRANCE

Cardiac orifice

STOMACH

Ruga

STOMACH EXIT

Pylorus

ALIMENTARY CANAL

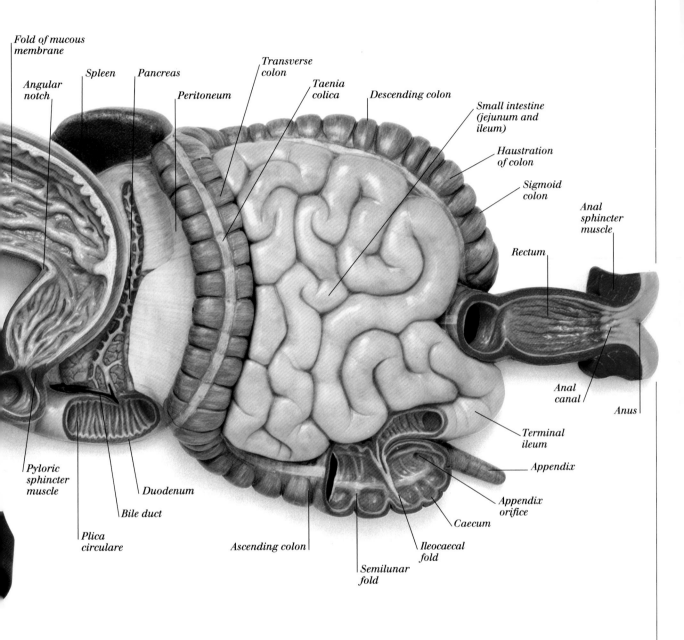

Fold of mucous membrane

Angular notch

Spleen

Pancreas

Peritoneum

Transverse colon

Taenia colica

Descending colon

Small intestine (jejunum and ileum)

Haustration of colon

Sigmoid colon

Anal sphincter muscle

Rectum

Anal canal

Anus

Terminal ileum

Appendix

Appendix orifice

Caecum

Ileocaecal fold

Semilunar fold

Ascending colon

Plica circulare

Bile duct

Duodenum

Pyloric sphincter muscle

DUODENUM

Plica circulare

ILEUM

Villi of mucosa

COLON

Semilunar fold

Blood vessel

RECTUM

Mucosa

Heart

THE HEART IS A HOLLOW MUSCLE in the middle of the chest that pumps blood around the body, supplying cells with oxygen and nutrients. A muscular wall, called the septum, divides the heart lengthways into left and right sides. A valve divides each side into two chambers: an upper atrium and a lower ventricle. When the heart muscle contracts, it squeezes blood through the atria and then through the ventricles. Oxygenated blood from the lungs flows from the pulmonary veins into the left atrium, through the left ventricle, and then out via the aorta to all parts of the body. Deoxygenated blood returning from the body flows from the vena cava into the right atrium, through the right ventricle, and then out via the pulmonary artery to the lungs for reoxygenation. At rest the heart beats between 60 and 80 times a minute; during exercise or at times of stress or excitement the rate may increase to 200 beats a minute.

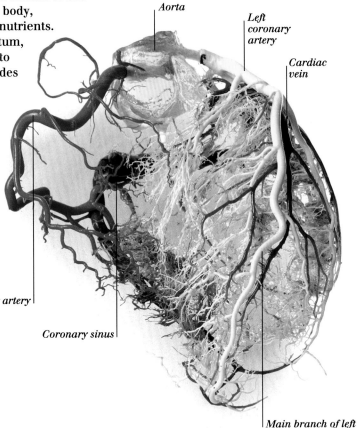

Aorta

Left coronary artery

Cardiac vein

Right coronary artery

Coronary sinus

Main branch of left coronary artery

SECTION THROUGH HEART WALL

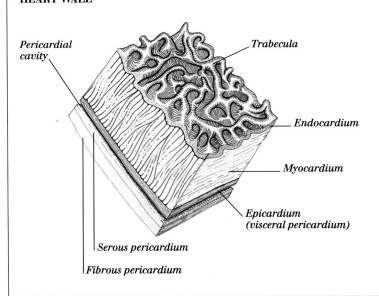

Pericardial cavity

Trabecula

Endocardium

Myocardium

Epicardium (visceral pericardium)

Serous pericardium

Fibrous pericardium

HEARTBEAT SEQUENCE

ATRIAL DIASTOLE

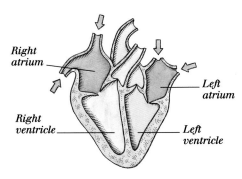

Right atrium

Left atrium

Right ventricle

Left ventricle

Deoxygenated blood enters the right atrium while the left atrium receives oxygenated blood.

STRUCTURE OF HEART

Brachiocephalic trunk

Superior vena cava

Ascending aorta

Right pulmonary artery

Fossa ovalis

Right pulmonary vein

Right atrium

Opening of inferior vena cava

Branch of coronary artery

Tricuspid valve

Chordae tendineae

Right ventricle

Trabecula

Left subclavian artery

Left common carotid artery

Left pulmonary vein

Pulmonary trunk

Pulmonary semilunar valve

Coronary artery

Chordae tendineae

Muscular part of interventricular septum

Left ventricle

Papillary muscle

Myocardium of left ventricle

ATRIAL SYSTOLE (VENTRICULAR DIASTOLE)

Right atrium contracts

Tricuspid valve opens

Right ventricle dilates

Left atrium contracts

Mitral valve opens

Left ventricle dilates

Left and right atria contract, forcing blood into the relaxed ventricles.

VENTRICULAR SYSTOLE

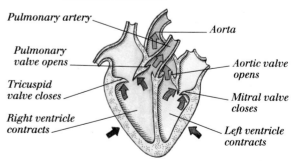

Pulmonary artery

Pulmonary valve opens

Tricuspid valve closes

Right ventricle contracts

Aorta

Aortic valve opens

Mitral valve closes

Left ventricle contracts

Ventricles contract and force blood to the lungs for oxygenation and via the aorta to the rest of the body.

Circulatory system

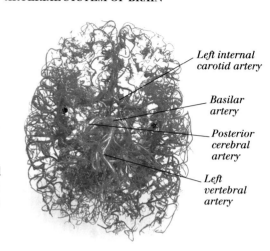

THE CIRCULATORY SYSTEM consists of the heart and blood vessels, which together maintain a continuous flow of blood around the body. The heart pumps oxygen-rich blood from the lungs to all parts of the body through a network of tubes called arteries, and smaller branches called arterioles. Blood returns to the heart via small vessels called venules, which lead in turn into larger tubes called veins. Arterioles and venules are linked by a network of tiny vessels called capillaries, where the exchange of oxygen and carbon dioxide between blood and body cells takes place. Blood has four main components: red blood cells, white blood cells, platelets, and liquid plasma.

Left internal carotid artery

Basilar artery

Posterior cerebral artery

Left vertebral artery

CIRCULATORY SYSTEM OF HEART AND LUNGS

Superior vena cava

Aorta

CIRCULATORY SYSTEM OF LIVER

Inferior vena cava

Portal vein

Common bile duct

Hepatic artery

Gallbladder

Right ventricle

Left ventricle

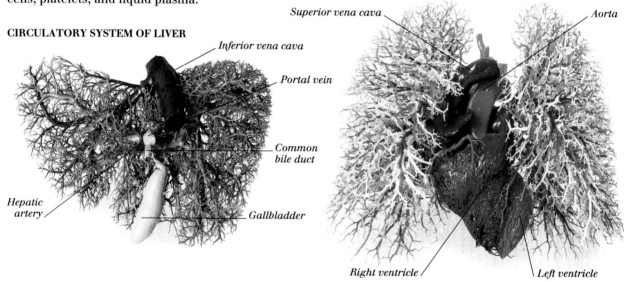

SECTION OF MAIN ARTERY

Tunica media

Collagen and elastic fibres

External elastic lamina

Tunica adventitia

Internal elastic lamina

Tunica intima

Endothelium

Arteriole

SECTION OF MAIN VEIN

Tunica media

Collagen and elastic fibres

External elastic lamina

Tunica adventitia

Valve cusp

Internal elastic lamina

Tunica intima

Endothelium

PRINCIPAL ARTERIES AND VEINS OF CIRCULATORY SYSTEM

Common carotid artery

Subclavian artery

Arch of aorta

Axillary artery

Pulmonary artery

Coronary artery

Brachial artery

Gastric artery

Hepatic artery

Splenic artery

Superior mesenteric artery

Radial artery

Ulnar artery

Palmar arch

Digital artery

Common iliac artery

External iliac artery

Internal iliac artery

Femoral artery

Popliteal artery

Peroneal artery

Anterior tibial artery

Posterior tibial artery

Lateral plantar artery

Dorsal metatarsal artery

Internal jugular vein

Brachiocephalic vein

Subclavian vein

Axillary vein

Cephalic vein

Superior vena cava

Pulmonary vein

Basilic vein

Hepatic portal vein

Median cubital vein

Inferior vena cava

Anterior median vein

Gastroepiploic vein

Palmar vein

Digital vein

Inferior mesenteric vein

Superior mesenteric vein

Common iliac vein

External iliac vein

Internal iliac vein

Femoral vein

Great saphenous vein

Short saphenous vein

Dorsal venous arch

Digital vein

TYPES OF BLOOD CELLS

RED BLOOD CELLS
These cells are biconcave in shape to maximize their oxygen-carrying capacity.

WHITE BLOOD CELLS
Lymphocytes are the smallest white blood cells; they form antibodies against disease.

PLATELETS
Tiny cells that are activated whenever blood clotting or repair to vessels is necessary.

BLOOD CLOTTING

Filaments of fibrin enmesh red blood cells as part of the process of blood clotting.

Respiratory system

THE RESPIRATORY SYSTEM supplies the oxygen needed by body cells and carries off their carbon dioxide waste. Inhaled air passes via the trachea (windpipe) through two narrower tubes, the bronchi, to the lungs. Each lung comprises many fine, branching tubes called bronchioles that end in tiny clustered chambers called alveoli. Gases cross the thin alveolar walls to and from a network of tiny blood vessels. Intercostal (rib) muscles and the muscular diaphragm below the lungs operate the lungs like bellows, drawing air in and forcing it out at regular intervals.

BRONCHIOLE AND ALVEOLI

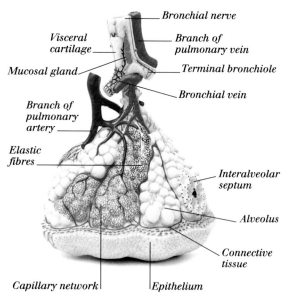

Bronchial nerve

Visceral cartilage

Branch of pulmonary vein

Mucosal gland

Terminal bronchiole

Bronchial vein

Branch of pulmonary artery

Elastic fibres

Interalveolar septum

Alveolus

Connective tissue

Capillary network

Epithelium

SEGMENTS OF BRONCHIAL TREE

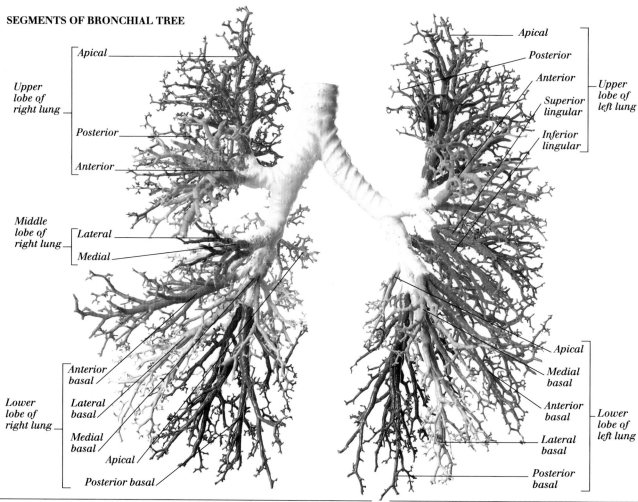

Apical

Upper lobe of right lung

Posterior

Anterior

Middle lobe of right lung

Lateral

Medial

Anterior basal

Lower lobe of right lung

Lateral basal

Medial basal

Apical

Posterior basal

Apical

Posterior

Anterior

Superior lingular

Upper lobe of left lung

Inferior lingular

Apical

Medial basal

Anterior basal

Lower lobe of left lung

Lateral basal

Posterior basal

STRUCTURES OF THORACIC CAVITY

Epiglottis

Hyoid bone

Thyroid cartilage

Thyroid gland

Cricoid cartilage

Apex of lung

Trachea

Superior vena cava

Aorta

Upper lobe of right lung

Upper lobe of left lung

Horizontal fissure

Pulmonary trunk

Oblique fissure

Left pulmonary artery

Heart

Lower lobe of left lung

Secondary bronchus

Tertiary bronchus

Lower lobe of right lung

Middle lobe of right lung

Right crus of diaphragm

Abdominal aorta

Left crus of diaphragm

Oesophagus

Muscular wall of diaphragm

GASEOUS EXCHANGE IN ALVEOLUS

Oxygen diffuses into blood

Oxygenated blood

Alveolus

Deoxygenated blood rich in carbon dioxide

Carbon dioxide diffuses from blood into alveolus

MECHANISM OF RESPIRATION
INSPIRATION

Lung expands

Air drawn into lungs

Diaphragm contracts and flattens

Intercostal muscles contract

EXPIRATION

Lung contracts

Air forced out of lungs

Diaphragm relaxes and moves up

Intercostal muscles relax

Urinary system

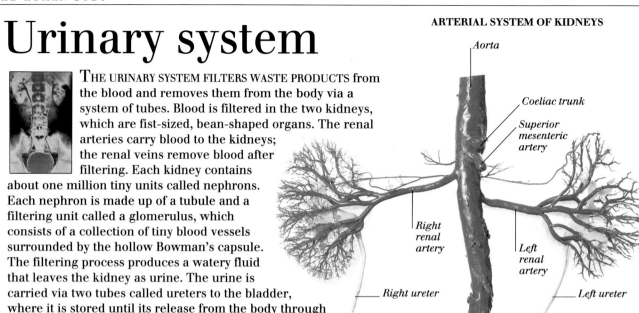

THE URINARY SYSTEM FILTERS WASTE PRODUCTS from the blood and removes them from the body via a system of tubes. Blood is filtered in the two kidneys, which are fist-sized, bean-shaped organs. The renal arteries carry blood to the kidneys; the renal veins remove blood after filtering. Each kidney contains about one million tiny units called nephrons. Each nephron is made up of a tubule and a filtering unit called a glomerulus, which consists of a collection of tiny blood vessels surrounded by the hollow Bowman's capsule. The filtering process produces a watery fluid that leaves the kidney as urine. The urine is carried via two tubes called ureters to the bladder, where it is stored until its release from the body through another tube called the urethra.

Aorta

Coeliac trunk

Superior mesenteric artery

Right renal artery

Left renal artery

Right ureter

Left ureter

SECTION THROUGH LEFT KIDNEY

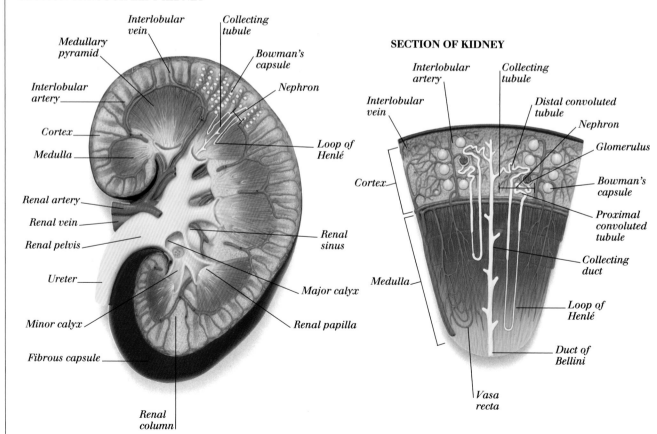

Interlobular vein

Collecting tubule

Medullary pyramid

Bowman's capsule

Nephron

Interlobular artery

Cortex

Medulla

Loop of Henlé

Renal artery

Renal vein

Renal pelvis

Renal sinus

Ureter

Major calyx

Minor calyx

Renal papilla

Fibrous capsule

Renal column

SECTION OF KIDNEY

Interlobular artery

Collecting tubule

Interlobular vein

Distal convoluted tubule

Nephron

Cortex

Glomerulus

Bowman's capsule

Proximal convoluted tubule

Medulla

Collecting duct

Loop of Henlé

Duct of Bellini

Vasa recta

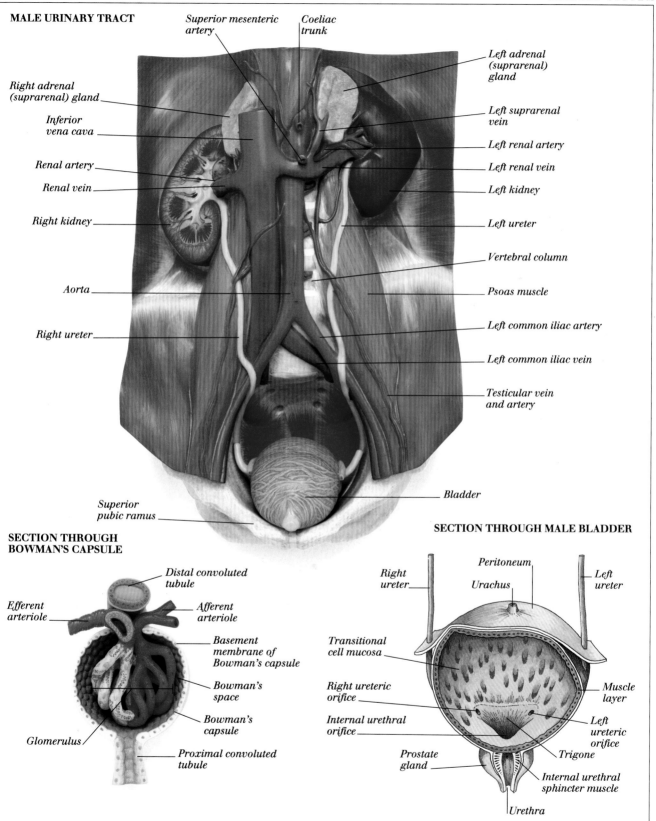

MALE URINARY TRACT

Superior mesenteric artery

Coeliac trunk

Left adrenal (suprarenal) gland

Right adrenal (suprarenal) gland

Inferior vena cava

Left suprarenal vein

Left renal artery

Renal artery

Left renal vein

Renal vein

Left kidney

Right kidney

Left ureter

Vertebral column

Aorta

Psoas muscle

Right ureter

Left common iliac artery

Left common iliac vein

Testicular vein and artery

Bladder

Superior pubic ramus

SECTION THROUGH BOWMAN'S CAPSULE

Distal convoluted tubule

Efferent arteriole

Afferent arteriole

Basement membrane of Bowman's capsule

Bowman's space

Bowman's capsule

Glomerulus

Proximal convoluted tubule

SECTION THROUGH MALE BLADDER

Right ureter

Peritoneum

Urachus

Left ureter

Transitional cell mucosa

Right ureteric orifice

Muscle layer

Internal urethral orifice

Left ureteric orifice

Prostate gland

Trigone

Internal urethral sphincter muscle

Urethra

257

Reproductive system

SEX ORGANS LOCATED IN THE PELVIS create new human lives. Each month a ripe egg is released from one of the female's ovaries into a fallopian tube leading to the uterus (womb), a muscular pear-sized organ. A male produces minute tadpole-like sperm in two oval glands called testes. When the male is ready to release sperm into the female's vagina, many millions pass into his urethra and leave his body through the fleshy penis. The sperm travel up through the vagina into the uterus and one sperm may enter and fertilize an egg. The fertilized egg becomes embedded in the uterus wall and starts to grow into a new human being.

SECTION THROUGH OVARY

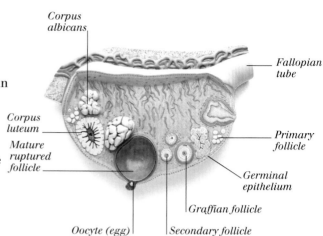

Corpus albicans

Fallopian tube

Corpus luteum

Mature ruptured follicle

Oocyte (egg)

Primary follicle

Germinal epithelium

Graffian follicle

Secondary follicle

SECTION THROUGH FEMALE PELVIC REGION

Ovary

Fundus of uterus

Uterus (womb)

Cervix (neck of uterus)

Os

Rectum

Vagina

Anus

Perineum

Introitus (vaginal opening)

Ureter

Ampulla of fallopian tube

Fimbria of fallopian tube

Isthmus of fallopian tube

Bladder

Pubic symphysis

Urethra

Clitoris

External urinary meatus

Labia minora

Labia majora

FEMALE REPRODUCTIVE ORGANS

Fallopian tube

Fundus of uterus

Isthmus of fallopian tube

Ampulla of fallopian tube

Ovarian ligament

Ovary

Body of uterus (womb)

Os

Vagina

Cervix (neck of uterus)

Fimbria of fallopian tube

MALE REPRODUCTIVE ORGANS

External spermatic fascia

Prostate gland

Ductus (vas) deferens

Seminal vesicle

Cremasteric fascia

Bulbourethral gland

Internal spermatic fascia

Urethra

Epididymis

Corpus spongiosum

Testis (testicle)

Corpus cavernosum

Scrotum

Prepuce (foreskin)

Glans penis

Urethral opening

SECTION THROUGH MALE PELVIC REGION

Intervertebral disc

Ureter

Colon

Sacrum

Seminal vesicle

Ejaculatory duct

Bladder

Pubis of pelvis

Prostate gland

Penis

Corpus cavernosum

Corpus spongiosum

Urethra

Epididymis

Glans penis

Testis (testicle)

Scrotum

EXTERNAL STRUCTURE OF SPERM

Acrosomal cap

Head

Mitochondrial sheath

Terminal ring

Tailpiece

Flagellum

Development of a baby

A FERTILIZED EGG IS NOURISHED AND PROTECTED as it develops into an embryo and then a fetus during the 40 weeks of pregnancy. The placenta, a mass of blood vessels implanted in the uterus lining, delivers nourishment and oxygen, and removes waste through the umbilical cord. Meanwhile, the fetus lies snugly in its amniotic sac, a bag of fluid that protects it against any sudden jolts. In the last weeks of the pregnancy, the rapidly growing fetus turns head-down: a baby ready to be born.

EMBRYO AT FIVE WEEKS

Rudimentary ear

Rudimentary eye

Rudimentary mouth

Heart bulge

Arm bud

Rudimentary liver

Tail bud

Leg bud

Rudimentary vertebra

Amniotic fluid

Umbilicus (navel)

Uterine wall

Fetus

SECTION THROUGH PLACENTA

Umbilical cord

Umbilical vein

Amnion

Umbilical artery

Fetal blood vessels

Chorionic plate

Chorion

Trophoblast

Chorionic villus

Pool of maternal blood

Septum

Decidual plate

Maternal blood vessel

Myometrium

SECTION THROUGH PELVIS IN NINTH MONTH OF PREGNANCY

THE DEVELOPING FETUS

Uterine wall

Placenta

Fallopian tube

SECOND MONTH
All the internal organs have developed by this stage.

Fetus

Intervertebral disc

Vertebra

Spinal cord

Umbilical cord

THIRD MONTH
The fetus is fully formed and now begins a period of rapid growth.

FIFTH MONTH
Although the fetus is here in breech (bottom down) position, it will probably turn by 180° before birth. By the fifth month the baby is moving actively and responds to sound.

Cervix

SEVENTH MONTH
The internal organs are maturing in preparation for life outside the uterus. The baby has grown to such a size that there is less room for movement within the uterus.

Bladder

Cervix

Rectum

Anus

Pubic bone

Placenta

Vagina

Urethra

Geology, Geography, and Meteorolgy

Earth's physical features

MOST OF THE EARTH'S SURFACE (about 70 per cent) is covered with water. The largest single body of water, the Pacific Ocean, alone covers about 30 per cent of the surface. Most of the land is distributed as seven continents; these are (from largest to smallest) Asia, Africa, North America, South America, Antarctica, Europe, and Australasia. The physical features of the land are remarkably varied. Among the most notable are mountain ranges, rivers, and deserts. The largest mountain ranges – the Himalayas in Asia and the Andes in South America – extend for thousands of kilometres. The Himalayas include the world's highest mountain, Mount Everest (8,848 metres). The longest rivers are the River Nile in Africa (6,695 kilometres) and the Amazon River in South America (6,437 kilometres). Deserts cover about 20 per cent of the total land area. The largest is the Sahara, which covers nearly a third of Africa. The Earth's surface features can be represented in various ways. Only a globe can correctly represent areas, shapes, sizes, and directions, because there is always distortion when a spherical surface – the Earth's, for example – is projected on to the flat surface of a map. Each map projection is therefore a compromise: it shows some features accurately but distorts others. Even satellite mapping does not produce completely accurate maps, although they can show physical features with great clarity.

EXAMPLES OF MAP PROJECTIONS

CYLINDRICAL PROJECTION

CYLINDRICAL-PROJECTION MAP

SATELLITE MAPPING OF THE EARTH

Satellite takes photographs of the Earth

Solar panel

Earth's rotation

Antenna

Earth

Polar orbit of satellite

Area of Earth's surface on each photograph

Composite picture of Earth created from thousands of separate images

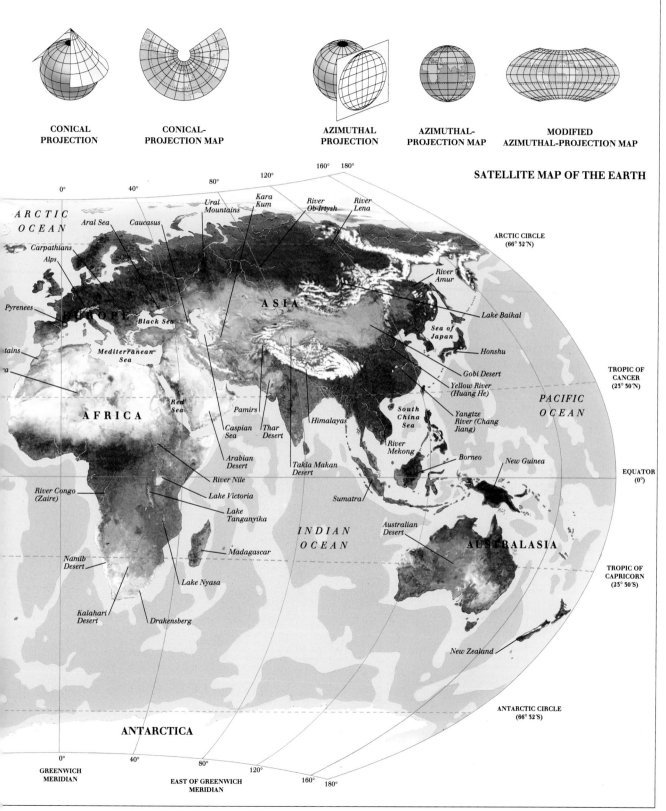

CONICAL PROJECTION

CONICAL-PROJECTION MAP

AZIMUTHAL PROJECTION

AZIMUTHAL-PROJECTION MAP

MODIFIED AZIMUTHAL-PROJECTION MAP

SATELLITE MAP OF THE EARTH

160° 180°
120°
80°
40°
0°

ARCTIC OCEAN

ARCTIC CIRCLE (66° 52'N)

Ural Mountains
Kara Kum
River Ob-Irtysh
River Lena

Aral Sea
Caucasus

Carpathians
Alps

River Amur

Pyrenees

EUROPE

Black Sea

ASIA

Lake Baikal

tains

Sea of Japan

Mediterranean Sea

Honshu

a

TROPIC OF CANCER (25° 50'N)

Gobi Desert

Red Sea

AFRICA

Yellow River (Huang He)

Pamirs

PACIFIC OCEAN

Caspian Sea
Thar Desert

Himalayas

South China Sea

Yangtze River (Chang Jiang)

Arabian Desert

Takla Makan Desert

River Mekong

Borneo

New Guinea

River Nile

EQUATOR (0°)

River Congo (Zaire)

Lake Victoria

Sumatra

Lake Tanganyika

INDIAN OCEAN

Australian Desert

AUSTRALASIA

Madagascar

Namib Desert

TROPIC OF CAPRICORN (25° 50'S)

Lake Nyasa

Kalahari Desert

Drakensberg

New Zealand

ANTARCTIC CIRCLE (66° 52'S)

ANTARCTICA

0°
40°
80°
120°
160° 180°

GREENWICH MERIDIAN

EAST OF GREENWICH MERIDIAN

The rock cycle

THE ROCK CYCLE IS A CONTINUOUS PROCESS through which old rocks are transformed into new ones. Rocks can be divided into three main groups: igneous, sedimentary, and metamorphic. Igneous rocks are formed when magma (molten rock) from the Earth's interior cools and solidifies (see pp. 274-275). Sedimentary rocks are formed when sediment (rock particles, for example) becomes compressed and cemented together in a process known as lithification (see pp. 276-277). Metamorphic rocks are formed when igneous, sedimentary, or other metamorphic rocks are changed by heat or pressure (see pp. 274-275). Rocks are added to the Earth's surface by crustal movements and volcanic activity. Once exposed on the surface, the rocks are broken down into rock particles by weathering (see pp. 282-283). The particles are then transported by glaciers, rivers, and wind, and deposited as sediment in lakes, deltas, deserts, and on the ocean floor. Some of this sediment undergoes lithification and forms sedimentary rock. This rock may be thrust back to the surface by crustal movements or forced deeper into the Earth's interior, where heat and pressure transform it into metamorphic rock. The metamorphic rock in turn may be pushed up to the surface or may be melted to form magma. Eventually, the magma cools and solidifies – below or on the surface – forming igneous rock. When the sedimentary, igneous, and metamorphic rocks are exposed once more on the Earth's surface, the cycle begins again.

HEXAGONAL BASALT
COLUMNS, ICELAND

THE ROCK CYCLE

Igneous
rock

Cooling and solidification (crystallization)

Heat and pressure (metamorphism)

Weathering, transport, and deposition

Weathering, transport, and deposition

Compression and cementation (lithification)

Weathering, transport,
and deposition

Sediment

Magma

Melting

Heat and pressure
(metamorphism)

Metamorphic
rock

Sedimentary
rock

STAGES IN THE ROCK CYCLE

*Magma extruded as lava,
which solidifies to form
igneous rock*

*Lava
flow*

Vent

*Main
conduit*

*Secondary
conduit*

Lava

Ash

*Rock surrounding
magma changed
by heat to form
metamorphic rock*

*Intense heat of rising
magma melts some of
the surrounding rock*

*Sedimentary rock
crushed and folded to
form metamorphic rock*

IGNEOUS ROCK

Pyroxene crystal

Olivine crystal

Plagioclase feldspar

PHOTOMICROGRAPH OF GABBRO

Coarse-grained texture

Dark pyroxene crystal

PIECE OF GABBRO

SEDIMENTARY ROCK

Mud groundmass (matrix)

Ammonite shell

PHOTOMICROGRAPH OF SHELLY LIMESTONE

Brown colouring from iron oxides

Fine-grained texture

Ammonite shell embedded in rock

PIECE OF SHELLY LIMESTONE

METAMORPHIC ROCK

Garnet crystal (pink)

Quartz and feldspar crystals (grey)

PHOTOMICROGRAPH OF GARNET-MICA SCHIST

Red garnet crystal

Wavy foliation

PIECE OF GARNET-MICA SCHIST

Mountain

Glacier erodes rocks and carries rock particles to river

Waterfall erodes rock

River erodes valley floor and carries rock particles downstream

Rock particles deposited as sediment in lake

Rock particles deposited by wind to form sand dunes

Rock particles deposited in delta

Heavier rock particles deposited on continental shelf

Continental shelf

Continental slope

Lighter rock particles collect on ocean floor to form layers of sediment

Layers of sediment compressed and cemented to form sedimentary rock

267

Minerals

A MINERAL IS A NATURALLY OCCURRING SUBSTANCE that has a characteristic chemical composition and specific physical properties, such as habit and streak (see pp. 270-271). A rock, by comparison, is an aggregate of minerals and need not have a specific chemical composition. Minerals are made up of elements (substances that cannot be broken down chemically into simpler substances), each of which can be represented by a chemical symbol. Minerals can be divided into two main groups: native elements and compounds. Native elements are made up of a pure element. Examples include gold (chemical symbol Au), silver (Ag), copper (Cu), and carbon (C); carbon occurs as a native element in two forms, diamond and graphite. Compounds are combinations of two or more elements. For example, sulphides are compounds of sulphur (S) and one or more other elements, such as lead (Pb) in the mineral galena, or antimony (Sb) in the mineral stibnite.

NATIVE ELEMENTS

Dendritic (branching) copper

Limonite groundmass (matrix)

**COPPER
(Cu)**

SULPHIDES

Cubic galena crystal

**GALENA
(PbS)**

Dendritic (branching) gold

Quartz vein

**GOLD
(Au)**

White diamond

Kimberlite groundmass (matrix)

**DIAMOND
(C)**

Hexagonal graphite crystal

**GRAPHITE
(C)**

OXIDES/HYDROXIDES

Milky quartz groundmass (matrix)

Smoky quartz crystal

**SMOKY QUARTZ
(SiO$_2$)**

Rounded bauxite grains in groundmass (matrix)

**BAUXITE
(FeO(OH) and Al$_2$O$_3$.2H$_2$O)**

Mass of specular haematite crystals

**SPECULAR HAEMATITE
(Fe$_2$O$_3$)**

Prismatic stibnite crystal

Quartz groundmass (matrix)

**STIBNITE
(Sb$_2$S$_3$)**

Perfect octahedral pyrites crystal

Quartz crystal

**PYRITES
(FeS$_2$)**

Parallel bands of onyx

**ONYX
(SiO$_2$)**

Kidney ore haematite

Specular crystals of haematite

**KIDNEY ORE HAEMATITE
(Fe$_2$O$_3$)**

PHOSPHATES

Limonite groundmass (matrix)

Rock groundmass (matrix)

Radiating wavellite crystals

WAVELLITE
$(Al_5(PO_4)_2(OH,F)_5.5H_2O)$

Prismatic pyromorphite crystals

PYROMORPHITE
$(Pb_5(PO_4)_5Cl)$

CARBONATES

Striated cerussite crystal

Dog tooth calcite crystal

CERUSSITE
$(PbCO_5)$

CALCITE
$(CaCO_5)$

SULPHATES

Rock groundmass (matrix)

Radiating crystal mass of daisy gypsum

Radiating cyanotrichite crystals

CYANOTRICHITE
$Cu_4Al_2(SO_4)(OH)_{12}.2H_2O)$

DAISY GYPSUM
$(CaSO_4.2H_2O)$

MOLYBDATE

Tabular wulfenite crystal

Dark rock groundmass (matrix)

WULFENITE
$(PbMoO_4)$

SILICATES

Feldspar groundmass (matrix)

Transparent bicolored tourmaline crystal

Dodecahedral sodalite crystal

SODALITE
$(Na_8Al_6Si_6O_{24}Cl_2)$

Striated surface of olivine crystal

TOURMALINE
$(Na(Mg,Fe,Li,Mn,Al)_5Al_6(BO_5)_5Si_6.O_{18}(OH,F)_4)$

OLIVINE
$(Fe_2SiO_4 - Mg_2SiO_4)$

Striated prismatic epidote crystal

Tabular muscovite crystal

EPIDOTE
$(Ca_2(Al,Fe)_5(SiO_4)_5(OH))$

Orthoclase crystal

MUSCOVITE
$(KAl_2(Si_5Al)O_{10}(OH,F)_2)$

ORTHOCLASE
$(KAlSi_5O_8)$

HALIDES

Cubic rock salt crystal

Cubic fluorite crystal

GREEN FLUORITE
(CaF_2)

ORANGE HALITE (ROCK SALT)
$(NaCl)$

Mineral features

MINERALS CAN BE IDENTIFIED BY STUDYING features such as fracture, cleavage, crystal system, habit, hardness, colour, and streak. Minerals can break in different ways. If a mineral breaks in an irregular way, leaving rough surfaces, it possesses fracture. If a mineral breaks along well-defined planes of weakness, it possesses cleavage. Specific minerals have distinctive patterns of cleavage; for example, mica cleaves along one plane. Most minerals form crystals, which can be categorized into crystal systems according to their symmetry and number of faces. Within each system, several different but related forms of crystal are possible; for example, a cubic crystal can have six, eight, or twelve sides. A mineral's habit is the typical form taken by an aggregate of its crystals. Examples of habit include botryoidal (like a bunch of grapes) and massive (no definite form). The relative hardness of a mineral may be assessed by testing its resistance to scratching. This property is usually measured using Mohs scale, which increases in hardness from 1 (talc) to 10 (diamond). The colour of a mineral is not a dependable guide to its identity as some minerals have a range of colours. Streak (the colour the powdered mineral makes when rubbed across an unglazed tile) is a more reliable indicator.

CLEAVAGE

Cleavage in one direction

CLEAVAGE ALONG ONE PLANE

Cleavage in three directions, forming a block cube

CLEAVAGE ALONG THREE PLANES

Horizontal cleavage

Vertical cleavage

CLEAVAGE ALONG TWO PLANES

Cleavage in four directions, forming a double-pyramid crystal

CLEAVAGE ALONG FOUR PLANES

CRYSTAL SYSTEMS

Cubic iron pyrites crystal

Tetragonal idocrase crystal

Representation of tetragonal system

TETRAGONAL SYSTEM

CUBIC SYSTEM

Representation of cubic system

Hexagonal beryl crystal

Representation of hexagonal/trigonal system

HEXAGONAL/TRIGONAL SYSTEM

Orthorhombic barytes crystal

Representation of orthorhombic system

ORTHORHOMBIC SYSTEM

FRACTURE

Fire opal with conchoidal (shell-like) fracture

Nickel-iron with hackly (jagged) fracture

CONCHOIDAL FRACTURE

HACKLY FRACTURE

Orpiment with uneven fracture

Garnierite with splintery fracture

UNEVEN FRACTURE

SPLINTERY FRACTURE

Monoclinic selenite crystal

Representation of monoclinic system

Triclinic axinite crystal

Representation of triclinic system

MONOCLINIC SYSTEM

TRICLINIC SYSTEM

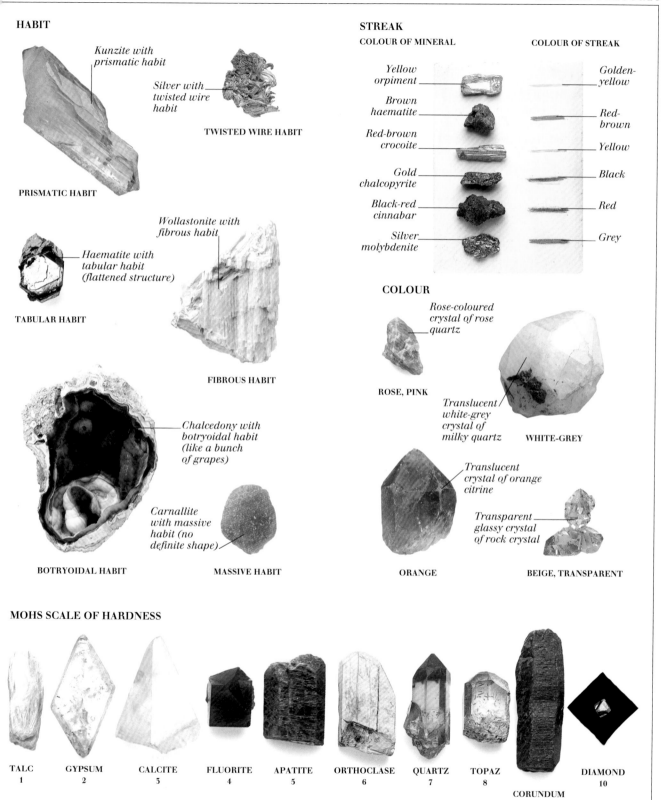

HABIT

Kunzite with prismatic habit

Silver with twisted wire habit

TWISTED WIRE HABIT

PRISMATIC HABIT

Wollastonite with fibrous habit

Haematite with tabular habit (flattened structure)

TABULAR HABIT

FIBROUS HABIT

Chalcedony with botryoidal habit (like a bunch of grapes)

Carnallite with massive habit (no definite shape)

BOTRYOIDAL HABIT

MASSIVE HABIT

STREAK

COLOUR OF MINERAL   **COLOUR OF STREAK**

Yellow orpiment — *Golden-yellow*

Brown haematite — *Red-brown*

Red-brown crocoite — *Yellow*

Gold chalcopyrite — *Black*

Black-red cinnabar — *Red*

Silver molybdenite — *Grey*

COLOUR

Rose-coloured crystal of rose quartz

ROSE, PINK

Translucent white-grey crystal of milky quartz

WHITE-GREY

Translucent crystal of orange citrine

Transparent glassy crystal of rock crystal

ORANGE

BEIGE, TRANSPARENT

MOHS SCALE OF HARDNESS

TALC	GYPSUM	CALCITE	FLUORITE	APATITE	ORTHOCLASE	QUARTZ	TOPAZ	CORUNDUM	DIAMOND
1	2	3	4	5	6	7	8	9	10

Volcanoes

VOLCANOES ARE VENTS OR FISSURES in the Earth's crust through which magma (molten rock that originates from deep beneath the crust) is forced on to the surface as lava. They occur most commonly along the boundaries of crustal plates; most volcanoes lie in a belt called the "Ring of Fire", which runs along the edge of the Pacific Ocean. Volcanoes can be classified according to the violence and frequency of their eruptions. Non-explosive volcanic eruptions generally occur where crustal plates pull apart. These eruptions produce runny basaltic lava that spreads quickly over a wide area to form relatively flat cones. The most violent eruptions take place where plates collide. Such eruptions produce thick rhyolitic lava and may also blast out clouds of dust and pyroclasts (lava fragments). The lava does not flow far before cooling and therefore builds up steep-sided, conical volcanoes. Some volcanoes produce lava and ash eruptions, which build up composite volcanic cones. Volcanoes that erupt frequently are described as active; those that erupt rarely are termed dormant; and those that have stopped erupting altogether are termed extinct. As well as the volcanoes themselves, other features associated with volcanic regions include geysers, hot mineral springs, solfataras, fumaroles, and bubbling mud pools.

Folded, rope-like surface

PAHOEHOE (ROPY LAVA)

HORU GEYSER, NEW ZEALAND

VOLCANO TYPES

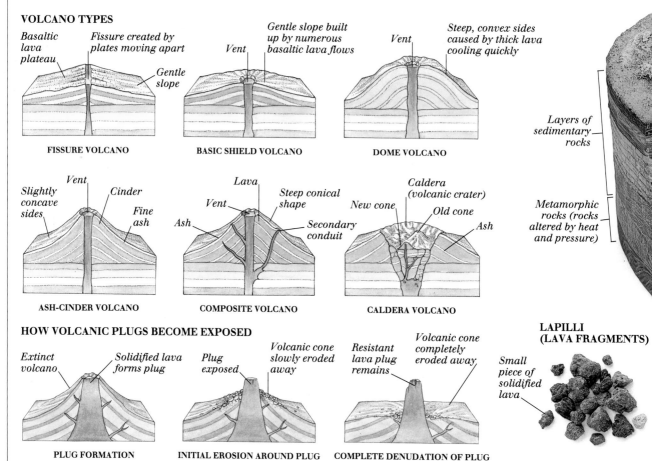

Basaltic lava plateau
Fissure created by plates moving apart
Gentle slope

FISSURE VOLCANO

Gentle slope built up by numerous basaltic lava flows
Vent

BASIC SHIELD VOLCANO

Vent
Steep, convex sides caused by thick lava cooling quickly

DOME VOLCANO

Slightly concave sides
Vent
Cinder
Fine ash

ASH-CINDER VOLCANO

Lava
Vent
Steep conical shape
Ash
Secondary conduit

COMPOSITE VOLCANO

Caldera (volcanic crater)
New cone
Old cone
Ash

CALDERA VOLCANO

Layers of sedimentary rocks

Metamorphic rocks (rocks altered by heat and pressure)

HOW VOLCANIC PLUGS BECOME EXPOSED

Extinct volcano
Solidified lava forms plug

PLUG FORMATION

Plug exposed
Volcanic cone slowly eroded away

INITIAL EROSION AROUND PLUG

Resistant lava plug remains
Volcanic cone completely eroded away

COMPLETE DENUDATION OF PLUG

LAPILLI (LAVA FRAGMENTS)

Small piece of solidified lava

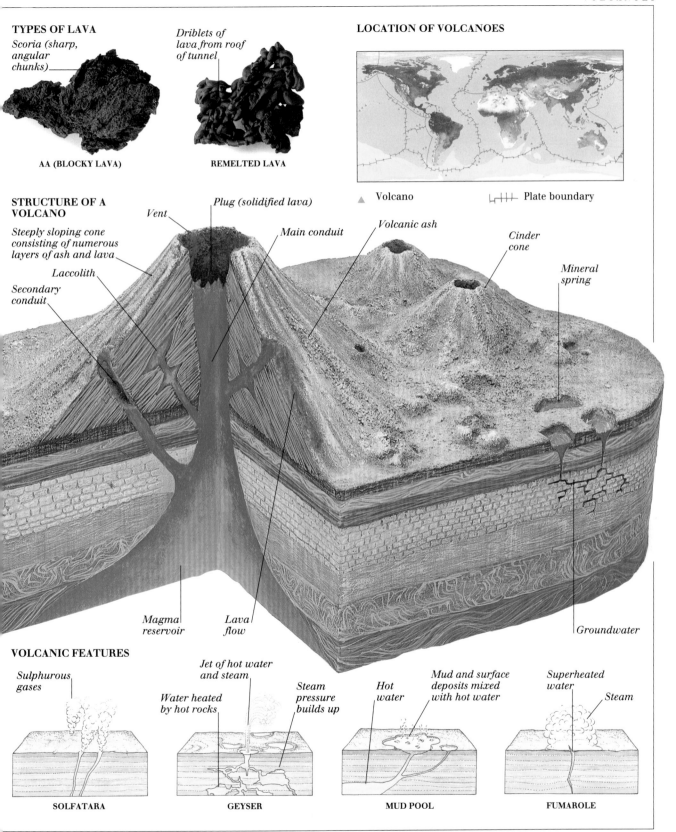

TYPES OF LAVA

Scoria (sharp, angular chunks)

AA (BLOCKY LAVA)

Driblets of lava from roof of tunnel

REMELTED LAVA

LOCATION OF VOLCANOES

▲ Volcano   ⊢⊣⊢⊢ Plate boundary

STRUCTURE OF A VOLCANO

Steeply sloping cone consisting of numerous layers of ash and lava

Laccolith

Secondary conduit

Vent

Plug (solidified lava)

Main conduit

Volcanic ash

Cinder cone

Mineral spring

Magma reservoir

Lava flow

Groundwater

VOLCANIC FEATURES

Sulphurous gases

Jet of hot water and steam

Water heated by hot rocks

Steam pressure builds up

Hot water

Mud and surface deposits mixed with hot water

Superheated water

Steam

SOLFATARA

GEYSER

MUD POOL

FUMAROLE

Igneous and metamorphic rocks

IGNEOUS ROCKS ARE FORMED WHEN MAGMA (molten rock that originates from deep beneath the Earth's crust) cools and solidifies. There are two main types of igneous rock: intrusive and extrusive. Intrusive rocks are formed deep underground where magma is forced into cracks or between rock layers to form structures such as sills, dykes, and batholiths. The magma cools slowly to form coarse-grained rocks such as gabbro and pegmatite. Extrusive rocks are formed above the Earth's surface from lava (magma that has been ejected in a volcanic eruption). The molten lava cools quickly, producing fine-grained rocks such as rhyolite and basalt. Metamorphic rocks are those that have been altered by intense heat (contact metamorphism) or extreme pressure (regional metamorphism). Contact metamorphism occurs when rocks are changed by heat from, for example, an igneous intrusion or lava flow. Regional metamorphism occurs when rock is crushed in the middle of a folding mountain range. Metamorphic rocks can be formed from igneous rocks, sedimentary rocks, or even from other metamorphic rocks.

BASALT COLUMNS

IGNEOUS ROCK STRUCTURES

Cinder cone
Large eroded lava flow
Cedar-tree laccolith
Butte
Plug
Cone sheet
Ring dyke
Batholith
Dyke
Sill
Dyke swarm
Lopolith

CONTACT METAMORPHISM

Metamorphic aureole (region where contact metamorphism occurs)
Hot igneous intrusion
Limestone
Shale
Marble (metamorphosed limestone)
Slate (metamorphosed shale)

REGIONAL METAMORPHISM

Mountain range
Slate, formed under low pressure and temperature
Compression
Compression
Schist, formed under medium pressure and temperature
Crust
Gneiss, formed under high pressure and temperature
Mantle
Magma

EXAMPLES OF METAMORPHIC ROCKS

Pale feldspar
Dark mica

GNEISS

Dark mineral band

FOLDED SCHIST

Pale calcite

SKARN

EXAMPLES OF EXTRUSIVE IGNEOUS ROCKS

Porphyritic texture

Fine-grained crystals

Elongated vesicles (gas cavities)

Fine-grained groundmass (matrix)

Conchoidal fracture

Glassy lustre

RHYOLITE

BASALT

PUMICE

PORPHYRITIC ANDESITE

OBSIDIAN

Mesa (flat-topped plateau)

Extinct geyser

Lake

Caldera

Sea

Lava flow

Vent

Active juvenile volcano

Parasitic volcano

Main conduit

Sagging caused by weight of volcano

Eroded plug of extinct volcano

Magma reservoir

Batholith

Laccolith

EXAMPLES OF INTRUSIVE IGNEOUS ROCKS

Dark groundmass (matrix)

KIMBERLITE

Plagioclase feldspar

OLIVINE GABBRO

Amphibole crystals

White feldspar

FELDSPAR PEGMATITE

Fine groundmass (matrix)

Pyrites crystal

Chiastolite crystal

Green calc-silicate mineral

High quartz content

Amphibole crystal

SLATE WITH PYRITES

CHIASTOLITE HORNFELS

GREEN MARBLE

HALLEFLINTA

SYENITE

275

Sedimentary rocks

SEDIMENTARY ROCKS ARE FORMED BY THE ACCUMULATION and consolidation of sediments (see pp. 266-267). There are three main types of sedimentary rock. Clastic sedimentary rocks, such as breccia or sandstone, are formed from other rocks that have been broken down into fragments by weathering (see pp. 282-283), which have then been transported and deposited elsewhere. Organic sedimentary rocks – for example, coal (see pp. 280-281) – are derived from plant and animal remains. Chemical sedimentary rocks are formed by chemical processes. For example, rock salt is formed when salt dissolved in water is deposited as the water evaporates. Sedimentary rocks are laid down in layers, called beds or strata. Each new layer is laid down horizontally over older ones. There are usually some gaps in the sequence, called unconformities. These represent periods in which no new sediments were being laid down, or when earlier sedimentary layers were raised above sea level and eroded away.

THE GRAND CANYON, USA

EXAMPLES OF UNCONFORMITIES

Early beds tilted and eroded *Later beds horizontal*

ANGULAR UNCONFORMITY

No bedding in early rocks *Later beds horizontal*

NONCONFORMITY

Early beds folded and eroded *Later beds horizontal*

DISCONFORMITY

SEDIMENTARY LAYERS OF THE GRAND CANYON REGION

Wasatch formation
Kaiparowits formation
Wahweap sandstone
Tropic formation
Dakota sandstone
Carmel formation
Pink Cliffs
Bryce Canyon
Zion Canyon
Gray Cliffs
Sevier fault
White Cliffs
Pipe Spring

Temple Cap sandstone
Navajo sandstone
Kayenta formation
Moenave formation
Chinle formation
Shinarump member
Moenkopi formation
Kaibab limestone
Toroweap formation
Coconino sandstone
Herm. shale

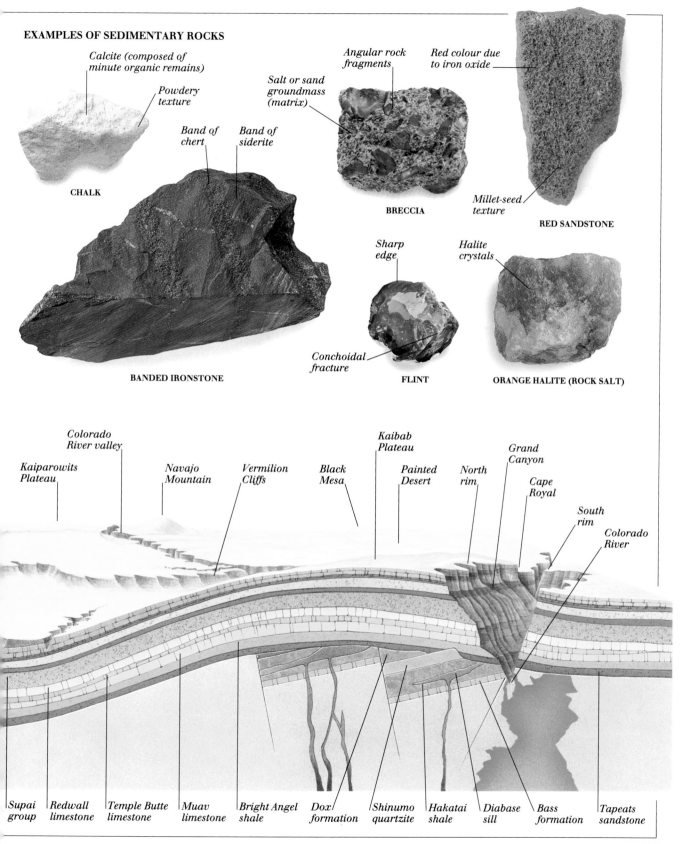

EXAMPLES OF SEDIMENTARY ROCKS

Calcite (composed of minute organic remains)

Powdery texture

CHALK

Band of chert

Band of siderite

BANDED IRONSTONE

Angular rock fragments

Salt or sand groundmass (matrix)

BRECCIA

Red colour due to iron oxide

Millet-seed texture

RED SANDSTONE

Sharp edge

Conchoidal fracture

FLINT

Halite crystals

ORANGE HALITE (ROCK SALT)

Kaiparowits Plateau

Colorado River valley

Navajo Mountain

Vermilion Cliffs

Black Mesa

Kaibab Plateau

Painted Desert

North rim

Grand Canyon

Cape Royal

South rim

Colorado River

Supai group

Redwall limestone

Temple Butte limestone

Muav limestone

Bright Angel shale

Dox formation

Shinumo quartzite

Hakatai shale

Diabase sill

Bass formation

Tapeats sandstone

Fossils

FOSSILS ARE THE REMAINS of plants and animals that have been preserved in rock. A fossil may be the preserved remains of an organism itself, an impression of it in rock, or preserved traces (known as trace fossils) left by an organism while it was alive, such as organic carbon outlines, fossilized footprints, or droppings. Most dead organisms soon rot away or are eaten by scavengers. For fossilization to occur, rapid burial by sediment is necessary. The organism decays, but the harder parts – bones, teeth, and shells, for example – may be preserved and hardened by minerals from the surrounding sediment. Fossilization may also occur even when the hard parts of an organism are dissolved away to leave an impression called a mould. The mould is filled by minerals, thereby creating a cast of the organism. The study of fossils (palaeontology) can not only show how living things have evolved, but can also help to reveal the Earth's geological history – for example, by aiding in the dating of rock strata.

PROCESS OF FOSSILIZATION

ANIMAL DIES

SOFT PARTS ROT

SHELL BURIED

SHELL FOSSILIZED

EXAMPLES OF FOSSILS

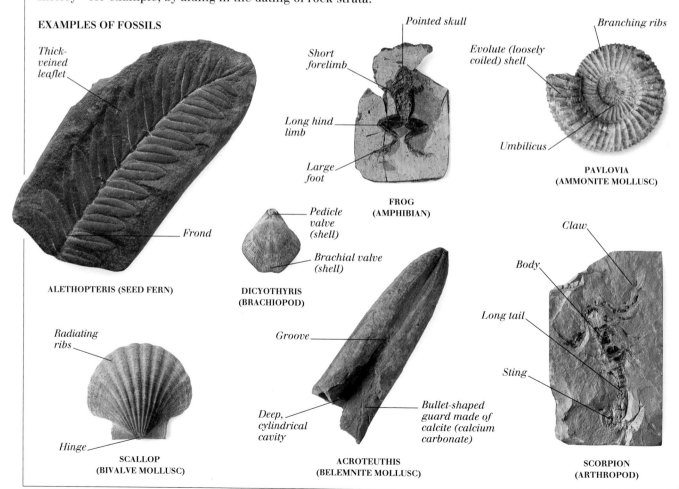

Thick-veined leaflet

Frond

ALETHOPTERIS (SEED FERN)

Short forelimb

Pointed skull

Long hind limb

Large foot

FROG (AMPHIBIAN)

Branching ribs

Evolute (loosely coiled) shell

Umbilicus

PAVLOVIA (AMMONITE MOLLUSC)

Pedicle valve (shell)

Brachial valve (shell)

DICYOTHYRIS (BRACHIOPOD)

Radiating ribs

Hinge

SCALLOP (BIVALVE MOLLUSC)

Groove

Deep, cylindrical cavity

Bullet-shaped guard made of calcite (calcium carbonate)

ACROTEUTHIS (BELEMNITE MOLLUSC)

Claw

Body

Long tail

Sting

SCORPION (ARTHROPOD)

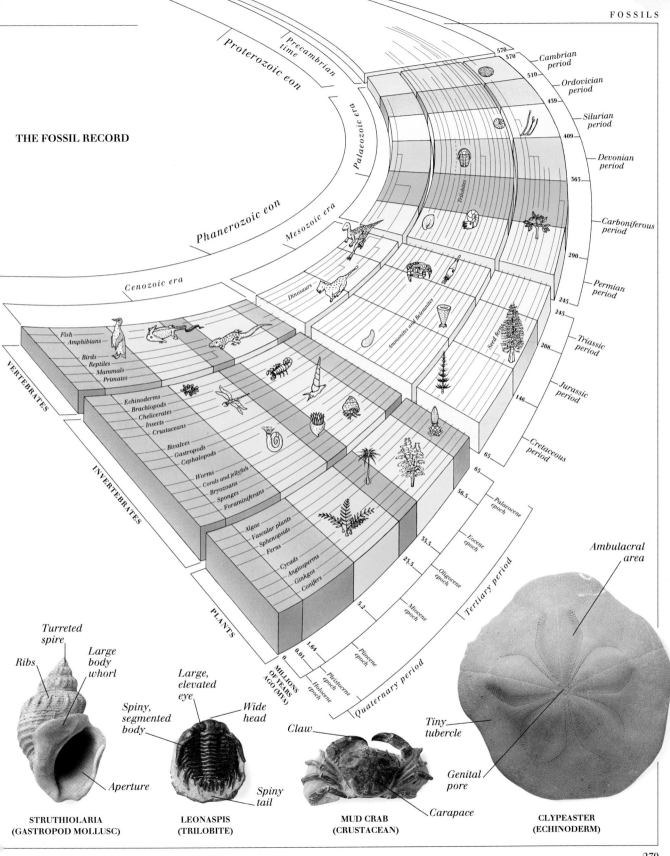

THE FOSSIL RECORD

Precambrian time

Proterozoic eon

Palaeozoic era

Phanerozoic eon

Mesozoic era

Cenozoic era

570
570 — Cambrian period
510 — Ordovician period
439 — Silurian period
409 — Devonian period
363 — Carboniferous period
290 — Permian period
245 — Permian period
245 — Triassic period
208 — Jurassic period
146 — Cretaceous period
65 — Cretaceous period

Dinosaurs

Trilobites

Ammonites and Belemnites

Seed ferns

VERTEBRATES

Fish
Amphibians
Birds
Reptiles
Mammals
Primates

INVERTEBRATES

Echinoderms
Brachiopods
Chelicerates
Insects
Crustaceans
Bivalves
Gastropods
Cephalopods
Worms
Corals and jellyfish
Bryozoans
Sponges
Foraminiferans

PLANTS

Algae
Vascular plants
Sphenopsids
Ferns
Cycads
Angiosperms
Ginkgos
Conifers

65
56.5 — Palaeocene epoch
35.5 — Eocene epoch
23.5 — Oligocene epoch
5.2 — Miocene epoch
1.64 — Pliocene epoch
0.01 — Pleistocene epoch
0 — Holocene epoch

Tertiary period

Quaternary period

MILLIONS
OF YEARS
AGO (MYA)

Ambulacral area

Turreted spire

Large body whorl

Ribs

Large, elevated eye

Wide head

Spiny, segmented body

Claw

Tiny tubercle

Genital pore

Aperture

Spiny tail

Carapace

STRUTHIOLARIA
(GASTROPOD MOLLUSC)

LEONASPIS
(TRILOBITE)

MUD CRAB
(CRUSTACEAN)

CLYPEASTER
(ECHINODERM)

279

Mineral resources

Stalk   *Leaf*

PLANT MATTER

MINERAL RESOURCES CAN BE DEFINED AS naturally occurring substances that can be extracted from the Earth and are useful as fuels and raw materials. Coal, oil, and gas – collectively called fossil fuels – are commonly included in this group, but are not strictly minerals, because they are of organic origin. Coal formation begins when vegetation is buried and partly decomposed to form peat. Overlying sediments compress the peat and transform it into lignite (soft brown coal). As the overlying sediments accumulate, increasing pressure and temperature eventually transform the lignite into bituminous and hard anthracite coals. Oil and gas are usually formed from organic matter that was deposited in marine sediments. Under the effects of heat and pressure, the compressed organic matter undergoes complex chemical changes to form oil and gas. The oil and gas percolate upwards through water-saturated, permeable rocks and they may rise to the Earth's surface or accumulate below an impermeable layer of rock that has been folded or faulted to form a trap – an anticline (upfold) trap, for example. Minerals are inorganic substances that may consist of a single chemical element, such as gold, silver, or copper, or combinations of elements (see pp. 268-269). Some minerals are concentrated in mineralization zones in rock associated with crustal movements or volcanic activity. Others may be found in sediments as placer deposits – accumulations of high-density minerals that have been weathered out of rocks, transported, and deposited (on river-beds, for example).

OIL RIG, NORTH SEA

Decayed plant matter

About 60% carbon   **PEAT**

About 70% carbon

Crumbly texture   **LIGNITE (BROWN COAL)**

Powdery texture

About 80% carbon

HOW COAL IS FORMED

Vegetation

Increasing layers of overlying sediment

Increasing pressure and temperature

Increasing layers of overlying sediment

Increasing pressure and temperature

Peat (about 60% carbon)

PEAT

Lignite (about 70% carbon)

LIGNITE (BROWN COAL)

Bituminous coal (about 80% carbon)

BITUMINOUS COAL

BITUMINOUS COAL

Shiny surface   **BITUMINOUS COAL**   *About 95% carbon*

ANTHRACITE COAL

EXAMPLES OF OIL AND GAS TRAPS

FAULT TRAP

Impermeable rock
Oil
Water-saturated permeable rock
Fault

PINCH-OUT TRAP

Pinch-out
Folded impermeable rock
Water-saturated permeable rock
Fault
Gas
Oil

ANTICLINE TRAP

Anticline
Folded impermeable rock
Water-saturated permeable rock
Gas
Oil

SALT-DOME TRAP

Folded impermeable rock
Water-saturated permeable rock
Oil
Impermeable salt dome

MAJOR COAL, OIL, AND GAS DEPOSITS

● Coal   ● Oil and gas

HOW AN ANTICLINE TRAP IS FORMED

Layer of sediment containing decayed plant and animal matter
Sea
Old seabed

Increasing layers of overlying sediment
Sea
Oil and gas formed by chemical reactions, heat, and pressure

DEPOSITION OF ORGANIC MATERIAL

FORMATION OF OIL AND GAS

Land
Sea
Anticline
Impermeable rock layer folded to form oil and gas trap
Gas
Oil
Water-saturated permeable rock

COLLECTION OF OIL AND GAS IN ANTICLINE TRAP

MINERALIZATION ZONES

Continental crust
Volcano
Subduction zone
Oceanic crust
Mid-ocean ridge

Tin, tungsten, bismuth, and copper
Copper, zinc, gold, and chromium
Copper, gold, silver, tin, lead, and mercury
Lead, zinc, and copper
Chromium
Manganese, cobalt, and nickel
Copper and zinc

281

Weathering and erosion

WEATHERING IS THE BREAKING DOWN of rocks on the Earth's surface. There are two main types: physical (or mechanical) and chemical. Physical weathering may be caused by temperature changes, such as freezing and thawing, or by abrasion from material carried by winds, rivers, or glaciers. Rocks may also be broken down by the actions of animals and plants, such as the burrowing of animals and the growth of roots. Chemical weathering causes rocks to decompose by changing their chemical composition – for example, rainwater may dissolve certain minerals in a rock. Erosion is the wearing away and removal of land surfaces by water, wind, or ice. It is greatest in areas of little or no surface vegetation, such as deserts, where sand dunes may form.

FORMATION OF A HAMADA (ROCK PAVEMENT)

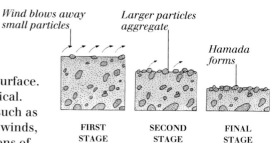

Wind blows away small particles

Larger particles aggregate

Hamada forms

FIRST STAGE **SECOND STAGE** **FINAL STAGE**

FEATURES PRODUCED BY WIND ACTION

Wind-blown sand

Mushroom-shaped rock

Neck

Rock base eroded by wind-blown sand

ROCK PEDESTAL

Wind-blown sand *Widened joint* *Soft rock*

Hard rock

ZEUGEN

Wind-blown sand

Furrow

Hard rock

Soft rock eroded by wind-blown sand

YARDANG

FEATURES OF WEATHERING AND EROSION

Mesa (flat-topped plateau)

Canyon

Zeugen

Joint

Hard rock

Soft rock

Shelf formed of hard rock

Talus (scree)

Alluvial fan (alluvial cone)

Bahada (gentle slope covered with loose rock)

Bolson (alluvium-filled basin)

EXAMPLES OF PHYSICAL WEATHERING PROCESSES

Heated rock surface expands

Exfoliation dome

Flaking rock

Fallen debris

EXFOLIATION (ONION-SKIN WEATHERING)

Joint expands and contracts due to temperature changes

Block of fallen rock

BLOCK DISINTEGRATION

Talus (scree)

Joint widened by frozen water

FROST WEDGING

Crack widened by tree root

Trunk

TREE ROOT ACTION

SECTION THROUGH A BARKHAN DUNE

Strong wind

Weak wind

Direction of wind-blown sand

Windward face

Direction of sand movement

Slip face

Foreset strata

Cross-bed set

Topset strata

Bottomset strata

EXAMPLES OF SAND DUNES

Wind direction

Crescent-shaped dune

BARKHAN DUNE

Wind direction

Dune at right angle to wind

TRANSVERSE DUNE

Wind direction

Point where sand ridges meet

STAR DUNE

Wind direction

Parallel dunes

SEIF (LINEAR) DUNE

Canyon

Wadi (dry wash)

Mesa (flat-topped plateau)

Talus (scree)

Butte (flat-topped mesa remnant)

Eroded arch

Residual hill on pediment

Hamada (rock pavement)

Rock pedestal

Barkhan dune

Parabolic dune

Transverse dune

Seif (linear) dune

Inselberg (isolated, steep-sided hill)

aya ry lake d of salt or siccated clay)

Faultline

Freshwater lake

Fertile oasis

Deflation hollow created by wind erosion

Hog's-back (steep ridge)

Hard sandstone

Faultline

Cuesta (asymmetric ridge)

Hard granite

Caves

CAVES COMMONLY FORM in areas of limestone, although on coastlines they also occur in other rocks. Limestone is made of calcite (calcium carbonate), which dissolves in the carbonic acid naturally present in rainwater, and in humic acids from the decay of vegetation. The acidic water trickles down through cracks and joints in the limestone and between rock layers, breaking up the surface terrain into clints (blocks of rock), separated by grikes (deep cracks), and punctuated by sink-holes (also called swallow-holes or potholes) into which surface streams may disappear. Underground, the acidic water dissolves the rock around crevices, opening up a network of passages and caves, which can become large caverns if the roofs collapse. Various features are formed when the dissolved calcite is redeposited; for example, it may be redeposited along an underground stream to form a gour (series of calcite ridges), or in caves and passages to form stalactites and stalagmites. Stalactites develop where calcite is left behind as water drips from the roof; where the drops land, stalagmites build up.

STALACTITE WITH RING MARKS

Ring mark

MERGED STALACTITES

SURFACE TOPOGRAPHY OF A CAVE SYSTEM

Doline (depression caused by collapse of cave roof)

Sink-hole

Porous limestone

Gorge where cave roof has fallen in

Resurgence

Limestone terrain with clints and grikes

Impermeable rock

STALAGMITE FORMATIONS

Calcite (calcium carbonate) crystallized under water

Thin encrustations of calcite (calcium carbonate)

CRYSTALLINE STALAGMITIC FLOOR

CALCAREOUS TUFA

Scar of bare rock

Former water table

Permeable limestone

Encrustations on dead stems of small plants

Calcite (calcium carbonate)

Calcite (calcium carbonate)

STALAGMITIC FLOOR

Resurgence

Encrustations with fungoid structure

STALAGMITIC BOSS

Layer of impermeable rock

Present water table

DEVELOPMENT OF A CAVE SYSTEM

Impermeable rock

Joint

Bedding plane

Impermeable rock

Permeable limestone

STRUCTURE OF LIMESTONE STRATA

Water seeps through cracks in rock

Stream enters permeable rock

Calcite (calcium carbonate) deposits begin to form

Resurgence

Tunnel

Underground stream

INITIAL CAVE

Doline caused by collapse of cave roof

Sink-hole

Stalactite

Stalagmite

Gorge

Resurgence

Cave

Dry gallery

EXTENDED CAVE SYSTEM

INTERCONNECTED CAVE SYSTEM

Stalactite

Pillar (column)

Gorge

Stalactite

Dry gallery (former course of underground stream)

Gour (series of calcite ridges) deposited by running water

Stalagmite

Joint in rock enlarged by water

Bedding plane

Curtain of deposited calcite (calcium carbonate)

Tunnel

Cave

Passage

Cavern

Gour (series of calcite ridges)

285

Glaciers

GLACIER BAY, ALASKA

A VALLEY GLACIER IS A LARGE MASS OF ICE that forms on land and moves slowly downhill under its own weight. It is formed from snow that collects in cirques (mountain hollows also known as corries) and compresses into ice as more and more snow accumulates. The cirque is deepened by frost wedging and abrasion (see pp. 282-283), and arêtes (sharp ridges) develop between adjacent cirques. Eventually, so much ice builds up that the glacier begins to move downhill. As the glacier moves it collects moraine (debris), which may range in size from particles of dust to large boulders. The rocks at the base of the glacier erode the glacial valley, giving it a U-shaped cross-section. Under the glacier, *roches moutonnées* (eroded outcrops of hard rock) and drumlins (rounded mounds of rock and clay) are left behind on the valley floor. The glacier ends at a terminus (the snout), where the ice melts as fast as it arrives. If the temperature increases, the ice melts faster than it arrives, and the glacier retreats. The retreating glacier leaves behind its moraine and also erratics (isolated single boulders). Glacial streams from the melting glacier deposit eskers and kames (ridges and mounds of sand and gravel), but carry away the finer sediment to form a stratified outwash plain. Lumps of ice carried on to this plain melt, creating holes called kettles.

VALLEY GLACIER

POST-GLACIAL VALLEY

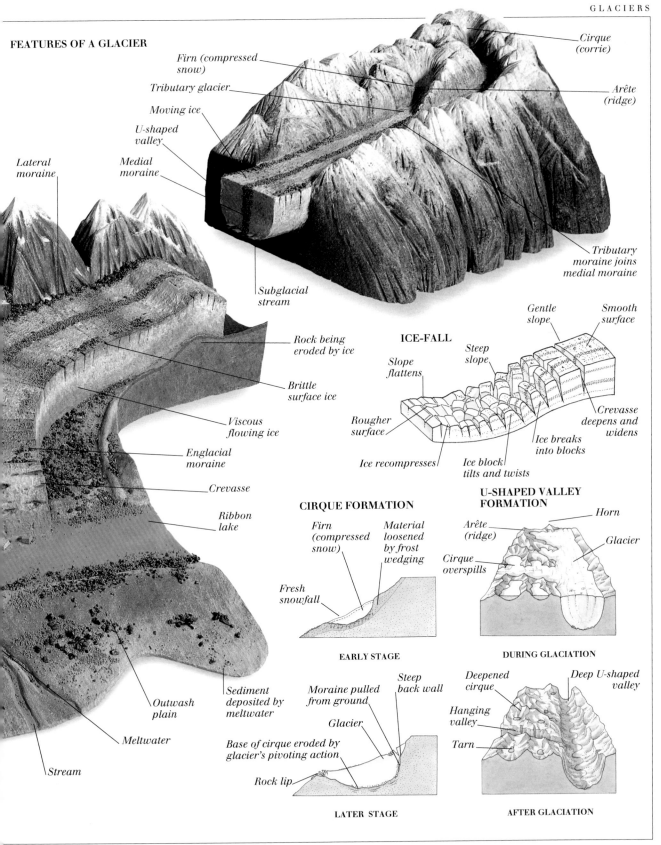

FEATURES OF A GLACIER

Cirque (corrie)

Firn (compressed snow)

Tributary glacier

Moving ice

U-shaped valley

Medial moraine

Arête (ridge)

Lateral moraine

Tributary moraine joins medial moraine

Subglacial stream

Rock being eroded by ice

Brittle surface ice

Viscous flowing ice

Englacial moraine

Crevasse

Ribbon lake

Sediment deposited by meltwater

Outwash plain

Meltwater

Stream

ICE-FALL

Gentle slope

Smooth surface

Steep slope

Slope flattens

Crevasse deepens and widens

Rougher surface

Ice breaks into blocks

Ice recompresses

Ice block tilts and twists

CIRQUE FORMATION

Firn (compressed snow)

Material loosened by frost wedging

Fresh snowfall

EARLY STAGE

Moraine pulled from ground

Steep back wall

Glacier

Base of cirque eroded by glacier's pivoting action

Rock lip

LATER STAGE

U-SHAPED VALLEY FORMATION

Horn

Arête (ridge)

Glacier

Cirque overspills

DURING GLACIATION

Deepened cirque

Deep U-shaped valley

Hanging valley

Tarn

AFTER GLACIATION

Rivers

RIVERS FORM PART of the water cycle – the continuous circulation of water between the land, sea, and atmosphere. The source of a river may be a mountain spring or lake, or a melting glacier. The course that the river subsequently takes depends on the slope of the terrain and on the rock types and formations over which it flows. In its early, upland stages, a river tumbles steeply over rocks and boulders and cuts a steep-sided V-shaped valley. Farther downstream, it flows smoothly over sediments and forms winding meanders, eroding sideways to create broad valleys and plains. On reaching the coast, the river may deposit sediment to form an estuary or delta (see pp. 290-291).

RIVER CAPTURE

EARLY STAGE

River

Tributary erodes headwards

River

LATER STAGE

Dry valley

River capture by tributary

River flow decreases

River flow increases

THE WATER CYCLE

Wind

Water vapour released into atmosphere by trees and other plants

Wind

Water vapour forms clouds

Precipitation falls on high ground

Water carried downstream by river

Water evaporates from sea

Water stored in sea

River flows into sea

Water seeps underground and flows to sea

Water evaporates from lake

Water seeps underground and flows to sea

SATELLITE IMAGE OF GANGES RIVER DELTA, BANGLADESH

River Ganges

Ganges delta

Infertile swampland

Distributary

Large volume of sediment

Seabed

Sea

Sediment layers

RIVER DRAINAGE PATTERNS

RADIAL

CENTRIPETAL

PARALLEL

DENDRITIC

DERANGED

TRELLISED

ANNULAR

RECTANGULAR

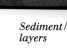

STAGES IN A RIVER'S DEVELOPMENT

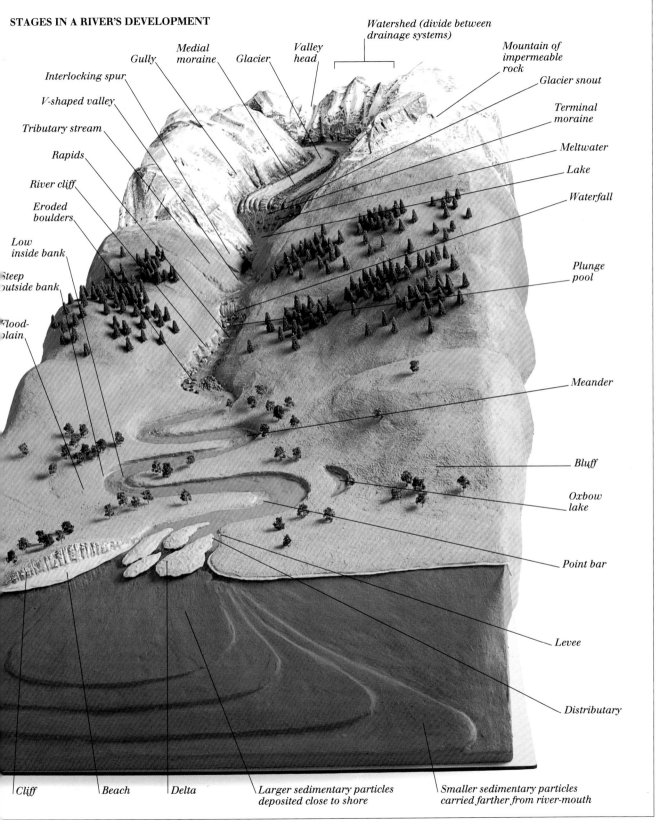

Watershed (divide between drainage systems)

Mountain of impermeable rock

Glacier snout

Medial moraine

Glacier

Valley head

Gully

Interlocking spur

V-shaped valley

Tributary stream

Rapids

River cliff

Eroded boulders

Low inside bank

Steep outside bank

Flood-plain

Terminal moraine

Meltwater

Lake

Waterfall

Plunge pool

Meander

Bluff

Oxbow lake

Point bar

Levee

Distributary

Cliff

Beach

Delta

Larger sedimentary particles deposited close to shore

Smaller sedimentary particles carried farther from river-mouth

River features

RIVERS ARE ONE OF THE MAJOR FORCES that shape the landscape. Near its source, a river is steep (see pp. 288-289). It erodes downwards, carving out V-shaped valleys and deep gorges. Waterfalls and rapids are formed where the river flows from hard rock to softer, more easily eroded rock. Farther downstream, meanders may form and there is greater sideways erosion, resulting in a broad river valley. The river sometimes erodes through the neck of a meander to form an oxbow lake. Sediment deposited on the valley floor by meandering rivers and during floods helps to create a flood-plain. Floods may also deposit sediment on the banks of the river to form levees. As a river spills into the sea or a lake, it deposits large amounts of sediment, and may form a delta. A delta is an area of sand-bars, swamps, and lagoons through which the river flows in several channels called distributaries – the Mississippi delta, for example. Often, a rise in sea level may have flooded the river-mouth to form a broad estuary, a tidal section where seawater mixes with fresh water.

A RIVER VALLEY DRAINAGE SYSTEM

290

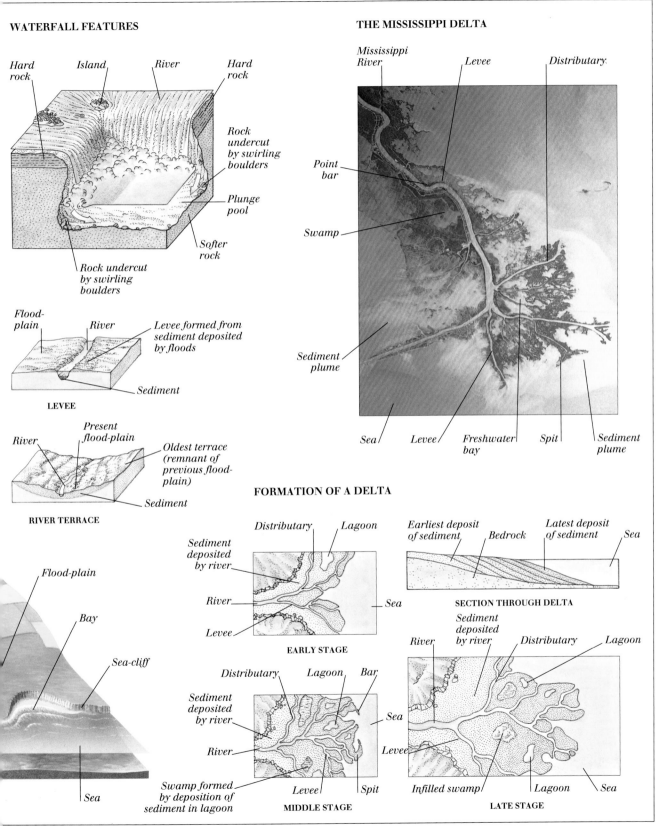

WATERFALL FEATURES

Hard rock

Island

River

Hard rock

Rock undercut by swirling boulders

Plunge pool

Softer rock

Rock undercut by swirling boulders

Flood-plain

River

Levee formed from sediment deposited by floods

Sediment

LEVEE

River

Present flood-plain

Oldest terrace (remnant of previous flood-plain)

Sediment

RIVER TERRACE

Flood-plain

Bay

Sea-cliff

Sea

THE MISSISSIPPI DELTA

Mississippi River

Levee

Distributary

Point bar

Swamp

Sediment plume

Sea

Levee

Freshwater bay

Spit

Sediment plume

FORMATION OF A DELTA

Distributary

Lagoon

Sediment deposited by river

River

Levee

Sea

EARLY STAGE

Earliest deposit of sediment

Bedrock

Latest deposit of sediment

Sea

SECTION THROUGH DELTA

Distributary

Lagoon

Bar

Sediment deposited by river

River

Levee

Sea

Spit

Swamp formed by deposition of sediment in lagoon

MIDDLE STAGE

Sediment deposited by river

River

Distributary

Lagoon

Levee

Infilled swamp

Lagoon

Sea

LATE STAGE

291

Lakes and groundwater

NATURAL LAKES OCCUR WHERE a large quantity of water collects in a hollow in impermeable rock, or is prevented from draining away by a barrier, such as moraine (glacial deposits) or solidified lava. Lakes are often relatively short-lived landscape features, as they tend to become silted up by sediment from the streams and rivers that feed them. Some of the more long-lasting lakes are found in deep rift valleys formed by vertical movements of the Earth's crust (see pp. 58-59) – for example, Lake Baikal in Russia, the world's largest freshwater lake, and the Dead Sea in the Middle East, one of the world's saltiest lakes. Where water is able to drain away, it sinks into the ground until it reaches a layer of impermeable rock, then accumulates in the permeable rock above it; this water-saturated permeable rock is called an aquifer. The saturated zone varies in depth according to seasonal and climatic changes. In wet conditions, the water stored underground builds up, while in dry periods it becomes depleted. Where the upper edge of the saturated zone – the water table – meets the ground surface, water emerges as springs. In an artesian basin, where the aquifer is below an aquiclude (layer of impermeable rock), the water table throughout the basin is determined by its height at the rim. In the centre of such a basin, the water table is above ground level. The water in the basin is thus trapped below the water table and can rise under its own pressure along faultlines or well shafts.

LAKE BAIKAL, RUSSIA

EXAMPLES OF SPRINGS

Permeable limestone *Water table* *Spring line* *Stream* *Spring* *Impermeable shale*

LIMESTONE SPRING

Permeable gravel *Water table* *Spring line* *Stream* *Spring* *Impermeable clay*

COASTAL (VALLEY) SPRING

Fault *Water table* *Permeable sandstone* *Spring line* *Spring* *Stream* *Impermeable shale*

FAULT SPRING

STRUCTURE OF AN ARTESIAN BASIN

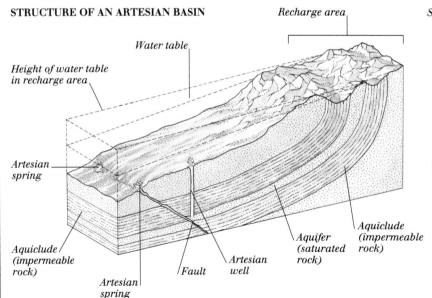

Recharge area *Water table* *Height of water table in recharge area* *Artesian spring* *Aquiclude (impermeable rock)* *Artesian spring* *Fault* *Artesian well* *Aquifer (saturated rock)* *Aquiclude (impermeable rock)*

Water table *Spring line* *Jointed, solidified lava* *Spring* *Jointed, solidified lava* *Stream* *Impermeable mudstone*

LAVA SPRING

FEATURES OF A GROUNDWATER SYSTEM

Lake

Stream

Zone of
aeration

Layer
of soil
moisture

Marsh

Zone of
aeration

Capillary
fringe

Water table

Saturated
zone

**CLOSE-UP OF
SURFACE LAYER**

*Dry-season
water table*

*Present water
table (wet season)*

*Temporarily saturated
zone (saturated only in
wet season)*

*Permanently
saturated zone
(saturated in wet
and dry seasons)*

EXAMPLES OF LAKES

*Glacial
deposits*

*Lake in kettle
(former site of
ice block)*

*Oxbow lake
(cut-off river
meander)*

River

KETTLE LAKE

OXBOW LAKE

*Caldera
(collapsed
crater)*

*Volcanic
lake*

*Movement
along strike-
slip (lateral)
fault*

*Strike-slip
(lateral) fault*

*Lake in
elongated
hollow*

VOLCANIC LAKE

STRIKE-SLIP (LATERAL) FAULT LAKE

Rift valley

*Steep back wall
eroded by frost
and ice*

*Moraine or rock
lip damming lake*

THE DEAD SEA, ISRAEL/JORDAN

*River
Jordan*

Dead Sea

*Steep rift-
valley walls*

*Salt left by
evaporation*

Israel

*High
valley
walls*

*Sinking graben
(block fault)*

*Tarn (circular
mountain lake)*

*Shallow
flats*

Jordan

GRABEN (BLOCK-FAULT) LAKE

TARN

Coastlines

COASTLINES ARE AMONG THE MOST RAPIDLY changing landscape features. Some are eroded by waves, wind, and rain, causing cliffs to be undercut and caves to be hollowed out of solid rock. Others are built up by waves transporting sand and small rocks in a process known as longshore drift, and by rivers depositing sediment in deltas. Additional influences include the activities of living organisms such as coral, crustal movements, and sea-level variations due to climatic changes. Rising land or a drop in sea level creates an emergent coastline, with cliffs and beaches stranded above the new shoreline. Sinking land or a rise in sea level produces a drowned coastline, typified by fjords (submerged glacial valleys) or submerged river valleys.

FEATURES OF A SEA-CLIFF

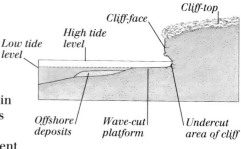

Cliff-top

Cliff-face

High tide level

Low tide level

Offshore deposits

Wave-cut platform

Undercut area of cliff

FEATURES OF WAVES

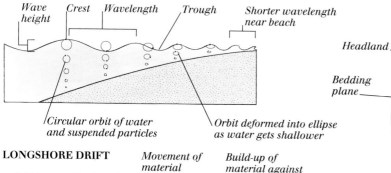

Wave height

Crest

Wavelength

Trough

Shorter wavelength near beach

Circular orbit of water and suspended particles

Orbit deformed into ellipse as water gets shallower

LONGSHORE DRIFT

Pebble

Backwash

Movement of material along beach

Build-up of material against groyne

Beach

Groyne

Waves approaching shore at an oblique angle

Swash zone

Swash

Mature river

Headland

Bedding plane

Sea-cliff

Remnants of former headland

Estuary

DEPOSITIONAL FEATURES OF COASTLINES

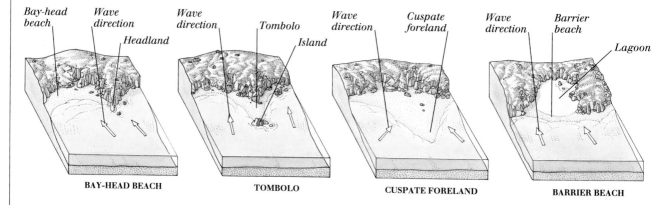

Bay-head beach

Wave direction

Headland

Wave direction

Tombolo

Island

Wave direction

Cuspate foreland

Wave direction

Barrier beach

Lagoon

BAY-HEAD BEACH

TOMBOLO

CUSPATE FORELAND

BARRIER BEACH

FEATURES OF A COASTLINE

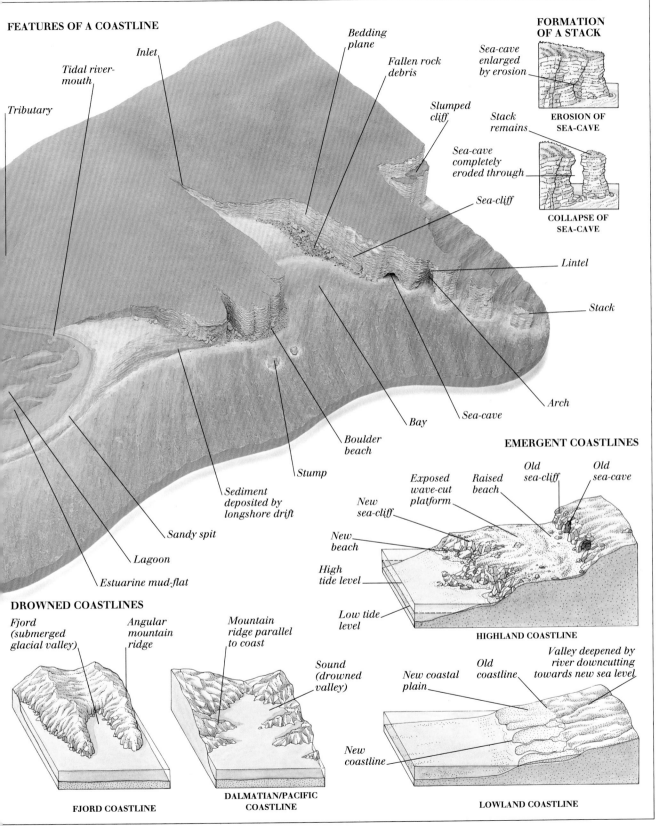

Bedding plane

Fallen rock debris

Slumped cliff

Inlet

Tidal river-mouth

Tributary

FORMATION OF A STACK

Sea-cave enlarged by erosion

EROSION OF SEA-CAVE

Stack remains

Sea-cave completely eroded through

COLLAPSE OF SEA-CAVE

Sea-cliff

Lintel

Stack

Arch

Sea-cave

Bay

Boulder beach

Stump

Sediment deposited by longshore drift

Sandy spit

Lagoon

Estuarine mud-flat

EMERGENT COASTLINES

Old sea-cliff

Old sea-cave

Exposed wave-cut platform

Raised beach

New sea-cliff

New beach

High tide level

Low tide level

HIGHLAND COASTLINE

DROWNED COASTLINES

Fjord (submerged glacial valley)

Angular mountain ridge

Mountain ridge parallel to coast

Sound (drowned valley)

Valley deepened by river downcutting towards new sea level

Old coastline

New coastal plain

New coastline

FJORD COASTLINE

DALMATIAN/PACIFIC COASTLINE

LOWLAND COASTLINE

Oceans and seas

OCEANS AND SEAS COVER ABOUT 70 PER CENT of the Earth's surface and account for about 97 per cent of its total water. These oceans and seas play a crucial role in regulating temperature variations and determining climate. Their waters absorb heat from the Sun, especially in tropical regions, and the surface currents distribute it around the Earth, warming overlying air masses and neighbouring land in winter and cooling them in summer. The oceans are never still. Differences in temperature and salinity drive deep current systems, while surface currents are generated by winds blowing over the oceans. All currents are deflected – to the right in the Northern Hemisphere, to the left in the Southern Hemisphere – as a result of the Earth's rotation. This deflective factor is known as the Coriolis force. A current that begins on the surface is immediately deflected. This current in turn generates a current in the layer of water beneath, which is also deflected. As the movement is transmitted downwards, the deflections form an Ekman spiral. The waters of the oceans and seas are also moved by the constant ebb and flow of tides. These are caused by the gravitational pull of the Moon and Sun. The highest tides (Spring tides) occur at full and new Moon; the lowest tides (neap tides) occur at first and last quarter.

SURFACE CURRENTS

OFFSHORE CURRENTS

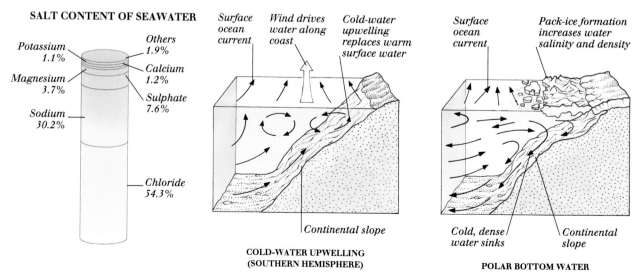

SALT CONTENT OF SEAWATER

Potassium 1.1%
Magnesium 3.7%
Sodium 30.2%

Others 1.9%
Calcium 1.2%
Sulphate 7.6%

Chloride 54.3%

Surface ocean current
Wind drives water along coast
Cold-water upwelling replaces warm surface water

Continental slope

COLD-WATER UPWELLING (SOUTHERN HEMISPHERE)

Surface ocean current
Pack-ice formation increases water salinity and density

Cold, dense water sinks
Continental slope

POLAR BOTTOM WATER

EFFECT OF CORIOLIS FORCE

North Pole

Coriolis
force

Winds and currents
deflected to right
in Northern
Hemisphere

Equator

Winds and
currents
deflected
to left in
Southern
Hemisphere

Original direction
of wind or current

Actual direction
of wind or current

South Pole

EKMAN SPIRAL (NORTHERN HEMISPHERE)

EQUATOR
(0°)

Wind

Surface current
caused by wind

Subsurface
current slightly
deflected by
Coriolis force

Deep current
at 180° to
surface current

Midwater current
further deflected
by Coriolis force

ARCTIC CIRCLE
(66° 32'N)

Oyashio Current

Kuroshio Current

North-east Monsoon Drift

North Equatorial Current

TROPIC OF
CANCER
(23° 30'N)

North Equatorial Current

Equatorial Countercurrent

Equatorial Countercurrent

South Equatorial Current

South Equatorial Current

Equatorial Countercurrent

South Equatorial Current

SOUTH
INDIAN
GYRE

West Australian Current

East Australian Current

TROPIC OF
CAPRICORN
(23° 30'S)

ANTARCTIC
CIRCLE
(66° 32'S)

HOW TIDES ARE CAUSED

HIGH
SPRING TIDE

New Moon

LOW
NEAP TIDE

Last
quarter

Moon's
gravitational
pull

HIGH
SPRING TIDE

Full Moon

Earth's orbit   Earth

Tidal bulge
caused by Sun's
gravitational pull

Tidal bulge
caused by Moon's
gravitational pull

Sun's
gravitational
pull

Sun

Sun's gravitational pull
reinforces centrifugal
effect, producing
large tidal
bulge

Sun's gravitational pull
diminishes Moon's effect

Tidal bulge where Moon's
gravitational pull is strongest

Equal and opposite tidal bulge
produced by centrifugal effect
due to Earth's spin

LOW
NEAP TIDE

First quarter

Moon's orbit

Moon

The ocean floor

THE OCEAN FLOOR COMPRISES TWO SECTIONS: the continental shelf and slope, and the deep-ocean floor. The continental shelf and slope are part of the continental crust, but may extend far into the ocean. Sloping quite gently to a depth of about 140 metres, the continental shelf is covered in sandy deposits shaped by waves and tidal currents. At the edge of the continental shelf, the seabed slopes down to the abyssal plain, which lies at an average depth of about 3,800 metres. On this deep-ocean floor is a layer of sediment made up of clays, fine oozes formed from the remains of tiny sea creatures, and occasional mineral-rich deposits. Echo-sounding and remote sensing from satellites has revealed that the abyssal plain is divided by a system of mountain ranges, far bigger than any on land – the mid-ocean ridge. Here, magma (molten rock) wells up from the Earth's interior and solidifies, widening the ocean floor (see pp. 58-59). As the ocean floor spreads, volcanoes that have formed over hot spots in the crust move away from their magma source; they become extinct and are increasingly submerged and eroded. Volcanoes eroded below sea level remain as seamounts (underwater mountains). In warm waters, a volcano that projects above the ocean surface often acquires a fringing coral reef, which may develop into an atoll as the volcano becomes submerged.

CONTINENTAL-SHELF FLOOR

Bedrock exposed by tidal scour

Shoreline

Parallel strips of coarse material left by strong tidal currents

Sand deposited in wavy pattern by weaker currents

Irregular patches of fine sand deposited by weakest currents

FEATURES OF THE OCEAN FLOOR

Sediment

Submarine canyon

Continental shelf

Course of mud river

Continental rise

Continental slope

Guyot (flat-topped seamount)

Seamount (underwater mountain)

Abyssal plain

Continental crust

Ooze (sediment consisting of remains of tiny sea creatures)

Layer of volcanic rock

Pillow lava

Volcanic crystalline rock

Oceanic crust

KEY

- Calcareous ooze
- Pelagic clay
- Glacial sediments
- Siliceous ooze
- Terrigenous sediments
- Continental margin sediments
- Metalliferous muds
- Major nodule fields

DEEP-OCEAN FLOOR SEDIMENTS

ECHO-SOUND PROFILE OF OCEAN FLOOR

Sand wave

Event mark indicates synchronization of survey equipment

Minor oscillations caused by ship's movement

Sand wave

Seabed profile

Velocity of sound in water (1,493 m/sec)

Reference code

Mid-ocean ridge

Magma (molten rock)

Ocean trench

Sediment

DEVELOPMENT OF AN ATOLL

Volcanic island

Sea level

Coral grows on shoreline

FRINGING REEF

Lagoon

Eroded volcanic island subsides

Coral continues to grow, forming barrier reef

BARRIER REEF

Coral continues to grow where waves bring food

Volcanic island becomes submerged

Lagoon

Dead coral

ATOLL

Coral submerged too deeply to grow

Volcanic island is submerged further

SUBMERGED ATOLL

The atmosphere

JET STREAM

THE EARTH IS SURROUNDED BY ITS ATMOSPHERE, a blanket of gases that enables life to exist on the planet. This layer has no definite outer edge, gradually becoming thinner until it merges into space, but over 80 per cent of atmospheric gases are held by gravity within about 20 kilometres of the Earth's surface. The atmosphere blocks out much harmful ultraviolet solar radiation, and insulates the Earth against extremes of temperature by limiting both incoming solar radiation and the escape of re-radiated heat into space. This natural balance may be distorted by the greenhouse effect, as gases such as carbon dioxide have built up in the atmosphere, trapping more heat. Close to the Earth's surface, differences in air temperature and pressure cause air to circulate between the equator and poles. This circulation, together with the Coriolis force, gives rise to the prevailing surface winds and the high-level jet streams.

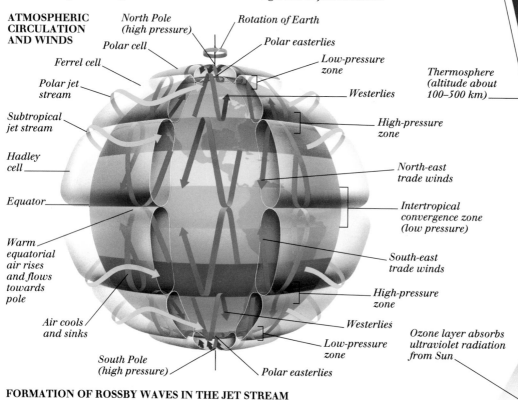

ATMOSPHERIC CIRCULATION AND WINDS

- North Pole (high pressure)
- Rotation of Earth
- Polar cell
- Polar easterlies
- Ferrel cell
- Low-pressure zone
- Polar jet stream
- Westerlies
- Subtropical jet stream
- High-pressure zone
- Hadley cell
- North-east trade winds
- Equator
- Intertropical convergence zone (low pressure)
- Warm equatorial air rises and flows towards pole
- South-east trade winds
- High-pressure zone
- Air cools and sinks
- Westerlies
- Low-pressure zone
- South Pole (high pressure)
- Polar easterlies

FORMATION OF ROSSBY WAVES IN THE JET STREAM

- Long Rossby wave develops in polar jet stream
- Cold air
- Rossby wave becomes more pronounced
- Fully developed Rossby wave
- Warm air

INITIAL UNDULATION

DEEPENING WAVE

DEVELOPED WAVE

- Exosphere (altitude above about 500 km)
- Corona
- Thermosphere (altitude about 100–500 km)
- Ozone layer absorbs ultraviolet radiation from Sun
- Mesosphere (altitude about 50–100 km)
- Stratosphere (altitude about 10–50 km)
- Troposphere (altitude up to about 10 km)

STRUCTURE OF THE ATMOSPHERE

GLOBAL WARMING

Solar radiation re-radiated as heat

Some re-radiated heat escapes into space

Sun

Some re-radiated heat reflected back to Earth

Incoming solar radiation

Earth

Atmosphere

NATURALLY MODERATED GREENHOUSE EFFECT

Meteor (shooting star) burns up as it passes through atmosphere

Less re-radiated heat escapes

Solar radiation re-radiated as heat

More re-radiated heat reflected back to Earth

Aurora

Surface temperature rises

"Greenhouse gases" accumulate in atmosphere

Incoming solar radiation

UNBALANCED GREENHOUSE EFFECT

14% of incoming solar radiation absorbed by atmosphere

7% of incoming solar radiation reflected by atmosphere

COMPOSITION OF THE LOWER ATMOSPHERE

Other elements less than 0.1%

24% of incoming solar radiation reflected by clouds

Argon 0.93%

Cosmic rays (high-energy particles from space) penetrate to stratosphere

Oxygen 21%

Some absorbed heat re-radiated by atmosphere

Nitrogen 78%

4% of incoming solar radiation reflected by oceans and land

51% of incoming solar radiation absorbed by Earth's surface

Some absorbed heat re-radiated by clouds

Weather

WEATHER IS DEFINED AS THE ATMOSPHERIC CONDITIONS at a particular time and place; climate is the average weather conditions for a given region over time. Weather is assessed in terms of temperature, wind, cloud cover, and precipitation, such as rain or snow. Fine weather is associated with high-pressure areas, where air is sinking. Cloudy, wet, changeable weather is common in low-pressure zones with rising, unstable air. Such conditions occur at temperate latitudes, where warm air meets cool air along the polar fronts. Here, spiralling low-pressure cells known as depressions (mid-latitude cyclones) often form. A depression usually contains a sector of warmer air, beginning at a warm front and ending at a cold front. If the two fronts merge, forming an occluded front, the warm air is pushed upwards. An extreme form of low-pressure cell is a hurricane (also called a typhoon or tropical cyclone), which brings torrential rain and exceptionally strong winds.

TYPES OF OCCLUDED FRONT

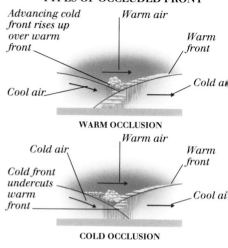

Advancing cold front rises up over warm front

Warm air

Warm front

Cool air

Cold ai

WARM OCCLUSION

Cold air

Warm air

Warm front

Cold front undercuts warm front

Cool ai

COLD OCCLUSION

FORMS OF PRECIPITATION

Water droplets less than 0.5 mm in diameter fall as drizzle

Water dropler coalesce t form raindrop 0.5–5.0 mm i diamete

Rising air

RAIN FROM CLOUDS NOT REACHING FREEZING LEVEL

Ice crystal

Snowflakes grown from ice crystals fall as snow

Coalesced water droplets fall as rain

Snowflakes melt to fall as rain

Rising air

RAIN AND SNOW FROM CLOUDS REACHING FREEZING LEVEL

Vertical air currents toss frozen water droplets up and down

Alternate freezing and meltin, builds up layers of ic

Rising air

Ice falls as hailstones

HAIL

TYPES OF CLOUD

Cirrus

Cirrostratus

Cirrocumulus

Freezing level, above which clouds consist of ice crystals

Cumulonimbus

Altocumulus

Altostratus

Nimbus

Stratocumulus

Cumulus

Nimbostratus

Stratus

Condensation level

13
12
11
10
9
8
7
6
5
4
3
2
1
0

Altitude in temperate regions (km)

STRUCTURE OF A HURRICANE

Outward-spiralling high-level winds

Outward-spiralling cirrus clouds

Descending dry air

10–15 km high

Storm moving at 15–40 km/h in direction of prevailing wind

Greatest windspeeds (up to 300 km/h) about 20 km from eye wall

Eye (calm, very low-pressure centre)

Precipitation greatest in eye wall

Spiralling bands of wind and rain

Water vapour picked up from sea feeds walls of cumulus clouds

Warm, moist air drawn in

WEATHER MAP

Centre of high-pressure area

Centre of low-pressure area

Very strong south-easterly wind

Cold front

Continuous rain

Cloudy sky

Light north-westerly wind

Obscured sky

Very cloudy sky

Air pressure 1026 millibars

Occluded front

Occluded front

Strong north-easterly wind

Slightly cloudy sky

Temperature 21°C

Overcast sky

Sea temperature 8°C

Cold front

Warm front

Calm

Very cloudy sky

Light southerly wind

PHYSICS AND CHEMISTRY

The variety of matter

PLANT AND INSECT (LIVING MATTER)

MATTER IS ANYTHING THAT OCCUPIES SPACE. It includes everything from natural substances, such as minerals or living organisms, to synthetic materials. Matter can exist in three distinct states – solid, liquid, and gas. A solid is rigid and retains its shape. A liquid is fluid, has a definite volume, and will take the shape of its container. A gas (also fluid) fills a space, so its volume will be the same as the volume of its container. Most substances can exist as a solid, a liquid, or a gas: the state is determined by temperature. At very high temperatures, matter becomes plasma, often considered to be a fourth state of matter. All matter is composed of microscopic particles, such as atoms and molecules (see pp. 308-309). The arrangement and interactions of these particles give a substance its physical and chemical properties, by which matter can be identified. There is a huge variety of matter because particles can arrange themselves in countless ways, in one substance or by mixing with others. Natural glass, for example, seems to be a solid but is, in fact, a supercool liquid: the atoms are not locked into a pattern and can flow. Pure substances known as elements (see p. 310) combine to form compounds or mixtures. Mixtures called colloids are made up of larger particles of matter suspended in a solid, liquid, or gas, while a solution is one substance dissolved in another.

TYPES OF COLLOID

HAIR GEL (SOLID IN LIQUID)

SHAVING FOAM (AIR IN LIQUID)

MIST (LIQUID IN GAS)

EXAMPLES OF MATTER

The element silicon in pure crystalline form

Polythene is made by combining natural materials in new ways

Low pressure gases

Streaks of plasma (mixture of electrons and charged atoms)

Voltage tears electrons from atoms of low pressure gases inside

Central electrode

POLYTHENE (SYNTHETIC POLYMER)

PURE SILICON (SEMICONDUCTOR)

BALL CONTAINING HIGH-TEMPERATURE GAS (PLASMA)

Obsidian is molten volcanic rock that cools quickly, so atoms cannot form a regular pattern

Solid crystals dissolve in liquid water

Water

Potassium permanganate crystals

Azurite is found naturally with deposits of copper ore

OBSIDIAN (NATURAL GLASS)

AZURITE (CRYSTALLINE MINERAL)

POTASSIUM PERMANGANATE AND WATER (SOLUTION)

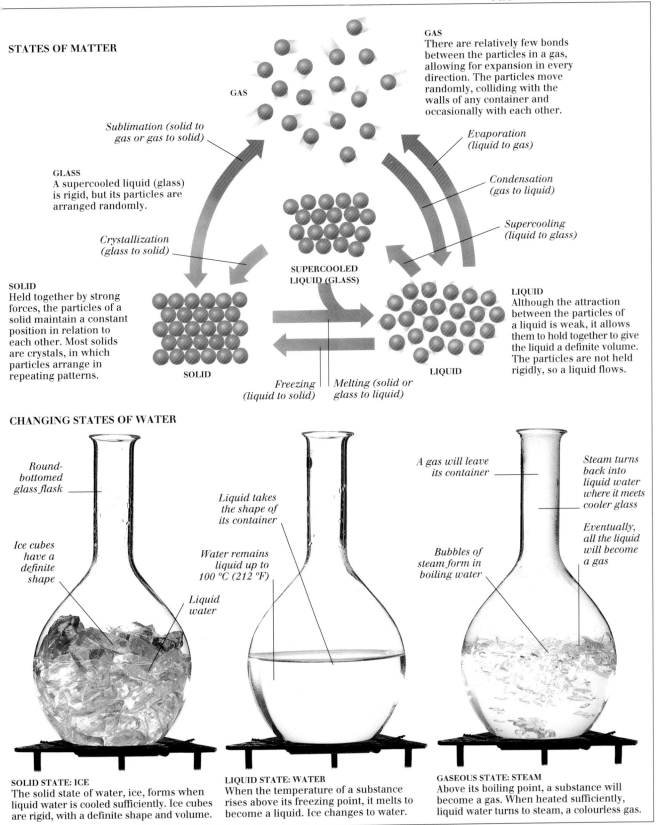

STATES OF MATTER

GAS

Sublimation (solid to gas or gas to solid)

GAS
There are relatively few bonds between the particles in a gas, allowing for expansion in every direction. The particles move randomly, colliding with the walls of any container and occasionally with each other.

Evaporation (liquid to gas)

Condensation (gas to liquid)

GLASS
A supercooled liquid (glass) is rigid, but its particles are arranged randomly.

Crystallization (glass to solid)

SUPERCOOLED LIQUID (GLASS)

Supercooling (liquid to glass)

SOLID
Held together by strong forces, the particles of a solid maintain a constant position in relation to each other. Most solids are crystals, in which particles arrange in repeating patterns.

SOLID

LIQUID
Although the attraction between the particles of a liquid is weak, it allows them to hold together to give the liquid a definite volume. The particles are not held rigidly, so a liquid flows.

LIQUID

Freezing (liquid to solid)

Melting (solid or glass to liquid)

CHANGING STATES OF WATER

Round-bottomed glass flask

Ice cubes have a definite shape

Liquid water

Liquid takes the shape of its container

Water remains liquid up to 100 °C (212 °F)

A gas will leave its container

Bubbles of steam form in boiling water

Steam turns back into liquid water where it meets cooler glass

Eventually, all the liquid will become a gas

SOLID STATE: ICE
The solid state of water, ice, forms when liquid water is cooled sufficiently. Ice cubes are rigid, with a definite shape and volume.

LIQUID STATE: WATER
When the temperature of a substance rises above its freezing point, it melts to become a liquid. Ice changes to water.

GASEOUS STATE: STEAM
Above its boiling point, a substance will become a gas. When heated sufficiently, liquid water turns to steam, a colourless gas.

Atoms and molecules

FALSE-COLOUR
IMAGE OF ACTUAL
GOLD ATOMS

ATOMS ARE THE smallest individual parts of an element (see pp. 310-311). They are tiny, with diameters in the order of one ten-thousand-millionth of a metre (10^{-10} m). Two or more atoms join together (bond) to form a molecule of a substance known as a compound. For example, when atoms of the elements hydrogen and fluorine join together, they form a molecule of the compound hydrogen fluoride. So molecules are the smallest individual parts of a compound. Atoms themselves are not indivisible – they possess an internal structure. At their centre is a dense nucleus, consisting of protons, which have a positive electric charge (see p. 316), and neutrons, which are uncharged. Around the nucleus are the negatively charged electrons. It is the electrons that give a substance most of its physical and chemical properties. They do not follow definite paths around the nucleus. Instead, electrons are said to be found within certain regions, called orbitals. These are arranged around the nucleus in "shells", each containing electrons of a particular energy. For example, the first shell (1) can hold up to two electrons, in a so-called s-orbital (1s). The second shell (2) can hold up to eight electrons, in s-orbitals (2s) and p-orbitals (2p). If an atom loses an electron, it becomes a positive ion (cation). If an electron is gained, an atom becomes a negative ion (anion). Ions of opposite charges will attract and join together, in a type of bonding known as ionic bonding. In covalent bonding, the atoms bond by sharing their electrons in what become molecular orbitals.

ATOMIC ORBITALS

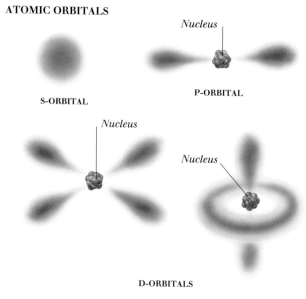

Nucleus

S-ORBITAL

P-ORBITAL

Nucleus

Nucleus

D-ORBITALS

MOLECULAR ORBITALS

Nucleus

Nucleus

Nucleus

Σ- (SIGMA) ORBITAL

Nucleus

π- (PI) ORBITAL

Nucleus

SP⁵-HYBRID ORBITAL

EXAMPLE OF IONIC BONDING

1s-orbital

2s-orbital

**1. NEUTRAL LITHIUM
ATOM (Li)**

1s-orbital   *1s-orbital*
*Second shell
holds seven
electrons*

2p-orbital

2s-orbital   *2p-orbital*

2p-orbital

**NEUTRAL FLUORINE
ATOM (F)**

*Electron
transfer*

*Lithium atom
loses 2s electron and
becomes positively
charged (Li⁺ ion)*

2. ELECTRON TRANSFER

*Second shell now
holds eight electrons,
and is "filled"*

*Charged atoms (ions)
held together by
electrostatic forces*

Li⁺ ion

F⁻ ion

*Fluorine atom gains
electron and becomes
negatively charged (F⁻ ion)*

**3. IONIC BONDING:
LITHIUM FLUORIDE MOLECULE (LiF)**

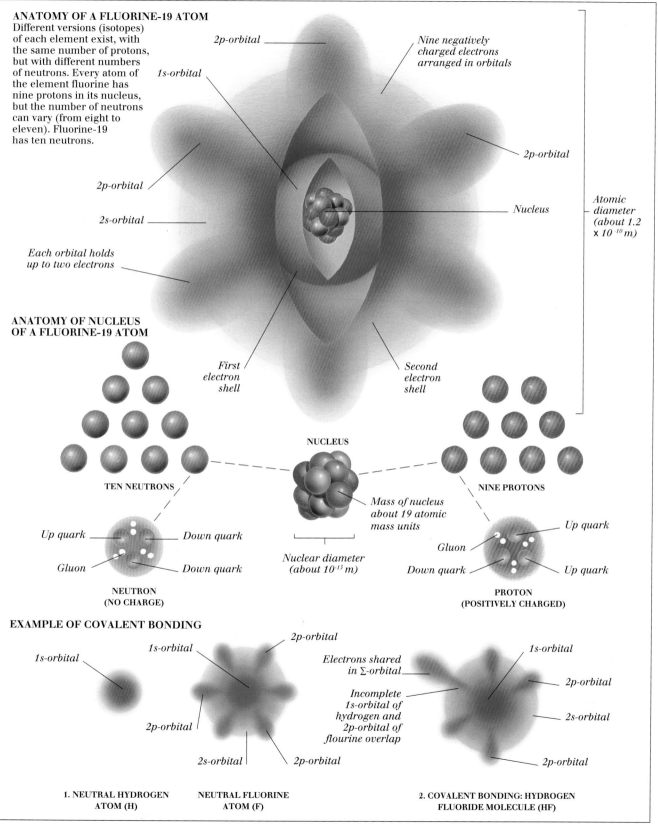

ANATOMY OF A FLUORINE-19 ATOM
Different versions (isotopes) of each element exist, with the same number of protons, but with different numbers of neutrons. Every atom of the element fluorine has nine protons in its nucleus, but the number of neutrons can vary (from eight to eleven). Fluorine-19 has ten neutrons.

2p-orbital

1s-orbital

2p-orbital

2s-orbital

Nine negatively charged electrons arranged in orbitals

2p-orbital

Nucleus

Atomic diameter (about 1.2 x 10⁻¹⁰ m)

Each orbital holds up to two electrons

ANATOMY OF NUCLEUS OF A FLUORINE-19 ATOM

First electron shell

Second electron shell

NUCLEUS

TEN NEUTRONS

NINE PROTONS

Mass of nucleus about 19 atomic mass units

Up quark

Gluon

Down quark

Down quark

Up quark

Gluon

Down quark

Up quark

Nuclear diameter (about 10⁻¹⁵ m)

**NEUTRON
(NO CHARGE)**

**PROTON
(POSITIVELY CHARGED)**

EXAMPLE OF COVALENT BONDING

1s-orbital

1s-orbital

2p-orbital

2p-orbital

2s-orbital

2p-orbital

Electrons shared in Σ-orbital

Incomplete 1s-orbital of hydrogen and 2p-orbital of flourine overlap

1s-orbital

2p-orbital

2s-orbital

2p-orbital

1. NEUTRAL HYDROGEN ATOM (H)

NEUTRAL FLUORINE ATOM (F)

2. COVALENT BONDING: HYDROGEN FLUORIDE MOLECULE (HF)

The periodic table

AN ELEMENT is a substance that consists of atoms of one type only. The 92 elements that occur naturally, and the 17 elements created artificially, are often arranged into a chart called the periodic table. Each element is defined by its atomic number – the number of protons in the nucleus of each of its atoms (it is also the number of electrons present). Atomic number increases along each row (period) and down each column (group). The shape of the table is determined by the way in which electrons arrange themselves around the nucleus: the positioning of elements in order of increasing atomic number brings together atoms with a similar pattern of orbiting electrons (orbitals). These appear in blocks. Electrons occupy shells of a certain energy (see pp. 308-309). Periods are ordered according to the filling of successive shells with electrons, while groups reflect the number of electrons in the outer shell (valency electrons). These outer electrons are important – they decide the chemical properties of the atom. Elements that appear in the same group have similar properties because they have the same number of electrons in their outer shell. Elements in Group 0 have "filled shells", where the outer shell holds its maximum number of electrons, and are stable. Atoms of Group I elements have just one electron in their outer shell. This makes them unstable – and ready to react with other substances.

METALS AND NON-METALS
Elements at the left-hand side of each period are metals. Metals easily lose electrons and form positive ions. Non-metals, on the right of a period, tend to become negative ions. Semi-metals, which have properties of both metals and non-metals, are between the two.

RELATIVE ATOMIC MASS
Atomic mass (formerly atomic weight) is the mass of each atom of an element. It is equal to the number of protons plus the number of neutrons (electrons have negligible mass). The figures given are the averages for all the different versions (isotopes) of each element, measured relative to the mass of carbon-12.

Atomic number
Chemical symbol
Chemical name
Relative atomic mass

Atomic number is number of protons in each nucleus

Atomic number goes up by one along each period

Group I
Group II
1st transition metals

s-block
d-block

Two series always separated out from the table to give it a coherent shape

Soft, silvery, and highly reactive metal

SODIUM: GROUP 1 METAL

Silvery, reactive metal

MAGNESIUM: GROUP 2 METAL

Hard, silvery metal

CHROMIUM: 1ST TRANSITION METAL

Radioactive metal

PLUTONIUM: ACTINIDE SERIES METAL

TYPES OF ELEMENT KEY:

 Alkali metals

 Alkaline earth metals

Transition metals

Lanthanides (rare earths)

 Actinides

Poor metals

Semi-metals

Non-metals

Noble gases

Bright yellow crystal

**SULPHUR:
GROUP 6 SOLID NON-METAL**

**IODINE:
GROUP 7
SOLID NON-METAL**

Purple-black solid turns to gas easily

ALLOTROPES OF CARBON
Some elements exist in more than one form – these are known as allotropes. Carbon powder, graphite, and diamond are allotropes of carbon. They all consist of carbon atoms, but have very different physical properties.

DIAMOND

GRAPHITE

CARBON POWDER

Boron and carbon groups

Nitrogen and oxygen groups

Halogens

Group 0

Group III	Group IV	Group V	Group VI	Group VII	
					2 **He** Helium 4.0

Period

| 5
B
Boron
10.8 | 6
C
Carbon
12.0 | 7
N
Nitrogen
14.0 | 8
O
Oxygen
16.0 | 9
F
Fluorine
19.0 | 10
Ne
Neon
20.2 |

Short period

| 13
Al
Aluminium
27.0 | 14
Si
Silicon
28.1 | 15
P
Phosphorus
31.0 | 16
S
Sulphur
32.1 | 17
Cl
Chlorine
55.5 | 18
Ar
Argon
40.0 |

2nd transition metals

3rd transition metals

26 **Fe** Iron 55.9	27 **Co** Cobalt 58.9	28 **Ni** Nickel 58.7	29 **Cu** Copper 63.5	30 **Zn** Zinc 65.4	31 **Ga** Gallium 69.7	32 **Ge** Germanium 72.6	33 **As** Arsenic 74.9	34 **Se** Selenium 79.0	35 **Br** Bromine 79.9	36 **Kr** Krypton 85.8
44 **Ru** Ruthenium 101.0	45 **Rh** Rhodium 102.9	46 **Pd** Palladium 106.4	47 **Ag** Silver 107.9	48 **Cd** Cadmium 112.4	49 **In** Indium 114.8	50 **Sn** Tin 118.7	51 **Sb** Antimony 121.8	52 **Te** Tellurium 127.6	53 **I** Iodine 126.9	54 **Xe** Xenon 131.5
76 **Os** Osmium 190.2	77 **Ir** Iridium 192.2	78 **Pt** Platinum 195.1	79 **Au** Gold 197.0	80 **Hg** Mercury 200.6	81 **Tl** Thallium 204.4	82 **Pb** Lead 207.2	83 **Bi** Bismuth 209.0	84 **Po** Polonium 210.0	85 **At** Astatine 210.0	86 **Rn** Radon 222.0
108 **Uno** Unniloctium (265)	109 **Une** Unnilennium (266)									

Long period

d-block

p-block

Atomic mass is estimated, as element exists fleetingly

Shiny semi-metal

NOBLE GASES
Group 0 contains elements that have a filled (complete) outer shell of electrons, which means the atoms do not need to lose or gain electrons by bonding with other atoms. This makes them stable and they do not easily form ions or react with other elements. Noble gases are also called rare or inert gases.

Unreactive, colourless gas glows red in discharge tube

Yellow, unreactive precious metal

Soft, shiny, reactive metal

**GOLD:
3RD TRANSITION METAL**

**TIN:
GROUP 4 POOR METAL**

**ANTIMONY:
GROUP 5 SEMI-METAL**

**NEON:
GROUP 0
COLOURLESS GAS**

61 **Pm** Promethium 147.0	62 **Sm** Samarium 150.4	63 **Eu** Europium 152.0	64 **Gd** Gadolinium 157.3	65 **Tb** Terbium 158.9	66 **Dy** Dysprosium 162.5	67 **Ho** Holmium 164.9	68 **Er** Erbium 167.3	69 **Tm** Thulium 168.9	70 **Yb** Ytterbium 175.0	71 **Lu** Lutetium 175.0
93 **Np** Neptunium 237.0	94 **Pu** Plutonium 242.0	95 **Am** Americium 243.0	96 **Cm** Curium 247.0	97 **Bk** Berkelium 247.0	98 **Cf** Californium 251.0	99 **Es** Einsteinium 254.0	100 **Fm** Fermium 253.0	101 **Md** Mendelevium 256.0	102 **No** Nobelium 254.0	103 **Lr** Lawrencium 257.0

f-block

Chemical reactions

A CHEMICAL REACTION TAKES PLACE whenever bonds between atoms are broken or made. In each case, atoms or groups of atoms rearrange, making new substances (products) from the original ones (reactants). Reactions happen naturally, or can be made to happen; they may take years, or only an instant. Some of the main types are shown here. A reaction usually involves a change in energy (see pp. 314-315). In a burning reaction, for example, the making of new bonds between atoms releases energy as heat and light. This type of reaction, in which heat is given off, is an exothermic reaction. Many reactions, like burning, are irreversible, but some can take place in either direction, and are said to be reversible. Reactions can be used to form solids from solutions: in a double decomposition reaction, two compounds in solution break down and re-form into two new substances, often creating a precipitate (insoluble solid); in displacement, an element (eg. copper) displaces another element (eg. silver) from a solution. The rate (speed) of a reaction is determined by many different factors, such as temperature, and the size and shape of the reactants. To describe and keep track of reactions, internationally recognized chemical symbols and equations are used. Reactions are also used in the laboratory to identify matter. An experiment with candle wax, for example, demonstrates that it contains carbon and hydrogen.

SALT FORMATION (ACID ON METAL)

Glass beaker

Hydrogen gas (H_2) given off

Zinc (Zn) replaces hydrogen in acid (HCl) to form zinc chloride solution ($ZnCl_2$)

Hydrogen in acid driven off when acid meets a reactive metal

Hydrochloric acid (HCl)

Effervescence

Zinc metal chippings (Zn)

Zinc metal chippings (Zn)

THE REACTION
Hydrochloric acid added to zinc produces zinc chloride and hydrogen.
$Zn + 2HCl \rightarrow ZnCl_2 + H_2$

DISPLACEMENT

Copper metal (Cu)

Copper (Cu) displaces silver ions (Ag^{2+}) from silver nitrate solution ($AgNO_3$)

Silver nitrate solution ($AgNO_3$)

Blue solution of copper nitrate ($Cu(NO_3)_2$) forms

Two metals compete for nitrate ions

Needles of silver metal (Ag) form

Glass flask

THE REACTION
Copper metal added to silver nitrate solution produces copper nitrate and silver metal.
$Cu + 2AgNO_3 \rightarrow Cu(NO_3)_2 + 2Ag$

BURNING MATTER

Ammonium dichromate ($(NH_4)_2Cr_2O_7$)

In this burning reaction, atoms form simpler substances and give off heat and light

Flame

Ammonium dichromate ($(NH_4)_2Cr_2O_7$) converts to chromium oxide (Cr_2O_3)

THE REACTION
When lit, ammonium dichromate combines with oxygen from air.
$(NH_4)_2Cr_2O_7 + O_2 \rightarrow Cr_2O_3 + 4H_2O + 2NO$

Nitrogen monoxide (NO) and water vapour (H_2O) given off as colourless gases

A REVERSIBLE REACTION

Flat-bottomed glass flask

Potassium chromate solution (K_2CrO_4)

Bright yellow solution contains potassium and chromate ions

1. THE REACTANT
Potassium chromate dissolves in water to form potassium ions and chromate ions.
$K_2CrO_4 \rightarrow 2K^+ + CrO_4^{2-}$

Pipette

Hydrochloric acid (HCl) added in drops

Acid causes reaction to take place

Chromate ions converted to orange dichromate ions

Potassium dichromate (KCr_2O_7) forms

2. THE REACTION
Addition of hydrochloric acid changes chromate ions into dichromate ions.
$2CrO_4^{2-} \rightarrow Cr_2O_7^{2-}$

Pipette

Sodium hydroxide (NaOH) added in drops

Sodium hydroxide (NaOH) neutralizes the acid

Solution turns to bright orange of potassium dichromate

Solution returns to original bright yellow colour

Potassium dichromate (KCr_2O_7) re-forms to potassium chromate (K_2CrO_4)

3. REVERSING
Addition of sodium hydroxide changes dichromate ions back into chromate ions.
$Cr_2O_7^{2-} \rightarrow 2CrO_4^{2-}$

FERMENTATION

Yeast converts sugar into alcohol (C_2H_5OH) and carbon dioxide gas (CO_2)

Airtight stopper

Flat-bottomed glass flask

Yeast mixed with warm water and sugar ($C_6H_{12}O_6$)

Carbon dioxide bubbles (CO_2)

THE REACTION
Yeast converts sugar and warm water into alcohol and carbon dioxide.
$$C_6H_{12}O_6 \rightarrow 2C_2H_5OH + 2CO_2$$

DOUBLE DECOMPOSITION

Potassium iodide solution (KI)

Lead nitrate solution ($Pb(NO_3)_2$)

Two solutions swap partners

Potassium iodide solution added to lead nitrate solution

Lead iodide (PbI_2), a yellow solid, forms

Potassium nitrate solution (KNO_3) forms

1. THE REACTANTS
Potassium iodide in water (KI) and lead nitrate in water ($Pb(NO_3)_2$) each form colourless solutions.

2. THE REACTION
When the solutions are mixed, lead iodide, a precipitate, and potassium nitrate solution are formed.
$$2KI + Pb(NO_3)_2 \rightarrow PbI_2 + 2KNO_3$$

TESTING CANDLE WAX, AN ORGANIC COMPOUND

Burning produces carbon dioxide gas (CO_2) and water vapour (H_2O)

Unburned carbon forms soot particles

Flame

Burning candle wax

Candle wax ($C_{18}H_{38}$), a hydrocarbon, contains the elements carbon and hydrogen

Delivery tube

Gases are trapped in funnel

Thistle funnel

Water vapour condenses to form liquid water (H_2O)

Water vapour trapped by solid drying agent, anhydrous copper sulphate ($CuSO_4$)

Anhydrous copper sulphate crystals ($CuSO_4$) combine with water vapour (H_2O) to form darker blue hydrated copper sulphate ($CuSO_4 . 10H_2O$)

Bung

Clamp

Anhydrous copper sulphate ($CuSO_4$)

Clamp stand

Delivery tube

Bung

U-tube

Carbon dioxide gas (CO_2) given off

Calcium hydroxide ($Ca(OH)_2$) and carbon dioxide (CO_2) form insoluble calcium carbonate ($CaCO_3$): lime water becomes milky

Tube connection to pump that sucks gases through

Bung

Test tube

Calcium hydroxide solution (lime water, $Ca(OH)_2$)

1. THE BURNING REACTION
Burning wax produces carbon dioxide gas and water vapour.
$$2C_{18}H_{38} + 55O_2 \rightarrow 36CO_2 + 38H_2O$$

2. TESTING FOR WATER VAPOUR
A solid drying agent traps water vapour, proving the presence of hydrogen in the candle wax.
$$CuSO_4 + 10H_2O \rightarrow CuSO_4 . 10H_2O$$

3. TESTING FOR CARBON DIOXIDE
Calcium hydroxide in solution reacts with carbon dioxide, forming a carbonate and turning milky.
$$Ca(OH)_2 + CO_2 \rightarrow CaCO_3 + H_2O$$

Energy

ANYTHING THAT HAPPENS – from a pin-drop to an explosion – requires energy. Energy is the capacity for "doing work" (making something happen). Various forms of energy exist, including light, heat, sound, electrical, chemical, nuclear, kinetic, and potential energies. The Law of Conservation of Energy states that the total amount of energy in the Universe is fixed – energy cannot be created or destroyed. It means that energy can only change from one form to another (energy transfer). For example, potential energy is energy that is "stored", and can be used in the future. An object gains potential energy when it is lifted; as the object is released, potential energy changes into the energy of motion (kinetic energy). During transference, some of the energy converts into heat. A combined heat and power station can put some of the otherwise "waste" heat to useful effect in local schools and housing. Most of the Earth's energy is provided by the Sun, in the form of electromagnetic radiation (see pp. 316-317). Some of this energy transfers to plant and animal life, and ultimately to fossil fuels, where it is stored in chemical form. Our bodies obtain energy from the food we eat, while energy needed for other tasks, such as heating and transport, can be obtained by burning fossil fuels – or by harnessing natural forces like wind or moving water – to generate electricity. Another source is nuclear power, where energy is released by reactions in the nucleus of an atom. All energy is measured by the international unit, the joule (J). As a guide, one joule is about equal to the amount of energy needed to lift an apple one metre.

SANKEY DIAGRAM SHOWING ENERGY FLOW IN A COAL-FIRED COMBINED HEAT AND POWER STATION

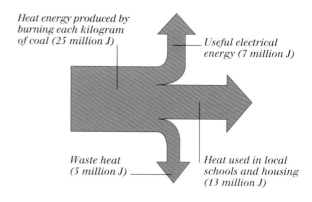

Heat energy produced by burning each kilogram of coal (25 million J)

Useful electrical energy (7 million J)

Waste heat (5 million J)

Heat used in local schools and housing (13 million J)

CROSS-SECTION OF HYDROELECTRIC POWER STATION WITH FRANCIS TURBINE

Transformer
Switch gear including circuit braker
Gate
Insulator
Bushing
High voltage cable
Rotor house
Generator unit
Generator rotor turned by turbine
Shaft
Francis turbine
Curved blade
Gate
Afterbay
Tailrace
Screen
Water in reservoir
Potential energy of water intake turns turbine
Penstock
Draft tube
Water that flows out has lost some energy

CROSS-SECTION OF NUCLEAR POWER STATION WITH PRESSURIZED WATER REACTOR

Steam generator
Concrete shielding
Water pressurizer
Steel girder framework
Control rod
Reactor core
Pump
Moderator (water)
Enriched uranium fuel
Coolant (water) takes heat from reactor core to heat exchanger
Heat exchanger
Water pumped back into steam generator
Water in heat exchanger turns to steam
Steam drives turbine
Turbine shaft turns generator
Generator produces electric current at 25,000 volts
Pump
Water cools used steam
Steam loses energy to turbine and condenses back to water
Transformer increases voltage to 300,000 volts
High voltage cable
Pylon carries high voltage electricity
Hot water to cooling tower
Cold water from cooling tower

ENERGY SYSTEMS

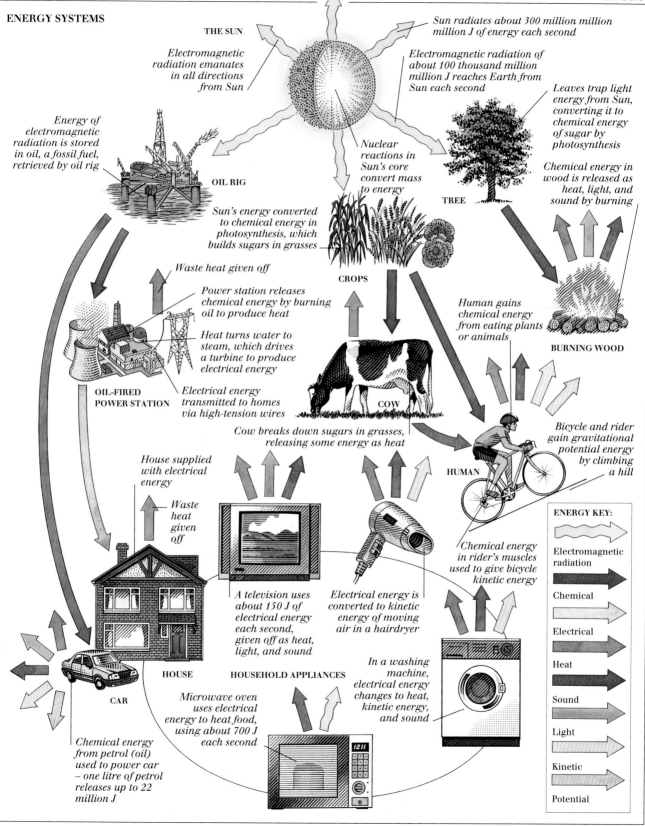

THE SUN

Electromagnetic radiation emanates in all directions from Sun

Sun radiates about 300 million million million J of energy each second

Electromagnetic radiation of about 100 thousand million million J reaches Earth from Sun each second

Leaves trap light energy from Sun, converting it to chemical energy of sugar by photosynthesis

Energy of electromagnetic radiation is stored in oil, a fossil fuel, retrieved by oil rig

OIL RIG

Nuclear reactions in Sun's core convert mass to energy

Chemical energy in wood is released as heat, light, and sound by burning

TREE

Sun's energy converted to chemical energy in photosynthesis, which builds sugars in grasses

Waste heat given off

Power station releases chemical energy by burning oil to produce heat

Heat turns water to steam, which drives a turbine to produce electrical energy

CROPS

Human gains chemical energy from eating plants or animals

BURNING WOOD

OIL-FIRED POWER STATION

Electrical energy transmitted to homes via high-tension wires

COW

Cow breaks down sugars in grasses, releasing some energy as heat

Bicycle and rider gain gravitational potential energy by climbing a hill

House supplied with electrical energy

HUMAN

Waste heat given off

Chemical energy in rider's muscles used to give bicycle kinetic energy

ENERGY KEY:

Electromagnetic radiation

Chemical

Electrical

Heat

Sound

Light

Kinetic

Potential

A television uses about 150 J of electrical energy each second, given off as heat, light, and sound

Electrical energy is converted to kinetic energy of moving air in a hairdryer

In a washing machine, electrical energy changes to heat, kinetic energy, and sound

HOUSE

HOUSEHOLD APPLIANCES

Microwave oven uses electrical energy to heat food, using about 700 J each second

CAR

Chemical energy from petrol (oil) used to power car – one litre of petrol releases up to 22 million J

315

Electricity and magnetism

ELECTRICAL EFFECTS result from an imbalance of electric charge. There are two types of electric charge, named positive (carried by protons) and negative (carried by electrons). If charges are opposite (unlike), they attract one another, while like charges repel. Forces of attraction and repulsion (electrostatic forces) exist between any two charged particles. Matter is normally uncharged, but if

LIGHTNING

electrons are gained, an object will gain an overall negative charge; if they are removed, it becomes positive. Objects with an overall negative or positive charge are said to have an imbalance of charge, and exert the same forces as individual negative and positive charges. On this larger scale, the forces will always act to regain the balance of charge. This causes static electricity. Lightning, for example, is produced by clouds discharging a huge excess of negative electrons. If charges are "free" – in a wire or material that allows

electrons to pass through it – the forces cause a flow of charge called an electric current. Some substances exhibit the strange phenomenon of magnetism – which also produces attractive and repulsive forces. Magnetic substances consist of small regions called domains. Normally unmagnetized, they can be magnetized by being placed in a magnetic field. Magnetism and electricity are inextricably linked, a fact put to use in motors and generators.

VAN DE GRAAFF (ELECTROSTATIC) GENERATOR

Positive charges at many thousands of volts

Metal dome

Rotation of belt

Positively charged belt strips negative charges (electrons) from dome via metal comb, giving dome a positive charge

Pulley wheel

Moving rubber belt gains a positive charge

Insulating column prevents charges leaking away

Positive metal comb strips negative charges (electrons) from belt

Negatively charged metal plate

Connection to positive electrical supply

Pulley wheel

Rotation of belt

Connection to negative electrical supply

CURRENT ELECTRICITY

Crocodile clip connector

Bulb receives 3 volts

Bulb holder

Metal wire (conductor) coated with plastic (insulator)

Bulb receives 3 volts

Bulb holder

Direction of current, opposite to electron flow by convention

Junction

Electrons flow from negative terminal to positive terminal

Switch completes or breaks circuit

Four 1.5 volt cells (total of 6 volts)

Negative terminal

Positive terminal

VOLTAGE
The higher the voltage, the greater the energy of electrical charges. One volt is one joule (unit of energy) per coulomb (unit of charge).

CURRENT
The greater the number of electrons moving around the circuit, the higher the current. Current is measured in amps (A). One amp equals one coulomb (unit of charge) per second.

Metal wire (conductor) coated with plastic (insulator)

Bulb holder

Bulb receives 6 volts

Bulb has high resistance

RESISTANCE
For a given voltage, the flow of current depends upon the resistance of a circuit. Resistance is the degree to which a substance resists electrical current. It is measured in ohms (Ω).

SERIES ELECTRICAL CIRCUIT   **SIMPLE ELECTRICAL CIRCUIT**

MAGNETIC FIELDS AND FORCES

Iron filings

Profile of magnetic field

Bar magnet

North-seeking pole

North-seeking pole

Like poles repel

North-seeking pole

Unlike poles attract

North-seeking pole

South-seeking pole of electromagnet

North-seeking pole

South-seeking pole

Unlike poles attract

Direction of force

South-seeking pole

South-seeking pole

Like poles repel

Electromagnet

Wire to battery

MAGNETIC DOMAINS

Domain

Direction of magnetization within domain is random

Direction of magnetization within domain has aligned

Domain aligned with magnetization has grown

Domain boundary

Domain not aligned with magnetization has shrunk

Direction of overall magnetization

UNMAGNETIZED IRON

MAGNETIZED IRON IN A MAGNETIC FIELD

GENERATING MAGNETISM FROM ELECTRICITY

Direction of magnetic field (from north pole to south pole)

Electric current produces magnetic field

Magnetic field

Coil carries electric current

Direction of current

Metal wire (conductor) coated with plastic (insulator)

Negative terminal

Positive terminal

Four 1.5 volt cells (total of 6 volts)

CIRCUIT WITH ELECTROMAGNET

GENERATING ELECTRICITY FROM MAGNETISM

Terminal box

Coil of wire

Permanent magnet

Bearing

Non-drive end

Coil of wire

Terminal

Stator

Main rotor turns in magnetic field produced by coil of wire in stator

Fan

Drive end

Coil of wire

Shaft

Secondary (exciter) rotor

ELECTRIC GENERATOR
In a generator, the rotor rotates within the magnetic field of the stator to produce an electric current.

Coil of wire rotates within magnetic field of permanent magnet

Permanent magnet

Steel casing

Iron core

Coated copper winding

Commutator

Terminal

Spindle

End of shaft

Terminal

ELECTRIC MOTOR
In a motor, magnetic forces between the winding and permanent magnet produce a rotary motion.

Light

LIGHT IS A FORM OF ENERGY. It is a type of electromagnetic radiation, like X-rays or radio waves. All electromagnetic radiation is produced by electric charges (see pp. 316-317): it is caused by the effects of oscillating electric and magnetic fields as they travel through space. Electromagnetic radiation is considered to have both wave and particle properties. It can be thought of as a wave of electricity and magnetism. In that case, the difference between the various forms of radiation is their wavelength. Radiation can also be said to consist of particles, or packets of energy, called photons. The difference between light and X-rays, for instance, is the amount of energy that each photon carries. The complete range of radiation is referred to as the electromagnetic spectrum, extending from low energy, long wavelength radio waves to high energy, short wavelength gamma rays. Light is the only part of the electromagnetic spectrum that is visible. White light from the Sun is made up of all the visible wavelengths of radiation, which can be seen when it is separated by using a prism. Light, like all forms of electromagnetic radiation, can be reflected (bounced back) and refracted (bent). Different parts of the electromagnetic spectrum are produced in different ways. Sometimes visible light – and infra-red radiation – is generated by the vibrating particles of warm or hot objects. The emission of light in this way is called incandescence. Light can also be produced by fluorescence, a phenomenon in which electrons gain and lose energy within atoms.

MAXWELLIAN DIAGRAM OF ELECTROMAGNETIC RADIATION AS WAVES

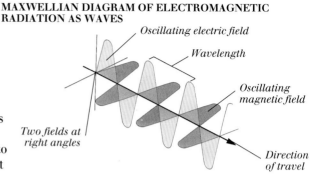

Oscillating electric field

Wavelength

Oscillating magnetic field

Two fields at right angles

Direction of travel

ELECTROMAGNETIC RADIATION AS PARTICLES

Photon thought of as wave packet of energy

Red light has long wavelength

Blue light has about twice the energy of red light

Blue light has shorter wavelength: waves are more tightly packed

PHOTON OF RED LIGHT   PHOTON OF BLUE LIGHT

SPLITTING WHITE LIGHT INTO THE SPECTRUM

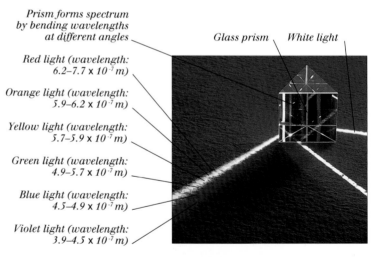

Prism forms spectrum by bending wavelengths at different angles

Glass prism   White light

Red light (wavelength: 6.2–7.7×10^{-7} m)

Orange light (wavelength: 5.9–6.2×10^{-7} m)

Yellow light (wavelength: 5.7–5.9×10^{-7} m)

Green light (wavelength: 4.9–5.7×10^{-7} m)

Blue light (wavelength: 4.5–4.9×10^{-7} m)

Violet light (wavelength: 3.9–4.5×10^{-7} m)

THE ELECTROMAGNETIC SPECTRUM

ENERGY (JOULES) 10^{-28} 10^{-27} 10^{-26} 10^{-25} 10^{-24} 10^{-23} 10^{-22} 10^{-21} 10^{-20}

WAVELENGTH (METERS) 10^{4} 10^{3} 10^{2} 10 1 10^{-1} 10^{-2} 10^{-3} 10^{-4} 10^{-}

Long-wave radio   Medium-wave radio   Short-wave radio   Very high-frequency (VHF) radio   Microwaves   Infra-red radiation

Radio waves

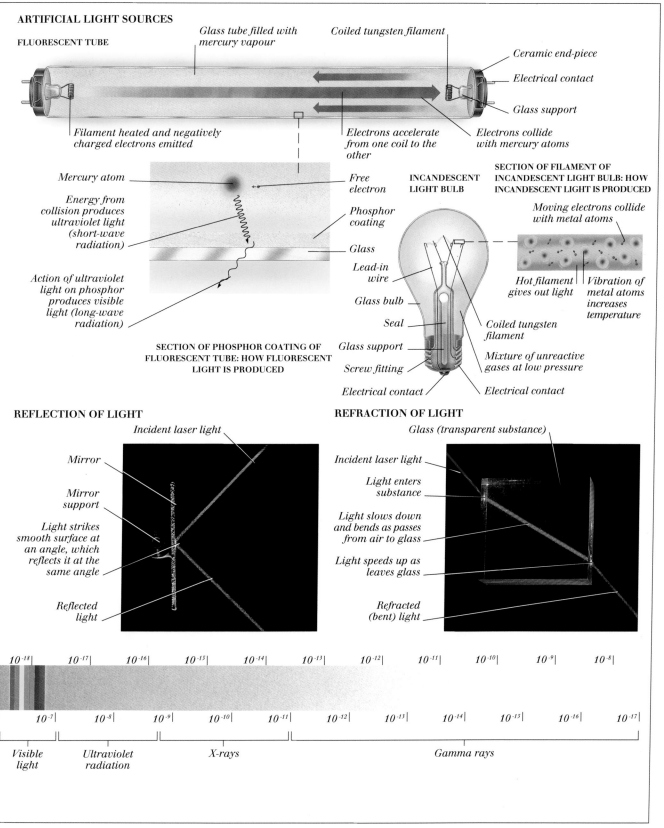

ARTIFICIAL LIGHT SOURCES

FLUORESCENT TUBE

Glass tube filled with mercury vapour

Coiled tungsten filament

Ceramic end-piece

Electrical contact

Glass support

Filament heated and negatively charged electrons emitted

Electrons accelerate from one coil to the other

Electrons collide with mercury atoms

Mercury atom

Energy from collision produces ultraviolet light (short-wave radiation)

Action of ultraviolet light on phosphor produces visible light (long-wave radiation)

Free electron

Phosphor coating

Glass

SECTION OF PHOSPHOR COATING OF FLUORESCENT TUBE: HOW FLUORESCENT LIGHT IS PRODUCED

INCANDESCENT LIGHT BULB

SECTION OF FILAMENT OF INCANDESCENT LIGHT BULB: HOW INCANDESCENT LIGHT IS PRODUCED

Moving electrons collide with metal atoms

Hot filament gives out light

Vibration of metal atoms increases temperature

Lead-in wire

Glass bulb

Seal

Glass support

Screw fitting

Electrical contact

Coiled tungsten filament

Mixture of unreactive gases at low pressure

Electrical contact

REFLECTION OF LIGHT

Incident laser light

Mirror

Mirror support

Light strikes smooth surface at an angle, which reflects it at the same angle

Reflected light

REFRACTION OF LIGHT

Glass (transparent substance)

Incident laser light

Light enters substance

Light slows down and bends as passes from air to glass

Light speeds up as leaves glass

Refracted (bent) light

10^{-18} | 10^{-17} | 10^{-16} | 10^{-15} | 10^{-14} | 10^{-13} | 10^{-12} | 10^{-11} | 10^{-10} | 10^{-9} | 10^{-8} |

10^{-7} | 10^{-8} | 10^{-9} | 10^{-10} | 10^{-11} | 10^{-12} | 10^{-13} | 10^{-14} | 10^{-15} | 10^{-16} | 10^{-17} |

Visible light

Ultraviolet radiation

X-rays

Gamma rays

Force and motion

FORCES ARE PUSHES OR PULLS that change the motion of objects. To make a stationary object move, or a moving object stop, a force is needed. A force is also required to change the speed or direction of an object. This change in speed or direction is known as acceleration. Acceleration depends on the size (magnitude) of the force, and on the mass of the object. The effects of forces were first summarized by Isaac Newton in his three laws of motion. The international unit of force, named after him, is the newton (N), which is approximately equal to the weight of one apple. Gravity – the force of attraction between any two masses – can be measured using a newton meter (spring balance). Forces are put to useful effect in machines. A simple machine, such as a wheel and axle, is a device that changes the size or direction of an applied force. It allows an applied force (the effort) to produce another force (the load). A lever uses a bar that turns on a fulcrum to exert force. In all simple machines, there is a relationship between force and distance. A small force (in a compound pulley, for instance) moves through a large distance to lift a heavy object a small distance. This is called the Law of Simple Machines.

SIMPLE MACHINES

Single-pulley system (simple pulley)

Pulley wheel

Simple pulley only changes direction of a force

Effort is the same size as the load (10 N) and is pulled the same distance

One rope attached to load

Load of 10 N

Two-pulley system (simple pulley)

Pulley wheel

Effort is half the load (5 N), but the rope must be pulled twice the distance

Two ropes share the force and distance

Pulley wheel

Load of 10 N

Four-pulley system (compound pulley)

Two pulley wheels

Effort is one quarter of the load (2.5 N), but the rope must be pulled four times the distance

Four ropes share the force and distance

SIMPLE AND COMPOUND PULLEYS

Two pulley wheels

Load of 10 N

NEWTON METERS (SPRING BALANCES)

Weight is measured using a spring

When weight pulls downwards, pointer moves along scale and measures force

Weight is 10 N

Weight is 20 N

Mass of 1 kg

Mass of 2 kg

WEIGHT AND MASS
The "mass" of an object is a measure of the quantity of matter that it possesses. Mass is usually measured in grams (g) or kilograms (kg). The "weight" of an object is the force exerted on the object's mass by gravity. Since weight is a force, its unit is the newton (N).

Wheel and axle multiplies the effort

Force is transmitted to the wheels by the chain

Pedal

Crank

Effort, provided by cyclist's muscles, is smaller than the load, but moves through a greater distance

A larger force, the load, is produced at the axle

WHEEL AND AXLE

A screw, acting like a wedge wrapped around a shaft, multiplies the effort

Effort, a turning force supplied through a screwdriver

Pitch (the angle of the screw thread)

The smaller the angle of pitch, the less force is required, but more turns are needed to move it through a greater distance

A larger force, the load, pulls the screw into wood

SCREW

Effort pushes axe into wood

Axe blade has wedge shape

Wedge multiplies effort

A larger force, the load, moves through a smaller distance to push wood apart

WEDGE

NEWTON'S THREE LAWS OF MOTION

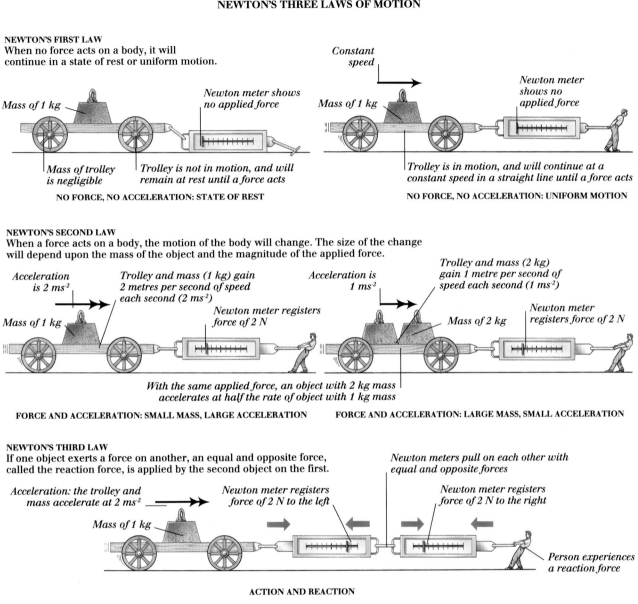

NEWTON'S FIRST LAW
When no force acts on a body, it will continue in a state of rest or uniform motion.

Newton meter shows no applied force

Mass of 1 kg

Mass of trolley is negligible

Trolley is not in motion, and will remain at rest until a force acts

NO FORCE, NO ACCELERATION: STATE OF REST

Constant speed

Mass of 1 kg

Newton meter shows no applied force

Trolley is in motion, and will continue at a constant speed in a straight line until a force acts

NO FORCE, NO ACCELERATION: UNIFORM MOTION

NEWTON'S SECOND LAW
When a force acts on a body, the motion of the body will change. The size of the change will depend upon the mass of the object and the magnitude of the applied force.

Acceleration is 2 ms⁻²

Trolley and mass (1 kg) gain 2 metres per second of speed each second (2 ms⁻²)

Newton meter registers force of 2 N

Mass of 1 kg

With the same applied force, an object with 2 kg mass accelerates at half the rate of object with 1 kg mass

FORCE AND ACCELERATION: SMALL MASS, LARGE ACCELERATION

Acceleration is 1 ms⁻²

Trolley and mass (2 kg) gain 1 metre per second of speed each second (1 ms⁻²)

Mass of 2 kg

Newton meter registers force of 2 N

FORCE AND ACCELERATION: LARGE MASS, SMALL ACCELERATION

NEWTON'S THIRD LAW
If one object exerts a force on another, an equal and opposite force, called the reaction force, is applied by the second object on the first.

Newton meters pull on each other with equal and opposite forces

Acceleration: the trolley and mass accelerate at 2 ms⁻²

Newton meter registers force of 2 N to the left

Newton meter registers force of 2 N to the right

Mass of 1 kg

Person experiences a reaction force

ACTION AND REACTION

THREE CLASSES OF LEVER

Fulcrum, between effort and load

Effort

Load is greater than effort, but moves through smaller distance

CLASS 1 LEVER
Pliers consist of two class 1 levers.

Fulcrum

Load, between effort and fulcrum

Effort is smaller than load, but moves through greater distance

CLASS 2 LEVER
Nutcrackers consist of two class 2 levers.

Load is applied at open end

Effort forces tongs together

Load is smaller than effort, but moves through greater distance

Effort, between fulcrum and load

Fulcrum

CLASS 3 LEVER
Tongs consist of two class 3 levers.

RAIL AND ROAD

Steam locomotives

WAGONS THAT ARE PULLED along tracks have been used to transport material since the 16th century, but these trains were drawn by men or horses until the invention of the steam locomotive. Steam locomotives enabled the basic railway system to realize its true potential. In 1804, Richard Trevithick built the world's first working steam locomotive in South Wales. It was not entirely successful, but it encouraged others to develop new designs. By 1829, the British engineer Robert Stephenson had built the "Rocket", considered to be the forerunner of the modern locomotive. The "Rocket" was a self-sufficient unit, carrying coal to heat the boiler and a water supply for generating steam. Steam passed from the boiler to force the pistons back and forth, and this movement turned the driving wheels, propelling the train forwards. Used steam was then expelled in characteristic "chuffs". Later steam locomotives, like "Ellerman Lines" and the "Mallard", worked in a similar way, but on a much larger scale. The simple design and reliability of steam locomotives ensured that they changed very little in 120 years of use, before being replaced from the 1950s by more efficient diesel and electric power (see pp. 326-329).

"ROCKET" STEAM LOCOMOTIVE, 1829

Chimney

Smokebox

Leaf spring

"Rocket" nameplate

Wooden buffer beam

Wooden driving wheel

Pipe takes steam from boiler to cylinder

Regulator (throttle)

Wrought iron boiler

Remains of firebox

Valve chest

Valve setting control

Metal tyre

Axle

Ballast

Rail chair

Wrought iron rail

Wooden sleeper

Piston rod

Cylinder

Carrying wheel

Driver's platform

Stay

"ELLERMAN LINES", 1949 (CUTAWAY VIEW)

Vacuum reservoir

Panel brace

Water filler

Panel sheeting

Water tank

Coal space

Tender hand brake

Cab

Firebox

Brick arch

Hand rail

Buffer

Brake vacuum pipe

Wheel guard

Axle

Axle box

Tender wheel

Brake rigging

Water float to indicate water level

Water float lever

Step

Axle box cover

Footplate

Coupling

Coil spring

Trailing wheel

Grate

Fire drawn into fire tubes

TENDER

CAB INTERIOR OF "MALLARD" EXPRESS STEAM LOCOMOTIVE, 1938

Steam sanding control
Blower isolator valve
Pressure gauge isolator valve
Vacuum brake isolator valve
Steam chest pressure gauge
Vacuum brake pressure gauge
Blower control
Regulator controls flow of steam to cylinders
Cab side-window
Vacuum brake lever
Live steam water injector control
Manual sanding lever
Reverser handle
Driver's seat
Steam-operated reversing shaft lock control
Steam heating isolator valve
Sliding roof vent
Boiler pressure gauge
Gauge glass to show level of water in boiler
Exhaust steam water injector control
Steam heating pressure gauge
Glass deflector
Whistle lever
Cylinder drain cock lever
Control valve for hot water hose
Fireman's seat
Steam heat safety valve
Oil can warming tray
Firebox
Firehole
Firebox door

Fire tube
Steam dome
Mechanical lubricator
Pipe takes steam from boiler to cylinder
Chimney
Thermal siphon
Regulator valve
Superheater tube inside flue tube
Boiler
Blast-pipe
Smokebox
Smokebox door
Lubricating pipe
Piston valve
Buffer
Brake shoe
Brake rigging
Coupling rod
Driving wheel
Crank
Expansion lever
Connecting rod
Combination lever
Slide bar
Piston, linked to connecting rod
Bogie frame
Cylinder
Leading wheel
Screw coupling

STEAM LOCOMOTIVE

Diesel trains

RUDOLF DIESEL FIRST DEMONSTRATED the diesel engine in Germany in 1898, but it was not until the 1940s that diesel locomotives were successfully established on both passenger and freight services, in the US. Early diesel locomotives like the "Union Pacific" were more expensive to build than steam locomotives, but were more efficient and cheaper to operate, especially where oil was plentiful. One feature of diesel engines is that the power output cannot be coupled directly to the wheels. To convert the mechanical energy produced by diesel engines, a transmission system is needed. Almost all diesel locomotives have electric transmissions, and are known as "diesel-electric" locomotives. The diesel engine works by drawing air into the cylinders and compressing it to increase its temperature; a small quantity of diesel fuel is then injected into it. The resulting combustion drives the generator (more recently an alternator) to produce electricity, which is fed to electric motors connected to the wheels. Diesel-electric locomotives are essentially electric locomotives that carry their own power plants, and are used worldwide today. The "Deltic" diesel-electric locomotive, similar to the one shown here, replaced classic express steam locomotives, and ran at speeds up to 160 kph (100 mph).

FRONT VIEW OF "UNION PACIFIC" DIESEL-ELECTRIC LOCOMOTIVE, 1950s

Exhaust vent
Windscreen wiper
Horn
Cab front window
Head-light
Cab door
Name of operating railroad
Illuminated locomotive unit number
Railroad crest
Cab step
Step
Motor-driven bogie axle
Air-brake coupling hose
Centre buck-eye coupler

PROTOTYPE "DELTIC" DIESEL-ELECTRIC LOCOMOTIVE, 1956

Engine room vent
Inspection hatch
Engine exhaust port
Radiator fan
Engine room window
Engine room vent

Fuel tank
Water for heating boiler
Inspection socket
Folding step
Drain for radiator coolant
Radiator coolant
Sand box
Telescopic damper
Drain for control reservoir

DIESEL ENGINE OF BRITISH RAIL CLASS 20 DIESEL-ELECTRIC LOCOMOTIVE

Exhaust vent

Cylinder head (V-four configuration)

Turbo-charged diesel engine drives generator

Generator cooling fan

Generator compartment vent

Auxiliary generator

Main generator produces electricity that drives wheels

Main chassis member

Innermost wheel set on cab-end bogie

Air brake pipe

Brake rigging

Battery box

Engine crankcase

Air reservoir and isolator valves

Lubricating oil primary pump and fuel supply pump

Cab door

Driver's seat

Cab

Warning horn

Windscreen

Windscreen wiper

Cab window

Manufacturer's logo

Cab vent

Indicator light

Sand box

Buffer

Brake cylinder

Roller-bearing axle box

Brake shoe

Brake actuating chain

Transverse leaf spring secondary suspension

Coil spring primary suspension

EXAMPLES OF FREIGHT CARS

BOX CAR

HOPPER CAR

REFRIGERATOR CAR

LIVESTOCK CAR

FLAT CAR WITH BULKHEADS

AUTOMOBILE CAR

Electric and high-speed trains

THE FIRST ELECTRIC LOCOMOTIVE ran in 1879 in Berlin, Germany. In Europe, electric trains developed as a more efficient alternative to the steam locomotive and diesel-electric power. Like diesels, electric trains employ electric motors to drive the wheels but, unlike diesels, the electricity is generated externally at a power station. Electric current is picked up either from a catenary (overhead cable) via a pantograph, or from a third rail. Since it does not carry its own power-generating equipment, an electric locomotive has a better power-to-weight ratio and greater acceleration than its diesel-electric equivalent. This makes electric trains suitable for urban routes with many stops. They are also faster, quieter, and less polluting. The latest electric French TGV (Train à Grande Vitesse) reaches 300 kph (186 mph); other trains, like the London to Paris and Brussels "Eurostar", can run at several voltages and operate between different countries. Simpler electric trains perform special duties – the "People Mover" at Gatwick Airport in Britain runs between terminals.

HOW ALTERNATING CURRENT (AC) ELECTRIC TRAINS WORK

Running rail for return current

Feeder station provides current

Catenary

Vacuum circuit breaker

Pantograph collects current

Thyristor converter converts current (ac) to direct current (dc)

Traction motor turns wheel

Control circuit

Transformer steps down voltage

Axle brush

FRONT VIEW OF PARIS METRO

Route number

Windscreen wiper

Unit number

Operator's initials (Régie Autonome des Transports Parisien)

Rubber running wheel

Guard for rubber wheel

Door open/shut indicator light

Driver's seat

Handle

Front light (white)

Rear light (red)

Buffing pad

Rubber guide wheel

FRONT VIEW OF ITALIAN STATE RAILWAYS CLASS 402 ELECTRIC LOCOMOTIVE

Collector strip for electric current

Double-arm pantograph

Head-light

Windscreen wiper

Italian State Railways crest

Number of electric (E) locomotive (class 402 No. 5)

Buffer

"Jumper" cable

Conventional hook-screw coupling

Front light (white)

Rear light (red)

SIDE VIEW OF GATWICK EXPRESS "PEOPLE MOVER"

Pneumatic rubber wheel

Concrete track

Automatic door

No driver (train controlled by central computer)

"EUROSTAR" MULTI-VOLTAGE ELECTRIC TRAIN

Cab window

Grille over warning horn

Rear light (red)

Head-light (white)

Fibreglass reinforced plastic cover

Fibreglass reinforced plastic cover

Aerofoil wheel guard

Aerofoil wheel guard

Sanding pipe

FRONT VIEW

Cab side-window

Electric equipment compartment

Cab door

Side vent

Cab front window

300?

Leading driven axle

Horizontal telescopic damper

Third (electric) rail collector shoe

Coil spring suspension

SIDE VIEW

TGV ELECTRIC HIGH-SPEED TRAIN

Luggage rack

Reading light

Double-glazed and tinted side-window

Sliding curtain

Seat

Main overhead lighting

Automatic electric carriage end door

Antimacassar

Headrest

Armrest

Centre gangway

INTERIOR OF TGV

Cab door

Hand rail

Side vent

Roof vent

Cab side-window

Cab front window

Windscreen wiper

Emergency exit door

Access panel for servicing

Nose air deflector dam

SNCF

306

SNCF PARTENAIRE OLYMPIQUE

Vertical damper

Horizontal damper

SIDE VIEW OF TGV

Train equipment

MODERN RAILWAY TRACK consists of two parallel steel rails clipped on to a support called a sleeper. Sleepers are usually made of reinforced concrete, although wood and steel are still used. The distance between the inside edges of the rails is the track gauge. It evolved in Britain, which uses a gauge of 1,435 mm (4 ft 8½ in), known as the standard gauge. As engineering grew more sophisticated, narrower gauges were adopted because they cost less to build. The loading gauge, which is equally important, determines the size of the largest loaded vehicle that may pass through tunnels and under bridges with adequate clearance. Safe train operation relies on following a signalling system. At first, signalling was based on a simple time interval between trains, but it now depends on maintaining a safe distance between successive trains travelling in the same direction. Most modern signals are colour lights, but older mechanical semaphore signals are still used. On the latest high-speed lines, train drivers receive control instructions by electronic means. Signalling depends on reliable control of the train by effective braking. For fast, modern trains, which have considerable momentum, it is essential that each vehicle in the train can be braked by the driver or by a train control system, such as Automatic Train Protection (ATP). Braking is achieved by the brake shoe acting on the wheel rim (rim brakes), by disc brakes, or, increasingly, by electrical braking.

MECHANICAL SEMAPHORE SIGNAL

Red, square-ended arm in raised position means "all clear"

Red glass

Green glass

Actuating lever system

Motor operating "home" stop signal

Green glass

Yellow glass

Yellow, "distant" warning arm in horizontal position means "caution"

Tubular steel post

Ladder

Electrical relay box

FOUR-ASPECT COLOUR LIGHT SIGNAL

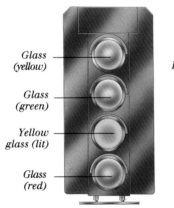

Glass (yellow)

Glass (green)

Yellow glass (lit)

Glass (red)

FRONT VIEW

Lifting lug

Lamp shield

Clip

Base

SIDE VIEW

HOW A MODERN MAIN-LINE SIGNALLING SYSTEM WORKS

Red "stop" light instructs next train not to enter this section of track

Green "all clear" light instructs train B to proceed into this section of track

Green "all clear" light instructs train B to proceed into this section of track

Green "all clear" light instructs train B to proceed into this section of track

Pantograph

Catenary

Train B

Track

EXAMPLES OF INTERNATIONAL TRACK GAUGES

1,000 mm
(3 ft 3¹/₂ in)
East Africa,
India,
Malaysia,
Chile, and
Argentina

1,067 mm
(3 ft 6 in)
Japan, Australia,
Sudan, West Africa,
South Africa, and
New Zealand

1,435 mm
(4 ft 8¹/₂ in)
US, Canada, China,
Egypt, Turkey, Iran,
Japan, Peru, Britain,
Europe, Australia,
Brazil, and Mexico

1,524 mm
(5 ft 0 in)
Russia, Spain,
Portugal, and
Finland

1,600 mm
(5 ft 3 in)
Ireland, Australia,
and Brazil

1,676 mm
(5 ft 6 in)
India, Pakistan,
and Argentina

EXAMPLES OF INTERNATIONAL LOADING GAUGES

Britain: 2.75 m (9 ft 0 in) x 3.95 m (12 ft 11 in)

Europe: 3.1 m (10 ft 2 in) x 4.5 m (14 ft 9 in)

US: 3.3 m (10 ft 10 in) x 4.9 m (16 ft 2 in)

Russia: 3.4 m (11 ft 2 in) x 5.3 m (17 ft 4 in)

1,435 mm
(4 ft 8¹/₂ in)
Standard track
gauge

1,524 mm
(5 ft 0 in)
Track gauge of Russia,
with largest loading gauge

FLAT-BOTTOMED RAIL

Flat-bottomed steel rail

Steel spring secures
rail to sleeper

Synthetic
insulating
pad

Sleeper supports
track and
maintains
gauge

BULL-HEAD RAIL

Wooden "key" secures
rail in chair

Steel tapered
screw fastens
chair to
sleeper

Bull-head pattern
steel rail

Cast-iron chair

Wooden
sleeper

DISC BRAKES ON MODERN WAGON BOGIE

Base of wagon

Airbag secondary
suspension

Damper

Hand
brake
wheel

Axle

Brake
disc

Brake calliper

Wheel

Two yellow "preliminary
caution" lights instruct train
B that it must stop in two
signals time

Yellow "caution" light
instructs train B that it
must stop at next signal

Green "all clear" light
instructs train A to proceed
into this section of track

Red "stop" light instructs
train B not to enter
this section of track

Braking distance

Train A

Trams and buses

METROLINK TRAM, MANCHESTER, BRITAIN

AS CITY POPULATIONS exploded in the 1800s, there was an urgent need for mass transportation. Trams were an early solution. The first trams, like buses, were horse-drawn, but in 1881, electric street tramways appeared in Berlin, Germany. Electric trams soon became widespread throughout Europe and North America. Trams run on rails along a fixed route, using electric motors that receive power from overhead cables. As road networks developed, motorized buses offered a flexible alternative to trams. By the 1930s, they had replaced tram systems in many cities. City buses typically have doors at both front and rear to make loading and unloading easier. Double-decker designs are popular, occupying the same amount of street space as single-decker buses but able to transport twice the number of people. Buses are also commonly used for inter-city travel and touring. Tour buses have reclining seats, large windows, luggage space, and toilets. Recently, as city traffic has become increasingly congested, many city planners have designed new tram routes to run alongside bus routes as part of an integrated transport system.

EARLY TRAM, c.1900

Trolley boom · Trolley head · Trolley base · Drop window · Upper deck · Quarter light · Brake · Stair · Lower deck · Underframe · Platform · Controller · Truck · Lifeguard · L.C.C.

MCW METROBUS, LONDON, BRITAIN

Upper deck air intake · Window vent · Upper deck windscreen · Route information · Destination screen · Offside mirror · Asymmetric windscreen · Windscreen wiper · Sidelight · Head-light · Fog light · Number plate · Manufacturer's badge · Nearside mirror · Licence holder · Turning indicator · Route number · LONDON NORTHERN · Hornsey Rise Crouch End · Turnpike Lane · West Green Road · 41 · ARCHWAY STN. · PAY DRIVER · mcw · KYV 739X

Square roof dome · Mirror for driver to see upstairs · Operator's logo · Destination screen · Nearside mirror · Front bumper · Entrance door · Emergency door control · Turning indicator · LONDON NORTHERN

FRONT VIEW

SINGLE-DECKER BUS, NEW YORK, US

Wheelchair access

Sliding window

Sloped roof dome

Tinted glass

Air intake

Tyre

Axle

Exit door

Access panel

Sidelight

Entrance door

Bumper

SIDE VIEW

Marker light

Repeater indicator

Entrance door

Side mirror

Route number

Head-light

Turning indicator

Number plate

Bumper

FRONT VIEW

DOUBLE-DECKER TOUR BUS, PARIS, FRANCE

Tinted glass

Air intake

Access panel

Skirt

Access door

Twin rear axle

Side entrance

Single front axle

Tyre

Raked windscreen

Panoramic window

Turning indicator

Bumper

Plug-style entrance door

Sliding window vent

Upper saloon window

Advertising panel

Air intake

Lower saloon window

Fleet number

Engine access panel

Rear bumper

Emergency door control

Two-leaf style exit door

Legal lettering

London Buses logo

Tyre

Skirt

Axle

SIDE VIEW

The first cars

THE EARLIEST ROAD VEHICLE powered by an engine, the Cugnot steam traction engine, was built in 1770. More practical steam carriages, such as the Bordino, were available in the early 19th century, but they were heavy and cumbersome. Restrictive laws and the introduction of railways, faster and able to carry more passengers, saw the decline of "cars" powered by steam. It was not until 1860 that the first practical power unit for road vehicles was developed, with the invention of the internal combustion engine by the Belgian Etienne Lenoir. By around 1890, Karl Benz and Gottlieb Daimler in Germany, and Albert de Dion and Armand Peugeot in France were building cars for sale to the public. These early cars, despite being primitive, expensive, and produced in limited numbers, heralded the age of the motor car.

STEAM-POWERED CUGNOT "FARDIER", 1770

Chimney

Steam pipe

Haystack boiler

Twin cylinder engine

Rocking beam

Steering tiller

Brake pedal

Seat

Wooden frame

Wooden wheel (artillery wheel)

Load space

Carrying fork

Piston rod

Ratchet wheel

Single front driving wheel

Step

Log basket

Broad, rough tyre

Chimney

BORDINO STEAM CARRIAGE, 1854

Hood iron (landau iron)

Landau body

Drop-down window

Leather hood

Fire-tube boiler

Sprung chassis

Water tank

Safety valve

Safety valve weight

Coke hopper

Chauffeur's seat (stoker's seat; spider seat; tiger seat)

Step

Tie bar

Full-elliptic leaf spring

Iron tyre

Wooden spoke

Wooden wheel (artillery wheel)

Hub

Unsprung chassis

Tie rod

Connecting rod

Steam chest

Twin-cylinder steam engine

Steam distributor valve

SIDE VIEW OF PETROL-DRIVEN BENZ MOTORWAGEN, 1886

Steering tiller
Brake quadrant
Brake lever
Cooling water tank
Full-elliptic leaf spring
Bevel gear
Final drive sprocket
Steering column
Steering rack
Steering link
Steering head
Seat spring
Driven pulley
Wheel fork
Tubular chassis
Driving chain
Hub
Solid rubber tyre
Tangent-spoked wire wheel
Driving sprocket

REAR VIEW OF BENZ MOTORWAGEN, 1886

Crown wheel
Pinion
Lubricator
Cooling tank
Driving pulley
Drive belt
Fuel tank
Big-end bearing
Groove for rope starter
Crankshaft
Flywheel

Seat squab

OVERHEAD VIEW OF BENZ MOTORWAGEN, 1886

Steering link
Footboard
Steering tiller
Brake lever
Tool and battery box
Trembler coil box
Intake pipe
Single cylinder
Fuel tank
Cooling water tank
Oil-filled lubricator
Flywheel
Crown wheel
Crankshaft
Driving pulley
Drive belt

Candle lamp
Driver's seat
Steering tiller
Brake lever
Dashboard
Headlamp
Round pin
Splinter bar
Towing hook
Forecarriage
Steam pipe
Spoke
Frame

Elegance and utility

DURING THE FIRST DECADE OF THIS CENTURY, the motorist who could afford it had a choice of some of the finest cars ever made. These handbuilt cars were powerful and luxurious, using the finest woods, leathers, and cloths, and bodywork made to the customer's individual requirements; some had six-cylinder engines as big as 15 litres. The price of such cars was several times that of an average house, and their yearly running costs were also very high. As a result, basic, utilitarian cars became popular. Costing perhaps one-tenth of the price of a luxury car, these cars had very little trim and often had only single-cylinder engines.

1904 OLDSMOBILE SINGLE-CYLINDER ENGINE

Oil bottle dripfeed
Crankcase
Exhaust pipe
Starting handle bracket
Cylinder head
Cylinder
Carburettor
Starter cog
Crankshaft
Engine timing gear
Gear band
Flywheel

FRONT VIEW OF 1906 RENAULT

Canopy
Mahogany framed windscreen
Cast aluminium wheel spider
Rear window
British Automobile Association badge
Bedford cord upholstery
Window blind
British Royal Automobile Club badge
Blind pull
Window lift strap
Rear-view mirror
Broad lace trim
Lamp bracket
Oil side lamp
Windscreen support
Dashboard radiator
Mudguard (wing)
Brass bevel
Access panel
Bonnet catch
Bail handle
Lifting handle
Mirror reflector
Acetylene headlamp
Steering spindle
Elliott steering knuckle
Chevron-tread tyre
Dumb iron
Screwdown greaser
Front axle
Starting handle
Track rod

SIDE VIEW OF 1906 RENAULT

Luggage grid
Button-quilted upholstery
Mahogany-framed plate glass window
Round-corner single limousine coachwork
Rear oil lamp
Shock absorber
Hub
Hub cap
Beaded edge tyre
Tyre security bolt

1904 OLDSMOBILE TRIM AND BODYWORK

1904 OLDSMOBILE CHASSIS

Reflector

Rear lamp

Engine cover handle

Engine cover

Mudguard

Mudguard stay

Seat back rest frame

Ignition switch

Seat squab

Dashboard

Tiller

Brake pedal

Throttle pedal

Mirror

Front steering track-rod

Front spring

Brake rod

Full-elliptic steering spring

Steering wiffletree

Rear spring

Starting handle bracket

Combined spring and chassis unit

Front axle

Non-skid tyre

Brass scrollwork

Blind pull

Canopy

Openable windscreen

Brass bevel

Division

Dashboard

Oil side lamp

Bonnet

Handbrake

Broad lace trim

Leather upholstery

Steering wheel

Gear lever

Water pipe

Plug lead conduit

Acetylene headlamp

Fuel/air intake pipe

Bi-block engine

Bulb horn

Spare tyre

Dashboard radiator

Jump seat (opera seat; strapontin)

Rim clamp

Tyre carrier

Running board

Leather valance

Tyre strap

Bonnet stay

Exhaust manifold

Starting handle

Wooden artillery wheel

Mass-production

THE FIRST CARS WERE HAND-ASSEMBLED from individually built parts, a time-consuming procedure that required skilled mechanics and made cars very expensive. This problem was solved, in America, by a Detroit car manufacturer named Henry Ford; he introduced mass-production by using standardized parts, and later combined these with a moving production line. The work was brought to the workers, each of whom performed one simple task in the construction process as the chassis moved along the line. The first mass-produced car, the Ford Model T, was launched in 1908 and was available in a limited range of body styles and colours. However, when the production line was introduced in 1914, the colour range was cut back; the Model T became available, as Henry Ford said, in "any colour you like, so long as it's black". Ford cut the production time for a car from several days to about 12 hours, and eventually to minutes, making cars much cheaper than before. As a result, by 1920 half the cars in the world were Model T Fords.

Throttle lever
Openable windscreen
Steering wheel
Ignition lever
Windscreen stay
Dashboard
Side lamp
Bulb horn
Spring shock absorber
Mudguard (wing)
Headlamp
Radiator
Front transverse leaf spring
Front axle
Number plate
Starting handle
Steering knuckle
Steering spindle connecting-rod

STAGES OF FORD MODEL T PRODUCTION

Left half of differential housing
Pinion
Rear leaf spring (cross-member)
Steering arm
King pin
Demountable wheel
Hub brake shoe
Track rod
Steering wheel
Hub bolt
Pinion housing
Front transverse leaf spring
Differential housing
Chassis frame
Rear spring perch
Radius rod
Rear axle
Front cross-member
Battery carrier
Body mount
Bearing sleeve
King pin
Half-shaft
Crown wheel
Bevel pinion
Front axle
Demountable wheel
Radius rod
Right half of differential housing
Rear axle bearing
Torque tube
Running-board stay
Hub brake shoe

SIDE VIEW OF 1913 FORD MODEL T

Hood

Rear seat

Hood frame

Rear door

Front seat

Steering wheel

Horn bulb

Steering column

Windscreen

Side lamp

Bonnet

Radiator filler cap

Radiator filler neck

Front mudguard

Spring shock absorber

Rear mudguard (rear wing)

Tyre valve

Wooden-spoked wheel

Hub cap

Running board

Valance

Spare tyre

Drain plug

Horn

Dummy front door

Radius rod

Steering column

Drag link

Demountable wheel

Bun lamp burner

Fuel sediment bowl

Running-board bracket

Light switch

Starter switch

Radiator shell

Headlamp rim

Headlamp

Track rod

Ruckstell axle

Bonnet clip

Steering gearbox

Handbrake

Radiator hose

Starter

Rear cross-member

Brake drum

Drop arm

Drag link

Crank handle

Cylinder block

Radiator apron

Torque tube

Greaser

Brake rod

Tank support

Front wing stay

Carburettor

Transmission casing

Demountable wheel

Radiator

Steering arm

Running-board support

Clincher wheel

Detachable rim

Battery strap

Reflector

Headlamp shell

Running board

Bonnet clip

Fender eye bolt

Handbrake quadrant

The "people's car"

**WORKING PARTS OF
VOLKSWAGEN BEETLE**

THE MOST POPULAR CAR in the history of car manufacture is the Volkswagen Beetle, originally called the KdF Wagen. The car was developed in Germany in the 1930s by Dr. Ferdinand Porsche. At that time, Germany had only half the number of cars of Britain or France, and Adolf Hitler took a personal interest in the development of the Volkswagen ("people's car"). The intention was to provide a new industry, new jobs, and a car so cheap that anyone in work could afford it. Dr. Porsche designed a car that was cheap to build and run; its rear-mounted, air-cooled engine cut down the number of parts needed and also reduced weight. However, few civilians managed to obtain the Beetle before the outbreak of the Second World War in 1939. After the war, the Beetle proved so popular that eventually more than 20 million were sold.

**CUSTOMIZED
VOLKSWAGEN
BEETLE**

Rear lamp
Air scoop
Quarter light
Bonnet
Tail pipe
Pressed steel wheel
Fuel filler cap
Indicator

**FLAT-FOUR
CYLINDER
ARRANGEMENT**

Counterweight
Piston
Crankshaft
Big end
Connecting rod (con-rod)

Fuel tank sender unit
Windscreen-wiper motor assembly
Steering idler
Brake back plate
Dust shroud
Front suspension top mount
Gear lever knob
Seat mount
Handbrake
Tyre
Sports wheel
Rear shock absorber
Transaxle (gearbox and final drive)
Clutch and flywheel
Flat-four engine
Air filter

Fuel tank
Steering tie-rod
Fuel filler neck
Steering box assembly
Frame head
Anti-roll bar
Track control arm
Pedal cluster
Suspension strut
Strut insert (shock absorber)
Front road spring
Front suspension top mount
Floor pan (platform chassis)
Torsion bar cover
Trailing arm
Rear brake drum
Drive shaft
Heat exchanger
Starter motor
Tail pipe

**BODY SHELL OF
VOLKSWAGEN BEETLE**

Front bumper

Bonnet release handle

Nearside headlamp unit

Offside headlamp unit

Nearside front indicator lens

Chrome trim strip

Bonnet

Offside front indicator lens

Nearside front mudguard (front wing)

Offside front mudguard (front wing)

Front wing piping

Spare-wheel well

Front wing piping

Bonnet hinge

Blade

Offside running board

Quarter light

Arm

Nearside running board

Mirror

Windscreen wiper

Door catch

Steering column

Wind deflector (baffle)

Sun roof

Quarter light

Door handle

Passenger door

Window winder handle

Body shell

Window winder regulator

Drop glass

Rear wing piping

Rear wing piping

Air intake vents

Nearside rear mudguard (rear wing)

Rear valance

Engine lid (engine cover)

Air intake vents

Offside rear mudguard (rear wing)

Number plate light

Nearside rear lamp cluster (rear lamp unit)

Number plate

Offside rear lamp cluster (rear lamp unit)

WRV 408L

Rear bumper

341

Early engines

STEAM AND ELECTRICITY were used to power cars until early this century, but neither power source was ideal. Electric cars had to stop frequently to recharge their heavy batteries, and steam cars gave smooth power delivery but were too complicated for the average motorist to use. A rival power source, the internal combustion engine, was invented in 1860 by Etienne Lenoir (see pp. 334-335). This engine converted the force of an explosion into rotary motion, to turn the wheels of a vehicle. Early variations on this basic model included sleeve valves, separately cast cylinders, and the two-stroke combustion cycle. Today, all combustion engines, including the Wankel rotary and diesels (see pp. 346-347), use the four-stroke cycle, first demonstrated by Nikolaus Otto in 1876. The Otto cycle, often described as "suck, squeeze, bang, blow", has proved the best method of ensuring that the engine turns over smoothly and that exhaust emissions are controllable.

TROJAN TWO-STROKE ENGINE, 1927

Port linking combustion chambers of upper and lower cylinders

Water connection

Upper paired cylinder

Spark plug

Wide piston-ring

Transfer port

Wire gauze pad

Upper piston

Flywheel

Flexible, forked connecting-rod

Counterweight

Big end

Crankcase

BERSEY ELECTRIC CAB, 1896

Mounting for tray of 40 batteries

Housing for electric motors

SECTIONED WHITE STEAM CAR, 1903

Steering wheel

Throttle wheel

Brake lever

Reverse lever

Flash steam generator

Automatic cylinder lubricator

Lamp bracket

High-pressure cylinder

Rocking lever

Exhaust pipe

Water pump

Condenser

Low-pressure cylinder

Fuel tank

Semi-elliptic spring

Brake drum

Spiral tubes

Flitch-plated wooden chassis

Drop arm

Water tank

Drag link

Dumb iron

CYCLE OF A FOUR-STROKE INTERNAL COMBUSTION ENGINE

INDUCTION STROKE ("SUCK")

Exhaust port closed
Inlet valve
Inlet port opens
Fuel and air (the "charge") sucked into cylinder
Piston moves downwards
Counterweight
Crankshaft
Crankpin

COMPRESSION STROKE ("SQUEEZE")

Exhaust port closed
Charge compressed by piston
Inlet port closed
Connecting rod (con-rod)
Piston moves upwards

POWER STROKE ("BANG")

Spark plug
Inlet port closed
Exhaust port closed
Charge ignited by spark plug
Explosion pushes piston downwards
Big end

EXHAUST STROKE ("BLOW")

Exhaust valve
Inlet port closed
Exhaust port opens
Burned gases forced out of cylinder
Piston moves upwards

16-HORSEPOWER HUMBER ENGINE, 1911

Brass housing for ignition cable
Inlet port
Water pipe
Valve cap
Spark plug
Side valve (inlet valve)
Pair-cast cylinder
Water jacket
Fan bracket
Tappet
Valve spring
Timing chain
Timing chest
Flywheel
Camshaft
Oil pump
Crankcase
Oil sump
Starting handle

DAIMLER DOUBLE-SLEEVE VALVE ENGINE, 1910

Spark plug socket
Junk ring
Cylinder head
Inlet port
Exhaust port
Inlet manifold
Outer sleeve valve
Water jacket
Cylinder wall
Inner sleeve valve
Piston
Carburettor
Engine bearer
Flywheel

OUTER SLEEVE VALVE

Oil groove

INNER SLEEVE VALVE

Sleeve port
Eye for connecting con-rods to secondary crankshaft

Modern engines

TODAY'S PETROL ENGINE WORKS on the same basic principles as the first car engines of a century ago, although it has been greatly refined. Modern engines, often made from special metal alloys, are much lighter than earlier engines. Computerized ignition systems, fuel injectors, and multi-valve cylinder heads achieve a more efficient combustion of the fuel/air mixture (the charge) so that less fuel is wasted. As a result of this greater efficiency, the power and performance of a modern engine are increased, and the level of pollution in the exhaust gases is reduced. Exhaust pollution levels today are also lowered by the increasing use of special filters called catalytic converters, which absorb many exhaust pollutants. The need to produce ever more efficient engines means that it can take up to seven years to develop a new engine for a family car, at a cost of many millions of pounds.

FRONT VIEW OF A FORD COSWORTH V6 12-VALVE

Idle control valve
Plenum chamber
Valve rocker
Power steering pump reservoir
Oil dipstick
Steering pump pulley
High-tension ignition lead (spark plug lead)
Cogged drive belt
Fan
Alternator
Crankshaft pulley
Viscous coupling
Oil sump

FRONT VIEW OF A FORD COSWORTH V6 24-VALVE

Idle control valve
Plenum chamber
Exhaust gas recirculation valve
Camshaft timing gear
Camshaft chain
Steering pump drive pulley
Belt tensioner
Air conditioning pump
Alternator cooling fan
Oil sump
Drive belt
Crankshaft pulley

SECTIONED VIEW OF A JAGUAR STRAIGHT 6

Cam follower (bucket tappet)
Valve spring
Cam lobe
Cam
Combustion chamber
Compression ring
Cam cover
Camshaft
Distributor
Cylinder head
Fan
Valve stem
Air conditioning refrigerant pipe
Exhaust valve
Suspension self-levelling pump
Cylinder liner
Power steering pump
Water jacket
Piston
Swash plate
Connecting rod (con-rod)
Drive belt
Main bearing housing
Big end
Compressor piston
Transmission adaptor plate
Crankshaft counterweight
Oil sump
Oil pick-up pipe
Anti-surge baffle
Crankcase
Oil-control ring (scraper ring)
Air conditioning compressor

FRONT VIEW OF A JAGUAR V12

Air cleaner

Camshaft sprocket

Distributor

Fuel injector nozzle

Piston

Crankshaft

Inlet manifold tract

Plenum chamber

Camshaft

Cam follower

Piston ring land

Piston ring groove

Exhaust manifold

Piston skirt

STRAIGHT 4 CYLINDER ARRANGEMENT

Coolant outlet

Cam cover

Viscous coupling

Gudgeon pin

Cooling fan

Fan drive shaft

Belt pulley

Counterweight

Connecting rod (con-rod)

V12 CYLINDER ARRANGEMENT

Alternator

Alternator pulley

SECTIONED VIEW OF A JAGUAR V12

Air inlet

Distributor drive shaft

Exhaust valve

Throttle butterfly

Fuel pipe

Inlet manifold

Ignition amplifier

Throttle linkage

Inlet valve

Timing chain

Piston crown

Piston ring land

Water pump

Piston

Cam cover

Oil feed pipe

Cylinder head

Coolant rail (water rail)

Exhaust heat shield

Exhaust manifold

Oil pipe banjo

Ancillary drive pulley

Timing chain drive sprocket

Connecting rod (con-rod)

Counterweight (balance weight)

Main bearing

Pipe to oil cooler

Crankcase

Sump

Drive plate

Starter ring

Oil filter

Alternative engines

THE MOST COMMON TYPE OF ALTERNATIVE ENGINE is the diesel engine, which, instead of igniting the compressed fuel/air mixture with a spark, uses compression alone, heating the mixture to the point where it explodes. A diesel engine's fuel consumption is low in comparison with similarly sized piston engines, despite its heavier, reinforced moving parts and cylinder block. Another type of engine is the rotary-combustion, first successfully developed by Felix Wankel in the 1950s. Its two trilobate (three-sided) rotors revolve in housings shaped in a fat figure-of-eight. The four sequences of the four-stroke cycle, which occur consecutively in a piston engine, occur simultaneously in a rotary engine, producing power in a continuous stream.

ROTARY-ENGINED MAZDA RX-7

Aerodynamic windscreen

Headrest

Hood bag

Front spoiler (chin spoiler)

Side marker lamp

Rubbing strake

Cast alloy wheel

WANKEL ROTARY ENGINE

OIL-PUMP HOUSING

FRONT SIDE HOUSING

Distributor fixing point (drive point)

Intake port

FRONT ROTOR CHAMBER

Trailing spark-plug hole

Dipstick tube

INTERMEDIATE HOUSING

Oil filler

Intake port

REAR ROTOR CHAMBER

Aluminium alloy backing

Oil-pump drive

Coolant passage

Exhaust port

Leading spark-plug hole

Water drain bolt

Trailing spark-plug hole

Leading spark-plug hole

THE WANKEL ROTARY CYCLE

Exhaust port

Intake port

Fuel/air mixture being compressed

Water passage

Gas continues to expand

Burning gas expands

Trilobate rotor

Exhaust port closed

Vacuum sucks in fuel/air mixture

Burnt gas exhausts

Rotor gear

Stationary gear (fixed gear)

Compression continues

Compressed gas ignites

Burnt gas continues to exhaust

Output shaft turns

Fuel/air mixture continues to enter

Burnt gas begins to expand

Compression begins

FORD TURBOCHARGED DIESEL ENGINE

Engine lifting eye

Rocker cover

Baffle plate

Inlet track

Turbo impeller (inlet rotor)

Turbo propeller (exhaust rotor)

Exhaust

Bell housing

Oil filler cap

Cam follower

Valve return spring

Water jacket

Water pump pulley

Compression ring

Oil-control ring

Piston

Ancillary drive belt

Water jacket

Oil cooler

Oil cooler matrix

Engine block

Oil filter

Oil sump pan

Oil return pipe for turbocharger

REAR SIDE HOUSING

Chrome plating

Exhaust port

ROTOR AND SEALS

Outer oil seal

Inner oil seal spring

Inner oil seal

Rotor bearing

Rotor gear

Side gear

Inner oil seal groove

Outer oil seal spring

Inner oil seal groove

Outer oil seal groove

Hole for output shaft

Side seal spring

Side seal

Side seal groove

Corner seal spring

Corner seal insert

Corner seal

Rotor

Balancing drilling

Apex seal

Apex seal spring

Apex seal groove

OUTPUT SHAFT

Front counterweight

Front eccentric rotor journal

Oil hole

Rear stationary gear (fixed gear)

V-belt pulley

Front stationary gear (fixed gear)

Main journal

Eccentric shaft

Oil jet

Rear eccentric rotor journal

Flywheel with balance weight

347

Modern bodywork

THE BODY OF A MODERN MASS-PRODUCED CAR is built on the monocoque (single-shell) principle, in which the roof, side panels, and floor are welded into a single integral unit. This bodyshell protects and supports the car's internal parts. Steel and glass are used to construct the bodyshell, creating a unit that is both light and strong. Its lightness helps to conserve energy, while its strength protects the occupants. Modern bodywork is designed with the aid of computers, which are used to predict factors such as aerodynamic efficiency and impact-resistance. High-technology is also employed on the production line, where robots are used to assemble, weld, and paint the body.

RENAULT LOGO

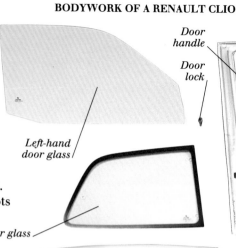

Door handle

Door lock

Left-hand door glass

Left-hand quarter glass

Tail-gate support

Window washer jet

Rear window glass

Heating element contact

Tail-gate support

Tail-gate

Rear bumper

Bodyshell

Fuel cap

Zinc phosphating

Degreased bare metal

Right-hand quarter glass

Primer

Base coat colour

Cataphoresic coating

Chrome passivation

Varnish

Right-hand door glass

Door key and lock

Door handle

Left-hand door

Left-hand mirror assembly

Door hinge

Electric window motor

Rear hatch

Aerial

Side marker lamp

SIDE VIEW OF A RENAULT CLIO

Spoiler bumper

Bonnet-release cable

Bonnet

Bonnet catch

Bonnet hinge

Window winder cable

Windscreen glass

Front bumper

Window winder handle

Door hinge

Right-hand door

Right-hand mirror assembly

Bonnet

Headrest

Headlamp

Spoiler bumper

Fog-lamp

H746 FBK

FRONT VIEW OF A RENAULT CLIO

Modern mechanics

A TYPICAL MODERN CAR has several thousand individual mechanical components. These are assembled to form the car's various mechanical systems: engine and exhaust, transmission, steering, suspension, and brakes. To ensure that each system functions properly, components are manufactured to extremely fine tolerances – to within a five-hundredth of a millimetre (about one ten-thousandth of an inch) in some cases.

Alloy wheel

Hub cap

Hub nut

Hub seal

Exhaust downpipe

Silencer

Catalytic converter

Suspension spring

Rear silencer

Fuel tank

Vent pipe

Shock absorber

Electric fuel pump

Fuel tank filler neck

Torsion bar

Nearside rear suspension arm

Anti-roll bar

Offside rear suspension arm

Handbrake

Gear lever

Steering wheel

Steering rack

Steering column

Brake cylinder

Brake shoe

Hub seal

Hub nut

Hub cap

Wheel trim

Steel wheel

Brake backplate

Hub and brake drum

Clutch pedal

Brake pedal

Throttle pedal

Clutch cable

Throttle cable

MECHANICAL COMPONENTS OF A RENAULT CLIO, 1991

Brake shield

Alloy wheel

Clutch release bearing

Brake disc

Hub

Nearside drive shaft

Clutch pressure plate

Track-rod end

Upper suspension arm

Brake hose

Top hose

Track rod

Brake pad

Power steering pump

Clutch centre plate

Gear-change rod

Bottom hose

Lower suspension arm

Gearbox (transmission)

Anti-roll bar

Starter motor

Flywheel

Fan motor

Electronic ignition unit

Subframe

Power steering belt

Exhaust Manifold

Brake cylinder

Intake manifold

Water pump

Brake servo

Fan motor support

Alternator

Alternator belt

Engine

Brake caliper fixing bolt

Distributor

Brake caliper locking plate

Suspension strut

Air cleaner

Brake caliper

Hub carrier

Brake hose

Offside drive shaft

Radiator

Lock nut and washer

Brake disc

Front hub bearing

Steel wheel

Wheel trim

Water bottle

Brake shield

Modern trim

A MODERN CAR HAS TWO TYPES OF TRIM, according to the materials used: hard (chrome and plastics) and soft (upholstery materials). Safety and comfort are priorities in the trim's design: seats help the occupants to maintain a comfortable posture, rubber seals keep out dirt and moisture, and headlamps light the way. Older cars had interior or leather panelling cut and fitted by craftsmen; modern cars use precisely moulded plastics and seat fabrics cut by robot-controlled lasers to reduce costs and production time. Doors are now trimmed off the production line so that complex wiring can be built in.

TRIM OF A RENAULT CLIO, 1991

Rear quarter trim panel

Inner roof trim

Roof seal

Quarter trim panel

Rear quarter trim panel

Quarter panel moulding

Rear seat belt

Split, folding rear seat assembly

Centre seat belt

Rear seat belt stalk (catch)

Rear shelf radio speaker

Rear shelf radio speaker

Gear lever surroun

Rear tyre

Rear shelf

Tail-gate trim

Rear wiper blade

Tail-gate seal

Rear wiper arm

Number plate lamp

Rear indicator and stop lamp assembly

Rear wheel embellisher (wheel trim)

Untrimmed headrest

Rear seat belt

Quarter panel moulding

HALOGEN HEADLAMP BULB

SPOTLAMP BULB

Filament

Rear tyre

MARKER LAMP BULB

Filament

FESTOON BULB

Rear quarter trim panel

Roof seal

Quarter trim panel

Inner roof trim

Roof moulding

Contact

Bayonet fixing

Contact

Contact

Window winder handle

Door seal

Door lock handle

Front tyre

Front wheel embellisher (wheel trim)

Door pull handle

Indicator lamp

Fog-lamp

Inner sill trim

Door moulding (rubbing strip)

Inner windscreen moulding

Front seat belt

Front door radio speaker

Front seat assembly

Dash radio speaker

Sun visor

Dash panel (instrument panel)

Headlamp

Windscreen wiper bracket and spindles

Windscreen wiper blade

Heater unit

Washer jet

Fan blade

Radio

Interior light

Rear-view mirror

Centre console

Steering wheel

Sun visor

Fascia (dash)

Windscreen seal

Headlamp

Front seat frame

Windscreen wiper arm

Dash radio speaker

Front seat belt

Control stalk

Front door radio speaker

Inner sill trim

Door moulding (rubbing strip)

Inner windscreen moulding

Door trim panel

Door seal

Fog-lamp

Door pull handle

Window winder handle

Door lock handle

Front tyre

Front wheel embellisher (wheel trim)

Indicator lamp

All-terrain vehicles

THE MODERN ALL-TERRAIN VEHICLE has its origins in
the US military Jeep of the 1940s and the British Land
Rover. Such vehicles have been used for a wide range of
purposes, from safari travel to fire-fighting. The principal
special features of such cars – including four- or six-wheel
drive, high ground clearance, and toughened braking,
suspension, and transmission systems – are designed
to enable driving under the most difficult off-road
conditions. The vehicle shown here is
equipped for safari travel and carries
a comprehensive range of
survival apparatus.

COOKING EQUIPMENT

**TWO-BURNER
ALCOHOL STOVE**

Handle
for all
pans

Flame
regulator

Wick

Cooking
pot

Zip

Mosquito netting

Ventilation
flap

Tie

**SIDE VIEW OF
PINZGAUER
TURBO D**

HAND WINCH

Folding
rooftop tent

Galvanized roof-rack

Locking
fuel filler
cap

Dust
trap

Raised
air
intake

Guard

Steel body

Jerrycan

Spare wheel
and tyre

Rubbing strip
(rubbing strake)

**TYRE
PUMP**

Pressure
gauge

TYRE LEVER

Heavy-duty shovel

Tubular backbone chassis

Fuel tank

Metal jerrycan for fuel

Plastic
jerrycan
for water

LEFT-HAND
TREAD PLATE

RIGHT-HAND
TREAD PLATE

TOW STRAP

HEAVY-DUTY
SHACKLE

SAFETY WINDSCREEN CLAMPS

WASHING BUCKET

Radio aerial

Observation
roof hatch

Grab
handle

Rear-view
mirror

Windscreen
washer
bottle

Wrap-
around
bumper

Access step

SECURITY
CHAIN

FRONT VIEW OF PINZGAUER TURBO D

Observation
roof hatch

Radio aerial

Galvanized
roof-rack

Laminated
windscreen

Rear-
view
mirror

Air vent

Radiator
grille

Indicator

Headlamp

Lamp
guard

Independent
portal swing axle

Locking
differential

Towing
pintle

External
step

Off-road
tyre

REAR VIEW OF PINZGAUER TURBO D

Roof-rack

Observation
platform

External
step for roof

Jerrycan

Jerrycan
carrier

Spare
wheel

Offset door
hinge

Rubbing strip
(rubbing
strake)

Rear
bumper

Rear lamp
cluster

Door and
wheel
support
frame

Mudflap

Off-road
tyre

Locking
differential

Independent portal swing axle

Racing cars

SINCE MOTORING BEGAN, racing cars have been a major focus of innovation in car design. Features that are now commonplace, such as disc brakes, turbochargers, and even safety belts, were used first on competition cars. Research into racing cars has contributed to a new understanding of engine performance, aerodynamics, and tyre adhesion, and has led to the development of ultra-light materials such as carbon-fibre for car bodies. Like the 1937 Bugatti Type 57S below, a modern Williams Formula One car has a low, streamlined body and an open cockpit, but, unlike its forerunner, it also has a front wing that pushes the front wheels firmly on to the track, huge slick tyres for extra grip, and electrical sensors that continually relay information to the pits about the car's performance.

OVERHEAD VIEW OF WILLIAMS 1990 FORMULA ONE RACING CAR

Diffuser

Bodywork bracket

Heat shield

Forward radius arm

Rear wing upper mainplane

Slot

Upper flap

Half shaft

Rear radius arm

Temperature-sensitive sticker

Aeroquip pipe union

Oil tank

Constant velocity joint cover

Rear wing end-plate

Diffuser

Rear brake duct

Oil feed to engine

1937 BUGATTI TYPE 57S

Fuel injection trumpet guard (debris guard)

Fuel injector

Cam cover

Cylinder head

Gearbox fixing stud

Mounting point

Electronic control-unit connector

Water outlet

Tail pipe

Stressed cylinder block

Harmonically-tuned exhaust pipe

ENGINE COWLING

Dzus fastener

RENAULT V10 RS1 ENGINE

SIDE FAIRING

Water rail

Engine cooling radiator

Master electrical switch

Anchor nut

Radiator air duct

Slick racing tyre

Steering link

Nose cover

Front wing end-plate

Front wing

Suspension push-rod

Rear-view mirror

Lower wishbone

Front lower wishbone

Brake pipe

Driver's radio aerial

Upper wishbone

Electrical connectors to engine

Lifting hook

Safety harness

Single-point safety harness release

Push-rod adjuster

Exhaust

Chassis electrical plug

Emergency electricity cut-off

Emergency air hose for driver

Fuel injection air-intake trumpet

Fuel filler

Fuel breather

Air intake

FRONT VIEW OF WILLIAMS 1990 FORMULA ONE RACING CAR

Rear wing upper mainplane

Engine air intake

Driver's radio aerial

Rear wing end-plate

Upper wishbone

Rear-view mirror

Rear brake duct

Suspension push-rod

Slick racing tyre

Front wing end-plate

Radiator air intake

Steering link

Front wing

End-plate aerodynamic skirt

Bicycle anatomy

THE BICYCLE IS A TWO-WHEELED, light-weight machine, which is propelled by human power. It is efficient, cheap, easily manufactured, and one of the world's most popular forms of transport. The first pedal-driven bicycle was built in Scotland in 1839. Since then the basic design – of a frame, wheels, brakes, handlebars, and saddle – has been gradually improved, with the addition of a chain, gear system, and pneumatic tyres (tyres inflated with air). The recent invention of the mountain bike (all-terrain bike) has been an important development. With its strong, rugged frame, wide tyres, and 21 gears, a mountain bike enables riders to reach rough and hilly areas that were previously inaccessible to cyclists.

Saddle

Seat post

Seat post quick-release bolt

Cable guide

Straddle wire

Seat tube

Rear cantilever brake

Seat stay

Front derailleur

REAR WHEEL

Tyre

Spoke

Hub

Rim

Rear drop-outs

Rear hub quick-release spindle

Bottom bracket shell

Bottom bracket axle

Crank bolt

Washer

Bottom bracket sleeve

Adjustable cup

17-tooth sprocket

13-tooth sprocket

Fixed cup

Caged ball bearings

Lock ring

Lock washer

Freewheel locknut

Jockey wheel

Chain

Lock washer

23-tooth sprocket

Rear derailleur

Derailleur cage plate

Jockey wheel

46-tooth chain ring

Toe clip

Sprocket spacer

GEAR SYSTEM

Spoke guard

30-tooth sprocket

Spider

FREEWHEEL SPROCKETS

Toe strap

Pedal

Gear cable

Gearshift

Gearshift

Handlebar
stem

Handlebar

Handlebar
grip

Expander
bolt

Lock
nut

Rear brake
cable

Top tube

Top race

Brake
lever

Brake lever

Lock
washer

Front brake
cable

Cable guide

Head
tube

Top cup

Caged ball
bearings

Hub

Spoke

**BICYCLE
FRAME**

Bottom
cup

Rubber
bearing
seal

Down
tube

Steerer
tube

Straddle wire

Bottom
race

Front
cantilever
brake

Toe clip

Cantilever
brake boss

Rim

Inner tube

Toe
strap

Pedal

Fork blade

Left crank
arm

Front hub
quick-release
spindle

24-tooth
chain ring

36-tooth
chain ring

Handlebar

Dust cap

Saddle

Frame

Brake lever
and gearshift

Valve

Pedal

Tyre

FRONT WHEEL

Chain

359

Bicycles

ALTHOUGH ALL BICYCLES are made up of the same basic components, they can vary greatly in design. A racing bike, such as the Eddy Merckx model, with its light frame and steep head- and seat-angles, is built for speed. Its design forces the rider to adopt the "aerotuck", a crouched, aerodynamic position. While a touring bike resembles the racing bike in many respects, it is designed for comfort and stability on long-distance journeys. Touring bikes are characterized by more relaxed frame angles, heavy chain stays that support the rear panniers, and a long wheelbase (the distance between the wheel axles) for reliable handling. All-round bicycles, known as "hybrids", combine the light weight and speed of sports bikes with the rugged durability of mountain bikes (see pp. 358-359). Bicycles that are not designed for conventional road use include time-trial bikes, which have a short head tube, sloping top tube, "aero" handlebars, and aerodynamic tubing. Most Human Powered Vehicles (HPVs) are recumbents – the rider has a recumbent position – which maximize power output and minimize drag (resistance). Essential to the safety of all riders are helmets, and both front and rear lights; locks protect against theft.

FRONT AND REAR LIGHTS

HELMET

Hard outer shell

Red rear light

White front light

Air vent

Polystyrene padding

Quick-release strap

EDDY MERCKX RACING BICYCLE

Saddle

Saddle clamp

Seat post

Seat-post bolt

Cable guide

Rear brake cable

Brake-block bolt

Top tube (crossbar)

Steel frame

Brake block

Seat stay

Seat tube

Tyre

Down tube

Tyre tread

Water-bottle cage

Tyre wall

Front derailleur

Wheel rim

Freewheel sprocket

STEEL LOCK

Key

Hardened steel

Pick-proof lock

Rear derailleur

Pulley bolt

Tension pulley

Chain

Chain stay

Chain ring

Crank bolt

Crank

Spider

Pedal

Toe clip

CANNONDALE SH600 HYBRID BICYCLE

Gel-filled saddle

Light-weight frame

Straight handlebar

Brake bridge

Cantilever brake

All-surface tyre

CANNONDALE ST1000 TOURING BICYCLE

Rear mudguard

Water bottle

Drop handlebar

Front mudguard

Rear pannier

Front pannier

Long chain stay

Large diameter aluminium tubing

Headset

Stem

Binder bolt

Handlebar

Front brake cable

Brake lever

Head tube

Brake pivot bolt

Brake pad

Fork

Hub quick-release lever

Spoke

Spoke nipple

Presta valve

Hub

ROSSIN ITALIAN TIME-TRIAL BICYCLE

Aero handlebar

Sloping top tube

Steep seat tube

Short head tube

Hollow disc wheel

Clipless pedal

Tri-spoke wheel

Narrow tyre

WINDCHEETAH SL MARK VI "SPEEDY" RACING HPV BICYCLE

Fleecy headrest

Fibreglass bucket seat

Joystick

Brake lever

53-tooth chain ring

Clipless pedal

7-speed freewheel

Aluminium tubing

Drum brake

Extended racing chain

The motorcycle

THE MOTORCYCLE HAS EVOLVED from a motorized cycle – a basic bicycle with an engine – into a sophisticated, high-performance machine. In 1901, the Werner brothers established the most viable location for the engine by positioning it low in the centre of the chassis (see pp. 364-365): the new Werner became the basis for the modern motorcycle. Motorcycles are used for many purposes – for commuting, delivering messages, touring, and racing – and different machines have been developed according to the demands of different types of riders. The Vespa scooter, for instance, which is small-wheeled, economical, and easy-to-ride, was designed to meet the needs of the commuter. Sidecars provided transport for the family until the arrival of cheap cars caused their popularity to decline. Enthusiast riders generally favour larger capacity machines that are capable of greater performance and offer more comfort. Four-cylinder machines have been common since the Honda CB750 appeared in 1969. Despite advances in motorcycle technology, many riders are attracted to the traditional looks of motorcycles like the twin-cylinder Harley-Davidson. The Harley-Davidson Glides exploit the style of the classic American V-twin engine, where the cylinders are placed in a V-formation.

1901 WERNER MOTORCYCLE

Vacuum-operated inlet valve
Fuel tank
Electric ignition control
Bicycle-type saddle
Inlet-over-exhaust (IOE) engine
Pulley rim rear brake
Alloy crankcase
Cast iron cylinder barrel
Twisted rawhide drive belt

1988 HARLEY-DAVIDSON FLHS ELECTRA GLIDE

1965 BMW R/60 WITH 1952 STEIB CHAIR

Handlebar
Head-light
Windscreen
Adjustable link
Mirror
Sidecar
Sidelight
Fuel tank
Mudguard
Horizontally opposed engine
Sidecar chassis rail
Sidecar wheel
Sidecar lower link
Exhaust pipe
Square-section tyre
FRONT VIEW
Indicator
Side reflector

Backrest
Passenger seat
Passenger grab rail
Pannier
Luggage rack
Licence plate
Tail-light

Mudguard
Canvas shroud
Speedometer
Ignition lock
Tail-light
Grab handle
Tool tray
Lockable luggage boot
Mudguard stay
Silencer
Silencer bracket
Disc brake
Suspension linkage
Bullet-shaped sidecar body
Drum brake
Crash bar
Exhaust clamp
Knock-off wheel nut
SIDE VIEW
Long leading-link fork (Earles fork)

1969 HONDA CB750

1963 VESPA GRAND SPORT 160 MARK 1

Tail-light

Seat

Mirror

Front brake lever

Seat strap

Indicator

Shock absorber

Oil tank

Telescopic fork

Mudguard stay

Disc brake

Clutch cover

Single overhead camshaft engine

Mirror

Heat shield

Passenger footrest

Exhaust pipe

Twist grip gear change

Monocoque chassis

Seat strap

Throttle

Front brake lever

Clutch lever

Engine cover

Seat

Head-light

Cooling grille

Horn

Tail-light

Choke

Shock absorber

Petrol tap

Kick-starter

Centre stand

Foot brake

Drum brake

Silencer

Rubber foot mat

Single-sided trailing-link fork

Brake master cylinder

Handgrip

Front brake lever

Windscreen

Clutch cable

Throttle cable

Padded seat

Light switch

Manufacturer's logo

Windscreen adjustor

Oil tank filler cap

Fuel tank

Head-light

Oil tank

Fog-lamp

Indicator

Telescopic fork

Side reflector

Mudguard

Gearbox

Air filter

Crash bar

Passenger footrest

45° V-twin engine

Exhaust pipe

Footrest

Duplex tubular cradle frame

Brake calliper

Cast alloy wheel

Brake pedal

Disc brake

The motorcycle chassis

THE MOTORCYCLE CHASSIS is the main "body" of the motorcycle, to which the engine is attached. Consisting of the frame, wheels, suspension, and brakes, the chassis performs various functions. The frame, which is built from steel or alloy, keeps the wheels in line to maintain the handling of the motorcycle, and serves as a structure for mounting other components. The engine and gearbox unit is bolted into place, while items such as the seat, the mudguards, and the fairing are more easily removable. Suspension cushions the rider from irregularities in the road surface. In most suspension systems, coil springs controlled by an oil damper separate the main mass of the motorcycle from the wheels. At the front, the spring and damper are usually incorporated in a telescopic fork; the rear employs a pivoted swingarm. The suspension also helps to retain maximum contact between the tyres and the road, necessary to effective braking and steering. Drum brakes were common until the 1970s, but modern motorcycles use disc brakes, which are more powerful.

1985 HONDA VF750 WITH BODYWORK

Racing number plate
Frame-mounted fairing
Fuel tank
Dual seat
Telescopic fork
Mudguard
Disc brake
Box-section swingarm
V4 engine unit
Box-section tubular cradle frame
Floating disc brake

1985 HONDA VF750 WITH BODYWORK REMOVED

Brake master cylinder
Headstock
Bracing tube
Shock absorber top mounting
Engine mounting plate
Square-section steel tubing
Rear sub-frame
Bodywork mounting point
Shock absorber
Exhaust mounting strap
Exhaust pipe
Light alloy wheel
Axle adjustor
Disc brake
Disc brake calliper
Box-section swingarm
Brake torque arm
Brake master cylinder
Footrest hanger
Brake pedal
Swingarm pivot
Multiplate clutch
Oil level window
Oil sump
Engine cover
Engine mounting bolt
V4 engine unit
Radiator
Oil cooler
Radiator pipe

DRUM BRAKE

EXTERIOR OF DRUM BRAKE

Bolt hole

Torque arm

Air cooling scoop

Axle hole

Cooling fin

Speedometer drive

Cable stop

Brake plate

Operating arm

INTERIOR OF DRUM BRAKE

Torque arm

Bolt hole

Brake shoe

Pivot

Brake shoe return spring

Operating cam

Axle hole

Brake shoe return spring

High-friction material

OPERATING PARTS OF DISC BRAKE SYSTEM

Brake fluid reservoir

Master cylinder

Push-rod

Piston

Hydraulic brake fluid

Wheel disc

Calliper assembly

Piston

Brake pad

Clutch cable

Hydraulic brake hose

Telescopic fork leg

Fork slide

Light alloy wheel

Floating disc brake

Brake calliper

Axle

SPRING/DAMPER UNIT

Rubber mounting bush

Twin rate spring

Damper rod

Damper body

Pre-load adjustor

Rubber mounting bush

HOW A SPRING/DAMPER UNIT WORKS

Rubber mounting bush

Spring

Damper rod

Non-return valve

Hydraulic fluid

Compressible gas

Hydraulic fluid chamber

Rubber mounting bush

TYPES OF TYRE

RACING SLICK TYRE

No tread pattern

TUBELESS SPORTS TYRE

Radial groove

TRIALS TYRE

Knobbly tread pattern

GENERAL -USE TYRE

Hard-wearing rubber compound

Motorcycle engines

MOTORCYCLE ENGINES must be light-weight and compact, and have a good power output. They have between one and six cylinders, can be cooled by air or water, and the capacity of the combustion chamber varies from 49cc (cubic centimetres) to 1500cc. Two types of internal combustion engine are common: the four-stroke, which is used in cars (see pp. 342-343), and the two-stroke. A basic two-stroke engine has only three moving parts – the crankshaft, the connecting rod, and the piston – but the power output is high. The engine fires every two strokes (rather than every four), giving a "power stroke" every revolution (see p. 343). Power is conveyed from the engine to the rear wheel by the transmission system. This usually consists of a clutch, a gearbox, and a final drive system. Clutches are multiplate devices, which run in oil. Gearboxes have five or six speeds and are operated by foot pedal. Shaft and belt drive systems are used in some cases, but chain drive to the rear wheel is most common.

EXTERIOR OF STANDARD TWO-STROKE ENGINE

Spark plug cap
Fuel tap
Carburettor mounting
Kick-starter
Carburettor
Cylinder head
Cooling fin
Exhaust port
Case screw
Clutch activating arm
Engine cover
Gear lever

TRANSMISSION SYSTEM

GEARBOX

1st gear
6th gear
4th gear
3rd gear
5th gear
2nd gear
Gear lever selector shaft
Input shaft
Splines for mounting gear lever
Bearing
Output shaft
Splines for mounting final drive sprocket
Gear tooth
Selector fork
Copper oil feed pipe
Aluminium outer casing

MULTIPLATE CLUTCH

Fibre plate
Key locks fibre plate to outer drum
Outer clutch drum, connected to engine
Pressure plate, connected to inner clutch drum
Springs force plates together
Metal plate
Straight-cut primary-drive gear

MODERN "O RING" DRIVE CHAIN

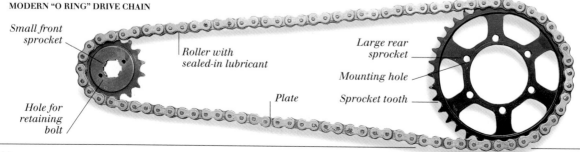

Small front sprocket
Roller with sealed-in lubricant
Large rear sprocket
Mounting hole
Sprocket tooth
Hole for retaining bolt
Plate

**VELOCETTE OVERHEAD
VALVE (OHV) ENGINE**

Screw and lock nut
tappet adjustor

Oil feed pipe

Inlet port

Spark plug lead

Cam follower

Magneto drive

Camshaft gear

Engine
mounting
bolt hole

Oil passageway

Crankcase

Oil pump

Mounting lug

Rocker arm

Rocker cover
retaining bolt

Cylinder head

Exhaust port

Cylinder head

Combustion chamber

Cooling fin

Piston

Push rod

Valve lifter

Timing gear

Engine
mounting
bolt hole

Crankshaft

Non-return valve

Oil sump

Competition motorcycles

THERE ARE MANY TYPES of motorcycle sport and in each, a specialist machine has evolved to perform to specific requirements. Races take place on roads or tracks or "off-road", in fields, dirt tracks, and even the desert. "Grand Prix" world championships in road-racing exist for 125cc, 250cc, and 500cc classes, as well as for sidecars. The latest racing sidecars have more in common with racing cars than motorcycles. The rider and passenger operate within an all-enclosing, aerodynamic fairing. The Suzuki RGV500 shown here, like other Grand Prix machines, carries advertising, which promotes the manufacturer and helps to cover the cost of developing motorcycle technology. In Speedway, which originated in the US in 1902, motorcycles operate without brakes or a gearbox. Off-road competition motorcycles have less emphasis on high power output. In Motocross, for example, which is held on rough terrain, they must have high ground clearance, flexible long-travel suspension, and tyres with a chunky tread pattern, to allow them to grip in sand or mud.

1992 HUSQVARNA MOTOCROSS TC610

Throttle cable · Hand protector · Flexible plastic mudguard · Handlebar brace · Radiator air vent · Long seat · Racing number · Light-weight exhaust system · Telescopic fork · Plastic guard · Axle · Knobbly tyre · Disc brake · Brake calliper · Overhead camshaft engine · Gear lever · Shock absorber · Alloy swingarm · Shock absorber linkage · Disc brake

1992 SUZUKI RGV500
SIDE VIEW

Exhaust pipe · Racing number · Air vent · One-piece seat and tail unit · Shock absorber · Minimal seat padding · Arched alloy swingarm

34

Exhaust pipe · Vent · Handlebar · Footrest · Rear brake pedal · Drive chain · Wide, slick tyre · **REAR VIEW** · Exhaust pipe · Silencer · Shock absorber mounting · Three-spoke alloy wheel · Exhaust pipe · Axle adjustor · Disc brake · Rear brake calliper · Slick racing tyre · Drive chain · Footrest · Brake pedal · Disc brake master cylinder · Light-weight alloy frame

1981 WESLAKE SPEEDWAY

Throttle

Throttle cable

Carburettor cover

Fuel tank filler cap

Oil filler cap

Mudguard

Seat

Fuel tank

Wheel cover

Mudguard

Telescopic fork

Narrow tyre

Wide tyre

Brakeless wheel hub

Silencer

Footrest

Oil pump

Overhead valve engine

Tubular open cradle frame

1968 KIRBY BSA RACING SIDECAR

FRONT VIEW

Rev counter

Windscreen

All-enclosing fairing

Fuel tank

Battery

Wheel guard

60

BSA

Square-section tyre

Passenger windscreen

Passenger grab rail

SIDE VIEW

Throttle cable

Exhaust pipe

Rev counter

All-enclosing fairing

60

Sidecar chassis

Engine

Fuel cap

Fibreglass wheel guard

Fairing stay

Throttle cable

Fuel tank breather

Fuel tank

MOTUL

Throttle

Front brake lever

Telescopic fork

Mudguard

TEAM LUCKY STRIKE SUZUKI MOTUL

Windscreen

Racing number

Clutch lever

Fairing

LUCKY STRIKE

34

Front brake lever

Radiator

Hydraulic brake hose

Mudguard

Axle

Slick tyre

Slick tyre

FRONT VIEW

Sponsor's logo

Air vent

Braided steel hydraulic hose

Brake calliper

Carbon-fibre disc brake

Three-spoke alloy wheel

Quickly detachable (QD) fairing

Sea and Air

Ships of Greece and Rome

ROMAN ANCHOR

Stock

Shank

Palm

Acutely
angled
arm

Ring

Crown

IN THE EXPANSIVE EMPIRES OF GREECE AND ROME, powerful fleets were needed for battle, trade, and communication. Greek galleys were powered by a sail and many oars. A new armament, the embolos (ram), was fitted on to the galley bow. As ramming duels required fast and manoeuvrable boats, extra rows of oarsmen were added, culminating in the trireme. During the fifth and fourth centuries B.C., the trireme dominated the Mediterranean. It was powered by 170 oarsmen, rowing with one oar each. The oarsmen were ranged on three levels, as the model opposite shows. The trireme also carried archers and soldiers for boarding. Galleys were pulled out of the water when not in use, and were kept in dockyard ship-sheds. The merchant ships of the Greeks and Romans were mighty vessels too. The full-bodied Roman corbita, for example, could hold up to 400 tons and carried a cargo of spices, gems, silk, and animals. The construction of these boats was based on a stout hull with planking secured by mortice and tenon. Some of these ships embarked on long voyages, sailing even as far as India. To make them easier to steer, corbitas set a fore sail called an "artemon". It flew from a forward-leaning mast that was a forerunner of the long bowsprits carried by the great clipper ships of the 19th century.

ATTIC VASE SHOWING A GALLEY

Double halyard **ROMAN CORBITA**

Roband
(rope band)

Ceruchi
(lift)

Bullseye

Fore mast

Heraldic device

Antenna
(yard)

Buntline

Ring

Brace

Ruden
(brail line)

Artemon
(fore sail)

Fore stay

Oculus
(eye)

Anchor

Tabling

Sheet

Bolt rope

Prow

Windlass

Bronze mast
truck

Keraia (yard)

Scala
(ladder)

Kalos
(brailing
rope)

Catena
(riding bitt)

Mast

Kubernetes
(helmsman)

Ancorale
(anchor rope;
anchor rode)

Embolos
(ram;
beak)

Sternpost

Pedalia
(twin rudder)

Hatch board

Ophthalmos
(eye)

Oar port sleeve

Deck beam

Zosteres (rubbing strake)

Kope (oar)

Cargo hold

Masthead

Single clump block

Malus (mast)

Rope parrel

Bullet block

Antenna (yard)

Brace block

Timber fairlead

Shroud

Leather reinforcing strip

Scala (ladder)

Velum (main sail)

Sheer pole

Deadeye

Lanyard

Poop break

Poop deck

Clew

Midships fence

Constratum (deck)

Bitt

Oar lanyard

Blade

ROWING POSITIONS ON A GREEK TRIREME (TRIERE)
The katastroma (deck) has been removed from this model to show the positions taken by oarsmen on a trireme.

Deck rail

Tropeter (leather grommet)

Paraxeiresia (outrigger)

Kope (oar)

Stanchion

Zugon (thwart; seat)

Thranite (upper level oarsman)

Zygian (middle level oarsman)

Thalamian (lower level oarsman)

Hyperesion (oarsman's cushion)

Pine hull

Main double halyard

Main brace

Main sheet

Hole and peg joint

Poop deck house

Clavus (tiller)

Swan neck ornament

Stern balustrade

Ring bolt

Sternpost

Gubernator (helmsman)

Wale

Planking

Shaft

Gubernacula (rudders)

MORTICE-AND-TENON FASTENINGS FOR HULL PLANKS

Mortice

Gomphoi (dowel)

Tenon

Hull plank

Viking ships

IN THE DARK AGES and early medieval times, the longships of Scandinavia were one of the most feared sights for people of northern Europe. The Vikings launched raids from Scandinavia every summer in longships equipped with a single steering oar on the right, or "steerboard", side (hence "starboard"). A longship had one row of oars on each side and a single sail. The hull had clinker (overlapping) planks. Prowheads adorned fighting ships during campaigns of war. The sailing longship was also used for local coastal travel. The karv below was probably built as transport for an important family, while the smaller faering (top right) was a rowing boat only. The fleet of William of Normandy that invaded England in 1066 owed much to the Viking boatbuilding tradition, and has been depicted in the Bayeux Tapestry (above). Seals used by port towns and royal courts through the ages provide an excellent record of contemporary ship design. The seal opposite shows how ships changed from the Viking period to the end of the Middle Ages. The introduction of the fighting platform – the castle – and the addition of extra masts and sails changed the character of the medieval ship. Note also that the steering oar has been replaced by a centred rudder.

BOATBUILDERS' TOOLS

Shave
Broad axe
Breast auger
Sheer
Master shipwright
Stempost
Hood end
Keel
T-handle auger
Axe
Strake
Tree cut for planking

Zoomorphic head
Eye
Tooth

Braiding
Serpentine neck
Lozenge-shaped recess
Rectangular cross-band

DRAGON PROWHEAD

Snake-tail ornament

VIKING KARV (COASTER)

Sternpost
Boss (rudder pivot)
Steering oar (side rudder)
Oar
Tiller
Starboard (steerboard) side

Tye halyard
Foot
Keel

Roband
Leather diagonal reinforcement
Square sail of homespun yarn
Leech (leach)

FAERING (VIKING ROWING BOAT)

Grommet

Tiller

Clench nail

Knee

Grommet

Kabe (oar pivot)

Plank scarf

Prow

Stepped sternpost

Stepped stempost

Pivot

Side rudder

Sheer strake

Oar

Keel

Thwart (seat)

Double-ended hull

Masthead

Masthead pulley for tye halyard

Yard

Head

Head earing

Parrel

COURT SEAL SHOWING A THREE-MASTED, SQUARE-RIGGED SHIP

Weaponry

Banner/ windvane

Topcastle

Main mast

Furled forecourse sail

Furled lateen mizzen sail

Jack staff

Mizzen mast

Fore mast

Aftercastle

Forecastle

Centred rudder

Stempost

Gudgeon

Main sail

Leechline

Anchor

Snake-head ornament

Mast

Sail foot control line used as a sheet or tack

Open, double-ended hull

Stempost

Main sheet

Oar port

Scroll work

Clinker-built oak planking (overlapping planking)

Stowage crutch for oars

Clench nail

Medieval warships and traders

FROM THE 16TH CENTURY, SHIPS WERE BUILT WITH A NEW FORM OF HULL, constructed from carvel (edge-to-edge) planking. Warships of the time, like King Henry VIII of England's Mary Rose, boasted awesome fire power. This ship carried both long-range cannon in bronze, and short-range, anti-personnel guns in iron. Elsewhere, ships took on a multiformity of shapes. Dhows transported slaves from East Africa to Arabia, their fore-and-aft rigged lateen sails allowing them to sail close to the wind around the lands of the Indian Ocean. The Chinese sailed to East Africa and Arabia in junks, trading goods that were carried in watertight compartments. New astronomical tools helped medieval sailors to find their way. Cross-staves and astrolabes were used to measure the altitude of the sun or stars. One of a choice of four cross-pieces was slid up or down the staff of the cross-stave – which was graduated in degrees of altitude – until its top aligned with the celestial body and its base with the horizon. The sighting rule of the astrolabe was simply lined up with a known body, and its altitude read from marks on the metal disc. With sundials, the sailor could use the shadow of the sun to show the time of day.

DHOW

Main yard
Furled lateen main sail
Mizzen yard
Parrel
Furled lateen mizzen sail
Main mast
Mizzen mast
Shroud
Parrel tackle
Tiller
Stem head
Rudder
Raking stempost
Eye

SAILING WARSHIP

Fore top yard
Fore topmast
Fore topcastle
Lift
Fore yard
Fore mast
Ratline
Shroud
Fore stay
Woolding
Forecastle
Forecastle castle-deck gunport
Beakhead
Rigging rail
Chain wale (channel)
Hawse hole
Anchor cable
Stempost

JUNK

Su-wei (fourth mast)
Topsail
Chung-ta-wei (main mast)
Fore topmast stay
Bowsprit
Wei-wei (mizzen mast)
Halyard
Erh-wei (second mast)
Sprit yard
Sail batten
T'on-wei (port fore-mast)
Lug sail
Rudder head
Transom
Rudder
Quarterdeck house
Cargo hatch
Oar
Grapnel-type anchor

Main topgallant mast

Main topgallant yard

Main topmast topcastle

Main top yard

Mizzen topmast

Mizzen top yard

Main topmast stay

Mizzen topcastle

Main topmast

Lift

Main topcastle

Bonaventure top yard

Lift

Bonaventure topmast

Main yard

30 degree cross-piece

Parrel

Tye

Jeer

Bonaventure topcastle

Brace

Bonaventure yard

Main stay

Mizzen mast

Bonaventure mast

Mizzen yard

Aftercastle

Main mast

Swifting tackle

Aftercastle castle-deck gunport

Upper deck gunport

Outrigger

Pivot

Lid

Chain wale (channel)

Gangway

Deadeye

Gun carriage

Transom

Rudder

Sternpost

Keel

Blindage (removable archery screen)

Wale

Main deck gunport

Carvel planking

Port bower anchor

CROSS-STAVE (CROSS-STAFF)

90 degree cross-piece (transversary)

Clamp

60 degree cross-piece

Boxwood staff

Altitude scale in degrees and minutes

Ocular end

10 degree cross-piece (dutch shoe)

SUNDIAL

Style of the gnomon (edge)

Gnomon

Needle

Pivot

Hour line

Dial

ASTROLABE

Swivel suspension ring

Graduated ring

Scale of degrees

Pivot

Alidade (sighting rule)

Bottom ballast

Scribed arc decoration

The expansion of sail

By THE 18TH CENTURY, SAILING SHIPS had become fast and effective floating fortresses. The navies of the north European powers competed with each other by building heavily-armed fighting ships called "men-of-war". The distinctive round stern of the ship below, with its open gallery, balcony, and elaborate wood carving is typical of the period. Hulls around this time were semicircular in cross section, although many boat designers were soon to return to the V-shaped hulls used by the Vikings. Ships of the period carried more sail than ever before. A labyrinth of rigging supported the masts and yards from which the profusion of square sails were set. Ships grew higher, as extra masts were fitted above the lower mast, and the bowsprit became longer to allow the ship to carry staysails, spritsails, and jibsails. Ships went into battle in single file, so that broadsides from the multiple decks of guns would have maximum effect. Ships were classified by rates, the rating of a vessel depending on how many guns it had. A first rate ship had more than 100 guns. The guns fired solid round shot, usually made of iron.

Gilded truck

Main topgallant mast

Main topgallant shroud

WOODEN SAILING SHIP

Bolster

Trestle trees

Main topmast

Main topmast backstay

Main topmast shroud

Cap

Main top

Mizzen topmast

Mizzen topmast stay

Mizzen top

Lift

Mizzen topmast shroud

Main top rail

Mast-head

Hounds

Futtock shroud

Mizzen yard

Mizzen backstay

Mizzen stay

Main shroud

BOW

Vang

Fiddle block

Mizzen shroud

Brace

Lift

Taffrail

Mizzen mast

Main shroud

Foot rope

Poop rail

Main mast

Studding sail boom

Main top rail

Studding sail yard (stuns'l yard)

Jacob's ladder

Rope preventer

Rudder chain

Rudder

Wash cant

Sternpost

Knee of the head

Hawse hole

Pintle strap

Gudgeon strap

Ship's wheel   Binnacle box   Keel   Channel   Chain   Step   Boat slide

SAIL PATTERN OF A 74-GUN SHIP

Main topgallant stay

Fore topgallant mast

Fore topgallant backstay

Gilded truck

Fore topgallant stay

Mouse and collar

Main topmast stay

Fore topmast shroud

Main topmast preventer stay

Ratline

Fore topmast

Fore topmast backstay

Fore shroud

Main stay

Mainstay tackle

Fore hatch tackle

Anchor buoy

Fore top

Fore mast

Rope woolding

Fish davit

Mainrail head

Fore topmast stay

Fore topmast preventer stay

Truck

Jack staff

Cap

Bee

Fore stay

Foot rope

Bowsprit

Bobstay

Figurehead

Rail

Trailboard

Draught (draft) mark

Bower anchor

Tallow coating

Capstan | Clewline | Gunport | Gun | Gripe

Main topgallant sail

Mizzen topgallant sail

Mizzen topsail

Mizzen course

Main topgallant sail

Fore mast topgallant sail

Fore mast topsail

Fore topsail

Jibsail

Sprit topsail

Spritsail course

Main course

Main topsail

Fore mast course

Fore staysail

Outer spritsail yard

Spritsail yard

Jib boom

STERN

Main topgallant yard

Fore topgallant yard

Main topsail yard

Yardarm

Fore topsail yard

Main yard

Fore yard

Mizzen topmast yard

Stern lantern

Captain's cabin (great cabin)

Upper gallery

Port

Balcony

Stern quarter gallery

A ship of the line

THE 74-GUN WOODEN SHIP WAS A MAINSTAY of British and French battlefleets in the late 18th and early 19th centuries. This "ship of the line" was heavy enough to fight with the most potent of rivals, yet nimble too. The length of such a ship was determined by the number of guns required for each deck, allowing enough room for crews to man them. The gun deck was about 52 m (170 ft) long. The decks had to be very strong to carry the weight of the guns. The deck planks have been removed on the vessel pictured below, to show just how close together the beams had to be to make the hull strong enough. Only timber with a perfect grain was used. The upper deck was open at the waist, but afore and abaft were officers' cabins. The forecastle and quarterdeck carried light guns and acted as platforms for working rigging and for reconnaissance. The ship's longboats (launches) were carried on booms between the gangways.

LONGBOAT

UPPER DECK OF A 74-GUN SHIP

Truck · Flag halyard · Mast · Backstay · Jib halyard · Topping lift · Fore stay halyard · Peak halyard · Shroud · Main sheet · Fore sail halyard · Gaff · Boom · Parrel · Bowsprit · Traveller · Stempost · Waterline · Deadeye · Oar · Side bench

Thole pin · Windlass bar · Transom · Tiller · Planking · Rabbit line · Sheerplank · Frame · Keel · Rudder · Floor · Thwart (seat)

Hoop · Stock · Steam grating · Cathead · Ring · Timber head · Galley stove chimney · Belfry · Waterway · Knighthead · Fore bitt · Deadeye · Gangway · Capstan · Heads (privy) · Figurehead · Head beam · Head rail · Roundhouse · Boomkin · Anchor cable · Arm · Sheave for cat tackle · Deck beam · Breastwork · Forked beam · Pawl · Skid beam · Fluke · Hoop · Stock · Foremast hole · Carling (carline) · Bulwark · Main companion way · Head · Forecastle (fo'c'sle) · Waist

BOW

Figurehead

Headboard

Head rail

Main rail

Middle rail

Lower rail

Supporter

Cat block

Ekeing

Cheek

Catted anchor

Riband

Hawse piece

Side step

Stempost

Deadwood

Hawse hole

Frame

Main wale

STERN

Cove

Taffrail

Screen bulkhead

Balcony

Upper counter rail

Drop

Lower counter rail

Gunport lid

Filling transom

Wing transom

Timber under transom

Side counter timber

Counter timber

Tuck

Tuck rail

After fashion piece

Cant frame

Eye bolt

Main bitt

Ledge

Hatch coaming/ shot garland

Spirketting

Backstay stool

Companion ladder

Master's sea cabin

Mizzen mast hole

Channel

Coaming

Great cabin (captain's cabin)

Pilaster

Ledge (batten)

Screen bulkhead

Standard knee

Stern carving

Taffrail

Necking

Wardroom

Upper finishing

Poop rail

Gunport drip (eyebrow; rigol)

Mizzen bitt

Clerk's cabin

Quarter gallery

Main mast hole

Mast partner

Grating

Lodging knee

Gunport lid

Rail at break of poop deck

Quarterdeck

Poop deck

Rigging

MOST SAILING SHIPS HAVE TWO TYPES OF RIGGING. Standing rigging – kept taut by rigging screws or old-fashioned lanyards and deadeyes – refers to the ropes, wires, and chains that support the masts and yards (horizontal spars). Running rigging, which includes types of block and tackle, halyards, and sheets, is used to hoist, lower, or trim sails.

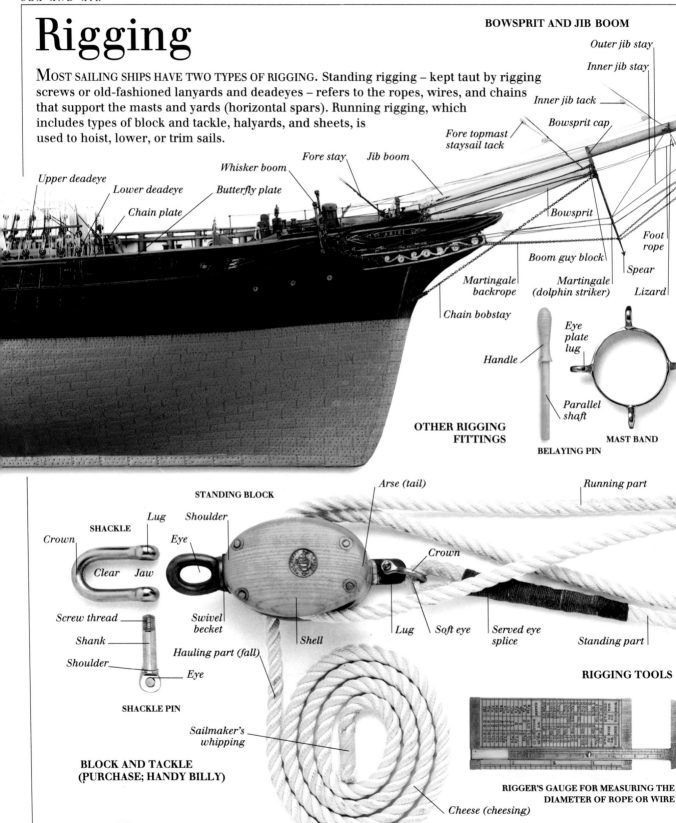

BOWSPRIT AND JIB BOOM

Outer jib stay

Inner jib stay

Inner jib tack

Bowsprit cap

Fore topmast staysail tack

Fore stay

Jib boom

Whisker boom

Upper deadeye

Lower deadeye

Chain plate

Butterfly plate

Bowsprit

Foot rope

Boom guy block

Spear

Martingale backrope

Martingale (dolphin striker)

Lizard

Chain bobstay

OTHER RIGGING FITTINGS

Handle

Eye plate lug

Parallel shaft

BELAYING PIN

MAST BAND

Arse (tail)

Running part

STANDING BLOCK

Lug

SHACKLE

Shoulder

Crown

Eye

Crown

Clear

Jaw

Swivel becket

Shell

Lug

Soft eye

Served eye splice

Standing part

Screw thread

Shank

Shoulder

Eye

Hauling part (fall)

SHACKLE PIN

RIGGING TOOLS

Sailmaker's whipping

BLOCK AND TACKLE (PURCHASE; HANDY BILLY)

RIGGER'S GAUGE FOR MEASURING THE DIAMETER OF ROPE OR WIRE

Cheese (cheesing)

Fore royal stay

Flying jib tack

Outer jib tack

Outer martingale stay

Middle martingale stay

Inner martingale stay

Eye

SCORED BULLSEYE FAIRLEAD

Eye

Strap

SHEET LEAD

Base

RUNNING BLOCK

Double rope becket

Flat seizing

Swallow

Strop

DUTCH TRIPLE FIDDLE BLOCK

Shoulder   Back   Shank

HOOK

Crown

Clear

Jaw

Fixed   Bill
lug

Cheek

Penny washer (pin cover plate)

HEAVER FOR WIRE SERVING

SPLICING FID

ROPE SERVING MALLET

PRICKERS

HOLLOW SPIKE FOR WIRE

MARLINSPIKE

LANYARD AND DEADEYES

RIGGING SCREW (TURNBUCKLE)

Leather pointing

Shroud

Spun yarn serving

Turk's head

Hitched hauling end

UPPER DEADEYE

Swallow

Sheave (shiver; shiv)

Standing part

LANYARD

LOWER DEADEYE

Grooving

Binding

Bolt

Flat wire seizing

Solid heart thimble

Cotter pin

Fork end

Tail

Right hand screw

Open body

Left hand screw

Safe working load mark

Seizing

Swallow

Shoulder

Face

Eye

Nut   Crown

383

PARREL
BEADS

Sails

THERE ARE TWO MAIN TYPES OF SAIL, often used in combination. Square sails are driving sails. They are usually attached by parrels to yards, square to the mast to catch the following wind. On fore-and-aft sails, such as lateen and lug sails, the luff (leading edge) usually abuts a mast or a stay. The head of the sail may abut a gaff, and the foot a boom. Around the world, a great range of rigs (sail patterns), such as the ketch, lugger, and schooner, have evolved to suit local needs. Sails are made from strips of cloth, cut to give the sail a belly and strong enough to resist the most violent of winds. Cotton and flax are the traditional sail materials, but synthetic fabrics are now commonly used.

SECTION OF A SAIL

Seizing LUFF (LEADING EDGE) Luff slide Bolt rope Head

Round thimble

Rope strand

Grommet

Head cringle

LEECH (LEACH)

Flat seam

Synthetic flax (duradon)

Tabling

Luff cloth

Rat's tail

SERVING MALLET

Sharp point

Groove for spunyarn rope

Flatboard

NEEDLES AND SEAMING TWINE

Handle

Seaming twine

Needle packet

Needle

Grip

SAILMAKER'S FID

SAILCLOTHS

KEVLAR ON FLEX FILM

HEAVYWEIGHT NYLON CLOTH

MYLAR

NYLON AND SILICON CLOTH

SYNTHETIC FLAX (DURADON)

WOVEN DACRON

SAIL HOOK

Crown

Bill

Shank

SAILMAKER'S PALM

Strap

Thumbhole

Metal needle pad

Cowhide face

BEESWAX

Handle

SAILMAKER'S MALLET

Cheek

Whipping

Hide grip

Seizing

Groove made by thread

SAILMAKING TOOLS

Copper face

384

Mizzen gaff topsail

Main sail

Main gaff topsail

Fore staysail

Jibsail

Mizzen sail

KETCH

Mizzen yard topsail

Dipping lug foresail

Standing lug mizzen

LUGGER

SAILING RIGS

Main gaff topsail

Fore topmast staysail

Fore sail

Fore staysail

Main sail

Jibsail

FISHERMAN'S SCHOONER (FORE-AND-AFT SCHOONER)

SAILS AND RUNNING RIGGING OF A DOUBLE TOPSAIL SCHOONER

Upper topsail lift

Lower topsail brace

Main topsail halyard

Flying jib halyard

Fore upper topsail

Triatic stay

Foot rope

Upper topsail brace

Outer jib halyard

Fore peak halyard

Lower topsail clewline

Fore yard lift

Fore lower topsail

Inner jib halyard

Fore throat halyard

Fore staysail halyard

Fore sail

Mast hoop

Inner jib downhaul

Outer jib downhaul

Outer jib sheet

Flying jib sheet

Inner jib sheet

Flying jib downhaul

Yard

Head

Gaff

Luff

Boom

Foot

Flying jib

Outer jib

Reef point

Fore staysail

Inner jib

Fore staysail sheet

Mooring and anchoring

FOR LARGE VESSELS IN OPEN WATER, ANCHORAGE IS ESSENTIAL. By holding a ship securely to the seabed, an anchor prevents the vessel from being at the mercy of wave, tide, and current. The earliest anchors were nothing more than stones. In later years, many anchors had a standard design, much like the Admiralty pattern anchor shown on this page. The Danforth anchor is somewhat different. It has particularly deep flukes to give it great holding power. On large sailing ships, anchors were worked by teams of sailors. They turned the drum of a capstan by pushing on bars slotted into the revolving cylinder. This, in turn, lifted or lowered the anchor chain. In calm harbours and estuaries, ships can moor (make fast) without using anchors. Berthing ropes can be attached to bollards both inboard and on the quayside. Berthing ropes are joined to each other by bends, like those opposite.

STONE ANCHOR (KILLICK)

Rope hole

TYPES OF ANCHOR

CLOSE-STOWING ANCHOR

CQR ANCHOR (SECURE ANCHOR; PLOUGH ANCHOR)

ADMIRALTY ANCHOR TYPE ACII

ADMIRALTY PATTERN ANCHOR

STOCKLESS ANCHOR

MUSHROOM ANCHOR (PERMANENT MOORING ANCHOR)

ANCHOR CHAIN

End link

Common link

Patent link

DANFORTH ANCHOR

Shank

Pea (bill)

Fluke

Stock

Tripping palm

Throat

Blade

Crown

SHACKLE, SWIVELS, AND LINK

Crown

Bolt

Lug

GALVANIZED "D" SHACKLE

MOORING SWIVEL

CHAIN SWIVEL

Screw thread

MAILLOT (SCREW LINK)

TWIN BOLLARDS WITH RAKED PILLARS AND A HAWSER (HEAVY ROPE)

Flat

Rim

Base

BERTHING ROPES (HAWSERS)

Stern rope
Ship
Twin bollards
Bar hole (pigeon hole)
Cap
Upper head (drumhead)
Head rope
Quayside
After breast rope
After spring rope
Bollard
Fore spring rope
Fore breast rope
Strengthening chock

MOORING ROPE BENDS

**HAWSER BEND
(TWO DOUBLE ROUND TURNS
AND DOUBLE HALF HITCHES)**

Standing part

Barrel

CARRICK BEND

Seizing

Seizing

Trenail (treenail)

Strengthening chock

Pawl slot

Lignum vitae bearing

Whelp

**SINGLE SHEET BEND
(SWAB HITCH)**

Bare end (fag end)
Standing part
Thin rope

Thick rope

Outboard end

Three-strand hawser belayed with figure of eight turns

Pillar

Foundry plug

**WOOD
CAPSTAN
WITH A
VERTICAL
SPINDLE**

Horn

Tapered spindle

Bolt hole

Cross piece

Bitter end (inboard end)

Spigot

Pin

Ropes and knots

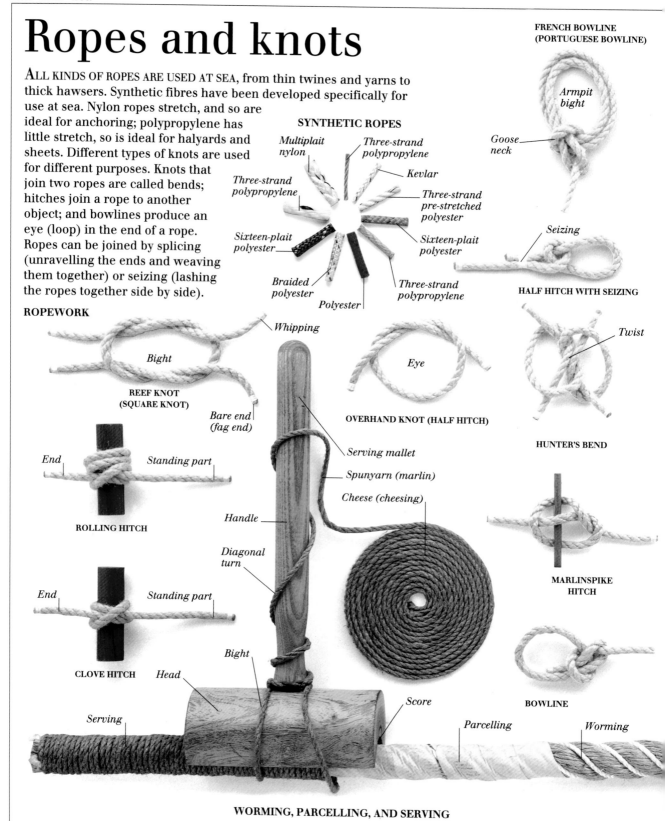

ALL KINDS OF ROPES ARE USED AT SEA, from thin twines and yarns to thick hawsers. Synthetic fibres have been developed specifically for use at sea. Nylon ropes stretch, and so are ideal for anchoring; polypropylene has little stretch, so is ideal for halyards and sheets. Different types of knots are used for different purposes. Knots that join two ropes are called bends; hitches join a rope to another object; and bowlines produce an eye (loop) in the end of a rope. Ropes can be joined by splicing (unravelling the ends and weaving them together) or seizing (lashing the ropes together side by side).

FRENCH BOWLINE (PORTUGUESE BOWLINE)

Armpit bight

Goose neck

Seizing

HALF HITCH WITH SEIZING

SYNTHETIC ROPES

Multiplait nylon

Three-strand polypropylene

Three-strand polypropylene

Kevlar

Three-strand pre-stretched polyester

Sixteen-plait polyester

Sixteen-plait polyester

Three-strand polypropylene

Braided polyester

Polyester

ROPEWORK

Whipping

Bight

REEF KNOT (SQUARE KNOT)

Bare end (fag end)

OVERHAND KNOT (HALF HITCH)

Eye

Twist

HUNTER'S BEND

End

Standing part

ROLLING HITCH

Serving mallet

Spunyarn (marlin)

Cheese (cheesing)

Handle

Diagonal turn

MARLINSPIKE HITCH

End

Standing part

CLOVE HITCH

Head

Bight

Score

BOWLINE

Serving

Parcelling

Worming

WORMING, PARCELLING, AND SERVING

SPANISH BOWLINE

THUMB KNOT

FLAT SEIZING
(ROUND SEIZING)

DOUBLE CARRICK BEND

End

*Frapped
turn*

*Heaving
line knot*

LIGHTERMAN'S HITCH

HEAVING LINE BEND

*Standing
part*

JURY MAST KNOT
(MAST HEAD BEND)

SHEET BEND (SWAB HITCH)

MANHARNESS KNOT
(BUTTERFLY KNOT;
ARTILLERY LOOP)

Cheese (cheesing)

Marlinspike

HEAVING LINE

PINNED SHEEPSHANK

Jaw

Rat tail

*Hawser laid three-strand manilla
rope with right-handed lay*

Paddle wheels and propellers

THE INVENTION OF THE STEAM ENGINE IN THE 18TH CENTURY made mechanically driven ships fitted with paddle wheels or propellers a viable alternative to sails. Paddle wheels have fixed or feathered floats, and the model shown below features both types. Feathered floats give more propulsive power than fixed floats because they are almost upright at all times in the water. Paddle wheels were superseded by the propeller on ocean-going vessels in the mid-19th century. Propellers are more efficient, work better in rough water, and are less vulnerable in collisions. The first propellers were two-bladed but later three- and four-bladed versions are more powerful; the shape and pitch of blades have also been refined over the years. At the beginning of the 18th century, tillers were superseded on many larger ships by the ship's wheel as a means of steering.

SHIP'S WHEEL

King spoke handle
Handle
Spoke
Rim plate
Felloe (rim section)
Maker's name
Nave plate
Nave

PADDLE WHEEL WITH FIXED FLOATS

Wrist pin
Limb
Fixed float
Hub
Deck beam

OSCILLATING STEAM ENGINE

Slip eccentric for slide valve
Ahead/astern controls
Slide valve
Main crank

THREE-BLADED PROPELLER

Blade
Tapered shaft hole
Hub
Keyway

Strut
Frame
Piston rod (tail rod)
Stuffing box
Oscillating cylinder
Bottom plate (bedplate)
Slide valve rod
Control platform

Propeller blade tip trace
Pitch
Blade
Propeller diameter
Hub
Propeller hub trace

PROPELLER ACTION

DESIGN FOR A STEAMBOAT WITH PADDLE WHEELS

Connecting rod

Truss

Rim

Paddle float

Safety valve

Funnel

Drive to air pump

Tiller

Boiler

Air pump

Flat bottom with no keel

Shallow, carvel-built hull

Bell crank (triangle)

Flywheel

Hub

Paddle shaft

PADDLE WHEEL WITH FEATHERED FLOATS

TYPES OF PROPELLER

Crank for air pipe

Outer rim

Drag link

Disengaging catch

Cylinder cover

Spoke

FROUDE'S EARLY TEST PROPELLER

Gland

Crankshaft

Inner rim

Paddle shaft

TUG PROPELLER

Hub

Paddle wheel box

Main steam supply pipe

Feathered float

THREE-BLADED PROPELLER

Eccentric rod (drive for pump)

Pump piston

Feed bilge pump

Guardrail

Exhaust

Shroud ring

Air pump

Kelson (keelson)

PROPULSION SYSTEM OF A 19TH CENTURY PADDLESTEAMER

SHROUD RING PROPELLER

Anatomy of an iron ship

IRON PARTS WERE USED IN THE HULLS OF WOODEN SHIPS AS EARLY AS 1675, often in the same form as the wooden parts that they replaced. Eventually, as on the tea clipper Cutty Sark (below), iron rigging was found to be stronger than the traditional rope. The first "ironclads" were warships whose wooden hulls were protected by iron armour plates. Later ironclads actually had iron hulls. The model opposite is based on the British warship HMS Warrior, launched in 1860, the first battleship built entirely of iron. The plan of the iron paddlesteamer (bottom), built somewhat later, shows that this vessel was a sailing ship; but it also boasted a steam propulsion plant amidships that turned two side paddlewheels. Early iron hulls were made from plates that were painstakingly rivetted together (as below), but by the 20th century vessels began to be welded together, whole sections at a time. The Second World War "liberty ship" was one of the first of these "production-line vessels".

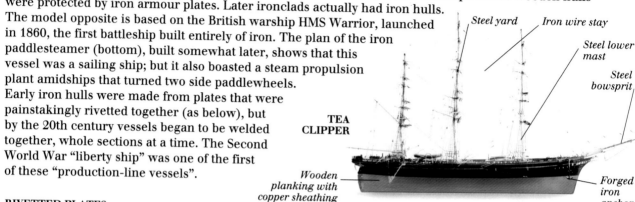

TEA CLIPPER

Steel yard
Iron wire stay
Steel lower mast
Steel bowsprit
Wooden planking with copper sheathing
Forged iron anchor

RIVETTED PLATES

Pan head rivet
Plate
Gun section
Button head rivet (snap head)
Seam

LIBERTY SHIP

Accommodation section
Cargo derrick
Weld line
Stern section
Midships section
Cargo hold
Bow section

PLAN OF AN IRON PADDLESTEAMER

Mizzen mast
Poop deck
Lounge
Deck lantern
Main mast
Steam whistle
Crankshaft
Guardrail
Paddle wheel
Steering position
Guardrail
Binnacle
State room
After funnel
Eccentric
Connecting rod
Steering gear
Skylight
Stern
Vertical frame ladder
Mast step
Rudder
Rudder post
Heel of rudder post
Bar keel
Afterpeak
Cabin
Stern framing
Tank
Main mast step
Donkey boiler
Box boiler
Foundation
Reversing wheel
Bottom plate
Side lever
Cylinder

CUTAWAY SECTION OF AN "IRONCLAD"

Bulwark cap

Waterway

Scupper

Deck planking

Upper deck stringer (tie) plate

Upper deck beam

Upper deck pillar (stanchion)

Main deck beam

Main deck pillar (stanchion)

Lower deck beam

Hold pillar (stanchion)

Centre line keelson

Bulwark

Upper sheer strake

Teak backing

Topside strake

Wrought iron armour plate

Main sheer strake

Main deck tie plate

Lower deck tie plate

Lighting hole

Angle bar (I bar)

Box sister keelson

Frame

Bilge stringer

Bilge strake

Bilge keelson

Side keelson

Bottom plating

Garboard strake

Keel

Limber hole

Floor

Forward funnel

Main deck

Fore mast

Skylight

Ventilator cowl

Capstan

Chimney

Hatch

Bowsprit

Hawse pipe

Stem

Beam

Chain locker

Bulkhead stiffener

Deep floor

Forefoot

Deck beam

Forepeak

Centre girder

Lower deck

'Tween decks ladder

Cabin

Combustion chamber

Smoke box

The battleship

IN THE EARLY YEARS OF THE 20TH CENTURY, sea warfare –
attacking enemy vessels or defending a ship – was
revolutionized by the introduction of Dreadnought-type
battleships like the Brazilian vessel below. These new
ships combined the latest advances in steam
propulsion, gunnery, and armour plating. The gun
turret was designed to fire shells over huge distances.
It was protected by armour 30 cm (12 in) thick. The
measurements given for the guns of this ship refer
to the bore diameter. Where "weight" is quoted, this
is the weight of the shell that the gun fires. Torpedoes –
as portrayed on the upper cigarette card (right) – were
self-propelled underwater missiles, often steered by gyro-
control. Depth charges were designed in the First World
War for use against submerged U-boats. They are
canisters filled with explosives that are detonated
by depth-sensitive pistols. The lower cigarette
card shows depth charges being fired by
a "thrower", fired from a torpedo tube,
and rolled from the stern. Ship's shields
were fitted to warships from the late
19th century onwards. The shield
shown opposite depicts a
traditional ship's cannon.

20TH CENTURY WEAPONRY

Torpedo tube

Sight

Warhead

TORPEDOES

DEPTH
CHARGES

Side-thrown
canister

Stern-rolled
canister

Torpedo-fired
canister

BRAZILIAN BATTLESHIP

Rangefinder

Light screen

Compass

Compass and rangefinder
platform

Ship's wheel

Navigating bridge

Conning tower

Captain's shelter/
chart house

Weather shutter
for gun

Forward
funnel

Lifeboat

Boat handling
derrick

Gunnery
spotting top

Purchase wire

Searchlight

Searchlight
platform

Leading block

Tripod mast

Boat
winch

"F" turret

Arms of
Brazil

Jack staff

30 cm (12 in)
gun

Skylight

Stem
(false ram bow)

Porthole

Belt
armour

Forward
accommodation
ladder

Sighting
hood

"A" turret

Turret barbette

Open gun mounting

12 cm (4.7 in) gun

Steam launch

Guest boat boom

SHIP'S SHIELD

Rope moulding

Muzzle moulding

Swell of muzzle

Chase

Reinforce

Ogee

Astragal

Trunnion

Radio antenna

Lion crest

Upper wireless and telegraphy yard (Upper W/T yard)

Topgallant mast

Wireless and telegraphy yard (W/T yard)

Lower yard

Signal gear

Ladder way

Brake slip

Davit

Clump cathead

Guardrail

Hawser fairlead

Sheet anchor

Starboard bower anchor

Lifeboat davit

Breakwater

Cable holder

Anchor chain

Bollard

Hawse pipe

Boat boom

Towing fairlead

Port bower anchor

Exhaust pipe

Searchlight

Vedette boat

Gig

After funnel

Funnel stay

Searchlight platform

After compass platform

After bridge

1.3 kg (3 pound) gun ("three pounder")

"X" turret

"Y" turret

Officer's accommodation ladder

Whaler

Davit for whaler

Flagmast

Stern walk

Scarph

Aft anchor

"P" turret

Ash chute

Hen coop

Bilge keel

Gun battery

Torpedo net boom

Turret roof rail

Propeller shaft boss

Torpedo net

Propeller shaft

Propeller

Rudder

Life buoy

Frigates and submarines

FROM THE MID-19TH CENTURY, ARMOURED SHIPS provided a new challenge to enemy craft. In response, huge revolving gun turrets were developed. These could fire in any direction, could be loaded from the breech very rapidly, and, instead of cannonballs, they discharged exploding shells. Modern fighting ships, like the frigate, combine heavy ship-borne armament with light helicopter weaponry. Submarines function below the surface of the sea. Their speed and ability to fire missiles from under water are their major assets. The nuclear submarine can stay under water for several years without refuelling.

Stabilizer fin

Aft hydroplane

Propeller

Lower rudder

Rangefinder

Look out periscope

Local control cabinet

Breech wheel

Breech block

Loading arm

Slide locking lever

Slide

Sighting hood

Recoil cylinder

Elevating wheel

Guide for gun loading cage

Blast bag (breeches)

Floor of gun house

Rammer lever

Gun loading cage

Turret roller

Roller path

Training rack gearing

Working chamber

Training gear

Rammer

Waiting position

Roller path support

Floor

"Walking pipe" (water supply)

GUN TURRET
In this turret for two 37 cm (15 in) guns, shells are carried in a hoisting cage. The shell is rammed into the gun, followed by the propellant (charge). Once the breech is closed, the gun is ready for firing. The whole operation requires around 70 sailors.

Barbette (armour)

Main hoisting cage

Turret trunk

Cordite handling room

Cordite supply shuttle

Ensign staff

FRIGATE

Lynx helicopter

SONAR torpedo decoy

Cordite case

Rudder

Variable pitch propeller

Practice projectile

High-explosive projectile

Shell bogie

Shell room

Hydraulic grab

Shell-handling gear

Ladder way

NUCLEAR "HUNTER-KILLER" SUBMARINE

Steam pipework

Machinery raft

Main turbine

Machinery control room

Switchboard room

Conning tower

Snort mast

Electronic warfare mast

Periscope

Control room

Sonar room

Galley

Officers' mess

SONAR transducer array

Torpedo tube

Forward hydroplane

Junior ratings' bunk space

Senior ratings' mess

Main engine steam condenser

Distiller

Diesel motor compartment

Reactor space

Wireless office

Junior ratings' mess

Carbon dioxide scrubber compartment

Torpedo compartment

Barrel

Muzzle

15 cm (6 in) SHELL
This shell is designed to burst in the air above its target.

Driving band

SHELL CASE

Bursting charge (explosive)

Flash tube

Body

Wooden packing

Transit plug

Expelling plate

CROSS-SECTION OF THE SHELL

Bullet

Seacat missile launcher

Stern gallery

Aerial

Motor whaler

Vent

Funnel

Surveillance RADAR

Mast

Aerial rig

Navigation/helicopter control RADAR antenna

RADAR for gunnery and missile control

Signalling lamp

Oerlikon gun position

Enclosed bridge

Exocet missile launcher

Gun turret

11 cm (4.5 in) gun

Jack staff

F174

RADAR for gunnery and missile control

Anti-submarine torpedo tube

Stabilizer

Liferaft cylinder

Triple "chaff" rocket launcher

Signal flag compartment

Bilge keel

Pennant number

Porthole

Reel

SONAR bulge

Bollard

Fairlead

Breakwater

Anchor

Draught (draft) mark

Pioneers of flight

FLIGHT HAS FASCINATED MANKIND for centuries, and countless unsuccessful flying machines have been designed. The first successful flight was made by the French Montgolfier brothers in 1783, when they flew a balloon over Paris. The next major advance was the development of gliders, notably by the Englishman Sir George Cayley, who in 1845 designed the first glider to make a sustained flight, and by the German Otto Lilienthal, who became known as the world's first pilot because he managed to achieve controlled flights. However, powered flight did not become a practical possibility until the invention of lightweight, petrol-driven internal combustion engines at the end of the 19th century. Then, in 1903, the American brothers Orville and Wilbur Wright made the first powered flight in their Wright Flyer biplane, which used a four-cylinder, petrol-driven engine. Aircraft design advanced rapidly, and in 1909 the Frenchman Louis Blériot made his pioneering flight across the English Channel (see pp. 400-401). The American Glenn Curtiss also achieved several "firsts" in his Model-D Pusher and its variants, most notably winning the world's first competition for airspeed at Reims in 1909.

FRONT VIEW OF WRIGHT FLYER, 1903

Biplane elevator

Pusher propeller (rear-mounted propeller)

Chain drive to starboard propeller

Fuel tank

Propeller-shaft bracing strut

Offset pilot's cradle

Take-off and landing skid

Side-mounted engine to balance pilot's weight

SIDE VIEW OF CURTISS MODEL-D PUSHER, 1911

Nine-cylinder Salmson radial engine

Pusher propeller (rear-mounted propeller)

Aileron operating arm

Wing strut

Body cradle that pivots to control ailerons

Fuel filler cap

Oil filler cap

Fuel and oil tank

Rudder control wheel

Elevator wire for diving

Lap strap

Control column

Throttle

Nose-wheel brake

Footrest

Aileron

Turnbuckle

Fuel pipe

Pneumatic tyre

Rubber-tyred nose-wheel

Seat support strut

Pilot's seat

Elevator wire for climbing

Wing-protecting skid

Thin, cambered lower wing

Starboard main landing gear

Engine and propeller thrust frame

SIDE VIEW OF WRIGHT FLYER, 1903

Plain cotton fabric

Interplane strut

Water-filled radiator

Front diagonal strut

Elevator drive wheel

Wing warping wire

Chain drive

Pusher propeller (rear-mounted propeller)

Rigid leading edge

Steel hub

Steel propeller shaft

Water pipe

Rudder

Front-mounted biplane elevator

Bracing wire

Braced rudder strut

Landing skid

Elevator control cable

Pilot's cradle

Magneto

Rudder control cable

Warping connection strut

Four-cylinder 12-HP engine

Propeller-shaft bracing strut

Softwood strut

Laminated wooden boom

Rudder bracing wire

Tailplane

Elevator control wire

Rudder

Elevator operating arm

Elevator

FRONT VIEW OF CURTISS MODEL-D PUSHER, 1911

Rudder control wheel

Anti-lift wire

Fuel and oil tank

Nine-cylinder Salmson radial engine

Elevator operating arm

Aileron operating arm

Starboard aileron

Port aileron

Carved interplane strut

Wing-protecting skid

Wing-protecting skid

Lift wire

Control column

Seat beam

Footrest

Axle

Tubular steel leg

Main landing gear lateral brace

Interplane strut pin-jointed to front spar

Early monoplanes

RUMPLER MONOPLANE, 1908

MONOPLANES HAVE ONE WING on each side of the fuselage. The principal disadvantage of this arrangement in early, wooden-framed aircraft was that single wings were weak and required strong wires to brace them to king-posts above and below the fuselage. However, single wings also had advantages: they experienced less drag than multiple wings, allowing greater speed; they also made aircraft more manoeuvrable because single wings were easier to warp (twist) than double wings, and warping the wings was how pilots controlled the roll of early aircraft. By 1912, the French pilot Louis Blériot had used a monoplane to make the first flight across the English Channel, and the Briton Robert Blackburn and the Frenchman Armand Deperdussin had proved the greater speed of monoplanes. However, a spate of crashes caused by broken wings discouraged monoplane production, except in Germany, where all-metal monoplanes were developed in 1917. The wings of all-metal monoplanes did not need strengthening by struts or bracing wires, but despite this, such planes were not widely adopted until the 1930s.

FRONT VIEW OF BLACKBURN MONOPLANE, 1912

Taut fabric

Carved wooden propeller

King-post

Hub bolted to propeller

Nose-ring

Pilot's viewing aperture

Exhaust valve push-rod

Gnome seven-cylinder rotary engine

Elevator hinge

Elevator

Landing gear rear cross-member

Wheel fairing

Rubber-sprung wheel

Landing gear front strut

Tailskid

Axle

Landing skid

Landing gear rear strut

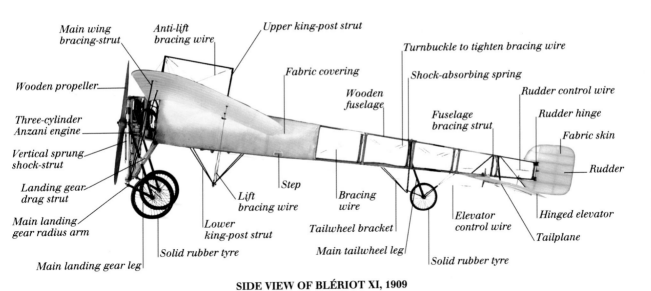

Main wing bracing-strut

Anti-lift bracing wire

Upper king-post strut

Wooden propeller

Three-cylinder Anzani engine

Vertical sprung shock-strut

Landing gear drag strut

Main landing gear radius arm

Main landing gear leg

Solid rubber tyre

Lift bracing wire

Lower king-post strut

Step

Fabric covering

Wooden fuselage

Bracing wire

Tailwheel bracket

Main tailwheel leg

Turnbuckle to tighten bracing wire

Shock-absorbing spring

Fuselage bracing strut

Solid rubber tyre

Elevator control wire

Rudder control wire

Rudder hinge

Fabric skin

Rudder

Hinged elevator

Tailplane

SIDE VIEW OF BLÉRIOT XI, 1909

Anti-lift bracing wire

Leading edge

Rib

Bracing wire anchor bolt

Turnbuckle to tighten bracing wire

Concave undersurface

Lift bracing wire

Warped wing

King-post

Anti-lift bracing wire

Lateral control wheel

Aluminium cowl

Carved wooden propeller

Rudder post

Tailplane

Large fin

Domed topdeck

Rudder

Elevator

Elevator-operating bracket

Tailskid

Diagonal bracing

Triangular-section rear fuselage

Lift bracing wire

Landing gear rear strut

Braced landing gear structure

Rubber-sprung wheel

Hub

Engine mount

Forward fuselage structure

Landing skid

SIDE VIEW OF BLACKBURN MONOPLANE, 1912

Biplanes and triplanes

BIPLANES DOMINATED AIRCRAFT DESIGN until the 1930s, largely because some early monoplanes (see pp. 400-401) were too fragile to withstand the stresses of flight. The struts between biplanes' wings made the wings strong compared with those of early monoplanes, although the greater surface area of biplanes' wings increased drag and reduced speed. Many aircraft designers also developed triplanes, which had a particular advantage over biplanes: more wings meant a shorter wingspan to achieve the same lifting power, and a shorter wingspan gave greater manoeuvrability. Triplanes were most successful as fighters during World War I, the German Fokker triplane being a notable example. However, the greater manoeuvrability of triplanes was no advantage for normal flying and so most manufacturers continued to make biplanes. Many other aircraft designs were attempted. Some were quadruplanes, with four pairs of wings. Some had tandem wings (two pairs of monoplane wings, one behind the other). One of the most bizarre designs was by the Englishman Horatio Phillips: it had 20 sets of narrow wings and looked rather like a Venetian blind.

LAMINATED PROPELLER

Rudder hinge

RAF Central Flying School badge

Rudder

Fin

Navigation light

K 3215

Elevator

Rudder cable

Tailplane

Tailwheel

Bracing strut

SIDE VIEW OF AVRO TRIPLANE IV, 1910

Valve rocker

Air cooling baffle

Magneto

Wing strut

Crankcase breather pipe

Fuel tank

Throttle

Harness

Directly driven propeller

Pilot's seat

AVRO

Main front strut to engine mount

Skid upper bracing strut

Limit of fuselage skin

Rubber cord suspension

Ash skid

Turnbuckle

Axle

Skid rear strut

Lateral bracing strut

Rubber tyre

Wheel rim

Wire wheel

**AVRO TUTOR
BIPLANE, 1931**

Navigation light

Pin joint

Aileron hinge strut

Slat-arm fairing

Aileron control wire

Lift bracing wire

Instructor's cockpit

Engine cowling

Wooden-domed deck

Padded coaming

Nose-ring

Pupil's cockpit

Propeller hub

RAF roundel

Laminated-wood, fixed-pitch propeller

Metal leading edge

3215

Exhaust pipe

Exhaust collector ring

Main landing gear leg

Aircraft registration code

Inspection cover

Radius rod

Inflation valve

Fabric-covered steel-tube fuselage

Fabric-covered aluminium and steel wing

Manufacturer's logo

Recessed nose of aileron

FRONT VIEW OF AVRO TRIPLANE IV, 1910

Unpainted, varnished fabric

Leading edge

Fuel filler and vent

Fixed-pitch wooden propeller

Anti-lift bracing wire

Top wing

Wing strut

Middle wing

Rib

Bottom wing

Landing skid

Lift bracing wire

Axle

Elevator

Tailplane

Triangular-section fuselage

Triangular-section fuselage

Fuselage bracing wire

Rudder control cable

Lateral bracing strut

Tailplane

Rudder

Metal plate anchorage

Elevator control cable

Longeron

Rubber cord suspension

Tailskid pivot

Tailskid

Elevator

World War I aircraft

FLYING HELMET

WHEN WORLD WAR I STARTED in 1914, the main purpose of military aircraft was reconnaissance. The British-built BE 2, of which the BE 2B was a variant, was well-suited to this duty; it was very stable in flight, allowing the occupants to study the terrain, take photographs, and make notes. The BE 2 was also one of the first aircraft to drop bombs.

One of the biggest problems for aircraft designers during the war was mounting machine-guns. On aircraft that had front-mounted propellers, the field of fire was restricted by the propeller and other parts of the aircraft. The problem was solved in 1915 by the Dutchman Anthony Fokker, who designed an interrupter gear that prevented a machine-gun from firing when a propeller blade passed in front of the barrel. The German LVG CVI had a forward-firing gun to the right of the engine, as well as a rear-cockpit gun, and a bombing capability. It was one of the most versatile aircraft of the war.

PORT WINGS FROM A BE 2B

Interplane-strut attachment
Intermediate leading-edge rib
Airspeed-indicator tube
Leading edge
Wingtip
Airspeed-indicator tube
Main rib
Root
Interplane strut
Trailing edge
Airspeed pitot tube
Interplane-strut attachment
Upper side of lower wing
Attachment lug

BE 2B, 1914

Observer's windscreen
Cabane strut fairing
Top-wing centre section
Engine air intake (ram scoop)
Cabane strut
Wooden propeller
Lift bracing wire
Pilot's windscreen
Air-cooled V8 engine
Plywood skin
Control column
Crankcase
Padded coaming
Buffed metal cowling
Silencing heat exchanger
Exhaust pipe
Landing gear front strut
Elevator rocking arm
Ash skid
Step
Step
Lateral control wire
Reconnaissance camera bracket
Pneumatic rubber tyre
Bomb rack
Wheel cover
V-strut
Lower-wing attachment
112 lb (51 kg) bomb

SIDE VIEW OF LVG CVI, 1917

Pilot's cockpit

Observer's cockpit

Starboard aileron

Cold-water pipe

Exhaust pipe

7.92-mm Parabellum machine-gun

230-HP Benz six-cylinder water-cooled engine

Fin

Rudder

Rudder control wire

Elevator

Steel drive bracket

Laminated wooden propeller

Pivoted, sprung tailskid

Air ventilator inlet

Pitot head

Aircraft registration code

Interplane strut

Pneumatic rubber tyre

Elevator control wire

Aircraft type

Aileron control cable

Axle

Bracing wire

Tyre inflation aperture

FRONT VIEW OF LVG CVI, 1917

Lozenge-patterned fabric

Forward-firing machine-gun

Exhaust stack

230-HP Benz six-cylinder water-cooled engine

Wooden propeller

Pitot head

Interplane strut

Anti-lift bracing wire

Lift bracing wire

Main fuel tank

Turnbuckle

Pneumatic rubber tyre

Axle

Gravity-feed fuel tank

Multiple rubber-cord suspension

Tailskid

Landing gear strut

Fabric lacing

Rib

Rudder

Fixed tailplane

Fabric covering

Elevator

Tailplane attachment

Rudder post

Steel lug

Elevator hinge

687

Aircraft registration code

Spar

Shock-absorbing spring

Steel V-strut

Trailing edge

Pivoted tailskid

National marking

Leading edge

Rib

HORIZONTAL TAIL OF A BE 2B

405

Early passenger aircraft

UNTIL THE 1930s, most passenger aircraft were biplanes, with two pairs of wings and a wooden or metal framework covered with fabric or, sometimes, plywood. Such aircraft were restricted to low speeds and low altitudes because of the drag on their wings. Many had an open cockpit, situated behind or in front of an enclosed – but unpressurized – cabin that carried a maximum of ten people. The passengers usually sat in wicker chairs that were not bolted to the floor, and the journey could be bumpy when flying through turbulence. Warm clothing, and ear plugs to reduce the effects of prolonged noise, were often required. During the 1930s, powerful, streamlined, all-metal monoplanes, such as the Lockheed Electra shown here, became widespread. By 1939, the advent of pressurized cabins allowed fast flights at high altitudes, where there is less turbulence.

Flying boats were still necessary on many routes until 1945 because of inadequate runways and the frequency of emergency sea-landings. World War II, however, resulted in enough good runways being built for land-planes to become standard on all major airline routes.

Green starboard navigation light

Flush-riveted metal-skinned wing

Leading edge

Fuel-jettison valve

Static discharge wick

Split flap in landing position

Roof trim panel

PASSENGER CABIN TRIM PANELS

Forward bulkhead upper panel

Passenger service-panel aperture

Ash-tray

Starboard wall forward panel

Cockpit door panel

Forward bulkhead lower panel

Starboard wall mid-forward panel

SIDE VIEW OF LOCKHEED ELECTRA, 1934

Cockpit windscreen

Sliding window

Emergency escape hatch

Steel firewall

Passenger window

Air intake

Ventilator exit

Oil tank

Nose

Propeller pitch-change cylinder

Blade counterweight

Spinner mounting disc

Variable-pitch propeller

Exhaust collector ring

Landing gear door

Exhaust pipe

Electrically driven split flap

Passenger door

Pratt & Whitney nine-cylinder radial engine

Red port navigation light

Brake pipe

Static discharge wick

Aileron

Main landing gear

Aluminium wheel

Mudguard

Metal-skinned wing

Cylinder-cooling gills

Variable-pitch propeller

Cockpit windscreen

High-visibility tip

Pratt & Whitney nine-cylinder radial engine

Valve push-rod tube

Inner wing containing fuel tank

Streamlined spinner

Fixed landing light

Red filter signal light

Exhaust pipe

Single-leg main landing gear

Pitot mast

Tank drain tap

Single-leg main landing gear

Landing gear door

Landing gear fork

Battery compartment

Electrical service compartment

Brake pipe

Axle

Pneumatic rubber tyre

Brake pipe

Inspection cover

Tailwheel

Disc brake

Landing gear fork

Axle

Pneumatic rubber tyre

Starboard wall aft panel

Roof trim

PASSENGER SEAT

Backrest

Seat button

Bulkhead starboard trim

Document panel

Lap strap

Armrest

Bulkhead port trim

Wall anchor

Floor anchor

Starboard wall mid-aft panel

Seat anchor bolthole

Interior cabin trim for aft bulkhead between cabin and luggage hold

Seat cushion

PORT ENGINE COWLINGS

Inspection door

Starboard rudder

Rotating beacon

Starboard trimtab

Tailplane

Port fin

120° nose-ring segment

Fixed tailplane

Aluminium flush-riveted skin

Propeller-hub spinner

Port trimtab

Ventilator exit

NC517IN

Tailplane tip

Aircraft registration code

Swivelling rubber-tyred tailwheel

120° cowling panel

Joining latch

World War II aircraft

WHEN WORLD WAR II began in 1939, air forces had already replaced most of their fabric-skinned biplanes with all-metal, stressed-skin monoplanes. Aircraft played a far greater role in military operations during World War II than ever before. The wide range of aircraft duties, and the introduction of radar tracking and guidance systems, put pressure on designers to improve aircraft performance. The main areas of improvement were speed, range, and engine power. Bombers became larger and more powerful – converting from two to four engines – in order to carry a heavier bomb load; the US B-17 Flying Fortress could carry up to 6.2 tonnes (6.1 tons) of bombs over a distance of about 3,200 km (2,000 miles). Some aircraft increased their range by using drop tanks (fuel tanks that were jettisoned when empty to reduce drag). Fighters needed speed and manoeuvrability: the Hawker Tempest shown here had a maximum speed of 700 kph (435 mph), and was one of the few Allied aircraft capable of catching the German jet-powered V1 "flying bomb". By 1944, Britain had introduced its first turbojet-powered aircraft, the Gloster Meteor fighter, and Germany had introduced the fastest fighter in the world, the turbojet-powered Me 262, which had a maximum speed of 868 kph (540 mph).

PROPELLER

High-visibility yellow tip

Light-alloy propeller spinner

Variable-pitch aluminium-alloy blade

COMPONENTS OF A HAWKER TEMPEST MARK V, c.1943

Radiator-access cowling

Lower side-cowling

Upper side-cowling

STARBOARD ENGINE COWLINGS

Cowling fastener

2,400-HP Napier Sabre 24-cylinder engine

Cartridge starter

Propeller governor

Radiator header tank

Propeller drive shaft

Distributor

Ejector exhaust

Magneto

Starter motor

Engine top cowling

Cowling fastener

Upper side-cowling

Lower side-cowling

Radiator-access cowling

PORT ENGINE COWLINGS

SECTIONED B-17G FLYING FORTRESS BOMBER, c.1943

Astronavigation dome

First pilot's seat

Oxygen bottle

Upper gun turret

1,000 lb (454 kg) bomb

Radio operator's seat

Ammunition belt

Ammunition box

Waist gun

Dorsal fin

Fin

VHF aerial

Rudder

"Cheyenne-type" tail-gun turret

Hand-held gun

Plastic nose

Bomb aimer's viewing panel

Chin gun turret

HF radio aerial

Bomb door

Direction-finding-aerial fairing

Navigator's seat

Sperry ball gun turret

Ammunition feed

Entrance door

Oxygen bottle

Retracted tailwheel

Tail gunner's compartment

Ammunition feed

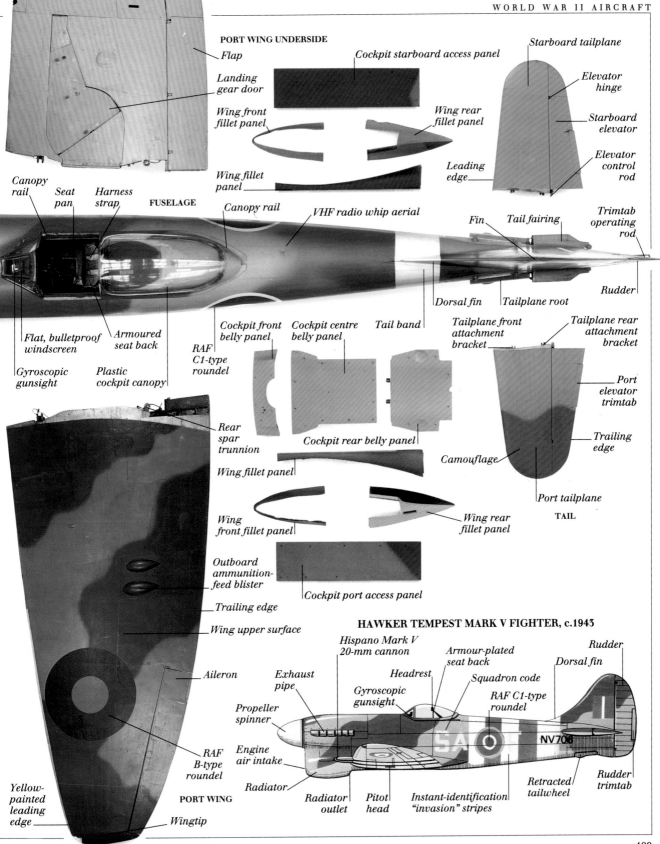

PORT WING UNDERSIDE

Flap

Landing gear door

Cockpit starboard access panel

Starboard tailplane

Elevator hinge

Starboard elevator

Elevator control rod

Wing front fillet panel

Wing rear fillet panel

Leading edge

Wing fillet panel

Canopy rail

Seat pan

Harness strap

FUSELAGE

Canopy rail

VHF radio whip aerial

Fin

Tail fairing

Trimtab operating rod

Rudder

Dorsal fin

Tailplane root

Flat, bulletproof windscreen

Armoured seat back

Gyroscopic gunsight

Plastic cockpit canopy

Cockpit front belly panel

Cockpit centre belly panel

Tail band

Tailplane front attachment bracket

Tailplane rear attachment bracket

RAF C1-type roundel

Port elevator trimtab

Rear spar trunnion

Cockpit rear belly panel

Wing fillet panel

Camouflage

Trailing edge

Wing front fillet panel

Wing rear fillet panel

Port tailplane

TAIL

Outboard ammunition-feed blister

Cockpit port access panel

Trailing edge

Wing upper surface

HAWKER TEMPEST MARK V FIGHTER, c.1943

Aileron

Hispano Mark V 20-mm cannon

Armour-plated seat back

Rudder

Dorsal fin

Exhaust pipe

Headrest

Squadron code

Gyroscopic gunsight

RAF C1-type roundel

Propeller spinner

RAF B-type roundel

Engine air intake

Radiator

Radiator outlet

Pitot head

Instant-identification "invasion" stripes

Retracted tailwheel

Rudder trimtab

Yellow-painted leading edge

PORT WING

Wingtip

NV7OB

SA

I

Modern piston aero-engines

MID WEST TWO-STROKE, THREE-CYLINDER ENGINE

PISTON ENGINES today are used mainly to power the vast numbers of light aircraft and microlights, as well as crop-sprayers and crop-dusters, small helicopters, and fire-bombers (which dump water on large fires). Virtually all heavier aircraft are now powered by jet engines. Modern piston aero-engines work on the same basic principles as the engine used by the Wright brothers in the first powered flight in 1903. However, today's engines are more sophisticated than earlier engines. For example, modern aero-engines may use a two-stroke or a four-stroke combustion cycle; they may have from one to nine air- or water-cooled cylinders, which may be arranged horizontally, in-line, in V formation, or radially; and they may drive the aircraft's propeller either directly or through a reduction gearbox. One of the more unconventional types of modern aero-engine is the rotary engine shown here, which has a trilobate (three-sided) rotor spinning in a chamber shaped like a fat figure-of-eight.

MID WEST 75-HP TWO-STROKE, THREE-CYLINDER ENGINE

Spark plug

Coolant outlet

Cylinder head

Piston

Cylinder barrel

Exhaust manifold

Exhaust port

Cylinder liner

Upper crankcase

Reduction gearbox

Driven gear

Propeller drive flange

Torsional vibration damper

Sprag clutch

Gearbox drive splines

Small end

Connecting rod (con-rod)

Big end

Counterweight

Crankshaft

Pump drive belt

Coolant pump

Generator rotor

Stator

Ignition trigger housing

Engine mounting plate

Gearbox mounting plate

Lower crankcase

ROTOR AND HOUSINGS OF A MID WEST SINGLE-ROTOR ENGINE

Propeller bolt hole

Propeller drive flange

Dowel

Stud

Roller

Eccentric-shaft bearing

Propeller shaft rear bearing

Coolant jacket

Dowel

Coolant jacket

Stud hole

Stud hole

Dowel hole

Rotor chamber

Inlet tract

Exhaust tract

GEARBOX CASE

FRONT HOUSING (FRONT END-PLATE)

TROCHOID HOUSING

MID WEST 90-HP TWIN-ROTOR ENGINE

Propeller-bolt collar
Propeller drive flange
Reduction gearbox
Lubricating oil feed
Engine front mounting plate
Blanking plate over air inlet
Carburettor
Upper rubber anti-vibration engine mount
Rotor-cooling air duct
Pipe clamp joint
Rotor-cooling air pump
Upper rotor-cooling air duct
Generator housing
Electric cable
Starter motor
Flywheel
Engine rear mounting plate
Exhaust pipe flange
Blanking plate over exhaust port
Fuel drip tray
Blanking plate over exhaust port
Fuel pipe inlet connection
Torsional vibration damper
Oil pump drive shaft cover
Front bearing mount
Lower rubber anti-vibration engine mount

OUTPUT SHAFT OF A MID WEST ROTARY ENGINE

Balance weight
Drive gear
Front bearing
Drive gear spline
Starter-ring teeth
Oil seal spacer ring
Flywheel retaining thread
Rear bearing
Eccentric shaft
Rotor bearing
Flywheel

Corner bolt
Fixed gear (stationary gear)
Engine mounting
Outlet manifold
Water pump cover and oil pump housing
Rotor tip seal
Rotor tip spring
Tip seal groove
Balancing drilling
Rotor gear teeth
Rotor side seal
Side seal spring
Pump drive shaft
Fixing stud
Bolt hole
Thermostat
Rotor bearing
Cooling fins
Side seal groove
Stud hole
Dowel hole
Coolant jacket
Inlet manifold
Oil pump

ROTOR AND SEALS   **REAR HOUSING (REAR END-PLATE)**   **WATER PUMP HOUSING**

Modern jetliners 1

BAE-146 JETLINER

MODERN JETLINERS HAVE ENABLED ordinary people to travel to places where once only the wealthy could afford to go. Compared with the first jetliners (which were introduced in the 1940s), modern ones are much quieter, burn fuel more efficiently, and produce less air pollution. These advances are largely due to the replacement of turbojet engines with turbofan engines (see pp. 418-419). The greater power of turbofan engines at low speeds enables modern jetliners to carry more fuel and passengers than turbojet aircraft; a modern Boeing 747-400 (popularly known as a "jumbo jet") can fly 400 people for 13,700 km (8,500 miles) without needing to refuel. Jetliners fly at high altitudes, typically cruising at 8,000-11,000 m (26,000-36,000 ft), where they can use fuel efficiently and usually avoid bad weather. The pilot always controls the aircraft during take-off and landing, but at other times the aircraft is usually controlled by an autopilot. Autopilots are complex on-board mechanisms that detect deviations from an aircraft's route and make appropriate adjustments to the flight controls. Flight decks are also equipped with radars that warn pilots of approaching hazards, such as mountain ranges, bad weather, and other aircraft.

Shoulder cowling

Engine pylon

Hinged cowling panel

Nose cowling

Fan duct nozzle

Fire-extinguisher discharge indicator

Core-engine jet pipe

Oil-filler door

Push-in door for hand-held fire-extinguisher

Drain mast

TURBOFAN ENGINE COWLING

STRUCTURAL COMPONENTS OF A BAE-146 JETLINER

Oil-filler door for integrated-drive generator

FUSELAGE NOSE-SECTION

FUSELAGE MID-SECTION

Electrically heated, birdproof windscreen

Side window

Anchor for open door

Rain gutter

Hinge

Peephole

Finger recess

Static air-pressure plate

Forward main door aperture

VHF omni-range and instrument-landing-system aerials

Passenger window aperture

Light-alloy door frame

Main external operating handle

Multiple-pinned lock

Floor level

Radome

Toilet service connector

Air temperature probe

Stall warning vane

Pitot head for dynamic air pressure

FORWARD MAIN DOOR

Anchor for open door

Systems connector

Overwing fuel-filler cap

Overwing fuel-filler cap

Fuel contents indicator

STARBOARD WING ASSEMBLY

Centre-line (spine) of aircraft

Single-piece skin over inboard wing

Rubber sealing strip

Rubber sealing strip

Trailing edge

Trailing edge of fixed wing

Spoiler anchorage

Hydraulic actuator attachment

Pivot point

Flap-track fairing

Screw joint

Aft section

Hinge

INBOARD LIFT SPOILERS

Stainless-steel flap seal

MOVABLE FLAP TRACK AND FAIRING

Track roller

Upper carriage attached to flap

Anchor bearing

Track

Tab-hinge line

FOWLER FLAP

Leading edge

Root

Gearbox mount

Bellcrank lever

Gearbox unit

Carriage drive nut

Flap drive screw

Lower carriage

Skin lap-joint

Main spar bridge

Leading edge

Wing-root mount containing central fuel tank

Root rib

Inboard tab

Attachment structure for wing-to-fuselage fairing

Cabin air-pressure discharge valve

Floor level

Fairing of landing gear bay

Fairing of landing gear pivot

Yellow anti-corrosion paint

413

Modern jetliners 2

Landing and taxiing light

Heated de-icing
leading edge

Roll-spoiler hinge

Roll-spoiler hydraulic actuator attachment

STARBOARD WING

Fixed trailing edge

Aileron hinge

Starboard
navigation
light

Hinge

Hydraulic actuator attachment

Spoiler arm

Aerodynamic
balance

Hinge
bracket

Horn
balance

Recessed hinge

INTERMEDIATE
LIFT SPOILER

Flap
seal

OUTBOARD ROLL SPOILER

AILERON

Trimtab

Servo-tab

MAIN FOWLER FLAP

Leading edge

Flap tip

Static discharge wick attachment

Outboard tab

Tab-hinge line

FUSELAGE SPINE FAIRING

Landing gear
door

Hydraulic brake pipe

Main pivot

Finger
recess

Peephole

Hot-air de-icing duct

Electrical harness

Oleo
lock-jack

Skin lap-joint

Passenger
window
aperture

Light-
alloy beam

Direction
bar

Hinge

Shock-strut bearing

Brake
pipe

Main
external
operating
handle

Pneumatic
tyre

Side brace
and retraction
jack trunnions

Outer
wheel
axle

Hinge

Lower pivot

Wheel hub

Pivoted
trailing-
link arm

Hydraulic
brake pipe

Anchor for open door

Cabin air-
discharge aperture

STARBOARD TWIN-WHEEL MAIN LANDING GEAR

AFT MAIN DOOR

BAE-146 MODERN JETLINER

Tailplane

Logo

Rudder

Fin

Starboard aft service door

Flap-track fairing

Core-engine jet pipe

Main landing gear fairing

Landing light

Starboard inboard engine

VHF radio aerial

Forward door for crew and service

Radome

VHF aerial

Water-drain mast

STARBOARD ELEVATOR

Horn balance

Tab hinge

Aerodynamic balance

Recessed hinge

Centre-line (spine)

Root

Trimtab

Servo-tab

TAILPLANE FAIRINGS

Intermediate fairing (fin tip)

Aft fairing

Fin trailing edge

Forward fairing

Side fairing

Elevator chassis box

Tailplane attachment bracket

Heated de-icing leading edge

FIN

Forward spar

Aft spar

Fairing panel

Fin-attachment skin

Access to yaw dampers and rudder trim jack

TAILPLANE

Rain gutter

Fin leading-edge attachment

Auxiliary power unit (APU) inlet

Heated de-icing leading edge

Operating arm

Elevator hinge

Hinge

Skin lap-joint

Trailing edge

Tailplane tip

Auxiliary power unit (APU) vent

Oil-cooler duct

STARBOARD AIR-BRAKE

Aft main door aperture

Heated drain mast

FUSELAGE TAIL-SECTION

Supersonic jetliners

SUPERSONIC AIRCRAFT FLY FASTER than the speed of sound (Mach 1). There are many supersonic military aircraft, but only two supersonic passenger-carrying aircraft (also called SSTs, or supersonic transports) have been produced: the Russian Tu-144, and Concorde, produced jointly by Britain and France. The Tu-144 had a greater maximum speed than Concorde but was withdrawn in 1978, after only seven months in service. Concorde has remained in service since 1976. It features many innovations, including a droop nose, which is lowered during take-off and landing to aid visibility from the cockpit, and the pumping of fuel between forward and aft trim tanks to help stabilize the aircraft. Concorde has a narrow fuselage and short-span wings to reduce drag during supersonic flight. Its noisy turbojet engines with afterburners enable it to carry 100 passengers at a cruising speed of Mach 2 at 15,000-18,000 m (50,000-60,000 ft). Once an aircraft is flying faster than Mach 1, it produces a continuous air-pressure wave, which is heard as a "sonic boom".

COMPUTER-DESIGNED SST

Strake
Fin
Standby pitot head
Starboard outboard engine air-intake
Inboard elevon-jack fairing
Nose-gear leg

FRONT VIEW OF CONCORDE

OVERHEAD VIEW OF CONCORDE

Variable nozzle
Leading edge

Toilets
Electrothermal de-icing panel
Starboard forward trim tank
Overhead hand-baggage bin
Passenger accommodation
Seat attachment rail
Underfloor air-conditioning duct
Life-raft
VHF aerial
Wardrobe
Forward galley
Additional crew's seat
Aluminium-alloy layers and insulation
Third pilot's seat
Erosion-resistant radome
Cockpit windscreen
Retractable visor
Lateral bracing strut
Telescopic strut
Nose-gear leg
Steering actuator
Port forward trim tank
"A" frame
Standby flight-control hydraulic jack
Plug-type passenger door
Nose-gear door
Multi-ply high-pressure tyre
Machined skin panel
Weather radar
Captain's seat
Upper rudder
Fin
Visor jack
Droop-nose hinge
Cockpit air-conditioning duct
Dorsal fin
Emergency exit
Pivoted retractable frame
Tail cone
Aft door
Elevon (combined elevator and aileron)
Hot-section steel and titanium skin
Engine cowling
Landing gear door
Bogie main landing gear

SECTIONED VIEW OF CONCORDE

Fire-suppression bottle access panel

Pressurized keel box

Fuel tank

Main air duct

Emergency exit

Cold-air unit

Static discharge wick

Elevon (combined elevator and aileron)

Cabin air duct

Inspection panel

Flight-control mixing unit

HF radio aerials fairing

Emergency oxygen cylinders

Upper rudder

Auxiliary power unit

VHF omni-range aerial

Lower-rudder power control unit

Servo control-unit fairing

Tail cone

Fuel-jettison pipe

Twin-wheel tail bumper

Air-conditioning duct

Rear bulkhead

Aft galley unit

Rear emergency door

Tank inspection access

Inboard elevon (combined elevator and aileron)

Landing gear hydraulics

Port main landing-gear leg well

Variable nozzle

Nozzle actuator

Heat-exchanger exhaust

Elevon power control unit

Spar

Rib

Leading edge

Middle passenger door

Fuel pipe

VHF aerial

Port engine fuel pumps

Four-wheel bogie

Port main landing gear leg

Forward ramp drive

Main landing gear cross-beam

Upper lip of port engine air intakes

Retraction jack

Engine front support link

Rolls-Royce Olympus Mark 610 turbojet

Heat exchanger

Fuel tank

Honeycomb elevon structure

SIDE VIEW OF CONCORDE

VHF aerial

Emergency exit

Passenger window

Flight deck windscreen

Retracted visor

Nose in drooped position

Standby pitot head

Nose-gear leg

Aerodynamic strake

Radome

Nose-leg telescopic strut

Starboard forward door

Steerable twin-wheel nose-gear

Jet engines

JET ENGINES ARE USED BY MOST MILITARY and heavy aircraft, and by many helicopters. The simplest type of jet engine, or gas turbine, is the turbojet. It works by continuously burning a mixture of fuel and air in a combustion chamber to produce a jet of hot exhaust gas that is expelled through a nozzle to produce thrust. The hot gas also spins turbine blades, which, in turn, spin the blades of an air compressor; the compressor forces air into the combustion chamber. Many of the fastest aircraft use turbojets, with additional booster units called afterburners, but their use is restricted by their high noise emission. Most jetliners use turbofan jet engines, which are quieter. An enormous fan, driven by a low-pressure turbine, feeds some air into the compressor but feeds most of it through bypass ducts to join the exhaust jetstream in the tail cone. The bypass stream produces most of the thrust. Many smaller, propeller-driven aircraft use turboprop jet engines, in which the engine powers a propeller.

NPT 301 MODERN TURBOJET

Fuel sprayer
Turbine rotor
Reverse-flow combustion chamber
Radial diffuser
Exhaust diffuser
Centrifugal compressor
Tail cone
Inducer
Jet pipe
Air intake
Exhaust nozzle
Nose cone
Igniter
Alternator
Nozzle guide vane
Air impingement starter
Combustion chamber casing

Temperature and pressure sensor

Low-pressure fan

Inlet cone (rotating spinner)

Pressure line

Fancase with special structure to contain broken fan

Electronic engine control and airframe interface connector

Electronic engine control (EEC) unit

Compressor front bearing

Plenum ring for hot anti-icing air

Flow splitter

Gearbox bevel drive

Integral oil tank

High-pressure compressor

Combustion chamber

High-pressure turbine

Fuel manifold

Fuel nozzle

Centrifugal compressor

Engine front mount

Electrical wiring harness

Fuel and oil heat exchanger

Oil filter

Fan duct

Compressor air-bleed connection

PRATT & WHITNEY CANADA PW120 SERIES MODERN TURBOPROP

Alternator mount pad
Propeller speed probe
Reduction gearbox
Propeller hub flange
Propeller brake pad
Engine front mount
Torquemeter mount
Gearbox oil scavenge line
Autofeather unit
Air intake
Electronic engine control (EEC) unit
Oil filter
Oil tank
Oil-pressure regulating valve
Intercompressor diffuser pipe
Accessory drive pad
Throttle lever
Fuel-cooled oil cooler
Fuel filter
Fuel heater
Fuel manifold
Intercompressor bleed valve
High-pressure bleed venturi connector
Turbine support case
Jet pipe connection
Oil pipe
Thermocouple bus-bar
Fuel nozzle
Igniter plug
Engine rear mount

HOW JET ENGINES WORK

TURBOFAN

Fan sucks air in
Fan blade
Rotating blades compress air
Outer drive shaft
Fuel inlet
Inner drive shaft
Exhaust gases provide extra thrust
Bypass air provides main thrust
High-pressure turbine spins outer drive shaft to drive compressor
Fuel/air mixture ignites

TURBOPROP

Compressor sucks air in
Propeller spins to provide main thrust
Reduction gearbox
Rotating blades compress air
Fuel inlet
Combustion chamber
Three-stage turbine driven by hot gas
Exhaust gases add a little thrust
Turbine shaft drives propeller and compressor

TURBOJET

Compressor sucks air in
Rotating blades compress air
Fuel inlet
Fuel/air mixture ignites
Combustion chamber
Turbine drives compressor via drive shaft
Turbine blades driven by hot gas
Exhaust gases provide all the thrust

Low-pressure turbine
Heat shield
Blade tip sealing shroud
Exhaust cone
Core jet pipe (exhaust fairing)
Scavenge oil line
Inter-module bolted joint
Fuel shut-off valve cable

SECTIONED PRATT & WHITNEY CANADA PW305 MODERN TURBOFAN

Modern military aircraft

MODERN MILITARY AIRCRAFT ARE AMONG THE MOST SOPHISTICATED and expensive products of the 20th century. Fighters need computer-operated controls for manoeuvrability, powerful engines, and effective air-to-air weapons. Most modern fighters also have guided missiles, radar, and passive, infra-red sensors. These developments enable today's fighters to engage in combat with adversaries that are outside visual range. Bombers carry a large weapon load and enough fuel for long-range flights. A few military aircraft, such as the Tornado and the F-14 Tomcat, have variable-sweep ("swing") wings. During take-off and landing their wings are fully extended, but for high-speed flight and low-level attacks the wings are pivoted fully back. A recent development is the "stealth" bomber, which is designed to absorb or deflect enemy radar in order to remain undetected. Earlier bombers, such as the Tornado, use terrain-following radars to fly so close to the ground that they avoid enemy radar detection.

FRONT VIEW OF A PANAVIA TORNADO

Instrument landing system aerial

Birdproof windscreen

Port variable-incidence air intake

Air data probe

Wing-root glove fairing

Starboard inboard stores pylon

Taileron

Starboard main landing gear door

Wing extended for take-off and landing

Wing pivoted back for high-speed flight

Main landing gear leg

Laser ranger and marked-target seeker

Starboard nose-gear door

Steerable twin-wheel nose-gear

Radome containing ground-mapping, attack, and terrain-following radars

Taxiing light

SWING-WING F-14 TOMCAT FIGHTER

SIDE VIEW OF A PANAVIA TORNADO GR1A (RECONNAISSANCE VERSION), 1986

Pilot's cockpit

Navigator's instrument console

Navigator's cockpit

Single canopy over both cockpits

Engine air intake

Navigation light

Flat, birdproof windscreen

High-velocity air duct to disperse rain

Upper "request identification" aerial

Air data probe

Radome containing ground-mapping, attack, and terrain-following radars

UHF aerial

Angle-of-attack probe

Tacan (tactical air navigation) aerial

Emergency canopy release handle

Nose-gear door

Steerable nose-gear leg

Pitot head

Twin nose-wheel

Hinged auxiliary air intake

Cold air intake (ram scoop)

Heat exchanger exhaust duct

Window covering infra-red reconnaissance camera

NORTHROP B-2 ("STEALTH" BOMBER), 1989

Starboard split rudder

Inboard elevons (combined elevators and ailerons)

Refractory (heat-resistant) skin behind exhaust outlet

Variable-incidence gust-alleviator

Wing leading edge coated with radar-absorbent material

Port wingtip rudder

Outboard elevon (combined elevator and aileron)

Leading-edge aerial

Engine aft bulkhead

Wing containing fuel tank

Weapon-bay rear bulkhead

Flight refuelling receptacle

Auxiliary air intake

Weapon-bay front bulkhead

Air intake coated with radar-absorbent material

Ejector-seat roof hatches

Port outboard stores pylon

Port navigation light

Space for extra crew member

Two-seater cockpit

Fin-tip aerial fairing

Radar warning receiver looking forwards

Instrument landing system aerial

Fin

Radar warning receiver looking rearwards

Heat exchanger air intake (ram scoop)

Extended port air-brake

Wing-root glove fairing

Rudder

Wing-root pneumatic seal

Heat exchanger hot-air exhaust

Fin-root aerial fairing

Air-brake jack

Spine end fairing

Thrust-reverser (closed)

Port fully-variable afterburner nozzle

Port flap

Port taileron (combined tailplane and aileron)

Wingtip aerial fairing

Port inboard stores pylon

Port navigation light

Hydraulic hand-pump

Lower "request identification" aerial

Powered leading-edge slat

Main-gear door

Port main landing gear

Port outboard stores pylon

Helicopters

HELICOPTERS USE ROTATING BLADES for lift, propulsion, and steering. The first machine to achieve sustained, controlled flight using rotating blades was the autogiro built in the 1920s by the Spaniard Juan de la Cierva. His machine had unpowered blades above the fuselage that relied on the flow of air to rotate them and provide lift as the autogiro was driven forwards by a conventional propeller. Then, in 1939, the Russian-born American Igor Sikorsky produced his VS-300, the forerunner of modern helicopters. Its engine-driven blades provided lift, propulsion, and steering. It could take off vertically, hover, and fly in any direction, and had a tail rotor to prevent the helicopter body from spinning. The introduction of gas turbine jet engines to helicopters in 1955 produced quieter, safer, and more powerful machines. Because of their versatility in flight, helicopters are today used for many purposes, including crop-spraying, traffic surveillance, and transporting crews to deep-sea oil rigs, as well as acting as gunships, air ambulances, and air taxis.

BELL 47G-3B1

BELL 47G-3B1

Droop stop
Blade counterweight
Main rotor hub
Blade-root attachment
Main rotor mast
Stabilizer-bar weight
Fuel vent pipe
Protective gaiter
Direct-vision panel
Fuel tank
Fuel tank cradle
Tail-rotor drive shaft
Frameless plastic canopy
Exhaust pipe
Air intake pipe
Radio
Electric fuel pump
Instrument panel
Cyclic-pitch lever
Battery
Battery overspill
Electrical inverter
Pitot head
Breather pipe
Anti-collision beacon
Oil tank
Landing light
Carburettor hot-air intake pipe
Landing skid
Air filter
VHF omni-range aerial
Navigation light
Ground handling wheel
Valve-rocker cover
Ventilator
Electric power socket
Lycoming six-cylinder engine
Collective-pitch lever
Riveted light-alloy forward fuselage section

Blade-root attachment

Three-blade main rotor

Ventilator

Flight-control rod

Outside air-temperature gauge

Anti-collision beacon

Anti-torque tail rotor

Magnetic compass

Main rotor mast

Automatic direction-finding aerial

Plastic canopy

Navigation aerial

Cyclic-pitch lever

Fuel tank

G-SAND

Tail boom

Engine air intake

Tubular bracing strut

Tail-rotor drive shaft

Vertical tail

Tail rotor guard

Pitot head

Tail-boom support strut

Anti-collision beacon

Exhaust silencer

SCHWEIZER 300C

Transmission drive-pulley cover

Landing skid

Landing gear damper

Landing light

Transponder aerial

Lycoming four-cylinder engine

High-visibility tip

Anti-torque tail rotor

Twin-blade main rotor

Tail rotor hub

Anti-collision beacon

Triangular-section, unskinned rear fuselage

Elevator upper control wire

Synchronized elevator

Tail rotor gearbox

Tubular tail rotor guard

G-BGID

Elevator lower control wire

Tail-rotor pitch control wire

Small fixed fin

Main rotor blade

Droop stop

Main rotor hub

Allison 250-C20J turboshaft engine

Anti-collision beacon

Blade-root attachment

Jet pipe

Main rotor mast

Horizontal stabilizer

Upper fin

VHF aerial

Anti-torque tail rotor

Air temperature probe

G-HUMT

Lower fin

Forward-hinged door

Tail boom

Transponder aerial

Flush-riveted aluminium fuselage

Boarding step

Baggage compartment door

BELL 206 JETRANGER

Landing skid

Rear cross-tube

Light aircraft

LIGHT AIRCRAFT, SUCH AS THE ARV SUPER 2 shown here, are small, lightweight, and of simple construction. More than a million have been built since World War I, mainly for recreational use by private owners. Virtually all light aircraft have piston engines, most of which are air-cooled, although some are liquid-cooled. Open cockpits, almost universal in the 1920s, have today been replaced by enclosed cabins. The cabins of high-wing aircraft have one or two doors, whereas those of low-wing aircraft usually have a sliding or hinged canopy. Most modern light aircraft are made of aluminium alloy, although some are made of wood or of fibre-reinforced materials. Light aircraft today also usually have navigational instruments, an electrical system, cabin heating, wheel brakes, and a two-way radio.

Port wingtip

Aileron mass balance

Aileron torque tube

Port aileron

PORT MAIN LANDING GEAR

Tyre · Inner tube · Hub · Brake disc · Stub axle · Landing gear leg · Brake mount · Brake pipe · Hydraulic brake calliper

Dorsal fin

TAILPLANE AND RUDDER

Elevator

Rudder tip fairing · Rudder mass balance · Fin tip fairing · Rudder · Fin · Elevator trimtab · Drive pillar · Attachment plate · Tailplane

Rear fuselage top skin

Rear attachment-bracket for wing

REAR FUSELAGE

Longeron · Frame · Battery box · Diaphragm · Side skin · "Skin-grip" pin

Coolant outlet · Aluminium radiator · Air scoop · Coolant inlet

Rear fuselage bottom skin

Elevator push-rod

CONTROL RODS AND CABLES

Flap torque tube · Aileron rod · Elevator push-rod · Rocking elevator arm · Aileron torque tube · Rudder cable · Flap drive-rod · Flap drive-rod

SIDE VIEW OF ARV SUPER 2

Spinner · Canopy · Wing · Communications aerial · Navigational aerial · Fin · Engine cowling · Dorsal fin · Rudder · G-BNHB · Elevator · Nose-gear · Tailplane · Tailskid · Aircraft registration code · Step · Radiator · Venturi for instruments · Wing strut · Main landing gear

STARBOARD MAIN LANDING GEAR

Brake mount · Brake calliper · Brake pipe · Landing gear leg · Brake disc · Stub axle · Inner tube · Hub · Tyre

PORT WING

Port top-wing fairing

Port underwing fairing

Headrest

Backrest

Wing strut

Port flap

Pitot head

Airspeed-indicator tube

COCKPIT

Fibreglass canopy frame

Fuel tank top skin

Rudder pedal

Cockpit coaming

Forward attachment bracket for wing

Control-column aperture

Semi-bulkhead

Fibreglass fuel tank

Bulkhead

Lap-strap attachment bracket

"Skin-grip" pin

Nose-leg upper mount

Firewall

SEAT ASSEMBLY

Seat cushion

Quick-release mechanism

Lap strap

Lap-strap length adjuster

Bolted anchor

THREE-CYLINDER ENGINE

Port engine cowling

Engine mount

Air intake box

Water outlet

Carburettor

Backplate

Fuel hose

Cylinder head

Gearbox

Propeller drive flange

Exhaust manifold

Starboard engine cowling

CANOPY

Direct-vision panel

Pressurized strut

Hinge

Leading-edge fairing

Canopy latch

Moulded plastic

Outside air-temperature gauge

PROPELLER

Spinner

Flanged plate

CONTROL COLUMN AND FLAP LEVER

Torque tube assembly

Throttle lever

Brake lever

Elevator arm

Control column

Elevator push-rod

Flap lever

Elevator trimtab lever

Flap lever detent box

Release button

Carburettor hot air lever

Bearing assembly

Pilot's handgrip

INSTRUMENT PANEL

Flight instruments

Engine instruments

Glove box

Radio plugs

NOSE-GEAR

Steering stop

Nose-leg down tube

Rubber bungee (elasticated cord) shock absorber

Damper unit

Pivoted fork

Hoop

Axle bolt

Nose-wheel

STARBOARD WING

Wing strut

Starboard underwing fairing

Starboard top-wing fairing

Gliders, hang-gliders, and microlights

NOSE SHELL

Grommet for front pylon strut

Instrument panel

HANG-GLIDER

MODERN GLIDERS ARE AMONG the most graceful and aerodynamically efficient of all aircraft. Unpowered but with a large wingspan (up to about 25 m, or 82 ft), gliders use currents of hot, rising air (thermals) to stay aloft, and a rudder, elevators, and ailerons for control. Modern gliders have achieved flights of more than 1,450 km (900 miles) and altitudes above 15,000 m (49,000 ft). Hang-gliders consist of a simple frame across which rigid or flexible material is stretched to form the wings. The pilot is suspended below the wings in a harness or body-bag and, gripping a triangular A-frame, steers by shifting weight from side to side. Like gliders, hang-gliders rely on thermals for lift. Microlights are basically powered hang-gliders. A small engine and an open fibreglass car (trike), which can hold a crew of two, are suspended beneath a stronger version of a hang-glider frame; the frame may have rigid or flexible wings. Microlight pilots, like hang-glider pilots, steer by shifting their weight against an A-frame. Microlights can reach speeds of up to 160 kph (100 mph).

King-post

Apex

PEGASUS XL SE MICROLIGHT

Stiffening rib

Centre-line beam

Main suspension

Rear-mounted propeller (pusher propeller)

Fuel tank

Spat (wheel fairing)

Main wheel

Trike nacelle

Apex wire

Nose shell

Nose-gear mount

Fixed nose-wheel

HANG-GLIDER BODY-BAG

Clip-in latch for pilot

Shoulder strap

Layers of insulating fabric

Armhole

Shoulder pad

Camera pouch

Body-bag

End of rib

Trailing edge

Dacron skin

SCHLEICHER K23 GLIDER

Down-turned wingtip acts as skid

Single pilot cockpit

Forward-opening canopy

Towing hook

Nose-wheel

Non-retractable main wheel

Aileron

Aluminium air-brake

Radio aerial

Fuselage of fibreglass and foam layers

Tailplane

Hinged elevator

EVW

T-type cantilevered fin

Rudder

Tailwheel

SOLAR WINGS PEGASUS QUASAR MICROLIGHT

TRIKE UNIT

Foot throttle

Pilot's steering bar

Pylon strut

Footbrake

Passenger's steering bar and footrest

Lap strap

Fuel tank filler nozzle

Pilot's seat

Hand throttle

Pylon-strut strap

Passenger's seat

Spat (wheel fairing)

Engine mount

Main wing-strut

Pylon fairing

Aircraft name

Air outlet

Rear engine cowling

TRIKE NACELLE

Sealed lid

Waterproof stowage box

TWIN-CYLINDER ENGINE

Trailing edge

Leading edge

Twin carburettors

Air filter

Propeller drive gearbox

Dual ignition plug

Air cooling fan

Exhaust connection

Engine rear mount

Metal hub

EXHAUST PIPE

PROPELLER

WINGFRAME

Eyelet tensioning trailing edge to rib

Bracing cable

Rib

Centre-line beam

Single spar

King-post

After silencer

Main exhaust silencer

Leading edge

Semi-rigid fibreglass skin

Lift bracing wire

THE
VISUAL ARTS

Drawing

DRAWINGS CAN BE FINISHED WORKS OF ART, or preparatory studies for paintings and other visual arts. They can be made using a wide variety of drawing instruments such as pencils, graphite sticks, chalks, charcoal, pens and inks, and silver wires. The most common drawing instrument is the graphite pencil. A graphite pencil consists of a thin rod of graphite mixed with clay, encased in wood. Charcoal is one of the oldest drawing instruments. It is produced by firing twigs of willow, vine, or other woods at high temperatures in airtight containers. Erasers can be used to rub out marks made by drawing materials such as graphite pencils or charcoal, or to achieve a particular effect – such as smudging. Fixative is often applied – using a mouth diffuser or aerosol spray fixative – to prevent smudging once a drawing is finished. Silver lines can be produced by drawing silver wire across specially prepared paper – a technique known as silverpoint. The lines are permanent and cannot be erased. In time the silver lines oxidize and turn brown.

FIXATIVE AND MOUTH DIFFUSER

Hinge

Liquid fixative consisting of dissolved resin

Fixative is sucked into tube and sprayed on to drawing

ERASERS

Hard texture

Medium-soft, light line

PLASTIC ERASER

Soft texture

Very soft, dark line

PUTTY ERASER

CHALK, CRAYON, AND CHARCOAL

Calcite (calcium carbonate) mixed with pigment

BLUE CHALK

Iron oxide mixed with chalk

SANGUINE CRAYON

Carbonized wood

WILLOW CHARCOAL

DRAWING INSTRUMENTS

2B GRAPHITE PENCIL

8B GRAPHITE PENCIL

SILVER WIRE IN A METAL HOLDER

DRAWING BOARD

Drawing board

Paper

Drawing clip

DRAWING MATERIALS

Coloured pencil

Graphite stick

Bulldog clip

Dip pen

Pencil sharpener

Sketch book

Ink bottle

Silver lines
oxidize to a
light brown
colour

Figures drawn
in ink on top
of lines

Line drawn
in silverpoint
using a rule

Complex perspective
drawing done as a
preparatory study
for a painting

Vanishing
point located
on head of
man riding
rearing horse

Lines of
squared
pavement slabs
recede toward
a single
vanishing
point

Paper prepared
with size (glue)
and pigment

EXAMPLE OF A SILVERPOINT DRAWING
The Adoration of the Magi, Leonardo da Vinci, 1481
Pen and ink over silverpoint on paper
16.5 x 29.2 cm (6½ x 11½ in)

One of a series
of drawings
recording
London during
1944–1945

Charcoal lines
softened by
rubbing and
smudging

Charcoal
gives strong,
expressive lines

Handmade, tinted
paper

Broad charcoal
mark

Lines rapidly
drawn on site

EXAMPLE OF A CHARCOAL DRAWING
St. Paul's and the River, David Bomberg, 1945
Charcoal on paper
50.8 x 65.8 cm (20 x 25⅛ in)

Tempera

**ILLUMINATED
MANUSCRIPT**

THE TERM TEMPERA is applied to any paint in which pigment is tempered (mixed) with a water-based binding medium – usually egg yolk. Egg tempera is applied to a smooth surface such as vellum (for illuminated manuscripts) or more commonly to hardwood panels prepared with gesso – a mixture of chalk and size (glue). Hog hair brushes are used to apply the gesso. A layer of gesso grosso (coarse gesso) is followed by successive layers of gesso sotile (fine gesso) that are sanded between coats to provide a smooth, yet absorbent ground. The paint is applied with fine sable brushes in thin layers, using light brushstrokes. Tempera dries quickly to form a tough skin with a satin sheen. The luminous white surface of the gesso combined with the overlaid paint produces the brilliant crispness and rich colours particular to this medium. Egg tempera paintings are frequently gilded with gold. Leaves of finely beaten gold are applied to a bole (reddish-brown clay) base and polished by burnishing.

MATERIALS FOR GILDING

Parchment for protecting gold leaf from draughts

Brush

Bowl containing diluted bole

Gold leaf

Gilder's knife

Gilder's tip for picking up gold leaf

Gilder's cushion

Gold leaf smoothed and polished with a burnisher

Surface prepared with gesso

Gold leaf applied in overlapping layers

Bole brushed on to gesso

Burnisher

Agate tip

MATERIALS FOR TEMPERA PANEL PAINTING

Yolk

EGG

White

SIZE (GLUE)

GESSO

MORTAR AND PESTLE

Mortar

Lip

Pestle for crushing and grinding pigments

EXAMPLES OF BRUSHES

FLAT HOG HAIR BRUSH

SABLE BRUSH SIZE 6

SABLE BRUSH SIZE 1

EGG YOLK BINDING MEDIUM

EXAMPLE OF A TEMPERA PAINTING
Presentation in the Temple, Ambrogio Lorenzetti, 1342
Tempera on wood, 257 x 168 cm (8 ft 5⅛ in x 5 ft 6⅛ in)

PIGMENTS FOR
FLESH-COLOUR
PAINTING

*Altarpiece
commissioned for
Siena Cathedral, Italy*

*Textured gold ornament made
by punching motifs into the
gilded surface*

*The red tinge of
the bole is just
visible beneath
the gold*

*Edge of a sheet
of gold leaf*

*Crisp edge
characteristic of
tempera painting*

*Vine black used
to create the
dim cathedral
interior*

*Highlights on
the beard made
by applying thin
layers of white
over dried paint*

*Red drapery
painted in
vermilion*

*Raised right hand
and pointing finger
is the gesture of
prophecy*

*Receding floor
tiles create the
impression of
depth*

*Patch of discoloured
varnish, left from
last cleaning*

PIGMENTS FOR FLESH-COLOUR PAINTING

VERDACCIO

**VERMILION AND
LEAD WHITE**

VERMILION

**RED EARTH
(IRON OXIDE)**

EXAMPLES OF PIGMENTS

MALACHITE

**ULTRAMARINE
LAPIS LAZULI**

VINE BLACK

LEAD TIN YELLOW

*Warm flesh
tones achieved
by layering
vermilion and
white over an
undercoat of
verdaccio*

*Patterned gold
halo glitters in
candlelight*

*Ultramarine
lapis lazuli, as
costly as gold,
was reserved for
significant
figures such as
the Virgin Mary*

*Craquelure
(pattern of
cracks in
the paint)*

**DETAIL FROM "PRESENTATION
IN THE TEMPLE"**

Fresco

FRESCO IS A METHOD OF WALL PAINTING. In buon fresco (true fresco), pigments are mixed with water and applied to an intonaco (layer of fresh, damp lime-plaster). The intonaco absorbs and binds the pigments as it dries making the picture a permanent part of the wall surface. The intonaco is applied in sections called giornate (daily sections). The size of each giornata depends on the artist's estimate of how much can be painted before the plaster sets. The junctions between giornate are sometimes visible on a finished fresco. The range of colours used in buon fresco are limited to lime-resistant pigments such as earth colours (below). Slaked lime (burnt lime mixed with water), bianco di San Giovanni (slaked lime that has been partly exposed to air), and chalk can be used to produce fresco whites. In fresco secco (dry fresco), pigments are mixed with a binding medium and applied to dry plaster. The pigments are not completely absorbed into the plaster and may flake off over time.

CROSS-SECTION SHOWING FRESCO LAYERS

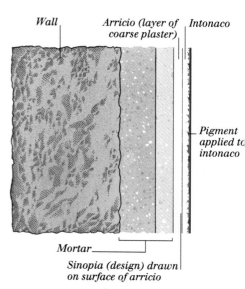

Wall

Arricio (layer of coarse plaster)

Intonaco

Pigment applied to intonaco

Mortar

Sinopia (design) drawn on surface of arricio

EXAMPLES OF EARTH COLOUR PIGMENTS

RAW UMBER

RED EARTH (IRON OXIDE)

GREEN EARTH

RAW SIENNA

EXAMPLES OF FRESCO BRUSHES

Round hog hair brush

Rust-resistant twine binding

Dome-shaped hog hair brush

Pointed hog hair brush

TONDO

MUCCINI

RIGA

INGREDIENTS FOR FRESCO WHITES

Marble slab for mixing ingredients

Bianco di San Giovanni

Slaked lime

Chalk

EXAMPLE OF A FRESCO
The Expulsion of the Merchants from the Temple, Giotto, c.1306
Fresco, 200 x 185 cm (78 x 72 in)

Temple acts as a backdrop for the action

Bianco di San Giovanni often used for fresco whites

Gold leaf applied to apostle's halo

Green earth pigment applied to robe

Child painted on top of apostle's robe

One of a series of frescoes in the Arena Chapel, Padua, Italy

Patches of azurite blue have turned green due to reaction with carbon dioxide

Hairline junction between giornate is visible

Red earth pigment applied in buon fresco has retained rich hue

Azurite blue applied in fresco secco has flaked off to reveal the plaster beneath

Dry, matt surface characteristic of buon fresco

Paint applied in buon fresco to child's face

White dove represents the Holy Ghost

Paint applied in fresco secco to child's body has flaked off

A fresco was generally worked in zones from the top down

Sinopia (design) sketched in red earth

Artist has to finish giornata before plaster dries

Junction between giornate

Area with little detail can be painted quickly, allowing a larger giornata to be completed

Highly detailed area takes a longer time to paint, restricting the size of the giornata

DETAIL FROM "THE EXPULSION"

GIORNATE (DAILY SECTIONS) IN "THE EXPULSION"

Oils

OIL PAINTS ARE MADE BY MIXING and grinding pigment with a drying vegetable oil such as linseed oil. The paint can be applied to many different surfaces and textures – the most common being canvas. Before painting, the canvas is stretched on a wooden frame and its surface is prepared with layers of size (glue) and primer. The two main types of brushes used in oil painting are stiff hog hair bristle brushes – generally used for covering large areas; and soft hair brushes made from sable or synthetic material – generally used for fine detail. Other tools, including painting knives, can also be used to achieve different effects. Oil paint can be applied thickly (a technique known as impasto), or can be thinned down using a solvent – such as turpentine or white spirit. Varnishes are sometimes applied to finished paintings to protect their surface and to give them a matt or gloss finish.

KIDNEY-SHAPED PALETTE

DAMMAR RESIN VARNISH

Crystals are dissolved and applied to painting to protect its surface

COMMERCIAL OIL PAINTS

CADMIUM RED

ULTRAMARINE

Lightfast opaque colour

Transparent colour

LINSEED OIL

Oil derived from seeds of flax plant

EXAMPLES OF PIGMENTS

CADMIUM RED

CERULEAN BLUE

DOUBLE DIPPER (PALETTE ATTACHMENT)

Screw-top lid

Container for storing solvent or drying oil

HOG HAIR BRISTLE BRUSHES

Flat hog hair brush

Flat hog hair brush

Filbert hog hair brush

Filbert hog hair brush

SYNTHETIC BRUSH

Round hog hair brush

EQUIPMENT FOR MAKING OIL PAINT

Airtight jar for storing paint

Palette knife for mixing drying oil and pigment

PAINTING KNIVES

TROWEL-SHAPED PAINTING KNIFE

DIAMOND-SHAPED PAINTING KNIFE

SABLE BRUSH

EXAMPLES OF BRUSHES

Long, wooden handle

Glass muller for grinding drying oil and pigment

Blade

Blade

Glass slab with abrasive surface

Cranked, steel shank

Cranked, steel shank

Protective, plastic case

EXAMPLE OF AN OIL PAINTING
Fritillarias, Vincent van Gogh, 1886
Oil on canvas, 73.5 x 60.5 cm (29 x 24 in)

Artist's signature
scratched in wet
paint with the
end of the brush

Each leaf
painted
in a single,
rapid stroke

Impasto
(deep ridges
of paint applied
in thick strokes)

Strong
directional
brushstrokes
on table draw
attention to
the vase

Features of vase highlighted
by generous touches of yellow

Background
enlivened by
dabs of white
and green

Orange and blue
(complementary
colours) placed
together to give
maximum contrast
and enhance
one another to
appear brighter

**RADIAL
STUDIO
EASEL**

Top sliding-
block adjusts
to canvas
height

Canvas
support

Height
adjustment
key

Angle
adjustment
key

Tripod

**CANVAS STRETCHED
ON WOODEN FRAME
(VIEWED FROM
THE BACK)**

Staple

Canvas prepared
with glue (size)
and primer

Wooden
frame

Unprimed
canvas

EXAMPLES OF CANVASES

COTTON DUCK

FINE LINEN

COARSE LINEN

Watercolour

WATERCOLOUR PAINT IS MADE OF GROUND PIGMENT mixed with a water-soluble binding medium, usually gum arabic. It is usually applied to paper using soft hair brushes such as sable, goat hair, squirrel, and synthetic brushes. Watercolours are often diluted and applied as overlaying washes (thin, transparent layers) to build up depth of colour. Washes can be laid in a variety of ways to create a range of different effects. For example, a wet-in-wet wash can be achieved by laying a wash on top of another wet wash. The two washes blend together to give a fused effect. Sponges are used to modify washes by soaking up paint so that areas of pigment are lightened or removed from the paper. Watercolours can also be applied undiluted – a technique known as dry brush – to create a broken-colour effect. Watercolours are generally transparent and allow light to reflect from the surface of the paper through the layers of paint to give a luminous effect. They can be thickened and made opaque by adding body colour (Chinese white).

GUM ARABIC

Natural sap from acacia tree

NATURAL SPONGE

ANATOMY OF A SABLE BRUSH

Soft red sable hair

Toe (tip)

Wooden handle

Hair trimmed and cemented into ferrule

SOFT HAIR BRUSHES

ROUND SABLE BRUSH (SIZE 6)

Round ferrule

Hair tied with clove hitch knot

ROUND SABLE BRUSH (SIZE 1)

TUBES OF WATERCOLOUR PAINT

WINSOR GREEN

SYNTHETIC WASH BRUSH

Winsor Green
Vert Winsor
Winsorgrün
Verde Winsor
Verde Winsor
0102 730 SL Series 1 A

Cadmium Yellow
Jaune de Cadmium
Kadmiumgelb
Amarillo de Cadmio
Giallo di Cadmio
0102 108 SL Series 4 A

SQUIRREL MOP
WASH BRUSH

PORTABLE BOX OF WATERCOLOUR PAINTS

CADMIUM YELLOW

Painted colour swatch

Chinese white

Pan of watercolour paint

ARTISTS' WATER COLOUR
Chinese White
Blanc de Chine
Chinesischweiss
Blanco de China

Lid can be used for mixing colours

LARGE GOAT HAKE
WASH BRUSH

EXAMPLE OF A WATERCOLOUR
Burning of the Houses of Parliament, Turner, 1834
Watercolour on paper, 29.2 x 44.5 cm (11½ x 17½ in)

Transparent washes laid on top of each other to create tonal depth

Transparent washes allow light to reflect off the surface of the paper to give a luminous effect

Highlight scratched out with a scalpel

Paper shows through thin wash to give flames added highlight

Crowd painted with thin strokes laid over a pale wash

Undiluted paint applied, then partly washed out, to create the impression of water

EXAMPLES OF WATERCOLOUR PAPERS

SMOOTH-TEXTURED PAPER

MEDIUM-TEXTURED PAPER

ROUGH-TEXTURED PAPER

EXAMPLES OF WASHES

WASH OVER DRY BRUSH
Wash laid over paint applied with dry brush gives two-tone effect

GRADED WASH
Strong wash applied to tilted paper gives graded effect

DRY BRUSH
Undiluted paint dragged across surface of paper gives broken effect

WET-IN-WET
Two diluted washes left to run together to give fused effect

COLOUR WHEEL OF WATERCOLOUR PAINTS

Yellow (primary colour)

Secondary colours made by mixing yellow and blue

Secondary colours made by mixing red and yellow

Blue (primary colour)

Red (primary colour)

Secondary colours made by mixing blue and red

Pastels

PASTELS ARE STICKS OF PIGMENT made by mixing ground pigment with chalk and a binding medium, such as gum arabic. They vary in hardness depending on the proportion of the binding medium to the chalk. Soft pastel – the most common form of pastel – contains just enough binding medium to hold the pigment in stick form. Pastels can be applied directly to any support (surface) with sufficient tooth (texture). When a pastel is drawn over a textured surface, the pigment crumbles and lodges in the fibres of the support. Pastel marks have a particular soft, matt quality and are suitable for techniques such as blending, scumbling, and feathering. Blending is a technique of rubbing and fusing two or more colours on the support using fingers or various tools such as tortillons (paper stumps), soft hair brushes, putty erasers, and soft bread. Scumbling is a technique of building up layers of pastel colours. The side or blunted tip of a soft pastel is lightly drawn over an underpainted area so that patches of the colour beneath show through. Feathering is a technique of applying parallel strokes of colour with the point of a pastel, usually over an existing layer of pastel colour. A thin spray of fixative can be applied – using a mouth diffuser (see pp. 430-431) or aerosol spray fixative – to a finished pastel painting, or in between layers of colour, to prevent smudging.

EQUIPMENT FOR MAKING PASTELS

Glass muller

Chalk

Glass slab with abrasive surface *Gum arabic* *Ivory-black pigment* *Cobalt-blue pigment*

EXAMPLES OF SOFT PASTELS

COBALT-BLUE HALF PASTEL

VERMILION HALF PASTEL

OLIVE-GREEN FULL PASTEL

MAUVE FULL PASTEL

BOXED PASTEL SET

Boxed set containing a mixture of portrait and landscape colours

Foam compartments protect the pastels

Soft pastel

Wooden tray

EQUIPMENT USED WITH PASTELS

PUTTY ERASER

BREAD

Soft bread suitable for erasing and blending

AEROSOL SPRAY FIXATIVE

SOFT HAIR BRUSH

TORTILLONS (PAPER STUMPS)

Soft point used for blending

Tight roll of paper

EXAMPLE OF A PASTEL PAINTING
Woman Drying her Neck, Edgar Degas, c.1898
Pastel on cardboard, 62.5 x 65.5 cm (24½ x 25½ in)

*Pastels
applied
directly to
support*

*Rich colour of
fabric created
by overlaying
yellows and
oranges*

*Broken colours,
characteristic
of scumbling
technique*

*Colours are
blended together
using fingers or
tools such as
tortillons*

*Built up
layers of
pastel*

*Toned colour
of paper visible
beneath thinly
applied pastels*

*Pure bright colours laid side by
side produce strong contrasts*

DETAIL FROM "WOMAN DRYING HER NECK"

*Feathering
technique
used to produce
skin tones*

EXAMPLES OF TEXTURED PAPERS AND PASTEL BOARDS

**WATERCOLOUR
PAPER (ROUGH
TEXTURE)**

GLASS PAPER

**WATERCOLOUR
PAPER (MEDIUM
TEXTURE)**

INGRES PAPER

**FLOCKED PASTEL
BOARD**

CANSON PAPER

EXAMPLES OF COLOURED AND TINTED PAPERS

Acrylics

ACRYLIC PAINT IS MADE BY MIXING PIGMENT with a synthetic resin. It can be thinned with water but dries to become water insoluble. Acrylics are applied to many surfaces, such as paper and acrylic-primed board and canvas. A variety of brushes, painting knives, rollers, air-brushes, plastic scrapers, and other tools are used in acrylic painting. The versatility of acrylics makes them suitable for a wide range of techniques. They can be used opaquely or – by adding water – in a transparent, watercolour style. Acrylic mediums can be added to the paint to adjust its consistency for special effects such as glazing and impasto (ridges of paint applied in thick strokes) or to make it more matt or glossy. Acrylics are quick-drying, which allows layers of paint to be applied on top of each other almost immediately.

EXAMPLES OF BRUSHES

Sable brush

Hog hair sash brush

Synthetic hog hair brush

Synthetic sable brush

Hog hair brush

Goat hair brush

Synthetic wash brush

Ox hair brush

EXAMPLES OF PAINTS USED IN ACRYLICS

Azo yellow

Phthalo green

Cerulean blue

Phthalo blue

Quinacridone red

Titanium white

Yellow ochre

Burnt umber

Burnt sienna

Pad of disposable paper palettes

Credit card

Paint spread evenly

Flexible, plastic blade

PAINTING TOOLS

Stippled effect achieved using thick paint

Striated effect

Glue spreader

PLASTIC PAINTING KNIFE

PLASTIC SCRAPERS

Blended tones

Paint cup

Main lever

Nozzle

AIR-BRUSH

Plastic handle

SPONGE ROLLER

Uniform tone

Air hose

EXAMPLE OF AN ACRYLIC PAINTING
A Bigger Splash, David Hockney, 1967
Acrylic on canvas, 242.5 x 243.8 cm (95½ x 96 in)

Paint applied evenly using a roller

Cotton duck canvas support (surface)

Flatness of rollered areas enhanced by adding gel medium to the paint

Masking tape stuck on to canvas to define main shapes, and paint applied within these areas using a roller

Thin strip of pool edge left unpainted

Splash painted using thicker paint and small brush

Imprecise edge on end of spring board where paint has seeped under masking tape

EXAMPLES OF ACRYLIC PAINTS AND TECHNIQUES

Opaque effect

Extruded (squeezed) effect

Paint applied using painting knife

PURPLE ACRYLIC PAINT

YELLOW ACRYLIC PAINT

ORANGE ACRYLIC PAINT

Transparent, watercolour effect

Translucent, impasto glaze

Thick impasto with coarse texture

BLUE ACRYLIC PAINT DILUTED WITH WATER

GREEN ACRYLIC PAINT MIXED WITH GEL MEDIUM

RED ACRYLIC PAINT MIXED WITH TEXTURE PASTE

Calligraphy

CALLIGRAPHY IS BEAUTIFULLY FORMED LETTERING. The term applies to written text and illumination (the decoration of manuscripts using gold leaf and colour). The essential materials needed to practise calligraphy are a writing tool, ink, and a writing surface. Quills are among the oldest writing tools. They are usually made from goose or turkey feathers, and are noted for their flexibility and ability to produce fine lines. A quill point, however, is not very durable and constant recutting and trimming is required. The most commonly used writing instrument in western calligraphy is a detachable, metal nib held in a penholder. The metal nib is very durable, and there are a wide range of different types. Particular types of nibs – such as copperplate, speedball, and roundhand nibs – are used for specific styles of lettering. Some nibs have integral ink reservoirs and others have reservoirs that are detachable. Brushes are also used for writing, and for filling in outlined letters and painting decoration. Other writing tools used in calligraphy are fountain pens, felt-tip pens, rotring pens, and reed pens. Calligraphy inks may come in liquid form, or as a solid ink stick. Ink sticks are ground down in distilled water to form a liquid ink. The most common writing surfaces for calligraphy are good quality, smooth -surfaced papers. To achieve the best writing position, the calligrapher places the paper on a drawing board set at an angle.

EQUIPMENT USED IN BRUSH LETTERING

Brush rest

Wolf hair brush

Goat hair brush

BRUSHES AND BRUSH REST

Liquid ink made by grinding down ink stick in distilled water

Solid carbon ink stick

Ink stone

INK STICK AND STONE

Feather

PENS, NIBS, AND BRUSHES USED IN CALLIGRAPHY

PENHOLDER

COPPERPLATE NIB

SPEEDBALL NIB

ROUNDHAND NIB AND DETACHABLE INK RESERVOIR

FELT-TIP PEN

ROTRING PEN

REED PEN

SQUARE SABLE BRUSH

POINTED SABLE BRUSH

Feather stripped for better handling

Barrel

Hand-cut point

GOOSE-FEATHER QUILL

GOAT HAIR BRUSH

WOLF HAIR BRUSH

FOUNTAIN PEN AND INK

Barrel

Bottle of permanent black ink

Clip

Nib

Outer cap

EXAMPLES OF LETTERING STYLES

Apex

Bowl

Curved stroke

Stem

Inner counter

Stem

Stem

Arm

Counter

A B C D E

Crossbar

Inner counter

Counter

Inner counter

ROMAN CAPITALS

Cap line

X line

Ascender

Curved stroke

Ear

Arch

Base line

Crossbar

Descender line

A b c g m p t

Serif

Neck

Descender

Height of letter determined by ladder of nib widths

ITALIC ROMAN

Slightly pinched (curved) vertical stroke

Letter filled in using brush

Inner counter

O R S W

Tail

Spine

Pointed apex

VERSAL

CHINESE LETTERING

Rice paper

Broad brush stroke

Chinese character meaning long life

Artist's stamped signature

ARTIST'S STAMP

Stamp

Stamped signature of the artist

Ink pad

DRAWING BOARD

Adjustable set square

Blade with parallel motion

AN ILLUMINATED MANUSCRIPT

Style of lettering called Gothic book script

Large decorative letter used to mark the opening of a chapter

Words written carefully by hand

Gold leaf

Grid lines provide guide to position of words and pictures

EXAMPLES OF CALLIGRAPHY PAPERS

Standard European paper

Indian handmade paper

Flecked, tinted paper

Imitation parchment paper

Printmaking 1

PRINTS ARE MADE BY FOUR BASIC printing processes – intaglio, lithographic, relief, and screen. In intaglio printing, lines are engraved or etched into the surface of a metal plate. Lines are engraved by hand using sharp metal tools. They are etched by corroding the metal plate with acid, using acid-resistant ground to protect the areas not to be etched. The plate is then inked and wiped, leaving the grooves filled with ink and the surface clean. Dampened paper is laid over the plate, and both paper and plate are passed through the rollers of an etching press. The pressure of the rollers forces the paper into the grooves, so that it takes up the ink, leaving an impression on the paper. Lithographic printing is based on the antipathy between grease and water. An image is drawn on a surface – usually a stone or metal plate – with a greasy medium, such as tusche (lihographic ink). The greasy drawing is fixed on to the plate by applying an acidic solution, such as gum arabic. The surface is then dampened and rolled with ink. The ink adheres only to the greasy areas and is repelled by the water. Paper is laid on the plate and pressure is applied by means of a press. In relief printing, the non-printing areas of a wood or linoleum block are cut away using gouges, knives, and other tools. The printing areas are left raised in relief and are rolled with ink. Paper is laid on the inked block and pressure is applied by means of a press or by burnishing (rubbing) the back of the paper. The most common forms of relief printing are woodcut, wood engraving, and linocut. In screen printing, the printing surface is a mesh stretched across a wooden frame. A stencil is applied to the mesh to seal the non-printing areas and ink is scraped through the mesh to produce an image.

THE FOUR MAIN PRINTING PROCESSES

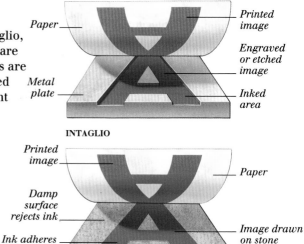

INTAGLIO
Paper · Printed image · Engraved or etched image · Metal plate · Inked area

LITHOGRAPHIC
Printed image · Paper · Damp surface rejects ink · Ink adheres to greasy image · Image drawn on stone with greasy medium

RELIEF
Paper · Printed image · Raised figure · Wood block · Inked surface

SCREEN
Ink forced through mesh · Paper · Wooden frame · Stencil · Printed image

LEATHER INK DABBER

EQUIPMENT USED IN INTAGLIO PRINTING

ROCKER · **SCRIBER** · **ROULETTE** · **SCRAPER** · **BURNISHER** · **CLAMP**

**ETCHING PRESS USED FOR
INTAGLIO PRINTMAKING**

Flywheel

Paper

*Felt blanket cushions and
distributes pressure
exerted by rollers*

Spoke

*Screw
pressure
adjustor*

Handle

*Top
roller*

Printed image

*Position
guide*

*Sliding bed (plank)
is wound between
steel rollers*

*Inked-up
copper plate*

GROUND

*Acid-resistant
ground rolled
on to metal
plate before
etching*

**EXAMPLES OF
PRINTING
PAPERS**

GROUND ROLLER

*Gelatine
roller*

*Wooden
handle*

EXAMPLE OF AN INTAGLIO PRINT
Annie with a Sun Hat, Jock McFadyen, 1993
Etched copper plate, 41 x 40 cm (16 x 15¾ in)

Printmaking 2

EXAMPLE OF A LITHOGRAPHIC STONE AND PRINT
Crown Gateway 2, Mandy Bonnell, 1987
Lithograph, 50 x 40 cm (19½ x 15¾ in)

IMAGE DRAWN ON STONE

LITHOGRAPIC PRINT

EXAMPLE OF A SCREEN PRINT
Sea Change, Patrick Hughes, 1992
Screen print, 77 x 94.5 cm (30 x 37 in)

SCREEN AND SQUEEGEE

Squeegee

Rubber blade

Mesh

Wooden frame

EQUIPMENT USED IN LITHOGRAPHIC PRINTING

CRAYON AND HOLDER

LITHOGRAPHIC PENCIL

TUSCHE (LITHOGRAPHIC INK) PEN

ERASING STICK

EXPANDABLE SPONGE

TUSCHE (LITHOGRAPHIC INK) STICK

INK ROLLER

RUBBING INK

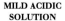

MILD ACIDIC SOLUTION

GUM ARABIC SOLUTION

WATER-BASED SCREEN PRINTING INKS

BLUE ACRYLIC INK

RED ACRYLIC INK

BROWN TEXTILE INK

EQUIPMENT USED IN RELIEF PRINTING

V-SHAPED GOUGE

INK ROLLER

Rubber roller

LINOLEUM AND WOODCUT BLOCK

U-SHAPED GOUGE

GRAVER

Linoleum

KNIFE

SCORPER

WOOD ENGRAVING

Side-grain wood block

END-GRAIN WOOD BLOCK

INKED-UP ENGRAVED BLOCK

WOOD ENGRAVING PRINT

RELIEF-PRINTING PRESS

Spiral spring

Crown

Tympan lowered on to printing block

Piston

Printed image

Staple (frame)

Bar (pressure handle)

Printing block

Bed is rolled under platen

Drum handle

Platen

Rail

Drum (rounce)

Leg

Counterweight

Pillar (post)

Foot

449

Mosaic

MOSAIC IS THE ART OF MAKING patterns and pictures from tesserae (small, coloured pieces of glass, marble, and other materials). Different materials are cut into tesserae using different tools. Smalti (glass enamel) and marble are cut into pieces using a hammer and a hardy (a pointed blade) embedded in a log. Vitreous glass is cut into pieces using a pair of nippers. Mosaics can be made using a direct or indirect method. In the direct method, the tesserae are laid directly into a bed of cement–based adhesive. In the indirect method, the design is drawn in reverse on paper or cloth. The tesserae are then stuck face-down on the paper or cloth using water-soluble glue. Adhesive is spread with a trowel on to a solid surface – such as a wall – and the back of the mosaic is laid into the adhesive. Finally, the paper or cloth is soaked off to reveal the mosaic. Gaps between tesserae can be filled with grout. Grout is forced into gaps by dragging a grouting squeegee across the face of the mosaic. Mosaics are usually used to decorate walls and floors, but they can also be applied to smaller objects.

EQUIPMENT FOR BREAKING MARBLE

Sawn strip of marble, ready for breaking into cubes

Mosaic hammer

NIPPERS

Hardwearing, tungsten carbide tip

Alicante (red marble) pieces

Hardy (pointed blade) embedded in a log

MOSAIC TOOLS

CEMENT-BASED ADHESIVE

GROUT

SMALTI (GLASS ENAMEL)

RED SMALTI

EXAMPLE OF A MOSAIC (DIRECT METHOD)
Seascape, Tessa Hunkin, 1993
Smalti mosaic on board
80 cm (31½ in) diameter

Handle with rubber grip

Gold-leaf smalti

YELLOW SMALTI

BLUE SMALTI

TROWEL

Notch

Wooden handle

Steel blade

Wooden handle

GROUTING SQUEEGEE

Wooden handle

Rubber blade

Nicobond

STAGES IN THE CREATION OF A MOSAIC (INDIRECT METHOD)

COLOUR SKETCH
A colour sketch is drawn
in oil pastel to give a clear
impression of how the finished
mosaic will look.

REVERSE IMAGE
Tesserae are glued face-down
on reverse image on paper.
Mosaic is then attached to solid
surface and paper is removed.

MOSAIC POT

Geometric design

Grout

MOSAIC MOSQUE DESIGN

Floral design

Geometric border

Andamenti (line along which tesserae are laid)

Grout fills the gaps between the tesserae

Mosaic mounted on board

Vitreous glass cut into triangular shape with nippers

Gold tessera with ripple finish

Gold tessera placed upside-down

FINISHED MOSAIC
Goldfish, Tessa Hunkin, 1993
Vitreous glass mosaic on board
35.5 x 25.5 cm (14 x 10 in)

Border of square vitreous glass

VITREOUS GLASS

GREEN VITREOUS GLASS WITH GOLD LEAF

Plain finish

Ripple finish

RED VITREOUS GLASS

BLUE VITREOUS GLASS

SHEETS OF VITREOUS GLASS

Sculpture 1

THE TWO TRADITIONAL METHODS OF MAKING SCULPTURE are carving and modelling. A carved sculpture is made by cutting away the surplus from a block of hard material such as stone, marble, or wood. The tools used for carving vary according to the material being carved. Heavy steel points, claws, and chisels that are struck with a lump hammer are generally used for stone and marble. Sharp gouges and chisels that are struck with a wooden mallet are used for wood. Sculptures formed from hard materials are generally finished by filing with rasps, rifflers, and other abrasive implements. Modelling is a process by which shapes are built up, using malleable materials such as clay, plaster, and wax. The material is cut with wire-ended tools and modelled with the fingers or a variety of hardwood and metal implements. For large or intricate modelled sculptures an armature (frame), made from metal or wood, is used to provide internal support. Sculptures formed in soft materials may harden naturally or can be made more durable by firing in a kiln. Modelled sculptures are often first designed in wax or another material to be cast later in a metal (see pp. 454-455) such as bronze. The development of many new materials in the 20th century has enabled sculptors to experiment with new techniques such as construction (joining preformed pieces of material such as machine components, mirrors, and furniture) and kinetic (mobile) sculpture.

EXAMPLES OF MARBLE CARVING TOOLS

1.1 kg (2½ lb) iron head

Ash handle

LUMP HAMMER

EXAMPLES OF WOODCARVING TOOLS

CABINET RASP

STRAIGHT GOUGE

SALMON BEND GOUGE

CHISEL

Stone for sharpening woodcarving tools

Cedar box

ARKANSAS HONE-STONE

CARVING MALLET

CALLIPERS

Curved leg

Gap measures distance between two points on a sculpture

Wing nut

EXAMPLES OF RIFFLERS (FOR STONE, MARBLE, AND WOOD)

30 CM (12 IN) RIFFLER

15 CM (6 IN) RIFFLER

Surface for sharpening stonecarving tools

WIDE MARBLE CLAW

NARROW MARBLE CLAW

POINT

FLAT CHISEL

BULLNOSE CHISEL

DIAMOND WHETSTONE

*Tiny holes along
the hairline made
with a point*

*Soft skin texture tooled
with a fine-toothed
marble claw*

**DETAIL OF
SLAVE'S HEAD**

EXAMPLE OF A CARVED MARBLE SCULPTURE
The Rebel Slave, Michelangelo, 1513-1516
Marble, height 213 cm (7ft)

*Hair worked
with a narrow
claw*

*Translucent white
marble, quarried at
Carrara, Italy*

*Surface rubbed
smooth with
rifflers and
pumice*

*Strut gives added
support to long
slender limb*

*Base scored with
jagged parallel
cuts made with
point and lump
hammer*

*Series of tiny
punch holes,
made with a
fine point,
outline the
form*

*The dimensions of the marble block
determine the size of the sculpture*

EXAMPLE OF A CARVED WOOD SCULPTURE
Mary Magdalene, Donatello, 1454-1455
Poplar wood, height 188 cm (6 ft 2 in)

*Delicately
modelled
hand carved
with a chisel*

*Hair
highlighted
with gold
leaf*

*Figure cut
from single
length of
poplar*

*Deep
ridges of
hair cut
with a
gouge*

*Wood prepared
with gesso
(chalk and glue)
and painted*

*Foot carved in
deep relief*

*Rough surface
made by driving
a point into the
marble at an
oblique angle*

DETAIL OF SLAVE'S FOOT

Sculpture 2

EXAMPLES OF MODELLING TOOLS

WIRE-ENDED CUTTING TOOL

CURVED MOULDING TOOL

SPATULA-ENDED WAX MODELLING TOOL

ROUNDED WAX MODELLING TOOL

EXAMPLES OF BRONZE FINISHING TOOLS

HOOKED RIFFLER   **POINTED RIFFLER**

SPIRIT LAMP (FOR HEATING WAX MODELLING TOOLS)

Wick

Brass holder

Glass bowl

Methylated spirit

STAGES IN THE LOST-WAX METHOD OF CASTING
Based on Mars, Giambologna, c.1546

Wax-covered wire armature

ORIGINAL MODEL
An original, solid wax model is made and preserved so that numerous replicas can be cast.

Wax riser (vertical, hollow rod)

Chaplet (iron nail)

Wax runner (horizontal, hollow rod)

HOLLOW WAX FIGURE IS CAST
A new, hollow wax model is cast from the original model. It is filled with a plaster core that is held in place with nails. Wax runners and risers are attached.

Fire-resistant clay

FIGURE IS BAKED IN CASTING MOULD
The model is encased in clay and baked. The wax melts away (through the channels made by the wax rods) and is replaced by molten bronze.

MODELLING STAND AND ARMATURE

Aluminium wire figure

Fixed iron armature support

Screw-hole for fastening the iron to modelling board

Marine ply modelling board

Aluminium table stand

Rotating table top

Height adjustor

Tripod

EXAMPLE OF A CLAY MODEL
Madonna and Child, Henry Moore, 1943
Terracotta, height 18.4 cm (7¼ in)

Clay smoothed to create the effect of soft skin

Maquette (small sketch) modelled from a solid lump of clay

Terracotta clay, fires at 1,000°C to 1,050°C (1,832°F to 1,922°F)

Incision made with serrated tool

Model for a much larger bronze sculpture

Strips of clay, added to the model, give the effect of folded drapery

Roughly worked clay

Metal riser

Metal runner

STATUE IS STRIPPED OF CLAY
When the bronze has cooled, the clay mould is broken open to reveal the bronze statue with solid metal runners and risers.

Golden brown colour of untreated bronze

Stump left by rod will be filed down

Hole left by nail will be plugged with bronze

STATUE IS FINISHED
The nails are pulled out and a large hole is made to remove the plaster core. When the metal rods have been sawn off, the sculpture is filed to refine the surface.

Dark brown patina

STATUE IS CLEANED
Finally the work is cleaned and polished. An artificial patina (colouring) is achieved by treating the surface with chemicals.

ARCHITECTURE

Ancient Egypt

FRONT VIEW OF HYPOSTYLE HALL, TEMPLE OF AMON-RE

Cornice decorated with cavetto moulding

THE CIVILIZATION OF THE ANCIENT EGYPTIANS (which lasted from about 3100 BC until it was finally absorbed into the Roman empire in 30 BC) is famous for its temples and tombs. Egyptian temples were often huge and geometric, like the Temple of Amon-Re (below and right). They were usually decorated with hieroglyphs (sacred characters used for picture-writing) and painted reliefs depicting gods, Pharaohs (kings), and queens. Tombs were particularly important to the Egyptians, who believed that the dead were resurrected in the after-life. The tombs were often decorated – as, for example, the surround of the false door opposite – in order to give comfort to the dead. The best-known ancient Egyptian tombs are the pyramids, which were designed to symbolize the rays of the sun. Many of the architectural forms used by the ancient Egyptians were later adopted by other civilizations; for example, columns and capitals were later used by the ancient Greeks (see pp. 460-461) and ancient Romans (see pp. 462-465).

Campaniform (open papyrus) capital

Architrave

Papyrus-bud capital

Socle

Side aisle *Central nave* *Side aisle*

Horus, the sun-god *Architrave* *Stone slab forming flat roof of side aisle*

SIDE VIEW OF HYPOSTYLE HALL, TEMPLE OF AMON-RE, KARNAK, EGYPT, c.1290 BC

Kepresh crown with disc

Chons, the moon-god *Amon-Re, king of the gods* *Hathor, the sky-goddess* *Papyrus motif* *Cartouche (oval border) containing the titles of the Pharaoh (king)* *Socle* *Aisle running north-south*

**LIMESTONE FALSE DOOR WITH HIEROGLYPHS,
TOMB OF KING TJETJI, GIZA, EGYPT, c.2400 BC**

Lintel

Hieroglyph representing a house

Disc representing sun or light

Eroded image of Tjetji

Limestone stela (slab)

Hoe-shaped hieroglyph representing "mr" sound

Head of false door

Image of Tjetji's wife

Image of Tjetji's daughter

**PLANT CAPITAL OF THE
PTOLEMAIC-ROMAN PERIOD,
EGYPT, 332-30 BC**

Palm leaf

Papyrus flower

Papyrus leaf

Papyrus stem

Lotus bud

Lotus stem

Cornice decorated with cavetto moulding

Bead moulding

Trellis window

Rectangular pier decorated with hieroglyphs

Elevated roof of central nave

Clerestory

Disc representing sun or light

Architrave

Square abacus

Papyrus-bud capital

Papyriform column

Shaft

Scene depicting a Pharaoh (king) paying homage to the god Amon-Re

Central nave

**ANCIENT EGYPTIAN
BUILDING DECORATION**

**DECORATED WINDOW,
MEDINET HABU, EGYPT,
C.1198 BC**

**ROPE AND PATERAE
DECORATION**

**CAPITAL WITH THE HEAD OF THE
SKY-GODDESS HATHOR, TEMPLE
OF ISIS, PHILAE, EGYPT, 285-47 BC**

**LOTUS AND PAPYRUS
FRIEZE DECORATION**

Ancient Greece

THE CLASSICAL TEMPLES OF ANCIENT GREECE were built according to the belief that certain forms and proportions were pleasing to the gods. There were three main ancient Greek architectural orders (styles), which can be distinguished by the decoration and proportions of their columns, capitals (column tops), and entablatures (structures resting on the capitals). The oldest is the Doric order, which dates from the seventh century BC and was used mainly on the Greek mainland and in the western colonies, such as Sicily and southern Italy. The Temple of Neptune, shown here, is a classic example of this order. It is hypaethral (roofless) and peripteral (surrounded by a single row of columns). About a century later, the more decorative Ionic order developed on the Aegean Islands. Features of this order include volutes (spiral scrolls) on capitals and acroteria (pediment ornaments). The Corinthian order was invented in Athens in the fifth century BC and is typically identified by an acanthus leaf on the capitals. This order was later widely used in ancient Roman architecture.

CAPITALS OF THE THREE ORDERS OF ANCIENT GREEK ARCHITECTURE

Abacus
Echinus
Annulet
Trachelion (neck)

DORIC CAPITAL, THE PROPYLAEUM (GATEWAY), THE ACROPOLIS, ATHENS, GREECE, 449 BC

Coussinet (cushion)
Abacus
Lesbian leaf pattern
Cyma reversa profile
Volute
Echinus with egg and dart decoration
Eye
Palmette

IONIC CAPITAL, THE PROPYLAEUM (GATEWAY), TEMPLE OF ATHENA POLIAS, PRIENE, GREECE, c.334 BC

Mask
Abacus
Volute
Cauliculus
Acanthus leaf
Bell-shaped core

CORINTHIAN CAPITAL FROM A STOA (PORTICO), PROBABLY FROM ASIA MINOR

TEMPLE OF NEPTUNE, PAESTUM, ITALY, c.460 BC

Raking cornice
Pediment
Trachelion (neck)
Taenia
Triglyph
Metope
Glyph (channel)
Doric entablature
Pteron (external colonnade)
Euthynteria
Drum
Stylobate
Column of the Doric order

PLAN OF THE TEMPLE OF NEPTUNE, PAESTUM

Pronaos (vestibule)

Naos wall

Anta (pilaster terminating naos wall)

Naos (cella)

Peristyle

Opisthodomos (rear portico)

Pteron (external colonnade)

Hexastyle pteron (colonnade of six columns)

ANCIENT GREEK BUILDING DECORATION

Volute

FACADE, TREASURY OF ATREUS, MYCENAE, GREECE, 1350-1250 BC

Meander

FRETWORK, PARTHENON, ATHENS, GREECE, 447-436 BC

ACROTERION, TEMPLE OF APHAIA, AEGINA, GREECE, 490 BC

Griffon (gryphon)

Raking cornice

ANTEFIXA, TEMPLE OF APHAIA, AEGINA, GREECE, 490 BC

Palmette

Volute

Regula (short fillet beneath taenia)   Eaves

Cornice

Frieze

Architrave

Capital

Shaft

Crepidoma (stepped base)

Entasis (slight curve of a column)   Intercolumniation   Fluting

461

Ancient Rome 1

IN THE EARLY PERIOD OF THE ROMAN EMPIRE extensive use was made of ancient Greek architectural ideas, particularly those of the Corinthian order (see pp. 460-461). As a result, many early Roman buildings – such as the Temple of Vesta (opposite) – closely resemble ancient Greek buildings. A distinctive Roman style began to evolve in the first century AD. This style developed the interiors of buildings (the Greeks had concentrated on the exterior) by using arches, vaults, and domes inside the buildings, and by ornamenting internal walls. Many of these features can be seen in the Pantheon. Exterior columns were often used for decorative, rather than structural, purposes, as in the Colosseum and the Porta Nigra (see pp. 464-465). Smaller buildings had timber frames with wattle-and-daub walls, as in the mill (see pp. 464-465). Roman architecture remained influential for many centuries, with some of its principles being used in the 11th century in Romanesque buildings (see pp. 468-469) and also in the 15th and 16th centuries in Renaissance buildings (see pp. 474-477).

ANCIENT ROMAN BUILDING DECORATION

FESTOON, TEMPLE OF VESTA,
TIVOLI, ITALY, C.80 BC

RICHLY DECORATED
ROMAN OVUM

INTERIOR OF THE PANTHEON, ROME, ITALY, 118-c.128

Inner dome, following the curve of a depressed arch

Outer saucer dome

Entablature

Curved cornice

Lesene

Cornice

Triangular pediment

Concave niche

Relieving arch

Marble veneer

Segmental pediment

Pedestal

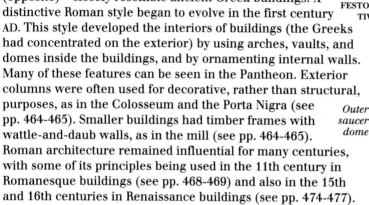

Oculus

Series of concentric, step-like rings

Dentil ornament

Engaged pediment

Raking cornice

Pediment

Rotunda

Outer saucer dome

Intermediate block

Entablature with inscription

Octastyle portico (eight-column portico)

FRONT VIEW OF THE PANTHEON

SIDE VIEW OF THE PANTHEON

Entablature

Pitched roof

Eaves

Intermediate block

Upper cornice

Relieving arch

Opening for ventilation

Cornice

Colonnade

Ornamental band decorated with festoons

Attached fluted pilaster

FRIEZE, FORUM OF TRAJAN, ROME,
ITALY, 98-113

KEYSTONE, ARCH OF TITUS,
ROME, ITALY, 81

TEMPLE OF VESTA, TIVOLI, ITALY, c.80 BC

Circular naos (cella)

Corinthian
entablature

Architrave

Ceiling

Fascia

Corinthian
capital

Pteron
(colonnade)

Naos (cella)
window

Opus incertum
(concrete wall
faced with
irregularly
shaped stones)

Egg and
dart
decoration

Upper
torus

Scotia

Lower torus

Jamb with
corrugated
surface

Naos
(cella)
door

Cornice

Threshold

Podium

Oculus illuminating
interior of rotunda

Coffer

Stepped side
of coffer

Step-like ring

Barrel vault

Passageway

Coffer

Frieze decorated
with arabesques,
urns, and
winged horses

Engaged
pediment

Monolithic shaft
(shaft made
from a single
stone)

Barrel vault

Raking cornice

Pediment

Entablature

Corinthian
column

Entablature

Aedicule (tabernacle)

Festoon

Fluting

Corinthian pilaster

Base

Corinthian
capital

Rotunda

Portico

Ancient Rome 2

SIDE VIEW OF A ROMAN MILL

Lath
Pantile
Principal rafter
Verge
Wall-plate
Eaves
Wall-post
Plain fascia
Top-plate
Plaster coating
Floorboard
Intermediate floor-joist
Sill
Stud
Foundation
Grille
Joist
Boarding

FRONT VIEW OF A ROMAN MILL, 1ST CENTURY BC

Half-round ridge tile
King-strut
Lath
Pitched roof
Principal rafter
Ashlar post
Tie-beam
Plain fascia
Wall-plate
Flat soffit
Intermediate floor-joist
Top-plate
Wall-post
Sill
Binder
Mill wheel
Wattle-and-daub wall with plaster coating
Supporting post
Floor-joist
Foundation post

THE COLOSSEUM (FLAVIAN AMPHITHEATRE), ROME, ITALY, 70-82

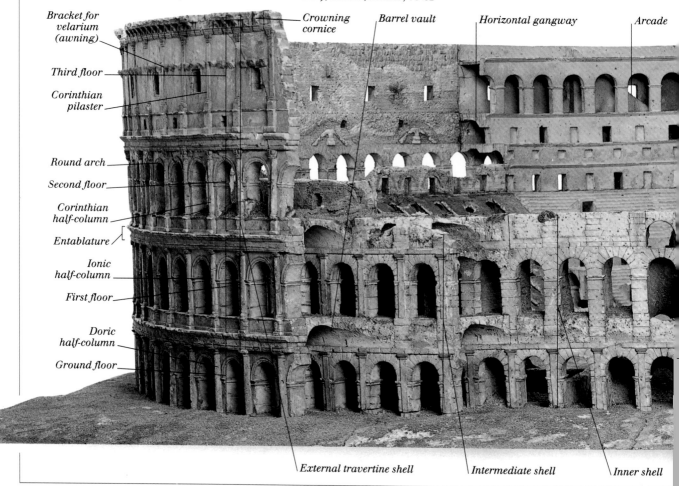

Bracket for velarium (awning)
Crowning cornice
Barrel vault
Horizontal gangway
Arcade
Third floor
Corinthian pilaster
Round arch
Second floor
Corinthian half-column
Entablature
Ionic half-column
First floor
Doric half-column
Ground floor
External travertine shell
Intermediate shell
Inner shell

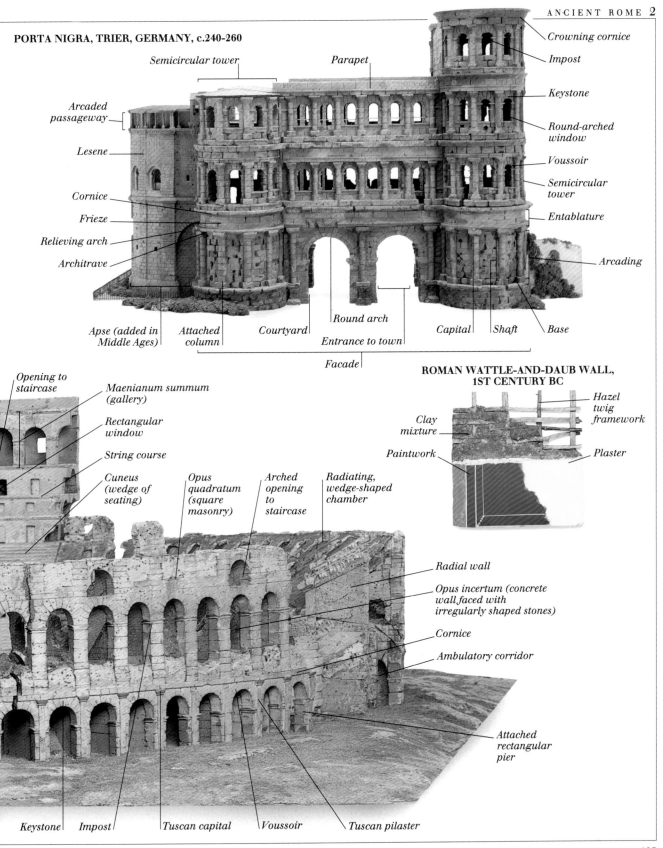

PORTA NIGRA, TRIER, GERMANY, c.240-260

Crowning cornice

Impost

Semicircular tower

Parapet

Keystone

Arcaded passageway

Round-arched window

Lesene

Voussoir

Cornice

Semicircular tower

Frieze

Entablature

Relieving arch

Architrave

Arcading

Apse (added in Middle Ages)

Attached column

Courtyard

Round arch

Entrance to town

Capital

Shaft

Base

Facade

ROMAN WATTLE-AND-DAUB WALL, 1ST CENTURY BC

Opening to staircase

Maenianum summum (gallery)

Rectangular window

Hazel twig framework

Clay mixture

String course

Plaster

Paintwork

Cuneus (wedge of seating)

Opus quadratum (square masonry)

Arched opening to staircase

Radiating, wedge-shaped chamber

Radial wall

Opus incertum (concrete wall, faced with irregularly shaped stones)

Cornice

Ambulatory corridor

Attached rectangular pier

Keystone

Impost

Tuscan capital

Voussoir

Tuscan pilaster

Medieval castles and houses

WARFARE WAS COMMON IN EUROPE in the Middle Ages, and many monarchs and nobles built castles as a form of defence. Typical medieval castles have outer walls surrounding a moat. Inside the moat is a bailey (courtyard), protected by a chemise (jacket-wall). The innermost and strongest part of a medieval castle is the keep. There are two main types of keep: towers called donjons, such as the Tour de César and Coucy-le-Château, and rectangular keeps ("hall-keeps"), such as the Tower of London. Castles were often guarded by salients (projecting fortifications), like those of the Bastille. Medieval houses typically had timber cruck (tent-like) frames, wattle-and-daub walls, and pitched roofs, like those on medieval London Bridge (opposite).

DONJON, TOUR DE CESAR, PROVINS, FRANCE, 12TH CENTURY

Oculus — Battlements (crenellations)
Loophole — Hemispherical cupola
Conical spire — Gallery
Flying buttress — Squinch
Hexahedral hall — Vaulted room
Semicircular turret — Main entrance
Fireplace — Staircase to chemise (jacket-wall)
Bailey —
Embrasure —
Chemise (jacket-wall) — Plain impost — Depressed cupola — Vaulted staircase — Motte

Loophole

SALIENT, CAERNARVON CASTLE, BRITAIN, 1283-1323

Timber cruck frame

CRUCK-FRAMED HOUSE, BRITAIN, c.1200

Blind, rounded relieving arch — Merlon — Battlements (crenellations)
Tetrahedral spire — Crenel — Loophole
Rectangular turret — Wooden staircase leading to entrance above ground level
Quoin — Timber-framed house
Cornice —
Buttress —
Round-arched window with twin openings — Cruck frame — Paling

TOWER OF LONDON, BRITAIN, FROM 1070

Curtain wall — Pointed relieving arch — Semicircular relieving arch — Plain string course — Bracket decorated with scroll moulding

Rectangular window — Sunken rectangular panel — Round-arched window — Semicircular salient — Loophole — Lateral circular salient

THE BASTILLE, PARIS, FRANCE, 14TH CENTURY

MEDIEVAL LONDON BRIDGE, BRITAIN, 1176 (WITH 14TH-CENTURY BATTLEMENTED BUILDING, NONESUCH HOUSE, AND TWO-TOWERED GATE)

Gate-house

Battlemented building

Chapel pier

Railing

Onion-shaped dome

Pitched roof

Shaped gable

Nonesuch House

Timber framing with ornamental woodwork

Crypt of Becket Chapel

Starling

Pier

Two-towered gate

Pointed Gothic stone arch

Oriel window

Timber framing

DONJON, COUCY-LE-CHATEAU, AISNE, FRANCE, 1225-1245

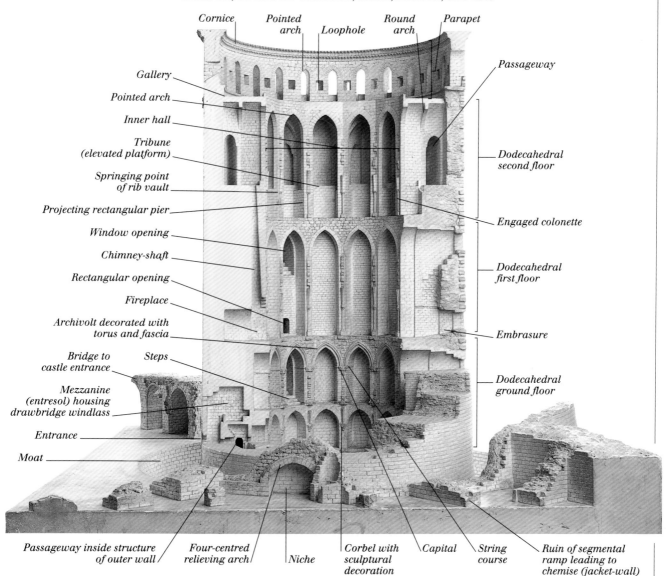

Cornice

Pointed arch

Loophole

Round arch

Parapet

Passageway

Gallery

Pointed arch

Inner hall

Tribune (elevated platform)

Springing point of rib vault

Projecting rectangular pier

Window opening

Chimney-shaft

Rectangular opening

Fireplace

Archivolt decorated with torus and fascia

Bridge to castle entrance

Steps

Mezzanine (entresol) housing drawbridge windlass

Entrance

Moat

Dodecahedral second floor

Engaged colonette

Dodecahedral first floor

Embrasure

Dodecahedral ground floor

Passageway inside structure of outer wall

Four-centred relieving arch

Niche

Corbel with sculptural decoration

Capital

String course

Ruin of segmental ramp leading to chemise (jacket-wall)

Medieval churches

DURING THE MIDDLE AGES, large numbers of churches were built in Europe. European churches of this period typically have high vaults supported by massive piers and columns. In the 10th century, the Romanesque style developed. Romanesque architects adopted many Roman or early Christian architectural ideas, such as cross-shaped ground-plans – like that of Angoulême Cathedral (opposite) – and the basilican system of a nave with a central vessel and side aisles. In the mid-12th century, flying buttresses and pointed vaults appeared. These features later became widely used in Gothic architecture (see pp. 470-471). Bagneux Church (opposite) has both styles: a Romanesque tower, and a Gothic nave and choir.

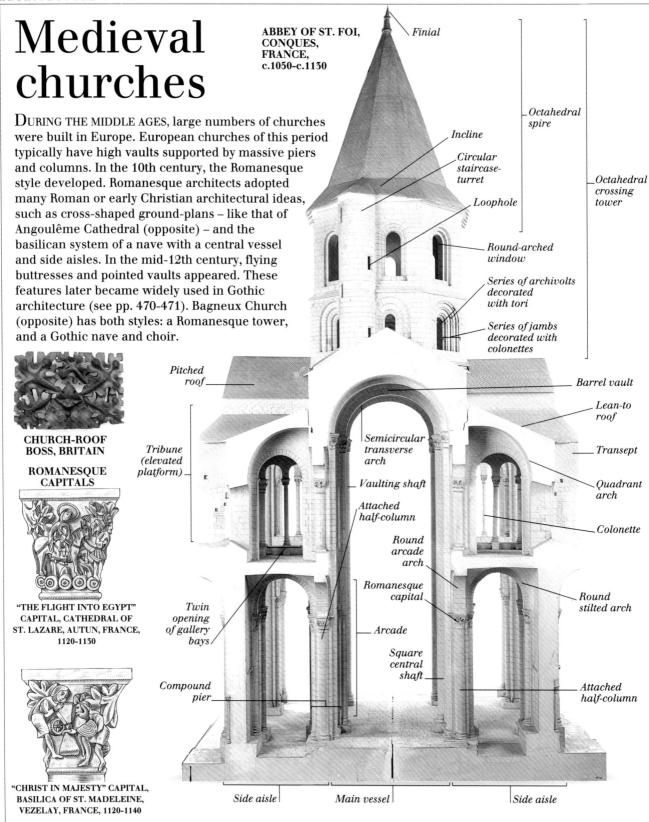

ABBEY OF ST. FOI, CONQUES, FRANCE, c.1050-c.1130

Finial

Incline

Circular staircase-turret

Loophole

Octahedral spire

Octahedral crossing tower

Round-arched window

Series of archivolts decorated with tori

Series of jambs decorated with colonettes

Pitched roof

Barrel vault

Lean-to roof

Tribune (elevated platform)

Semicircular transverse arch

Vaulting shaft

Attached half-column

Transept

Quadrant arch

Colonette

Round arcade arch

Romanesque capital

Round stilted arch

Twin opening of gallery bays

Arcade

Compound pier

Square central shaft

Attached half-column

Side aisle

Main vessel

Side aisle

CHURCH-ROOF BOSS, BRITAIN

ROMANESQUE CAPITALS

"THE FLIGHT INTO EGYPT" CAPITAL, CATHEDRAL OF ST. LAZARE, AUTUN, FRANCE, 1120-1150

"CHRIST IN MAJESTY" CAPITAL, BASILICA OF ST. MADELEINE, VEZELAY, FRANCE, 1120-1140

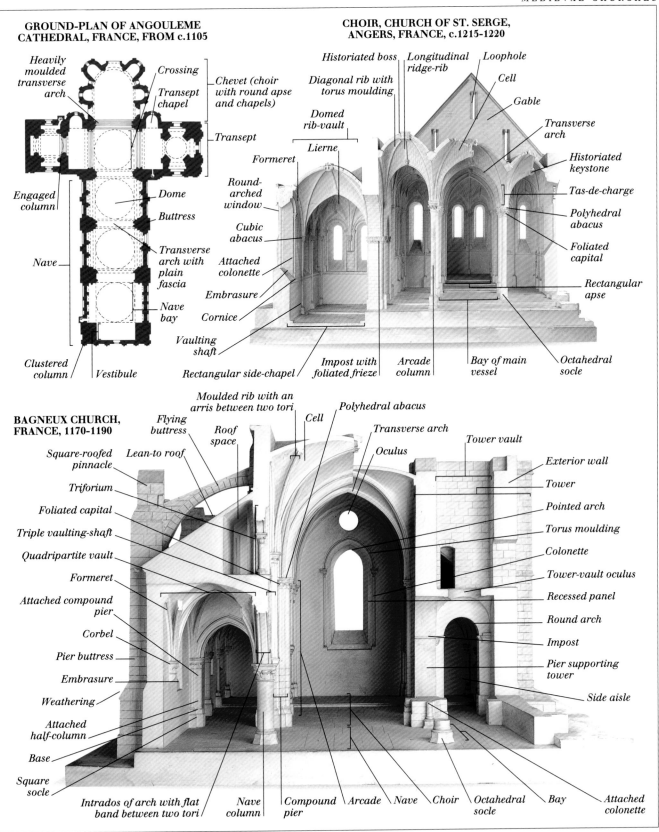

GROUND-PLAN OF ANGOULEME CATHEDRAL, FRANCE, FROM c.1105

Heavily moulded transverse arch
Crossing
Transept chapel
Chevet (choir with round apse and chapels)
Transept
Engaged column
Dome
Buttress
Nave
Transverse arch with plain fascia
Nave bay
Clustered column
Vestibule

CHOIR, CHURCH OF ST. SERGE, ANGERS, FRANCE, c.1215-1220

Historiated boss
Longitudinal ridge-rib
Loophole
Cell
Diagonal rib with torus moulding
Gable
Domed rib-vault
Transverse arch
Lierne
Historiated keystone
Formeret
Tas-de-charge
Round-arched window
Polyhedral abacus
Cubic abacus
Foliated capital
Attached colonette
Embrasure
Rectangular apse
Cornice
Vaulting shaft
Rectangular side-chapel
Impost with foliated frieze
Arcade column
Bay of main vessel
Octahedral socle

BAGNEUX CHURCH, FRANCE, 1170-1190

Moulded rib with an arris between two tori
Polyhedral abacus
Flying buttress
Cell
Transverse arch
Roof space
Tower vault
Square-roofed pinnacle
Lean-to roof
Oculus
Exterior wall
Triforium
Tower
Foliated capital
Pointed arch
Triple vaulting-shaft
Torus moulding
Quadripartite vault
Colonette
Formeret
Tower-vault oculus
Attached compound pier
Recessed panel
Corbel
Round arch
Pier buttress
Impost
Embrasure
Pier supporting tower
Weathering
Side aisle
Attached half-column
Base
Square socle
Intrados of arch with flat band between two tori
Nave column
Compound pier
Arcade
Nave
Choir
Octahedral socle
Bay
Attached colonette

Gothic 1

GOTHIC STAINED
GLASS WITH FOLIATED
SCROLL MOTIF, ON
WOODEN FORM

GOTHIC BUILDINGS are characterized by rib vaults, pointed or lancet arches, flying buttresses, decorative tracery and gables, and stained-glass windows. Typical Gothic buildings include the Cathedrals of Salisbury and old St. Paul's in England, and Notre Dame de Paris in France (see pp. 472-473). The Gothic style developed out of Romanesque architecture in France (see pp. 468-469) in the mid-12th century, and then spread throughout Europe. The decorative elements of Gothic architecture became highly developed in buildings of the English Decorated style (late 13th-14th century) and the French Flamboyant style (15th-16th century). These styles are exemplified by the tower of Salisbury Cathedral and the staircase in the Church of St. Maclou (see pp. 472-473), respectively. In both of these styles, embellishments such as ballflowers and curvilinear (flowing) tracery were used liberally. The English Perpendicular style (late 14th-15th century), which followed the Decorated style, emphasized the vertical and horizontal elements of a building. A notable feature of this style is the hammer-beam roof.

GROUND-PLAN OF SALISBURY CATHEDRAL

- Altar
- Square east end
- Trinity Chapel (Lady Chapel)
- Monument
- High altar
- Reredos (choir-screen)
- Processional path
- Side chapel
- South choir-aisle
- Choir
- East transept
- Sacristy
- Choir-stall
- Crossing
- Organ
- Transept aisle
- West transept
- Crossing pier
- Staircase
- Pier buttress
- Arcade pier (nave pier)
- Arcade
- North porch
- Main vessel
- Nave
- South aisle
- North aisle
- Facade wall
- Turret

GOTHIC TORUS WITH BALLFLOWERS

- Limestone block
- Block members carved into rolls
- Block members cut polygonally
- Pencil guideline
- Early stage of ballflower carving

BLOCK AFTER INITIAL CUTTING

BLOCK WITH MEMBERS CUT INTO ROLLS

- Torus
- Ballflower
- Fillet
- Mason's mark

FINISHED BLOCK

- Trinity Chapel (Lady Chapel)
- Choir
- Finial
- Octahedral pinnacle with small spire
- Blind semi-arch
- Staggered triple lancet windows
- Turret-like pinnacle
- Parapet decorated with blind arches filled with trefoils
- Mullion
- Stained glass
- Base
- Cornice
- Buttress
- Lean-to roof
- East transept facade

Weather-vane

Orb

NORTH SIDE, SALISBURY CATHEDRAL, BRITAIN, 1220-1280 (STEEPLE AND SPIRE ADDED DURING 14TH CENTURY)

WEST FACADE, SALISBURY CATHEDRAL

Spire

Band with lozenge decoration

Semi-attached gable with small pilasters

Turret-like pinnacle

Ballflower decoration

Traceried parapet with lozenge decoration

Octahedral turret

Row of blind arches filled with trefoils

Battlemented cornice

Cinquefoil moulding

Spire-like pinnacle

Blind gabled arch

Gable

Octafoil

Angle buttress

West transept facade

Weathering

Pier buttress

Blind lancet

Flying buttress

Trefoil decoration

North porch

Archivolt

Twin lancet window under pointed arch, crowned by a quatrefoil

Trefoil in a spandrel

Aureole

Gable

Blind rhombus tracery filled with a quatrefoil

Staggered triple lancet window

Finial

Spire

Parapet

Pitched roof

Row of blind trefoil arches

Staggered triple lancet window

Blind pointed arches filled with twin lancets and quatrefoils

Parapet

Small gable crowning buttress

Projecting turret

Angle buttress

Row of gabled niches under trefoil arches

North porch

Blind semi-arch

Lateral porch

Crocket

Main porch

Niche under small gabled roof

Nave

Spire

Moulded side of gable

Spire-like pinnacle

Pitched roof

Flying buttress

Lateral turret

Small gable crowning buttress

Crocket

Buttress

Gothic 2

CURVILINEAR (FLOWING) TRACERY FROM A BALUSTRADE, 14TH OR 15TH CENTURY

Cyma reversa (reversed ogee curve)

Cavetto moulding

Plain fascia

Moulded cornice

Cavetto moulding with elongated lower part

Mouchette (curved dagger)

Ogee curve

Cusp

Drop shape

Cavetto moulding

SPIRAL STAIRCASE TO ORGAN, CHURCH OF ST. MACLOU, ROUEN, FRANCE, c.1519

Trefoil

Mouchette (curved dagger)

Foliated scrollwork

Pointed arch

Winding cornice

Rectangular buttress

Attached gable

Gabled canopy

Statue

Base

Basket arch

Socle

Cross motif

Flamboyant tracery

Cherub

Crocket

Figure

Niche

Attached gable

Square pillar

Dagger

Round arch

Base decorated with ovolo mouldings

TOWER AND PART OF THE NAVE AND CHOIR, OLD ST. PAUL'S CATHEDRAL, LONDON, BRITAIN, 1087-1666

Octahedral spire

Parapet

Turret-like pinnacle

Angle buttress

Lancet window with twin lancets and crowned with a quatrefoil

Tower

Niche

Pointed arch filled with geometrical tracery

Turret-like pinnacle

Flying buttress

Mullion

Pitched roof

Lancet window

Blind lancet arch

Window filled with early English Perpendicular-style tracery

Buttress

Octahedral chapter-house

Oculus

Cloister

Early English-style window

Gable

Couronnement

Parapet decorated with quatrefoils

Pointed arch filled with tracery and three lancet windows

Clerestory wall

Lean-to roof

Outer wall of side aisle

Weathering

Oculus filled with multifoil

Nave

Transept facade

Choir

Ridge

Common rafter

Architrave of window zone, also acting as collar-beam

SPIRE AND TRANSEPT ROOF, CATHEDRAL OF NOTRE DAME DE PARIS, FRANCE, c.1163-1250

Principal

Attached baluster

Attached column

Strut

Raised surface

Hammer-post

Bevelled edge

Arched brace

Wooden panel

Hammer-beam

Gothic window tracery

Collar-beam decorated with pearl motif

Gothic window

Arched brace

Bracket

Brace

Impost

TRUSS OF HAMMER-BEAM ROOF, THE UPPER FRATER (LATER BLACKFRIARS' PLAYHOUSE), LONDON, BRITAIN, PROBABLY 14TH CENTURY

TYPICAL GOTHIC FEATURES

Rafter

Straight brace

Beam

Gable

Round arch

Pinnacle

Oculus

Blind trefoil

Lancet arch

Trefoil arch

Cusp

Quatrefoil

Colonette

Pointed arch

Lesene

Lancet arch

Balustrade

Mullion

Triangular cornice

Cornice with chamfered edge

Geometrical tracery

Trefoil arch

Balustrade

Stud

Upper collar

Scissor brace

Ridge-board

Principal rafter

Common rafter

FLYING BUTTRESS OVER SIDE AISLES, MILAN CATHEDRAL, ITALY, C.1385-1485

GARGOYLE, HORSLEY CHURCH, DERBYSHIRE, BRITAIN, C.1450

Octahedral spire

Roof truss of nave and transept

Vertical strut

Intermediate collar

Raised valley-rafter

Beam

Jack-rafter

Clasped purlin

Lower collar

King-post

Queen-post

Scissor-beam

Tie-beam

Passing brace

HAMMER-BEAM ROOF, CHURCH OF ST. BOTOLPH, TRUNCH, NORFOLK, BRITAIN, 1360-1380

Renaissance 1

THE RENAISSANCE was a European movement – lasting roughly from the 14th century to the mid-17th century – in which the arts and sciences underwent great changes. In architecture, these changes were marked by a return to the classical forms and proportions of ancient Roman buildings. The Renaissance originated in Italy, and the buildings most characteristic of its style can be found there, such as the Palazzo Strozzi shown here. Mannerism is a branch of the Renaissance style that distorts the classical forms; an example is the Laurentian Library staircase. As the Renaissance style spread to other European countries, many of its features were incorporated into the local architecture; for example, the Château de Montal in France (see pp. 476-477) incorporates aedicules (tabernacles).

FACADE ON TO PIAZZA, PALAZZO STROZZI

Crowning cornice

Arched window

Round arch

Light

Rustication

Arched doorway

Rectangular window

SIDE VIEW OF PALAZZO STROZZI, FLORENCE, ITALY, 1489 (BY G. DA SANGALLO, B. DA MAIANO, AND CRONACA)

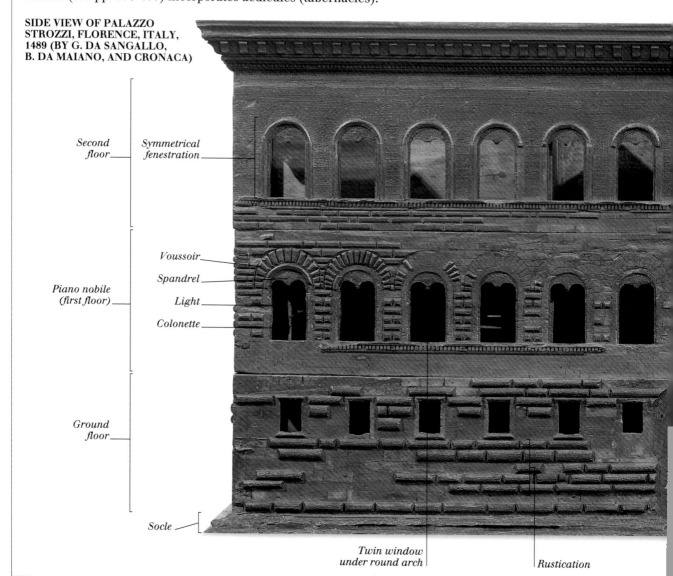

Second floor

Symmetrical fenestration

Voussoir

Spandrel

Light

Colonette

Piano nobile (first floor)

Ground floor

Socle

Twin window under round arch

Rustication

DETAILS FROM ITALIAN RENAISSANCE BUILDINGS

**PANEL FROM DRUM OF DOME,
FLORENCE CATHEDRAL, 1420-1436**

**COFFERING IN DOME,
PAZZI CHAPEL,
FLORENCE, 1429-1461**

**STAIRCASE,
LAURENTIAN LIBRARY,
FLORENCE, 1559**

**PORTICO, VILLA ROTUNDA,
VICENZA, 1567-1569**

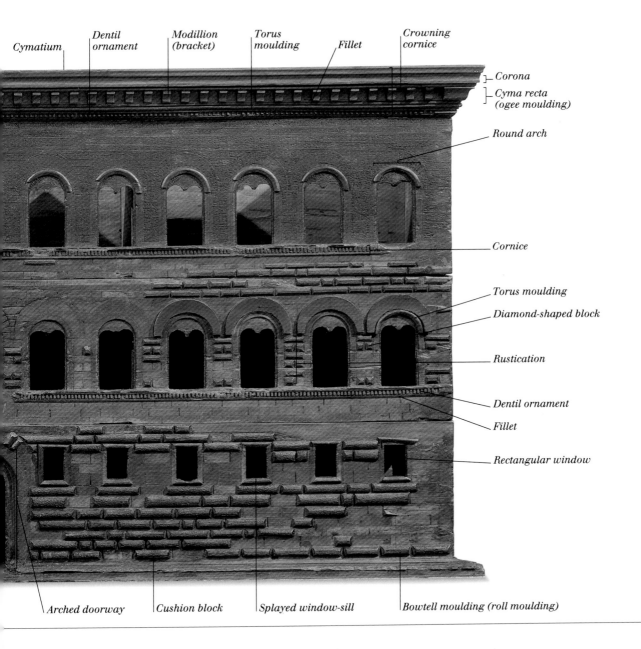

Cymatium

Dentil ornament

Modillion (bracket)

Torus moulding

Fillet

Crowning cornice

Corona

Cyma recta (ogee moulding)

Round arch

Cornice

Torus moulding

Diamond-shaped block

Rustication

Dentil ornament

Fillet

Rectangular window

Arched doorway

Cushion block

Splayed window-sill

Bowtell moulding (roll moulding)

Renaissance 2

NORTH WING, CHATEAU DE MONTAL, LOT, FRANCE, FROM 1523

DETAILS FROM EUROPEAN RENAISSANCE BUILDINGS

STONE WALL, QUOINS, AND SHELL DECORATION, CASA DE LAS CONCHAS, SALAMANCA, SPAIN, 1475-1483

SPIRAL-STAIRCASE TOWER, CHATEAU DE BLOIS, FRANCE, 1514-1530

CONICAL DOME, CHATEAU DE CHAMBORD, FRANCE, 1519-1547

PAIR OF CHIMNEY-STACKS, PALAIS DE FONTAINEBLEAU, FRANCE, FROM 1528

Hipped roof

Conical spire of turret

Fish-scale tile

Belvedere

Chimney-stack

Ridge of half-round tiles

Pitched roof

Finial

Medallion

Pinnacle

Foliated volute with dolphin head

Gable

Head-shaped keystone

Dormer window

Frieze with shell-pattern decoration

Finial

Ionic capital with head-shaped decoration

Putto holding candelabrum

Blind pediment

Grotesque figure

Medallion with bust of Robert de Montal

Lesene decorated with paterae

Frieze decorated with sculptural wreaths, tendrils, and grotesque figures

Lesene

Pedestal

Dado

Keystone decorated with scroll ornament

Cornice decorated with fascias and an ogee moulding

Rectangular window

Transom

Aedicule (tabernacle)

Double pilaster

Mullion

Shell

Concave, arched niche

Small pier decorated with statuette in concave niche

Cornice

Frieze with scroll motif

Pseudo-Corinthian capital

Plinth   Cornice   Architrave   Portal   Pilaster

NORTH-WING STAIRCASE, CHATEAU DE MONTAL

Hipped roof

Conical spire

Turret

Eaves with oversailing fascias and fillets

Loophole

Cornice with fascias and ogee mouldings

Rib vault

Column

Second-floor landing

Conical corbel

First-floor landing

Flight of stairs

Lesene

Pier supporting flight of stairs

Handrail

Pier supporting first-floor landing

Riser

Tread

CAMPANILE, CHURCH OF ST. EUSTACHE, PARIS, FRANCE, 1532-1640

Weather-vane

Orb

Fish-scale tile

Hemispherical dome

Semicircular torus moulding

Weathering

Fillet

Ogee moulding

Plain fascia

Small architrave

Archivolt

Plain fascia

Volute

Cavetto moulding

Emphasized keystone

Capital

Cincture

Fillet

Zinc plating

Square pillar

GLOBE THEATRE, LONDON, BRITAIN, 1599

Hipped roof

Timber-framed hut, housing windlass

Turret

Balustrade

Ornamental panelling

Pitched roof

Thatched roof

Balcony stage

Stage cover

Music gallery

Ornamental panelling with concave brace decoration

Light curtain

Loft used as storage room

Door to dressing-rooms

Window stage

Box (gentlemen's room)

Outer wall

Upper gallery (twopenny gallery)

Railing

Post supporting bay window

Middle gallery

Upper-gallery support

Stage-door

Lower gallery

Standing room

Bench

Round pillar (stage-post)

Square, carved base

Study (inner stage) with traverse (crossing)

Platform stage

Low balustrade

Paling

Door to tiring-house

Partition separating galleries from boxes

Baroque and neoclassical 1

THE BAROQUE STYLE EVOLVED IN THE EARLY 17TH CENTURY in Rome. It is characterized by curved outlines and ostentatious decoration, as can be seen in the Italian church details (right). The baroque style was particularly widely favoured in Italy, Spain, and Germany. It was also adopted in Britain and France, but with adaptations. The British architects Sir Christopher Wren and Nicholas Hawksmoor, for example, used baroque features – such as the concave walls of St. Paul's Cathedral and the curved buttresses of the Church of St. George in the East (see pp. 480-481) – but they did so with restraint. Similarly, the curved buttresses and volutes of the Parisian Church of St. Paul-St. Louis are relatively plain. In the second half of the 17th century, a distinct classical style (known as neoclassicism) developed in northern Europe as a reaction to the excesses of baroque. Typical of this new style were churches such as the Madeleine (a proposed facade is shown below), as well as secular buildings such as the Cirque Napoleon (opposite) and the buildings of the British architect Sir John Soane (see pp. 482-483). In early 18th-century France, an extremely lavish form of baroque developed, known as rococo. The balcony from Nantes (see pp. 482-483) with its twisted ironwork and head-shaped corbels is typical of this style.

SCROLLED BUTTRESS,
CHURCH OF ST. MARIA DELLA
SALUTE, VENICE, 1631-1682

STATUE OF THE ECSTASY OF
ST. THERESA, CHURCH OF ST. MARIA
DELLA VITTORIA, ROME, 1645-1652

PROPOSED FACADE, THE MADELEINE (NEOCLASSICAL), PARIS, FRANCE, 1764 (BY P. CONTANT D'IVRY)

CIRQUE NAPOLEON (NEOCLASSICAL), PARIS, FRANCE, 1852 (BY J.I. HITTORFF)

EXTERIOR

Rectangular panel

Small polyhedral roof

Attached colonette

Polyhedral iron roof

Projecting entablature

Palmette

Sculpted frieze

Cornice

Pedestal

Smooth, vertical rustication

Statue of Amazon on horseback

Hanging wreath

Dado (die)

Plinth

Smooth rustication

Projecting pedestal

Eagle carrying festoons

INTERIOR

King-post

Statue of Minerva

Tie-beam

Orb

Painted inner roof

Brace

Polyhedral lantern

Roll moulding

Strut

Straight brace

Projecting entablature

Crest

Projecting socle

Outer wall

Attached Corinthian column

Frieze painted with scenes from classical mythology

Circle (auditorium)

Finial with cavetto moulding

Foliated panel

Transverse arch

Crowning cornice

Window hood-mould

Volute

Fascia

Barrel vault

Dentil

Clerestory level

Rectangular door leading to roofed space

Groin vault

Raised window jamb

Semi-parabolic curve

Short pilaster

Curved buttress

Gallery level

Modillion (bracket)

Cornice

Semicircular arched window

Pier-shaped pinnacle

Corinthian capital

Architrave decorated with oversailing fascias

Gallery

Cornice

Depressed arch

Foliated frieze

Small cupola

Pendentive

Oeil-de-boeuf ("ox-eye") window

Balustrade

Archivolt

Keystone decorated with scroll ornament

Formeret (wall rib)

Cornice

Archivolt decorated with plain fascias

Window jamb

Arcade level

Arcade

Round arch

Window-sill

Outer wall

Buttress

Round arch

Re-entrant corner

Base

Socle

Doorway connecting chapels

Side chapels

Main vessel

Side chapels

NAVE, CHURCH OF ST. PAUL-ST. LOUIS (FRENCH BAROQUE), PARIS, FRANCE, FROM 1627 (BY E. MARTELLANGE)

Baroque and neoclassical 2

ARABESQUE

Volute
Palmette
Tendril
Cornucopia

BAY-LEAF GARLAND

Bayberry
Bay leaf

PATERA

Petal
Fillet
Rosette
Ovolo (quarter-round) moulding

DECORATIVE MOULDINGS FROM ENGLISH NEOCLASSICAL BUILDINGS

Raking cornice
Representation in bas-relief of conversion of St. Paul

TRIANGULAR PEDIMENT, WEST FACADE, ST. PAUL'S CATHEDRAL

Cross
Orb
Small dome
Entablature
Pedestal
Gallery with balustrade
Arcade
Convex moulding
Lantern
Circular lucarne window
Dome
Plat lesene
Curved buttress
Round arch
Corinthian pilaster
Rectangular pier
Sunken lunette
Sunken panel
Plain pilaster
Raking cornice
Pediment
Attic storey
Entablature
Architrave
Cornice
Small pilaster
Pedestal
Semicircular cornice
Plinth
Concave, arched niche
Attached Corinthian column
Free-standing Corinthian column
Projecting side portal

CHURCH OF ST. GEORGE IN THE EAST (ENGLISH BAROQUE), LONDON, BRITAIN, 1714-1734 (BY N. HAWKSMOOR)

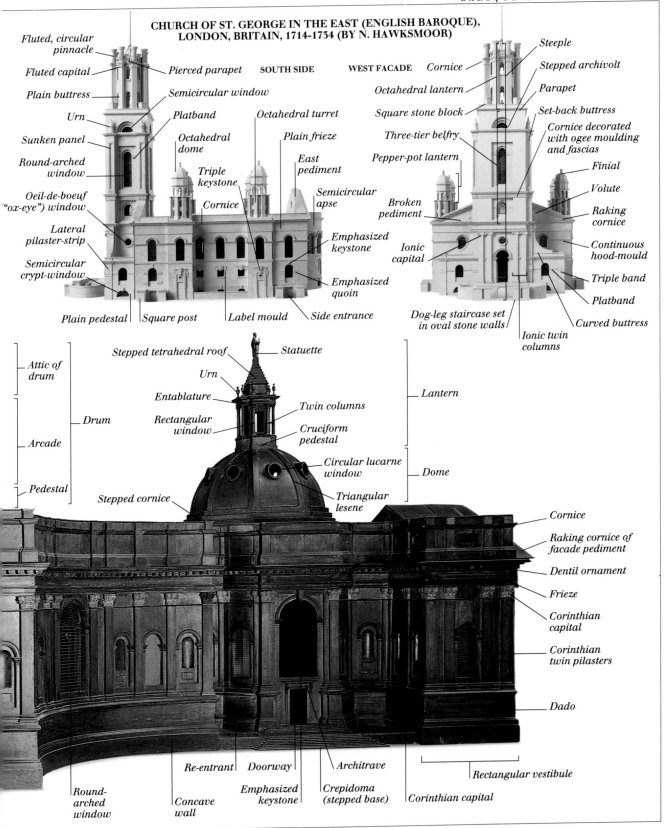

SOUTH SIDE

WEST FACADE

Fluted, circular pinnacle

Fluted capital

Plain buttress

Urn

Sunken panel

Round-arched window

Oeil-de-boeuf ("ox-eye") window

Lateral pilaster-strip

Semicircular crypt-window

Plain pedestal

Square post

Pierced parapet

Semicircular window

Platband

Octahedral dome

Triple keystone

Cornice

Label mould

Octahedral turret

Plain frieze

East pediment

Semicircular apse

Emphasized keystone

Emphasized quoin

Side entrance

Steeple

Cornice

Stepped archivolt

Octahedral lantern

Parapet

Square stone block

Set-back buttress

Three-tier belfry

Cornice decorated with ogee moulding and fascias

Pepper-pot lantern

Finial

Broken pediment

Volute

Ionic capital

Raking cornice

Continuous hood-mould

Triple band

Platband

Dog-leg staircase set in oval stone walls

Curved buttress

Ionic twin columns

Attic of drum

Drum

Arcade

Pedestal

Stepped tetrahedral roof

Statuette

Urn

Entablature

Rectangular window

Lantern

Twin columns

Cruciform pedestal

Circular lucarne window

Dome

Triangular lesene

Stepped cornice

Cornice

Raking cornice of facade pediment

Dentil ornament

Frieze

Corinthian capital

Corinthian twin pilasters

Dado

Round-arched window

Concave wall

Re-entrant

Doorway

Emphasized keystone

Architrave

Crepidoma (stepped base)

Corinthian capital

Rectangular vestibule

481

Baroque and neoclassical 3

DETAILS FROM BAROQUE, NEOCLASSICAL, AND ROCOCO BUILDINGS

PORTICO, THE VYNE, HAMPSHIRE, BRITAIN, 1654 (NEOCLASSICAL)

GILT IRONWORK FROM SCREEN, PALAIS DE VERSAILLES, FRANCE, 1669-1674 (FRENCH BAROQUE)

WINDOW, PALAZZO STANGA, CREMONA, ITALY, EARLY 18TH CENTURY (ROCOCO)

ATLAS (MALE CARYATID), UPPER BELVEDERE, VIENNA, AUSTRIA, 1721 (GERMAN-STYLE BAROQUE)

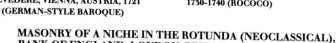

BALCONY, NANTES, FRANCE, 1730-1740 (ROCOCO)

MASONRY OF A NICHE IN THE ROTUNDA (NEOCLASSICAL), BANK OF ENGLAND, LONDON, BRITAIN, 1794 (BY J. SOANE)

Frieze

Spandrel

Scoop-pattern concave moulding

Keystone

Semi-dome

Voussoir

Rotunda wall

Flat, rectangular niche

Rounded niche

Flat, square niche

CORNER OF THE NEW STATE PAPER OFFICE (NEOCLASSICAL), LONDON, BRITAIN, 1830-1831 (BY J. SOANE)

Classical-style entablature

Cornice

Frieze

Architrave

Pantile (S-shaped roofing tile)

Fascia

Curved corbel

Eaves

Scroll-shaped corbel

Smooth rustication

Second-floor window

Cornice

Drip-cap

Cornice

Frieze

Window architrave

Window jamb

First-floor window

Window-sill in the form of a frieze

Ground-floor window

Splayed window-sill

Vermiculated rustication

TYRINGHAM HOUSE (NEOCLASSICAL), BUCKINGHAMSHIRE, BRITAIN, 1793-1797 (BY J. SOANE)

ROOF LEVEL (ATTIC LEVEL)

Space for illumination above unroofed central hall

Chimney-stack

Space above unroofed main staircase

Flat roof

Oculus illuminating secondary staircase

Parapet rail

Balustrade

Baluster

Cornice

Attic storey of convex portico

Cornice

FIRST-FLOOR LEVEL (CHAMBER FLOOR)

Upper level of central hall, open to floor below

Main staircase

Secondary staircase

Abacus

Pilaster capital

Triangular pilaster

Attached Tuscan twin pilasters

First-floor storey of convex portico

Window-sill

Bow front

GROUND-FLOOR LEVEL (PRINCIPAL FLOOR)

Withdrawing-room

Central hall

Library and breakfast-room

Main staircase

Water-closet (toilet)

Eating-room

Secondary staircase

Segmented lintel course

Band incised with Greek-style fret ornament

Window-sill

Window jamb

Window architrave

Basement

Base

Plinth

Horizontal rustication

Vestibule (entrance hall)

Ground-floor storey of convex portico

FACADE OF TYRINGHAM HOUSE

Chimney-stack

Voussoir

Basement window

Entrance door

Circular entrance steps

Rail

Baluster

Parapet

Balustrade

Cornice

Entablature

Capital

Shaft

Ionic column

Base

PROSTYLE COLONNADE

Arches and vaults

PARTS OF AN ARCH

Voussoir Keystone Crown Abutment

Keystone

Abutment

Extrados

Intrados (soffit)

Haunch

Impost

Abutment

Springing point

Intrados (soffit)

Span

Abutment

FRONT **SIDE**

ARCHES ARE CURVED STRUCTURES used to bridge spans and to support the weight of upper parts of buildings, such as domes, as in St. Paul's Cathedral (below) and the antique temple (opposite). The voussoirs (wedge-shaped blocks) that form an arch (right) support each other and convert the downward force of the weight of the building into an outward force. This outward force is in turn transferred to buttresses, piers, or abutments. A vault is an arched roof or ceiling. There are four main types of vault (opposite). A barrel vault is a single vault, semicircular in cross-section; a groin vault consists of two barrel vaults intersecting at right-angles; a rib vault is a groin vault reinforced by ribs; and a fan vault is a rib vault in which the ribs radiate from the springing point (where the arch begins) like a fan.

ARCHES AND BASE OF DOME, ST. PAUL'S CATHEDRAL, LONDON, BRITAIN, 1675-1710 (BY C. WREN)

Pendentive

Pilaster

Base

Opening to passageway

Inner dome

Colonnade

Passageway

Cornice

Pedestal of outer dome

"Whispering Gallery"

Triangular buttress

Moulded bracket

Semi-dome

Upper barrel-vaulted passage opening on to side aisle

Abutment

Strut built into masonry to strengthen pier (added in the 20th century)

Upper arch (concealing difference in heights between main arch and minor arches)

Round arch

Extrados

Intrados (soffit)

Springing point

Impost

Barrel vault

Passage leading to side aisle

Minor arch leading to side aisle

Main arch leading to nave

Pier

Minor arch

TYPES OF ARCH

HORSESHOE ARCH (MOORISH ARCH), GREAT MOSQUE, CORDOBA, SPAIN, 785

BASKET ARCH (SEMI-ELLIPTICAL ARCH), PALATINE CHAPEL, AIX-LA-CHAPELLE, FRANCE, 790-798

TUDOR ARCH, TOWER OF LONDON, BRITAIN, C.1086-1097

LANCET ARCH, WESTMINSTER ABBEY, LONDON, BRITAIN, 1503-1519

TREFOIL ARCH, BEVERLEY MINSTER, YORKSHIRE, BRITAIN, C.1300

TYPES OF VAULT

BARREL VAULT (TUNNEL VAULT; WAGON VAULT)

Transverse rib
Temporary brace
Horizontal abutment
Temporary structure used to centre vault

GROIN VAULT

Barrel vault
Transverse ridge-rib
Transverse arch
Voussoir
Right-angled intersection
Groin
Diagonal rib
Longitudinal ridge-rib

RIB VAULT

FAN VAULT

Tierceron (secondary rib)
Ridge-rib
Springing point
Concave-sided lozenge
Panel

ENGLISH BOND BRICKWORK OF GROIN VAULT AND RIB VAULT

Right-angled intersection
Groin
Header
Stretcher
Cell of barrel vault
Springing point

EXTRADOS OF GROIN VAULT

Stretcher
Header
Cell
Extrados of diagonal rib
Springing point

EXTRADOS OF RIB VAULT

COMPOSITE MODEL OF ANTIQUE FRENCH TEMPLE

Coved dome
Pedestal of lantern
Lesene
Archivolt decorated with plain fascias
Lantern
Abutment
Dentil
Coved dome
Pedestal of dome
Entablature
Fluted Ionic column
Pedestal of column

Series of plain fascias
Re-entrant angle
Cavetto moulding
Fillet
Cornice
Plain frieze
Architrave
Ionic capital
Chamfered corner
Keystone decorated with scroll
Plain Ionic column
Shaft
Scotia
Plinth
Dado
Base

Round arch
Cornice
Horizontal band
Twisted vertical band
Naos (cella)

Intercolumniation
Ionic column with twisted vertical bands (wreaths) and horizontal bands

INTERIOR DECORATION OF COFFERED VAULT

Compass
Square
Hammer
Chamfered edge
Arris moulding
Coffer (square sunken panel)
Mason's tools

Domes

A DOME IS A CONVEX ROOF. Domes are categorized according to the shapes of both the base and the section through the centre of the dome. The base may be circular, square, or polygonal (many-sided), depending on the plan of the drum (the walls on which the dome rests). The section of a dome may be the same shape as any arch (see pp. 484-485). Various types of dome are illustrated here: a hemispherical dome, which has a circular base and a semicircular section; a saucer dome, which has a circular base and a segmental (less than a semicircle) section; a polyhedral dome, which is a dome on a polygonal base whose sides meet at the top of the dome; and an onion dome, which has a circular or polygonal base and an ogee-shaped section. Many domes have a lantern (a turret with windows) to provide light inside.

LANTERN AND UPPER DOME TIMBERING, ST. PAUL'S CATHEDRAL

DOME TIMBERING, CHURCH OF THE SORBONNE, PARIS, FRANCE, 1635-1642 (BY J. LEMERCIER)

Ogee-curved dome
Window zone
Pedestal
Floorboard
Ashlar piece
Pin
Short strut
Mortise-and-tenon joint
Principal rafter
Straight brace
Vertical post
Tie-beam
Circular baseplate

Straight brace
Deeply projecting pier buttress
Cornice
Depressed hood-mould
Circular lucarne window
Floor-joist
Hood-mould
Waisted-oval lucarne window
Ogee-curved window-frame
Common rafter
Shaft connecting lantern and church interior

ROOF WITH LANTERN AND ONION DOME

Weathercock
Ellipsoid orb
Keeled lesene
Onion dome
Fish-scale tile
Octahedral base
Sloping roof
Oversailing fascia
Round arch
Attached pillar
Tetrahedral capital
Vertical band
Return
Window
Oversailing fascia
Torus
Fillet
Octahedral base of lantern
Lantern
Tetrahedral roof

REPRESENTATION OF DOME METALLING, CHURCH OF THE SORBONNE

Cross
Orb
Square rib
Inverted ovolo (quarter-round)
Astragal
Fillet
Volute
Plain fascia
Roll moulding
Round-arched window
Buttress
Lantern
Volute
Ovolo (quarter-round)
Cornice
Fillet
Projecting pier buttress
Dome on a circular base
Fish-scale tile
Inverted demi-heart torus moulding
Hood-mould
Waisted-oval lucarne window
Small volute
Gutter
Parapet
Small roll
Fillet
Plain fascia
Triple lesene
Semicircular torus moulding

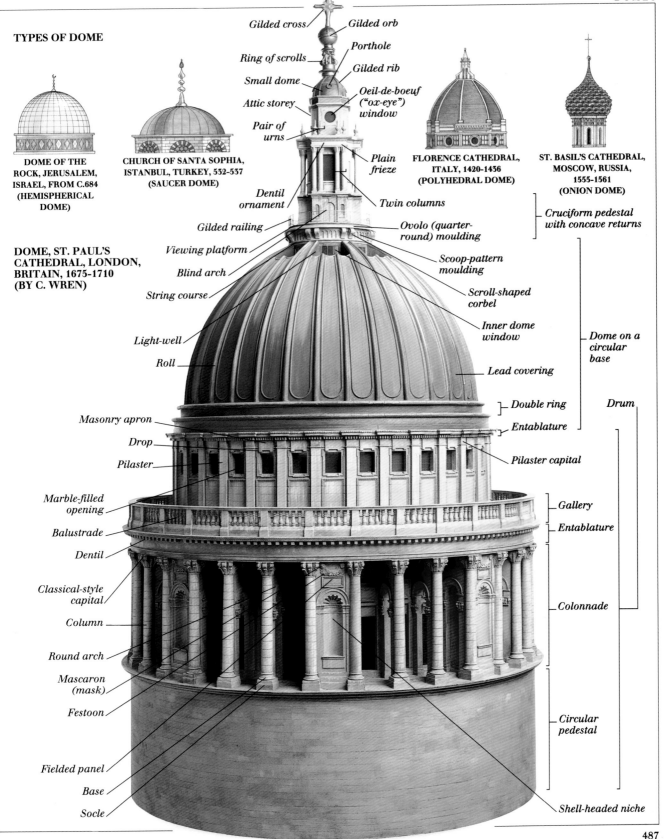

TYPES OF DOME

DOME OF THE ROCK, JERUSALEM, ISRAEL, FROM C.684 (HEMISPHERICAL DOME)

CHURCH OF SANTA SOPHIA, ISTANBUL, TURKEY, 532-537 (SAUCER DOME)

Gilded cross

Gilded orb

Porthole

Ring of scrolls

Gilded rib

Small dome

Attic storey

Oeil-de-boeuf ("ox-eye") window

Pair of urns

Plain frieze

FLORENCE CATHEDRAL, ITALY, 1420-1456 (POLYHEDRAL DOME)

ST. BASIL'S CATHEDRAL, MOSCOW, RUSSIA, 1555-1561 (ONION DOME)

DOME, ST. PAUL'S CATHEDRAL, LONDON, BRITAIN, 1675-1710 (BY C. WREN)

Dentil ornament

Gilded railing

Viewing platform

Blind arch

String course

Light-well

Roll

Twin columns

Ovolo (quarter-round) moulding

Scoop-pattern moulding

Scroll-shaped corbel

Inner dome window

Cruciform pedestal with concave returns

Dome on a circular base

Lead covering

Double ring

Entablature

Pilaster capital

Drum

Masonry apron

Drop

Pilaster

Marble-filled opening

Balustrade

Dentil

Classical-style capital

Column

Round arch

Mascaron (mask)

Festoon

Fielded panel

Base

Socle

Gallery

Entablature

Colonnade

Circular pedestal

Shell-headed niche

Islamic buildings

OPUS SECTILE MOSAIC DESIGN

THE ISLAMIC RELIGION was founded by the prophet Mohammed, who was born in Mecca (in present-day Saudi Arabia) about 570 AD. In the following three centuries, Islam spread from Arabia to North Africa and Spain, as well as to India and much of the rest of Asia. The worldwide influence of Islam remains strong today. Common characteristics of Islamic buildings include ogee arches and roofs, onion domes, and walls decorated with carved stone, paintings, inlays, or mosaics. The most important type of Islamic building is the mosque – the place of worship – which generally has a minaret (tower) from which the muezzin (official crier) calls Muslims to prayer. Most mosques have a mihrab (decorative niche) that indicates the direction of Mecca. As figurative art is not allowed in Islam, buildings are ornamented with geometric and arabesque motifs, and inscriptions (frequently Koranic verses).

Bud-like onion dome

Depressed arch surrounding mihrab

Painted roof pavilion

Lotus-flower pendentive

Turkish-crescent finial

Arabic inscription

Crest

Painted minaret with censer (incense burner)

Spandrel

Series of recessed arches

Semi-dome

Arched niche within a niche

Mural resembling tomb

Polyhedral niche

Recessed colonettes

MIHRAB, JAMI MASJID (PRINCIPAL OR CONGREGATIONAL MOSQUE), BIJAPUR, INDIA, c.1636

Tablet flower

Shield

Herring-bone pattern

Spandrel with floral design

Ogee arch

Carved stone

Undulating band

Cusp

Volute

Impost

Capital with stylized floral design

Panel with fret pattern

Jali (latticed screen) with geometrical patterns

Band with Arabic inscriptions praising Allah (God)

Attached colonette

ARCH, THE ALHAMBRA, GRANADA, SPAIN, 1333-1354

Enamelled turquoise earthenware tile

Cube with chamfered corners

Trigon

Polygonal capital

Niche

Enamelled white earthenware tile

Column shaft

Arabesques of stylized plants

Enamelled lapis blue earthenware tile

MIHRAB WITH COLUMN, EL-AINYI MOSQUE, CAIRO, EGYPT, 15TH CENTURY

EXAMPLES OF ISLAMIC MOSAICS, EGYPT AND SYRIA

Star-shaped motif

Triangle of yellow marble

Rhombus of black marble

Stone band

Greek cross of red marble

STAR AND GREEK-CROSS MOSAIC

Mosaic tessellation

Stone

Black marble

Turquoise glass

Tessera (small mosaic piece)

FRET-PATTERN MOSAIC

Greek cross of black and yellow marble

Star-shaped motif

Stone band

Rhombus of red marble

STAR AND GREEK-CROSS MOSAIC

Parallelogram of black marble

Triangle of yellow marble

Rhombus of red marble

Symmetrical quadrilateral of stone

Star-shaped motif

MOSAIC OF HEXAGONS, TRIANGLES, AND SYMMETRICAL QUADRILATERALS

Hexagonal design

Band of black marble

Band of stone

HEXAGON AND BAND MOSAIC

Triangle of turquoise glass

Parallelogram of mother-of-pearl

DANCETTE-PATTERN MOSAIC

Symmetrical quadrilateral of black marble

Hexagon of red marble

Triangle of stone

MOSAIC OF HEXAGONS, TRIANGLES, AND SYMMETRICAL QUADRILATERALS

MARBLE TOMB OF ITIMAD-UD-DAULA, AGRA, INDIA, c.1622-1628

Kalasa finial (finial with orbs)

Padmakosa (lotus petal)

Ogee-curved roof

Chajya (deep eaves)

Domed roof

Parapet decorated with lattice-work

Balcony

Roof pavilion

Cusped arch

Circular top of minaret

Pietra dura inlay (slices of semi-precious stone laid in sockets)

Cornice

Bracket

Octahedral base of minaret

Spandrel decorated with arabesque

Star-pattern inlay

Sandstone plinth

Sandstone parapet decorated with lattice-work

Jali (latticed screen) with geometrical patterns

Depressed entrance arch

Sandstone stairway

Opus sectile mosaic (geometric mosaic) of stone, tile, glass, and enamel

South and east Asia

THE TRADITIONAL ARCHITECTURE of south and east Asia has been profoundly influenced by the spread from India of Buddhism and Hinduism. This influence is shown both by the abundance and by the architectural styles of temples and shrines in the region. Many early Hindu temples consist of rooms carved from solid rock-faces. However, free-standing structures began to be built in southern India from about the eighth century AD. Many were built in the Dravidian style, like the Temple of Virupaksha (opposite) with its characteristic antarala (terraced tower), perforated windows, and numerous arches, pilasters, and carvings. The earliest Buddhist religious monuments were Indian stupas, which consisted of a single hemispherical dome surmounted by a chattravali (shaft) and surrounded by railings with ornate gates. Later Indian stupas and those built elsewhere were sometimes modified; for example, in Sri Lanka, the dome became bell-shaped, and was called a dagoba. Buddhist pagodas, such as the Burmese example (right), are multistoreyed temples, each storey having a projecting roof. The form of these buildings probably derived from the yasti (pointed spire) of the stupa. Another feature of many traditional Asian buildings is their imaginative roof-forms, such as gambrel (mansard) roofs, and roofs with angle-rafters (below).

SEVEN-STOREYED PAGODA IN BURMESE STYLE, c.9TH-10TH CENTURY

Gilded band

Gilded iron hti (crown)

Dubika (mast)

Arrow motif

Torus moulding with spiral carving

Decorative eaves board

Ogee-arched motif with decorative carvings

Ogee-arched motif forming horn

Hip-rafter

Pentroof

Undulating moulding

Baluster finial

Balustrade

Pillar

Engaged pillar

Arched entrance

Rectangular window

Baluster

Straight brace

DETAILS FROM EAST ASIAN BUILDINGS

KASUGA-STYLE ROOF WITH SUMIGI (ANGLE-RAFTERS), KASUGADO SHRINE OF ENJOJI, NARA, JAPAN, 12TH-14TH CENTURY

TERRACES, TEMPLE OF HEAVEN, BEIJING, CHINA, 15TH CENTURY

GAMBREL (MANSARD) ROOF WITH UPSWEPT EAVES AND UNDULATING GABLES, HIMEJI CASTLE, HIMEJI, JAPAN, 1608-1609

CORNER CAPITAL WITH ROOF BEAMS, POPCHU-SA TEMPLE, POPCHU-SA, SOUTH KOREA, 17TH CENTURY

PERFORATED STONE WINDOWS, TEMPLES OF VIRUPAKSHA AND MALLIKARJUNA, PATTADAKAL, INDIA, 8TH CENTURY

Tablet flower

Fret motif

Chain motif

Floral pattern

Sickle motif

Leaf

Scroll motif

Semicircle

DAGOBA STUPA, KANDY, SRI LANKA, c.2ND CENTURY BC–7TH CENTURY AD

Chattra (umbrella)

Hanging ornament

Chattravali (shaft)

Ring with indentations symbolizing chattras

Yasti (tee; pointed spire)

Harmika (stylized square railing)

Ornamental metalwork

Auda (bell-shaped dome)

Trimala (series of three circular courses)

Circular base

SIDE VIEW AND PLAN VIEW, TEMPLE OF VIRUPAKSHA, PATTADAKAL, INDIA, c.746

Stupica (small stupa) of the Dravidian order

Dravidian finial

Blind chataya arch

Perforated window

Gopuram finial (wagon-like finial)

Bracketed capital

Small gopuram (gate-head)

Parapet

Roll cornice

Antarala (terraced tower)

Niche with statue

Gate

Panel with bas-relief carving

Pillar

Mandapa (pillared hall)

Plan view

Twin pilasters

Pradakshina (circumambulatory passage around shrine)

Shrine

Shrine chamber

Niche

Gate

491

The 19th century

BUILDINGS OF THE 19TH CENTURY are characterized by the use of new materials and by a great diversity of architectural styles. From the end of the 18th century, iron and steel became widely used as alternatives to wood for the framework of buildings, as in the flax-spinning mill shown here. Built in Britain in 1796, this mill exemplifies an architectural style that became common throughout the industrialized world for more than a century. The Industrial Revolution also brought mass-production of building parts – a development that enabled the British architect Sir Joseph Paxton to erect London's Crystal Palace (a building made entirely of iron and glass) in only nine months, ready for the Great Exhibition of 1851. The 19th century saw a widespread revival of older architectural styles. For example, in the USA and Germany, Neo-Greek architecture was fashionable; in Britain and France, Neo-Baroque, Neo-Byzantine, and Neo-Gothic styles (as seen in the Palace of Westminster and Tower Bridge) were dominant.

SECTION THROUGH A FLAX-SPINNING MILL

Cast-iron wall-plate
Pitched roof
Ridge
Machinery space
Verge
Gutter
Cast-iron mortise-and-tenon joint
Anchor-joint
Inverted T-section cast-iron beam
Drain-pipe
Segmentally arched brick vault
End flange
Concrete floor
Tapering part of column
Paved ground floor
Strengthened central column

FLAX-SPINNING MILL, SHREWSBURY, BRITAIN, 1796 (BY C. BAGE)

Multi-gabled roof (ridge and furrow roof)
Ridge
Furrow
Verge
Timber rafter
Cast-iron wall-plate
Gutter
Gable
Drain-pipe
Tapering part of column
Three courses of stretchers
Segmentally arched brick vault
Course of headers
Cast-iron mortise-and-tenon joint
Course of decorative headers
Tie-rod
Cast-iron lattice window
Cast-iron cruciform column
Cast-iron tenon
Inverted T-section cast-iron beam
Anchor-joint
Strengthened central column
Bonded brick wall
Stone foundation
Quoin
Jamb
Gauged arch (segmental arch of tapered bricks)

CLOCK TOWER ("BIG BEN"), PALACE OF WESTMINSTER, LONDON, BRITAIN, 1836-1868 (BY C. BARRY AND A.W.N. PUGIN)

Finial
Spire
Skylight
Iron tracery
Dormer window
Cornice decorated with shields
Round arch filled with open tracery
Tetrahedral spire
Iron railing
Bell chamber
Small orb
Balustrade
Orb
Ogee tracery arch filled with trefoil
Flying buttress
Pinnacle
Spandrel
Octahedral shaft with billet decoration
Dial
Cornice
Moulded corbel
Star-shaped corner buttress
Panelled field filled with tracery
Slender diagonal buttress
Narrow window
String course
Carved panel
Stepped storeys

DETAILS FROM BUILDINGS IN REVIVALIST STYLES

CUPOLA, MERCHANTS' EXCHANGE, PHILADELPHIA, USA, 1832-1834 (NEO-GREEK)

SCULPTURE AND PEDIMENT, OPERA HOUSE, PARIS, FRANCE, 1861-1874 (NEO-BAROQUE)

DOMED TURRET, WESTMINSTER CATHEDRAL, LONDON, BRITAIN, 1894-1903 (NEO-BYZANTINE)

Tetrahedral spire
Finial
Finial
Dormer head (gable) filled with blind tracery
Parapet
Parapet of balcony
Spire
High-level footbridge
Cornice
Octahedral upper turret
Lattice-work
Heraldic shield
Wedge-shaped corbel
Cast-iron tracery
Cast-iron panelling
Archway
Moulded corbel
String course
Drawbridge (bascule)
Steel brace
Stone panel
Circular turret/buttress
Archway
Pier

TOWER BRIDGE, LONDON, BRITAIN, 1886-1894 (BY H. JONES)

CRYSTAL PALACE EXHIBITION HALL, LONDON, BRITAIN, 1851 (BY J. PAXTON)

Longitudinal girder
Window
Cast-iron ornamental arch-plate
Arched facade
Ridge and furrow glass roof-windows
Crest
Semicircular barrel vault
Cast-iron trapezium
Octahedral column
Side exit
Sheet-iron louvre
Strengthened support
Entrance

The early 20th century

ARCHITECTURE OF THE EARLY 20TH CENTURY is notable for radical new types of steel-and-glass buildings – particularly skyscrapers – and the widespread use of steel-reinforced concrete. The steel-framed skyscraper was pioneered in Chicago in the 1880s, but did not become widespread until the first decades of the 20th century. As construction techniques were refined, skyscrapers became higher and higher; for example, the Empire State Building (right) of 1929-1931 has 102 storeys. Many buildings of this period were constructed from lightweight concrete slabs, which could be supported by cantilever beams or by pilotis (stilts), as in the Villa Savoye (below). The early 20th century also produced a great variety of architectural styles, some of which are illustrated opposite. Despite their diversity, the styles of this period generally had one thing in common: they were completely new, with few links to past architectural styles. This originality is in marked contrast to 19th-century architecture (see pp. 492-493), much of which was revivalist.

EMPIRE STATE BUILDING, NEW YORK, USA, 1929-1931 (BY R. H. SHREVE, T. LAMB, AND A. L. HARMON)

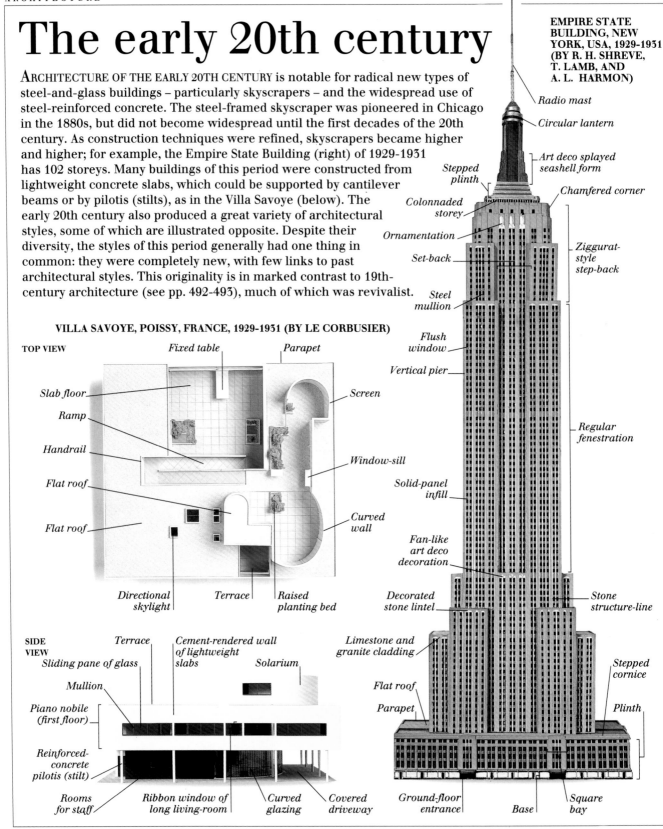

VILLA SAVOYE, POISSY, FRANCE, 1929-1931 (BY LE CORBUSIER)

TOP VIEW

- Fixed table
- Parapet
- Slab floor
- Ramp
- Handrail
- Flat roof
- Flat roof
- Screen
- Window-sill
- Curved wall
- Directional skylight
- Terrace
- Raised planting bed

SIDE VIEW

- Terrace
- Cement-rendered wall of lightweight slabs
- Solarium
- Sliding pane of glass
- Mullion
- Piano nobile (first floor)
- Reinforced-concrete pilotis (stilt)
- Rooms for staff
- Ribbon window of long living-room
- Curved glazing
- Covered driveway

Empire State Building labels:
- Radio mast
- Circular lantern
- Stepped plinth
- Art deco splayed seashell form
- Chamfered corner
- Colonnaded storey
- Ornamentation
- Ziggurat-style step-back
- Set-back
- Steel mullion
- Flush window
- Vertical pier
- Regular fenestration
- Solid-panel infill
- Fan-like art deco decoration
- Decorated stone lintel
- Stone structure-line
- Limestone and granite cladding
- Flat roof
- Parapet
- Stepped cornice
- Plinth
- Ground-floor entrance
- Base
- Square bay

494

MIDWAY GARDENS, CHICAGO, USA, 1914 (BY F. L. WRIGHT)

Flagpole

Plain coping-stone

Main floor

Orchestra shell

Tiled, shallow pitched roof

Decorated cement frieze

Terrace

Steps

Stage

Ridge

Projecting balustrade

Hip

Ornamental light

Main pavilion

Arcade

Terrace

Octagonal window

Ornamental sculpture

Flat roof

Stone plinth

EAST SIDE

Cantilevered, latticed shade

NORTH SIDE

Tiled frieze

Planting bed

Deep-set window

Slit window

Brick pier

Terrace

Stepped flat-roofs

Ornamented coping-stone

EARLY 20TH-CENTURY ARCHITECTURAL STYLES

DORMER WINDOW, STUDIO ELVIRA, MUNICH, GERMANY, 1902 (ART NOUVEAU)

AEG TURBINE HALL, BERLIN, GERMANY, 1909 (DEUTSCHER WERKBUND)

ROBIE HOUSE, CHICAGO, USA, 1909-1910 (PRAIRIE STYLE)

GRUNDTVIG CHURCH, COPENHAGEN, DENMARK, 1920 (EXPRESSIONIST)

VERTEX, CHRYSLER BUILDING, NEW YORK, USA, 1928-1930 (ART DECO)

TOWER, TOWN HALL, HILVERSUM, NETHERLANDS, 1930 (DUTCH CUBIST)

CASA DEL FASCIO, COMO, ITALY, 1932-1936 (GRUPPO SEVEN CUBIST)

MOTIF ABOVE DOORWAY, HOOVER FACTORY, LONDON, BRITAIN, 1933 (ART DECO)

Modern buildings 1

ARCHITECTURE SINCE ABOUT THE 1950s is generally known as modern architecture. One of its main influences has been functionalism – a belief that a building's function should be apparent in its design. Both the Centre Georges Pompidou (below and opposite) and the Hong Kong and Shanghai Bank (see pp. 498-499) are functionalist buildings: on each, elements of engineering and the building's services are clearly visible on the outside. In the 1980s, some architects rejected functionalism in favour of post-modernism, in which historical styles – particularly neoclassicism – were revived, using modern building materials and techniques. In many modern buildings, walls are made of glass or concrete hung from a frame, as in the Kawana House (right); this type of wall construction is known as curtain walling. Other modern construction techniques include the intricate interlocking of concrete vaults – as in the Sydney Opera House (see pp. 498-499) – and the use of high-tension beams to create complex roof shapes, such as the paraboloid roof of the Church of St. Pierre de Libreville (see pp. 498-499).

Solar panel

Concrete frame

Pile foundation

Raft   Composite cladding-panel

SIDE VIEW

Rocker-beam

Curtain walling

Lattice-beam

Floor-beam connection   Floor

FRONT VIEW

SERVICES FACADE, CENTRE GEORGES POMPIDOU, PARIS, FRANCE, 1977 (BY R. PIANO AND R. ROGERS)

Metal-faced, fire-resistant panel

Air-conditioning duct

Cooling tower

Water-pipe

Grand gallery level

Main gallery levels

Library level

Administrative level

Mezzanine gallery level

Reception level

Staircase to grand hall

Electrical plant

Water-cooled, fire-resistant column

Continuous glazing

Tinted glass

Services entrance

PRINCIPAL FACADE, CENTRE GEORGES POMPIDOU

Gallery space

External walkway

Electronically operated roller-blind

Cooling tower

Continuous glazing

Steel lattice-beam

Terrace

Main truss

Cradle support for escalator

Gerberette (cast-steel rocker-beam)

Cross-bracing

Suspended fire-resistant glass curtain

Double fire-escape staircase

Reinforced-concrete and steel floor-plate

Double floor-height

Main entrance

Glazed escalator tube

Node

Water-cooled, fire-resistant steel column

Exposed "plug-in" services

Steel lattice-beam

Dual air-conditioning unit for roof

Elevator

Elevator-motor room

Vertical-duct distribution zone

Metal sandwich-panel (insulating panel)

Gerberette (cast-steel rocker-beam)

Rose connection

Outer tension-column

External steel-lattice mullion

Water-cooled, fire-resistant cross-beam

Double fire-escape staircase

Water storage tank

Cross-bracing

Open gallery floor

Water-pipe

Steel-framed services column

Double cross-bracing

Modern buildings 2

HONG KONG AND SHANGHAI BANK, HONG KONG, 1981-1985 (BY N. FOSTER)

Inverted top-truss

Soffit

Mast

Illuminated fascia

Curved glazing

External maintenance crane

Cockpit

Counterweight

Boom

Circular access platform

Steel column

Sun-shade louvre

Mullion

Face panel

Hanger

Handrail

Composite cladding-panel

Top beam

Outer diagonal beam

Escalator

Outer bottom boom

Inner diagonal beam

Fire-escape staircase

External staircase

Inner bottom boom

Pin joint

Double floor-height

Refuge terrace

Hanger

Full-height glazing

Sun scoop

Two-storey stability truss (coathanger truss)

Glazed curtain wall

Flange

Lightweight, column-free, steel and concrete floor

Vertical, glazed typhoon screen

Entrance lobby

Plaza

Glazed soffit

SOUTH FACADE

Soffit

Helicopter landing-pad

Navigation light

Stepped elevation

Face panel

Horizontal window

Vertical window

External maintenance crane

Cross-bracing

Service shaft

Double floor-height

Sun scoop

10-floor-high atrium

Internal bridge

EAST SIDE

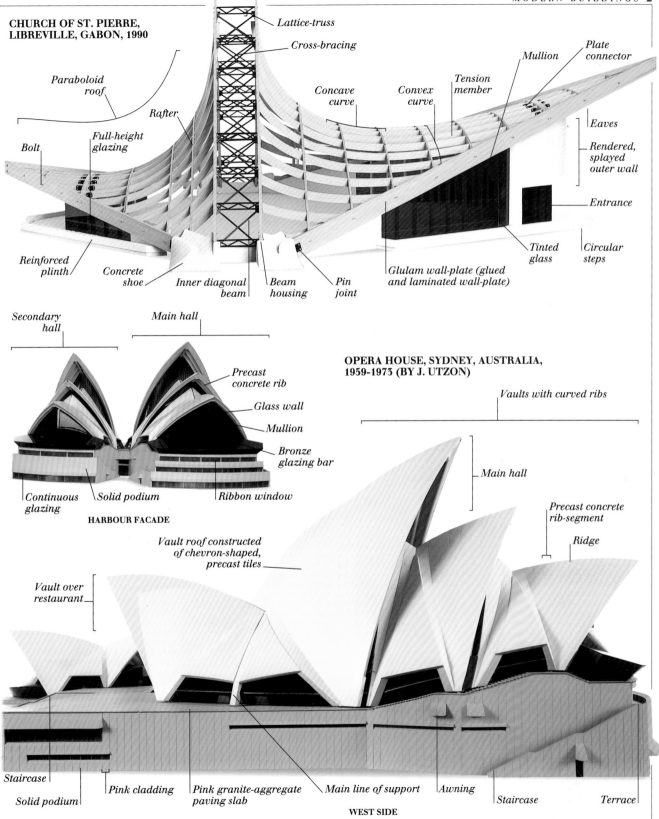

CHURCH OF ST. PIERRE, LIBREVILLE, GABON, 1990

Lattice-truss

Cross-bracing

Paraboloid roof

Rafter

Concave curve

Convex curve

Tension member

Mullion

Plate connector

Bolt

Full-height glazing

Eaves

Rendered, splayed outer wall

Entrance

Reinforced plinth

Concrete shoe

Inner diagonal beam

Beam housing

Pin joint

Tinted glass

Circular steps

Glulam wall-plate (glued and laminated wall-plate)

Secondary hall

Main hall

OPERA HOUSE, SYDNEY, AUSTRALIA, 1959-1973 (BY J. UTZON)

Precast concrete rib

Glass wall

Mullion

Bronze glazing bar

Vaults with curved ribs

Main hall

Precast concrete rib-segment

Ridge

Continuous glazing

Solid podium

Ribbon window

HARBOUR FACADE

Vault roof constructed of chevron-shaped, precast tiles

Vault over restaurant

Staircase

Solid podium

Pink cladding

Pink granite-aggregate paving slab

Main line of support

Awning

Staircase

Terrace

WEST SIDE

MUSIC

Musical notation

MUSICAL NOTATION IS ANY METHOD by which sounds are written down so that they can be read and performed by others. The present-day conventional system of notation uses a five-line stave (staff) – divided by vertical lines into sections known as bars – on which notes, rests, clefs, key signatures, time signatures, accidentals, and other symbols are written. A note indicates the duration of a sound and, according to its position on the stave, its pitch. Notes can be arranged on the stave in order of pitch to form a scale. A silence in the music is indicated by a rest. The clef, which is placed at the begininng of a stave, fixes the pitch. The key signature, which is placed after the clef, indicates the key. The time signature, placed after the key signature, shows the number of beats in a bar. Accidentals are used to indicate the raising or lowering of the pitch of a note.

**EXAMPLE OF AN ORIGINAL MANUSCRIPT:
THE PRODIGAL SON, ARTHUR SULLIVAN, 1869**

ELEMENTS OF MUSICAL NOTATION

CLEFS

TIME SIGNATURES

NOTES

RESTS

SCALE

ACCIDENTALS

FLUTES

OBOES

CLARINETS IN A

BASSOONS

Accidental sharp

Tie (bind)

Accidental natural

Unison (both clarinets play the same note)

Semibreve

Crotchet

HORNS IN D

TRUMPETS IN D

TIMPANI IN D AND A

FIRST AND SECOND VIOLINS

VIOLAS

VOICES

ORGAN

Slur

Crotchet rest

Semibreve rest

Accidental sharp

Piano (play softly)

Pianissimo (play very softly)

CELLOS

DOUBLE BASSES

Orchestras

AN ORCHESTRA IS A GROUP of musicians that plays music written for a specific combination of instruments. The number and type of instruments included in the orchestra depends on the style of music being played. The modern orchestra (also known as a symphony orchestra) is made up of four sections of instruments – stringed, woodwind, brass, and percussion. The stringed section consists of violins, violas, cellos (violoncellos), double basses, and sometimes a harp (see pp. 510-511). The main instruments of the woodwind section are flutes, oboes, clarinets, and bassoons – the piccolo, cor anglais, bass clarinet, saxophone, and double bassoon (contrabassoon) can also be included if the music requires them (see pp. 508-509). The brass section usually consists of horns, trumpets, trombones, and the tuba (see pp. 506-507). The main instruments of the percussion section are the timpani (see pp. 518-519). The side drum, bass drum, cymbals, tambourine, triangle, tubular bells, xylophone, vibraphone, tam-tam (gong), castanets, and maracas can also be included in the percussion section (see pp. 516-517). The musicians are usually arranged in a semi-circle – strings spread along the front, woodwind and brass in the centre, and percussion at the back. A conductor stands in front of the musicians and controls the tempo (speed) of the music and the overall balance of the sound, ensuring that no instruments are too loud or too soft in relation to the others.

TUBULAR BELLS

TAM-TAM (GONG)

VIBRAPHONE

XYLOPHONE

CASTANETS

TAMBOURINE

MARACAS

TRIANGLE

TRUMPETS

HORNS

CLARINETS

BASS CLARINET

HARP

SAXOPHONE

PICCOLO

SECOND VIOLINS

FIRST VIOLINS

CYMBALS SIDE DRUM BASS DRUM

TIMPANI

EXAMPLE OF A LAYOUT OF THE
INSTRUMENTS FOR A MODERN
(SYMPHONY) ORCHESTRA

TROMBONES

TUBA

DOUBLE BASSES

BASSOONS

DOUBLE BASSOON

FLUTES

OBOES

COR ANGLAIS

VIOLAS

Score

CONDUCTOR'S
STAND

CELLOS

505

Brass instruments

BUGLE

BRASS INSTRUMENTS ARE WIND INSTRUMENTS that are made of metal, usually brass. Although they appear in many different shapes and sizes, all brass instruments have a mouthpiece, a length of hollow tube, and a flared bell. The mouthpiece of a brass instrument may be cup-shaped, as in the cornet, or cone-shaped, as in the horn. The tube may be wide or narrow, mainly conical, as in the horn and tuba, or mainly cylindrical, as in the trumpet and trombone. The sound of a brass instrument is made by the player's lips vibrating against the mouthpiece, so that the air vibrates in the tube. By changing lip tension, the player can vary the vibrations and produce notes of different pitches. The range of notes produced by a brass instrument can be extended by means of a valve system. Most brass instruments, such as the trumpet, have piston valves that divert the air in the instrument along an extra piece of tubing (known as a valve slide) when pressed down. The total length of the tube is increased and the pitch of the note produced is lowered. Instead of valves, the trombone has a movable slide that can be pushed away from or drawn toward the player. The sound of a brass instrument can also be changed by inserting a mute into the bell of the instrument.

Brace

Tuning slide

Counterbalancing weight

SIMPLIFIED DIAGRAM SHOWING HOW A PISTON VALVE SYSTEM WORKS

Piston valves at rest

Air bypasses piston valves

PISTON VALVES AT REST

First piston valve pressed down

Second and third piston valves at rest

Air diverted through first valve slide

PISTON VALVE PRESSED DOWN

TRUMPET

Finger button

First piston valve

Spring returns piston valve to rest position

Second piston valve

Third piston valve

Holes divert air into valve slides

Cup-shaped mouthpiece

Mouthpiece receiver

Little finger support

Music stand holder

Narrow, cylindrical tube

Flared bell

Tuning slide

Tuning slide water key

First valve slide

First valve slide thumb hook

Second valve slide

Third valve slide finger ring

Third valve slide

Third valve slide water key

SECTIONS OF A TROMBONE

EXAMPLES OF MUTES

Flared bell

CUP MUTE

TENOR MUTE

ALTO MUTE

Inner tube

Outer tube of slide

Cup-shaped mouthpiece

Mouthpiece brace held by the left hand

Slide brace held by the right hand

Narrow, cylindrical tube

Water key

TROMBONE

Flared bell

Outer tube of slide

Cup-shaped mouthpiece

FLUGELHORN

Little finger support

Piston valves

Flared bell

Cup-shaped mouthpiece

Conical tube

Valve slide

HORN

Cone-shaped mouthpiece

Finger key

Rotary valves

CORNET

Piston valves

Little finger support

Flared bell

Cup-shaped mouthpiece

Bore widens after valves

Valve slide

Narrow, conical bore

Large, flared bell

TUBA

Large, flared bell

Piston valves

Cup-shaped mouthpiece

Valve slide

Wide, conical tube

Woodwind instruments

WOODWIND INSTRUMENTS ARE wind instruments that are generally made of wood, although some are made of metal or plastic. The sound of a woodwind instrument is produced by the vibration of air in a hollow tube. The air is made to vibrate by blowing across a blow hole – as in the flute and piccolo – or by blowing through a single reed – as in the clarinet and saxophone – or a double reed – as in the bassoon, cor anglais, and oboe. The pitch of a woodwind instrument can be changed by opening or closing holes cut into the tube of the instrument.

Bell

Double reed

Bell joint

Curved crook

Double reed

Cylindrical, metal tube

Conical, wooden tube

Tenor joint

Key

Body joint

Crook

Conical, wooden tube

Upper joint

Blow hole

Head joint

Lip plate

PICCOLO

Bass joint

Right-hand rest

Key

Double reed

Foot joint

Finger hole

Key

Butt

Key

Key

Middle joint

Upper joint

Cork

Mouthpiece with single reed

Ligature

Barrel joint

BASSOON

Key

Middle joint

Cylindrical, metal tube

Body joint

Finger hole

Cylindrical, wooden tube

Bell joint

Conical, wooden tube

Lip plate

Head joint

Key

Upper joint

Bulb-shaped bell

COR ANGLAIS

Blow hole

Bell joint

Bell joint

Middle joint

FLUTE

Flared bell

OBOE

Flared bell

CLARINET

TENOR SAXOPHONE

Mouthpiece with single reed

Conical, metal tube

Upturned, flared bell

Mouthpiece with single reed

SECTIONS OF A TENOR SAXOPHONE

Ligature

Neck

Upper octave key

Key rod

KEYS FOR THE LEFT THUMB

Lower octave key

Key

Key

KEYS FOR THE LEFT HAND

Key rod

Key

Mother-of-pearl touchpiece (button)

Key rod

KEYS FOR THE LEFT PALM

KEYS FOR THE RIGHT HAND

Key

Key rod

MAIN BODY OF SAXOPHONE

Conical, metal tube

KEYS FOR THE RIGHT PALM

Upturned, flared bell

Tonehole

Mother-of-pearl touchpiece (button)

Tonehole

Pad made up of layers of felt and cork

Roller

Cup

Key guard

Key rod

Key

Key guard

Metal centre of pad reflects sound

Key guard

KEYS FOR THE RIGHT LITTLE FINGER

Padded key

Key guard

KEYS FOR THE LEFT LITTLE FINGER

Stringed instruments

STRINGED INSTRUMENTS PRODUCE SOUND by the vibration of stretched strings. This may be done by drawing a bow across the strings, as in the violin; or by plucking the strings, as in the harp and guitar (see pp. 512-513). The four modern members of the bowed string family are the violin, viola, cello (violoncello), and double bass. Each consists of a hollow, wooden body, a long neck, and four strings. The bow is a wooden stick with horsehair stretched across its length. The vibrations made by drawing the bow across the strings are transmitted to the hollow body, and this itself vibrates, amplifying and enriching the sound produced. The harp consists of a set of strings of different lengths stretched across a wooden frame. The strings are plucked by the player's thumbs and fingers – except the little finger of each hand – which produces vibrations that are amplified by the harp's soundboard. The pitch of the note produced by any stringed instrument depends on the length, weight, and tension of the string. A shorter, lighter, or tighter string gives a higher note.

Scroll eye

Scroll

Peg-hole

Ebony tuning-pegs

Neck made of maple wood

Fingerboard

Rounded shoulder

Belly (soundboard)

Strings

Waist

Sound-hole

Rib

Purfling

Bridge

Tailpiece

Chin rest

Tailpiece loop fits around end-pin

End-pin (tail-pin)

SECTIONS OF A VIOLIN

Head

Point

Stick

Horsehair

Frog

Screw

VIOLIN BOW

Scroll

Scroll eye

Peg-box

Tuning-peg

Nut

String

Fingerboard

Rounded shoulder

Belly (soundboard)

Purfling

Waist

Sound-hole

Bridge

Tuning adjustor

Tailpiece

Chin rest

VIOLIN

Crown

Tuning-peg

Neck (string arm)

Shoulder

String

Soundboard

Pillar

Pedestal

Foot

Pedal

HARP

Scroll

Scroll eye

Peg-box

Tuning-peg

Nut

Fingerboard

String

Belly (soundboard)

Rounded shoulder

Waist

Sound-hole

Bridge

Tuning adjustor

Tailpiece

Spike

CELLO (VIOLONCELLO)

Belly (soundboard)

Scroll

Tuning-peg

Scroll eye

Peg-box

Nut

Fingerboard

String

Rounded shoulder

Belly (soundboard)

Purfling

Waist

Bridge

Sound-hole

Chin rest

Tailpiece

VIOLA

Head

Point

Inward-curving stick

Horsehair

Frog

Screw

DOUBLE BASS BOW

Scroll

Scroll eye

Tuning-pegs at back of peg-box

Nut

Fingerboard

String

Sloping shoulder

Belly (soundboard)

Purfling

Waist

Bridge

Rib

Sound-hole

Tailpiece

Spike

DOUBLE BASS

Guitars

THE GUITAR IS A PLUCKED stringed instrument
(see pp. 510-511). There are two types of guitar –
acoustic and electric. Acoustic guitars have hollow
bodies and six or twelve strings. Plucking the strings
produces vibrations that are amplified by their hollow
bodies. Electric guitars usually have solid bodies and
six strings. Pick-ups placed under the strings convert
their vibrations into electronic signals that are magnified
by an amplifier, and sent to a loudspeaker where they are
converted into sounds (see pp. 520-521). Electric bass
guitars are very similar in structure to electric guitars,
and produce sound in the same way, but have four
strings and play bass notes.

ACOUSTIC GUITAR

Hollow body

String

Fret

Machine head

Neck

Headstock

Sound-hole

B string

Bridge

G string

D string

A string

Low E string

Maker's label

Rib

Lining glued along top and bottom edge of rib

End block

Strap peg

Joint

Transverse (crosswise) strut strengthens back

Back made of two pieces of cherry wood joined together

Saddle

Bridge pin

Bridge

Binding

EXAMPLES OF ACOUSTIC GUITARS

Rose
Sound-hole
Machine head
Hollow body
String
Bridge
Neck
Headstock
Scratchplate

WASHBURN TWELVE-STRING

Hollow, metal body
Sound-hole
Machine head
Tailpiece
String
Neck
Headstock
Resonator

DOBRO RESONATOR

COMPONENTS OF AN ACOUSTIC GUITAR

Machine heads
Top E string
Truss rod cover
Nut
Screws
Headstock
Machine head
Truss rod slot
Fingerboard
Truss rod
Fretwire slot
Position dots
Fretwire
Sound-hole
Bracing
Soundboard made of two pieces of spruce joined together

EXAMPLES OF ELECTRIC GUITARS

Pick-up
Scratchplate
Machine head
Solid body
String
Bridge
Neck
Headstock
Output socket
Vibrato arm

FENDER STRATOCASTER

Pick-up
Toggle switch
Machine head
Solid body
String
Bridge
Neck
Headstock
Scratchplate

GIBSON LES PAUL

Pick-up
Machine head
Solid body
String
Bridge
Neck
Headstock
Output socket
Scratchplate

FENDER JAZZ BASS

Keyboard instruments

KEYBOARD INSTRUMENTS are instruments that are sounded by means of a keyboard. The organ and piano are two of the principal members of the keyboard family. The organ consists of pipes which are operated by one or more manuals (keyboards) and a pedal board. The pipes are lined up in rows (known as ranks or registers) on top of a wind chest. The sound of the organ is made when air is admitted into a pipe by pressing a key or pedal. The piano consists of wire strings stretched over a metal frame, and a keyboard and pedals that operate hammers and dampers. The piano frame is either vertical – as in the upright piano – or horizontal – as in the grand piano. When a key is at rest, a damper lies against the string to stop it vibrating. When a key is pressed down, the damper moves away from the string as the hammer strikes it, causing the string to vibrate and sound a note.

ORGAN PIPE

UPRIGHT PIANO

Muffler felt
Pressure bar
Tuning pin
Pin block
Hammer
Hamme rail
88–note keyboard
Woode case
Keybed
Soundboard
Metal frame
String
Hitch pin
Treble bridge
Bass bridge
Una corda (soft) pedal
Sostenuto pedal
Damper (sustaining) pedal

ORGAN CONSOLE

Pipe
Pedal stop
Music stand
Swell stop
Choir stop
Swell manual (keyboard)
Great stop
Great manual (keyboard)
Thumb piston
Choir manual (keyboard)
Toe piston
Pedal board
Foot pedal
Swell pedal

UPRIGHT PIANO ACTION

KEY AT REST

String
Hammer
Damper lies against string, and stops it vibrating
Hammer rest
Back check
Damper lever
Action lever
Jack
Capstan screw
Key released

KEY PRESSED DOWN

String
Hammer strikes string
Damper moves away from string, allowing it to vibrate
Hammer rest
Back check
Damper lever
Action lever
Jack
Capstan screw
Key pressed down

CONCERT GRAND PIANO (VIEWED FROM ABOVE)

CONCERT GRAND PIANO (FRONT VIEW)

Soundboard

Bass bridge

Hitch pin

Metal frame

Single bass note string

Long bridge

Lid

String

Wooden case

Keyboard

Una corda (soft) pedal

Sostenuto pedal

Damper (sustaining) pedal

Tenor note strings (two strings for each note)

Treble note strings (three strings for each note)

Wooden case

Hammer

Tuning pin

Wrest plank

Keyboard lid

STEINWAY & SONS
NEW YORK HAMBURG

STEINWAY

88-note keyboard

Percussion instruments

TUBULAR BELLS

PERCUSSION INSTRUMENTS are a large group of instruments that produce sound by being struck, shaken, scraped, or clashed together. Most percussion instruments – such as the tam-tam (gong), cymbals, and maracas – do not have a definite pitch and are used for rhythm and impact, and the distinctive timbre (colour) of their sound. Other percussion instruments – such as the xylophone, vibraphone, and tubular bells – are tuned to a definite pitch and can play melody, harmony, and rhythms. The xylophone and vibraphone each have two rows of bars that are arranged in a similar way to the black and white keys of a piano. Metal tubes are suspended below the bars to amplify the sound. The vibraphone has electrically operated fans that rotate in the tubes and produce a vibrato (wavering pitch) effect.

TEMPLE BLOCKS

Tube struck with mallet

Hollow, metal tube

Damper bar

Metal frame

Mechanism linking pedal and damper bar

Row of tubes graduated in length and pitch

Damper pedal

EXAMPLES OF BEATERS

SOFT-HEADED BEATER   *Felt-covered head*

HARD-HEADED BEATER   *Rosewood head*

MALLET   *Leather-covered head*

Tam-tam struck in centre with soft-headed beater

TAM-TAM (GONG)

Cord

Metal frame

PAiSTe

Row of bars graduated in length and pitch   **XYLOPHONE**

Wooden bar struck with hard-headed beater

Hollow, metal tube

Metal stand

Rim

Large, metal disc

CYMBALS

Leather strap fits around player's hand

Pad protects hands from vibrations

Thin, convex disc of copper and tin alloy

SECTIONS OF A MARACA

Wooden handle

Lead shot

Hollow, wooden head

CLAVES

Hardwood sticks clashed together to give a sharp crack

TRIANGLE

Steel rod bent into triangular shape

Steel beater

CASTANETS

Cord

Hollowed wood

VIBRAPHONE

Row of bars graduated in length and pitch

Metal bar struck with soft-headed beater

Metal frame

Damper pedal

Metal tube containing electrically operated fan that produces vibrato (wavering pitch) effect

Electric cable

Drums

A DRUM IS A percussion instrument that consists of a drumhead, made of skin or plastic, stretched over one or both ends of a hollow vessel (the body-shell). Drums are played in most parts of the world and are made in a number of different shapes and sizes. They can be divided into three groups according to the shape of the body-shell: frame drums (e.g., tambourines), bowl-shaped drums (e.g., timpani), and tubular drums (e.g., congas). Drums are usually sounded by striking the drumhead with the hands or with beaters, such as a hard-headed stick. The drumhead vibrates, and its vibrations are amplified by the hollow body-shell. The snare drum has wires – known as snares – stretched across the lower drumhead; the snares vibrate against the lower drumhead when the drum is played. Most drums, such as congas, do not have a definite pitch and can play only rhythms (see pp. 516-517). Other drums, such as timpani, have a definite pitch and can play melody, harmony, and rhythms. They can be tuned by adjusting the tension of the drumhead. Different types of drum can be combined together with other percussion instruments to form a drum kit. The basic components of the drum kit are bass drum, tom-toms, floor tom (tenor drum), snare drum, and cymbals.

TAMBOURINE

Crash cymbal

Tension key

DRUM KIT

Tension rod

Tom-tom

Lug

Hi-hat cymbal

Snare drum

SNARE DRUM (VIEWED FROM BELOW)

Snare mounting

Adjustable damper

Lug

Transparent lower drumhead

Tripod stand

Chain

Tension screw

Upper drumhead

Snare

Felt-covered beater

Stick

Pedal

Snare release lever

Pedal

Ride cymbal

Tension key

Tom-tom

Tension rod

Lug

Floor tom
(tenor drum)

Height
adjustment key

EXAMPLES OF BEATERS

Acorn

Taper

HARD-HEADED STICK

SOFT-HEADED STICK

Felt-covered
head

WIRE BRUSH

Wire bristles

CONGAS

Metal hoop

Drumhead

Tension rod

Wooden
body-shell

Tension rod

Lug

Wooden
body-shell

Leg

Tripod
stand

TIMPANUM (KETTLE DRUM)

Drumhead

Tension rod

Metal hoop

Tuning
gauge

Copper
body-shell

Strut

Height
adjustment key

Leg

Tension rod

Crown

Bass
drum

Tuning pedal

Rubber foot

Castor

Electronic instruments

ELECTRONIC INSTRUMENTS generate electronic signals
that are magnified by an amplifier, and sent to a loudspeaker
where they are converted into sounds. Synthesizers, and other
electronic instruments, simulate the characteristic sounds of
conventional instruments, and also create entirely new sounds.
Most electronic instruments are keyboard instruments, but electronic
wind and percussion instruments are also popular. A digital sampler
records and stores sounds from musical instruments or other sources.
When the sound is played back, the pitch of the original sound can be
altered. A keyboard can be connected to the sampler so that a tune can
be played using the sampled sounds. With a MIDI (Musical Instrument
Digital Interface) system, a computer can be linked with other electronic
instruments, such as keyboards and electronic drums, to make sounds
together or in sequence. It is also possible, using music software, to
compose and play music on a home computer.

ELECTRONIC DRUMS

Drum pad

Height
adjustment key

Tripod

HOME KEYBOARD

Power button

Volume control

Function display

Memory record button

Tone editor control

Demonstration tune button

Pitch modulator

Multi-accompaniment system control

Tone and rhythm pattern selector

Key

SYNTHESIZER

Memory card slot

Joystick

Function display

Edit control

Data entry key pad

Sound structure guide

Volume control

Pitch modulator

Sound selection control

Key

WIND SYNTHESIZER

Keys for left hand

Mouthpiece

WIND CONTROLLER

Keys for right hand

DIGITAL SAMPLER

Contrast control

Function display

Power button

Data increment control

POWER PACK

MIDI (Musical Instrument Digital Interface) cable

Connecting cable

SOUND MODULE

Record trigger

Floppy-disc drive

Play button

Data entry key pad

Microphone input

Store button

Data entry key pad

Input connector socket

Volume control

HOME COMPUTER SYSTEM

Edit control

Play button

Function display

Effect balance control

VISUAL DISPLAY UNIT

Music sequencing software

Score for harpsichord

SPEAKER

Hard-disc drive

Floppy-disc drive

SOUND MODULE

SPEAKER

Volume control

Volume and tone controls

Volume control

KEYBOARD

Data entry key pad

Mouse pad

Mouse

521

SPORTS

Soccer

GAMES INVOLVING KICKING A BALL have a long history and were recorded in China as early as 300 BC; in medieval Europe, street football was banned as a menace to the public; only in 1863 were the rules established, specifically banning carrying the ball for all players except the goalkeeper, and separating rugby from soccer. Soccer, officially termed association football, is a team sport in which players attempt to score goals by passing and dribbling the ball down the field past opposing defenders, and kicking or heading the ball into the goal net, outwitting the defending goalkeeper. Each team consists of ten outfield players (defenders, midfielders, and strikers) and a goalkeeper. Players from the opposing team may challenge the player in possession of the ball, but an illegal or foul tackle results in a penalty if a foul occurs inside the penalty area or a free kick if outside the penalty area. The round ball used in soccer is more easily controlled than the oval balls used in American, Canadian, and Australian rules football and in rugby. The result is a more "open" or flowing game which is played and watched by millions of people worldwide.

LINESMAN'S FLAG

Lightweight, brightly coloured fabric

Handle with rubber grip

REFEREE'S EQUIPMENT

Red card

Yellow card

Referee's whistle

Stop-watch

PITCH MARKINGS

Halfway line

1.5 m
(5 ft)

HALFWAY-LINE FLAG

Corner arc

CORNER FLAG

7.3 m
(24 ft)

Goal-line

GOAL

SOCCER PITCH

46–91 m
(150–300 ft)

Goal-line

Corner flag

Corner arc

Penalty area

Penalty mark

Referee

Halfway-line flag

Striker

Striker

Left midfielder

Central midfielder

Left back

Touch-line

Central defender

Penalty arc

Linesman

Centre circle

Centre spot

Halfway line

Striker

Right midfielder

Right back

Central defender

Goal area

Goal

Goalkeeper

GOALKEEPER

Goalkeeper's shirt

Glove

Shin guard

Shorts

Sock

Soccer boot

SOCCER STRIP

Open-neck collar

Lightweight, man-made fabric team shirt

Team logo

Manufacturer's logo

Ribbed welt

Sponsor's logo

Manufacturer's name

Edge cut to fit perfectly

MAKING A SOCCER BALL

Hole punched in panel for stitching

Ball size number

Waxed thread

22–23 cm (8¹⁄₂–9 in)

Needle

Bladder valve

Bladder made from latex rubber

Long cotton sock

Club crest

Team shorts

Panels sewn together with ball inside out

Laminated panel

Synthetic bootlace

Interchangeable nylon stud

SOCCER BOOT

American football

IN AMERICAN AND CANADIAN FOOTBALL, the object of the game is to get the ball across the opponent's goal line, either by passing or carrying it across (a touch-down), or by kicking it between their goalposts (a field goal). An American football team has 11 players on the field at a time, although up to 40 players can appear for each side in a single game. The agile "offence" tries to score points, and the heavy hitting "defence" holds back the opposition. When in possession of the ball, a team has four chances ("downs"), to move it at least ten yards (nine metres) up the field to make a "first down". The opposition gains possession if they fail, or by tackling and intercepting the ball. Canadian football is played on a larger field, with 12 men on each side. A team has only three chances to achieve a first down. Otherwise, the game is very similar to American football. Helmets, face masks, and layers of body padding are worn by the players for protection.

AMERICAN FOOTBALL FIELD

Goalpost — End-line
Goal-line
Inbound line
Side-line
Line judge
Players' bench
Referee
Umpire
9.2 m (30 ft)
Back judge
End zone
GOALPOST
49 m (160 ft 6 in)

AMERICAN FOOTBALL PLAYING FORMATION

Right safety — Middle linebacker — Left safety
Right defensive tackle
Left defensive tackle
Right cornerback
Inside linebacker
Left cornerback
Outside linebacker
Left defensive end
Right defensive end — Centre
Tight end — Split end
Left tackle — Right tackle
Right guard
Left guard — Quarter back
Left half-back — Right half-back
Full back

CANADIAN FOOTBALL PLAYING FORMATION

Right defensive back — Middle linebacker — Safety — Left defensive back
Left defensive tackle
Right cornerback
Left cornerback
Left outside linebacker
Right outside linebacker
Left defensive end
Right defensive end
Wide receiver
Wide receiver
Right defensive tackle
Right tackle
Flanker
Left guard
Running back — Centre
Left tackle — Quarter back
Full back — Half back
9.2 m (30 ft)
GOALPOST

CANADIAN FOOTBALL FIELD

Goalpost
Goal-line
Players' bench
Yardsman
Referee
Umpire
Field judge
Head linesman
Yardsman
Side-line
End zone
59.5 m (195 ft)

PLAYER

Team logo

Helmet

Wrist pad

Player's number

Thigh pad

Pants

Tie to shoulder pads

Studded shoe

PROTECTIVE EQUIPMENT

28 cm (11 in)

Painted white ring

Lace

Brown pebbled leather

FOOTBALL

195

HELMET

Non-breakable plastic

Rubber-coated plastic

Shock absorber

SHOULDER PAD

BIKE

BIKE

AIR·LITE

BLUE LASER 40-42

Chest protector weight up to 2.5 kg (5 lb 8 oz)

REFEREE'S SIGNALS

TIME OUT

TOUCH-DOWN OR FIELD GOAL

PERSONAL FOUL

OFFSIDE OR ENCROACHMENT

HOLDING

ILLEGAL MOTION

FIRST DOWN

PASS INTERFERENCE

BIKE

UPPER ARM PAD

BIKE

ELBOW PAD

FINGERLESS GLOVE

Screw-in stud

BOOT

Fold-over leather tongue

RIB PADS

Strap ties on to shoulder pad

Groin pad

Foam-sponge filling

BIKE AL60

HIP PAD

BIKE AL60

Rigid plastic covering

BIKE AL82

PANTS

BIKE AL82

THIGH PAD

KNEE PAD

527

Australian rules and Gaelic football

VARIETIES OF FOOTBALL have developed all over the world and Australian rules football is considered to be one of the roughest versions, allowing full body tackles although participants wear no protective padding. The game is played on a large, oval pitch by two sides, each of 18 players. Players can kick or punch the ball, which is shaped like a rugby ball, but cannot throw it. Running with the ball is permitted, as long as the ball touches the ground at least once every ten metres. The full backs defend two sets of posts. Teams try to score "goals" (six points) between the inner posts or "behinds" (one point) inside the outer posts. Each game has four quarters of 25 minutes, and the team with the most points at the end of the allotted time is the winner. In Gaelic football, an Irish version of soccer (see pp. 524–525), a size 5 soccer ball is used. Each team can have 15 players on the field at a time. Players are allowed to catch, fist, and kick the ball, or dribble it using their hands or feet, but cannot throw it. Teams are awarded three points for getting the ball into the net, and one point for getting it through the posts above the crossbar. Gaelic football is rarely played outside of Ireland.

START OF PLAY

Field umpire

Centre circle

SCORING

GOAL (6 POINTS)

BEHIND (1 POINT)

AUSTRALIAN RULES FOOTBALL FIELD

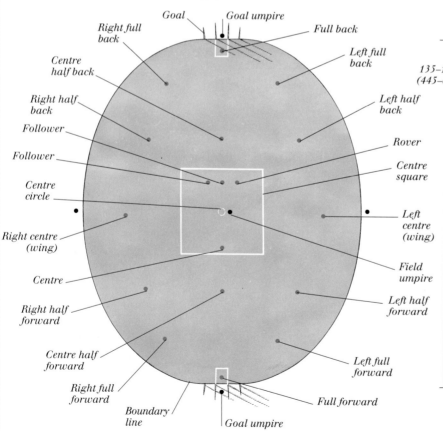

Goal

Goal umpire

Right full back

Full back

Centre half back

Left full back

Right half back

Left half back

Follower

Follower

Rover

Centre circle

Centre square

Right centre (wing)

Left centre (wing)

Centre

Field umpire

Right half forward

Left half forward

Centre half forward

Left full forward

Right full forward

Full forward

Boundary line

Goal umpire

135–185 m (445–610 ft)

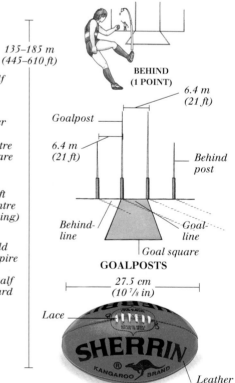

6.4 m (21 ft)

Goalpost

6.4 m (21 ft)

Behind post

Behind-line

Goal-line

Goal square

GOALPOSTS

27.5 cm (10 7/8 in)

Lace

SHERRIN

KANGAROO BRAND

Leather covering

AUSTRALIAN RULES FOOTBALL

AUSTRALIAN RULES FOOTBALL SKILLS

RUNNING WITH THE BALL

KICKING

TACKLING

TAKING A MARK

PASSING THE BALL

AUSTRALIAN RULES FOOTBALL DRESS

Australian Football League logo

Team colours

Sleeveless team guernsey

Sock

Shorts

GAELIC FOOTBALL PITCH

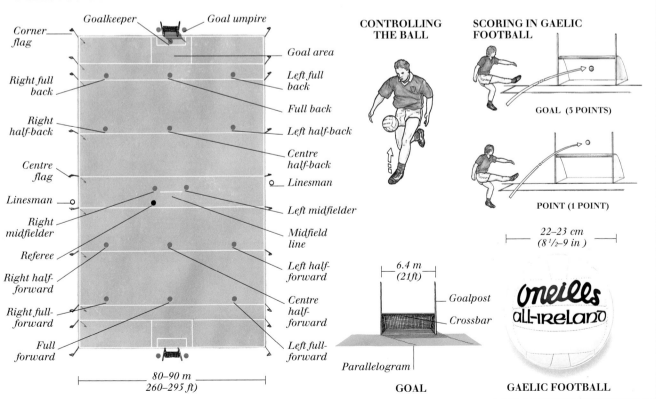

Goalkeeper

Goal umpire

Corner flag

Right full back

Right half-back

Centre flag

Linesman

Right midfielder

Referee

Right half-forward

Right full-forward

Full forward

Goal area

Left full back

Full back

Left half-back

Centre half-back

Linesman

Left midfielder

Midfield line

Left half-forward

Centre half-forward

Left full-forward

80–90 m
260–295 ft)

CONTROLLING THE BALL

SCORING IN GAELIC FOOTBALL

GOAL (3 POINTS)

POINT (1 POINT)

22–23 cm
(8 1/2–9 in)

6.4 m
(21ft)

Goalpost

Crossbar

Parallelogram

GOAL

oneills
all-ireland

GAELIC FOOTBALL

Rugby

RUGBY IS PLAYED WITH AN OVAL BALL which may be carried, thrown, or kicked. There are two codes of rugby. Rugby Union is an amateur game played by two teams of 15 players. They can score points in two ways: by placing the ball by hand over the opponents' goal-line (a try, scoring four points) or by kicking it over the crossbar of the opponent's goal (a conversion of a try, scoring two points; a penalty kick, scoring three points; or a drop-kick, scoring three points). Rugby League developed from the Union game but is played by 13 players at amateur and professional levels. In League games, a try scores four points; a conversion of a try scores two points; a drop goal scores three points, and a penalty kick scores two points. Scrummages occur in both forms of the game when play stops following an infringement.

RUGBY UNION PITCH

Goal · Dead-ball line · Touch in-goal line · Goal-line · 5 m line · Scrum-half · 10 m line · Loose-head prop · Flanker · Lock forward · Centre · Left wing · Centre · Full back · Touch-line · Referee · Hooker · Tight-head prop · Linesman · Flanker · Lock forward · Right wing · Number 8 · Fly-half · In-goal area

68 m (225 ft) maximum

RUGBY UNION SCRUMMAGE

Loose-head prop · Hooker · Tight-head prop · Scrum-half · Flanker · Flanker · Lock forward · Lock forward · Number 8

RUGBY UNION GOALPOST

5.5 m (18 ft) · Upright · Crossbar · Protective padding · 3 m (9 ft 10 in)

RUGBY LEAGUE PITCH

Goal · Dead-ball line · Touch in-goal · Touch in-goal line · Goal-line · Touch-line · 10 m line · Hooker · Referee · Open-side prop · Linesman · Linesman · Blind-side prop · Second-row forward · Second-row forward · Scrum-half · Loose forward · Stand-off half · Left wing · Centre · Full back · Centre · Right wing

68 m (225 ft) maximum

RUGBY LEAGUE SCRUMMAGE

Hooker · Open-side prop · Scrum-half · Blind-side prop · Second-row forward · Second-row forward · Loose forward

RUGBY LEAGUE GOALPOST

5.5 m (18 ft) · Upright · Crossbar · Protective padding

**RUGBY SCORING
AND SKILLS**

GOAL

*Goal-
line*

TRY

PASS

PLACE KICK

FLYING TACKLE

*Circular
stud*

RUGBY BOOT

*Ankle
support*

RUGBY UNION PLAYER

*Shirt
in team
colour*

*Laminated leather
panel covered with
textured plastic*

*Four-panel
construction*

*Knee-high
sock*

*Team
shorts*

*Studded
boot*

RUGBY UNION BALL

28–30 cm (11–12 in)

RUGBY LEAGUE BALL

*Four-panel
construction*

*Laminated leather
panel covered with
smooth plastic*

28 cm (11 in)

*Official logo of the
British Rugby Football
League*

*Button-up
collar*

*Three-quarter
sleeve*

RUGBY UNION SHIRT

RUGBY LEAGUE SHIRT

*Team
crest*

*Team
crest*

Team colour

Long sleeve

RUGBY SHIRTS

531

Basketball

BASKETBALL IS A BALL GAME for two teams of five players, originally devised in 1890 by James Naismath for the Y.M.C.A. in Springfield, Massachusetts, U.S.A. The object of the game is to take possession of the ball and score points by throwing the ball into the opposing team's basket. A player moves the ball up and down the court by bouncing it along the ground or "dribbling"; the ball may be passed between players by throwing, bouncing, or rolling. Players may not run with or kick the ball, although pivoting on one foot is allowed. The game begins with the referee throwing the ball into the air and a player from each team jumping up to try and "tip" the ball to a team-mate. The length of the game and the number of periods played varies at different levels. There are amateur, professional, and international rules. No game ends in a draw. An extra period of five minutes is played, plus as many extra periods as are necessary to break the tie. In addition to the five players on court, each team has up to seven substitutes, but players may only leave the court with the permission of the referee. Basketball is a non-contact sport and fouls on other players are penalized by a throw-in awarded against the offending team; a free throw at the basket is awarded when a player is fouled in the act of shooting. Basketball is a fast-moving game, requiring both physical and mental coordination. Skilful tactical play matters more than simple physical strength and the agility of the players makes the game an excellent spectator sport.

CHEST PASS

DRIBBLE

OVERHEAD PASS

INTERNATIONAL BASKETBALL COURT

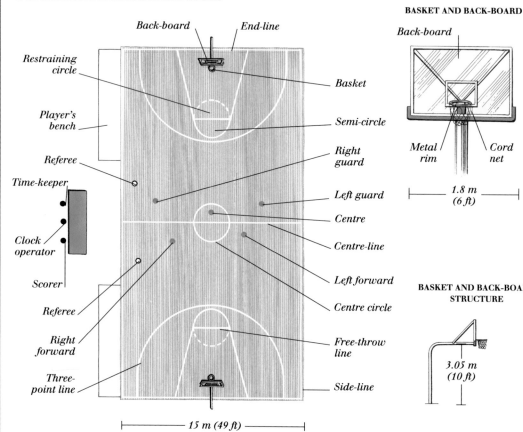

Back-board · End-line · Restraining circle · Player's bench · Referee · Time-keeper · Clock operator · Scorer · Referee · Right forward · Three-point line · Basket · Semi-circle · Right guard · Left guard · Centre · Centre-line · Left forward · Centre circle · Free-throw line · Side-line

— 15 m (49 ft) —

BASKET AND BACK-BOARD

Back-board · Metal rim · Cord net

1.8 m (6 ft)

BASKET AND BACK-BOARD STRUCTURE

3.05 m (10 ft)

LAY-UP SHOT

JUMP SHOT

LONG PASS

ZONE DEFENCES

AMERICAN BASKETBALL VEST

Cool, lightweight fabric

Team name

Player's number

Free-throw line

Point man

1 – 2 – 2 ZONE

1 – 3 – 1 ZONE

2 – 3 ZONE

24–5 cm
(9$\frac{1}{2}$–9$\frac{3}{4}$ in)

Textured surface for good grip

Low heel profile

Cushioned sole

BASKETBALL

BASKETBALL SHOE

INTERNATIONAL REFEREE'S SIGNALS

TECHNICAL FOUL

INTENTIONAL FOUL

JUMP BALL

STOP CLOCK FOR FOUL

SUBSTITUTION

PERSONAL FOUL: NO FREE THROWS

TRAVELLING

ILLEGAL DRIBBLE

CHARGING WITH THE BALL

ONE FREE THROW

STOP CLOCK

Volleyball, netball, and handball

VOLLEYBALL, NETBALL, AND HANDBALL are fast-moving team sports played with balls on courts with a hard surface. In volleyball, the object of the game is to hit the ball over a net strung across the centre of the court so that it touches the ground on the opponent's side. The team of six players can take three hits to direct the ball over the net, although the same player cannot hit the ball twice in a row. Players can hit the ball with their arms, hands or any other part of their upper body. Teams score points only while serving. The first team to score 15 points, with a two-point margin over their opponent, wins the game. Netball is one of the few sports played exclusively by women. Similar to basketball (see pp.532–533), it is played on a slightly larger court with seven players instead of five. A team moves the ball towards the goal by throwing, passing, and catching it with the aim of throwing the ball through the opponents' goal net. Players are confined by their playing position to specific areas of the court. Team handball is one of the world's fastest games. Each side has seven players. A team moves the ball by dribbling, passing, or bouncing it as they run. Players may stop, catch, throw, bounce, or strike the ball with any part of the body above the knees. Each team tries to score goals by directing the ball past the opposition's goalkeeper into the net, which is similar to a soccer net.

VOLLEYBALL SHOTS

OVERHAND SERVE   SPIKE (SMASH)

UNDERHAND SERVE   FOREARM PASS
(DIG)

VOLLEYBALL KIT

Team colours

Ribbed cuff

Cotton-knit jersey

Elasticated waist

Mizuno

Shorts

Mizuno

VOLLEYBALL COURT

End-line

Linesman

Clear space

Leather covering

21 cm (8¼ in)

Linesman

Side-line

Attack zone

Players' bench

Attack line

Referee

Umpire

VOLLEYBALL

Scorer

Centre forward

Net

Left forward

Right forward

Back zone

Centre back

Left back

Linesman

Service area

Linesman

Server

9 m (29 ft 6 in)

Elasticated knit fabric

Injected moulded padding

Tape   Net   Antenna

Men's: 2.4 m (8 ft)
Women's: 2.2 m (7 ft 4 in)

Post

VOLLEYBALL NET

KNEE PADS

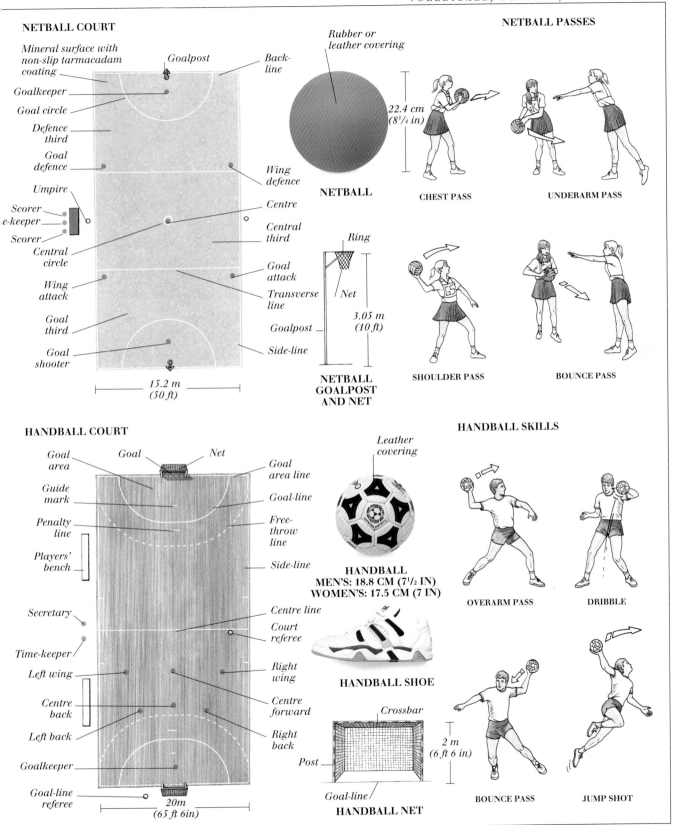

NETBALL COURT

Mineral surface with non-slip tarmacadam coating

Goalpost

Back-line

Goalkeeper

Goal circle

Defence third

Goal defence

Wing defence

Umpire

Scorer

e-keeper

Scorer

Central circle

Centre

Central third

Goal attack

Transverse line

Wing attack

Goal third

Goal shooter

Side-line

15.2 m (50 ft)

NETBALL PASSES

Rubber or leather covering

22.4 cm (8³⁄₄ in)

NETBALL

CHEST PASS

UNDERARM PASS

Ring

Net

Goalpost

3.05 m (10 ft)

NETBALL GOALPOST AND NET

SHOULDER PASS

BOUNCE PASS

HANDBALL COURT

Goal area

Goal

Net

Guide mark

Penalty line

Players' bench

Secretary

Time-keeper

Left wing

Centre back

Left back

Goalkeeper

Goal-line referee

Goal area line

Goal-line

Free-throw line

Side-line

Centre line

Court referee

Right wing

Centre forward

Right back

20m (65 ft 6in)

HANDBALL SKILLS

Leather covering

HANDBALL
MEN'S: 18.8 CM (7¹⁄₂ IN)
WOMEN'S: 17.5 CM (7 IN)

OVERARM PASS

DRIBBLE

HANDBALL SHOE

Crossbar

2 m (6 ft 6 in)

Post

Goal-line

HANDBALL NET

BOUNCE PASS

JUMP SHOT

Baseball

BASEBALL IS A BALL GAME for two teams of nine players. The batter hits the ball thrown by the opposing team's pitcher, into the area between the foul lines. He then runs round all four fixed bases in order to score a run, touching or "tagging" each base in turn. The pitcher must throw the ball at a height between the batter's armpits and knees, a height which is called the "strike zone". A ball pitched in this area that crosses over the "home plate" is called a "strike" and the batter has three strikes in which to try and hit the ball (otherwise he is "struck out"). The fielding team tries to get the batting team out by catching the ball before it bounces, tagging a player of the batting team with the ball who is running between bases, or by tagging a base before the player has reached it. Members of the batting team may stop safely at a base as long as it is not occupied by another member of their team. When the batter runs to first base, his team-mate at first base must run on to second – this is called "force play". A game consists of nine innings and each team will bat once during an inning. When three members of the batting team are out, the teams swap roles. The team with the greatest number of runs wins the game.

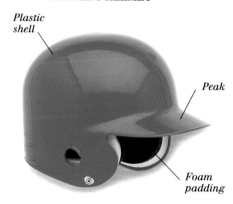

BATTER'S HELMET

Plastic shell

Peak

Foam padding

Wire coated in strong nylon

Plastic-coated foam padding

CATCHER'S MASK

BASEBALL PITCH

Centre field

Centre fielder

Warning track

Right fielder

Left fielder

Left field

Second baseman

Right field

Foul line

Outfield

Shortstop

First baseman

Umpire

Third baseman

First base

Third base

Infield

Coach's box

Home run

Second base

Dugout

100 m (325 ft) minimum

On-deck circle

Pitcher's mound

Pitcher

Pitcher's rubber

PITCHER'S MOUND

Batter

Home plate

Catcher

Home-plate umpire

HOME PLATE

MAKING A BASEBALL

Woollen yarn

Rubber inner casing

Horsehide strip

CUSHION CORK
5 oz
TAIWAN
LEATHER COVER

Cooper
63

Cork centre

Cotton thread outer casing

Woollen strand

Red outer stitching

THE PITCHING SEQUENCE

THE WIND-UP 1

THE WIND-UP 2

THE WIND-UP 3

THE WIND-UP 4

THE RELEASE

THE FOLLOW-THROUGH

UMPIRING SIGNALS

BALL

INFIELD

STRIKE

FAIR BALL

RUNNER IS SAFE

FOUL TIP

BASEBALL EQUIPMENT

Webbed pocket

Fingers laced together

Strap

Thumb

STEERHIDE LEATHER

Palm

Willie Randolph

Leather stitching

Heel

FIELDER'S GLOVE AND BALL

PONY

Metal heel plate

AMERICAN BASEBALL BOOT

Metal toe plate

Batter's helmet

Bat

Batting glove

Team shirt

Undershirt

Pants

Spiked shoe

BATTER

Hitting area

Official Baseball

Crest

1.1 m (3 ft 6 in) maximum

Handle

Knob

BAT

Cricket

CRICKET IS A BALL GAME PLAYED by two teams of eleven players on a pitch with two sets of three stumps (wickets). The bowler bowls the ball down the pitch to the batsman of the opposing team, who must defend the wicket in front of which he stands. The object of the game is to score as many runs as possible. Runs can be scored individually by running the length of the playing strip, or by hitting a ball which lands outside the boundary ("six"), or which lands inside the boundary but bounces or rolls outside ("four"); the opposing team will bowl and field, attempting to dismiss the batsmen. A batsman can be dismissed in one of several ways: by the bowler hitting the wicket with the ball ("bowled"); by a fielder catching the ball hit by the batsman before it touches the ground ("caught"); by the wicket-keeper or another fielder breaking the wicket while the batsman is attempting a run and is therefore out of his ground ("stumped" or "run out"); by the batsman breaking the wicket with his own bat or body ("hit wicket"); by a part of the batsman's body being hit by a ball that would otherwise have hit the wicket ("leg before wicket" ["lbw"]). A match consists of one or two innings and each innings ends when the tenth batsman of the batting team is out, when a certain number of overs (a series of six balls bowled) have been played, or when the captain of the batting team "declares" ending the innings voluntarily.

CRICKET STROKES

FORWARD DEFENSIVE STROKE

BACKWARD DEFENSIVE STROKE

ON-DRIVE

OFF-DRIVE

PULL

HOOK

SQUARE CUT

LEG GLANCE

Wicket-keeper

Batsman

Wicket

Bowling crease

CRICKET PITCH

20 m (66 ft)

Bowler

Return crease

Umpire

Non-striking batsman

POSSIBLE FIELD POSITIONS FOR AN AWAY SWING BOWLER TO A RIGHT-HANDED BATSMAN (IN RED) AND OTHER FIELD POSITIONS

Long on

Umpire

Long off

Boundary line

Bowler

Deep mid-wicket

Non-striking batsman

Mid-on

Extra cover

Silly mid-on

Mid-off

Forward short leg

Silly mid-off

Square leg

Cover

Deep square leg

Point

Square-leg umpire

Gulley

Batsman

Third man

Long leg

Second slip

Leg slip

First slip

Wicket-keeper

Fine leg

Sight screen

CRICKET BALL AND WICKET

Leather skin

Seam

BALL

Bail

WICKET

Stump

MAKING A BAT HANDLE

Sarawak cane

Twine wrapped around handle

Rubber strip

LAMINATING THE WOOD

BINDING THE HANDLE

PROTECTIVE CLOTHING

Slit in leather for greater flexibility

Padding protects knuckles from injury

Dimpled rubber improves grip

Polycarbonate shell with cloth covering

Mesh covering for ventilation

Wrist strap

Peak

Foam cheek-piece for comfort and good fit

Protective plastic ear piece

BATTING GLOVE

WICKET-KEEPER'S GLOVES

HELMET

MAKING A BAT BLADE

V-shaped splice

ADDING THE HANDLE TO THE BAT

Rubber grip

Shoulder of bat

Grip rolled onto handle

Handle glued into splice

Scoop

Bat

BATSMAN

Padded glove

Cap

Wristband

White shirt

White sweater

Stripes in team colours

Thigh pad under white trousers

Knee roll

Cricket shoe

Leg pad

Kiln-dried willow

Blade planed by hand

Toe of the bat shaped

Sanded and polished bat

Dimpled rubber sole

SEASONING THE TIMBER

CUTTING THE SPLICE

FITTING THE HANDLE

FINISHING TOUCHES

Hockey, lacrosse, and hurling

ALL OVER THE WORLD, TEAM GAMES have evolved which require that a ball be struck or carried, and tossed at the end of a stick. Early forms of these games include hurling, shinty, bandy, and pelota. Hockey is played by men and women: two teams of eleven players try to gain and keep possession of the ball and score goals by using the hockey stick to propel the ball into their opponents' goal net. Skills such as passing, pushing, or hitting the ball by slapping or lifting it in a flicking movement, and shooting at goal are crucial. Hockey is played indoors and outdoors on grass or synthetic pitches. Lacrosse is played internationally as a 12-a-side game for women and as 10-a-side game for men. The women's pitch has no absolute boundaries but the men's pitch has clearly defined side-lines and end-lines. The ball is kept in play by being carried, thrown or batted with the crosse, and rolled or kicked in any direction. In men's and women's lacrosse, play can continue behind the marked goal areas. Similar skills are required in hurling – a Gaelic field game played on the same pitch as Gaelic football (see pp. 528–529), using the same goalposts and net. In hurling, the ball may be struck with or carried on the hurley and, when off the ground, may be struck with the hand or kicked. Goals (three points) are scored when the ball passes between the posts and under the crossbar; one point is scored when it passes between the posts and over the crossbar.

GOALKEEPER'S EQUIPMENT

Air vent

Hard shell

Face mask

Cooper XL7

HELMET

Strap

Rigid palm

Padded wrist

GAUNTLET

Stitched seam

HOCKEY STICK AND BALL

STICK

Handle

Tape

Steam-bent ash head

Blade

Slazenger FLEX!

91 cm (3 ft)

7–7.5 cm (2³/₄–3 in)

BALL

HOCKEY FIELD

Side-line

Centre forward

Inside right

Right wing

Right half

Right back

Corner flag

Shooting circle

Goal

Penalty spot

Five yard mark

Goal-line

Inside left

Left wing

Umpire

Centre half

Left half

Left back

Goalkeeper

55 m (180 ft)

Protective overshoe

Padding protects toes against the hard ball

Strap

GOALKEEPER'S KICKER

2.1 m (7 ft)

HOCKEY GOAL

MEN'S LACROSSE FIELD

Defender
Goalkeeper
Defender
Corner flag
Goal
Goal circle
Defender
Midfielder
Chief bench official
Scorer
Midfielder
Midfielder
Referee
Penalty time-keeper
Attacker
Attacker
Attacker
Time-keeper
55m (180 ft)

LACROSSE SKILLS

CRADLING
THROWING
SIDE-SHOOTING

LACROSSE GOALKEEPER

Goalkeeper's stick
Leather glove
Sweat trousers
Helmet
Face mask
Team shirt
Player's number
Solid rubber lacrosse ball

WOMEN'S LACROSSE FIELD

Centre
Third man
15 m fan
Hash mark
Goalkeeper
Goal circle
Point
Cover point
Right wing defence
Left wing defence
Left wing attack
Time-keeper
Scorer
Third home
Penalty time-keeper
Second home
First home
Right wing attack
Umpire
60 m (200 ft) approx

1.8 m (6 ft)
Crossbar
Post
Peg

LACROSSE NET

Net made from gut, rawhide, or cord
Throat
Lacing
Guardstop
Pocket
Wall
Head

CROSSE AND BALL

Butt
Handle

HURLER

Helmet
Team shirt
Hurley
Shorts
Sock
Boot

SCORING AT HURLING

7 m (23 ft)

GOAL (3 POINTS)
POINT (1 POINT)

Leather cover around a cork centre

HURLING BALL

HURLEY AND HURLING BALL

Grip
HURLEY
Boss
91 cm (3 ft)

Athletics

THE SPORTS that make up athletics are divided into two main groups: track events – which include sprinting, middle, and long distance running, relay running, hurdling, and walking – and field events which require jumping and throwing skills. Contests designed to test the speed, strength, agility, and stamina of athletes were held by the ancient Greeks over 4,000 years ago. However, the abolition of the Olympic Games in 393 AD meant that athletics were neglected until the revival of large-scale competitions in the mid-nineteenth century. Modern stadia offer areas reserved for the long jump, triple jump, and pole vault usually situated outside the running track. The javelin, shot, hammer, and discus are thrown within the track area. Most athletes specialize in one or two events but, in the heptathlon, women compete in seven events, held over two days: 200 m and 800 m races, 100 m hurdles, javelin, shot put, high jump, and long jump. In the decathlon, men compete in ten events over two days: 100 m, 400 m, and 1,500 m races, 110 m hurdles, javelin, discus, shot put, pole vault, high jump, and long jump.

FIELD EVENT EQUIPMENT

Steel wire

Head

Body

Swivel

HAMMER 7 KG (16 LB)

Metal rim

Centre weight

DISCUS MEN: 2 KG (4 LB 7 OZ) WOMEN: 1 KG (2 LB 3 OZ)

Hammer handle

Rubber coating

Shot-pellet filling

12.7 cm (5 in)

10 cm (4 in)

MEN'S SHOT 7 KG (16 LB)

WOMEN'S SHOT 4 KG (8 LB 12 OZ)

JAVELIN

Cord grip

Shaft

Tip

Men: 2.6 m (8 ft 6 in)
Women: 2.3 m (7 ft 6 in)

ATHLETICS TRACK AND FIELD

Finishing post

Pole-vault mat

Pole-vault runway

100 m starting line

Finishing line

Hammer circle

Javelin fan

Discus circle

Steeplechase water jump

Javelin runway

Lane

One lap is 400 m

Shot-put fan

High-jump fan

Shot-put circle

High-jump mat

Discus fan

Hammer fan

Triple-jump take-off board

Triple-jump take-off line

Indicator board

Triple-jump runway

Long-jump take-off board

Landing area

RELAY BATONS

Hollow plastic tube

TYPES OF SHOE

Lightweight construction

Spiked sole

TRACK SHOE

Air "pumping" device for comfort and fit

Reflective side strip

Wedge heel

Air-cushioned sole

RUNNING SHOE

DISCUS THROW

Swing

Shift

Twist

Release

SHOT PUT

Crouch

Shift

Release

Thrust

HAMMER THROW

Swing

Entry

Lift

Release

JAVELIN THROW

Withdrawal stride

Half turn

Step

Drive forward

Release

LONG JUMP

Take-off

Flight

Hitch-kick

Stretch

Landing

Take-off board

TRIPLE JUMP

Take-off

Hop

Skip

Jump

Take-off board

Land on foot used for take-off

Land on opposite foot

HIGH JUMP

Drive

Arch

Take-off

Approach

Landing

POLE VAULT

Handstand

Push-pull

Release

Rock-back

Hang

Take-off

Plant

Landing

543

Racket sports

PROTECTIVE EYEWEAR

THE OBJECT OF ALL RACKET SPORTS is to make shots the opponent cannot return. Games are played by two players (singles) or four players (doubles). Racket shape and size is tailored to each sport, but all rackets are constructed of wood, plastic, aluminium, or high-performance materials such as fibreglass and carbon graphite. Racket strings are usually synthetic, although natural gut is still used. Tennis is played on a court divided by a low net. Opposing players serve alternate games. At least six games must be won to gain a set, and two or sometimes three sets are needed to win a match. Tennis courts may be concrete, grass, clay, or synthetic, each surface requiring a different style of play. Badminton is an indoor sport that is played with light, flexible rackets and a feather shuttlecock on a court with a high net. Players can score points only on their serve. The first to reach 15 points (11 points for women's singles) wins the game. Two games are needed to win a match. Squash and racketball are both played in enclosed courts. One player hits the ball against the front wall, and the other tries to return it before it bounces on the floor more than once. Squash rackets have smaller, rounder heads and stiffer frames than badminton rackets. In America, the game is played on a narrower court than an international court using a much harder ball. Squash games are played to nine points (international) or 15 points (American). In racketball, players use a ball that is larger and bouncier than a squash ball. The racket is thick and sturdy, with a large head, short handle, and a thong that loops around the wrist. Points can be won only when serving, and the first player to reach 21 points wins.

TENNIS RACKET

- Synthetic string
- Frame
- Head
- Logo
- Throat
- Grip
- Butt

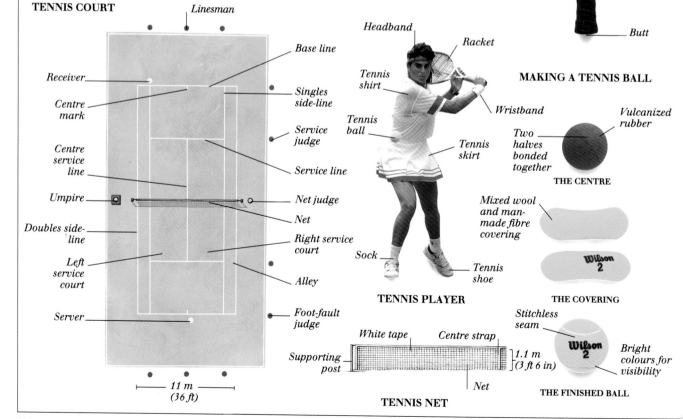

TENNIS COURT

- Linesman
- Base line
- Receiver
- Singles side-line
- Centre mark
- Service judge
- Centre service line
- Service line
- Umpire
- Net judge
- Net
- Doubles side-line
- Right service court
- Left service court
- Alley
- Server
- Foot-fault judge

11 m (36 ft)

TENNIS PLAYER

- Headband
- Racket
- Tennis shirt
- Wristband
- Tennis ball
- Tennis skirt
- Sock
- Tennis shoe

TENNIS NET

- White tape
- Centre strap
- Supporting post
- Net
- 1.1 m (3 ft 6 in)

MAKING A TENNIS BALL

- Vulcanized rubber
- Two halves bonded together

THE CENTRE

- Mixed wool and man-made fibre covering

THE COVERING

- Stitchless seam
- Bright colours for visibility

THE FINISHED BALL

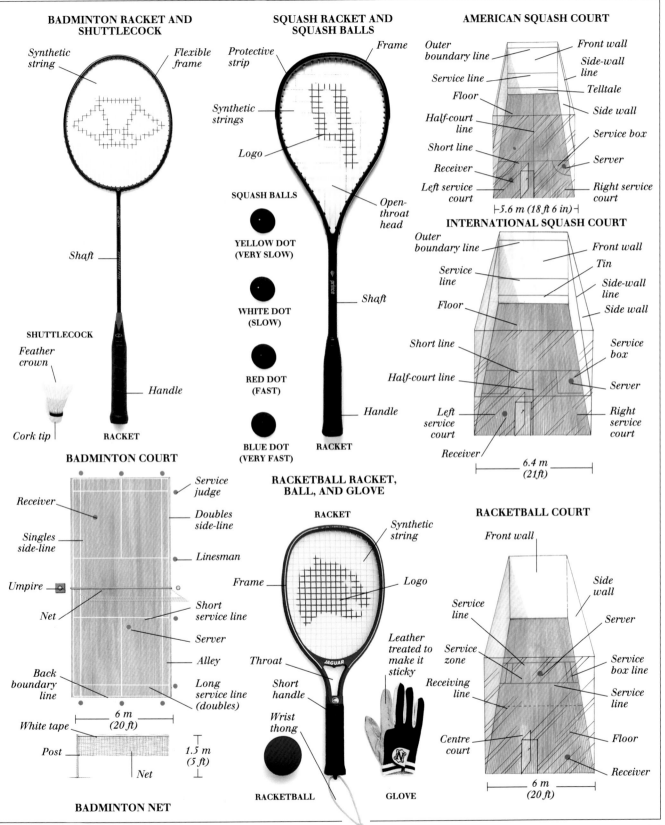

BADMINTON RACKET AND SHUTTLECOCK

Synthetic string
Flexible frame
Shaft

SHUTTLECOCK
Feather crown
Cork tip

Handle

RACKET

SQUASH RACKET AND SQUASH BALLS

Protective strip
Frame
Synthetic strings
Logo
Open-throat head
Shaft
Handle

RACKET

SQUASH BALLS

YELLOW DOT (VERY SLOW)

WHITE DOT (SLOW)

RED DOT (FAST)

BLUE DOT (VERY FAST)

AMERICAN SQUASH COURT

Outer boundary line
Front wall
Service line
Side-wall line
Floor
Telltale
Half-court line
Side wall
Short line
Service box
Receiver
Server
Left service court
Right service court

⊢5.6 m (18 ft 6 in)⊣

INTERNATIONAL SQUASH COURT

Outer boundary line
Front wall
Service line
Tin
Floor
Side-wall line
Side wall
Short line
Half-court line
Service box
Left service court
Server
Right service court
Receiver

6.4 m (21ft)

BADMINTON COURT

Receiver
Service judge
Singles side-line
Doubles side-line
Linesman
Umpire
Net
Short service line
Server
Alley
Back boundary line
Long service line (doubles)

6 m (20 ft)

White tape
Post
Net
1.5 m (5 ft)

BADMINTON NET

RACKETBALL RACKET, BALL, AND GLOVE

RACKET
Synthetic string
Frame
Logo
Leather treated to make it sticky
Throat
Short handle
Wrist thong

RACKETBALL
GLOVE

RACKETBALL COURT

Front wall
Side wall
Service line
Server
Service zone
Service box line
Receiving line
Service line
Centre court
Floor
Receiver

6 m (20 ft)

Golf

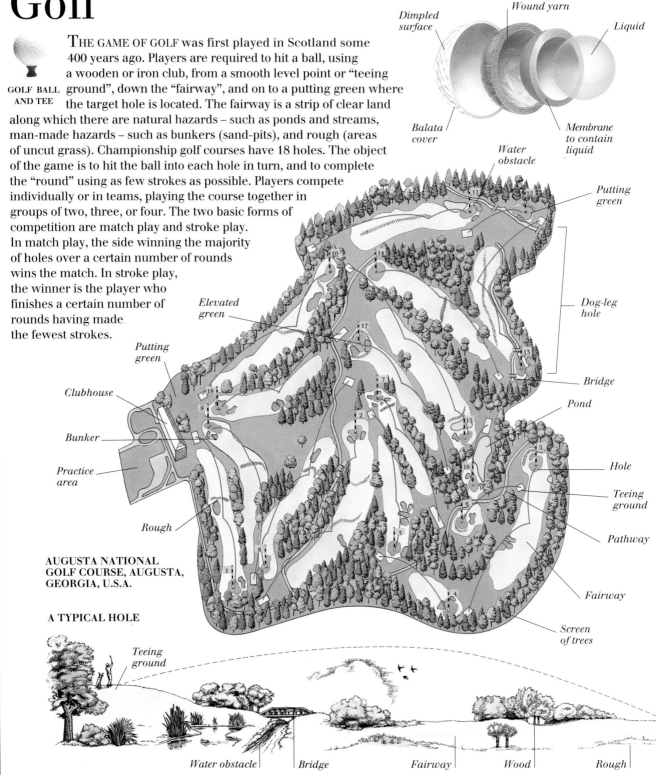

**GOLF BALL
AND TEE**

THE GAME OF GOLF was first played in Scotland some 400 years ago. Players are required to hit a ball, using a wooden or iron club, from a smooth level point or "teeing ground", down the "fairway", and on to a putting green where the target hole is located. The fairway is a strip of clear land along which there are natural hazards – such as ponds and streams, man-made hazards – such as bunkers (sand-pits), and rough (areas of uncut grass). Championship golf courses have 18 holes. The object of the game is to hit the ball into each hole in turn, and to complete the "round" using as few strokes as possible. Players compete individually or in teams, playing the course together in groups of two, three, or four. The two basic forms of competition are match play and stroke play. In match play, the side winning the majority of holes over a certain number of rounds wins the match. In stroke play, the winner is the player who finishes a certain number of rounds having made the fewest strokes.

GOLF BALL WITH BALATA SURFACE

Dimpled surface

Wound yarn

Liquid

Balata cover

Membrane to contain liquid

Water obstacle

Putting green

Dog-leg hole

Bridge

Pond

Hole

Teeing ground

Pathway

Fairway

Screen of trees

Elevated green

Putting green

Clubhouse

Bunker

Practice area

Rough

**AUGUSTA NATIONAL
GOLF COURSE, AUGUSTA,
GEORGIA, U.S.A.**

A TYPICAL HOLE

Teeing ground

Water obstacle   *Bridge*   *Fairway*   *Wood*   *Rough*

MAKING A WOODEN CLUB

Close grain of wood

Streamlined back

Plastic insert on face

Sand, stain, and varnish finish

Persimmon wood

Slot cut for plate

Metal sole plate protects the wood

Outline of head

RAW MATERIAL

CREATING THE BASIC SHAPE

ADDING THE LEAD WEIGHT

THE FINISHED CLUB HEAD

RANGE OF WOODEN CLUBS

10 degree loft

15 degree loft

21 degree loft

DRIVER

3-WOOD

5-WOOD

30 degree loft

34 degree loft

38 degree loft

42 degree loft

46 degree loft

50 degree loft

56 degree loft

5-IRON

6-IRON

7-IRON

8-IRON

9-IRON

PITCHING WEDGE

SAND WEDGE

RANGE OF IRON CLUBS

22 degree loft

26 degree loft

3-IRON

4-IRON

GOLF ACCESSORIES

SCORECARD AND PENCIL

BALL MARKERS

TEE PEGS

PITCHMARK REPAIRER

PRACTICE BALL

Spiked sole

LIGHTWEIGHT SHOE

Flag pole or pin

Green

Bunker (sand -pit)

PUTTER, WOOD, AND IRON

IRON

Textured vulcanized rubber grip

WOOD

PUTTER

Shaped pistol grip

Stainless steel shaft

Steel shaft

Steel shaft

84 cm (33 in)

94 cm (37 in)

109 cm (43 in)

Neck

Neck

Face

Angled neck

Heel

Toe

Heel

Toe

Groove

Sole

Heel

Blade

547

Archery and shooting

TARGET SHOOTING AND ARCHERY EVOLVED as practice for hunting and battle skills. Modern bows, although designed according to the principles of early hunting bows, use laminates, fibreglass, dacron, and carbon, and are equipped with sights and stabilizers. Competitors in target archery shoot over distances of 30 m (100 ft), 50 m (165 ft), 70 m (230 ft), and 90 m (300 ft) for men, and 30 m (100 ft), 50 m (165 ft), 60 m (200 ft), and 70 m (230 ft) for women. The closer the shot is to the centre of the target, the higher the score. The individual scores are added up, and the archer with the highest total wins the competition. Crossbows are used in match competitions over 10 m (33 ft), and 30 m (100 ft). Rifle shooting is divided into three categories: smallbore, bigbore, and air rifle. Contests take place over a variety of distances and further subdivisions are based on the type of shooting position used: prone, kneeling, or standing. The Olympic biathlon combines cross-country skiing and rifle shooting over a course of approximately 20 km (12$\frac{1}{2}$ miles). Additional magazines of ammunition are carried in the butt of the rifles. Bigbore rifles fitted with a telescopic sight can be used for hunting and running game target shooting. Pistol shooting events, using rapid-fire pistols, target pistols, and air pistols, take place over 10 m (33 ft), 25 m (82 ft), and 50 m (165 ft) distances. In rapid-fire pistol shooting, a total of 60 shots are fired from a distance of 25 m (83 ft).

CROSSBOW AND BOLT

Laminated fibreglass bow

Bolt

Bolt rest

45 mm (1^3/$_4$ in)

Stirrup held between feet when drawing bow

Sight

CROSSBOW TARGET

Hardwood laminate limb

Dacron string

Sight

MODERN BOW

Pressure button

Grip

V-bar stabilizers

Magnesium riser

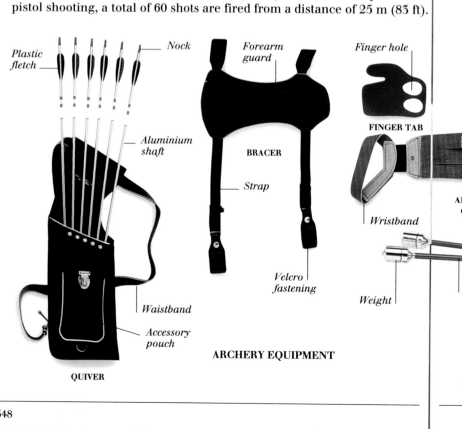

Plastic fletch

Nock

Forearm guard

Finger hole

Aluminium shaft

BRACER

FINGER TAB

Strap

ARCHER'S GLOVE

Wristband

Weight

Velcro fastening

Waistband

Accessory pouch

ARCHERY EQUIPMENT

QUIVER

**SMALLBORE
BIATHLON RIFLE**

*Rifle sight without
magnifying lens*

Fore sight

Barrel

Trigger

*Trigger
guard*

*Extra magazine
stored in rifle butt*

*5.6 mm (0.22 in)
calibre bullet*

Magazine

*155 mm
(6 in)*

**SMALLBORE
FREE RIFLE
TARGET FOR
50 M (165 FT)
RANGE**

**BIGBORE
HUNTING RIFLE**

Bolt

*Bolt
handle*

Telescopic sight

Open sight

Open sight

Sling fixing point

*7.62 mm
(0.3 in)
calibre
bullet*

*1 m
(39 in)*

**BIGBORE RIFLE
TARGET FOR
300 M (1000 FT)
RANGE**

AIR PISTOL

*Wooden grip
shaped to fit
the hand*

*Cocking
lever and
barrel*

Piston

*155 mm
(6 in)*

TARGET PISTOL

Back sight

Fore sight

Hammer

*Firing
pin*

Sight pin

*Sight ring
attachment*

Magazine

*9 mm
(0.35 in)
calibre
bullet*

*197 mm
(7¼ in)*

**PISTOL
TARGET FOR
18 M (60 FT)
RANGE**

Trigger

*Air-pistol
pellet*

**AIR-PISTOL
TARGET FOR
10 M (33 FT)
RANGE**

Nock

FIELD ARROW

Metal tip

Feathering

Wooden shaft

Straw butt

*White inner
2 points*

*Aluminium
longrod stabilizer*

*Blue outer
5 points*

*Yellow inner 10
points (bull's-eye)*

ARCHERY TARGET

Ice hockey

ICE HOCKEY IS PLAYED by two teams of six players on an ice rink, with a goal net at each end. The object of this fast, and often dangerous, game is to hit a frozen rubber puck into the opposing team's net with a ice hockey stick. The game begins when the referee drops the puck between the sticks of two players from opposing teams, who "face off". The rink is divided into three areas: defending, neutral, and attacking zones. Players may move with the puck and pass the puck to one another along the ice, but may not pass it more than two zones across the rink markings. A goal is scored when the puck entirely crosses the goal-line between the posts and under the crossbar of the goal. A team may field up to 20 players although only six players are allowed on the ice at one time; substitutions occur frequently. Each game consists of three periods of 20 minutes, divided by breaks of 15 minutes.

GOALKEEPER

Helmet
Face mask
Throat protector
Team shirt
Butt end
Catch glove
Pants
Blocking pad
Goalkeeper's pad
Blade
Skate
Blade
Goalkeeper's stick
Heel

ICE HOCKEY RINK

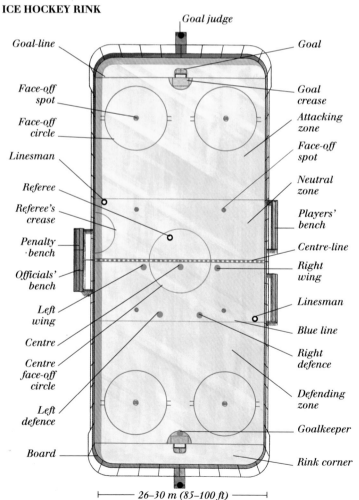

Goal judge
Goal-line
Goal
Face-off spot
Goal crease
Face-off circle
Attacking zone
Linesman
Face-off spot
Referee
Neutral zone
Referee's crease
Players' bench
Penalty bench
Centre-line
Officials' bench
Right wing
Left wing
Linesman
Centre
Blue line
Centre face-off circle
Right defence
Left defence
Defending zone
Board
Goalkeeper
Rink corner

├─── 26–30 m (85–100 ft) ───┤

THE FACE-OFF

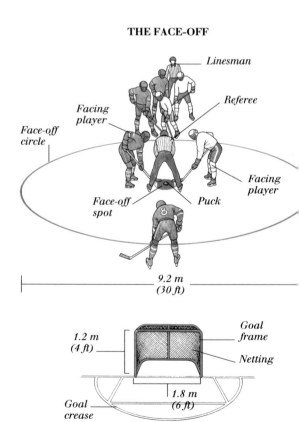

Linesman
Facing player
Referee
Face-off circle
Facing player
Face-off spot
Puck

├──── 9.2 m ────┤
(30 ft)

1.2 m (4 ft)
Goal frame
Netting
1.8 m (6 ft)
Goal crease

ICE HOCKEY GOAL

GOALKEEPER'S HELMET

Customized paintwork

Face guard

Chin protection

PLAYER'S BODY ARMOUR

Air vents

Rigid plastic shell

Manufacturer's logo

Chin strap

PLAYER'S HELMET

Foam padding

ICE HOCKEY STICKS

GOALKEEPER'S STICK

SHOULDER AND CHEST PADDING

Shoulder padding

OUTFIELD PLAYER'S STICK

MADE IN FINLAND

TORSPO

Pro 5000

TORSPO

Pro 500

147 cm (4 ft 9 in)

ELBOW PADS

DAIGNAULT ROLLAND
3075N
GRAND/LARGE

Heavy padding

Flexible gusset

Rigid finger cap

TORSPO
20

Strap

Wrist protection

DR
Daignault · Rolland
4355 M
DÉFENSE-**PRO**-DEFENCE

Chest padding

LEG PROTECTOR

Knee protection

Rigid plastic casing

DR
Daignault · Rolland
16.5" **CENTURION-J** 43cm

Thick foam backing

Leg pad

GLOVE

Ankle support

Wide lower shaft

TORSPO

Thin shaft

Vulcanized rubber

7.6 cm (3 in)

FROZEN PUCK

TORSPO

39 cm (15 in)

32 cm (12½ in)

Safety heel tip

Blade **SKATE**

Puck stopper

Thick blade

Heel

Alpine skiing

COMPETITIVE ALPINE SKIING is divided into four disciplines: downhill, slalom, giant slalom, and super-giant slalom (Super-G). Each one tests different skills. In downhill skiing, competitors race down a slope marked out by control flags, known as "gates", and are timed on a single run only. Competitors wear crash helmets, one-piece Lycra suits, and long skis with flattened tips to minimize air resistance. Slalom and giant slalom skiers negotiate a twisting course requiring balance, agility, and quick reactions. Courses are defined by pairs of gates. Racers must pass through each pair of gates to complete the course successfully. Competitors are timed on two runs over different courses, and the skier who completes the courses in the shortest time wins. The equipment and protective guards used by slalom skiers are shown opposite. In Super-G races, competitors ski a single run that combines the technical challenge of slalom with the speed of downhill. The course requires skiers to complete medium-to-long radius turns at high speed, and contain up to two jumps. Clothing is the same as for downhill, but slightly shorter skis are used.

DOWNHILL SKIER

Ski goggles · Helmet · One-piece lycra ski suit · Wrist strap · Ski pole · Basket · Safety binding · Tail · Ski boot · Ski glove

ALPINE SKI SLOPE COURSES

Downhill start · Downhill racing control flag · Super-G start · Pine forest · Giant slalom start · Giant slalom gate · Slalom start · Slalom gate · Finish line · Safety barrier

Polyamide inner boot · Tongue · Upper cuff · Upper strap · Buckle · Energy-distributing bonnet · Power bar · Adjusting catch · Tension control · Sole · Lower shell of boot · Heel grip

SKI BOOT

Wing · Toe-piece · Blind release lever · Heel-piece · Anti-friction pad · Housing · Release adjustment screw · Base plate · Brake arm

SAFETY BINDING

SLALOM CLOTHING AND EQUIPMENT

Elasticated strap

Anti-glare lens

GOGGLES

Hard nylon shell

Padding

Strap

Chin guard

SLALOM HELMET

Extended cuff

Wrist strap

Rigid pad for hand protection

SKI GLOVE

Adjustable shoulder strap

High collar

Double-knit wool and polyester fabric

Ribbed cuff

Zip pocket

Front zip fastening

Waterproof fabric

Wrist strap

Grip

Shock-absorbing platform under boot

Edge

Moulded polypropylene

PADDED SWEATER

HAND GUARD

188–203 cm (74–80 in)

Tough polypropylene shell deflects the shaft of the slalom gate

Shaft

Velcro strap

Basket

Cuff fits over ski boot

LEG GUARD

PADDED SKI TROUSERS

SLALOM SKI POLE

SLALOM SKI

Tail

Tip

Equestrian sports

EQUESTRIAN SPORTS HAVE TAKEN place throughout the world for centuries: events involving mounted horses were recorded in the Olympic Games of 642 BC. Showjumping, however, is a much more recent innovation, and the first competitions were held at the beginning of the 1900s. In this sport, horse and rider must negotiate a course of variable, unfixed obstacles, making as few mistakes as possible. Showjumping fences consist of wooden stands, known as standards or wings, that support planks or poles. Parts of the fence are designed to collapse on impact, preventing injury to the horse and rider. Judges penalise competitors for errors, such as knocking down obstacles, refusing jumps, or deviating from the course. Depending on the type of competition, the rider with the fewest faults, most points, or fastest time wins. There are two basic forms of horse racing – flat races and races with jumps, such as steeplechase or hurdle-races. Thoroughbred horses are used in this sport, as they have great strength and stamina and can achieve speeds of up to 65 kph (40 mph). Jockeys wear "silks" – caps and jackets designed in distinctive colours and patterns which help identify the horses. In harness racing, the horse is driven from a light, two-wheeled carriage called a sulky. Horses are trained to trot and to pace, and different races are held for each of these types of gait. In pacing races, the horses wear hobbles to prevent them from breaking into a trot or gallop. Breeds such as the Standardbred and the French Trotter have been developed especially for this sport.

SHOWJUMPING SADDLE

High cantle
Deep seat
Pommel
Forward-cut flap
Knee roll

SHOWJUMPING FENCES

Standard
Foot
Plank

UPRIGHT PLANKS

Standard
Foot
Pole

UPRIGHT POLES

Back pole
Standard
Foot
Pole

TRIPLE BAR (STAIRCASE)

Standard
Pole
Foot

HOG'S-BACK

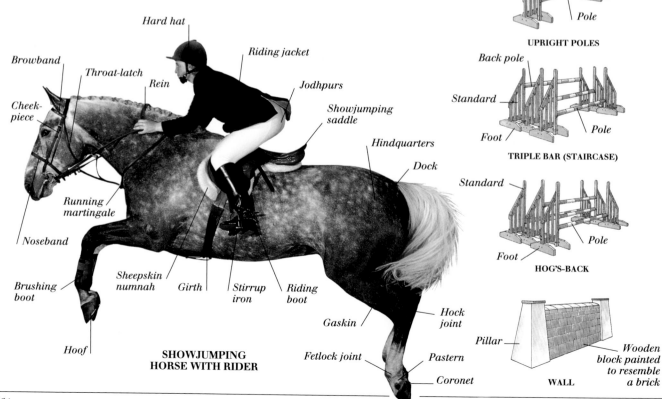

Hard hat
Browband
Throat-latch
Rein
Riding jacket
Jodhpurs
Cheek-piece
Showjumping saddle
Hindquarters
Dock
Running martingale
Noseband
Brushing boot
Sheepskin numnah
Girth
Stirrup iron
Riding boot
Hoof
Gaskin
Hock joint
Fetlock joint
Pastern
Coronet

SHOWJUMPING HORSE WITH RIDER

Pillar
Wooden block painted to resemble a brick

WALL

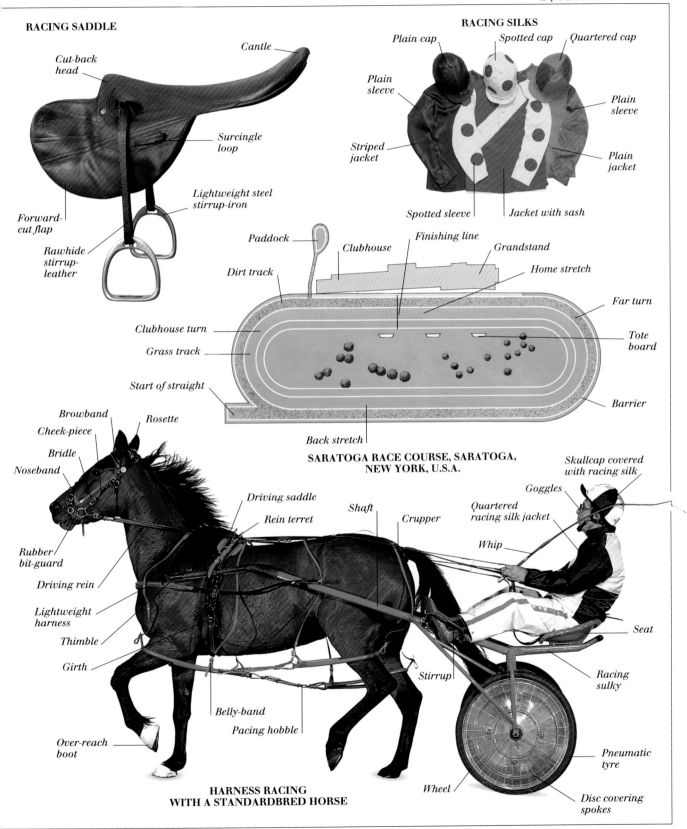

RACING SADDLE

Cut-back head

Cantle

Surcingle loop

Lightweight steel stirrup-iron

Forward-cut flap

Rawhide stirrup-leather

RACING SILKS

Plain cap

Spotted cap

Quartered cap

Plain sleeve

Plain sleeve

Striped jacket

Plain jacket

Spotted sleeve

Jacket with sash

Paddock

Clubhouse

Finishing line

Grandstand

Home stretch

Dirt track

Far turn

Clubhouse turn

Tote board

Grass track

Start of straight

Barrier

Back stretch

SARATOGA RACE COURSE, SARATOGA, NEW YORK, U.S.A.

Browband

Rosette

Cheek-piece

Bridle

Noseband

Driving saddle

Rein terret

Shaft

Crupper

Skullcap covered with racing silk

Goggles

Quartered racing silk jacket

Whip

Rubber bit-guard

Driving rein

Lightweight harness

Thimble

Seat

Girth

Stirrup

Racing sulky

Over-reach boot

Belly-band

Pacing hobble

Pneumatic tyre

Wheel

Disc covering spokes

HARNESS RACING WITH A STANDARDBRED HORSE

Judo and fencing

COMBAT SPORTS ARE BASED ON THE SKILLS used in fighting. In these sports, the competitors may be unarmed – as in judo and boxing – or armed – as in fencing and kendo. Judo is a system of unarmed combat developed in the East. Translated from the Japanese the name means "the gentle way". Students learn how to turn an opponent's force to their own advantage. The usual costume is loose white trousers and a jacket, fastened with a cloth belt. The colour of belt indicates the student's level of expertise, from white-belted novices to the expert "black belts". Competitions take place on a mat or "shiaijo", 9 or 10 m (30 or 33 ft) square in size, bounded by "danger" and "safety" areas to prevent injury. Competitors try to throw, pin, or master their opponent by applying pressure to the arm joints or neck. Judo bouts are strictly monitored, and competitors receive points for superior technique, not for injuring their opponent. Fencing is a combat sport using swords, which takes place on a narrow "piste" 14 m (46 ft) long. Competitors try to touch specific target areas on their opponent with their sword or "foil" while avoiding being touched themselves. The winner is the one who scores the greatest number of hits. Fencers wear clothing made from strong white material, which affords maximum protection while allowing freedom of movement, steel mesh masks with padded bibs to protect the fencer's neck, and a long white glove on their sword hand. Fencing foils do not have sharpened blades, and their tips end in a blunt button to prevent injuries. Three types of swords are used – foils, épées, and sabres. Official foil and épée competitions always use an electric scoring system. The sword tips are connected to lights by a long wire that passes underneath each fencer's jacket. A bulb flashes when a hit is made.

JUDO HOLDS AND THROWS

SIDE FOUR QUARTER HOLD

SINGLE WING

BODY DROP

ONE ARM SHOULDER THROW

SHOULDER WHEEL

SWEEPING LOW THROW

STOMACH THROW

KNEE WHEEL

JUDO MAT

16 m
(52 ft 6 in)

Judge

Scorer

Holding time-keeper

Time-keeper

Danger area

Contestant

JUDO KIT

Draw-string

Contestant

Referee

Contest area

Safety area

Cotton trousers

Black belt

Heavy-duty cotton jacket

FENCING PISTE

Rear limit line

14 m (46 ft)

Scorer

Time-keeper

Sabre and épéé warning line

Electrical scoring apparatus

Centre line

President

On-guard line

Body wire

Reel

FENCING TARGET AREAS

SABREUR

FOILIST

EPEEIST

FENCING EQUIPMENT

Steel wire mesh

Padded bib

MESH MASK

Woven metal thread

METAL JACKET

Cuff

Glove

GAUNTLET

THE SABRE

THE FOIL

Martingale

THE EPEE

Button

Blade

PARTS OF THE SWORD

Guard

Tang

Leather pad

Alternative pistol-grip handle

Brass screw

Steel foil pommel

TARGET AREAS ON THE UPPER BODY

Mask

Wire mesh

Bib

Under plastron

Tierce

Sixte

Quinte

Quarte

Gauntlet

Seconde

Octave

Prime

Septime

Metal over-jacket

Breeches

Stocking

Fencing shoe

Swimming and diving

SWIMMING GOGGLES

SWIMMING WAS INCLUDED in the first modern Olympic Games in 1896 and diving events were added in 1904. Swimming is both an individual and a team sport and races take place over a predetermined distance in one of the four major categories of stroke – freestyle (usually front crawl), butterfly, breaststroke, and backstroke. Competition pools are clearly marked for racing and anti-turbulence lane lines are used to separate the swimmers and help keep the water calm. The first team or individual to finish the race is the winner. Competitive diving is divided into men's and women's springboard and platform (highboard) events. There are six official groups of dives: forward dives, backward dives, armstand dives, twist dives, reverse dives, and inward dives. Competitors perform a set number of dives and after each one a panel of judges awards marks according to the quality of execution and the degree of difficulty.

STYLES OF DIVES

Starting position

Hands above head

Legs fully stretched

Flight

Arched back

Toes pointed

Entry

Feet together

Hands close together

FORWARD DIVE

BACKWARD DIVE

SWIMMING POOL

Latex rubber moulds to shape of head

CAPS

Rubber-covered wire

NOSE CLIP

Moulded rubber

EARPLUG

SWIMWEAR

High neckline

Man-made stretch fabric

Drawstring

High-cut leg

Strong seam

SWIMSUIT

TRUNKS

Swimmer

Lane number

Starting block

Chief time-keeper

Placing judge

Recorder

Backstroke marker 15 m (49 ft) from end of pool

Referee

Backstroke turn indicator 5 m (16 ft) from end of pool

Turning judge

Lane time-keeper

End wall

Starter

Side wall

Anti-turbulence lane line

Stroke judge

Bottom line

Turning wall

Lane

23 m (75 ft 6 in)

Perfectly steady armstand

Arms and legs align throughout flight and entry

ARMSTAND DIVE

Arms spread wide apart

Body and legs straighten for flight and entry

TWIST DIVE

Pike position

Height of dive

Shoulders fall backwards for vertical entry

REVERSE DIVE PIKED

Pike position

Hands touch toes

Feet lift up for straight entry

INWARD DIVE PIKED

FRONT CRAWL
Flutter kick

Arm pulls like a paddle

Arrow-like position

Body rolls on a central axis

FULL BODY STRETCH   **LOWER ARM PULL**   **STREAMLINED ARM ENTRY**   **SIDE-TO-SIDE BODY ROLL**

BREASTSTROKE
Straight leg

Knees together

Elbows tucked in

Arm fully extended

BODY GLIDE   **DOUBLE ARM PULL**   **SQUEEZING THE WATER**   **FROG KICK**

BACKSTROKE   Little finger enters first

Arm comes up straight

Recovering hand

Shoulder exits water first

BODY ROLL   **PULLING THROUGH**   **STRAIGHTENING OUT**   **SHOULDER LIFT**

BUTTERFLY   Palm turned outwards

Legs ready to kick down

Head clears the water

Shoulders power the stroke

CATCHING THE WATER   **DOUBLE ARM PULL**   **KICKING DOWN**   **WHOLE BODY UNDULATION**

Canoeing, rowing, and sailing

WATERBORNE SPORTS are as varied as the crafts used. There are two disciplines in rowing; sweep rowing, in which each rower has one oar and sculling, in which rowers use two oars. There are a number of different Olympic and competitive rowing events for both men and women. The number of rowers and weight classes vary. Some rowing events use a coxswain; a steersman who does not row but directs the crew. Kayaks and canoes are used in straight sprint and slalom races. Slalom races take place over a course consisting of 20 to 25 gates, including at least six upstream gates. In yacht racing, competitors must complete prescribed courses, organized by the race committees, in the shortest possible time, using sail power only. Olympic events include classes for keel boats, dinghies, and catamarans.

SAILING GEAR

Sleeveless long johns

Buoyancy aid

Long-sleeved jacket

Neoprene material

Belt

GLOVE

Bootlace

Ribbed top

Non-slip sole

BOOT

ONE-PERSON KAYAK AND PADDLE

Blade

Rim

Shaft

Right rail

Cockpit

Back strap

Stern

High density polythene

Nose cone

Toggle

Bow

Left rail

Seat

Cockpit rim

**SINGLE SCULL AND OARS
(WITH CLOTH DECKING REMOVED)**

Adjusting screw

Gate clamp

Gate

Spoon

Blade

Colours

Neck

Shaft

Stroke-side oar

Rigger

Grip

Bow-side oar

Button

Loom

Stretcher

Sycamore beam

Keel

Water shoot

Shoe

Sternpost

Spruce beam

Diagonal frame

Aluminium beam

Bung

Aft shoulder

Kelson (keelson)

LIFEJACKET

Backstrap/ rescue strap

Reinforced seam

SAILING DINGHY

Elastic control line

Neck opening

Boom

Rudder

Whistle

Topping-up valve

Mast

Mainsheet

Lanyard

Standing rigging

Waistband

Spreader

Bow

Stern

Tiller

Toestrap

Centre-board

Cockpit

Shroud

SCULLS

Jib fairlead

DOUBLE SCULL

SINGLE SCULL

Non-slip deck surface

SWEEP-ROWING BOATS

Slide track

Wheel

Sliding seat

COXLESS FOUR

COXED PAIR

COXLESS PAIR

Main deck

Saxboard

Forward deck

EIGHT

COXED FOUR

Wheel spacer

Hatch

Breakwater

In-board

Bowball

Bowpost

Angling

ANGLING MEANS FISHING WITH A ROD, reel, line, and lure.
There are several different types of angling: freshwater
coarse angling, for members of the carp family and pike;
freshwater game angling, for salmon and trout; and sea
angling, for sea fish such as flatfish, bass, and mackerel.
Anglers use a variety of methods of catching fish. These
include bait fishing, in which bait (food to allure the fish)
is placed on a hook and cast into the water; fly fishing, in
which a natural or artificial fly is used to lure the fish;
and spinning, in which a lure that looks like a small fish
revolves as it is pulled through the water. The angler uses
the rod, reel, and line to cast the lure over the water. The
reel controls the line as it spills off the spool and as it is
wound back. Weights may be fixed to
the line so that it will sink. Swivels
are attached to prevent the line
from twisting. When a fish bites,
the hook must become embedded
in its mouth and remain there
while the catch is reeled in.

Keeper ring

Drag spindle

Handgrip

Disk drag

Drag washer

Disk spring

Gear retainer

Dual click gear

Retaining screw

Check slide

Check pawl cover

Check pawl

Check spring

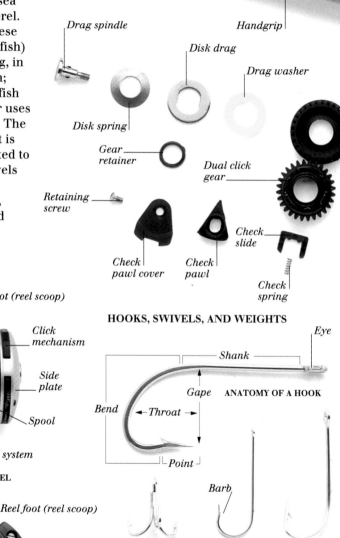

REELS

Plate-nut

Spool-release button

Reel foot (reel scoop)

Click mechanism

Mechanical brake

Centrifugal brake

Side plate

Spool

Handle

Star drag

Level-wind system

MULTIPLIER REEL

Line

Unskirted spool

Reel foot (reel scoop)

Handle

Tension nut (drag adjustment)

Ratchet (anti-reverse device)

Handgrip

Reel

Bail arm

FIXED-SPOOL REEL

HOOKS, SWIVELS, AND WEIGHTS

Eye

Shank

Gape **ANATOMY OF A HOOK**

Bend

Throat

Point

Barb

TREBLE HOOK

ABERDEEN HOOK

REVERSED BEND HOOK

EXAMPLES OF BARREL SWIVELS

HILLMAN ANTI-KINK WEIGHT

FLY ROD AND REEL

Intermediate ring

TIP SECTION

Reel seat

Screw locking nut

Tip ring

Butt cap

Disk drag housing

Reel foot (reel scoop)

Line

Drag knob screw

Butt extension

DragonFly 100

Disc Drag

Release lever

Spool screw

Clicker plate

Drag knob

Line guide

ARTIFICIAL FLIES

DUNKELD WET FLY

Release spring

Spool cover

Spool-release button

Handle

Line guide cover

Tail

Body

Cheek

Head

ARTIFICIAL LURES

Retaining screw

Hackle

Ribbing

DEVON MINNOW   *Fin*

Eye

Treble hook

DEER HOPPER DRY FLY

Swivel

Tulip mount

Front hackle

JOINTED PLUG

Eye

Tail

Hook

Adjustable vane

Joint

Treble hook

Head

Wing

EVERYDAY THINGS

Drills

THE ELECTRICALLY POWERED MOTOR OF A POWER DRILL, cooled by a fan, turns a shaft at high speed. The shaft connects, in turn, to a system of gears that rotates a chuck even faster. Clamped by the chuck, a sharp bit cuts out the hole, and at the same time the bit's screw-shaped grooves channel the waste out of the hole. For drilling hard materials, many power drills have a hammer mechanism: when this is operated a ratchet in the gearcase causes the chuck and bit to pound in and out as they drill. A hand drill, although slower and less forceful than a power drill, is easier to control. For cutting wide holes, carpenters often prefer a brace-and-bit. This acts like a lever: the bowed handle of the brace moves a larger distance than the bit, turning the bit with extra force.

MOTOR ASSEMBLY

Commutator

Armature

Armature spindle

Fan

Motor case

Field coils

Motor case

Spring

Screw

Washer

Brush

Lead wire

Brush holder

Top insert blank

Hammer mechanism actuator

Electromagnetic induction capacitor

Screw hole

Chuck key holder

Triac device

Hammer actuator position

Gearcase position

Screw

INTERNAL VIEW OF CLAMSHELL

Motor position

Lock button

On/off trigger

Trigger position

TRIGGER MECHANISM

Washer

Cable

Spring

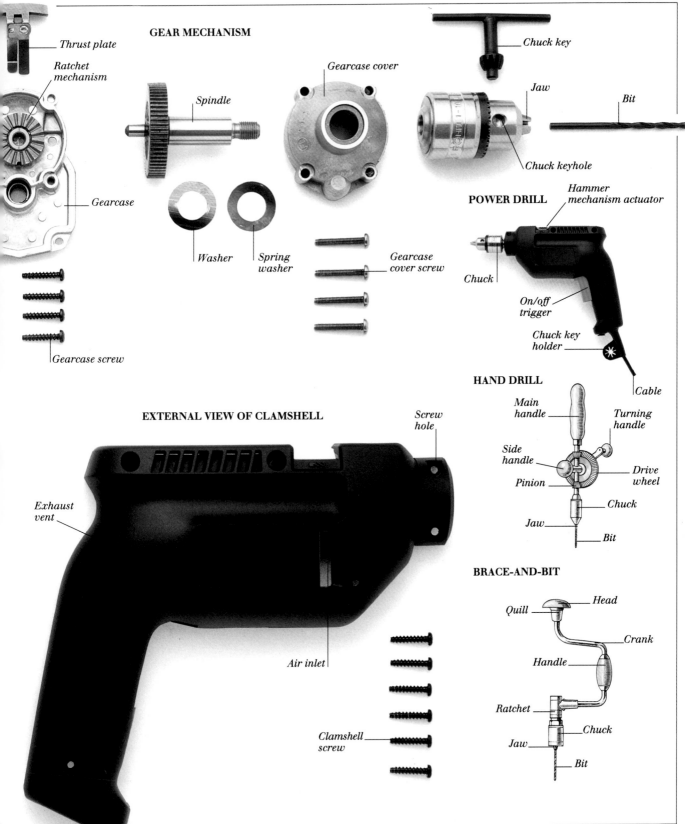

GEAR MECHANISM

Thrust plate

Ratchet mechanism

Spindle

Gearcase cover

Chuck key

Jaw

Bit

Gearcase

Washer

Spring washer

Gearcase cover screw

Chuck keyhole

POWER DRILL

Hammer mechanism actuator

Chuck

On/off trigger

Chuck key holder

Gearcase screw

Cable

HAND DRILL

Main handle

Turning handle

Side handle

Pinion

Drive wheel

Chuck

Jaw

Bit

EXTERNAL VIEW OF CLAMSHELL

Screw hole

Exhaust vent

Air inlet

Clamshell screw

BRACE-AND-BIT

Quill

Head

Crank

Handle

Ratchet

Chuck

Jaw

Bit

Shoes

WELL-MADE SHOES PROTECT THE FEET and are also comfortable and long-lasting. The best shoemakers use a wooden or plastic mould, called a last, which matches the shape of the customer's foot. The different parts of a shoe are stitched and glued together around the last; rivets and nails are used only in the heel, which is built up from layers of leather and rubber. The steel shank gives support to the arch of the foot and, with the seat lift, helps the wearer maintain posture. The layers of the sole give strength, while the soft insole cushions the foot. The leather welt sewn between the leather uppers and the sole ensures a strong join.

Inside quarter

Quarter lining

Wing cap and vamp lining

Quarter backer

Inner sock

Counter

Tongue

Shoelace

Outside quarter

Vamp

Punchhole

Welt

Perforated wing cap

Wing cap

Wing cap backer

Toe puff

Vamp

Tongue

Tongue lining

CROSS SECTION OF FINISHED SHOE

Tongue

Vamp

Wing cap

Welt

Insole

Bottom filler

Outsole

Lining

Cuff

Heel grip

Counter

Seat lift

Heel

Steel shank

Quarter
backer

Outside quarter

Shoelace

Eyelet

Tag

Counter

Counter stiffener

Quarter and
counter lining

Cone

LAST

Thimble (jack-
locating hole)

Vamp backer

Counter
backer

Hinge

Bottom
filler

Outsole

Shank

Seat lift

Inner sock

Quarter tip

Insole with
ribbing

Welt

Thread

Seat rivet

Heel nail

Heel

Clock

MECHANICAL CLOCKS HAVE TWO essential elements: a mainspring and a pendulum. When the clock is wound with the key, the mainspring is tightened. As the mainspring unwinds, it turns the gears, which move the minute and hour hands at different speeds around the face of the clock. The pendulum ensures that the hands move at a regular pace. At the top of the pendulum are two hooks called pallets. As the pendulum swings, the pallets allow the escape wheel to turn slowly and evenly.

CLOCK CASE

Steady pin hole

Screw hole

Pallet arbour position

Barrel pivot hole

Wooden peg

Fusee pivot hole

Pillar

Winding key

Ratchet screw

Ratchet pawl

Click wheel

Barrel arbour hook

PENDULUM ASSEMBLY

Pallet cock screw

Mainspring barrel arbour

Pallet cock

CLOCK TRAIN

Crutch screw

Pallet arbour

Pallet screw

Suspension spring

Crutch

Pallet

Mainspring

Mainspring barrel cap

Escape wheel

FRONT PLATE

Pinion

Pendulum rod

Third wheel

Pinion

Pinion

Centre wheel

Mainspring barrel

Fusee

Fusee chain

Lenticular bob

Fusee stop screw

Pivot hole

Fusee stop

Tension spring screw

Tension spring

Rating nut

CLOCK FACE

Side inspection door

Wooden bezel

Hinged brass bezel

Wooden peg

Back plate

Bottom door key

Minute track

Hour marker

Back box

Bottom door

Minute hand

Roman numeral

Screw hole

Minute wheel cock

Cock screw

Minute wheel

Dial washer

Hour hand screw

CAMERER. KUSS & C°. 56 New Oxford St

Hand collet

Maker's name

Centre hole

Cannon pinion

Hour wheel

Pin

Winding hole

Bridge

Dial

LONDON

Bridge screw

Pin

Hour hand

Dial foot hole

Pillar hole

Lamp

THE FIRST SPRING-TENSIONED, adjustable work lamp was designed in 1934 by George Carwardine. This type of lamp imitates the human arm in the way that it can be kept in a fixed position or moved easily and precisely. In the arm, such control is achieved by coordinating the opposing action of paired muscles (e.g., when the biceps contracts, the triceps relaxes and the arm bends). In the work lamp, one muscle of a pair is represented by the springs that pull on the rigid bars of the lamp; the other muscle is represented by the nuts, bolts, screws, and washers in the lamp's joints that resist the pull of the springs. By balancing the pull of the springs against the resistance in the joints, the lamp's height and angle can be adjusted with minimal pressure.

Cap nut

Switch enclosure cover

Push switch

Terminal screw

Bushing

Mains lead

Insulation

End cap

Copper conductor

Switch enclosure

Pivot plate

Bracket

Metal shade

Dome

Body

Cap

LIGHT BULB

Connecting wire

Terminal screw

Nut

Fuse enclosure

Plunger contact

LAMP HOLDER

Support wire

Glass envelope

Skirt

Filament

Wing nut

SUPPORT ARM ASSEMBLY

Cheese head screw

Washer

Nut

Locking nut

Mains lead

Pivot plate

End cap

Cheese head screw

Washer

Hexagon nut

Bushing

Metal arm

Spring attachment

Coil tension spring

Clamping screw

Arm coupling

Metal arm

Lamp holder coupling

Pivot

Spigot

Mains lead

Metal shade

Pivot plate

Metal arm

Washer

Shade coupling

Socket

Spring attachment

Threaded rod

Clamp upper jaw

TABLE CLAMP ASSEMBLY

Coil tension spring

Adjustment locking nut

Metal arm

Coil tension spring

Cheese head screw

Washer

Nut

Threaded rod

Table clamp

Wing nut

Clamp lower jaw

End cap

Spring attachment bolt

573

Mini-television

MINIATURIZED TELEVISION SETS are small enough to be held in the hand while being watched. A signal sent by a broadcast transmitter is picked up by the television aerial and passed to an electron gun at the back of the television set. In response to the signal this gun produces an electron beam that is passed through a deflection yoke. The yoke contains magnets and coils that cause the beam to scan across the screen in a series of lines. The screen is coated with phosphor, which glows when hit by the beam. As the beam scans the screen, its strength is varied so that the phosphor glows with different intensities in different parts of the screen. A continuous sequence of 25 black-and-white pictures per second appears on the screen so rapidly that the illusion of a moving picture is created.

CATHODE RAY TUBE (CRT)

CRT cover

Dial pointer

Tuning drive gear

Keystone (East-West) amplifier integrated circuit

Antenna connector

Tuner

Rear cabinet

Electrolytic capacitor

Earphone jack

Direct current jack

Metal shield

Tuning knob

Battery compartment

Screw

Tuning printed circuit board

Deflection coil

CRT bracket

Battery case lid

Tape

Positive pole

Electron gun

Mounting bracket

TUBE NECK

Nipple

Scan coil clamp

SCAN COIL DEFLECTION YOKE

BATTERY CONTACTS

Connecting pin

Centring magnet

Positive pole

CRT socket

Negative pole

Positive pole

Screw

Intermediate frequency coil

Choke

PRINTED CIRCUIT BOARD

Plastic sheath

Antenna holder

Ornamental strip

Coil

Glue

Horizontal frequency adjustment

Capacitor

Window

Volume control knob

Power switch

Power knob

Filter

Fly back transformer

Plastic cap

SONY

Focus control

Extra-high tension lead

21 30 40 50 60 68 UHF

Filter ornament

Speaker

Front cabinet

Chair

A TRADITIONALLY MADE DINING CHAIR, such as the Regency-style carver shown here, is held together, not by nails or bolts, but by snugly fitting joints, screws, dowels, and glue. Its curved arms and top splats, as well as its tapering legs, are cut from seasoned – that is, dried – mahogany. Mortice slots in the back legs receive the tenon tongues of the top and bottom splats; angled grooves at the top of the back legs, called rebates, take the curved arm rail. Though the various joints are so tight-fitting that they could produce a solid frame on their own, screws and glue are used to give the joints added strength. The comfortable, upholstered seatpad shown here consists of a patterned cover, calico lining, and foam stuffing that has been treated for fire safety; it is supported by webbing stretched across a wooden frame.

Top splat

Cross stick

Arm

Bottom splat

Head

Seatpad

Front rail

Back leg

Left sabre leg

Square brass line

Tenon

Tenon

Mortice

Arm

Washer

Groove

Top splat

Washer

Dowel screw

Screw

Diamond

Screw

Wooden plug

Wooden plug

Splat mortice

Head

Cross stick

Bottom splat

Tenon

Side rail

Tenon

Dowel

Back rail

Dowel

Dowel hole

Dowel

Screw

Dowel

Right sabre leg

Dowel

Dowel hole

Back leg

Front rail

CHAIR FRAME

SEAT UPHOLSTERY

Seat cover

Mortice

Webbing

Arm

Dowel screw

Splat mortice

Head

Tenon

Side rail

Screw

Dowel hole

Back leg

Left sabre leg

Foam stuffing

Calico lining

Seat back rail

Bottom lining

Tacks

SEAT FRAME

Seat side rail

Seat side rail

Dowel hole

Seat front rail

Toaster

MOST ELECTRIC TOASTERS NOT ONLY GRILL slices of bread, they also pop them up when ready. While the slices rest on a spring-loaded rack, electric heating elements toast the bread. At the same time, a bimetallic strip heats and expands. One of the two metals in this strip expands more quickly than the other, causing the strip to curve. As it bends, it completes an electrical circuit and activates an electromagnet. The magnet attracts a catch, releasing the spring that holds the rack down in the toaster. The elements switch off, and the toasted slices pop up.

Connecting wire

Ejector bracket

Time switch

Variable time control knob

Selector switch

Screw

Screw

Switch end casting

Crumb tray

End baffle plate

Screw

Screw

Earth connection point

Cable entry point

End element connecting link

End element

Foot

Baseplate

End element wire guard

Screw

Washer

Mains input lead

Bolt

Nut

Cable retaining gland

Ejector knob

Screw

Spring

Nut

Ejector bracket

Ejector assembly

Centre element
wire cage

Inner cage
assembly

End baffle
plate

Screw

Element
retaining stop

Nut

Washer

Screw

Element
connecting
link

Centre element

End element

End element
wire guard

Plain end
casting

Switch end
casting

Stainless steel
cover

Selector switch

Ejector knob

Variable time
control knob

Foot

Crumb tray

Fixing screw

Screw

Foot

Stainless steel
cover

Plain end
casting

Foot

Screw

Nut

Washer

Screw

Lawnmower

THE SHARP BLADES OF A LAWNMOWER – whether driven by electrical, petrol, or human power – shave grass close to the ground. The petrol-powered type shown here has a small engine that is electrically ignited by a battery and spark plug. This engine rotates a horizontal blade at the base of the lawnmower that slices the grass against a fixed blade. A grass bag at the back of the machine collects the cuttings. As the engine rotates the blades, it also turns the rear wheels, moving the lawnmower forwards. Gears ensure that the horizontal blade spins faster than the wheels so that all of the grass is cut neatly before the lawnmower moves on.

Rear tyre

Wheel cover

Rear wheel

GEAR CASE ASSEMBLY

Upper gear case

Wheel bolt

Blower shroud

Fuel tank

Spring

Drive-shaft

Door

Half pulley

Belt guard

Chain drive-belt

Screw

Cap

Screw

Oil dipstick

Door seal

Bolt

ENGINE AND RECOIL ASSEMBLY

Oil fill tube

Screw

OHV

Recoil case

Flywheel

Screw

Housing

Starter cup

Screw

Muffler cover

Air filter

Muffler

Throttle guard

Screw

Blade cover

Engine pulley

Air filter cover

Front tyre

Height adjuster

Shoulder screw

Front wheel

53 cm

TORO

Handle

Control panel

Grass bag

Fuel tank cap

Recoil case

Muffler cover

Latch handle

Rear wheel

Housing

Front wheel

Handle

Traction lever

Ground speed control knob

Throttle control knob

Mower drive-handle

Control lever

Traction cable support

Control panel

Vertical panel

Cable support bracket

Latch handle

Battery

Battery retainer

HANDLE AND TRACTION CONTROL ASSEMBLY

Screen panel

Door discharge

Grass bag

Traction cable

Blade

Screw

Blade retainer

Washer

Blade bolt

Grass bag frame

Battery connection

Wheel bolt

Saddle

THE FIRST HORSE RIDERS HAD NO SADDLES; they sat bareback, clinging to the animal's mane. Next came a simple cloth saddle. The leather saddle, which was invented about 2,000 years ago by the warriors of the Asian steppes, revolutionized horse riding. On this saddle, horsemen could gallop towards the enemy, fire arrows in all directions, and stay on their horses. Modern saddles are of two main types. The Western saddle is a heavy, working saddle used mainly by ranch hands in the United States. It has a metal horn at the front for securing a lasso and a high cantle at the back to keep the rider on the horse. The English saddle is a much lighter affair. Designed for sport, it allows the horse to gallop fast. Its drawback is that it provides less stability; to stay on the horse, the rider must grip the animal with the knees.

Cantle

Leather seat

Pommel

Sloped head

Dee

Surcingle

Block flap

Girth

Stirrup leather

Stirrup iron

Facing

Strap bearing

Gullet

Web

Gullet plate

Tree

Stirrup bar

Point pocket

Stuffing hole

Cantle

Knee roll

Metal reinforcement

Web

Copper rivet

Top leather

Spring tree

Flexible leather point

Point cover

Facing

Rivet

Belly nail

Lining of underside of saddle

Brass nameplate nail

Tack

Knee cover

Screw

Gullet lining

Nylon rope

Stirrup buckle

Stirrup leather

Flock stuffing

ATHERSTONE GIRTH

Girth buckle

Chape

Stirrup iron

Block flap

Buckle guard

Plated nail

Dee

Girth strap

Surcingle

Name-plate

Stirrup buckle

Bar leather

Belly nail

Forepiece

Dee

Skirt

Stirrup leather

Welt

Back

Webbing

Leather seat

Canvas

Canvas

Leather

Rubber seat

Canvas

Welt

Back

Buckle guard

Skirt

Leather belly

Buckle guard

Bar leather

Lacing thread

3-cord linen thread

Belly nail

Nameplate

Beeswax

4-cord linen thread

Surcingle

Dee

Stirrup leather

Stirrup iron

Block flap

Plated nail

CD-ROM

A CD-ROM IS A TYPE OF COMPACT DISC (CD) that can be used to produce images on a computer screen. ROM stands for Read Only Memory, which means that the digitally recorded data registered in pits on the surface of the disc is fixed and cannot be altered or replaced. The CD is loaded into the CD-ROM player, where the data on the spinning disc is read by a laser. CD-ROMs are different from vinyl records in that they are not read along a spiral groove, from outer circumference to inner edge: instead each image or piece of information has a co-ordinate on the disc, which is located by the laser. Information picked up by the laser is relayed to the computer, where it is translated into the text and images that appear on screen. The information is relayed through a SCSI (Small Computer System Interface), which processes the electronic impulses between the disc drive and the computer system. The user can move around the program by clicking on different parts of the screen with a mouse (a hand-held tool with a clicking button whose movement on its pad is mimicked by an icon on the screen). The image in the viewing area (see opposite) can be changed by clicking on the active scrolling button: this moves a rectangular panel down the scrolling figure in the navigational panel. Clicking on active text will provide a new screen with more information, either in the form of text and diagrams, or as narrated animated sequences.

CD-ROM drive

CD loading tray

Caddy cover flap

Front bezel

Push button

CD-ROM CASING

CD-ROM drive motor

Film strip connector

Laser

Connector

Washer

Gearing mechanism

Spring

Roller bearing

Guide post

Insulating grommet

Power connector to CD-ROM

SCSI connectors

Earth connection to case

Connector clasp

SCSI selector switch

Mains switch

Washer

Earth wire

Surface-mounted integrated circuit

Power supply screening cover

Mounting post

Power on/off LED (Light Emitting Diode)

Transistor

CD-ROM DISC DRIVE

Screws

CD-ROM disc

CD-ROM LOADING MECHANISM

CONTENTS PAGE

THE ULTIMATE HUMAN BODY

BODY MACHINE | BODY ORGANS | BODY SYSTEMS

External speaker

Keyboard

Disc

Display monitor

Mouse

Mouse pad

CD-ROM PLAYER

COMPUTER HARDWARE

SCREEN FROM A CD-ROM PROGRAM

Dorling Kindersley MULTIMEDIA

Navigational panel

Help button

Index button

Back button

Pronunciation button on/off

Options button

Navigational figures

BODY MACHINE | BODY ORGANS | BODY SYSTEMS

Scrolling figure

BODY MACHINE

Active scrolling button

FIND OUT MORE

BODY MACHINE

Picon (pictorial icon)

BODY MACHINE

ABOUT THE BODY MACHINE

What happens when you sleep?

Why do you blink?

How do you hear?

How do you swallow?

Why do you chew your food?

How do reflex actions work?

How often does your heart beat?

Active text

What are you made of?

How do your joints move?

ZOOMING INTO MULTI-LAYERED INFORMATION

Viewing area

HEAD

YOUR HEAD contains your brain, which is protected by the strong interlocking bones of your skull. Most of your sensory organs are located in your head: these include your eyes, ears, mouth, and nose.

Hair, skull and scalp

Brain

Eye

Ear

Nose

Mouth and lip

INITIAL SCREEN UNDER BODY ORGANS MENU

EYES

THESE DELICATE ORGANS lie in pads of fat protected within bony sockets called orbits. On the outside they are protected from injury by your eyelids, thin folds of skin that can close rapidly. Each eye is moved by six muscles which are attached around the eyeball.

Around the eye

Inside the eye

Skin

Blood vessels

Bone

CLICKING ON "EYES" LABEL PRODUCES MORE INFORMATION

INSIDE THE EYE

THE EYE is a hollow sphere filled with gel-like fluids that help keep the eye in shape. Light rays entering the eye through the pupil, are focused by the cornea and lens to form an image on the retina. Here, millions of cells enable you to detect light and colours. The cells send messages to the brain, which then makes sense of what you see.

Conjunctiva (Thin, clear layer covering cornea)

Vitreous humous (Clear jelly that fills the space behind the lens)

Lens

Iris

Cornea

Vein

Optic nerve

Retina

EACH LABEL PRODUCES A FURTHER SCREEN

LENS

THE LENS of your eye is on the front surface of your eyeball. It is transparent and light passes through it to be focused onto the back of your eye. To focus on both objects that are near and those far away, the lens must change its shape. The many fibres around the lens allow this by pulling against the outer rim of the lens.

Lens

Fibres

THE FINAL IMAGE SHOWS MICROSCOPIC DETAIL

Books

THOUGH THE PROCESS OF BOOKBINDING today is usually mechanized, some books are still bound by hand. The pages of a book are printed on large sheets of paper called sections, or signatures. When folded, sections usually make 8, 16, or 32 pages. To assemble a hand-bound hardback book, the binder first places the folded sections in the correct order within the endpapers. Next, he or she sews the sections together along the spine edge using strong thread and then pastes them with glue for extra strength. After trimming the pages, the binder puts the book in a press and hammers the spine to round it. The binder then glues one or more linings to the spine. The cover, or case, comes last. To make this, the bookbinder sticks cover boards to the endpapers, front and back, and then covers them with cloth or leather.

HALF-BOUND BOOK

Corner piece

Spine

Fore-edge

Tail

Marbled paper

LEATHER-BOUND BOOK

Joint

Leather cover

Rib

Spine

Ribbon

Tail

Gold embossing

HALF-BOUND BOOK

Buckram corner piece

Board paper (endpaper)

Lining

Headband

Spine piece

Section (signature)

Mull

Marbled paper

Tape

Tailband

Front cover board

Manila

LEATHER-BOUND BOOK

Board paper (endpaper)

Headband

Rib

Tape

Leather cover

Back cover board

Section (signature)

Frontispiece

Thread

Front cover board

Ribbon

Lining

Tailband

Mull

Flyleaf (endpaper)

Buckram corner piece

Back cover board

Reverse of marbled paper

Buckram corner piece

Board paper (endpaper)

LEATHER-BOUND BOOK

Joint

Ribbon

Headband

Mull

Tape

Rib

Lining

Spine

Gold embossing

Fore-edge

Flyleaf (endpaper)

Board paper (endpaper)

Front cover board

Leather cover

Camera

A CAMERA IS AN INSTRUMENT for recording images on photographic film. It consists of a light-tight box with a shutter, a lens containing a diaphragm, and a viewing system. When the shutter is released, the film is exposed to light from the subject that is being photographed. Adjusting the shutter speed alters the time for which the film is exposed to light. The diaphragm, by altering the aperture of the lens, controls the intensity of light entering the camera. The total amount of light entering the camera is called the exposure. The lens focuses the light on to the film. When there is insufficient light to produce an adequate image, a flashgun may be used to give extra light.

FRONT VIEW OF CAMERA

Shutter release button
Shutter speed dial
Film rewind/back cover release knob
Exposure counter
Strap lug
Lens lock release lever
X-flash sync terminal

FRONT BOARD ASSEMBLY

Mount
Left body covering
Right body covering
Lens lock release lever
X-flash sync cap

BOTTOM COVER ASSEMBLY

Tripod socket hole
Bottom cover
Battery
Battery chamber cap

REAR VIEW OF CAMERA

Film rewind crank
Viewfinder eyepiece
Film take-up spool
Film rewind/ back cover release knob
Film roller
Film chamber
Back cover
Film pressure plate
Film rail
Film guide rail
Shutter curtain
Film sprocket spool

LENS BARREL ASSEMBLY

Ornament ring
Cover frame
Nameplate ring
Front lens frame retainer plate
Front lens group
Installing ring retainer plate
Retainer screw
Washer
Retainer screw
Retainer screw

TOP COVER ASSEMBLY

Shutter dial knob spring

Film speed indicator

Speed dial knob

Shutter speed dial

Retainer screw

Counter dial cover

Exposure counter dial

Counter dial housing

Film wind lever

Top cover

X-contact

Rewind shaft

Film rewind/ back cover release knob

Wind lever install spring

Wind lever collar

Hot shoe

Retainer screw

Washer

Window

Prism retainer plate

Shutter release button

Shutter speed index

Rewind shaft collar

Prism retainer spring

Film rewind crank

Pentaprism

Cover frame

Retainer screw

MAIN BODY

Strap lug

Viewfinder eyepiece

TOP VIEW OF CAMERA

Focusing ring

Distance scale (focal length scale)

Depth-of-field guide

Aperture/distance index

Lens alignment node

Aperture auto-lock button

Hole for film rewind button

Lens lock release lever

Shutter release button

Cocked indicator

Exposure counter

Retainer screw

Film rewind crank

Film rewind/back cover release knob

Hot shoe

X-contact

Shutter speed index

Film speed indicator

Shutter speed dial

Film wind lever

Supporter ring retainer plate

Supporter ring

Diaphragm blade

Installing ring

Main barrel assembly

Rear lens group

Opening and closing plate

Appendix: useful data

Metric unit	Equivalent
Length	
1 centimetre (cm)	10 millimetres (mm)
1 metre (m)	100 centimetres
1 kilometre (km)	1,000 metres
Mass	
1 kilogram (kg)	1,000 grams (g)
1 tonne (t)	1,000 kilograms
Area	
1 square centimetre (cm²)	100 square millimetres (mm²)
1 square metre (m²)	10,000 square centimetres
1 hectare	10,000 square metres
1 square kilometre (km²)	1,000,000 square metres
Volume	
1 cubic centimetre (cc)	1 millilitre (ml)
1 litre (l)	1,000 millilitres
1 cubic metre (m³)	1,000 litres
Capacity (liquid and dry measures)	
1 centilitre (cl)	10 millilitres (ml)
1 decilitre (dl)	10 centilitres
1 litre (l)	10 decilitres
1 decalitre (dal)	10 litres
1 hectolitre (hi)	10 decalitres
1 kilolitre (kl)	10 hectolitres

Imperial unit	Equivalent
Length	
1 foot (ft)	12 inches (in)
1 yard (yd)	3 feet
1 rod (rd)	5.5 yards
1 mile (mi)	1,760 yards
Mass	
1 dram (dr)	27.344 grains (gr)
1 ounce (oz)	16 drams
1 pound (lb)	16 ounces
1 hundredweight (cwt) (long)	112 pounds
1 hundredweight (cwt) (short)	100 pounds
1 ton (long)	2,240 pounds
1 ton (short)	2,000 pounds
Area	
1 square foot (ft²)	144 square inches (in²)
1 square yard (yd²)	9 square feet
1 acre	4,840 square yards
1 square mile	640 acres
Volume	
1 cubic foot	1,728 cubic inches
1 cubic yard	27 cubic feet
Capacity (liquid and dry measures)	
1 fluidram (fl dr)	60 minims (min)
1 fluid ounce (fl oz)	8 fluidrams
1 gill (gi)	5 fluid ounces
1 pint (pt)	4 gills
1 quart (qt)	2 pints
1 gallon (gal)	4 quarts
1 peck (pk)	2 gallons
1 bushel (bu)	4 pecks

TEMPERATURE SCALES

To convert from Celsius (C) to Fahrenheit (F): $F = (C \times 9 \div 5) + 32$
To convert from Fahrenheit to Celsius: $C = (F - 32) \times 5 \div 9$
To convert from Celsius to Kelvin (K): $K = C + 273$
To convert from Kelvin to Celsius: $C = K - 273$

Celsius	-20	-10	0	10	20	30	40	50	60	70	80	90	100
Fahrenheit	-4	14	32	50	68	86	104	122	140	158	176	194	212
Kelvin	253	263	273	283	293	303	313	323	333	343	353	363	373

AREAS AND VOLUMES

Radius r
Diameter
d = 2 x r

CIRCLE
Circumference = 2 x π x r
Area = π x r²
(π = 3.1416)

Height h
Sides a, b, c

TRIANGLE
Perimeter = a + b + c
Area = ½ x b x h

Sides a, b

RECTANGLE
Perimeter = 2 x (a + b)
Area = a x b

Height h
Radius r

CYLINDER
Surface area = 2 x π x r x h
(excluding ends)
Volume = π x r² x h

Height h
Radius r
Side l

CONE
Surface area = π x r x l (excluding base)
Volume = ⅓ x π x r² x l

Sides a, b, c

RECTANGULAR BLOCK
Surface area = 2 x (a x b + b x c + a x c)
Volume = a x b x c

METRIC - IMPERIAL CONVERSIONS

To convert	Into	Multiply by
Length		
Centimetres	inches	0.3937
Metres	feet	3.2810
Kilometres	miles	0.6214
Metres	yards	1.0940
Mass		
Grams	ounces	0.0352
Kilograms	pounds	2.2050
Tonnes	long tons	0.9843
Tonnes	short tons	1.1025
Area		
Square centimetres	square inches	0.1550
Square metres	square feet	10.7600
Hectares	acres	2.4710
Square kilometres	square miles	0.3861
Square metres	square yards	1.1960
Volume		
Cubic centimetres	cubic inches	0.0610
Cubic metres	cubic feet	35.3100
Capacity		
Litres	pints	1.7600
Litres	gallons	0.2200

IMPERIAL - METRIC CONVERSIONS

To convert	Into	Multiply by
Length		
Inches	centimetres	2.5400
Feet	metres	0.3048
Miles	kilometres	1.6090
Yards	metres	0.9144
Mass		
Ounces	grams	28.3500
Pounds	kilograms	0.4536
Long tons	tonnes	1.0160
Short tons	tonnes	0.9070
Area		
Square inches	square centimetres	6.4520
Square feet	square metres	0.0929
Acres	hectares	0.4047
Square miles	square kilometres	2.5900
Square yards	square metres	0.8361
Volume		
Cubic inches	cubic centimetres	16.3900
Cubic feet	cubic metres	0.0283
Capacity		
Pints	litres	0.5683
Gallons	litres	4.5460

NUMBER SYSTEMS

Roman	Arabic
I	1
II	2
III	3
IV	4
V	5
VI	6
VII	7
VIII	8
IX	9
X	10
XI	11
XII	12
XIII	13
XIV	14
XV	15
XX	20
XXI	21
XXX	30
XL	40
L	50
LX	60
LXX	70
LXXX	80
XC	90
C	100
CI	101
CC	200
CCC	300
CD	400
D	500
DC	600
DCC	700
DCCC	800
CM	900
M	1,000
MM	2,000

PHYSICS SYMBOLS

Symbol	Meaning
α	alpha particle
β	beta ray
γ	gamma ray; photon
ϵ	electromotive force
η	efficiency; viscosity
λ	wavelength
μ	micro-; permeability
ν	frequency; neutrino
ρ	density; resistivity
σ	conductivity
c	velocity of light
e	electronic charge

MATHEMATICS SYMBOLS

Symbol	Meaning
$+$	plus
$-$	minus
$\pm$	plus or minus
$\times$	multiplied by
$\div$	divided by
$=$	equals
$>$	is greater than
$<$	is less than
$\geq$	is greater than or equal to
$\leq$	is less than or equal to
$\%$	per cent
$\sqrt{}$	root
π	pi (3.1416)
$°$	degree
∞	infinity
	is approximately equal to
$\angle$	angle
$\parallel$	parallel to

CHEMISTRY SYMBOLS

Symbol	Meaning
$+$	plus; together with
$-$	single bond
	single bond; single unpaired electron; two separate parts or compounds regarded as loosely joined
$=$	double bond
$\equiv$	triple bond
R	group
X	halogen atom
Z	atomic number

BIOLOGY SYMBOLS

Symbol	Meaning
$\circ$	female individual (used in inheritance charts)
$\square$	male individual (used in inheritance charts)
♀	female
♂	male
$\times$	crossed with; hybrid
$+$	wild type
F_1	offspring of the first generation
F_2	offspring of the second generation

POWERS OF TEN USED WITH SCIENTIFIC UNITS

Factor	Name	Prefix	Symbol
10^{18}	quintillion	exa-	E
10^{15}	quadrillion	peta-	P
10^{12}	trillion	tera-	T
10^{9}	billion	giga-	G
10^{6}	million	mega-	M
10^{3}	thousand	kilo-	k
10^{2}	hundred	hecto-	h
10^{1}	ten	deca-	da
10^{-1}	one tenth	deci-	d
10^{-2}	one hundredth	centi-	c
10^{-3}	one thousandth	milli-	m
10^{-6}	one millionth	micro-	μ
10^{-9}	one billionth	nano-	n
10^{-12}	one trillionth	pico-	p
10^{-15}	one quadrillionth	femto-	f
10^{-18}	one quintillionth	atto-	a

NOTE: The American system of numeration for denominations above one million is used in this book. In this system, each of the denominations above one billion (1,000 millions) is 1,000 times the preceding one.

Index

610

624

627

Acknowledgments

Dorling Kindersley would like to thank (in order of sections):

The Universe
(consultant editors – Sue Becklake, Gevorkyan Tatyana Alekseyevna):
John Becklake; the Memorial Museum of Cosmonautics, Moscow; The Cosmos Pavilion, Moscow; The United States Space and Rocket Centre, Alabama; Broadhurst, Clarkson and Fuller Ltd; Susannah Massey

Prehistoric Earth
(consultant editors – William Lindsay, Martyn Bramwell, Dr Ralph E. Molnar, David Lambert):
Dr Monty Reid, Andrew Neuman, and the staff of the Royal Tyrrell Museum of Palaeontology, Drumheller, Alberta; Dr Angela Milner and the staff of the Department of Palaeontology, the Natural History Museum, London; Professor W. Ziegler and the staff, in particular Michael Loderstaedt, of the Naturmuseum Senckenburg, Frankfurt; Dr Alexander Liebau, Axel Hunghrebüller, Reiner Schoch, and the staff of the Institut und Museum für Geologie und Paläontologie der Universität, Tübingen; Rupert Wild of the Institut für Paläontologie, Staatliches Museum für Naturkunde, Stuttgart; Dr Scheiber of the Stadtmuseum, Nördlingen; Professor Dr Dietrich Herm of Staatssammlung für Paläontologie und Historische Geologie, München; Dr Michael Keith-Lucas of the Department of Botany, University of Reading; Richard Walker; American Museum of Natural History, New York

Plants
(consultant editor – Richard Walker):
Diana Miller; Lawrie Springate; Karen Sidwell; Chris Thody; Michelle End; Susan Barnes and Chris Jones of the EMU Unit of the Natural History Museum, London; Jenny Evans of Kew Gardens, London; Kate Biggs of the Royal Horticultural Society Gardens, Wisley, Surrey; Spike Walker of Microworld Services; Neil Fletcher; John Bryant of Bedgebury Pinetum, Kent; Dean Franklin

Animals
(consultant editor – Richard Walker):
David Manning's Animal Ark; Intellectual Animals; Howletts Zoo, Canterbury; John Dunlop; Alexander O'Donnell; Sue Evans of the Royal Veterinary College, London; Dr Geoff Potts and Fred Frettsome of the Marine Biological Association of the United Kingdom, Plymouth; Jeremy Adams of the Booth Museum of Natural History, Brighton; Derek Telling of the Department of Anatomy, University of Bristol; the Natural History Museum, London; Andy Highfield of the Tortoise Trust; Brian Harris of the Aquarium, London Zoo; the Invertebrate Department, London Zoo; Dr Harold McClure of the Yerkes Regional Primate Research Center, Emory University, Atlanta, Georgia; Nielson Lausen of the Harvard Medical School, New England Regional Primates Research Centre, Southborough, Massachusetts; Dr Paul Hopwood of the Department of Veterinary Anatomy, University of Sydney; Dean Franklin

The Human Body
(consultant editors – Dr Frances Williams, Dr Fiona Payne, Richard Cummins FRCS):
Derek Edwards and Dr Martin Collins, British School of Osteopathy; Dr M.C.E. Hutchinson of the Department of Anatomy, United Medical and Dental Schools of Guy's and St Thomas' Hospitals, London. Models – Barry O'Rorke (Bodyline Agency) and Pauline Swaine (MOT Model Agency)

Geology, Geography, and Meteorology
(consultant editor – Martyn Bramwell):
Dr John Nudds of the Manchester Museum, Manchester; Dr Alan Wooley and Dr Andrew Clark of the Natural History Museum, London; Graham Bartlett of the National Meteorological Library and Archive, Bracknell; Tony Drake of BP Exploration, Uxbridge; Jane Davies of the Royal Society of Chemistry, Cambridge; Dr Tony Waltham of Nottingham Trent University, Nottingham; staff of the Smithsonian Institute, Washington; staff of the United States Geological Survey, Washington; staff of the National Geographic Society, Washington; staff of Edward Lawrence Associates (Export Ltd), Midhurst; John Farndon; David Lambert

Rail and Road
Rail (consultant editor – John Coiley)
Michael Ashworth of the London Transport Museum

Road (consultant editors – David Burgess-Wise, Hugo Wilson)
The National Motor Museum, Beaulieu; Alf Newell of Renault UK Ltd; David Suter of Cheltenham Cutaway Exhibits Ltd; Francesca Riccini of the Science Museum, London. Signore Amadelli of the Museo dell' Automobile Carlo Biscaretti di Ruffia; Paul Bolton of the Mazda MCL Group; Duncan Bradford of Reg Mills Wire Wheels; John and Leslie Brewster of Autocavan; David Burgess-Wise; Trevor Cass of Garrett Turbo Service; John Corbett of The Patrick Collection; Gary Crumpler of Williams Grand Prix Engineering Ltd; Mollie Easterbrooke and Duncan Gough of Overland Ltd; Arthur Fairley of the Vauxhall Motor Company; Paul Foulkes-Halbard of Filching Manor Motor Museum; Frank Gilbert of I. Wilkinson and Son Ltd; Paolo Gratton of Gratton Museum; Colvin Gunn of Gunn and Son; Judy Hogg of Ecurie Bertelli; Milton Holman of Dream Cars; Ian Matthews of IMAT Electronics; Eric Neal of Jaguar Cars Ltd; Paul Niblett, Keith Davidson, Mark Reumel, and David Woolf of Michelin Tyre plc; Doug Nye; Kevin O'Keefe of O'Keefe Cars; Seat UK; Roger Smith; Jim Stirling of Ironbridge Gorge Museum, Staffordshire; Jon Taylor; Doug Thompson; Martyn Watkins of Ford Motor Company Ltd; John Cattermole, Customer Services Manager at London Northern Buses; F. W. Evans Cycles Ltd; Trek UK Ltd (Bicycle); Sam Grimmer

Physics and Chemistry
(consultant editor – Jack Challoner)

Sea and Air
Sea (consultant editors – Geoff Hales and Harvey B. Loomis):
David Spence, Gillian Hutchinson, David Topliss, Simon Stephens, Robert Baldwin, Jonathan Betts, all of the National Maritime Museum, London; Ian Friel; Simon Turnage of Captain O.M. Watts of London Ltd; Davey and Company Ltd, Great Dunmow; Avon Inflatables Ltd, Llanelli; Musto Ltd, Benfleet; Peter Martin of Spencer Rigging Ltd, Southampton; Peter Rowson of Ratseys Sailmakers, Southampton; Swiftech Ltd, Wallingford; Colin Scattergood of the Barrow Boat Company Ltd, Colchester; Professor J.S. Morrison of the Trireme Trust, Cambridge; The Cutty Sark Maritime Trust; Adrian Daniels of Kelvin Hughes Marine Instruments, London; Arthur Credland of Hull City Council Museums and Art Galleries; The Hull Maritime Society; Gerald Clark; Peter Fitzgerald of the Science Museum, London; Alec Michael of HMB Subwork Ltd, Great Yarmouth, and Ray Ward of the OSEL Group, Great Yarmouth; Richard Bird of UWI, Weybridge; Walker Marine Instruments, Birmingham; The International Sailing Craft Association; The Exeter Maritime Museum; Jane Wilson of the Trinity Lighthouse Company, London; The Imperial War Museum Collections; Thorn Security Ltd; Michael Bach

Air (consultant editor – Bill Gunston):
Aeromega Helicopters, Stapleford; Aero Shopping, London; Avionics Mobile Services Ltd, Watford; Roy Barber and John Chapman of the RAF Museum, Hendon; Mitch Barnes Aviation, London; Mike Beach; British Caledonian Flight Training Ltd; Fred Coates of Helitech (Luton) Ltd; Michael Cuttell and CSE Aviation Ltd, Oxford; Dowty Aerospace Landing Gear, Gloucester; Guy Hartcup of the Airship Association; Anthony Hooley, Chris Walsh, and David Cord of British Aerospace Regional Aircraft Ltd; Ken Huntley of Mid-West Aero Engines Ltd; Imperial War Museum, Duxford; The London Gliding Club, Dunstable; Musée des Ballons, Calvados; Noel Penny Turbines Ltd; Andy Pavey of Aviation Scotland Ltd; Tony Pavey of Thermal Aircraft Developments, London; the Commanding Officer and personnel of RAF St Athan; the Commanding Officer and personnel of RAF Wittering; The Science Museum, London; Ross Sharp of the Science Museum, Wroughton; The Shuttleworth Collection; Skysport Engineering; Mike Smith; Solar Wings Ltd, Marlborough; Julian Temple of Brooklands Museum Trust Ltd; Kelvin Wilson of Flying Start

Architecture
(consultant editor – Alexandra Kennedy):
Stephen Cutler for advice and text; Gavin Morgan of the Museum of London, London; Chris Zeuner of the Weald and Downland Museum, Singleton, Sussex; Alan Hills and James Putnam of the British Museum, London; Dr Simon Penn and Michael Thomas of the Avoncroft Museum of Buildings, Bromsgrove,

Worcestershire; Christina Scull of Sir John Soane's Museum, London; Paul Kennedy and John Williamson of the London Door Company, London; Lou Davis of The Original Box Sash Window Company, Windsor; Goddard and Gibbs Studios Ltd, London, for access to stained glass windows; The Royal Courts of Justice, Strand, London; Charles Brooking and Peter Dalton for access to the doors and windows in the Charles Brooking Collection, University of Greenwich, Dartford, Kent; Clare O'Brien of the Shakespeare Globe Trust, Shakespeare's Globe Museum, Bear Gardens, Southwark, London; Ken Teague of the Horniman Museum, London; Canon Haliburton, Mike Payton, Ken Stones, and Anthony Webb of St Paul's Cathedral, London; Roy Spring of Salisbury Cathedral; Reverend Gillean Craig of the Church of St George in the East, London; the Science Museum, London; Dr Neil Bingham; Lin Kennedy of Historic Royal Palaces; Katy Harris of Sir Norman Foster and Partners; Production Design, Thames Television plc, London, for supplying models; Dominique Reynier of Le Centre Georges Pompidou, Paris; Denis Roche of Le Musée National des Monuments Français, Paris; Franck Gioria and students of Les Compagnons du Devoir, Paris, for access to construction models; Frank Folliot of Le Musée Carnavalet, Paris; Dr Martina Harms of Hessische Landesmuseums, Darmstadt; Jefferson Chapman of the University of Tennessee, Knoxville, for access to the model of the Hypostyle Hall, Temple of Amon-Re; staff of the Palazzo Strozzi, Florence; staff of the Sydney Opera House, Sydney; staff of the Empire State Building, New York; Nick Jackson; Ann Terrell

The Visual Arts
(consultant editor – Pip Seymour):

Rosemary Simmons; Michael Taylor of Paupers Press, London; Tessa Hunkin and Emma Biggs of Mosaic Workshop, London; John Tiranti, Jonathan Lyons of Alec Tiranti Ltd, London; Chris Hough; Dr Ashok Roy; Satwinder Sehmi of Alphabet Soup, London; Phillip Poole of Cornelissens, London; George Weil and Sons Ltd, London; The National Gallery, London; Chris Webster of the Tate Gallery, London; China Art Cultural Centre, London; London Graphic Centre, London; A.P. Fitzpatrick, London; Flowers Graphics, London; Intaglio Printmaker, London; Falkiner Papers, London; Edgar Udny and Co, London; John Green

Music
(consultant editor – Susan Sturrock):

Boosey and Hawkes Music Publishers Ltd, London, for permission to reproduce extract from The Prodigal Son by Arthur Sullivan; The Bass and Drum Cellar, London; Empire Drums and Percussion, London; Argents (part of World of Music), London; Bill Lewington Ltd, London; Frobenius organ at Kingston Parish Church, Surrey; Yamaha-Kemble Music (UK) Ltd, Tilbrook, Milton Keynes; Yamaha Atelier, London; Akai (UK) Ltd, Hounslow, Middlesex; Casio Electronics Co. Ltd, London; Roland (UK) Ltd, Fleet, Hampshire; Richard Schulman

Sports

The Sports Council Information Centre, London; The British Olympic Games Committee; Brian Crennell of Black's Leisure Group (First Sport); Lillywhites of Piccadilly, London; Mitre Sports International Ltd, Huddersfield; David Bloomfield of the Football Association; Denver Athletics Ltd, Norfolk; Greg Everest and Keith Birley of the British League of Australian Rules Football; Peter McNally of the Gaelic Athletic Association; Rex King of the Rugby Football Union, Twickenham; Neil Tunnicliffe of the Rugby Football League, Leeds; Wayne Patterson of the Basketball Hall of Fame, Springfield, Connecticut; Brian Coleman of the English Basketball Association; All American Imports, Northampton; George Bulman of the English Volleyball Association; Julie Longdon of Mizuno Mallory (UK) Ltd; Juliet Stanford of the All-England Netball Association; Jeff Rowland of the British Handball Association; Cally Melin of Adidas UK Ltd; Patrick Donnely of the Baseball Hall of Fame, Cooperstown, New York; Ian Lepage and Stephen Barlow of the Hockey Association, Milton Keynes; Alison Taylor and Anita Mason of the All England Women's Lacrosse Association, Birmingham; David Shuttleworth of the English Lacrosse Union; Les Barnett and Jock Bentley of the British Athletic Federation Ltd, Birmingham; Mike Gilks of the Badminton Association of England; Gurinder Purewall for advice on archery; Chris McCartney of the US Archery Association; Geoff Doe of the National Smallbore Rifle Association, Bisley, Surrey, for information and reference material on shooting; Fagan Sports Goods Distributors, Surrey; Konrad Bartelski for advice on skiing; The British Ski Federation, Edinburgh; Mike Barnett of Snow and Rock of London; Sally Spurway of Mast-Co. Ltd, Reading; Sarah Morgan for advice on equestrian sports; Steve Brown and the New York Racing Association Inc, New York; Danrho of London; Alan Skipp and James Chambers of the Amateur Fencing Association, London; Carla Richards of the US Fencing Association; Hamilton Bland and John Dryer of the Amateur Swimming Association, Loughborough; Cotswold Camping Ltd, London; Tim Spalton of Glyn Locke (Racing Shells) Ltd, Chalgrove; Terry Friel of the US Rowing Association; House of Hardy; Leeda Fishing Tackle

Everyday Things

City Clocks (Clocks); Christopher Cullen of Babber Electronics; Sony UK Ltd (Mini-television); Black and Decker Ltd (Drills); British Footwear Manufacturing Federation; Grenson Shoes Ltd (Shoes); The Folio Society; R S Bookbinders (Books); Pentax UK Ltd (Camera); F E Murdin of the Decorative Lighting Association; Habitat (Lamp); Chingford Reproductions Ltd (Chair); Dualit Ltd (Toaster); J B Dove; Toro Wheelhorse UK Ltd (Lawnmower); WandH Gidden Ltd (Saddle)

PHOTOGRAPHY:

M. Alexander; Peter Anderson; Charles Brooks; Jane Burton; Peter Chadwick; Simon Clay; John Coiley; Andy Crawford; Geoff Dann; Philip Dowell; John Downs; Mike Dunning; Torla Evans; David Exton; Robert and Anthony Fretwell of Fretwell Photography Ltd.; Philip Gatward; Anna Hodgson; Gary Kevin; J. Heseltine; Cyril Laubscher; John Lepine; Lynton Gardiner (American Museum of Natural History, New York); Steve Gorton; Michelangelo Gratton; Judith Harrington; Peter Hayman; Anna Hodgson; Colin Keates; Gary Kevin; Dave King; Bob Langrish; Brian D.Morgan; Nick Nicholls; Nick Parfitt; Tim Parmenter and Colin Keates (Natural History Museum, London); Tim Ridley; Dave Rudkin; Philippe Sebert; James Stevenson; Clive Streeter; Harry Taylor; Matthew Ward; Jerry Young

PHOTOGRAPHIC ASSISTANCE:

Kevin Zak; Gary Ombler

ILLUSTRATORS:

Julian Baum; Rick Blakeley; Kuo Kang Chen; Karen Cochrane; Simone End; Ian Fleming; Roy Flooks; Mark Franklin; David Gardner; Will Giles; Mick Gillah; David Hopkins; Selwyn Hutchinson; Mei Lim; Linden Artists; Nick Loates; Chris Lyon; Kathleen McDougall; Coral Mula; Sandra Pond; Dave Pugh; Colin Rose; Graham Rosewarne; John Temperton; John Woodcock; Chris Woolmer

MODEL MAKERS:

Roby Braun; David Donkin; Morrison Frederick; Gordon Models; John Holmes; Graham High and Jeremy Hunt of Centaur Studios; Richard Kemp; Kelvin Thatcher; Paul Wilkinson

ADDITIONAL DESIGN ASSISTANCE:

Stefan Morris; Ulysses Santos; Suchada Smith

ADDITIONAL EDITORIAL ASSISTANCE:

Helen Castle; Colette Connolly; Camela Decaire; Nick Harris; Andrea Horth; Stewart McEwen; Damien Moore; Melanie Tham

INDEX: Kay Wright